C'a[...]
(Please return.)

ROBERT R. BLAKE
JANE SRYGLEY MOUTON
Scientific Methods, Inc.

CONSULTATION
A Handbook for Individual
and Organization Development

SECOND EDITION

**ADDISON-WESLEY
PUBLISHING COMPANY**

Reading, Massachusetts
Menlo Park, California
London • Amsterdam
Don Mills, Ontario • Sydney

Library of Congress Cataloging in Publication Data

Blake, Robert Rogers, 1918–
   Consultation.

   Includes bibliographies and indexes.
   1. Social systems.   2. Counseling.   3. Consultants—
United States.   I. Mouton, Jane Srygley.   II. Title.
H91.B46   1982   302   82–6746
ISBN 0–201–10165–3   AACR2

Copyright © 1983, 1976 by Scientific Methods, Inc.

All rights reserved. No part of this publication may be reproduced, stored in a retrieval system, or transmitted, in any form or by any means, electronic, mechanical, photocopying, recording, or otherwise, without the prior written permission of the publisher. Printed in the United States of America. Published simultaneously in Canada.

ISBN 0–201–10165–3
ABCDEFGHIJ–AL-898765432

Preface

Education and consultation are probably two of the most important factors behind the forward movement of society. Consultation may be more meaningful than education in focusing on actual "here and now" problems. When these problems are resolved, people can make real progress in the way they live and work.

This book provides a comprehensive exploration of the nature and scope of the consulting field. A systematic approach is employed to ensure broad and in-depth coverage of the subject. Only highly specialized kinds of consultation that are not of general interest have been excluded.

The field of consultation is in many respects unlimited, ranging as wide as there are knowledge to be used and problems to be solved. The varieties and sub-varieties of consultation are so great that the person wishing to become competent faces a bewildering array of possibilities. Within each particular intervention, however, there are underlying uniformities. Once the uniformities are identified, it becomes possible to recognize that the field of consultation is premised on relatively few basic assumptions as to how a client can best be helped to solve a problem.

The barrier to seeing these basic assumptions has been our inability to get above the field and look down on it in its entirety. The analogy is that of a satellite picture showing the various patterns of weather and their interrelationships when viewed from a continent-wide perspective. This second edition also discusses the Consulcube, a tool that makes it possible for the student of consultation to look upon any particular intervention in such a way as to identify its underlying assumptions and to see it in relation to others. Thus, this book provides a basis for comparing, contrasting, and evaluating all major approaches applied in the field. Patterns of similarities and differences become visible, and the reader is enabled to examine choices for intervention most likely to be successful or unsuccessful.

This book examines five major approaches to consultation from the standpoint of their underlying assumptions in such a way as to demonstrate their relative richness or shallowness. Observations are made as to what conditions are favorable to each approach and likely to produce desired results as well as when and where the approach would be inappropriate. Emphasis throughout is on the dynamics of the interaction between consultant and client. Numerous concrete examples are cited to illuminate representative client-consultant interactions. Each example describes techniques employed by the consultant to the degree necessary for learning about the approach and its "how to do it" aspects.

In Chapter 1 a cube of 100 cells is introduced which serves as the orienting framework for the book. Thereafter the text illustrates the application of various consultation strategies for dealing with a variety of problems and describes the client who receives the intervention. Illustrative case studies were selected primarily for their utility in demonstrating an approach, not for the content of the intervention. The examples within any cell of the cube are intended to be representative of innumerable illustrations, all of which have common characteristics. An individual consultant's interventions with the same client may be represented in one or more cells of the cube, depending on the number of strategies used.

The Consulcube has proven to be an effective way to integrate the field of consultation, and two changes have been introduced in this edition. The order in which the intervention modes are presented is reversed. In response to several requests, theory/principle interventions are presented first. This strategy provides a basis for interweaving consultation and education in many modern applications. The development and change which occur offer an important and powerful way of breaking through barriers to effectiveness that previously resisted penetration. Prescriptive, confrontation, catalytic, and the acceptant modes follow. The other change in this edition is that the system for designating cells in the cube has been modified slightly.

Some see consultation as a *performing art* that can neither be described in the specific instance nor characterized in systematic terms. A performing art is difficult to learn except as one is tutored in it by a master. Others see consultation as a behavioral science discipline; that is, as an activity which can be described and characterized in systematic terms and applied in a deliberate way in specific instances.

Granted that effective consultation is based on a complex of factors, the goal of learning about consultation skills and theory is to increase the utilization of systematic insights, thereby creating a discipline to replace a performing art. Though an intervention entails a delicate and subtle relationship characterized by a performing-art quality, there is little question but that systematic insights can do much to strengthen the effectiveness of help-giving beyond that possible when consultation is regarded only as a performing art.*

This book will be of interest to a number of audiences. Consultants, whether internal organization development (OD) persons or external consultants retained by clients for specific purposes, will find it a useful basis for evaluating their own approaches and for seeing possible benefits of alternative approaches and of new opportunities for application. Corporate executives and industrial managers will find the presentation helpful in assessing what kinds of consultative assistance are likely to be useful in solving their particular problems. Undergraduate and graduate behavioral sciences or MBA students who wish to explore a career in consultation will find this book a useful orientation to the full range of possibilities.

This way of treating consultation provides a number of benefits for the student of consultation or the practitioner in the field.

1. A comprehensive orientation to the field permits all the interrelated aspects to be seen in the context of the whole.

2. The strengths and limitations of one intervention mode can be compared and evaluated against others.

3. The points of application are so numerous that the reader is able to see opportunities of consultation beyond what he or she has been able to learn from direct experience.

4. A systematic approach to the field provides a basis for aiding the student or practitioner to learn why one kind of consultation is more likely and another kind less likely to be helpful in solving the same problem.

5. Sometimes a needless mistake is made because inexperienced consultants are unaware of a valid way of dealing with the problem. Needless mistakes can be avoided through a deeper understanding of the field.

The book may be used in several ways, but learning the Consulcube framework in Chapter 1 is basic. Once this is understood the book can be studied, a segment at a time, beginning with theory/principles interventions in Chapter 2. Practicing consultants will not only find the book useful as a basis for evaluating their own interventions, but also for seeing the richness of the field and how they may extend their own practices. The best way for a practicing consultant to do this is to locate the cell most characteristic of his or her own work and then test options as to how interventions from other cells might be used. For the practicing consultant it can be a useful reference work.

Chapter 32 is of particular value and may be used in sequence after Chapter 1. It is a summary but it also provides the beginning of a more general theory of consultation.

---

* P. B. Vaill, "From the Bookshelf," a review of *Consultation* by Robert R. Blake and Jane S. Mouton, in *Journal of Applied Behavioral Science* 13, no. 1 (1977): 117–20.

Reginald C. Tillam has provided invaluable support in the preparation of the first edition of *Consultation,* and Delores Thomas the same for this second edition. Along with our experiences as consultants over a period of thirty years, these collaborations have led to this integrated presentation. Also, our close personal acquaintance with other consultants has aided us in interpreting the various writings about consultation that are reviewed here. Appreciation is expressed to the many authors included in the text who have sought to reveal their approaches.

Austin, Texas   R.R.B.
January, 1983   J.S.M.

Contents

1

Consultation

Consultation is useful in seeking solutions to many of the complex issues and problems that people and organizations face today. Consultants offer assistance by *intervening*—that is, by taking some action to help a client solve his or her problem(s). These interventions may involve much more than simply telling a client what to do or applying "common sense" remedies to a situation.

The range of situations encountered by today's consultant is as varied and distinctive as are the behavioral dilemmas people face in modern times. In addition to classical consulting areas, the field has expanded to include individual and group therapy, rehabilitative efforts and community action initiatives. In business and government, consultation is no longer limited to aspects involving managerial competence. Firms and agencies now recognize that alcoholism and drug addiction, for example, are as much organizational problems as they are personal problems. Thus numerous organizations are seeking assistance in understanding and coping with such varied dilemmas as helping an individual relieve pent-up tensions; consulting someone who has lost patience with subordinates; dealing with teamwide frustrations; or launching a major effort to increase productivity and enhance organizational effectiveness. In the latter sense, management development and organization development also are fields of intervention, as are vocational counseling, mid-career "retreading," and retirement planning. Consultation now extends even to helping nations grapple with a range of issues from border disputes to ideological conflicts. Despite the seeming uniqueness of these situations, they are linked by a common framework of underlying principles—principles that will become clear as our discussion progresses.

REASONS FOR SEEKING CONSULTATION

An endless number of conditions may cause a client to seek consultant help. Some are genuine problems for which the consultant can help develop solutions. Other calls for consultant help are motivated by what the client may think are real needs, but in point of fact, they arise from goals other than increasing effectiveness. The consultant can satisfy these motivations if he or she wishes, but little improvement in problem solving will result from doing so and many ethical issues will crop up. Genuine motivations are of the following sort:

Bafflement. One of the conditions that causes clients to seek consultative help is a sense of bafflement. This means that things are not as they should be but the client is unable to figure out why. An expert's perception of the situation will hopefully result in a reduction of bafflement and production of insight into what really is going on in the situation, and how it should be handled.

Uneasy feelings. Uneasy feelings are not of the same quality as bafflement, yet they fall in the same area. A person may have an uneasy feeling that things are not as they appear, but may be unable to penetrate the situation in order to test the true state of affairs. Uneasy feelings are usually more specific than the sense of bafflement, and discrepancy is more likely to be perceived between what the client thinks the situation ought to be and what he or she infers it to be.

Check-up. Many clients find interest in employing consultants on the basis of conducting a check-up. Check-ups are useful because they compare the analysis of a situation by an outsider to that of the insider(s). An outsider can often identify adverse factors that insiders have come to take for granted. This, in itself, is a useful contribution.

Standards of performance excellence. Clients seek the help of consultants because of constantly changing standards for judging the quality of performance. What constituted a standard of performance excellence ten years ago, for example, no longer provides a measure of what is theoretically possible in today's environment. Realizing that standards of excellence change and perhaps having a perception of what would be excellent, a client may seek consultation assistance in order to shift the level of performance to a higher degree of excellence.

Change motivations. A client may feel that change is in order and be interested in exploring the possibilities of change. The conclusion may be that changes are unnecessary or even undesirable or it may be that an effort to change could be highly rewarding and satisfying. The point is that the client is motivated to explore the possibilities without necessarily having a sense of any dire need for change or even a basic sense of direction.

Conflicts. Organizations and individuals experience many and sometimes very deep, severe, and destructive conflicts. These conflicts may be interpersonal, intergroup, or interdivisional, but the end result is that they reduce cooperation and interfere with performance. Sometimes an uncooperative individual or group duplicates the personnel and services that the other could have provided if cooperation was available. Consultants can do much to bring conflict resolution about and great benefits can then be realized by individuals, groups, intergroups, and organizations.

Behavioral science knowledge. The behavioral sciences have been creating a revolution in management by aiding organizations gain to insight into principles of behavior. Through these insights, the general structure of management is strengthened and awareness of the possible need for consultation may be increased.

Morale and cohesion. A client may be aware that morale and cohesion within his or her group or organization is at a lower than optimal level. He or she may request the services of a consultant to diagnose the situation, and, if findings are adverse, to recommend steps by which morale and cohesion might be improved.

Human resources management. Clients may find themselves in need of assistance or support in personnel decisions.

Competence deficiency. Organizations find themselves needing help when the skills necessary to solve problems are simply unavailable within the organization. A consultant may contribute temporary problem-solving skills under such circumstances.

All of the above reasons for employing a consultant are real in the sense of being genuine, even though they may be symptomatic of deeper problems.

There are other reasons for employing consultants that have a somewhat questionable and even cynical character, either because there is no real problem to be solved or the real problem does not lend itself to resolution by the help of a consultant. These pseudo needs must be reviewed and understood in order to be recognized. Consultants who respond to requests for services based on these kinds of motivations are taking a great risk.

Saving face. The client may employ a consultant to get answers that the client then "confirms" as being consistent with his or her own judgment. The consultant is really covering up the client's lack of knowledge by giving answers which are then taken by the client and projected as his or her own.

Snubbing inside competitors. Insiders may have a point of view on how to deal with a situation, but clients may perceive themselves as displaying weakness by permitting other insiders to take the lead. The client is reluctant to show internal and external competitors that he or she does not know how to deal with the situation. The solution is to employ a consultant who may develop the same solution as an insider, but allows the client to avoid "bowing" to the inside competitor.

Keeping up with the Joneses. Another reason for employing a consultant is that other persons with whom one is in comparison also are employing consultants. If the client were not to employ consultants while competitors do, this might reflect negatively on his or her openness to new ideas or to self-examination. It becomes important for one not to fall behind, so managers may develop a stable of consultants, primarily to compete or impress rather than to gain the consultant's experiences or resources for resolving problems.

Rigid organization lines of reporting. In many bureaucracies, expert resources may be available, but not immediately accessible. When internal sources of assistance are not responsible to the person needing help, they may be perceived as unavailable. A client may contact outside consultants who can provide the services that others within the organization could contribute, but because they are in other reporting lines it is impossible to make contact with them.

Objectivity. Frequently consultants are asked to provide an "objective" assessment in terms of establishing a credible premise. A recommendation from within a company may be regarded as biased or self-serving, while the same recommendation arrived at independently has the apparent legitimacy of expert outside judgment. The motivation in this case is not to gain the benefits of another view but to create that appearance—the kind of appearance that can make a recommendation more appealing.

Taking the heat. Sometimes when an unpopular or disturbing decision is called for, a consultant is employed for the purpose of making and/or implementing the recommendation. In this way, management is not seen as being responsible for the adverse or harsh decision. By implication and innuendo, it can be rationalized that the consultant's recommendations were impartial and unbiased and therefore fair and appropriate.

Beating the Peter Principle. The Peter Principle is operating when individuals are promoted beyond their talents or competence to perform. As a result, organizational decisions are made by incompetent persons. The "smart" person who is limited in performance can "cover up" by relying on consultant assistance to "tell him or her what to do."

Disposing of funds. Sometimes organizations, or departments within government agencies or universities, find themselves with unspent funds toward the end of a budgeting period. It is thought better to spend the funds than return them, so consulting services are procured.

All of the above involve questionable underlying motivations. Though some deep problem is usually indicated, a consultant needs to be aware of a client's underlying motivations. The issues here are spelled out quite well by Kelley.[1] In summary, clients retain consultants for any number of reasons, such as to

- help them think (or feel)
- think (or feel) for them
- help them improve their thinking (or feelings)
- hide their poor thinking (or negative feelings)
- test their thinking
- supplement their thinking (or feelings)
- deny their thinking (or feelings)
- teach them to think (in subject areas where they have no previous knowledge or to feel in areas where they have become detached).

When emphasis is placed on the word "thinking" it should be understood that thinking and feeling are two sides of the same coin. Both are aspects of a single process.

CYCLICAL NATURE OF BEHAVIOR

Behavior, whether that of a solitary individual, members of a group, or people in a larger social setting, tends to be cyclical in character. In other words, a sequence of behavior repeats its main features, within specific time periods or within specifiable settings. For example, an alcoholic might start each day with a drink. The first is not necessarily at exactly the same time every day and he or she may depart from this pattern occasionally by skipping a day or two. But such deviations are variations on a regular theme. The same holds true with smoking: the smoker consumes, say, one or two packs per day on the average, even though there may be temporary intermissions. Likewise, the heroin addict may shoot up daily, except for foregoing a fix when out of funds. Poor people around the world find themselves repeating day-to-day routines comprising the "cycle of poverty." A business or government executive often establishes a behavioral routine in the work place. He or she arrives at work each day about the same time, attends similar meetings with familiar people, week after week. Often, the executive finds the same kinds of recurring problems. The boss may respond predictably whenever problems of one or another particular category surface. A corporate management group may never finish its meetings' agendas even though session time is increased. In the broader corporate setting, one fiscal quarter may follow another with one year's annual report being very similar to the previous year's publication. A few old problems may be solved, a few new ones developed to take their place, but the major themes will recycle from period to period.

Cyclical behavior can become so habitual as to be beyond the conscious control of the person, group, organization, or community whose performance it characterizes. As long as this repetition stays within certain situational bounds, it can be advantageous. For example, many such cycles help to free intellectual and emotional resources for concentration on less programmable aspects of behavior. Outside these bounds, however, patterned behavioral response can be harmful, even dangerous. Take a simple example. An American in London who looks to the left before crossing the street may be headed for trouble. In most cases, fortunately, he or she gets immediate feedback—via squealing tires and tooting horns—which enables him or her to snap out of a stateside behavior cycle and construct a different pattern for crossing streets. Unfortunately, most of life's situations give no immediate warning of inappropriateness. Individuals, groups, or organizations may perform behavior cycles without explicit awareness or by the force of habit, unsuspecting of possibly harmful and self-defeating consequences. The consultant's function is to aid a person, a group, an organization, or a larger social system by helping the client identify and break out of these damaging kinds of cycles.

Some object to the concept of "change" on the grounds that no one should seek to change another; these people prefer the term "influence" instead. Used in behavioral science applications, the concept of change is neutral: change is a phenomenon that is constantly occurring. We know, for example, that group cohesion rises with victory over another group and falls with defeat. This is change and no one objects to the use of the term in this context.

Consultation is an intervention calculated to bring change about in a deliberate way. While it may be undertaken in a manipulative way, there is nothing inherent in consultation that lends itself to manipulation more than any other human interaction. Indeed, the fact that the client seeks consultation and can terminate it at will may lessen that likelihood.

The concept of change, then, is preferable to influence, or persuasion, or helping. All of these processes may be employed in the induction of change, but as will be seen, much more is implicit in change based on consultation than in these processes of influence or persuasion.

CYCLE-BREAKING INTERVENTIONS

An intervention occurs whenever one individual or group does something with a client in the context of a cycle-breaking endeavor. Who does what to whom for what purpose, of course, involves a whole spectrum of interactions. A teacher may criticize a student's essay so that the pupil will stop making the same grammatical, stylistic, or spelling mistakes. A therapist may interpret a patient's "transference" (i.e., positive or negative feelings toward the therapist) in order to enable the patient to identify the basis of certain impacting feelings that are likely to be characteristic of the patient's relationship with other authority figures as well.

In other kinds of interventions, an encounter-group leader may suggest arm wrestling to two participants who are antagonistic toward one another in order for them to experience their relationship under an unusual circumstance. A management consultant may tell a corporate president that the repetitive pattern of low profit margins should be broken by carrying out a 15-percent manpower reduction. A team-building practitioner may suggest that a boss and his or her subordinates examine problems existing within their patterns of decision making, difficulties that may be caused to some extent by lack of openness and candor in their discussions. An organization development consultant may confront members of a company with evidence of how their reliance on precedent and past practice hampers problem solving. Suggestions for moving outside of their corporate selves to take a "fresh look" at problem areas may lead to discovering new directions for improvement within the company. Also, a social worker may show a prospective client how to complete applications and negotiate with a government agency for assistance.

Lippitt sums up the consultant-client relationship in the following way:

> Consultation, like supervision, . . . is a general label for many variations of relationship. The general definition of consultation . . . assumes that
>
> 1. The consultation relation is a voluntary relationship between

2. a professional helper (consultant) and help-needing system (client)
3. in which the consultant is attempting to give help to the client in the solving of some current or potential problem,
4. and the relationship is perceived as temporary by both parties.
5. Also, the consultant is an "outsider," i.e., is not a part of any hierarchical power system in which the client is located.

Some additional clarification of this condensed definition is needed. The client is conceived to be any functioning social unit, such as a family, industrial organization, individual, committee, staff, membership association, governmental department, delinquent gang, or hospital staff. The consultant is usually a professional helper, such as a marriage counselor, management consultant, community organizer, minister, social worker, human relations trainer, psychiatrist, applied anthropologist, group therapist, or social psychologist. The role of psychological "outsider" may sometimes be taken by a consultant located within the client system, such as a member of the personnel department.[2]

Any language for identifying the intervention participants has some emotional coloring, but a sound working rule is to use language that does not get in the way of understanding. For the purposes of this study, the person who is intervening is called the *consultant*. The person, group, or other intervention recipient is spoken of as the *client*. The problem to be solved is referred to as the *focal issue*.

Though the consultant is usually an individual, the consultant-team approach is also well accepted and widely used. Consultant teams are usually comprised of two or more consultants simultaneously working together or working in tandem, one after the other. Team consultation is a topic of special study by Steele.[3] Additional considerations concerning team consultation are discussed in Chapter 32.

Until a few years ago, the description of a consultant presumed outstanding academic or experience-based qualifications. Consultants had demonstrated their expertise through career and personal success, and displayed unusual knowledge and capacity for assisting clients with specific problems in one or several areas. If not a university professor, the consultant was likely to be employed by a consulting firm.

Today, effective consultants are neither necessarily employed by a consulting firm nor by a university. With accrediting agencies setting standards and accepting experience-based credentials as evidence of individual competence, it is impractical to try to identify who a consultant is by reference to his or her employer. It is equally impractical to try to identify what a consultant's qualifications are by inspecting academic degrees. Even if it were possible to do so, the task would be infinitely complex given two new trends of recent years.

One such trend is the use of "internal consultants," individuals employed on a full-time salaried basis by the organizations with which they consult. The internal consultant is not an outsider coming in, but rather is an inside member of the firm. Dynamics of consultation involving external and internal interventions respectively have been evaluated by Beckhard and Shepard.[4] By comparison, Davey[5] describes successful interventions in terms of the character of the client/external consultant relationship.

The other, and certainly no less important, trend is the emergence after World War II of the paraprofessional and the so-called indigenous nonprofessional. A paraprofessional is a person with a limited degree of specialized training but without the full range of professional qualifications. The indigenous nonprofessional is someone embedded within the client situation who is working effectively to bring about change. The work of these newly emerging consultants has been evaluated from a number of different perspectives (Hines,[6] Lynch and Gardner,[7] Nolan and Cooke[8]). Other evidence of the changing character of the consultant comes from a number of fields, some quite remote from "classical" consultation and others that are not customarily thought of as consultation at all. Yet all the examples introduced below are documented in clinical work, field studies, or through practical experiments.[9] Since there is little or no evidence to demonstrate that the paraprofessional or indigenous nonprofessional is more or less successful than the certified or formally qualified consultant, equivalence of effectiveness is presumed.

For example, other things being equal, "dry" alcoholics are often better equipped to help other alcoholics control their behavior than are psychiatrists, ministers, or other counselors.[10] Working together, ex-drug addicts are equally or more effective in assisting active drug addicts to solve their problems than are medical personnel, psychiatrists, or ministers.[11] Ghetto residents who have succeeded in commercial, educational, or upwardly mobile social lines of endeavor are found to be equally or possibly more effective in helping other ghetto residents break out of the poverty cycle than are ministers, social workers, and so on.[12] Though relevant data are somewhat more difficult to interpret, it appears that people who have themselves been prone to neurotic reactions are sometimes as capable of helping one another to gain insight into and increase their mastery over neurotic symptoms as are psychologists, psychiatrists, or other professionals.[13] Criminals in prison, halfway houses, or on probation can be capably assisted in thinking through their pasts and in discovering more constructive modes of behavior by ex-criminals who have successfully gone straight.[14] Programs for adult literacy development have an equal or greater impact when taught by those who share a common cultural heritage yet who have overcome illiteracy than when taught by experts for whom literacy has never been a problem.[15]

When intervening with university students, dormitory counselors who also are students achieve as good or better results than do university counselors who are members of the administration or teaching faculty. Similarly, freshman orientation has been found to be at least as beneficial, or more so, when carried out by upperclassmen as when implemented by the professional/administrative group.[16]

Equally significant are industrial research findings, where internal consultants either cooperate on a team basis with external consultants or replace them, and the now-emerging academic experiments in education. Both demonstrate that one student can tutor another student with results that are equal to or better than results obtained by professional educators.[17]

Correct generalization from these findings is important in understanding consultation processes. The basic proposition appears to be that the wider the gap between consultant and client, the more numerous and intractable the difficulties encountered in bridging it. By the same reasoning, the narrower the gap—particularly when creative ways are found to enable people of equal status to help in bringing about change—the more effective are the changes that result.

The task of characterizing the consultant is further complicated by another factor, however. In many paraprofessional consultant-client contacts, a consultant who does meet professional standards of competence, for example, a psychiatrist or an organization-development expert, may be in the picture but *not* visible to the client. This happens because the paraprofessional consultant— a person comparable to the client in socioeconomic, ethnic, and other characteristics—serves as intermediary. He or she *interprets* the client's situation to the professional consultant and, in turn, gains insight from the professional consultant-expert as to the next steps of intervention he or she might consider taking with the client. This intermediary role appears to be no less effective and, in fact, even more efficient than when an outsider consults directly with the client. One professional consultant-expert may advise or supervise ten, twelve, or more paraprofessionals, each of whom may carry a client load of ten, twenty, or thirty clients. In other words, representing the situation arithmetically—in a conservative circumstance, $1 \times 10 \times 10$—one professional consultant can have an impact on 100 clients. In direct professional consultant-client contact the load would be far less and there is not much evidence that outcomes would be superior.

The strengths and limitations inherent in the concept of paraprofessional or internal consultation have yet to be worked out fully. An obvious and significant conclusion is that the capacity for intervening on a consultation basis has little to do with academic credentials, employment by a prestigious consulting firm, accumulated experience, or demonstrated success. As will be seen, in each of these interactions there is a keyed matching in the who-does-what-to-whom relationship between consultant and client. The match often is based on the fact that those involved have experienced common symptoms and so can "understand" one another.

THE CONSULCUBE

Three dimensions—focal issues, modes of consultation, and the client—form the Consulcube in Figure 1.1. Within it are a hundred cells, each representing the characteristics of a particular kind of intervention that might be employed with a particular client who is facing a particular problem resulting from an unproductive or self-defeating cycle of behavior. Using the Consulcube, then, any given intervention can be described in three ways; *what issue* the intervention is intended to help resolve, *who* is defined as the client, and what the consultant *does*.

The coding system illustrated in Figure 1.1 is to be utilized throughout this book. On the front of the cube an alphabetical letter designates each intervention/focal issue combination: for example, *A-1* denotes a theory/principles intervention with power/authority as the focal issue, *B-2* a prescriptive intervention with morale/cohesion as the focal issue, and so on. The numbers along the third dimension (from front to back) represent the different ways for viewing the question "who is the client?" As affixed to any letter, the numbers refer to any one of the hundred cells. Thus *C-3-3*, for example, means "a confrontational intervention to help resolve a norms/standards problem within an intergroup situation"; *E-3-5* "an acceptant intervention to help resolve a problem of norms/standards in a larger social system"; and so on.

The Consulcube provides a framework within which various consultant-client interactions can be categorized, compared, and evaluated in terms of their

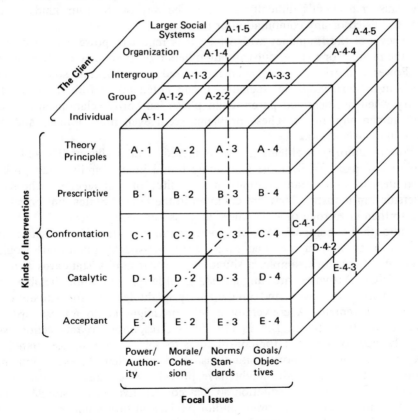

Figure 1.1 The Consulcube

richness, variety, and utility. These main features now will be briefly described and discussed. In general, consultant effectiveness depends on the consultant's ability to identify the focal issue correctly, to employ the most suitable intervention, and to deal with the real client.

FOCAL ISSUES FOR INTERVENTION

The focal issue of an intervention is the problem the client is seeking help to solve. The first kind involves the exercise of *power/authority*. The second relates to *morale/cohesion*. The third is centered in problems that arise from *norms/standards* of conduct. The fourth comprises any issue in the *goals/objectives* area.

Power/authority, morale/cohesion, norms/standards, and goals/objectives are interdependent. This means that when change is initiated in any one of them, changes may be observed in one or more of the other three, whether at that moment or later. For example, reduction of a boss's unilateral use of authority may increase morale/cohesion among subordinates. Other similar interactions will suggest themselves. Thus, the *focal issue* is that aspect of a situation presently causing a client's difficulty and may be any of the four kinds of focal issues just listed or any combination of them.

In view of the frequency with which it is reported, power/authority seems to be the number one issue, outstripping others by a frequency of about three to one. Power/authority has long been recognized as an endemic source of social disease in modern industrial societies. Freud noted this before the turn of the century when he identified parent-child power/authority relationships as basic to all human adjustment. These problems seem even more intense and widespread in today's world.

Power/authority problems are encountered in all walks of life and among people of all ages. While most commonly found in the family, such problems repeat themselves in many settings later in life: in marriage, in schools and universities, in industry. They are common in the United States, but possibly no more so than in Europe or Asia where they also abound.

Although by comparison with power/authority other focal issues might seem less important, such a conclusion (while statistically supported) would be misleading. Take, for example, a situation in which norms/standards appear to be the issue. Activities are unplanned, disorderly, and unpredictable—even though plans, orderliness, and predictability might lead to the situation's all-around improvement. A conventional solution might be to impose order via power/authority methods. But in due course, responses to this action would probably lead to the need for consultation to solve problems associated with unacceptable power/authority situations. Had the client foreseen impending adverse reactions, he or she might have provided structured opportunities for participants to discuss the situation so that constructive norms/standards could emerge without exercise of power/authority. This in turn could provide a basis for establishing order through behavior regulating norms/standards in terms acceptable to all, thus bringing predictability to the situation. Had the client seen the situation in this light, he or she might not have approached the situation coercively. Power/authority, in other words, was the surface problem under these conditions, but norms/standards constituted the real issue.

Similar explanations may clarify situations in which the real problem is not power/authority but rather the absence of satisfactory goals/objectives. A client's immediate power/authority solution might be to impose goals, thereby creating the power/authority problem for which consultation is sought. However, if the client had first created opportunities for subordinate involvement, both in setting and working toward demanding yet mutually accepted goals/objectives, the initial goals/objectives problem might have been solved. Alternatively, if a client's skill in engendering goals/objectives is insufficient, then the consultation might deal with helping this client increase his or her leadership effectiveness through a theory/principles intervention. The focus is on the properties of goals and the motivational conditions essential for gaining the involvement of others in the process of goal setting and implementation.

Occasionally, low morale/cohesion may derive from *anomie*—widespread normlessness and an accompanying lack of shared goals/objectives—which may in turn be an historic consequence of inappropriate or unacceptable exercises of power/authority.

One of the risks of consultation, therefore, is that the consultant perceives the focal issue as being power/authority while the deeper problem, of which the power/authority problems are but symptoms, continues unrecognized and untreated.

The consultant centers attention on what he or she thinks the focal issue to be, even though other issues may in some way be linked to it. Skill in identifying the focal issue(s) is one of the important competencies of an effective consultant. Interventions are not useful if they fail to deal with the critical problem that is the barrier to effectiveness.

An example of consultants not identifying the key problem, with the intervention failing as a result, is provided by Luke et al.[18] Working with a grocery chain, they assisted the organization in changing its structure to facilitate headquarters giving consultative assistance to outlets. This change involved the norms/standards for operating the organization structure.

Looking back on this intervention from a decade's perspective, the consultants are struck by their failure to recognize power/authority as the organization's critical focal issue. Because the power/authority issue was not dealt with, the intervention did not bring about expected results. Had the intervention focused on the power/authority issue, then consultative help in the context of a power and authority system might have provided a basis for shifting the norms/standards as a second step.

Why were these four dimensions chosen as focal issues rather than others? First, they seem to be inclusive. No others are needed to characterize behavior in its entirety. Second, the entire literature on consultation can be classified using this schema. No other variables or substitutes for any of these seem to provide a better framework. Third, the authors, with Muzafer Sherif from the

University of Oklahoma, conducted a year-long graduate seminar, designed to develop a framework for identifying the range of variables essential for characterizing behavior in organized settings. These four variables were identified and have been subsequently tested through research and clinical literature to verify, reject, or modify this initial classification.[19] Independent confirmation of these focal issues is found in Cartwright and Zander's use of them as the basis for structuring the field of social psychology.[20]

KINDS OF INTERVENTIONS

Five consulting modes can be identified which differ in character from one another as ways of dealing with focal issues. Interventions can be related to one of the categories described here. No other definition of an intervention mode is needed to bring similar ways of intervening together or to separate unlike methodologies into different modes.

Theories and principles. By making theories and principles that are pertinent to the client's situation evident, the consultant aids the client to internalize systematic and empirically tested ways of understanding and acting. When learned so well as to be personally useful, these principles permit the client to view his or her situation in a more analytic, cause-and-effect fashion than has hitherto been possible. Thus the client becomes able to diagnose and deal with present and future situations in more valid ways. From the outset he or she can correct an immediate problem or can plan for long-range improvements on the basis of proven effective approaches. Interventions that bring theories and principles into use involve an integration between education and consultation.

Prescription. The consultant tells the client what to do to rectify a given situation or else does it for him or her. The consultant assumes responsibility for formulating the solution as a recommendation to be followed.

Confrontation. This mode challenges a client to examine how the present foundations of his or her thinking—usually value-laden assumptions—may be coloring and distorting the way situations are viewed. Possible alternatives that might lead to more effective solutions may then come clearly into view.

Catalytic. A catalytic intervention assists the client in collecting data and information to evaluate and possibly reinterpret his or her perceptions as to how things are, based on better or more extensive knowledge of the situation. In this way, the client may arrive at a better awareness of underlying causes of a problem and how to address or resolve it.

Acceptant. The intention is to aid the client to develop a basic sense of personal security so that he or she will feel free to express personal thoughts without fear of being judged or rejected. The client may be helped to sort out his or her emotions and in this way get a more objective view of the situation.

The consultant may fail even though he or she correctly diagnoses the focal issue by adopting an incorrect intervention mode. Sebring and Duffee provide an example of what can result when an incorrect intervention mode is adopted.[21] Dealing with a key problem that involved interrelations between departmental groups within a prison system, the consultants' initial intervention was catalytic and involved getting and feeding information to the groups. The intervention was inappropriate. The tensions and hostilities within the interrelationships were so intense that the catalytic mode of expanding the available information had insufficient strength to bring the clients themselves to awareness of the deeper emotions at the roots of their conflict.

When the catalytic mode of intervention failed and the intensity of the conflict increased, the consultants, again inappropriately, shifted their intervention from a catalytic to a prescriptive mode. The prescriptive mode is demonstrated by the consultants' action in writing a report of their diagnosis and delivering it to the key parties in the conflict through registered mail (in order to have validated evidence of delivery, should the protagonists accuse them of not having followed through on a commitment).

The consultants who were responsible for this intervention understood the focal issue and they dealt with the real client. Their failure came from reliance on the catalytic mode to reestablish functional communication across lines of conflict. Intergroup confrontation, described in later chapters, might have been the sound approach.

Consultant interventions may be "pure" acceptant or "pure" catalytic, "pure" confrontation, and so on. Some consultants employ combinations, taking an acceptant stance at one point, shifting to a catalytic one at another and to a confrontational one at still another. An example of combinations of intervention modes is provided by Blumberg and Weiner.[22] Two units of a larger organization had been instructed by their headquarters to merge. As interventionists, the authors utilized the standard intergroup confrontation design to bring similarities and differences in the operating characteristics of the two units into better focus. This exercise revealed significant differences in the client units' leadership characteristics. It identified a dilemma as to how to merge two different value systems. Once these differences became clear, the intervention mode shifted to a theory-based approach. Each group was helped to plot out what they regarded as ideal leadership for the merged organization. Likert's System 4 turned out to be the preferred theory of leadership for the future. An implementation was then outlined that permitted the client groups to bring System 4 into use in the merged organization.

In this example, a confrontational intervention was used to identify the key problem, and then a shift to a theory-based intervention provided a basis for reaching a valid solution.

This example demonstrates that no one kind of intervention is necessarily better than any other. Given a specific problem, however, there is one most effective way of handling it, but that way may be totally inappropriate for dealing with a different problem. In the same sense, one intervention mode may be desirable for a certain phase of consultation with a given client, but a different intervention may be called for in the next phases with the same client. Nevertheless, most consultants appear to develop one intervention style and rely on it exclusively. The intervention approach employed should not be based on the consultant's favorite techniques but rather on the dynamic features of the intervention setting and the client's real needs for increased effectiveness.

WHO IS THE CLIENT?

The social context of an intervention is determined by the target for the consultation. An *individual* may be the client. Another target may be a *group* or *team*—whether a husband-wife couple, a small working group, or some larger assemblage—whose members share some primary basis for their current or continued association. A broader level of intervention is an *intergroup* relationship between, for example, two divisions or departments, or management and the union with which it bargains. A fourth possibility is an entire *organization,* such as a corporate body, a government agency, a school, a hospital, or a church. The fifth category comprises *larger social systems,* such as a community, a city, or a grouping of states or even nations.

"Who is the client?" may appear to be an unimportant question with an obvious answer. In reality, it is among the most critical, for when a consultant deals with the "wrong" client the consequence is at best unproductive, at worst, destructive. The individual can be identified as the client when he or she is reacting out of personal history, values, and so on, in response to current problems. Client identification becomes more complex when the following happens. The consultant may be contacted by an individual who complains about situational problems that pose barriers to personal effectiveness. In this case the individual may be the initial client, but further investigation might reveal inherent constraints over which the individual has no control, constraints subject to resolution only if others involved in the situation simultaneously participate in solution seeking. The client then becomes a group or a team whose members are experiencing a common interactional problem.

The question of "Who is the client?" becomes even more complex when the consultant is approached by an individual whose difficulty involves interaction with another person of equal rank who, for example, heads another division. The real client may be the person himself, his or her group, or the intergroup relationship. The following question is a way of testing these possibilities. If the individual were to change toward the other person, how would these changes in behavior, attitudes, and conduct be perceived by others within the immediate membership group? Would he or she be seen as a traitor, or as a hero because he or she is now acting differently toward the other person? If this kind of reaction occurs, the likelihood is that the real client in this situation is the intergroup relationship itself. An illustrative example may be helpful.

Consider two departments within a large university—a department of psychology and one of educational psychology. It is likely that the department of psychology, housed in the College of Arts and Sciences, is seen by the educational psychology department, housed in the College of Education, as "pure," engaging in rigorous research but dealing with trivial problems in a "holier-than-thou" manner. By comparison, the educational psychology department may be seen as "loose" in the sense of not being rigorously experimental. To the purists, it seems clinically oriented, even tainted by "mentalism."

Now, if the chairpersons of these two departments were to come together, and the chair of the department of "pure" psychology were to agree to a joint professorship for one of the professors of educational psychology, he or she would likely be seen as "selling out" to the chair of the department of educational psychology. Likewise, if the educational psychology chair were to agree to a joint professorship for one of the "purist" psychology department members, whose life had been devoted to problems of visual discrimination in the monkey, for example, the educational faculty might view this behavior as "selling out."

It is clear that both decisions might facilitate the overriding objective of aiding students in learning the fundamentals of psychology. The educational psychology professor teaching in the College of Arts and Sciences might make a beneficial contribution by helping experimental psychologists understand "real world" problems that they may approach in an experimental vein. At the same time the pure psychology professor operating in the educational psychology department could engender an increased understanding and respect for experimental methods.

When decisions about client identity result in win-lose attitudes between two departments, it is clear that the client is the two departments considered jointly and in their interrelationship. Both need the opportunity of studying their relationship and confronting the emotion-based reactions to their differences so that, based on shared understanding, they can reach mutually agreed upon solutions to the problem of collaboration.

The same line of reasoning applies when the organization is considered as a whole. If the organization is even as old as two or three years, it already has built a climate and a culture of reactions and attitudes based upon tradition, precedents and past practices, ritual, sacred cows, and so on. These are widely recognized and rarely discussed, but serve as the boundary conditions that define what is acceptable for people to do and what is beyond the limits of proper responsibility. In such cases the client is the organization as a system rather than the intergroup relationships or the working groups of teams or the separate individuals who comprise the organization.

Sometimes the problems are in the larger social system within which the organization's groups and individuals operate. In the case of a school, for example, these involve issues of community support; taxation; and relationships with parents and interested citizens, law enforcement authorities, and so on. When these interrelationships are among the sources of school problems, then the client is the larger social system, including the school as a subsystem within that larger social system. The interventions necessary must then deal with this broader context.

Thus the question, "Who is the client?" is far more complicated than might appear at first glance. To reiterate, an analytical approach to answering "Who is the client?" leads to a separation of individuals who approach a consultant into two categories. Sometimes the individual is the real client, i.e., the entire problem that he or she confronts is within his or her capacity to resolve. Sometimes, however, the individual should be seen not as *the* client but as the entry person, that is, an individual through whom access to the *real* client may be possible.

A demonstration of how interventions are doomed to failure if the consultant is involved with the wrong client is provided by Nadler,[23] who offers a core study of an intervention calculated to strengthen a quality-of-work project in a hospital.

All but one significant group in the hospital participated in the effort—nurses, administrators, nonprofessional employees, and so on, including interns and residents. The only nonrepresented group was the physicians, those most directly responsible for the work of the hospital itself, including teaching, research, and medical care. Without participation of the senior staff (in this case, the physicians), commitment to basic change was unlikely. Eventually, even the interns and residents withdrew participation and the project stopped.

Another example of the adverse consequences from dealing with the wrong client is provided by Boss. Catalytic team building was undertaken with six work groups. In all but one the leader did not participate. After six months the five leaderless teams either had regressed or else showed no change by comparison with the one intact team, which reported significant change. Boss concludes that a leader's presence is an essential condition for any prospect of success. An incomplete team, particularly when the leader is excluded, is not a "valid" client.[24]

Another example of the consultant dealing with the "wrong" client is presented by Lewicki and Alderfer.[25] The goal of the intervention was to reduce the likelihood of strike recurrence through research to diagnose the causes of a recently concluded strike. Senior corporate staff executives and the top leadership of an international union reached agreement which affirmed the desirability of the suggested research program and provided a funding base. The intervention never materialized, however, because the "real" client whose collaboration was essential in order to put the effort into motion included the local union leadership where the strike had occurred. These key persons were not contacted until several months after the initial formulation and approval of the study. The union leadership resented their exclusion from the proposal phase and when they took the proposal to the membership, it was rejected out of hand. The client definition in this case was the reverse of what has been found in other interventions to be more valid. Gaining cooperation first from the local union leadership and the business representatives, and then, if necessary, going to higher levels, i.e., the international officers, would have been the sound approach. Starting at the top with the international union leadership and eventually approaching the local level, as was done by Lewicki and Alderfer, fails because it does not involve the real client. Rather than accurately diagnosing who had to be involved for effective collaboration, the consultants may have unwittingly colluded with power figures in the hierarchy on the incorrect assumption based in managerial thinking that local union leadership took its orders from above.

It is important for a consultant to determine "who" the real client is. Trying to focus change on an individual as a *separate* entity is only likely to generate resistance if such a personal change would make the client a deviant, rejected by other group members who have no understanding and even less sympathy for his or her observable behavior shift. Under these conditions, the client is the group and its members need to change simultaneously and together if that change in behavior is to be supported. Consultants must focus their efforts on the real client in order to intervene effectively. The *real* client is that individual, group, or relationship in which change is expected to occur.

ORGANIZATION OF THE BOOK

In addition to having produced some basic research investigations, the field of consulting is rich in case studies, clinical reports, and field research. The Consulcube serves to organize these many disparate reports into a systematic and coherent whole in such a way that the respective consultants' assumptions can be identified and the particular interventions evaluated.

To summarize, the Consulcube identifies:

WHO   —the *consultant*

WHAT   —does some kind of *intervention* such as
        —Theory and Principles
        —Prescriptive
        —Confrontational
        —Catalytic
        —Acceptant

WHY   —to address and/or resolve a *focal issue* such as
        —Power/Authority
        —Morale/Cohesion
        —Norms/Standards
        —Goals/Objectives

TO WHOM—the *client* as
        —Individual
        —Group
        —Intergroup
        —Organization
        —Larger Social System, which is capable of solving the problem in its entirety

The various consultant reports that fit together because they share underlying assumptions characteristic of a specific cell are summarized to provide the gist of what took place and a basis for seeing the strengths and limitations of each. Not all cells are represented by examples, because certain focal issues coupled with certain kinds of intervention result in circumstances where consultation is unlikely to be sought by the client system.

Interventions reported throughout the wide-ranging consultation field have been reviewed and are presented as representative of one (or more) of the Consulcube cells. In each instance, an attempt is made to include enough detail from the original work to afford the reader both a flavor for the intervention, the rationale for its use, and the consequences resulting from it. Occasionally the original author(s) may not have been sufficiently explicit to ensure that interpretations of their work are complete and accurate in all significant aspects. Nonetheless, with each report selected, we have endeavored to represent the intervention as accurately and completely as possible.

The Consulcube schema enables comprehensive definition and pertinent focusing on the dynamics of consultation, and represents an integration and extension of earlier work.[26,27] Alternative ways of characterizing consultant interventions include those of Lippitt, Watson, and Westley;[28] Lippitt,[29] Nadler,[30] Miles and Schmuck;[31] Golden,[32] Lieberman, Yalom, and Miles;[33] Morrill, Oetting, and Hurst;[34] and Geis.[35] Recent studies, not of interventions but of traditional management consulting, by Hollander[36] and Fuchs,[37] might also be mentioned.

Other books dealing with consultation have appeared since the first edition of *Consultation.* One by Bell[38] offers brief collections on many different details of consultation. Other sources that amplify the catalytic mode are by Goodstein[39] and Lubin.[40] A third, by Block, examines the confrontational approach to consultation.[41] Kelley[42] provides a practical guide to "how to do it" but he does not deal with such matters as focal issues, client identity, or intervention modes. A critique of consultation practices and processes is provided by Steele.[43] A book centered on mental health consultation, but with a very wide-ranging and historically oriented bibliography, is edited by Mannino et al.[44]

This book seeks to encompass the entire field of consultation by analogy in much the same way as a satellite provides a picture of inclusive weather patterns. The cube allows us to examine and evaluate the field from a perspective that encompasses its full scope. In this way, the reader is assisted to examine any particular problem from a range of perspectives before concluding that any one approach may prove more successful than any other.

Notes

1. R. E. Kelley, *Consulting: The Complete Guide to a Profitable Career* (New York: Charles Scribner's Sons, 1981).
2. R. Lippitt, "Dimensions of the Consultant's Job," *Journal of Social Issues* 15, no. 2 (1959): 5–12. Reprinted by permission.
3. F. Steele, *Consulting for Organizational Change* (Amherst: University of Massachusetts Press, 1975).

4. L. Porter, "An Interview with Beckhard and Shepard—OD: Some Questions, Some Answers," *OD Practitioner* 6, no. 3 (1974): 1–8.
5. N. G. Davey, *The External Consultant's Role in Organizational Change* (East Lansing, Mich.: Michigan State University Studies, 1971).
6. L. Hines, "A Nonprofessional Discusses Her Role in Mental Health," *American Journal of Psychiatry* 126, no. 10 (1970): 111–16.
7. M. Lynch and E. A. Gardner, "Some Issues Raised in the Training of Paraprofessional Personnel as Clinic Therapists," *American Journal of Psychiatry* 126, no. 10 (1970): 117–23.
8. K. J. Nolan and E. T. Cooke, "The Training and Utilization of the Mental Health Paraprofessional within the Military: The Social Work/Psychology Specialist," *American Journal of Psychiatry* 127, no. 1 (1970): 114–19.
9. F. Reissman, "The Helper Therapy Principle," *Social Work* 10, no. 2 (1965): 27–32.
10. *Alcoholics Anonymous,* new and rev. ed. (New York: AA Publishing, Inc., 1955).
11. J. B. Enright, "On the Playing Fields of Synanon," in L. Blank, G. B. Gottsegen, and M. G. Gottsegen, eds., *Confrontation: Encounters in Self and Interpersonal Awareness* (New York: Macmillan, 1971), pp. 147–77.
12. E. Hallowitz, "The Expanding Role of the Neighborhood Service Center," in F. Reissman and H. R. Popper, eds., *Up from Poverty: New Career Ladders for Nonprofessionals* (New York: Harper & Row, 1968), pp. 92–105.
13. A. A. Low, *Mental Health through Will-Training: A System of Self-Help in Psychotherapy as Practiced by Recovery, Incorporated* (Boston: The Christopher Publishing House, 1978).
14. M. Buckley, "Enter: The Ex-Con," *Federal Probation* 36, no. 4 (1972): 24–30.
15. F. C. Laubach and R. I. Laubach, *Toward World History* (Syracuse: Syracuse University Press, 1960).
16. W. F. Brown, "Student-to-Student Counseling for Academic Adjustment," *Personnel and Guidance Journal* 43, no. 8 (1965): 811–17.
17. A. Gartner, M. Kohler, and F. Reissman, *Children Teach Children* (New York: Harper & Row, 1971).
18. R. A. Luke, Jr., P. Block, J. M. Davey, and V. R. Averch, "A Structural Approach to Organization Change," in Bernard Lubin, Leonard D. Goodstein, and Alice W. Lubin, eds., *Organizational Change Sourcebook I: Cases in Organization Development* (San Diego: University Associates, Inc., 1979), pp. 125–47.
19. R. R. Blake, H. A. Shepard, and J. S. Mouton, *Managing Intergroup Conflict in Industry* (Houston: Gulf Publishing Co., 1964).
20. A. Cartwright and A. Zander, eds., *Group Dynamics: Research and Theory* (Evanston, Ill.: Row Peterson, 1953, 1960).
21. R. H. Sebring and D. Duffee, "Who Are the Real Prisoners? A Case of Win/Lose Conflict in a State Correctional Institution," *Journal of Applied Behavioral Science* 13, no. 1 (1977): 23–40.
22. A. Blumberg and W. Weiner, "One from Two: Facilitating an Organizational Merger," *Journal of Applied Behavioral Science* 7, no. 1 (1971): 87–102.
23. David A. Nadler, "Hospitals, Organized Labor and Quality of Work: An Intervention Case Study," *Journal of Applied Behavioral Science* 14, no. 3 (1978): 366–81.
24. R. W. Boss, "The Effects of Leader Absence on a Confrontation Team-Building Design," *Journal of Applied Behavioral Science* 14, no. 4 (1978): 469–78.
25. R. J. Lewicki and C. P. Alderfer, "The Tensions Between Research and Interventions in Intergroup Conflict," *Journal of Applied Behavioral Science* 9, no. 4 (1973): 424–49.

26. R. R. Blake and J. S. Mouton, *Group Dynamics—Key to Decision Making* (Houston: Gulf Publishing Co., 1961).
27. R. R. Blake and J. S. Mouton, "The D/D Matrix," in J. D. Adams, ed., *Theory and Method in Organization Development: An Evolutionary Process* (Washington, D.C.: NTL Institute for Applied Behavioral Science, 1974), pp. 3–36. (Originally published Austin, Texas: Scientific Methods, Inc., 1972.)
28. R. J. Lippitt, J. Watson and B. Westley, *Planned Change: A Comparative Study of Principles and Techniques* (New York: Harcourt, Brace, 1958).
29. G. L. Lippitt, *Organization Renewal: Achieving Viability in a Changing World* (New York: Appleton-Century-Crofts, 1969).
30. L. Nadler, *Developing Human Resources* (Houston: Gulf Publishing Co., 1970).
31. M. B. Miles and R. A. Schmuck, "Improving Schools through Organization Development: An Overview," in R. A. Schmuck and M. B. Miles, eds., *Organization Development in Schools* (Palo Alto, Calif.: National Press Books, 1971), pp. 1–27.
32. W. P. Golden, "On Becoming a Trainer," in W. G. Dyer, ed., *Modern Theory and Method in Group Training* (New York: Van Nostrand Reinhold, 1972), pp. 3–29.
33. M. A. Lieberman, I. D. Yalom and M. B. Miles, *Encounter Groups: First Facts* (New York: Basic Books, 1973).
34. W. H. Morrill, E. R. Oetting and J. C. Hurst, "Dimensions of Counselor Functioning," *Personnel and Guidance Journal* 52, no. 6 (1974): 355–59.
35. H. J. Geis, "Toward a Comprehensive Framework Unifying All Systems of Counseling," *Educational Technology,* March 1969, pp. 19–28.
36. S. C. Hollander, *Management Consultants and Clients* (East Lansing, Mich.: Michigan State University Studies, 1972).
37. J. H. Fuchs, *Making the Most of Management Consulting Services* (New York: AMACOM, 1975).
38. C. R. Bell and L. Nadler, eds., *The Client-Consultant Handbook* (Houston: Gulf Publishing Co., 1979).
39. L. D. Goodstein, B. Lubin and A. W. Lubin, eds., *Organizational Change Sourcebook II: Cases in Conflict Management* (San Diego: University Associates, 1979).
40. B. Lubin, L. D. Goodstein and A. W. Lubin, eds., *Organizational Change Sourcebook I: Cases in Organization Development* (San Diego: University Associates, 1979).
41. P. Block, *Flawless Consulting* (Austin, Texas: Learning Concepts, 1981).
42. Kelley, *Consulting.*
43. Steele, *Consulting for Organizational Change.*
44. F. V. Mannino, B. W. MacLennan and M. F. Shore, eds., *The Practice of Mental Health* (New York: Gardner Press, 1975).

Part I

THEORY-PRINCIPLES INTERVENTIONS

2

THEORY-PRINCIPLES INTERVENTIONS

Theory-Principles Interventions: An Introduction

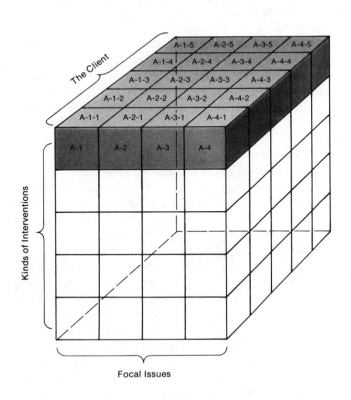

Focal Issues

A significant intervention approach was identified when consultants realized that theory could be learned and subsequently used by clients to bring about systematic changes in self-defeating cycles of behavior. In other words, a client could be aided, through theory-based interventions, to comprehend *and* shift the cause-and-effect variables operating in his or her situation. Through awareness of what causes things to be as they are, the client could predict the consequences of specific anticipated changes and plan accordingly.

THE THEORY SPECTRUM

Theory-based consultation should not be confused with interventions in which the consultant uses theory solely to guide him- or herself during interaction with the client. A purely prescriptive consultant, for example, neither reveals to nor helps the client understand the systematic insights that the consultant may rely upon to guide the intervention.

As used in everyday conversation the word "theory" has little to do with theory as employed in theory-based consultation. When someone says, "I've got a theory about that. . . ," he or she may only mean having a hunch or playing an angle. A person might develop an abstract philosophical doctrine that he or she describes by saying, "That's my theory. . . ." In neither case is the word *theory* being used in the same way it is used when describing theory-based interventions. Theory in the behavioral science sense is quite different.

The Theory Spectrum shown in Table 2.1 helps to clarify what theory does and does not mean. Nontheoretical bases of action, including trial and error, hunch, and intuition are listed on the Spectrum's left side. Toward the middle of the Spectrum are subjective or empirical explanations. The first of these involves common-sense accounts of what is happening expressed in scientific terms. Often, conclusions and actions are based on sensible generalizations that correspond to preconceived notions or hoped-for outcomes. Another basis of action includes attitudes, beliefs, and convictions. These are often unstated propositions people act upon when deciding what to do or not to do to solve given situations. Such attitudes, beliefs, and convictions are based upon accumulated personal experiences and, as practical guides to action, may never have been empirically verified or tested.

Another degree nearer the Spectrum's theory end are *cognitive maps* and *conceptual systems.* A cognitive map is a provisional picture a person creates to explain the character of a problem and develop approaches to its solution. Such a map is likely to be a complex of common-sense explanations, subjective attitudes, beliefs and convictions, as well as bits and pieces of theory, all of which are put together and expected to match the real problem. A cognitive map for a complex problem sometimes has a correlate in the New World maps produced after Columbus's voyage. Although these early maps bear some resemblance to the shoreline of the east coast of America, the lack of accuracy precludes their use as a sound basis for navigation.

Table 2.1 The theory spectrum

Nontheoretical basis for action		Subjective or empirical explanations				Theoretical basis for action	
Trial and error	Hunch and intuition	Common-sense expla-nations	Attitudes, beliefs, and con-ventional wisdom	Cognitive maps and conceptual systems	Plans and planning	Theory expressed in the form of explicit hypotheses that can be tested	Principles as expres-sions of lawfulness underlying human behavior

Source: R. R. Blake and J. S. Mouton, *Corporate Excellence Through Grid Organization Development,* 2nd ed. (Houston: Gulf Publishing Company, 1968, 1983), p. 283.

Also close to theory, but still not meeting criteria of a genuine theory-based approach, is a conceptual system, the set of ideas a person uses to account for things. Harrison has explained the importance of conceptual systems in supporting effective problem solving.

> Let us consider how we understand the world we live in, and particularly those parts of it concerning ourselves and our relations with other people. First of all, we organize the world according to *concepts,* or categories. We say that things are warm or cold; good or bad; simple or complex. Each of these concepts may be considered a dimension along which we can place events in the world—some closer to one end of the dimension, some closer to the other.
>
> Actually, we can't really think about using these categories or dimensions to organize our thoughts. Any time we consider the qualities of ourselves, other persons, or events in the inanimate world, we have to use categories to do it. We are dependent for our understanding of the world on the concepts and categories we have for organizing our experiences. If we lack a concept for something which occurs in the world, we either have to invent one or we cannot respond to the event in an organized fashion. How, for example, would a person explain his or her own and others' behavior without the concept of love and hate? Think how much behavior would simply puzzle or confuse him or her or, perhaps, just go by without really being perceived at all, for lack of this one dimension.
>
> Concepts do not exist in isolation; they are connected to one another by a network of relationships. Taken all together, the concept we use to understand a situation, plus the relationships among the concepts, are called a *conceptual system.* For example, we may say, "People who are warm and friendly are usually trusting, and hence, they are often deceived by others." Here we have a conceptual system linking the concepts of *friendly warmth, trust in others,* and *ease of deception.* Because concepts are linked one to another, the location of an event on one concept usually implies something about where the event is located on each of a whole network of concepts. It is thus almost impossible to take in a small bit of information about a characteristic of a person or event without its having a whole host of implications about other characteristics.[1]

Planning and operational blueprints represent still another degree of precision approaching the theory end of the Spectrum. This is particularly so when plans are created from data that involve forecasting the future rather than simply projecting based on the past. Such plans represent educated guesses geared to predict specific situations. Although they can be very useful, they are not theory. When nontheoretical bases for action and subjective or empirical explanations are utilized in interventions (even though labeled *theory*), these are still premised on prescientific concept formation and were therefore included in other sections of this book.

Behavioral science theories are more comprehensive and qualitatively different from cognitive maps or conceptual systems in the sense Harrison uses that term. A theory is a specific set of explicit statements as to what will or will not occur. Predictions are made that can be tested in action under particular conditions. The degree of the prediction's accuracy is subject to experimental post-evaluation with prior confidence in the prediction expressed in statistical terms. Sometimes referred to as hypotheses, and, sometimes less accurately as axioms or principles, these statements provide the user a basis for preevaluating actions in terms of their soundness. Once the client has learned theories and knows how to employ them in concrete situations, he or she no longer has to rely solely on intuition or hunch, common sense, or his or her own subjective conceptual system.

Some consultants reject theory as of little or no use in guiding behavior. Kingsbury provides an apt description of the "anti" point of view regarding those positions on the Spectrum tending toward the theory end of the continuum.

> In the past, I have been more strongly committed than I am now to the idea that it is important for a person to talk through his experiences in a group in order to develop cognitive clarity and a personal theory about the meaning of the experiences he has. Recently, however, I have found myself suspecting that some pretty good things were being talked to death, and that an experience which involved the whole person—mind and body, head and heart, reason and emotion—became so intellectualized that the feeling component of the insight was dulled or lost; the reality, intensity, and, I have suspected, the transferability of the insight to other situations was drained away.
>
> Perhaps all I am doing is criticizing the state of the science, but I think something more than that is going on—something that has to do with the denial of the reality of feeling on the irrational ground that is not rational. A lot of "objective" research published in the field of applied behavioral science has the quality of talking valid experience to death. The notion that reason and emotions are mutually exclusive pervades our society. I want reason and emotion unified in my own behavior and experience, and I want to do something better than I know how to do now with these issues in the groups I lead.[2]

In preference to theory-based interventions Kingsbury seems to favor an acceptant orientation, where emotions are felt and expressed as the necessary and sufficient basis for development of new skills or for breaking out of self-defeating cycles.

The opposite point of view is succinctly presented by Lewin, who popularized the famous statement, "Nothing is so practical as a good theory." We see this point of view amplified by McGregor, who points to the contribution that theory can make in fostering development.

> The basic point is that some knowledge of existing theory can guide a group engaged in self-development, not alone by the discussion it provokes but by providing generalizations to be tested by the group both in selecting the strategies it uses for carrying out its primary tasks and in attempting to improve group maintenance.[3]

The theory end of the Spectrum identifies circumstances in which cause-and-effect relationships between action and reaction can be specified. Thus the consequences of any given action can be predicted with a relatively high degree of accuracy. Such theory derives from experiments and field research, mostly in the behavioral sciences. Kingsbury's "complaint" notwithstanding, this kind of theory has reached a degree of sophistication such that quite reliable predictions can be made.

There have been a number of recent formulations by academic personnel who are joining the ranks of those who recognize the importance of theory and principle as the undergirding structure for consultation.

One of these is Vaill. Paraphrasing Trist, he comes to the following position as a way of clarifying the meaning of systems.

> Basically a work system is some organized collection of people and things. The "things" may be tools and machinery from the simplest to the most complex elements. The people may function as individuals and/or in twos and threes and/or in groupings of a dozen or so and/or in large organizations to make the system work just right. The problem is to get the things whose behavior is governed by one set of laws to interface effectively with the people whose behavior is governed by another set of laws. The laws which govern the behavior of things are physical laws; for instance, laws of mechanics, thermodynamics, hydraulics, and electronics. The laws which govern the behavior of people are the laws of psychology, sociology, and anthropology, as well as, perhaps, better established laws of biology. Each set of laws (one for inanimate, one for animate) has its own limits, imparities, and opportunities. Each is discoverable and manageable by its own particular brands of scientific investigation.
>
> A simple example: an automobile may be capable within the laws which govern it of going 200 m.p.h. but a particular person may not be capable within the laws which govern him/her of driving that fast. Therefore, at 200 m.p.h., a condition of joint optimization does not exist. The system is unstable and probably cannot endure at that level of performance. Conversely, the person may be capable of controlling an automobile at 200 m.p.h. but the particular car she/he is driving may not be capable of that sustained speed. Therefore at or near 200 m.p.h. joint optimization is again not occur-

ring. Thus, the problem of joint optimization here would be "what is the optimal level of performance for a particular person in a particular car under a particular set of road conditions?"

Studying the problem in this way results in the generalization that intervention is a process of dealing with systems, either on the social side, the technical side, or in sociotechnical terms in ways that bring theory and principle of the system itself into alignment with one another and into alignment with scientific law.[4]

Theory-based interventions engage a consultant in those activities necessary to assist a client in acquiring a theoretical basis for governing action. The client is freed from blind reliance on intuition and hunch or on common sense and conventional wisdom and is enabled to see situations more objectively. The distortions that subjective attitudes, beliefs, and untested convictions can produce are avoided. Plans and planning can be helpful, but unfortunately they frequently are premised on pragmatic concerns rooted in history only, without sufficient regard for scientifically derived and experimentally validated theory. When valid theory is relied upon, actions can be taken with assurance that the anticipated consequences will, in fact, occur.

INTELLECTUAL VERSUS EMOTIONAL PROBLEMS

A common reaction to theory interventions is that, although they might contribute to the solution of intellectual problems, they would not be pertinent for handling emotion-based difficulties. However, since ideas and emotions are simultaneous aspects of experience rather than different processes, theory applies equally to both. For example,

Sometimes facts are not enough because the problem is not one of fact. It may lie in the emotional attitudes of two persons toward one another which result in stereotypical thinking, persuasive argument, not listening, reacting defensively, closed minded attitudes, and so on. When barriers are present which prevent the use of fact to solve problems the 9,9 approach is to get directly to the cause of the barriers. Then solution of the conflict is to face the emotions that are beneath the surfaces, examine them objectively, and probe for causes beneath them. In order to do this people must be committed to revealing their reactions of frustration, the reasons they feel misunderstood, and the ways in which their expectations or aspirations have been violated. Equally, they must be prepared to identify and to face up to the inherent limitations of competence which may be preventing them from making an effective contribution rather than to cover up or to pass the buck. When this kind of genuine behavior which can only be based upon open and unobstructed communication is achieved, the conditions are right for the surface problems causing disagreement to be resolved. When these highly personal attitudes can be forthrightly identified and discussed, presumed injustices and misunderstandings can be cleared up and genuine injustices and misunderstandings rectified. This way of confronting the emotions of disagreement and conflict provides a key for the creative resolution of conflict.[5]

The power of theory to direct technological change, such as aerodynamic theory to build airplanes, is unquestioned. The same is true for biological applications as evidenced in the dramatic strides in medicine that have occurred during the past hundred years. Behavioral theories per se have been clarified for only a hundred or so years, and only at an increased rate since World War II, but already they have proved powerful in increasing behavioral efficacy.

HOW CAN THEORY BE MADE USABLE?

The development of theories pertinent for solving everyday kinds of human problems blossomed after World War II as researchers and practitioners alike began to learn how to communicate theories for problem-solving purposes. What caused this shift toward the actual *use* of theory? There are many explanations, including the following.

1. Methods for "internalization" of theory. In ordinary classroom learning the teacher may tell a student(s) how things should be but provide little insight as to how the desired conditions can be achieved. No positive change in student behavior is likely under these circumstances. The post–World War II difference is a distinction between theory taught in the abstract and theory learned by the client and internalized for personal use and guidance. A student might get classroom exposure to various theoretical concepts but might not incorporate them into his/her own behavioral repertoire. Internalization, on the other hand, permits the client to become so familiar with theory as to actually apply it to given situations he or she encounters. Then he or she can test such theories against more characteristic ways of thinking—trial and error, or hunch and intuition, for example. In this way poor mental practices can be replaced with better ones.

2. Strategies for helping a client understand theory sufficiently to be able to apply it in given situations are different from traditional classroom methods. These learning strategies involve several fairly basic steps. The following are employed by theory-oriented consultants in assisting clients to shift their thinking to a theoretical basis.

Step 1. The client is presented with some kind of typical situation likely to be met in daily activities. His or her reaction, either written or acted out, is elicited. Such reactions define the client's natural bent. This activity is completed *before* any theory is introduced.

Step 2. The client then studies pertinent theories of behavior, either through a textbook or lecture approach, by the use of audio cassettes, by viewing a movie, or engaging in discussions that introduce the theoretical orientation. Questions and test examples enable the client to check out how well the theory is being understood.

Step 3. The client participates in simulated problem situations where "best" solutions can be reached by using theories learned in Step 2.

Step 4. Postsimulation critiques enable the client to evaluate the degree to which he or she understood and was able to use the theories. These critiques also reveal any inaccurate client assumptions or possible limitations in the theory itself.

Step 5. Through an additional series of simulations the client is repeatedly provided the opportunity to compare his or her natural bent for dealing with situations against theoretical specifications. Such self-confrontations enable the client to understand theory in a personally useful way and recognize the extent to which his or her second-nature assumptions surface under pressure. Confidence is built and the client gains awareness of the distance between optimal and actual performance.

Step 6. When theories have been learned, further practice enables the client to perfect his or her capacity to identify and execute the actions and practices the theory requires for breaking self-defeating cycles.

Step 7. Theory is then employed by the client to reevaluate his or her learned methodology for solving problems in comparison with the natural inclination as revealed in Step 1. He or she reevaluates the Step 1 circumstances, this time from the theory-based orientation.

Step 8. Generalizations regarding natural bent are further clarified and differentiated to prevent the client from slipping into habitual patterns of behavior. This enhances the client's ability to approach and handle situations from a theory-based perspective.

Step 9. Consultant support and an implementation plan for using a theory-based approach on the job or in social or personal situations are available to assist the client's changeover from the left side to the right side of the Theory Spectrum.

Though educational tactics vary from case to case, these steps are as useful with a team, an organization, or a larger social system as with an individual client. A successful theory intervention is likely to include each of these basic steps. Many theory-based approaches, however, bypass significant elements of this internalization process. As a result, the theory is rejected or is not used by the client because he or she has not experienced its practicality.

WHY THEORY IS A USEFUL INTERVENTION

Science-based theories and principles are fundamental for facilitating a change from current practices to a more systematic way of doing things. There are a number of reasons why behavioral approaches provide such a powerful basis for changing behavior. First, theories are written out and thus are open to public examination. They are objective in the sense of being subject to external validation and verification not only against research and experimental evidence but in personal terms as well. In other words, they derive strength from demonstrated utility.

Theory can aid behavior change in a number of ways.

Values. Theory, with its explicit formulations, brings individuals face to face with their subjective values. What each thinks is right, sound, and valid as a means of relating to subordinates, colleagues, and bosses is subject to testing, common sharing, and review.

Defensiveness. Defensiveness ceases to serve a functional purpose when a person can see and understand that what he or she previously accepted as "right" or "sound" or "valid" is actually untenable in the light of systematic evidence. Theory-based understanding of personal modes of managing and their consequences reduces or eliminates defensiveness.

Perspective. Theory provides individuals a social microscope for viewing the present as well as a social telescope for seeing how the past or a possible future is affecting here-and-now behavior. People are motivated to think through not only short-term consequences but the longer-term implications of various courses of action. This is an effective curb on impulsive actions and their possibly negative effects.

Communication. Theory-based language facilitates dialogue between individuals and their friends, spouses, subordinates, colleagues, and bosses as to the soundest approaches for getting results.

Motivation. Theory specifies the properties of a model of excellence that an individual can aspire to reach.

Creativity. Theory increases people's curiosity about what they observe and they become more imaginative in pursuing creative solutions to managerial problems.

Autonomy. Theory increases an individual's capacity for self-direction. It is less necessary to consult with others because a person can consult with him- or herself as to the implications of various actions being considered.

Not all theories are of equal significance. Some are overly simple in the sense that so few behavioral distinctions are made that dissimilar behaviors are artificially grouped together. Therefore predictive value is severely limited. Others are so overelaborate that users lose their way in attempting to understand them and dismiss most theory as irrelevant. Still others, although called theories, are little more than philosophical speculations as to the nature of man and his motivations. Their appeal is in common-sense terms, but the scientific evidence for validity is lacking.[6,7]

Summary _____

A key difference between academic theory and theory for use in problem solving is not found in the concepts per se, but in the teaching methodology employed by the consultant. Theory can be communicated in such a way that the client first internalizes the concepts, then evaluates them against his or her natural bents. Thereafter the client demonstrates two critical habit-altering patterns: (1) he or she rejects inclinations when they are inconsistent with sound behavior, and (2) practices sound theory-indicated behaviors in order to reinforce the learning and build greater confidence.

The Theory Spectrum aids in distinguishing the deeper meaning of theory as employed in a consultation context. Trial and error, and hunch and intuition, clearly do not involve the use of theory. Often confused with theory are subjective or empirical assertions that are little more than common-sense explanations; or reported attitudes, beliefs, and convictions intended to account for behavior. Conceptual systems or cognitive maps are more elaborate ideas that are put together by consultants to guide the behavior of their clients, or as the basis for explaining differences between the actions of people facing essentially the same situation. Plans and planning are also examples of the use of common sense at the empirical level, but here for the first time can be seen an emphasis on anticipating the future consequences of present actions. Thus plans and planning are calculated to anticipate consequences that are wanted and to provide a basis for taking actions that will permit those consequences to be reached.

The theory end of the Spectrum is represented by systematic behavioral science formulations that have been experimentally determined to have significant implications for predicting the consequences of behavior. They have emerged from extensive behavioral science research concerned with power/authority, morale/cohesion, norms/standards, and goals/objectives. Once the client has learned these theories, has tested his or her natural bents against them, and has learned not only to reject natural-bent activities that lead to difficulties but also to strengthen his or her use of theory as the basis for determining action, the theory-based intervention has had its effect. The client is now able to make the shift to a systematic theory-based set of orientations that explain and give predictive value to behavior. At the far right end of the Spectrum are principles as expressions of lawfulness underlying human behavior; these represent the highest level of using systematic thinking as the basis for identifying and reshaping behavior in optimally effective ways.

Notes

1. R. Harrison, "Defenses and the Need to Know," in W. B. Eddy, W. W. Burke, V. A. Dupre and O. P. South, eds., *Behavioral Science and the Manager's Role* (Washington, D.C.: NTL Institute for Applied Behavioral Science, 1969), pp. 64–70. Reprinted by permission.
2. S. Kingsbury, "Dilemmas for the Trainer," from W. Dyer, ed., *Modern Theory*

and Method in Group Training (New York: Litton, 1972), pp. 107–15. © 1972 by Litton Educational Publishing, Inc. Reprinted by permission of Van Nostrand Reinhold Company.

3. D. McGregor, *The Professional Manager* (New York: McGraw-Hill, 1967).
4. P. B. Vaill, "Towards the Behavioral Description of High Perfoming Systems," in M. W. McCall and M. M. Lombardo, eds., *Leadership: Where Else Can We Go?* (Durham, NC: Duke University Press, 1978), p. 106.
5. R. R. Blake and J. S. Mouton, *Corporate Excellence Through Grid Organization Development* (Houston: Gulf Publishing Co., 1968). Copyright © 1968 by Gulf Publishing Company, Houston, Texas, 2nd ed., 1983, in press. Used with permission.
6. A. Maslow, *Motivation and Personality* (New York: Harper, 1954).
7. P. G. Hersey and K. H. Blanchard, *Management of Organizational Behavior: Utilizing Human Resources,* 3d ed. (Englewood Cliffs, N.J.: Prentice-Hall, 1977).

3

THEORY-PRINCIPLES
INTERVENTIONS

Power/
Authority

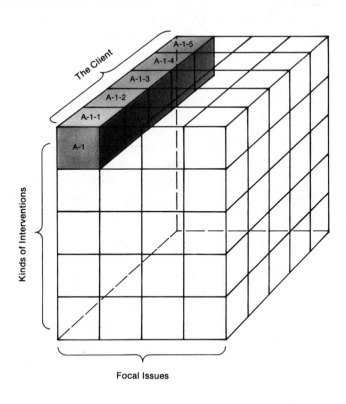

A number of behavioral science theories deal with power/authority as a central concept, and there are a number of published examples of theory interventions. The consultant's objective is to aid the client in internalizing a pertinent theory and then applying it to his or her own situation.

INDIVIDUAL (A-1-1)

Power/authority can only be exercised in the context of interpersonal relationships, yet an individual is often the target of theory-based power/authority interventions. The individual client can be engaged in self-examination as to his or her own assumptions about using power/authority apart from relations taking place with others. Many interventions fit into this category.

The Managerial Grid[1] provides a set of contrasting theories depicting different ways of dealing with others. Grid concepts enable individuals to gain insight into their own power/authority dynamics. A typical first step in this process involves the client in describing his or her managerial behavior in boss-subordinate situations. Secondly, the individual studies the Managerial Grid in order to gain insights regarding the systematic issues it clarifies. This is initially accomplished through reading, but recurs later in an organized seminar situation where participants, through intensive team interactions, have an opportunity to observe one another's Grid styles.

Finally, participants feed back observations on one another's Grid styles by preparing Grid-oriented paragraph descriptions of evidenced behavior. These paragraph descriptions aid participants to carry their self-examination through to meaningful conclusions.

The Managerial Grid, then, provides a framework (Figure 3.1) for comparative thinking about alternative approaches to management and supervision. It identifies thirteen such approaches that are being used in organizations today. Five of these theories—9,1; 1,9; 1,1; 5,5; and 9,9—are "basic." Eight additional possibilities are 9,5; 5,9—"consultative"; and combinations such as 9,1/1,9—"paternalism"; 9,1–1,9 to-and-fro "wide-arc pendulum"; intermittent 9,1 line/1,9 staff "counterbalancing"; the splitting "two-hat" approach, the 9,1–1,1 "win-leave cycle"; and the reactive-around-the-Grid "statistical 5,5," or situationalism.

Once internalized through a theory/principle intervention, Grid concepts provide both a foundation for exercising sound leadership and a system for exploring and addressing interpersonal conflicts. How a boss deals with a subordinate is largely determined by his or her Grid mode of response to conflict. The 9,1 method of conflict resolution is suppression; 1,9 involves smoothing over the differences; 1,1 entails withdrawing into neutrality. 5,5, on the other hand, is an effort to encompass the difference through accommodation and compromise on a "half-a-loaf-is-better-than-none" basis. The 9,9 approach is to confront differences by exploring reservations and doubts and by reviewing the facts, data, and logic bases of the difference. The 9,9 mode of confrontation may involve surfacing and working through any underlying emotional tensions that exist between a boss and a subordinate, thereby restoring a functional problem-solving

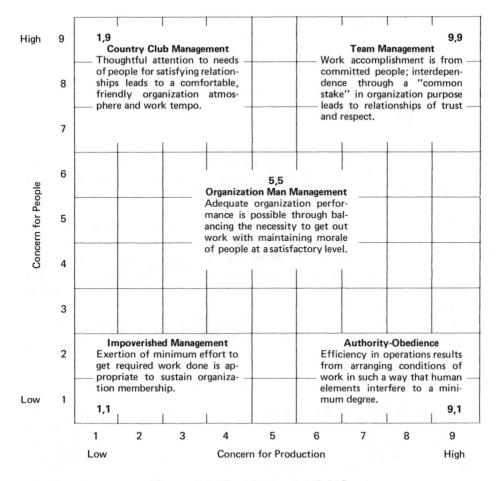

High 9 | **1,9** | | | | | | | **9,9**
Country Club Management | **Team Management**
Thoughtful attention to needs | Work accomplishment is from
of people for satisfying relation- | committed people; interdepen-
ships leads to a comfortable, | dence through a "common
friendly organization atmos- | stake" in organization purpose
phere and work tempo. | leads to relationships of trust
and respect.

5,5
Organization Man Management
Adequate organization performance is possible through balancing the necessity to get out
work with maintaining morale
of people at a satisfactory level.

Impoverished Management | **Authority-Obedience**
Exertion of minimum effort to | Efficiency in operations results
get required work done is ap- | from arranging conditions of
propriate to sustain organiza- | work in such a way that human
tion membership. | elements interfere to a mini-
mum degree.

Figure 3.1 The Managerial Grid®

Source: Blake, Robert R., and Jane S. Mouton. *The New Managerial Grid*. Houston: Gulf Publishing Company. Copyright © 1964, 1978, p. 11. Reprinted by permission.

relationship. These approaches have been further described by Thomas[2] and Filley[3] and researched by Burke.[4]

One way of evaluating the Grid intervention's impact on behavior is in terms of quantitative studies reflecting participants' own post-seminar reports of behavioral or perceptual change. Results of such studies are shown in Table 3.1 where comparison is made between how 3,590 individual participants described themselves before attending a seminar and after completing it. For example, 66 percent of the participants described themselves in pre-seminar exercises as operating from a 9,9 orientation. Participants' post-seminar descriptions reflect

Table 3.1 Personal grid style descriptions pre- and post-seminar

Style	9,9	9,1	5,5	1,9	1,1
Pre-seminar	66.3	14.3	17.3	1.7	0.4
Post-seminar	19.4	38.1	35.9	5.6	1.0
Difference	−46.9	+23.8	+18.6	+3.9	+0.6

only 19 percent 9,9 responses to the same set of exercises. This 46.9 percent reduction in 9,9 choices reflects the pervasiveness of self-deception. What participants thought was 9,9 prior to the seminar was in fact partly the 5,5, partly the 9,1 (and partly the paternalistic) orientations.

These data are based on reactions by many managers from different companies. The results demonstrate that self-deception is a general characteristic of people, and therefore of organizations. The frequency of individual reactions related to self-reappraisal is presented in Table 3.2. The nature of reported changes can be drawn from interviews conducted in one company with fourteen members of the same department.

Table 3.2 indicates that all participants initiate some degree of self-reappraisal following a Grid intervention. The following quotations from seminar participants clarify what is meant by *some self-reappraisal* in comparison with *searching self-reappraisal*.

A typical *some self-reappraisal* reaction follows:

> I can't say that I have changed much. At least I haven't modified my approach to people and their ideas too far. I have not shifted away from the direction in which I was already operating. However, I do think I have changed in degree. I am doing a better job now than I was doing previously. I feel more confident that I am on the right track. Therefore, I am working more diligently to increase my skill, but I'm moving in the same direction.

An example of self-reappraisal which is in the *searching self-reappraisal* category is as follows:

> After I got rocked and knocked on my heels a half dozen times at the laboratory and had spent two sleepless nights, I decided something was basically wrong. A serious, deep review of my own performance was in order. I spent considerable thought afterward in reviewing what I had heard about my own approach and attitudes during the laboratory. I looked into each of the major areas where it seemed to me important suggestions had been made. I set a concrete plan of personal improvement for myself. As a result I have been able to keep constant check on my own progress. While I feel I have not come too far, I remain convinced that it is possible for me to change. I intend to continue my effort.

Another reaction is typical of those categorized as making a *searching self-reappraisal*. This person remarked:

I continuously use stored-up bits of information gleaned from the laboratory to appraise myself. I do this in terms to understand why I am not
so effective in certain situations. I keep in view the question, 'How, through
better understanding, might I make a more adequate contribution?' It
seems I have been able to make some progress up to this time.

Table 3.2 The degree of self-reappraisal produced by the seminar

Initiated no self-reappraisal of my personal behavior	Initiated some self-reappraisal of my personal behavior	Initiated a searching self-reappraisal of my personal behavior
Percent* reporting 0	40	60

* For ease of reading, numbers in all tables have been converted to percents.

The general conclusion drawn from these reactions is that widespread self-
reappraisal may have contributed to actual increased effectiveness. The effectiveness issue is addressed in Table 3.3.[5]

Table 3.3 Changes in managerial effectiveness after the seminar as judged by interviewers

Less effective	No significant change	More effective
Percent reporting 7	20	73

To fully explain such changes one must understand that more effective
performance resulted to a significant degree from altered personal attitudes
toward conflict and how best to deal with it. The 9,9 way of dealing with conflict
involves confronting differences and working them through to achieve understanding and agreement. Table 3.4 reflects trends observed through interviews
regarding personal perceptions as to the significance of managing conflict.

From Table 3.4, it is apparent that one significant area of rethinking directly
involves seminar principles associated with managing conflict. The individuals
who pointed to no change in thinking about conflict reported that their characteristic way of dealing with conflict always had been to confront it so, in effect,
they learned nothing new. For those who did report a change, the prevailing
direction was toward confronting conflict and working it through. Eighty-six
percent of the respondents indicated that significant shifts in their attitudes
toward dealing with conflict had taken place.

It is increasingly apparent that conflict is a pivotal area upon which managerial effectiveness hinges. Once people who work together learn to deal effectively with conflict, problem-solving energies can be focused on discovering and
implementing better ways of integrating people into production.

Table 3.4 Significance of understanding situation conflict and "working it
through"

Dealing with conflict has become less important in my thinking	No change	Dealing with conflict has become more important in my thinking
Percent reporting 0	14	86

Another theory/principle intervention with individual managers utilized
Likert's System 4 theory for dealing with issues of style and behavior. The aim
of the intervention was to aid internal consultants to deal more effectively with
their line manager clients as they attempted to solve problems and make work-
related decisions. Each line manager was assigned one or more internal consultants. Together they attended five-day T-group laboratories. Instruments
based on Likert's theory were completed in advance of the laboratory by the
line manager's subordinates and during the laboratory by other managers to
describe individual, team, and organization behavior. The internal consultant/
line manager pairings collaborated with one another in analyzing, coordinating,
and integrating these several sources of data for personal and organizational
implications.

Dyer et al.[6] reevaluated this project several years after it was completed
and concluded that while it had benefits, one limitation was in the internal consultant's intermediary role. He concluded that line managers themselves should
have had increased responsibility for the entire process of change. The implication is that internal consultants impeded line managers in their efforts to gain
systematic understanding of processes of change and then to exercise personal
responsibility for their implementation. Dyer seems to recommend the alternative of managers learning directly to implement change without reliance on inside intermediaries.

Another limitation of this intervention was the lack of programmed follow-
up between line manager participants and their bosses to gain the upper level
management's ownership of the program, rather than its being a staff training
responsibility. The issue is that the client focused on, the individual, perhaps
was the incorrect target for inducing change by the use of a T-group intervention. Had the organization itself been defined as the unit of change, more real
impact on the organization might have resulted.

Argyris and Schön have concerned themselves with theory-based interventions, recognizing that without internalization, nothing much happens in the way
of change.[7] They refer to the advocated but not internalized theory as the
espoused theory, while they call the prevailing theory the theory-in-use. The two
beliefs may differ without the client sensing any contradiction. Argyris's goal
is to aid people in distinguishing between their espoused theory and their theory-
in-use.

This is done by having a person write, in more or less story form, the details of some important managerial, administrative, or supervisory event, telling what he or she was thinking during conversations, while completing a parallel dialogue reflecting as closely as possible what originally took place. Then the story's author and other students in the program evaluate discrepancies between the two accounts and evaluate the extent to which Argyris's Models I and II are in evidence. The author receives minimal evaluative feedback and is confronted with any inconsistency, incongruity, and ineffectiveness. Models I and II are essentially equivalent to the 9,1 and 9,9 orientations.

An example that demonstrates how this intervention is conducted follows.

MINISTER

The Sunday after President Nixon's decision to invade Cambodia, 50 members of the church met to determine what response they could make. One response was to hold a protest demonstration on the front lawn of the church. That meant seeking the permission of the executive committee, which is responsible for use of the property, or bringing the matter before the congregation for approval. The latter course of action would have required a lapse of several days so members of the congregation could be notified, whereas the executive committee was scheduled to meet the following night. It was decided that a representative group would appear before the executive committee to make an unprecedented request to use the church property for a public protest of U.S. policy in Indochina.

The chairman of the 12-member executive committee is a conservative man who has, in the past, indicated great discomfort when people get upset. He has been told of the unusual request to be made. On entering the meeting room, the chairman found 35 other church members in addition to the executive committee.

This was a pressure setting. It intimidated the chairman, who had not demonstrated flexibility and the capacity to be at ease under pressure in the past.

Chairman: Good evening. I am impressed by the unusual number of our good members who have come here tonight. [The chairman reflects considerable nervousness. After a few opening remarks, he asks the minister to lead the group in prayer.]

The members of the executive committee were assumed to favor the proposal; most people thought it would be passed. To bring the matter before the executive committee rather than to call a special meeting of the congregation made an immediate response to the Cambodian invasions possible, but it

Minister: Lord, these are momentous and agonizing days. Tonight we reflect the anguish that grips our nation and divides its citizens. We need the wisdom of Your spirit as we face hard questions before us. Enable us to be open and compassionate toward one another as we wrestle with left the majority of the church members, particularly the dissenters, with the realization that they had no opportunity to participate in an important decision.

It is clear that I am not neutral regarding the proposal to be made. The institutional church must be responsive to critical current moral issues like this one.

I was convinced that the outcome of the vote would not have been affected whether the executive committee continued in open meeting or in executive session. I did desire full participation by all present, however.

I did not feel that the chairman wanted to hide anything in an executive session but rather that he simply could not cope in the pressure-cooker situation in which he found himself.

I took the position that the chairman's feelings of inadequacy had to be endured by him and that open participation was a goal to be pursued. But, in that room of almost

these questions in the light of our own faith. Amen.

Chairman: We have a group of visitors with us to make a request. After hearing from them, we may want to go into executive session to consider the matter.

Minister: Mr. Chairman, we all know this is a most unusual situation. Everyone in this room is a member of this church. We might want to consider remaining together throughout the evening as we sort out the ramifications of the request that will be set before us.

Chairman: I brought with me tonight *Robert's Rules of Order,* which makes provision for a committee like this to go into executive session.

Minister: You are quite right in pointing up that provision. I think we need to think through, however, how this congregation can best deal with the situation that is before us, and the implications of the action that will be proposed here tonight. Our by-laws indicate that all meetings of the church are open to all members.

Chairman: I thought we might make a more careful, considered judgment if, after hearing the request, we went into executive session.

Minister: We are faced with a matter that is going to be thoroughly aired by church members in the days ahead no matter what decision is made. If our discussion to-

50 people, no more than two or three would have been able to disagree with the proposal. An overwhelming majority favored the proposal, a heavy imbalance which did not represent the feelings of the entire congregation. The chairman moved that an executive session be held and was defeated; the proposal to use the church lawn for a public demonstration was carried by a vote of 10 to 2.

The immediate objective was achieved, but the price was creating a win/lose situation and making many church members feel that they had not been allowed to share in one of the most momentous decisions that had ever been before the church.

night is open to all who are present, we'll have the advantage of hearing all opinions first-hand rather than second-hand.

In reacting to the case description, Argyris and Schön emphasize the following points made by way of feedback.

1. The minister did little to alleviate the chairman's discomfort from the pressures of the meeting.
2. The minister's desire to act quickly precluded participation in the decision by other church members. Ironically, President Nixon had used the same strategy of intervention—he had announced his plans for Cambodia in a way that precluded participation in the decision and made resistance difficult. The minister was shocked to realize that he had used the same tactics by saying there had been so little time. Another participant pointed out that President Nixon had probably used the same excuse. Other participants suggested that the minister should at least have been aware of the dilemma, admitting it to the executive committee.
3. The minister consciously avoided discussing some of his assumptions in order to win. For example, he did not discuss openly the problem of acting quickly versus broader participation.

In a paper the minister wrote after the discussion, he stated:

The comparison to Nixonian tactics hit me very hard; both of us enforcing our will and using our power to accomplish our purposes upon a constituency that contains a significant segment of dissenters. Both of us are convinced that our aims and actions are right and good; both of us create a closed system that leads to self-fulfilling prophecy. That is not my self-conscious aim, *but that is my action.* I own it—painfully.

> The dilemmas remain. At the personal level, it has been a case of survival for me. I have prided myself on my political acumen (Nixon again), and I have survived. Many of my professional peers have not survived and/or have quit the ministry. Over the years when it has come to the moment of the political votes, I have been quite sure in advance that I would "win," and I have staked my ministry upon the church going in a particular direction—the direction I deemed proper and right.

The following week, the minister wrote another paper as a result of reading and thinking about his theory-in-use as constructed in class.

> I am persuaded that my behavior generates a closed system, with nontestable, self-fulfilling results. It is not a self-conscious design, but a result of my doing what comes naturally. That scares me, for it means that my spontaneous behavior produces a system that perpetuates mistrust and diplomacy—and that does not match my self-image of what I want to be and what I want to do.
>
> I know how to win. I have a decade of data in the Church. . . . I don't have to learn how to be 'successful,' but the gap between what I really want to be and what my present behavior now reveals is enormous.[8]

This theory-based intervention is carried out in such a way as to enable the client to penetrate his own rationalizations, justifications, and power tactics. The key element, however, is internalization; the client "tests" the theory against his own "spontaneous" conduct and becomes aware of significant discrepancies and the consequences for himself and others of his reliance on a destructive theory-in-use.

Another intervention with individual managers used two decision-making models to provide rules for alternative degrees of subordinate participation in a manager's decision. As described by Vroom and Yetton the theory focuses on power/authority as the central issue; that is, whether the boss uses his or her own power to make a decision independently or whether and under what conditions others are involved. Model A is economical in the use of time and minimizes participation; Model B allows for maximum participation but places no weight on time consumed. If decision *quality* is all-important the boss must determine whether or not there is sufficient information to reach a decision or if he or she needs the information of others. If *acceptability* is all-important, those who must implement the decision may be invited to participate in order to gain their endorsement of the eventual position. A manager's judgment of the priorities in a given situation determines the model he or she uses.

Part of the model is introduced in the intervention itself and then participants are asked to indicate how they would handle thirty typical managerial dilemmas. An example follows.

> Sharply decreasing profits for the firm have resulted in a directive from top management that makes it impossible to take on any new personnel even to replace those who leave. Shortly after this directive is issued, one of your

five subordinates resigns to take a job with another firm. Your problem is how to rearrange the work assignments among the remaining four subordinates without reducing the total productivity of the group.[9]

Using a series of eight criteria, the client learns to evaluate the recommended ways to go about making decisions regarding these standardized situations. Examples of criteria employed are: "Does the boss have sufficient information?" . . . "Will subordinates accept the boss's decision and implement it well?" Feedback is provided via a computer printout that contrasts each client's resolution of the dilemmas with those of his or her colleagues and with solutions recommended by the consultants. The model of decision quality/acceptance is close to being theory based for it provides an ordered framework for thinking. The client is helped to internalize the framework as a basis for predicting the consequences of actions taken, as well as for comparing his or her natural bent with the requirements of "good" management as conceived by Vroom and Yetton and as incorporated into their model. Empirical evaluations of the model are unavailable.

Transactional Analysis is derived from psychoanalytic theory. It is a theory/principles intervention utilized mostly at the individual level. Its underlying premise is that each person has three basic yet alternative orientations that may operate as he or she relates with other people.

One of these orientations is referred to as Parent. The Parent reflects judgmental "should" and "shouldn't" attitudes that typify evaluations of self and others. A second orientation, the Adult, comprises a problem-solving attitude for dealing with situations encountered in the process of everyday living. This orientation is based on empirical data and the assumption that the individual's problems are solvable. The third orientation is referred to as the Child. The Child orientation involves spontaneity, impulsiveness, and, more generally speaking, reactions that are emotionally rooted.

When any two individuals interact both may be operating from the Parent orientation, or both may be responding from the Adult orientation, or from their respective Child orientations. These are "complementary" transactions, that is, the "lines" between the two persons' orientations do not "cross." Communication between one individual's Parent state and another's Child are also complementary. Asymmetrical "crossed" transactions, as where one person is relating to another out of the Adult orientation and the second is responding from the Child orientation, can lead to significant difficulties in the relationship. Certain consequences follow, depending on which of the three orientations is being employed by each person.

As a consultation-based intervention, Transactional Analysis can be approached in a number of ways. Using it as a basis of self-examination, an individual indicates what his or her characteristic response is to certain described situations. Comparison of these natural reactions with the theoretical model of transactional analysis can now be made. Internalized theory can then be used to identify and implement needed changes. The individual gains insight into the kinds of behavior he or she "naturally" displays as compared with the kinds of behavior, defined according to transactional analysis, that would be a more effective basis for mature adjustment.

Transactional Analysis was originated by Berne[10] and has been popularized through the work of Harris,[11] Steiner,[12] Bennett,[13] and others. Jongeward[14] provides a series of exercises designed to aid an individual in this kind of self-examination. James describes the application of transactional analysis to the boss-subordinate relationship.[15]

Once an individual has learned the basic orientations of transactional analysis and the resulting interactions, he or she has available a systematic framework through which to view and review situations as they happen. In this manner, he or she can become a self-consultant by asking such questions as, "How does transactional analysis apply in this situation and what are my options for improving this situation?"

Blansfield describes his use of Transactional Analysis as a theory intervention with individuals.

In beginning a program using transactional analysis, I usually explain that I am proposing a more structured beginning methodology than group members may have anticipated. I say that, with their concurrence, I will teach them something about a rather new psychiatric theory and ask them to use this lesson for self-analysis and reporting, and that we will then pursue whatever course the group wishes. At this point I always ask for expressions of feeling about the proposals. It seems very important to uncover feelings of resistance to the intervention and to explore them until the whole group selects another beginning methodology or the resistance is overcome. The possibility that one or more members of the group will withdraw has not occurred in my experience to date. (By the beginning of 1969 I had used this methodology with at least twenty-five groups over a four-year period. Groups of mixed sex and professional background, averaging twelve per group, met usually for a week.) The groups to which I have proposed this approach have generally been enthusiastic about trying something new. Our verbal contract has always contained the clear understanding that during the process group members may ask questions or express resistance. Perhaps four persons of some three hundred have actually done so. Questions arise almost exclusively about Berne's theory, not its use in the group.

I next informally poll the group to confirm that we agree about our immediate methodology. If we do, we proceed to a simplified presentation of the theory, a lecture-dialogue that usually lasts about three hours. I try to cover the information and characteristics of the three ego states, their functioning, and the concepts of age fixation in the Child, executive power, contamination, and decommissioning. Berne's theory of transactions is not referred to at this point; it is dealt with later if appropriate. In this initial phase, I try to convey only enough about transactional analysis to enable each participant to describe himself in terms of his understanding of the theory. Nor do I deal extensively at this point with psychopathology or pathogenesis, for the populations I work with are relatively stable and self-selecting and want increased insight and understanding, not psychotherapy.

An early emphasis on neurosis or psychosis might cause them to conceal data they viewed as excessively deviant from group norms.[16]

Blansfield comments that his theory-based interventions with individuals are "concerned with organized self-understanding and, where appropriate and possible, with the alleviation of nonfunctional behavior."

The four approaches described here (Grid, System 4, Models I and II, and Transactional Analysis) are widely employed for helping a given individual gain insight into how he or she subjectively perceives his or her own personal behavior or the behavior of others. Though other people may be actively drawn into the discussions and may offer feedback to help the client clarify thoughts, the theory intervention focuses on individual examination of personal attitudes toward utilizing power/authority. Other equally pertinent theories are not introduced at this time because examples of their use at the individual level are lacking.

GROUP (A-1-2)

Theory/principles interventions have been used to enable several people who interact with one another in group settings to pursue some common objective. The issue of power/authority often is central because in organized groups, such as are found in an industrial setting, the real boss and his or her actual subordinates comprise the work group.

The general strategy of intervention using a theory/principles approach is to involve participants first in learning the theory/principles (as discussed in Chapter 2) and then in utilizing these theories to diagnose, evaluate, and eventually to shift their own bases of interaction.

In team building, using the Grid as the theory basis of intervention, participants first engage in self-learning and self-examination through Grid Seminar participation as already described. Thereafter, when each of the individual members of the team has acquired this basic understanding, they convene for the purpose of studying their own teamwork.

Although this study covers the entire range of dimensions, including power/authority, morale/cohesion, norms/standards, and goals/objectives, a central part of it concentrates upon the power/authority issues.[17] A client's description of the impact of Grid-based team building is provided by the president of a company.

WORK TEAM DEVELOPMENT

The next step was Phase II. These are work team seminars of three days or more as necessary. Our first Phase II involved myself, the executive vice president, vice president for finance, vice president and corporate secretary, vice president for marketing, corporate controller, and director of engineering. This group constitutes the top work team in the company. The tasks undertaken enable each individual in the work team to see how he is viewed as a manager by his immediate associates. This gives him insight into the ways in which he might change to operate more effectively. The group also, as in Phase I, determines what are the barriers to improved effectiveness of the work team. This first Phase II seminar was a most rewarding experience. For a majority of the seven it was even more valuable than the Phase I, and for all of us either confirmed or reconfirmed the validity of the Grid concepts.

BARRIERS TO TEAM EFFECTIVENESS

My work team decided that the greatest barrier to our improved effectiveness was the lack of candor. In our work team and within the company there were certain subjects that were considered too delicate or sensitive to be discussed between us. We defined these as the "sacred cows" of the organization. During our three-day seminar, the environment was critiqued in which all of these sacred cows were flushed out. As a result, action decisions were made to deal with the sacred cows, whose demise will save the company nearly one million dollars in operating costs in the next 12 months.

The second most serious barrier to improved team effectiveness was seen as the lack of creativity. We concluded that, as a team, the lack of candor was also the principal limitation on creativity. If people feel more free to be candid because the right environment for it exists, the flow of managerial innovation, experimentation, and creativity will increase. We are now seeing increasing candor in the work team situation.

When one considers the lack of candor which characterizes many work relationships, it is worth recognizing that we grow up learning never to be totally candid. As children there are things we feel unable to discuss with our parents. As pupils there are things we cannot discuss with the minister, and in business there are things we cannot discuss with our bosses. Unfortunately, in so many instances it is the things that we feel unable to discuss that are the subjects in most urgent need of discussion and so often of critical nature. It will not be easy to break down the habits of a lifetime which inhibit candor, but if corporations really want to solve their most delicate and sensitive problems, we all need to learn to talk about them. At Simmonds we at least feel we have taken our first steps in the right direction.[18]

Another example of Grid team building involving a top team of a major supermarket chain is described in the following.

This is the team development seminar. It starts the same way as the Phase I, [but] with the boss and his immediate subordinates exploring their managerial styles and operating practices as a work team. They work within the 9,9 management style. Taken together, Phase I & II unblock communication barriers between people, amongst other things. Here's how the Grid worked for Gerry Spitzer.

"In the past, when we would set budgets, I would calculate what each department would get. For example, say we had a budget of $300 million. I would say to the fellows: 'You Max Grossner (produce sales manager), you get $30 million'—or however it works out. Then they would yell and complain, 'Why did you give me this?' I would say, 'This is the way it is boys, I'm the boss.' "

"Now, since we went to Grid last year, there's no such happening. I say, 'This is the pie. How are we going to divide it.' Perhaps we've got to reduce our margin in meat. We know we've got to make it up somewhere else. The groups comes to a decision. This year it took us an hour-and-a-half to set our budget. Before Grid, we were in there for eight solid hours of table-pounding. But now we were committed. . . ."[19]

McGregor has postulated two theories, X and Y, identifying opposing views of human motivation.[20] When used as a theory intervention for group self-study purposes, members are asked first to indicate their characteristic ways of interaction prior to the presentation of Theories X and Y. Theories are introduced and then can be further employed to evaluate whether or not members see their interactions in the same way after the theory is understood. Sound and unsound behavior is subject to identification. The final step is to plan how to move toward a more desirable interaction mode.

The characteristics of Theories X and Y are summarized in Table 3.5.

Table 3.5 McGregor's Theories X and Y

Assumptions	
Theory X	**Theory Y**
1. Work is inherently distasteful to most people.	1. Work is as natural as play if conditions are favorable.
2. Most people have little ambition or desire for responsibility and prefer to be directed.	2. For achieving organizational goals, self-management is often indispensable.
3. Most people have little capacity for creativity involving organization problems.	3. Creativity for solving an organization's problems is widely distributed throughout its membership.
4. Motivation occurs at a bread-and-butter survival level.	4. Rewards which satisfy ego and social needs as well as bread-and-butter needs, conduce to self-control in line with organizational objectives.
5. Most people must be closely controlled and often coerced to achieve organizational objectives.	5. The capacity for creativity is underutilized in organizations.

Implications for teamwork	
Theory X	**Theory Y**
1. Authority flows unilaterally from superior to subordinate.	1. Authority flows from formal and informal sources, up, down, and across the team.
2. Span of control is narrow and supervision is close.	2. Span of control is wide, with supervision being general rather than detailed.
3. The individual is considered as an isolated unit, and work is organized primarily in terms of his physiological being.	3. The individual is considered as a social-psychological-physiological being and the structuring of his work does not ignore the fullness of man.
4. Work is routinized.	4. The task is a meaningful whole, providing some variety and requiring some skill and judgment.

Using these two models McGregor also developed a set of scales for use in group development. The left side of each scale represents X, the right side, Y. At the beginning of an intervention, members rate the team on these seven-point scales. Then the team members discuss the situation as indicated by an average score for any item of less than 5, or for any scale where there is a wide range of differences in individual ratings. Finally team members consider and identify causative factors operating in certain situations. In using scales such as these McGregor points out that "it is important to agree in advance of any individual rating, [that] although any member may *volunteer* comment about his own rating, [he or she is not compelled to do so]."[21] If the consultant knows the team by virtue of having worked with its members previously, he or she also may complete the scales. These ratings may also be used as data, either as a part of the statistical summary or as a basis of comparison in order to give the team the benefits of an "expert" outside view. McGregor's experience is that ratings by most groups using these kinds of scales tend to be unrealistically high, particularly upon the first attempt. He therefore suggests that, after an initial discussion, it is better to wait a week or two and then readminister the scales, this time in a regular meeting dealing with normal operating problems.

One of the advantages of such a set of scales is that the consultant, by including certain items, can ask the team to deal with issues it might not have recognized as being important. For example, McGregor's scales include questions concerned with mutual trust and mutual support, communications, listening, team objectives, conflict, use of member resources, how control is exercised, and

Table 3.6

Scale	Theory X						Theory Y
Trust	High suspicion						High trust
	1	2	3	4	5	6	7
Support	Every man for himself				Genuine concern for each other		
	1	2	3	4	5	6	7
Communication	Guarded, cautious				Open and authentic		
	1	2	3	4	5	6	7
Listening	We don't listen to each other				We understand and are understood		
	1	2	3	4	5	6	7
Team Objectives	Not understood				Clearly understood		
	1	2	3	4	5	6	7
Conflicts	Deny, avoid, or suppress				Accepted and "worked through"		
	1	2	3	4	5	6	7

"organization climate." Most of these are not issues that managers spontaneously raise in day-to-day work in such clearcut terms. These particular questions are not the only ones that might be asked; indeed, team members might be asked to invent their own scales. McGregor points out that managers may then become too preoccupied with mechanics rather than data. The main purpose is to provide each member with information about how others perceive the team in comparison with his or her own team perceptions. Evidence of perceptual discrepancies yields important clues as to how group effectiveness can be improved.

Power/authority problems abound in husband/wife interactions. Unless the conflict involved in working out power/authority differences is resolved, morale/cohesion is likely to be adversely affected with the probable consequence of either further intense combativeness or mutual withdrawal.

A theory-based intervention designed to aid husband-wife pairs to study their approaches to resolving power/authority problems is offered by Bach and Wyden. They have originated a "fight training" approach for improving relations between couples. The idea is this: it is more or less natural for couples to fight; but many, in doing so, do not make their relationships more livable. "Clean" fighting can be part of a healthy basis for living together because it provides a means of clearing tensions away and enables partners to maintain a fresh and vital relationship. The thesis is, "intelligent fighting regulates the intensity of intimate involvement by occasionally creating relief from it. It makes intimacy controllable."[22]

Fight training utilizes the value system presented in Table 3.7, which shows the nine categories of interaction present in ongoing behavior. These categories can be scored by each member of a couple or by the couple together to indicate how "clean" or "dirty" some specific fight they have had has been. The diagram shown can be used as a comparison model by plotting data submitted by both husband and wife. The higher "positive" end of the column for each category represents the kind of *constructive* fighting that helps the relationship to grow and change; the lower end denotes more and more "negative" fighting, or fighting that leaves bitterness in its wake.

Fight-training participants learn how to use the Fight Elements Profile diagram by attending sessions where several couples, meeting with the consultant, reenact earlier or recent fights, or get into spontaneous fights during the session itself. Through alternately observing and/or participating in these, giving feedback to other couples, and getting feedback from other participants and the consultant over a three-month period, clients learn to accurately describe various kinds of behavior throughout the range of each of the nine categories. They learn to "pilot" themselves and to study changes in their fight styles as the seminar proceeds.

Mastering the scoring system (usually after only six fight-group sessions) and then using it to score tape-recorded fights at home and live fights in front of a trainee group (who independently score and later compare) enables trainees to reinforce the all-important belief that they can learn to fight fair and informatively with a minimum of injury.[23]

Table 3.7 The fight elements profile

Category of interaction	1 Reality	2 Injury	3 Involvement	4 Responsibility	5 Humor	6 Expression	7 Communication	8 Directness	9 Specificity
+ or bonding	Authentic, realistic	Fair, above belt	Active, reciprocal	Owning up	Laugh with relief	Open, leveling	High, clear, reciprocal feedback	Direct focus	Specific
0 or neutral									
− or alienating	Imaginary	Dirty, below the belt	Passive, or one-way	Anonymous or group	Ridicule, clowning or laugh-at	Hidden or camouflaged	Static, one-way, no feedback	Displaced focus	General "analysis"

Source: G. R. Bach and P. Wyden, *The Intimate Enemy: How to Fight Fair in Love and Marriage* (New York: Avon Books, 1970), p. 163. Reprinted by permission of William Morrow & Co., Inc., New York.
The "plus" (+) positions on the profile represent good (or "bonding") styles of aggression.
The "minus" (−) positions represent poor (or "alienating") styles of aggression.
The middle (0) positions indicate styles rated as neutral, irrelevant, or unobservable.
The profile is complete when one line is drawn to connect all nine dimensions, intersecting each dimension at the appropriate level. (+ or − or 0). When the line stays predominantly above the "0" level, the fight was fought in a predominantly bonding style. When the line stays predominantly below the "0" level, the fight was fought in predominantly alienating style.

The scoring system is devised so as to avoid the conclusion that either partner has won or lost. Bach's axiom is that learning how to fight in the context of an intimate relationship is like learning how to dance, not how to box. If *both* don't win, both lose.

Bach and Wyden point out that a man and a woman who live together get to know each other's sensitive and weak points ("Achilles' heel"). This enables either person to "hit" the other where it will hurt most. For example, a doctor's wife knew

> that he felt guilty because he treated relatively few nonpaying clinic patients. So she needled him by calling him "money mad." Yet she refused to listen when he tried to level with her. He attempted to find out how she might feel about living on a reduced income, but she would not discuss it.[24]

Couples may find themselves leveling with each other regarding their motives for "going for the Achilles' heel." The doctor's wife mentioned earlier explained her motivations to their fight-training group,

> Sure I fought dirty! But only when you overwhelmed me and had me in a corner. I got tired of losing practically all the time. Anybody would! So the only way I knew how to slow you down was to get at you with a sort of fifth-column approach.[25]

Before entering fight training the husband had been unaware of how he had actually prompted her needling tactics. Similarly, she had been misreading his valuation of her as well as his behavior toward her. With these and other mutual misconceptions removed, their fighting could progress to levels that have a positive, health-promoting effect on their relationship.

As already described, transactional analysis has other points of application beyond self-examination. One is concerned with aiding husbands and wives in the study of their interaction in order to move more in the direction of Adult-Adult communication. In addition, there are examples of how transactional analysis can be employed with parents and children in family group development.[26]

Parents and children are in power/authority relationships in the sense that society expects parents to exercise authority in behalf of their children's growth and development. As in management or husband/wife relations, power/authority conflicts often become win-lose struggles. Gordon[27] describes a theory-based intervention designed to help parents use the power/authority available to them in ways that solve rather than create or aggravate parent-child problems. He describes three contrasting ways of resolving conflict: "Parent wins" (Method I); "Child wins" (Method II); and "Both win" (Method III). Unfortunately, paternalism, wherein the parent wins but the child's defeat is appeased or smoothed over, is not dealt with, yet it is one of the most common and often destructive ways of resolving differences.

In the following example, a father and his twelve-year-old daughter resolve conflict by Methods I and II respectively. First, a conflict is generated.

> *Jane:* 'Bye. I'm off to school.
> *Parent:* Honey, it's raining and you don't have your raincoat on.
> *Jane:* I don't need it.
> *Parent:* You don't need it! You'll get wet and ruin your clothes or catch a cold.
> *Jane:* It's not raining that hard.
> *Parent:* It is too.
> *Jane:* Well, I don't want to wear a raincoat. I hate to wear a raincoat.

Then one of the two win-lose outcomes is reached. One outcome is as follows.

> *Parent:* Now, honey, you know you'll be warmer and drier if you wear it. Please go get it.
> *Jane:* I hate that raincoat—I won't wear it!
> *Parent:* You march right back to your room and get that raincoat! I will not let you go to school without your raincoat on a day like this.
> *Jane:* But I don't like it. . . .
> *Parent:* No "buts"—if you don't wear it your mother and I will have to ground you.
> *Jane* (angrily): All right, you win! I'll wear the stupid raincoat!

Another possibility for an outcome is:

> *Parent:* I want you to.
> *Jane:* I hate that raincoat—I won't wear it. If you make me wear it, I'll be mad at you.
> *Parent:* Oh, I give up! Go on to school without your raincoat, I don't want to argue with you anymore—you win.

Either or both types of resolution are familiar yet unsatisfying. The first is a 9,1 parent orientation. The second is the 1,1 parental withdrawal from the problem. One of the consultant's initial interventions is to trace and compare the different working principles that have operated so as to produce each outcome.

METHOD I

Parent and child encounter a conflict-of-needs situation. The parent decides what the solution should be. Having selected the solution, the parent announces it and hopes the child will accept it. If the child does not like the solution, the parent may first use persuasion to try to influence the child to accept the solution. If this fails, the parent usually tries to get compliance by employing power and authority.

This is a classical description of the 9,1 orientation.

METHOD II

Parent and child encounter a conflict-of-needs situation. The parent may or may not have a preconceived solution. If he does, he may try to persuade the child to accept it. It becomes obvious that the child has his own solution and is attempting to persuade the parent to accept it. If the parent resists, the child might then try to use his power to get compliance from the parent. In the end the parent gives in.[28]

Though the particular theory being employed by the parent is not clear, this situation depicts either a 1,1 or 1,9 orientation.

In effect, the Method I and Method II summaries serve as simple models that help clarify the dynamics of win-lose conflicts. Furthermore, as the assembled parents-as-client compare the two win-lose models and discuss with the consultant various longer-term consequences of employing either of them, the "structured ineffectiveness" of both Methods I and II probably becomes even more apparent. Such insights are way stations rather than end objectives from the consultant's point of view, for

> The dilemma of almost all parents who come to our P.E.T. classes seems to be that they are locked in to either Method I or Method II, or oscillate between the two, *because they know of no other alternative to these two ineffective "win-lose" methods.* We find that most parents not only know which method they use most frequently; they also realize both methods are ineffective. It is as if they know they are in trouble, whichever method they use, but do not know where else they can turn. Most of them are grateful to be released from their self-imposed trap.[29]

As a further contrast to Methods I and II, and an alternative to them, at this point the consultant introduces Method III. The summary of this "model" is as follows:

> Parent and child encounter a conflict-of-needs situation. The parent asks the child to participate with him in a joint search for some solution acceptable to both. One or both may offer possible solutions. They critically evaluate them and eventually make a decision on a final solution acceptable to both. No selling of the other is required after the solution has been selected, because both have already accepted it. No power is required to force compliance, because neither is resisting the decision.

For illustration, here is how the raincoat issue might be resolved by Method III, as reported by the parent involved.

Jane: 'Bye, I'm off to school.
Parent: Honey, it's raining outside and you don't have your raincoat on.
Jane: I don't need it.
Parent: I think it's raining quite hard and I'm concerned that you'll ruin your clothes or get a cold, and that will affect us.
Jane: Well, I don't want to wear my raincoat.
Parent: You sure sound like you definitely don't want to wear that raincoat.
Jane: That's right, I hate it.
Parent: You really hate your raincoat.
Jane: Yeah, it's plaid.

Parent: Something about plaid raincoats you hate, huh?

Jane: Yes, nobody at school wears plaid raincoats.

Parent: You don't want to be the only one wearing something different.

Jane: I sure don't. Everybody wears plain-colored raincoats—either white or blue or green.

Parent: I see. Well, we really have a conflict here. You don't want to wear your raincoat 'cause it's plaid, but I sure don't want to pay a cleaning bill, and I will not feel comfortable with you getting a cold. Can you think of a happy solution that we both could accept? How could we solve this so we're both happy?

Jane: (Pause) Maybe I could borrow Mom's car coat today.

Parent: What does that look like? Is it plain-colored?

Jane: Yeah, it's white.

Parent: Think she'll let you wear it today?

Jane: I'll ask her. [Comes back in a few minutes with car coat on; sleeves are too long, but she rolls them back.] It's okay by Mom.

Parent: You're happy with that thing?

Jane: Sure, it's fine.

Parent: Well, I'm convinced it will keep you dry. So if you're happy with that solution, I am too.

Jane: Well, so long.

Parent: So long. Have a good day at school.[30]

It is noteworthy that Jane's actual reason for not wanting to wear her raincoat failed to emerge during either the Method I or Method II disputes. In the polarized conflict she did not find it a useful missile to hurl at her parents. In the joint-search Method III or 9,9-oriented discussion, however, it was identified as information that had a bearing on both the problem and a solution.

While parents may quickly perceive Method III as a promising new alternative, this by no means implies that they accept it or are capable of putting it to work. Further stages of training are devoted to developing and strengthening Model III skills. These excerpts illustrate the usefulness of contrasting models of conflict resolution in bringing to clients' awareness the principal working parts of defective yet established systems of conflict resolution.

The several theories used as the basis of intervention in power/authority problems have both differences and similarities. The most characteristically shared feature is their common emphasis upon the importance of conflict as a significant issue that can strengthen or weaken relationships, depending on how it is dealt with. The Grid, which identifies a number of different ways of dealing with conflict, is the approach which most concentrates on conflict resolution. Bach's fight training appears the next most concerned with issues of conflict, with Gordon's approach third. While transactional analysis recognizes the importance of conflict, it is not treated as straightforwardly as in these other three approaches. Finally, implications regarding the importance of conflict can be observed in McGregor's Theories X and Y, but the management of conflict is not central in this approach. Argyris does not single out conflict resolution as a central concept.

The most significant differences among these several theories involve the extent to which they examine and attempt to change correlated aspects of behavior that also influence the quality of relationships. The Grid is a theory-based approach to intervention, not only in terms of its use for unraveling dilemmas in the area of power/authority but also for solving problems of interaction that relate to morale/cohesion, norms/standards, and goals/objectives. It is a tested theory in terms of its applicability to various kinds of group settings. For example, it can be applied to management teams,[31] salesman/customer problems,[32] or husband/wife interactions.[33] The Grid has also been utilized in school settings to evaluate administrator interactions,[34] and so on.

Transactional analysis also has numerous applications. The writings of Berne show its utility in mental-health problem situations. A number of adaptations illustrate its relevance for dealing with managerial and family situations as well.

McGregor's Theories X and Y, Gordon's methods of problem solving, and Bach's fight training are of a more or less comparable order, albeit with a somewhat narrower scope.

INTERGROUP (A-1-3)

Win/lose (i.e., 9,1-oriented) power struggles between groups also are susceptible to resolution through theory-based interventions.[35] The strategy already has been described in connection with both group development and self-examination at the individual level and this section extends its application to situations between groups.

Grid approaches are available that enable participants to characterize the situation between their own and a contending group as it currently exists and as it would be if it were sound. Once this kind of description has been completed by group members, the contending groups are convened and asked to describe what would constitute their ideal intergroup relationship. The two groups then meet together to share with each other their ideal-relationship formulations. Once these images have been presented, the two groups, working through representatives but in the hearing of everyone, reach agreement as to what the future ideal relationship should be.

Returning to work as separate groups, each next characterizes the actual here-and-now intergroup relationship. Once completed the two groups again reconvene in a general setting, as intact groups. Through representatives they exchange their images of the present state of intergroup affairs. As a final step, the two groups set goals as to the steps necessary for shifting their relationship from what it is to what it should become.

Theory is basic. Without theory there would be little possibility of achieving 9,9 win-win conditions wherein both groups are able to cooperate more effectively. With theory translated into practice, groups can form a healthy and productive relationship. Adherence to Grid principles precludes being separated by a win-lose fight of the 9,1 sort, or in a 1,9 way avoiding interaction on matters that would produce conflict, or maintaining walls of isolation in a 1,1 sense, or even collaborating but on a 5,5 compromise-accommodation basis. With theory for what constitutes a sound relationship widely shared it becomes more possible for group members to behave in terms congruent with theoretical specifications. Integration is strengthened in order that group interdependence become productive rather than destructive.

Intergroup relations can be improved by group members on both sides of a cleavage committing themselves to superordinate goals. This is further enhanced by threat from external forces as was seen in the 1982 renegotiations of contracts in the U.S. automobile industry, when both unions and managements made concessions in the interests of increasing the competitiveness of the automobile industry.

An example of intergroup problem solving involving a headquarters-field relationship is described below. The headquarters manufacturing vice-president and his group were trying to modernize the entire manufacturing operations of the company. However, the particular plant involved was seen as having a parochial and narrow perspective, paying attention to its own problems but not seeing the larger opportunities for growth and development occasioned by the rapid changes occurring in the company as a whole.

Steps as outlined above were introduced. A picture of reactions is provided by a participant in the situation.

> Looking back six months after the headquarters-field team training session, relationships between the headquarters officers, and the biggest plant, are close to being beautiful to observe. Before, they were pretty good, and we bragged about them, but we now see that they were beset by many of the doubts and questions and skepticisms that do so much to undermine real understanding. Furthermore, we uncovered and resolved one shipping issue that was having an adverse effect on profit, but before the training we didn't know how to bring the issue into focus so that we could work on it.
>
> Both the headquarters and the plant personnel speak frequently about how much better things are as a result of the team training. Really, for the first time, I can say that our headquarters and plant people are collaborating effectively on a basis of mutual assistance. This is something I have been striving for over a period of years and this kind of result is therefore extremely gratifying.[36]

Another example of intergroup development using theory-based interventions, but now involving lateral rather than vertical groups, is illustrated in the following.

> Phase III concerns intergroup relations and lasts three days. It might bring together sales with manufacturing, or warehousing [or any other groups whose relationships are characterized by disrupting tensions].
>
> At first, the groups meet in separate rooms. Zeke Ferley's group (he's director of distribution) would discuss:
>
> How does our department relate to sales?

How do we see ourselves operating now?

Can we improve?

Then Ferley's people sit down with Spitzer's people and explain their answers. (There's either tacit agreement or heated discussion.) They exchange papers and go off to separate rooms.

"When they return," says Suffrin, "hopefully they'll have reached agreement on key points. If not, they'll set up task force committees to report back to the group on what progress they've made."[37]

The two examples, one of a vertical and one of a horizontal intergroup situation, demonstrate how theory-based interventions can be used to strengthen the integration between groups that must collaborate if they are to contribute to the larger purposes of the organization.

As briefly mentioned earlier, when two subsidiaries of the same parent organization were instructed to merge themselves into a single unit,[38] conflict arose over integrating the efforts of people who formerly had belonged to two independent subsystems into one organization. Called in for another purpose, the consultants first focused attention on the merger dilemma and, as the initial step, used the standard Blake-Mouton intergroup intervention design to define problems of the merger.[39] This confrontation was centered on how power and authority are exercised in the subsystems as they currently exist. The theory intervention that followed involved use of the Likert system to measure actual in contrast with ideal ways of leading, with all members of each client organization participating. Participants found that System 4 was desired as the future basis of leadership and one organization had less change to make to reach System 4 as members of the merged organization than did the other. With these agreements in hand, the new chief executive, formerly one of the merging organization's leaders, was appointed. Presumably the new organization emerged along the lines of management specified as ideal during the intervention, but this is not a conclusion that is verified in a commentary on the intervention published eight years later.[40]

An example of a partly theory-based intervention at the intergroup level is by Lorsch and Lawrence, who formulated a contingency theory of organization structure. They base their interventions on a "cognitive map" that is explained to managers prior to intergroup problem analysis. The following are its main points.

1. Any complex social system, such as a company, is composed of differentiated parts.
2. These differentiated parts must be integrated into a unified effort to accomplish corporate purpose.
3. Any part, because of the tasks it performs, develops at least four distinctive attributes, (a) time orientation, (b) interpersonal orientation, (c) internal formal structure, and (d) goal orientation.

The more unlike one another any two interdependent groups are along these four dimensions, the greater the likelihood of difficulties in achieving an effective integration between them. A case example in which this cognitive map was used is presented in Chapter 23. While the authors maintain that a 9,9 kind of approach to conflict resolution is prerequisite to sound intergroup relationships, the intervention as a whole was more catalytic than theory/principle. The consultants first gathered and summarized interview and questionnaire information, and then interpreted their findings in terms of the cognitive map, as follows.

> We explained that the high differentiation in interpersonal and structural attributes was related to the problems of achieving integration, but that the fact the units were occupying the same task and time space seemed to be intensifying the difficulties in achieving collaboration. In this discussion the managers recognized that two things were needed; first a clearer differentiation of the role of the laboratories and second the development of improved integrative devices.[41]

This may have the ring of theory, but no effort is reported for aiding managers to experience the concepts or dynamics underlying intergroup theory. While theory may have guided the consultant's approach, the client was not made privy to the theoretical framework or operation. Internalization under these conditions is impossible. Another limitation of this approach is its emphasis on role specificity. When members of different groups share a superordinate goal and are committed to its achievement, it is less necessary to have a specialized role such as "integrator." Members themselves are alert to and capable of designing appropriate differentiations and achieving desirable integrations. In other words, if the intervention helps participants learn intergroup relations theory, it is less necessary to seek solutions through special role assignments.

ORGANIZATION (A-1-4)

The idea that the power/authority basis of management and supervision might be changed on an organization-wide basis through the use of theory-based interventions is of recent date, tracing back no earlier than the 1950s.

The Grid is a major approach used to strengthen the effective exercise of power/authority throughout an organization. Participants learn Grid theory in the manner described previously except that most organization members gain their basic Grid experience through in-company seminars. Study teams are composed of higher- and lower-ranking organization members on a cousin basis and, therefore, members of teams are not direct bosses and subordinates of one another. This diagonal slice rather than vertical basis of organizing study teams makes it unnecessary for boss and subordinates to face their power/authority difficulties at a time when they are learning theory-based models of excellence for integrating boss-subordinate relationships.

Team building utilizes the Grid in functional settings to solve actual power/authority problems; since this step has been described above, it will not be considered further.[42] When the intergroup situations where interdependence needs to be strengthened in order for the two or more groups to work more effectively together have been worked through, significant progress has been made. Those who manage and supervise an organization can then use power/ authority in a more constructive manner.

Duffin et al. describe an organizational intervention designed to change the use of hierarchy from a boss-dominated approach to one of more participatory planning and problem solving. A county-wide school system had been formed by a forced merger of smaller school boards. The resulting organization "had all the classic behaviors and attitudes of any large-scale merger: mutual suspicion, cries for autonomy, generalized hostility toward the head office, competition for resources, and a collection of principals who were clustered in groups that were somewhat isolated from each other and from the total system."[43] The Board of Trustees down to the elementary school principal level took part in the intervention. Participative management was seen as an approach to alleviating merger related difficulties. The primary intervention was a voluntary organization development laboratory patterned on Grid organization development where participants were first exposed to a Grid-oriented theory base regarding alternative approaches to the use of power/authority. Once learned, this was then applied to the diagnosis, discussion, and resolution of real organizational problems.

> . . . the educational phase of the OD program, a one-week course designed for learning concepts, skills, theory and a specific methodology is to establish . . . such a climate that the individual manager, with his work teams, has an opportunity to confront the assumptions which underlie habitual approaches to management, to establish levels of effectiveness; and to create new alternatives to replace older habits which might be less effective.
>
> The second week the groups identify the significant issues influencing their activities and apply the learnings to the practical problems of managing within and between their specific work groups. During the two-week course, many actions have been identified that need to and can be done to improve the organization. Through joint planning of the boss, his subordinates, with the assistance of the internal consultants, the OD unit, these needed actions become goals and the bases for building a culture for continuing follow-up—learning—action, and organizational improvement . . . through the OD unit's follow-up services and resources, they are now widely viewed as important and as making significant contributions to achieving the system's goals.[44]

Key results are expected. They include: development of team identity; improved vertical communication which facilitates planning and decision making; more effective planning, problem solving, and conflict resolution; and concrete plans and decisions for solving job enrichment issues.

The translation of theory-based learning to job application reported in this case was enhanced by two important factors. First, participants were not asked to apply theory to someone else's problems. By owning the problem, participants had vested interests in working toward identification and application of optimal solutions. Secondly, solutions were sought through the best efforts of the team which was actually experiencing the problem. Not only did the participants own

the problem, they owned the solution as well. In addition, a pattern of cooperation and commitment to participative problem solving was established and reinforced. When evaluated by Croft[45] several years later, it is reported that this
theory-centered organization-wide intervention had proven to have strong positive impact on the school system's effectiveness.

Another major approach to organization development via strengthening the
use of power/authority makes use of Likert's System 1-4 theory. No explicit
effort is made to enable organization members to internalize the concepts involved. Understanding of them on the basis of verbal presentation is presumed
and self-deception disregarded. Combined with survey research and feedback,
the Likert model assists the organization-as-client to assess and change the
character of its human organization. Likert has concluded that differences in
managerial leadership can be reduced to four different categories which are expressed on a continuum from: "exploitive authoritative," "benevolent authoritative," "consultative," and "participative group." Scales such as those illustrated
in Table 3.8, which are designed to indicate variations in boss power from
unilateral to shared power, are used by members to "picture" their management
situation. Summarized, these data are fed back and evaluated against the theory
so as to identify the current character of the human organization. Since the
theory and the scales describe what is required to move toward a "participative
group" style—demonstrated empirically to be the most facilitating for productivity and satisfaction—it becomes possible to plot the steps essential for change.
The direction for improvement is toward the right end of the continuum (shown
on Table 3.8).

This use of data is based on assumptions in the theory/principles approach
in the sense of interpreting data in the light of theory, coupled with assumptions
from the catalytic area regarding consultant interventions. When education-based
interventions beyond "data feedback" are required to strengthen managerial
effectiveness, Likert[46] points out that training via the sensitivity or Grid approaches can serve to reinforce System 4 values and actions. Though Likert's
approach skips the critical steps for internalization, by this caveat he acknowledges that managers must learn to internalize theory before they can use it in a
more fully effective way.

An analysis of the use of System 4 in two General Motors plants provides
an interesting case study, concluding that significant change took place as one
plant sought to move from System 2 to 4. These changes are not specified in
quantitative terms, however, and the report is vague as to whether efforts at
internalization of the theory were involved. Much emphasis is placed on the role
of performance feedback, however.[47]

Research on the validity of System 4 conducted primarily at the Institute of
Social Research of the University of Michigan is of both a statistical and a direct
experimental nature.[48] The statistical evidence can be interpreted in the following way: the closer a work group's leadership is to System 4, the higher the
productivity. This conclusion has been verified in a wide range of studies involving more than 20,000 managers and 200,000 employees.[49] Similar results

Table 3.8 Profile of organizational characteristics

Instructions:

1. On the lines below each organizational variable (item), please place an *n* at the point which, *in your experience*, describes your organization at the present time (*n* = now). Treat each item as a continuous variable from the extreme at one end to that at the other.

2. In addition, if you have been in your organization one or more years, please also place a *p* on each line at the point which, *in your experience*, describes your organization as it was one to two years ago (*p* — previously).

3. If you were not in your organization one or more years ago, please check here ___ and answer as of the present time, i.e., answer only with an *n*.

Organizational variable				Item No.
1. Leadership processes used				
a. Extent to which superiors have confidence and trust in *subordinates*	Have no confidence and trust in subordinates	Have condescending confidence and trust, such as master has in servant	Substantial but not complete confidence and trust; still wishes to keep control of decisions	Complete confidence and trust in all matters	1
. . .				
2. Character of motivational forces a. Underlying motives tapped	Physical security, economic needs, and some use of the desire for status	Economic needs and moderate use of motives, e.g., desire for status, affiliation, and achievement	Economic needs and considerable use of ego and other major motives, e.g., desire for new experiences	Full use of economic, ego, and other major motives, as, for example, motivational forces arising from group goals	6

Source: R. Likert, *The Human Organization* (New York: McGraw-Hill, 1967), pp. 197–98. Reprinted by permission.

have been reproduced in nonbusiness fields such as school systems,[50] hospitals,[51] and government organizations.[52]

Herzberg's motivational concepts[53] focus on working relationships from the standpoint of how management and supervision use power/authority to create a productive work climate. The approach aligns sound and unsound motivations toward productivity in the industrial situation with actual output. Premised on the idea that man's "Animal-Adam" nature is concerned with avoiding "pain from environment," organizations are taught to deal constructively with "hygiene/maintenance" factors such as work layout and physical job demands, wages and salaries, supervisors' fairness and other aspects of personal security, social climate, matters of job orientation, personal status, and so on. When these factors are deficient or absent they detract from production motivation. When present, however, they do not directly enhance production motivation or output. The best their fulfillment can be expected to do is to lessen the individual's preoccupation with the work environment and the accompanying tendencies to find fault with it. A further basic need of man, according to Herzberg,[54] stems from his "Human-Abraham" nature which seeks growth from tasks. Thus the direct "motivators" are task-centered and are largely influenced by a person's immediate boss, with positive motivational variables that include relevant job information, recognition, responsibility, advancement, and intrinsically interesting work. Then the theory points to the productivity motivations as being embedded within the work itself. Research-based evidence for these conclusions is extensive.

Myers has worked as a consultant to increase the alignment between motivational theory and managerial practices in Texas Instruments.[55] His ground rules are that to become fully effective in supporting productivity, motivational theories must (1) find expression in the day-to-day behavior and decisions of supervisors, and (2) be used to design the environment within which work takes place. To accomplish the latter, the corporation as a system was restructured to fit motivation-maintenance concepts by analyzing functions performed by personnel in terms of the function's potential for serving either maintenance or motivation needs. The theory was then explained to managers through large group meetings where they were informed of the company's theory implementation plan.

To meet the first-mentioned criterion—that of strengthening the alignment between theory and supervisory practice—consultant/education interventions were introduced. How the theory was internalized is not indicated but supervisors, in small seminars of from six to ten participants, were given skill practice in applying the theory within their own supervisory jobs and they received direct feedback from their subordinates as one way of deepening the impact. An attitude-measurement program was structured around the motivation-maintenance framework and used to assess progress in satisfying various maintenance-need and motivation-need areas. The following are conclusions regarding this organization-wide program.

It can be useful as a practical framework for codifying intuitive effectiveness and for guiding the inexperienced, but it will not correct a management failure which, for example, permits the appointment of immature or unscrupulous supervisors. The management philosophy which sparked the growth of TI created a fertile environment for introducing motivation-maintenance theory as a mechanism for achieving company goals by providing opportunities for employees to achieve personal goals.[56]

Another theory-based intervention designed to generate organizational change involves altering the organizational structure. The idea that one organization structure of power/authority is necessary but may not provide a sufficient basis for effectively managing an organization has led to the idea that two power/authority structures may be essential. The first organizational structure is used to operate the production system. The second is designed to stimulate, implement, and manage change. One is hierarchical and directive; the other, flat and participative. The same personnel may operate both systems, but in different group compositions and with different reporting relationships.

There are several versions of this basic idea, but the original is by Zand[57] and is called Collateral organization. Without apparent awareness of the work of Zand, Stein and Kanter[58] have recently described the development of a parallel organization in very much the same terms.

The Stein and Kanter version is said to be deduced from Kanter's structural theory. More a cognitive map than a theory, it centers upon the following notions.

1. Individual job effectiveness is partly determined by job description.
2. Relevant aspects of a job description are:
   a. opportunity (advancement, challenge, contribution, and development of competence and skills)
   b. power (access to resources, capacity to mobilize them and tools to apply them).
3. The greater the opportunity and motivation, the greater the productivity.
4. The greater the power, the more effective the performer; the greater the readiness to empower others.

A structural intervention with a high technology firm in the electrical equipment field was intended to create a collateral organization that is in parallel to the production system but that can offer opportunity and provide access to powerful resources and relationships.

The intervention is in five stages and is concerned first with teaching the four points in the conceptual model described above. This instruction, however, does little by way of aiding participants to internalize the insights necessary for changing their own personal effectiveness. This is followed by diagnostic interviews with organization members and with questionnaire data gathered throughout the organization. The third step involves construction of a parallel organization to deal with the diagnostic data and led by a steering committee. In the fourth step, action groups (task forces) take problem-solving initiatives. The final step, integration and diffusion, entails changing performance evaluations to include such things as parallel organization activities and modification of job descriptions.

This intervention is reported to have been successful, but difficulties of diffusion from this location to other locations within the company are acknowledged.

By setting up a parallel organization along the lines of a more participative model in order to promote change the production system is reported over time also to have become more participative. This finding, also reported by Zand,[59] leads to the conclusion that the collateral organization is unnecessary.

The more direct solution is to shift the organization directly rather than through the roundabout approach of a collateral organization. Beyond communicating with the top and revision of job descriptions and performance appraisals, no explicit interventions for integrating the parallel model into the prevailing power/authority system are provided. Team building, intergroup confrontation, and so on are not mentioned as ways of bringing this about. The Kanter model, without the cognitive map she provides, is characteristic of many quality-of-work life projects.[60]

LARGER SOCIAL SYSTEM (A-1-5)

Every social system deals in some way or another with the power/authority problem, for it is central to the maintenance of order. Examples are furnished throughout of interventions at the larger-social-system level that have shifted the power/authority basis of interaction among members of the system. None of these, however, have involved changes induced by theory intervention. Indeed, there appears to be no extant example of theory/principles interventions applied to a larger social system to strengthen the effective utilization of power/authority.

One consideration is whether or not a theory/principle basis of intervention is even possible at this level. Such an intervention would permit members of the larger social system to share common ideas for "best" ways of using power/authority. For example, there is widespread intuitive comprehension of the value of the 9,9 way of managing the power/authority problem, as demonstrated in the following discussion. Participants from many different national groupings and cultures have attended Grid seminars under uniform conditions and have provided the data reported below.

GRID SEMINAR SUBJECTS

The managers completing the instruments are from the middle and higher levels of business, industry, and government organizations. Most are men. All have at least a high school education or its equivalent. The subjects, by geographical breakdown, are from:

■ the United States, 1,477 managers from 607 organizations;

- Canada, 166 managers from 144 organizations;
- England, 326 managers from 106 organizations;
- South Africa, 72 managers from 37 organizations;
- Australia, 146 managers from 50 organizations;
- Japan, 178 managers from 52 organizations;
- South America, 59 managers from 32 organizations (Spanish-speaking countries);
- Middle East, 65 managers from 42 organizations in Iran, Lebanon, Saudi Arabia, Iraq, Jordan, and Yemen.

SETTING

Seminars were conducted over a four-year period according to the same basic design. Translations made it possible for most managers to use their native languages.[61]

Given these conditions, it was found possible to explore a number of questions related to power/authority that are embedded in different larger social systems. Three issues of managerial thinking, attitudes, and performance are represented by the following questions.

1. What is viewed as effective management across various national groupings? (If there are differences in concepts of effectiveness, a manager working outside of the home country faces values that are in conflict with his or her own.)
2. What similarities or differences are there in managerial attitudes and actions across national groupings?
3. Can educational methods be applied to increase understanding between managers from different countries who work together within the same company?

WHAT CONSTITUTES SOUNDNESS?

Organization practices. Managers internalize Grid theory in prework and during the seminar. They are then engaged in experiments designed to answer the question, "What is the best way for a company to operate?" while putting actual practices aside. What managers see as ideal is significant, for actions consistent with ideal concepts are bound to be more acceptable than those that are not.

In seminars, managers are divided into small study teams to debate twenty questions on particular aspects of business, behavior, and organization performance. Five answers (representing the five Grid theories) are supplied. Managers rank the answers from "most sound" to "least sound," selecting responses that represent what they think would be sound practice in an effective organization, not what currently happens in their organizations. If for each of the twenty questions the answer chosen as "most sound" is one representing the same Grid

Table 3.9 Agreement across nations on 9,9 Grid theory as soundest for operating a corporation

Grid theory for operating a corporation	Seminar participant scores for least to most sound (range 20–100)							
	United States	South Africa	Canada	England	Australia	Middle East	South America	Japan
9,9	98.2	99.9	99.8	99.9	100.0	97.6	100.0	99.9
9,1	66.7	65.8	62.4	66.3	65.4	67.0	66.0	65.4
5,5	66.0	65.2	66.3	66.5	64.0	60.0	68.0	65.6
1,9	44.1	44.2	46.5	44.5	46.3	47.6	44.5	46.9
1,1	23.4	24.9	25.0	22.8	24.3	27.8	21.5	22.2

theory or style, the score for that style is 100. If the answers chosen for each of the twenty questions as "least sound" represent the same Grid style, the score for that style is 20.

Data shown in Table 3.9 indicate that, regardless of national grouping, managers agree that the 9,9 orientation represents the soundest way to manage. Differences between one country or another do not have statistical significance. The 9,1 and 5,5 ways of managing were chosen as second best with about equal frequency. Next selected was the 1,9 orientation while the 1,1 approach was selected as the "least sound" for operating a company on an across-country basis.

Managerial values. Along with the issue of how a company should be operated for soundness is the question of how a manager should manage as a boss. Each manager identifies what he or she sees as the best way to solve problems with subordinates. Forty forced-choice questions pair each of the five Grid styles with each other style four times. The managerial behavior described involves boss-subordinate interactions in planning, organizing, directing, and controlling work. Managers select the answer they prefer as representing the more effective way to manage. A weight of three points is assigned each pair. The highest score available for any Grid theory is 48, the lowest is 0. Data in Table 3.10 show that 9,9 again is the theory preferred most. Here 5,5 is second and the others in order are 9,1; 1,9; and 1,1.

When complex aspects of management are evaluated, the 9,9 orientation is endorsed as the theory that makes the most productive use of an organization's members. The data above indicate strongly that theory-based interventions for strengthening the use of power/authority in larger social systems is a practical possibility. That such a theory-based intervention might have practical utility in an actual larger social system remains to be demonstrated, however.

Table 3.10 Agreement across nations on 9,9 Grid theory as soundest basis for individual managerial values

Grid theory for individual managerial values	Seminar participant scores for preference for Grid theories (range 0–48)							
	United States	South Africa	Canada	England	Australia	Middle East	South America	Japan
9,9	41.3	40.8	40.6	40.9	40.1	39.5	41.0	40.3
9,1	25.6	26.1	24.0	26.4	23.2	28.6	25.9	27.2
5,5	30.7	31.5	31.1	30.7	32.5	29.1	32.2	29.8
1,9	17.5	18.1	18.3	17.4	18.6	18.4	17.5	17.1
1,1	4.9	3.5	6.0	4.6	5.6	4.4	3.4	5.6

Source: J. S. Mouton and R. R. Blake, "Organization Development in the Free World," *Personnel Administration* 32, no. 4 (1969): 16–17.

Summary

Use of theory/principles interventions to deal with focal issues involving power/authority is shown to be a post–World War II development. While theories of power/authority were available earlier, they were rarely examined and when examined they were taught in academic rather than functional ways that might permit their internalization. This classical teacher-tell manner enabled the student-as-client to understand what the theories were, but did not aid him or her to test their utility for changing his or her own situation. One of the first of such theories was developed by Mary Parker Follett[62] in 1924. The initial critical experiment was conducted in the late 1930s by Lewin, Lippitt, and White. This experiment identified autocratic, democratic, and laissez-faire styles. It permitted the testing of predictions as to consequences on the performance of children when these approaches were exercised. Empirical results led to the conclusion that democratic practices made a more positive contribution and had fewer adverse side effects than did either the autocratic or laissez-faire leadership models.

It was only after World War II, with the advent of instrumented team learning, that consultants learned how to communicate theory to clients to internalize their learning so as to help them strengthen personal effectiveness. The steps essential for effective internalization of theory are indicated in Chapter 2. They need not be reconstructed here, beyond saying that theory/principles interventions appear to be most effective when individuals are enabled not only to understand the concepts inherent in the theory but also to use the theories to examine their own assumptions about leadership by stripping away self-deception. These appear to be the essential preconditions for actual change in power/authority relationships.

Much theory-based consultation in the power/authority area involves either individual self-examination, or group development or team building with internalization. This takes place in primary work groups and most often on an in-company basis. Such group development as a second step, therefore, involves an actual boss and his or her working interactions with actual subordinates. Theory-based consultation on power/authority issues in such a setting can be an effective way of bringing into focus interaction issues that are causing behavior to be unproductive, thereby encouraging more positive team participation.

The use of theory-based interventions for dealing with lateral and vertical intergroup relationships is less common than is its use for strengthening power/authority throughout an organization in a vertical, or downward, direction.

Basic to the power/authority problem as the focal issue is how protagonists deal with conflicts. All theory-based approaches deal with this fundamental issue in one way or another, either explicitly or incidentally. The basic approaches for dealing with conflict involve five possibilities: suppression, smoothing, withdrawal, compromise and accommodation, or confrontation. The Grid approach, fight training, and Parent Effectiveness Training are direct strategies for grappling with conflict resolution. Theories such as transactional analysis makes no distinction between confrontation and compromise, and theories such as McGregor's X and Y deal only with suppression as contrasted with confrontation. Transactional analysis and Likert's System 4 are not explicit in identifying alternative ways of approaching conflict situations. Thus, although the theories differ in the degree to which they center upon conflict resolution as the basic power/authority issue, and though they differ in the vividness with which they make alternative possibilities explicit to the client, this feature is basic to each of them.

Notes

1. R. R. Blake and J. S. Mouton, *The Managerial Grid* (Houston: Gulf Publishing Co., 1964). Copyright © 1964 by Gulf Publishing Company, Houston, Texas. Used with permission: R. R. Blake and J. S. Mouton, *The New Managerial Grid* (Houston: Gulf Publishing Co., 1978), p. 11.
2. W. I. Thomas and F. Znaniecki, "Three Types of Personality," in C. W. Mills, ed., *Images of Man* (New York: George Braziller, 1960).
3. A. C. Filley, *Interpersonal Conflict Resolution* (Glenview, Ill.: Scott, Foresman, 1975).
4. R. J. Burke, "Methods of Resolving Superior-Subordinate Conflict: The Constructive Use of Subordinate Differences and Disagreements," *Organizational Behavior and Human Performance* 5 (1970): 393–411.
5. R. R. Blake and J. S. Mouton, "Improving Organizational Problem Solving through Increasing the Flow and Utilization of New Ideas," *Training Directors Journal* 17, no. 9 (1963a): 48–57. Reprinted by permission. R. R. Blake and J. S. Mouton, "Improving Organizational Problem Solving through Increasing the Flow and Utilization of New Ideas," *Training Directors Journal* 17, no. 10 (1963b): 38–54. Reprinted by permission.
6. W. G. Dyer, R. F. Maddocks, J. W. Moffit and W. S. Underwood, "A Laboratory-

Consultation Model for Organization Change," in B. Lubin, L. D. Goodstein and A. W. Lubin, eds., *Organizational Change Sourcebook I: Cases in Organizational Development* (San Diego: University Associates, 1979), pp. 23–40.

7. C. Argyris and D. A. Schön, *Theory in Practice: Increasing Professional Effectiveness* (San Francisco: Jossey-Bass, 1974).

8. Ibid., pp. 42–47.

9. V. H. Vroom and P. W. Yetton, *Leadership and Decision-Making* (Pittsburgh: University of Pittsburgh Press, 1973). Reprinted by permission.

10. E. Berne, *Transactional Analysis in Psychotherapy* (New York: Random House, 1961).

11. T. A. Harris, *I'm OK—You're OK* (New York: Harper & Row, 1967).

12. C. Steiner, *Scripts People Live: Transactional Analysis of Life Scripts* (New York: Bantam Books, 1974).

13. D. Bennett, *TA and the Manager* (New York: AMACOM, 1976).

14. D. Jongeward, ed., *Everybody Wins: Transactional Analysis Applied to Organizations* (Reading, Mass.: Addison-Wesley, 1973).

15. M. James, *The OK Boss* (Reading, Mass.: Addison-Wesley, 1975).

16. M. G. Blansfield, "Transactional Analysis as a Training Intervention," in W. G. Dyer, ed., *Modern Theory and Method in Group Training* (New York: Van Nostrand Reinhold Co., 1972), pp. 149–54. Reprinted by permission.

17. Dyer, "A Laboratory-Consultation Model for Organizational Change."

18. G. R. Simmonds, "Organization Development: A Key to Future Growth," *Personnel Administration* 30, no. 1 (1967): 19–24. Reprinted by permission.

19. "Steinberg's: People Are the Pulse," *Food Topics* 22, no. 7 (1967): 9–23.

20. D. McGregor, *The Human Side of Enterprise* (New York: McGraw-Hill, 1960).

21. D. McGregor, *The Professional Manager* (New York: McGraw-Hill, 1967).

22. G. R. Bach and P. Wyden, *The Intimate Enemy: How to Fight Fair in Love and Marriage* (New York: Avon Books, 1970). First published by William Morrow & Co., Inc., 1968. Reprinted by permission of William Morrow & Co., Inc., New York.

23. Ibid., pp. 350–51.

24. Ibid., p. 84.

25. Ibid., p. 84.

26. Harris, *I'm OK—You're OK,* chapters 8, 9, and 10.

27. T. Gordon, *Parent Effectiveness Training* (New York: David McKay, 1970). Reprinted by permission.

28. Ibid., pp. 153–63.

29. Ibid., p. 163.

30. Ibid., pp. 196–97.

31. Blake and Mouton, *The Managerial Grid* (Houston: Gulf Publishing, 1964).

32. R. R. Blake and J. S. Mouton, *The Grid for Sales Excellence* (New York: McGraw-Hill, 1970).

33. R. R. Blake and J. S. Mouton, *The Marriage Grid* (New York: McGraw-Hill, 1972).

34. R. R. Blake and J. S. Mouton, *The Academic Administrator Grid* (San Francisco: Jossey-Bass, 1981).

35. R. R. Blake, J. S. Mouton, and H. S. Williams, "Lateral Conflict," in D. W. Johnson and D. Tjosvold, eds., *Conflicts in Organizations* (Beverly Hills: Sage Publications, 1982).

36. R. R. Blake and J. S. Mouton, "Headquarters-Field Team Training for Organizational Improvement, *Training Directors Journal* 16, no. 3 (1962): 3–11.

37. "Steinberg's: People are the Pulse," *Food Topics* 22, no. 7 (1967): 9–23.
38. A. Blumberg and W. K. Wiener, "One from Two: Facilitating an Organizational Merger," *Journal of Applied Behavioral Science* 7, no. 1 (1971): 87–102.
39. M. G. Blansfield, R. R. Blake, and J. S. Mouton, "The Merger Laboratory: A New Strategy for Bringing One Corporation into Another," *Training Directors Journal* 18, no. 5 (1964): 2–10.
40. A. Blumberg and W. K. Wiener, "The Authors Comment on 'One from Two: Facilitating an Organizational Merger,' " in L. D. Goodstein, B. Lubin and A. W. Lubin, eds., *Organizational Change Sourcebook II: Cases in Conflict Management* (San Diego: University Associates, 1974), pp. 74–76.
41. J. W. Lorsch and P. R. Lawrence, "The Diagnosis of Organizational Problems," in N. Margulies and A. P. Raia, eds., *Organizational Development: Values, Process, and Technology* (New York: McGraw-Hill, 1972), pp. 218–28. Reprinted by permission.
42. R. R. Blake and J. S. Mouton, *Building a Dynamic Corporation Through Grid Organization Development* (Reading, Mass.: Addison-Wesley, 1969).
43. R. Duffin, A. Falusi, P. Lawrence and R. B. Morton, "Increasing Organizational Effectiveness," *Training and Development Journal* (April 1973): 37. Copyright 1973, *Training and Development Journal,* American Society for Training and Development. All rights reserved. Reprinted with permission.
44. Ibid., pp. 38–39.
45. J. C. Croft, "Thornlea Ten Years Later," in L. D. Goodstein, B. Lubin and A. W. Lubin, eds., *Organizational Change Sourcebook I: Cases in Organization Development* (San Diego: University Associates, 1979), pp. 19–23.
46. R. Likert, *The Human Organization* (New York: McGraw-Hill, 1967). Reprinted by permission.
47. W. F. Dowling, "At General Motors: System 4 Builds Performance and Profits," *Organizational Dynamics* (Winter 1975): 23–38.
48. R. Likert, *The Human Organization: Its Management and Value* (New York: McGraw-Hill, 1967).
49. R. G. Likert and J. G. Likert, *New Ways of Managing Conflict* (New York: McGraw-Hill, 1976).
50. B. Cullers, C. Hughes, and T. McGreal, "Administrative Behavior and Student Dissatisfaction: A Possible Relationship," *Peabody Journal of Education,* January 1973: 155–63. F. Feitler and A. Blumberg, "Changing the Organization Character of a School," *The Elementary School Journal* (January 1971): 206–15.
51. B. S. Georgopoulos and F. C. Mann, *The Community General Hospital* (New York: Macmillan, 1962). B. S. Georgopoulos and A. Matejko, "The American General Hospital as a Complex Social System," *Health Service Research* 2, no. 1 (1967): 76–112.
52. D. P. Warwick, M. Meade and T. Reed, *A Public Bureaucracy: Politics, Personality, and Organization in the U.S. State Department* (Cambridge, Mass.: Harvard University Press, 1975).
53. F. Herzberg, B. Mausner, and B. B. Snyderman, *The Motivation to Work* (New York: John Wiley, 1959).
54. F. Herzberg, *Work and the Nature of Man* (Cleveland: The World Publishing Co., 1966).
55. M. S. Myers, "Who Are Your Motivated Workers?" *Harvard Business Review* 42, no. 1 (1964): 73–88.
56. Ibid.
57. D. E. Zand, *Information, Organization, and Power: Effective Management in the Knowledge Society* (New York: McGraw-Hill, 1981).

58. B. A. Stein and R. M. Kanter, "Building the Parallel Organization: Creating Mechanisms for Permanent Quality of Work Life," *Journal of Applied Behavioral Science* 16, no. 3 (1980): 371–88.

59. Zand, *Information, Organization, and Power.*

60. J. A. Drexler and E. E. Lawler, "A Union-Management Cooperative Project to Improve the Quality of Work Life," *Journal of Applied Behavioral Science* 13, no. 3 (1977): 373–87.

61. J. S. Mouton and R. R. Blake, "Organization Development in the Free World," *Personnel Administration* 32, no. 4 (1969): 13–23.

62. L. Urwick, *Dynamic Administration: The Collected Papers of Mary Parker Follett* (New York: Harper, 1940).

4

THEORY-PRINCIPLES INTERVENTIONS

Morale/ Cohesion

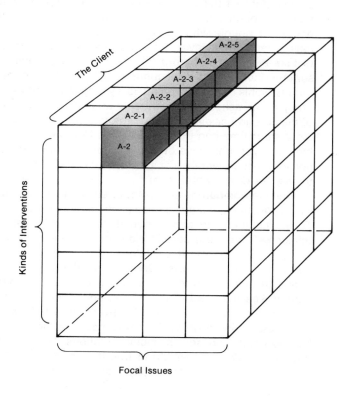

While the importance of morale/cohesion is widely recognized, it is relatively rare to find theory-based interventions used to resolve a morale/cohesion focal issue. The reason may be that morale/cohesion is usually easier and more fundamentally changed by changing something else. For example, if power/authority is being misused, it can cause lowered morale/cohesion and the more basic approach is to solve the morale/cohesion problem by dealing with the power/authority problem first. Nevertheless, there are approaches that use a theory basis for intervention.

INDIVIDUAL (A-2-1)

Transactional analysis was discussed in Chapter 3 and its basic features need not be elaborated upon further. An example of its use to help an individual test the potential cohesion of a possible husband/wife relationship is reported by Harris, who provides an example of consultant-assisted evaluation of a prospective husband.

> One of the most helpful ways to examine similarities and dissimilarities is the use of Transactional Analysis in premarital counseling to construct a personality diagram of the couple contemplating marriage. The aim is to expose not just the obvious similarities or dissimilarities but to undertake a more thorough inquiry of what is in the Parent, Adult, and Child of each partner. A couple who enters into such an inquiry might be said to already have a lot in their favor, inasmuch as they take marriage seriously enough to take a long look before they leap. However, one of the partners, having serious doubt about the soundness of the alliance, may undertake such an inquiry on his own. An example is a young lady who was in one of my treatment groups. She asked me to schedule an individual hour for her for the purpose of discussing her dilemma over the fact that a young man she had been dating a short time had proposed to her. Her Child was immensely attracted to him, and yet there was other data coming into her computer which caused her to question whether or not marriage was a good idea. She had learned to use P-A-C in each of them.
>
> First we compared the Parent of each. We found she had a strong Parent which contained countless rules of conduct and many "shoulds" and "oughts." These included the admonition that you don't rush into marriage without thinking. There were certain elements of self-righteousness, like "our kind" are the best people. It contained ideas such as "you are judged by the company you keep" and "don't do anything that is beneath you." It contained the early imprints of a home life that was highly organized, where mother was the head of the house, and where father worked hard and late at the office. There was a great store of "how to" material: How to celebrate a birthday, how to dress the Christmas tree, how to bring up children, and how to handle oneself in social situations. Her Parent came on as an important influence in her life in that the impressions had been more or less consistent. Although its rigidity was sometimes oppressive and produced

considerable NOT OK feelings in her Child, her Parent nonetheless continued to be a constant source of data in all her transactions in the present.

We then turned to an examination of the Parent in the young man. His parents had been divorced when he was seven years old, and he had been raised by his mother, who indulged him in material possessions and gave him sporadic attention. She herself was Child-dominated and emotional and acted out her feelings in impetuous displays of spending, with intermittent spells of sulking, withdrawal, and vindictiveness. Father did not come through on the tape at all except as the imprint that he was a "rotten bastard, like all men." The boy's Parent was so disintegrated and fragmented and inconsistent that it did not come through in present transactions as a controlling or modifying influence over his impulsive, Child-dominated behavior. Her Parent and his Parent not only had nothing in common; her Parent also highly disapproved of his. It was readily seen that little basis existed for a Parent-Parent transaction about any subject, thus ruling out anything complementary at this level.*

The couple's "Adult" and "Child" orientations were then diagnosed and contrasted in a similar manner, after which the development of the relationship was traced in terms of the Parent-Adult-Child model.

As their relationship progressed there became less and less to talk about. Nothing existed Parent-Parent, little existed Adult-Adult, and what did exist on the Child-Child level soon produced major disturbances in the girl's Parent. The relationship then began to settle in a Parent-Child pattern with her assuming the role of the responsible and critical partner and he assuming the role of the manipulative, testing Child, reproducing his original situation in childhood.†

On the basis of what she now saw to be characteristic of the current relationship pattern and the prospects of its continuation in marriage, she finally decided that she didn't want the young man as a husband and broke off the relationship.

Herzberg's theories of motivation,[1,2] also introduced in Chapter 3, demonstrate how power/authority relations can either stimulate or stifle productivity and achievement. It can be noted here that "hygiene/maintenance" provisions of the theory are related to morale/cohesion as a focal issue. Hygiene/maintenance provisions at best only prevent declines in current performance levels. Failure to deal with these can have disrupting effects on morale/cohesion, and indirectly on performance, but this set of connections appears not to have served as the basis for significant interventions.

---

* From pp. 128–129 in *I'm OK—You're OK* by Thomas A. Harris. Copyright © 1967, 1968, 1969 by Thomas A. Harris. Reprinted by permission of Harper & Row, Publishers, Inc.

† Ibid., p. 131.

Summary

The paucity of examples may lead to one or more of several conclusions. It may be that morale/cohesion theory is insufficiently developed to make it functionally useful in day-to-day affairs. Alternatively, the theories may be satisfactory, but they may have not been converted from academic to practical meaning through better modes of communication. A third possibility is that theory is of little utility in bringing morale/cohesion to a higher level, though Myers' work (Chapter 3) suggests that this may not be true. A fourth possibility is that the best way to deal with low morale/cohesion is to solve underlying causes first rather than trying to arouse a high degree of morale/cohesion directly.

Notes

1. F. Herzberg, B. Mausner and B. B. Snyderman, *The Motivation to Work* (New York: Wiley, 1959).
2. F. Herzberg, *Work and the Nature of Man* (Cleveland: The World Publishing Co., 1966).

5

THEORY-PRINCIPLES
INTERVENTIONS

Norms/
Standards

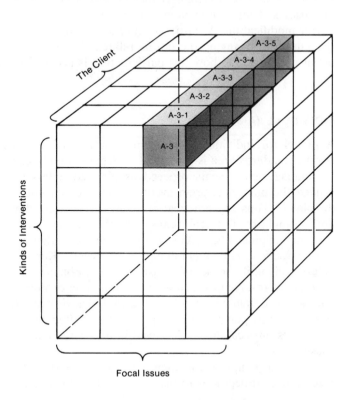

The Client

Kinds of Interventions

A-3-5
A-3-4
A-3-3
A-3-2
A-3-1

A-3

Focal Issues

Norms/standards are those shared expectations to which people desire or to which they are expected to conform. One's adherence to prevailing norms/standards, particularly the more important ones, tends to be rewarded in various ways while violations of established codes of behavior tend to be punished. Social regulation, then, can be a powerful perpetuating influence whether or not the particular norms/standards are pertinent to effectiveness. This source of control derives more from horizontal than from vertical influences.

When norms/standards that relate to a group, an organization, or even larger social systems have been internalized by an individual, they become a basis for self-regulation of behavior; thus any improvement in effectiveness may require that the person's internalized norms/standards be surfaced and examined. Several different theory-based interventions have been employed to accomplish this kind of change.

The Grid[1] has proved to be an effective norms/standards intervention, at team, intergroup, and organizational levels. After the Grid has been learned and members are prepared to confront conflict, they use instruments on an open, participative basis to evaluate "what is," in contrast to "what is ideal," and then design strategies for shifting from actual to the ideal. This method of intervention enables members themselves, without further consultation, except on highly technical problems, to engineer their own processes of change. Another approach that uses a theory-based model to intervene with individuals makes use of behavior modification. A third, which relates to organization as the unit of change, is focused on changing the norms related to who participates in solving operational problems and how this participation is accomplished.

INDIVIDUAL (A-3-1)

A model for individual development of reasoning skills and their use in the norms/standards area is presented by Kepner and Tregoe. The basic idea is that "in management, events proceed as planned unless some force, not provided *against* the plan, acts upon events to produce an outcome not contemplated in the plan."[2] Thus any practical problem can be viewed as a deviation from some norm/standard. The real "cause" of the problem, therefore, is an unplanned and unanticipated change away from "standard" that has been brought about by some specific event or combination of events. Kepner and Tregoe assert that unless and until the actual cause of the problem is precisely determined, any attempts to resolve it—such as by treating one or more of its symptoms—represent no more than guesswork and have a high probability of failing. The authors emphasize this point with examples of the ineffectiveness, wasteful expense, and sometimes physical danger involved in making a managerial decision based on a "false cause."

Rational management, then, consists of valid problem analysis followed by specific related decisions to institute problem-solving action. Kepner and Tregoe offer a model of this process. It involves seven initial steps of problem analysis and seven additional steps of formulating the best course of action for solving the problem. Briefly stated, these are:

Problem Analysis

1. As a prerequisite, the manager has expectations of what the standards of performance in areas of his or her responsibility should be. He or she observes what is actually going on, and compares various aspects of the situation against expectations.

2. Noticing discrepancies between "is" and "should be," the manager selects one out of several problems to work on. This choice is made according to priorities of (a) the problem's urgency, (b) its seriousness, and (c) its potential for growth if left unattended.

3. The manager specifies "what the problem *is*"—in terms of its deviation from a standard of performance—by describing accurately its dimensions of "identity," "location," "time," and "extent." To draw a boundary around it, he or she may also specify what in general the problem does *not* include.

4. Comparing what *has* and what *has not* been affected as deviation from standard, the manager identifies specific *effects* of the real cause.

5. In each "area of distinction" uncovered in the previous step, the manager looks for relevant changes that have taken place and which can be logically connected to the unwanted effect(s).

6. From the array of relevant changes the manager deduces possible causes of the deviation. Each such conclusion is put in the form of a testable statement or hypothetical proposition.

7. Each "possible cause" is tested against the facts of the problem specification (established in Step 2). The "most likely" cause of the deviation is described by that tested hypothesis which exactly explains *all* the facts of "what the problem is" (Step 3), not only of what *has* been affected as deviation from standard, but also of what *has not* (see Step 4).

Decision making to solve the problem is possible on completion of the steps above, according to the additional steps enumerated below.

1. Now that the problem's cause has been identified and verified, the manager lists the objectives to be accomplished by clearing up the problem.

2. The manager classifies these objectives into (a) "Musts"—requirements that cannot be compromised, and (b) "Wants"—aspects of "best possible performance out of the decision," not all of which can be realized in combination. The latter are ranked and weighed.

3. A number of alternative ways of attaining the established objectives are devised.

4. Each alternative is evaluated against the objectives, assessing it in terms of how well it satisfies each of the "Musts" and "Wants."

5. A tentative decision is made, by choosing whichever alternative (or combination of alternatives) appears best able to achieve all the objectives.
6. The tentative decision is evaluated for any future possible adverse consequences that might be inherent in it.
7. The final decision includes (a) specific problem-solving actions to be taken, (b) whatever additional actions are considered necessary for avoiding adverse consequences that might create new problems, and (c) ways of making sure that the actions decided on are carried out.

When this model has been presented and internalized, an individual can be helped to test his or her current characteristic modes of problem solving against it, thereby learning to reject hasty and nonrational "snap judgments." This is particularly crucial in dealing with pressure situations where, although time is short, a positive outcome is dependent on the quality of the problem-solving analysis. Sound information gathering and logical checking procedures are an absolute necessity in making the best possible decisions.

Overall, the Kepner-Tregoe intervention sequence is used with individuals. The client begins by studying the model itself and its inherent problem-analysis and decision-making requirements. Next, in a five-day, off-the-job training program, he or she (along with others) learns to internalize the model and practices using the model to identify and solve, under time pressure, complex problems of a simulated business enterprise as well as selected real-life problems of the back-home situation.

In doing so the individual may indicate his or her natural bent by slipping into characteristic ways of dealing with problems, without regard for what the logic of the model suggests. By monitoring each exercise or simulation, the consultant is in a position to observe the quality of an individual's contribution and to help him or her see "spontaneous" departures from the model that limit its effective use.

In the sessions scheduled to follow each exercise, each participant is aided by colleagues and consultant to critically evaluate his or her performance in *using,* for the purpose of arriving at the cause of the problem and making the appropriate decision, the *information* he or she has been given. This almost immediate feedback aids each individual in comprehending the extent to which personal norms and standards are revealed in his or her ways of thinking about problems and the degree to which decisions conform with or deviate from the model. Follow-up interventions provide opportunities for individuals to further strengthen their own problem-solving and decision-making skills in the back-home job situation.

This entire rational process may also be installed throughout the organization, starting with the top managers, not only to solve specific problems but also to modify and redesign organizational systems and procedures. Shifting the reward system to encourage the model's use, as well as continued monitoring and evaluation of the results, help reinforce continued application of the rational process.[3]

Changing behavior by aiding the individual client to internalize behavior-modification principles in order to apply them to changing personal norms and standards of conduct is a theory-based intervention. The clients who then design their own application programs are using an innovative approach. Four basic considerations underlie this approach.

Commitment. This is an absolutely essential precondition for change. No change is possible unless the person is genuinely committed to making a change. Also, such commitments tend to be stronger when made publicly than when made in private.

Observable behavior. The restatement of the goals to which one is committed in terms of behavior (instead of feelings, thoughts, or other phenomena) has the advantage of making the goal more specific and less ambiguous and will often suggest in and of itself a solution to the problem. Furthermore, when other helping persons are available, the description of the problem, with examples of specific behaviors in specific situations, facilitates communications with the helping person and makes it possible for the helper to provide observations and suggestions and to reinforce desired changes when they occur.

A hierarchical approach to goal attainment. Frequently individuals fail to execute a desired change in behavior because they attempt to change a total pattern of complex responses all at once rather than beginning with those aspects of the problem that are easy to change and gradually moving in the direction of those that are most resistant to modification. In lay terms, the idea is sometimes expressed in the maxim "Learn to crawl before you attempt to walk." Skinner's concept of "shaping," Wolpe's "desensitization," Gagne's "learning programs," and task analysis procedures in the human factors area all constitute examples of the value of this approach to applied psychologists. Altogether, there is impressive evidence for the value of this principle of change.

Changing behavior by reinforcement rather than insight. Much of the success of the behaviorist approach seems attributable to the behaviorists' observation that change is relatively unrelated to insight. In order to increase the strength of a desired response, the response must be reinforced rather than understood. Before it can be reinforced, it must occur. Practicing being what you want to be (or some small part of what you want to be) is the best way to become a fully functioning person.[4]

An intervention that exemplifies this approach was structured as follows:

> Students were required to apply the model to their own behavior to see for themselves if it was a valid tool for producing behavior change. Class activities and grading procedures were based on the behaviorists' translation of the "Know thyself" maxim. That is, some class activities directed students to careful observation and recording of their behavior, while other assignments required analysis and manipulation of the environment.

Two class activities focused on the objective "Know thy behavior." First, the students . . . write a two-page statement describing the problem behavior, its longevity, its frequency, and how difficult they felt it would be to change. At this stage, a very wide range of problems was cited by the students, e.g., study problems, obesity, anxiety about taking exams, shyness, dating problems, depression, lack of motivation, etc. Many of the problems were stated in terms of feelings or emotions and frequently appeared to the student not to involve any overt observable behaviors.

In a second assigned paper students were required to reduce their problem to some overt, observable behavior, to propose a means of measurement, and to collect base rate data. At this point a problem such as "I can't study" might be expanded to focus on the amount of time engaged in study, the allocation of time to different subjects by "copying notes," "getting organized," or "staring at a book without reading." One ingenious student in an anatomy course measured the number of definitions she was able to memorize in a given period of time. In another project a student who complained initially that she was "too inflexible," that she did "very few things spontaneously," measured a wide range of behaviors related to the problem, including how often she laid her clothes out at night (an activity that interfered with other, more spontaneous behaviors), the number of study breaks she took with friends, the number of times she departed from her rigid study schedule to "have fun with others," and how often she checked ahead of time with her date to find out what he had planned to do. In all projects, base rate was compared to similar data taken at the end of the semester.

A second series of class procedures focused on the objective of knowing the environment and the relationship between the environment and behavior. Reading and lectures on environment factors in study and concentration, anxiety, and tensions were accompanied by class exercises in the identification of environmental reinforcers and relaxation training. The students were required to write weekly papers describing ways they applied these ideas to their projects. Many interesting environmental manipulations resulted from this stage of the project. One student made seeing or talking to her boyfriend contingent on studying. Another student asked his wife and a friend to provide regular feedback when he became abstract and vague in his speech. (His wife loved the job.) For many, the mere act of recording their own behavior provided enough feedback and reinforcement to induce change without additional environmental manipulation.[5]

Client reactions twelve months later reveal what aspects of the approach were considered particularly significant.

. . . listing certain behavior patterns which I consider damaging to my overall personality when I find myself acting them out, and then referring to the notes later on to compare the feelings involved during both the deviant and "normal" behavior.

The most important thing to me . . . was the idea of subgoals being so important to achieve before long range goals could be achieved. I had known this before, but had never really applied it to a specific problem.

To me, this project was a real catalyst into a total new self-awareness program for myself. I actually started to be honest with myself—for the first time. I learned techniques; however, I have transcended into deeper self-analysis. I've used many techniques in my teaching of children.

. . . that any behavior can be altered or at least changed to a more acceptable form of behavior by employing the behavior modification steps. . . .[6]

It is doubtful that this intervention is an example of behavior modification at work. The reason, as the author indicates, is that client commitment to the goal of self-change through cycle breaking is "absolutely essential." "Commitment" is a "mentalistic" concept and is without operational meaning in modification methodologies that focus exclusively on producing specific and externally observable behavior. A motivational concept must be introduced to account for the observed behavior and behavior change, thus bringing this approach toward other dynamic orientations.

GROUP (A-3-2)

The importance of negative norms in reducing group effectiveness and the kinds of interventions essential for moving toward more positive norms is described by de la Porte.[7] He maintains that individuals adhere to and, therefore, are controlled by group norms, sometimes doing so without conscious awareness. Thus increased effectiveness is possible only when those susceptible to such norms become aware of and reject them. Negative norms can then be replaced with those that promote greater productivity through a series of interventions that include:

- Creating understanding and appreciation of the significance of norms, how they influence organizational effectiveness, and how they contribute to both the creation and the solution of key organizational problems. Group members are taught to think in normative terms and to identify and state norms. The process starts at the top of the company and permeates downward as each organizational level becomes involved in change.

- Establishing positive norm goals through cooperative action. A group can establish acceptable norm goals just as it would establish functional goals.

- Determining the excellence point of norms for the company concerned, and therefore the improvement distance to be covered.

- Establishing normative change priorities. The size of the normative gap is only one factor. More important is the relationship of the norm area to the effectiveness and profitability (or other problems) of the organization. This leads to weighting—and gives more urgent attention to—those norm clusters that have more direct impact than others on the given problem, even though the gap may be narrower than average.

- Developing systematic change strategies by examining and modifying ten specific (and crucial) areas, among which are management commitment to change; information, communication, and feedback on and about results;

recognition and reward of consistent employee behavior; and recruitment and selection of new employees. Inclusion of the last recognizes the fact that newcomers can introduce negative norms, just as they can be trained to conform to positive norms.

■ Implementing the change strategy. Here, the essential point is to begin at the top of the organization and move downward, with the assurance of top management commitment, support, and modeling behavior.

■ Providing follow-through and maintenance on a continuous basis. The emphasis here is on assigning responsibilities for change programs (often best accomplished by setting up a task force or change committee).

■ Providing for continuous evaluation of the effectiveness of change strategies, and standing ready to modify plans, by reviewing change strategies if and when they fall short of expectations.[8]

How participants internalize the concept of norms is not indicated. However, among the advantages claimed is that it does not expose individuals to criticism by their peers, for all are equally "guilty" of adhering to the same negative norm(s).

INTERGROUP (A-3-3)

An example of the collateral system notion was introduced in Chapter 3 but now is applied to the union/management relationship at the plant level by Duckles, Duckles, and Maccoby. In this case study, contract bargaining takes place in the traditional manner while a collateral system, referred to as a Work Improvement Program, is introduced. Issues that develop around contract negotiations often create conflict and tension in management/union relationships. The collateral system is based on an integrating orientation. The collateral system notion seeks, through cooperation, to create conditions of work that are more equitable, democratic, responsive to individuals as individuals, and promotive of a greater sense of security. The aim of the collateral system is to make work better and more satisfying for all employees, salaried and hourly, while maintaining the necessary productivity to ensure job security. This approach shares some properties resembling the European notion of joint or co-management, with the union and management mutually responsible for profit through productivity, performance, security, and satisfaction.

Management and organized labor are seldom seen operating from a basis of collaborative cooperation such as might be required by a collateral systems approach. Management at Harmon International Industries and the United Auto Workers Union joined together in this intervention to develop and implement new norms/standards through a Work Improvement Program at the Bolivar, Tennessee plant.

The interventionists were members of the third-party project staff. They helped get the Bolivar project started. Two members of the team had on-site roles, providing behavioral science resources to labor and management.

... the "third-party" staff ... analyze work with people at all levels of the organization and help them to develop their ideas into specific changes that are to be implemented. Such changes may include job rotation, job enlargement, and autonomous or semiautonomous work groups, but only if this is the decision reached by the people involved and approved by management and the union in the Working Committee. ...[9]

This intervention is applied through voluntary experimental work groups that meet at least weekly to examine and critically discuss their work and to explore more productive, satisfying alternatives.

The role of project staff in this process was to raise questions aimed at providing a full description of the nature of the work, its purpose, methods, and organization, ... materials and supplies. Where gaps in the participant's knowledge about their own work existed, the staff sought out the people in the plant who could provide the answers and scheduled them to meet with the group.[10]

In one of the experimenting groups, for example, an area foreman suggested providing workers an opportunity to experience supervision on a firsthand basis. A two-phase process was developed where participants began with a four-hour observation session designed to gain exposure to the supervisor's daily activities and responsibilities. Each employee-volunteer received training from the supervisor in terms of job specifics.

The second phase allowed each participant to spend five consecutive half-days executing the foreman's role. Except for disciplining fellow employees, the participant was directly involved in aspects of supervision.

When the foreman coincidentally transferred to another job, the experimenting group gained approval on a trial basis to operate their area without a foreman. A group coordinator was selected, and the group leader function rotated among the workers. After a one-month period, it was found that the group had effectively handled the human relations aspects of supervision. Nevertheless, a permanent foreman was needed to handle technical problems and to relate to other interdependent groups.

The participants in the experiment, while disappointed they could not fully supervise themselves, gained an understanding of the processes in which they are involved and dialogue about the work continues to take place.

This case study demonstrates the potential benefits of a management/union partnership in strengthening norms/standards related to quality-of-work-life issues. Increased morale and job satisfaction are said to be achieved through the kind of cooperative effort illustrated. Contributions of an objective third party appear to help bridge the traditional management/labor gap while providing the kind of collateral system that facilitates creative thinking and innovative action in shifting norms/standards.

The interventionists see this activity as being based on principles of security, democracy, equality, and individuality. Basically this intervention deals with intergroup relations and the focal issue is norms and standards, with the structure of working relationships as well as the processes and practices being applied to the work itself subject to change.

It is unclear whether theory/principles were used to guide the consultants' interventions or whether the principles were taught to participants. It does not appear that the participants internalized the theory for future independent application to understanding and evaluating specific organization practices in terms of theory/principles.

The collateral system notion itself needs to be more deeply examined in order to clarify the assumptions that underlie its use. The idea that two systems should co-exist, one premised on authority-obedience assumptions and the other on collaborative assumptions, can be reinterpreted as follows. Because the authority-obedience production system causes problems, it is necessary to have a different system to solve them. The converse interpretation is that because the authority-obedience production system causes problems, it is the appropriate target of change itself. In this sense the collateral system seeks to solve the power-authority issue through creating a normative system of collaboration that exists side by side with the intact authority-obedience system. From a Grid perspective, use of the collateral system represents the two-hat managerial theory: "solve production problems on Monday; deal with human problems on Wednesday."[11]

ORGANIZATION (A-3-4)

Penetrating and Changing Organization Culture Norms

A theory-based approach to shifting norms/standards has recently become available. The theory identifies why norms arise, how they are maintained, and describes interventions showing how they can be changed; conformity dynamics are pictured as are issues related to maintaining the interdependent factors of independence and creativity.

Several examples of how norms/standards can be shifted are provided. The first example depicts an intervention in which conformity theory is used to resolve a safety problem in a large plant.

> There are a variety of ways to analyze accidents, their causes, and the techniques for preventing accidents or keeping them at a minimum.
>
> One approach centers on accident-proneness. Some people have career records of accidents while others, working under comparable conditions, seem never to have a problem. The difference is within the individual people involved. Therefore, an important part of the management of safety is selection—bringing employees with the maximum likelihood of being able to work in a safe manner into work situations that pose some hazard.
>
> Another approach is to ensure that those who work under conditions of potential risk are adequately protected by safety equipment—goggles when welding or using drilling equipment, hard hats whenever there is a risk of falling objects, gloves when the hands can be hurt, heavy shoes or boots

when the feet need to be protected. Safety equipment can significantly cut down the hazards present in many kinds of work.

Another approach to safety is to make and enforce safety rules. These rules are expected to be respected by those who are at risk. An area in which walking is risky is marked "Dangerous"; so is an area where heavy equipment is moving and operators may not see pedestrians because they are concentrating on their equipment.

Still another approach to safety focuses on state and federal safety regulations that are applied on an industry-wide basis. These are necessary because many companies, each competing with one another, won't implement them unless all do so in a uniform way. The reason, of course, is that if only one were to introduce some of the safety rules, the expense of doing so would make that company noncompetitive. Therefore, it is essential that government regulate on an across-industry basis.

Each of these approaches has an important contribution to make in the overall management of safety, yet none of them can make much of a contribution if employees share attitudes that involve needless risk taking. The following is a description of how one organization approached this basic attitude problem.

STATEMENT OF THE PROBLEM

A task paragraph was produced that clearly stated the problem and then asked, "What is the cause of our poor safety record? How can it be improved?" A total of 800 employees, both supervisory and wage and salaried personnel, participated. The study consisted of two parts: a preparatory segment and a seminar discussion period of eight hours, leading to crystallization of a new safety norm. Seminars consisted of 80 people assembled in leaderless discussion groups of 10. Each seminar was conducted over a two-day period. The ratio of supervisors to wage and salaried personnel in the discussion groups was the same as in the organizational population. No effort was made to put supervisors and those whom they directly supervised in the same groups, but no effort was made to separate them either.

Each seminar commenced after lunch on the first day and continued until the end of the workday. It picked up the morning of the second day and ended at noon. All sessions were conducted in the plant itself. Leaders of the several unions participated, not as union representatives but as employees of the company.

The preparatory work consisted of examining background materials related to previous accidents, with the past 25 lost-time accidents reviewed. The accidents were described and richly illustrated with pictures, the cause(s) identified, and conclusion drawn as to how each problem might have been avoided and how it could be corrected in the future. Participants were expected to study the prework document and to be prepared to discuss the material during the seminars.

The seminars began with a discussion of the question posed in the task paragraph. Even a casual observer would recognize that all participants in the discussion were deeply concerned with the problem. The entire session was serious business. The groups were so comparable that the following description is sufficient to indicate what the discussions entailed.

In group after group, statements made by participants—primarily wage and salaried personnel (although supervisors quickly joined in, once the issue developed)—centered on "them-ism": "The 'real cause' of all these accidents is 'them.' We get pushed for productivity these days in a way that was never true before the new management took over. That's the cause of the problem—pressure."

Another point of view was, "They don't care. It's not like the old days. It used to be that when any risk was involved, the safety inspector would check it out first. He'd tell us what to do and what not to do. They don't do that any more. As a matter of fact, we used to have 15 safety inspectors and we could call on them any time. Nowadays two people in the personnel department are responsible for safety, and that's it. It's become a line responsibility and the line doesn't know how to study the situation and really determine what the factors of risk are."

A third point of view frequently expressed was, "It's the equipment, it's getting old." Still another: "It's the new people. They come in and are not given adequate training. Before you know it, an accident has happened."

The point here is that the tension people felt from being under pressure and subject to the risk of accidents had produced substantial anger, and a target of these angry reactions was "them"—that is, management.

EMERGENCE OF THE NEW NORMS

After the catharsis and ventilation period, someone in a group, or occasionally a higher-level manager who was responsible for monitoring the discussions, intervened. Members were asked whether the "explanations" of accidents given by participants squared with the facts of 25 accident synopses examined in the preliminary phase. The prework document had been written to illuminate the reality of the situation and to increase objectivity.

Most participants initially preferred their own explanations to the conclusions from the accident studies. Yet there was enough concern about exploring the problem in greater depth for the synopses of accidents to come to the fore. What the study demonstrated, by and large, was that very few of the accidents could be traced to faulty equipment or to lack of safety rules or safety equipment. More often than not, the accident was the personal responsibility of the employee who had suffered it.

For example, an eye accident that resulted in lost time had happened when an employee was sweating and took his goggles off because of difficulties he was having in seeing the work. An electrical burn resulted when an employee was making a fine adjustment and found it difficult to do so with the heavy gloves on. By taking off his gloves, he placed himself at an increased risk and suffered the burn. Another accident was caused by an employee walking in an area marked "Dangerous" and slipping on grease, with a resultant bone injury.

As the discussion continued through the afternoon of the first day, it became clear that two alternative explanations were under examination. Only one of them could be valid. Either it was the "them" norm, as evidenced in equipment, rules, pressure, and so on, or it was the "us" norm. The accident results clearly indicated that shortcutting and trying to solve a problem by convenience were, far more often than not, suggestive of the real problem.

When the discussions resumed at the beginning of day 2, some of the "them-ism" returned, and a new but far briefer period of catharsis and ventilation was necessary in some groups to get back to a problem-solving orientation.

By the end of the first hour of day 2 most groups had arrived at an entirely different notion than anyone had had at the beginning of the discussions. Typical comments were, "When you come right down to it, it's not them; it's us. We can blame them, but we put ourselves at risk." "We've developed sloppy work habits; we cut corners, not because we have to or because we're pressured to, but because we've become sloppy." "We don't look out for one another. I see you entering an area marked 'Dangerous' when you've got no good reason to be there, and I say nothing. You slip. They didn't cause your broken hip. You and I did."

By this time, the old norm of blaming problems on management and re- fusing to be personally responsible had become visible and was beginning to crumble. A new norm began to replace it. The new norm might be de- scribed in the following way: "We are the last link on the safety chain. You can't blame rules if the rules are okay but we don't follow them. You can't even blame supervisors, though they could do more to chew us out when they see an infraction. You can't blame safety equipment if it's not in place and in use when the accident occurs. We can only take the responsibility for our accident situation ourselves."

COMMITMENT TO THE NEW NORMS

Translated into practice, the new norm resulted in supervisors and wage and salaried personnel committing themselves to being responsible for themselves and for one another. Each person was committed to adhering to safety practices, and employees who didn't know what the practices were would ask others for help. All employees agreed on the importance of being mutually responsible. In other words, "I will call your hand, as one employee to another, whenever I see you involved in a foolish action. I ex- pect you to call my hand the same way. If we're the last link on the safety chain, we can solve the problem only by strengthening the link. Being self- responsible and mutually responsible are the only possible ways for strength- ening that link."

With all employees whose activities placed them at risk committed to personal and mutual responsibility for safe practices, the poor safety record in the plant was quickly reversed in the 12-plant comparison. The plant rapidly moved up in safety. Within nine months it led the other 11.

The solution the workers reached was based on the readiness of indi- viduals to converge on a norm that squared with experiential reality. Once the strategy of discussion made it possible for the participants themselves to define the problem, the old norm, characterized by "them-ism," was re- jected as an unsatisfactory basis of behavior. The new norm of personal and mutual responsibility was quickly implemented and served beautifully to rectify the problem.[12]

SHIFTING NORMS OF ORGANIZATIONAL PROBLEM SOLVING

A norms/standards intervention dealing with the entire faculty and supporting staff of one school organization, fifty-four participants in all, is described by Schmuck, Runkel, and Langmeyer.[13] The example is described here because a structured model was taught to participants as the basis for improving their problem-solving procedures. The attempt was to change the norms/standards for problem solving within the faculty. The intervention began with a six-day interpersonal laboratory for internalization in which administrators and faculty practiced using a group problem-solving approach. The model of the problem-solving sequence involved the following steps: (1) identifying the problem; (2) completing a force-field diagnosis; (3) brainstorming for reducing restraining forces; (4) designing steps to solve the problem; (5) simulating the solution's soundness. The first two days were applied to structured group exercises on simulated problems to demonstrate, through firsthand data gathering, the importance of clear communication and to evaluate the experience in terms of its pertinence for dealing with real-life school situations. This stimulated shared interpersonal feedback.

During the last four days a problem-solving sequence using "real" school problems was introduced to gather data and test the sequence for its utility. Identified problems included: (1) insufficient clarity of job responsibility; (2) inadequate use of staff resources; (3) limited involvement and participation of faculty and school decision makers. Working in subgroups organized around identified problems provided members with practice in using the problem-solving sequence. Five training consultants, each assigned to one of the five groups, provided interventions based primarily on sensitivity training methods, including observation of group processes, with feedback of observations, as well as development of skills to reinforce new behavior. The consultants sought to enhance task-oriented activity as contrasted with personal growth. "Family" team building was not involved.

Participants received day-and-a-half-long "booster shot" training sessions during the school year. The first "refresher" stimulated discussion of the faculty's insufficient use of what they had learned in the first six-day session. The second involved stock-taking in further efforts to revive deteriorating skills. The intervention's operational impact included: (1) classroom application projects; (2) increased influence on school operations from an advisory committee; (3) better interpersonal relations among faculty and administrators; (4) setting up a new internal "facilitator" to serve as a liaison between groups and to help interpersonal relationships, and so on.

The causes of deterioration from earlier post-seminar levels of performance are not specified but may have been due, among other possibilities, to (1) inadequate internalization of the concepts, (2) insufficient attention to school culture, or (3) overreliance on consultants.

Summary

Much is known from behavioral-science research about the extent to which behavior is controlled and regulated by norms/standards. Most of this theory, however, remains at the academic level—in other words, internalization methodologies have not been used to convert it to functional use.

The "actual versus ideal" methodology is one illustration of a wide range of possibilities. The behavior-modification-theory intervention based both upon insight into the process of and personal commitment to change is another example of the potential value of helping clients learn how to replace counterproductive norms and standards with more positive ones. A theory intervention that focuses on practical problem solving may also contribute to phasing out inappropriate norms/standards.

The advantage of shifting norms in this theory/principles-based manner is that changes in norm-referenced behavior can come about without provoking the intense resistance that is almost inevitable when the same kinds of changes are attempted by prescriptive interventions which disregard individual insight and involvement.

Notes

1. R. R. Blake and J. S. Mouton, *Corporate Excellence Through Grid Organization Development* (Houston: Gulf Publishing Co., 1968).
2. C. H. Kepner and B. B. Tregoe, *The New Rational Manager* (Princeton, N.J.: Princeton Research Press, 1981).
3. Ibid.
4. R. A. Mencke, "Teaching Self-Modification in an Adjustment Course," *Personnel and Guidance Journal* 52, no. 2 (1973): 98. Copyright 1973 American Personnel and Guidance Association. Reprinted with permission.
5. Ibid., pp. 98–99.
6. Ibid., p. 101.
7. P. C. A. de la Porte, "Group Norms: Key to Building a Winning Team," *Personnel* 51, no. 5 (1974): 60–67.
8. Ibid., pp. 65–66. Reprinted by permission of the publisher.
9. M. M. Duckles, R. Duckles and M. Maccoby, "The Process of Change at Bolivar," *Journal of Applied Behavioral Science* 13, no. 3 (1977): 390. See also M. Maccoby, *The Leader: A New Face for American Management* (New York: Simon and Schuster, 1981).
10. Ibid., p. 392.
11. R. R. Blake and J. S. Mouton, *The New Managerial Grid* (Houston: Gulf Publishing Co., 1978).
12. R. R. Blake and J. S. Mouton, *Productivity: The Human Side* (New York: AMACOM, 1981), pp. 81–87.
13. R. A. Schmuck, P. Runkel and D. Langmeyer, "Using Group Problem-Solving Procedures," in R. A. Schmuck and M. B. Miles, eds., *Organization Development in Schools* (Palo Alto, Calif.: National Press Books, 1971), pp. 51–69.

6

THEORY-PRINCIPLES INTERVENTIONS

Goals/ Objectives

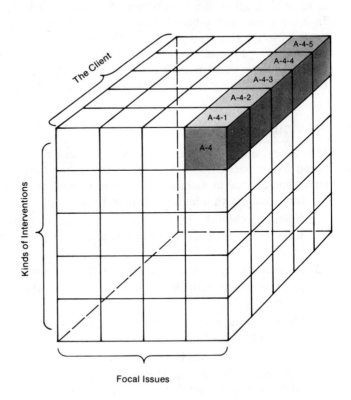

It is difficult to overestimate the extent to which goals/objectives give character and direction to human endeavors. Goals and objectives offer a meaningful orientation to any activity; they lend it purpose. Many activities in modern society are already structured in goals/objectives terms. College education is an example. An educated mind is a goal of schools and universities. Graduation represents completion of a planned cycle of activity. Planned activities are calculated to reach the goal of profit in business by increasing the return on investment from certain products or by reducing the expense of producing or marketing them. Family life and healthy children constitute the goals of numerous marriages.

Oftentimes, however, goals are expressed in such abstract terms or are so remote from the activities in which people are engaged that they exert little or no influence on behavior. Graduation may be the completion of a college activity cycle, but for the first several years of education this goal may be too far removed to affect conscious endeavor. The same is true with regard to corporate profit. Certain higher layers in the organization's hiearchy may consider profit crucial, and allow their decisions to be influenced by it. At other levels an individual's contribution to profit is so difficult to see, feel, and evaluate as to be altogether disregarded in decision making.

The dearth of theory-based interventions with a goals/objectives focal issue is surprising, given the importance of goals in promoting meaningful behavior. In a complete theory-based intervention focused on setting and accomplishing goals/objectives, a consultant aids the client in any one or possibly all four of these ways: (1) goal clarification; (2) goal redefinition; (3) restructuring activities so as to make pursuit of goal-oriented actions possible; (4) setting goals in situations where it is possible to designate *what* the goals should be.

INDIVIDUAL (A-4-1)

McClelland and colleagues have identified and researched a motivation termed "need for achievement" (*n* Ach). In turn, they have designed theory-based interventions aimed at increasing individual capacity for achievement.

Individuals with a high motivation to achieve:

1. Calculate carefully what it is they must do to gain a sense of mastery in a situation where the effort put out can influence whether they are successful or not.
2. Set moderately difficult, but potentially achievable goals for themselves.
3. Are concerned with the achievement itself rather than the rewards of success per se.
4. Show a strong preference for work situations in which they get concrete feedback on how well they are doing.

This research-derived model provides a basis of intervention for teaching participants how to increase their achievement motivation. The general rationale on which the intervention is based is as follows.

A quest for personal achievement is or can be a continuing stimulus to an individual's financial and economic progress. Comparably, the general or particular population's level of motivation to achieve may be crucial for the financial and social health of a nation. Some individuals, as well as communities and nations, seem naturally to strive toward goals of achievement while others—the vast majority—are far less motivated to do so.[1]

Why one person is perennially motivated to achieve while his or her neighbor is more or less satisfied to be one of the pack is, of course, a complicated question. To answer it in terms of a particular individual entails much research into personal history and environmental influences. A more pertinent question, however, is whether or not a presently low level of achievement motivation can be raised through consultant-based interventions. The intervention varies from circumstance to circumstance, but its basic outline includes the following steps.

First, clients are taught how people with a high need to achieve think, talk, and act. This includes demonstrations of how achievement motivation is revealed in imaginative stories as well as how it is reflected in personal goal setting. For example, those highest in need to achieve (a) when given a choice, elect to *work* at a problem-solving task designed to give them about a 1-in-3 chance of succeeding, rather than risk rolling dice in a relatively effortless *game of chance* with similar odds,[2] (b) when participating in a *game of skill* (such as throwing darts), they set moderately challenging goals for themselves (which also tend to have about a 1-in-3 chance of being achieved). Apparently, achievement-motivated people prefer to plan and *themselves* take the actions leading up to success-or-failure outcomes. They enjoy stretching their capabilities, but are careful to set realistic and attainable goals. Therefore, interventions are designed to stimulate participants to set higher but carefully planned and operational work goals for themselves.[3]

As a second step, the role of feedback in achievement motivation is clarified. Participants learn that achievement-motivated individuals display a strong preference for situations in which they receive ongoing information on how well they are doing.

Small group discussions are then used as the third step in the internalization process. Opportunities are provided for participants to evaluate and critique one another's achievement motivations under circumstances where each individual is obligated to explain to the others why the goals he or she set are realistic in terms of his or her present situation, performance, and aptitudes. Other discussions stimulate much broader sharing of life goals and achievement. This step is calculated to free participants from old habits and attitudes, i.e., their natural bents. The small-group atmosphere may produce a cohesiveness among members that provides mutual encouragement and support for future striving.

Many participants gain systematic comprehension of the dynamics of achievement from the intervention. Numerous applications have shown that the motive to achieve can be increased over and above its previously established level. It has also been demonstrated that such changes in personal motivation translate into improved performance and achievement.

McClelland[4] points out, but offers no wider basis for solution than the on-going mutual-support group of clients, that one of the important deterrents to achievement motivation is the surrounding cultural norms and attitudes. If these are stagnant or negative, the impact of achievement training is likely to be significantly less than if the motivation to achieve within the culture itself is high. Possibly the limited impact of some achievement-motivation projects is due to failure of those responsible for the intervention to address the content and normative context of economic and financial realities.

In a more recent analysis, McClelland[5] has identified goal-oriented behavior relative to the need for power (9,1) and the need for affiliation (1,9) as two uncorrelated and independent dimensions of leadership. He concludes that these two dimensions cannot be drawn together except through religious arousal. An interpretation of this is that McClelland is identifying paternalism, i.e., power and affiliation as the resultant leadership style, not 9,9 team-oriented leadership.

GROUP (A-4-2)

Participants who attend Grid seminars often are motivated to apply teamwork skills in solving organizational problems. Working in the Internal Revenue Service, O'Rourke identified key points describing a team approach used for setting and achieving specific goals and objectives.[6] These include:

1. The problems worked on must be those participants themselves identify.
2. The teams are organized around members' commitments to overcome a specific obstacle in which they have a stake.
3. The nominated projects need to have properly defined parameters with necessary resources for success and endorsement coming from top management.
4. The projects must be achievable, and attainable within a specified time frame.
5. The results anticipated should be identified, measured, and evaluated in terms of some behavioral objectives or end result.
6. Considerable latitude is extended to these teams, with creativity the premium sought.
7. An orderly process or framework for attacking the problem is helpful, but not essential.
8. Progressively planned team project meetings and reports on them are organized, with starting and target completion dates.
9. Top management support and encouragement of necessary or recommended actions enhances team motivation.
10. Due publicity and recognition—even rewards—are appropriate, where justified.

O'Rourke evaluates the impact of team-oriented problem solving on 14 different aspects of organizational performance. Typical results included improvement in the suggestion awards program, incentive awards program, security system, employment placement, as well as the development of additional training programs concerned with job duties, counseling and coaching, special efforts to increase coordination among branches, and supervisory planning.

ORGANIZATION (A-4-4)

Another theory-based intervention designed to enhance group functioning occurred in a hospital setting. Viewed from the patients' perspective, living in a hospital involves experiences with a number of specialists, supporting services, and housekeeping groups. Many times the patient recognizes that only nominal coordination exists among these many providers of treatment and services. This state of affairs is traceable to the administrative and professional structure of most hospitals, where reporting relationships within various specialties are vertical and where the practice of medicine itself is sometimes little more than nominally connected with the rest of the administrative and support structure.

An alternative structure for hospital staff coordination is the ward team. This MbO-based intervention is related to coordination of ward activities and can be introduced on a group-by-group sequence.

The specific intervention reported here took place in Australia.[7] Members of the work team included junior medical staff, senior nursing staff, physiotherapists, occupational therapists, social workers, a ward pharmacist, and the ward clerk. All were initially invited to meet once a week to discuss care and progress of each specific patient and to overview the ward's activities. The ward resident convened the meetings and led the discussions. During the first ten weeks of the intervention, principles of MbO were introduced. Additional meeting time was used to define ward team objectives and develop performance measures. A deeper purpose was to use these MbO discussions for team building.

Based on this successful pilot effort, the idea for team-based ward management was extended throughout the hospital, with the diffusion completed over an eighteen-month period. Overall hospital performance during the project period showed significant improvement. A five-year trend of increasing costs was reversed by a 13.3-percent cost reduction while average length of patient stay declined by 10 percent.

While this intervention is primarily a theory-based one, it is also an example of a combination of interventions. Management by Objectives was introduced based on theory/principles. Team building and intergroup coordination aspects were based on more or less standard catalytic assumptions as described later in this text. In comparison with so many unsuccessful change efforts in hospitals, this one may have been more successful because it actively involved the medical staff.

A reorganization at the end of a seven-year period of unprecedented growth resulted in a new service and installation division in the Diebold organization. The organization had spent three years working with different external consultants to strengthen management skills at all levels. Like most technically oriented organizations, Diebold had invested in technical rather than managerial training and development. To broaden its managerial base, the company offered a nationwide workshop to its entire managerial workforce; service and installation managers were provided a structured way to review their basic management skills of communication, motivation, understanding people, and leadership.

The theory/principles intervention introduced at Diebold dealt with concepts of participation based on the work of McGregor, reinforced by Maslow's need hierarchy, Herzberg's concepts of work enrichment, and Varney's goal setting. Thus, MbO as a management technique was presented with the precaution that successful MbO implementation typically requires three to five years. In workshop settings, participating managers practiced setting goals and objectives through an MbO-oriented approach. This practical application of MbO theory provided the basis for internalization and subsequent MbO implementation. An internal resource person coordinated implementation.

This initial series of workshops helped establish an organizational climate receptive to and supportive of initiating an organization-wide development program based on Management by Objectives.

> To help assure a uniform approach throughout the organization, we decided to offer to all levels of management a seminar which would not only define Management by Objectives . . . but would explain to them that MBO is more than just goal-setting; it is an entire system of management.[8]

Particular emphasis was placed on the participative aspects of MbO as well as practical application of the theories and principles communicated through training. At this stage in the introduction of MbO, many organizations fall into the trap of expecting immediate, overnight results. Since expectations are unrealistic, failure, frustration, and disappointment often result. Then organizations blame "the system" (MbO) for failing to produce desired organizational change.

> After we had repeated the seminar throughout the country, area managers forward to the home office the objectives they had worked out with their local management groups. Although the goals differed, a significant common thread was that every area established improvement objectives.[9]

To provide organizational reinforcement for the successful implementation of MbO, Diebold established a highly visible reward system that recognized area and individual contributions to goal attainment. Systematically rewarding outstanding performance translated to improved organizational results for this company.

Regardless of the content of a theory/principles intervention, the organizational context may ultimately determine the degree of an intervention's eventual success. As in this case, the client's commitment and the organization's climate were congruent with the intervention's theoretical orientation. Its practices and procedures supported participative application of the theories provided and expectations were tempered by the realistic awareness that change, even for the better, is often long in coming. Finally, when change is organizationally re-warded, results are likely to be dramatic, as seems true in this case.

> The results have been impressive: volume has more than doubled. We have given award winners a symbol of their achievement that they can hang on the wall, a symbol to spur them to even greater accomplishment; and everyone wants to be next year's winner.[10]

Positive results like those reported by Diebold are not always attributable to the intervention per se. Oftentimes, confounding variables (e.g. increased attention, heightened expectations, etc.) are operating simultaneously with the intervention.

The success of one organization in an effort to change through the use of Grid OD as a multiphase theory/principles organization-wide approach is shown in Figure 6.1. The six interventions that comprise Grid OD are summarized below.

Individual development. Executives, managers, and supervisors learn Grid theories in weeklong seminars conducted by line management and supported by the training department or outsiders.

Team development. Starting at the top, the management of the organization uses Grid theories, particularly those related to conflict management, as the basis for examining the character, quality, consistency, and soundness of the organization's leadership.

Intergroup development. Those components of the organization that have working relationships examine the effectiveness of problem solving and productivity across interdepartmental lines.

Strategic modeling. The top team designs an ideal strategic corporate model based on six considerations. These are (1) key financial objectives, (2) nature of the business, (3) nature of the markets, (4) organization structure, (5) policies, and (6) development requirements.

The top management may spend a considerable amount of time creating an ideal strategic model. When the model is finally in hand, it is actually an organizational blueprint. It should be based on such thorough analysis that the organization can test its effectiveness in resolving the inevitable conflicts that will arise in shifting the organization to fit its requirements.

Implementation. The model is implemented. This process involves defining the maximum number of profit centers within the organization and evaluating each one's performance relative to the model's requirements.

Stabilization and critique. In this final phase efforts are made to stabilize the processes of change already brought into use and to ensure that goals, standards,

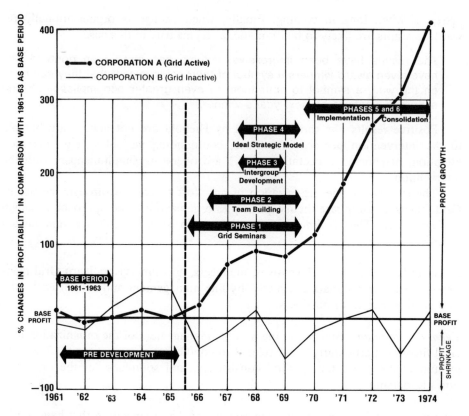

Figure 6.1 Comparison of the profitability of two matched corporations; Corporation A is involved in Grid development, but Corporation B is not.

and morale are developing in a sound way. Corrective steps are taken to rectify any difficulties that have arisen.

The study compared profitability of two autonomous corporations operating nationwide on opposite sides of an international border. Corporation A engaged in Grid development. Corporation B did not. They are owned by the same parent located in a third country, and both have access to the same capital support, same research and development, same trademarks, brand names, and so on. The corporations are engaged in similar businesses and face the same character of competition in comparable markets.

The comparisons that end in 1974 began fourteen years earlier. They are based on published annual reports and show that for the five years prior to the introduction of Grid development, the experimental corporation, A, and the control corporation, B, appeared to be hovering around the expected economic performance, with differences well within the range of chance fluctuations. After introduction of Grid organization development, Corporation A experienced a continuous and rising curve of profitability during the following decade. By

1974, the cumulative impact on profitability in the Grid-oriented company is 400 percent greater than in Corporation B, which is not engaged in Grid organization development. Corporation B has only managed to hold its own over the entire fourteen-year period.

When his company had been engaged in Grid OD for six years, the president of corporation A offered the following evaluative comments.

> . . . there is no doubt that OD has had a significant and positive effect on profits. . . . A major objective of the Grid was to change behavior and values within the organization in the direction of showing a high concern for both task accomplishment and human motivation, and then to sustain these changes and institutionalize them . . . there has undoubtedly been a substantial transformation in this area, with positive effects accruing through improved communication, the use of critique, profit or cost consciousness, some aspects of planning, the handling of conflict, meaningful participation in a group, and commitment among key managers. . . . there is one other most important benefit that has accrued from the OD program and that is a substantial improvement in the working relationships between management and union officials.
>
> Much of the work involving the union can be considered as a breakthrough in the application of OD principles and there is little doubt as to its success.[11]

LARGER SOCIAL SYSTEM (A-4-5)

Further use of McClelland-innovated training as a precursor to a community development workshop, where participants could begin applying achievement-motivation learnings in an actual social setting, is reported by Berlew and LeClere. While outcomes did not match objectives, the project itself provides an interesting case study of a community development attempt.

The activity took place in Curacao, one of the islands in the West Indies which has been self-governing within the Dutch Commonwealth since 1954. Curacao has a population of about 140,000. In the spring of 1969, a heavy and costly outbreak of community violence occurred on the island. Almost simultaneously the Curacao Chamber of Commerce intensified its exploration of possible community building opportunities. Berlew was one of the applied behavioral scientists contracted. He traveled to Curacao for discussions with the Chamber and his suggestion that achievement motivation was pertinent to the island's needs resulted in the more or less "crash project" that followed.

> At 8 p.m. (a few hours after my arrival) I met with the Board of Directors of the Chamber of Commerce and Industry. The President listed four objectives to which the Chamber was committed: (1) to encourage Antilleans to become associated with existing businesses, (2) to increase the amount of commercial activity on Curacao by encouraging Antillean business activity, (3) to create new jobs, and (4) to give Antilleans a sense of participation in their community.

We spent the next two hours reviewing current business and social conditions on Curacao and the prerequisites of an effective small-business development program. I emphasized that while we believe achievement motivation training to be one essential element, the availability of capital and training in business skills are also critical. We ended the Board meeting by planning strategy for a meeting scheduled the next morning with 40 government, community, labor, and business leaders. Our approach, we decided, would be (a) to describe "new behavioral science technologies" such as achievement training; (b) to engage those present in a discussion of how these technologies might relate to the problems of Curacao; and (c) to discuss how we might proceed to apply these technologies, if they were perceived as relevant.

Although the morning meeting was held in the Chamber building (hardly neutral turf), nearly everyone invited showed up. I introduced myself as a "technologist"—someone who did not know much about their specific situation but who was knowledgeable about some new social or change technologies which they should know about and might find useful in solving their problems. During my initial presentation I described achievement motivation training, various types of group training, and "psychological education" . . .; in response to questions, I also discussed community and organization development. Fearing that people might too readily see "cures" to their problems, I tried to be very objective and factual, presenting research findings whenever I could. The meeting lasted over four hours, and each group present appeared to find something relevant to its specific needs, which went well beyond the business development needs of the Chamber. The meeting ended with what seemed to be a general feeling that these new "technologies" were highly relevant and an effort should be made to apply them to the problems on Curacao.[12]

A special organization, representative of the various factions and neutral in terms of the different vested community interests, was set up to spearhead this broad intervention. In due course, several hundred of the island residents participated in either or both the achievement-motivation or community-development activities.

While the achievement-motivation program followed along lines generally comparable to those described earlier in this chapter, the community-development workshop dealt with content issues, such as what the participants would like to see Curacao become, and demonstration projects involving "intergroup competition and cooperation" aspects of community problem solving. Little emphasis was placed upon team-building skills or the capability of individual members to handle interpersonal or group-based conflict.

The overall impact of the intervention, which had as one of its primary objectives an increase in the number of entrepreneurs and the number of jobs available in Curacao, fell short of its targets. Nor did it stimulate continued support by the community and business leadership of Curacao. It is unclear as to why this is so, but the character of the interventions themselves may be at fault as explained below.

The Curacao intervention may have been unusual in that it was based more on a motivational model derived from psychology or sociology. The motivational model seemed particularly relevant for a number of reasons. First, during initial interview, black Antillean leaders expressed great concern over the lack of an Antillean identity. Specifically, they worried about an almost total lack of initiative by black Antilleans, which they attributed to centuries of dependency, first as slaves, then as Dutch subjects. It was this information that led us to the concept of efficacy and deCharm's distinction between "origins" and "pawns." Second, the lack of an entrepreneurial tradition among black Antilleans suggested that achievement motivation and the development of entrepreneurial spirit should play an important part in the intervention.

It was obvious that the use and distribution of power would have to be a major concern of the intervention. . . .

Unfortunately, we never fully understood the complexities of power on Curacao, although we did come to appreciate its singular importance.[13]

The relative lack of success could be partly attributable to the strategies by which the interventions were introduced and carried forward.

This intervention asks people to analyze what they want, when they want to do it, and then to do it, or try to do it. That can create revolutionaries as well as solutions. But unless *some* of the people start thinking in these terms, nothing in the system is going to improve anyway.[14]

More fundamentally, though, there appears to have been little in the way of foresighted consultant-client efforts to address the culture-based influence of norms/standards as evidenced in long-established traditions, precedents, and past practices that run counter to achievement training. Instead, the following serendipitous currents may have helped launch the intervention, move it awhile, and then leave it "dead in the water."

. . . Consultants are accepted because of a funny cross-mixture of the voodoo culture and the Dutch educational system where the people basically believe in voodoo, in magic, in fortune telling, in destiny, and all those things. The motivation training course is seen as something that gives people increased mental powers to control the directions of their lives. And to that extent it's consonant with what I call the voodoo cult. On the other hand, anyone who is a university professor is, by definition, the master. . . . People don't even question the validity of the ideas. So I think the consultant's initial speeches to the community were accepted immediately, whereas they wouldn't be necessarily in other systems.[15]

The Berlew-LeClere intervention provides an example of an effort to introduce the members of a large community to theories and concepts, several of which aimed to shift the cultural basis of interaction in the community to a new and more entrepreneurial orientation.

This intervention may be an example of consultants diagnosing and dealing with the wrong focal issue—that of goals/objectives, and failing to deal with critical focal issues—those of power/authority and norms/standards. The intervention might have been more successful if issues of power/authority and norms/standards had been addressed before trying to deal with goals/objectives.

Summary

Strategies for theory-based interventions designed to aid the client in setting and achieving goals and objectives are only beginning to be employed in systematic and quantifiable terms. The result is that relatively little is known about how to take advantage of the theory/principles that are available. The interventions that have been reported are suggestive, but there are significant indications that goals/objectives setting, given the broader norms/standards control over individual behavior, is not sufficient to bring about "permanent" change. Evidence to date indicates that when individual members participate in resolving power/authority issues, they begin to feel an increased commitment to finding solutions. Furthermore, when norms/standards are consonant with striving, it becomes a practical possibility for members to set goals for their own achievement or for the achievement of the group or organization of which they are members. However, if these other basic dimensions are disregarded, goals/objectives that are set, even as a result of theory-based interventions, are not likely to be achieved.

Notes

1. D. C. McClelland, *The Achieving Society* (Princeton, N.J.: Van Nostrand, 1961).
2. D. C. McClelland, "That Urge to Achieve," *THINK Magazine* 32, no. 6 (1966): 19–23.
3. J. Aronoff and G. H. Litwin, "Achievement Motivation Training and Executive Advancement," *Journal of Applied Behavioral Science* 7, no. 2 (1971): 215–29.
4. McClelland, "That Urge to Achieve," pp. 19–23.
5. D. C. McClelland, *Power: The Inner Experience* (New York: Irvington Publishers, 1975).
6. P. O'Rourke and L. Peterson, "Why Won't OD Phase II Just Happen?" *Training and Development Journal* 27, no. 1 (1973): 22–28.
7. J. U. Stoelwinder and P. S. Clayton, "Hospital Organization Development: Changing the Focus from 'Better Management' to 'Better Patient Care,'" *Journal of Applied Behavioral Science* 14, no. 3 (1978): 400–414.
8. R. E. Calhoun, "Results: Five Years with MBO," *Training and Development Journal* (October 1977): 8–10.
9. Ibid., p. 9.
10. Ibid., p. 10.
11. R. R. Blake and J. S. Mouton, *The New Managerial Grid* (Houston: Gulf Publishing Co., 1978), pp. 178–79.
12. D. E. Berlew and W. E. LeClere, "Social Interventions in Curacao." Reproduced by special permission from *Journal of Applied Behavioral Science* 10, no. 2 (1974): 30–31.
13. Ibid., p. 50.
14. Ibid., p. 52.
15. Ibid., pp. 50–51.

7

THEORY-PRINCIPLES INTERVENTIONS

Summary and Implications

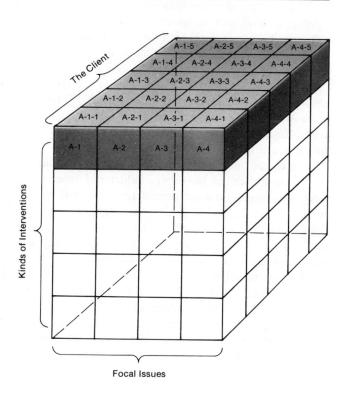

In each intervention described in this section the client has been taught theories pertinent to his or her behavior and has been aided in applying these theories to solving whatever difficulties he or she may be encountering. A significant issue bearing upon the use of theory-based interventions is how to help the client internalize theory so that it becomes a personally useful source of guidance.

The dynamics of internalization include the following:

1. Prior to being introduced to theories that may be pertinent, the client is enabled to indicate his or her natural bent in approaching a given problem.

2. Theories are then introduced to the client in any number of ways, but the general strategy is that the mode of theory presentation should permit the client to learn through active involvement and participation rather than through passive listening.

3. Opportunities for developing skill in using theory for diagnosis and problem solving are then provided. Along the way the client is afforded the opportunity to test his or her inclinations in the light of the theory, particularly with regard to behaviors that should be rejected while learning to utilize theory to strengthen new kinds of behavior.

These steps of internalization can be used when the client is an individual, a group, several groups, or an organization. As yet there are no good examples of successful theory interventions at the larger social-system level.

Power/authority is the focal issue that has drawn the greatest attention from those utilizing theory-based interventions. There are a number of theory-based approaches, including the Grid, Theories X and Y, Systems 1–4, transactional analysis, and Parent Effectiveness Training. Many unsuccessful interventions fail to deal with the focal issue of power/authority prior to trying to resolve other focal issues. Morale/cohesion has barely been approached from the standard of theory-based interventions, and the use of theory-based intervention to shift norms/standards is largely unexplored territory.

Goals/objectives have been addressed from a theory-intervention point of view. The interventions reported to date provide a model for what is possible, but are of limited value in demonstrating that this mode of theory intervention can be expected to have significant impact. The exception lies in its application after participants have resolved power/authority and norms/standards issues that otherwise block successful accomplishment of established goals/objectives.

Theory/principles is a sound and promising method of implementing positive behavioral change and strengthening effectiveness.

The most significant deficiency in theory/principles interventions arises from failure to deal with the basic requirement that clients internalize a theory before attempting to solve problems with it. Proven, effective ways of facilitating internalization have been suggested throughout the discussion of theory-based interventions.

These approaches to development are among the most important reported in this book. When successful, the client's thinking undergoes permanent change. Utilizing behavioral science ideas, he or she can now see things in a different light and sound perspective, and this altered perspective applies to a far wider range of events than the ones involved in the original learning.

Part II

PRESCRIPTIVE INTERVENTIONS

8

**PRESCRIPTIVE
INTERVENTIONS**

Prescriptive Interventions: An Introduction

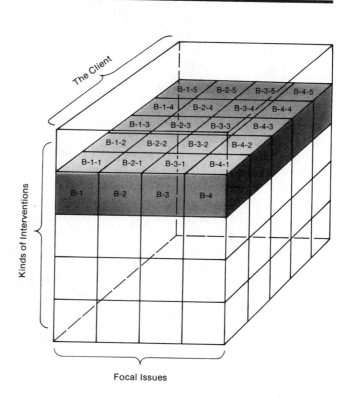

Bafflement, frustration, depression, and hopelessness are descriptions of how people may respond when facing situations which they cannot deal with effectively. All of these responses are amenable to a prescriptive approach. Under these conditions, the client is likely to find a prescribed solution both useful and attractive.

Prescription is probably the oldest approach for dealing with problems, and its character is most easily seen in the field of medicine. A physician usually listens to what a patient has to say about his or her symptoms, and then conducts an independent examination in an effort to establish the true nature of the problem, the client's real needs. Once the diagnosis is completed, the physician tells the patient what he or she needs to do or what needs to be done. This may include treatment designed to help in the restoration of health.

A formulation, as it applies in industrial consulting, based on doctor-patient assumptions of the prescriptive model, is provided by Cash and Minter. It includes the following:

1. The consultant is hired to identify the problem, diagnose it, and recommend a solution.

2. The consultant has more expertise regarding the specific problem than does the client.

3. The consultant is not expected by management to train the client in diagnostic and problem-solving skills.

4. The client expects the consultant to solve the problem in a relatively short period of time with minimal disruption and involvement of the work force.

5. The client can be just as committed to implement the recommended solution and to follow up on its progress if the procedures and reward structure for doing so exist.[1]

The prescriptive consultant relies on skills acquired from a body of knowledge or from years of practical experience. The consultant acts on the premise that he or she is sufficiently expert to discern the client's *actual* needs as contrasted with *felt* needs. The presumption is that the client lacks the necessary knowledge, skill, or objectivity to make a sound diagnosis and to design a plan of corrective action. A prescriptive consultant not only identifies what the real need is but also specifies the actions necessary if the client is to escape from self-defeating cycles.

A prescription-oriented consultant creates a relationship with the client that in many respects parallels that between doctor and patient. A significant feature is that perscriptions are possible even when clients are at their "wits' ends" or have thrown up their hands in despair. The consultant's aim is to give the client needed guidance or the impetus to take action. Recommendations may have the greatest impact when the client surrenders his or her self-will and unquestioningly accepts and follows the consultant's expert recommendations. The prescriptive consultant may or may not offer a rationale for what he or she recommends. When one is provided, the "answer" may become even more acceptable because the client understands, or at least appreciates in some degree, the problem-solving strategy involved. Readiness of consultants to explain answers makes them no less prescriptive, since a prescriptive consultant operates on the assumption that the client's request for consultation is prima facie evidence that the client either will not or cannot act on his or her own initiative.

A useful distinction that highlights a significant aspect of prescription can be drawn between a client on the one hand and a customer in a selling situation on the other. A customer is also a purchaser of goods or services, but customers generally act on the assumption that they know their own needs and have sufficient knowledge to make a choice between alternative possibilities for satisfying these needs. By contrast with the client, therefore, he or she does not want to be "told" but rather usually wants to be informed about the various available possibilities.

The exercise of options under client conditions belongs to the consultant. The consultant viewing the client as a "customer" is more typical of the catalytic approach to be discussed in later chapters.

The prescriptive consultant listens to the client's remarks and, without rejecting them, does not necessarily accept them at face value either. The client's expression of felt needs serves as a useful point of departure for the consultant in initiating diagnostic activities. The consultant then interrogates, observes, interviews, and investigates. After being satisfied that the real problem has been identified, the consultant says something like, "Here is your problem," and "This is the best thing for you to do to solve it."

The prescriptive consultant:

1. Interrogates for what he or she needs to know about the client's situation and in a professional manner cuts through to the heart of the matter, sometimes without much concern for social delicacies.

2. Controls the situation by telling the client how he or she perceives the problem.

3. Tells the client in a confident, authoritative way the "best" solution to implement.

4. Expresses confidence in the plan and often offers to supervise its implementation.

5. If the client procrastinates, or tries to avoid acting on recommendations, the consultant may say, "I don't think we can work together now, but feel free to call for an appointment whenever you feel seriously committed to having your problem resolved."

6. Weakens the client's defensiveness through undermining his or her claims or explanations, or establishes a relationship based on feelings of dependency (positive transference) which can result in the client doing what he or she has been told in order to enjoy the consultant's approval.

The basic premise of prescriptive interventions is that the consultant is an expert authority and the client is prepared to accept answers the consultant provides. This situation of authority/dependency is fraught with difficulties. Even though the consultant may know what is best for the client, prescription may be inappropriate as the intervention strategy for certain types of problems. The client may be unwilling, or not prepared by insight or competence, to act according to prescribed behavior or shift attitudes according to prescription. This can be partly because the client feels incapable of implementing the recommended actions, and partly because implementing them may be problematic in an interpersonal sense. It should be noted that the prescriptive approach may prescribe *what* to do in solving a technical problem of operations, as well as how to behave in the "process" sense. Prescription is far more likely to be successful in the former case, but even here the advice may prove unacceptable.

Another common feature of the prescriptive mode of consultation, particularly as it relates to group, intergroup, organization, or larger social-system applications, is that answers usually are directed to the top of the system so that the system's power/authority-obedience structure can be used to mandate the changes. Under these circumstances, implementation is more likely to occur, but resistance will almost certainly be generated at lower levels. Perceived coercion will eventually cause the prescribed changes to become distorted, watered down, or simply ignored.

The main source of resistance to prescriptive consultation arises when the client culture is adverse to recommended changes or the consultant fails to recognize and help the client to deal with these resistances in a constructive manner.

The prescriptive mode of intervention is found to be particularly effective when the client has reached "the end of the rope" and, though action is imperative, is unable to select the best course of action from the available alternatives. This inability may be due to emotional turmoil, or to having reached a hopeless impasse, or to ignorance of the salient variables impacting the situation. Under any of these conditions, the client is sufficiently dependent to be governed by the consultant's expertise. The inherent weakness in this approach is the fact that the consultant provides a ready-made solution, but the client may not possess enough competence to implement it.

Note

1. W. B. Cash and R. L. Minter, "Consulting Approaches: Two Basic Styles," *Training and Development Journal* 33, no. 9 (1979): 26–38.

9

PRESCRIPTIVE
INTERVENTIONS

Power/
Authority

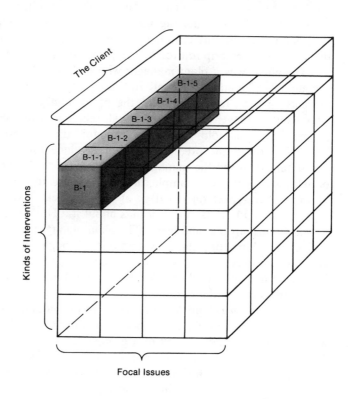

Prescriptive interventions are used frequently when the focal issue is power/authority. The intervention might aid a person to exercise his or her power/authority more effectively with another person, such as a consultant trying to help a parent deal with a child. Or, in organizational systems where power/authority relationships are hierarchical in character, a consultant may identify the problem inherent in a faulty organizational structure. Prescriptions for changing the power/authority relationships in order to enhance organizational effectiveness are then offered by the consultant.

INDIVIDUAL (B-1-1)

A major use of prescriptive consultation is to bolster the client's assertiveness. Whatever the reason, the individual is presently weak in the power/authority area. In some cases, the actions of the client who is expected to exercise power/authority need strengthening; in other cases, the client is a subordinate who should increase his or her power in the particular situation.

Ineffective Performance by a Subordinate

An example of prescription to bolster individual effectiveness in exercising power/authority is described by Flory.[1] The consultant involved was asked by his client for help in dealing more effectively with a "problem" subordinate. Responding to this invitation, the consultant first diagnosed the problem and then offered a prescription for boosting the client's use of power/authority.

The client was a plant manager who had been having trouble with his chief accountant, a "cold and formal" individual. To obtain better results than he was presently getting from this man, the plant manager—a genial fatherly person who liked to develop warm personal relations with his subordinates [i.e., a paternalist]—was told to take a forceful, direct, and impersonal approach. This, the consultant predicted, would produce much better results with the accountant than did the manager's more typical "soft" approach. On the matter of delayed reports, for example, the manager was instructed to say the following, "I want your report on my desk at nine o'clock Friday morning, complete in every detail, and no ifs, ands, or buts about it." Having delivered that ultimatum, he was to turn around and leave. The plant manager did just that, although it was difficult for him. But the new approach brought striking results. The report came in on schedule and was one of the finest the plant manager had received. The client had been told specifically how he should act and he followed through in accordance with the consultant's plan.

A similar kind of prescription given to individuals, but this time by a group-as-consultant, is described by Cohen and Smith. This intervention is said to be most suitable toward the end of a group's learning experience. At that time the total group is divided into subgroups of four or five members each. Each subgroup is given instructions as to how to proceed. One person from each subgroup leaves the room for ten minutes or so, while those who remain are instructed

[to] first diagnose this person's typical style of interacting with others, and secondly try to pinpoint definite, specific, helpful suggestions as to how he [or she] might be helped to engage in atypical but productive behavior both for himself and the group. I must stress the terms 'definite' and 'specific' . . . give him definite and specific prescriptions to carry out that are generally atypical but productive. Thus, one person might be told to express anger toward the group more directly and verbally instead of remaining quiet.[2]

At the end of this feedback session, participants have a prescription for what they should do to increase their effectiveness.

Behavior Modeling for Supervisory Effectiveness

Behavior modeling is an approach targeted to changing individual behavior. It entails explicit displays of exemplary behavior before the learner who is then encouraged to replicate or imitate the modeled behavior in his or her own performance. Application of what has been imitated to real-life operational or personal problems is the ultimate aim. Rationale as to why the modeled behavior is desirable is sometimes provided to increase acceptability.

An intervention designed to shift first-line supervisors' approaches to supervising through behavioral modeling took place in a manufacturing operation of a major forest products corporation and is described by Porras and Anderson.[3] The intervention came about because of substandard performance by employees. This was routinely reacted to by supervisors who "would typically either attack the employee with hostile and abusive language [9,1] or ignore the problem to avoid a confrontation [1,1]." Furthermore, supervisors complained of powerlessness and helplessness to deal with substandard performance in the face of an increasingly powerful union.

Supervisors were surveyed and asked to identify the most difficult problems faced in managing subordinates. Results were provided to the plant manager, who then discussed the data and decided on the intervention's content. The ten most difficult and frequently encountered incidents chosen were as follows.

1. Motivating an employee who is having a performance problem.
2. Handling employee complaints.
3. Reducing resistance to change.
4. Gaining the cooperation of another supervisor.
5. Achieving a commitment to performance goals.
6. Taking formal corrective action.
7. Problem solving with the boss.
8. Recognizing safe work practices.
9. Improving performance through recognition.
10. Improving attendance.

The intervention took place in seven workshop sessions, each lasting approximately six hours and each a week apart, enabling members to apply what had been learned on the job between sessions. Each session focused on a particular supervisory incident and was designed to help participants develop the skills necessary to deal with these situations. Discussion leaders were selected from line management positions, usually second- or third-level supervisors.

Each workshop session was based on learning and using motivational procedures derived from social learning theory. Six separate phases were included: (1) a conceptual presentation, (2) a videotape demonstration of the skills being taught, taped in company plants and using organizational members as actors, with each new tape introduced by a well-known company executive, (3) a rehearsal period for practicing the prescribed behaviors, (4) a feedback and reinforcement period for refining the behaviors, (5) the establishment of commitments to use learned skills to deal with specific problems on the job, and (6) follow-up discussion at the beginning of the next session to determine how well the skills had worked on the job.

An added feature was to hold one- to two-day meetings of the top-level managers in order to gain their commitment, and to demonstrate how they could reinforce and encourage others to use the newly developed skills.

The program's impact was evaluated by outside investigators. In the opinions of their subordinates, supervisors significantly changed their behavior. Changes in plant performance and labor relations indices imply that the new orientation of supervisors also led to improvements in plant efficiency and effectiveness.

This prescriptive intervention was applied to aid supervisors in solving practical problems of supervision. The prescriptive character of the intervention is in the fact that supervisors were "told" the correct handling of problems, given practice in its execution, and reinforced by socioemotional rewards for doing so in a successful way.

Daughter-Mother Conflict

One of the roots of prescriptive behavioral science interventions is J. L. Moreno's work with psychodrama, an approach patterned in some respects after Greek tragedy.[4] The method uses dramatic portrayals to help a client deal with some significant life situation. This may relate to feelings of being rejected by parents, issues of marriage, concerns about work, or other emotion-provoking situations that can block effective action.

Psychodrama takes place on an open, often circular, stage around which ten to thirty or more people may be seated. Lighting arrangements can either turn the stage into a kind of "room" where the audience is set apart from participants, or can create a setting where actors and audience interact with one another. The psychodrama proceeds through three stages: warm-up, enactment, and wrap-up. During the warm-up, the consultant-director provides background information, such as how the Greeks built their plays around a central protagonist whose contest with his circumstances—the tragedy—purged the audience of violent and overpowering emotions. Then someone in the audience is invited to volunteer to act out his or her circumstances. Others in the audience participate by taking roles of significant persons in the actor-client's life. There are many technical terms for the supporting cast members, such as "alter ego" ("other self") or "auxiliary ego," and for the processes that take place, such as role reversal and soliloquy, but knowledge of these is not essential for understanding how psychodrama works in practice.

The following is an account of the opening of the warm-up phase of a psychodrama conducted by a psychodramatic consultant. Judy is the volunteer client.

"What do you do, Judy?"

Judy shrugged. "Nothing . . . I guess."

"Nothing?" The director's voice had a hint of sarcasm. "You mean you sit around all day and stare at the walls?"

The girl smiled. "Well . . . no."

"Do you go to school?"

"No."

"You graduated?"

"I went to art school for six months and dropped out," Judy revealed.

"How did your parents feel about it?"

"They didn't like it very much."

"Show us," the director said.

A table and a couple of chairs were brought on stage and, under Judy's direction, arranged in an approximation of her family's living room. Then the director invited a woman from the audience to come up on the stage and portray Judy's mother.

"All right, Judy," she said. "Now show us what happened."

Judy looked self-conscious as she walked into the make-believe room, but she made her announcement in a strong clear voice. "Well, I've done it," she said, "I've told them I'm not going back to art school."

Before Judy's "mother" had a chance to reply, the director stepped in and suggested that the two characters switch roles. Now Judy stood in her mother's place; the volunteer from the audience walked in and repeated Judy's announcement.

"How do you feel, Mother?" the director asked Judy.

The girl seemed confused. Her voice faltered. "I'm angry, I'm disappointed. I'm hurt," she said.

"And what are you going to say to your daughter?"

"How could you do such a thing?" Judy said sharply. "Your father and I have worked hard to give you the things we never had. But you won't take them. You keep refusing our kindness."

"How do you feel about that, Judy?" Mrs. Moreno cut in. "This time answer her as yourself."

"You aren't very kind. You're selfish!" Judy cried. "You don't care about me at all. You just want your children to go to school and graduate because it makes you look good to the neighbors."[5]

This episode suggests the richness of expression made possible through psychodramatic presentation. The director supervises the entire process and both stimulates and supports the expression of emotions that have been aroused under client "protagonist" circumstances. Moreover, the director supervises the expression of feelings by *others* who represent "real life" people. The prescriptive nature of the consultation is in the *process* interactions. That is, the consultant tells the client what to do to release feelings and how to set up a situation, rather than giving answers to specific problems. Prescription comes externally but impacts upon internal or subjective problems the consultant judges to be of central importance to the client.

During the wrap-up, reactions toward the protagonist's problem and toward one another are shared between audience members and actors. Participants often describe their feelings toward the circumstances enacted and sometimes relate their own similar or related experiences for reactions and comments. This third give-and-take step, usually in the catalytic but also in the acceptant vein, permits the central character to see his or her situation in the perspective of similar problems experienced by others. While the outcome for the client may be *cathartic,* the prescriptiveness inherent in psychodrama makes it very different from an acceptant approach. A critical difference between the two is related to what the client learns. In an acceptant intervention the client learns *how* to express his or her emotions and feelings, and, at least theoretically, this learning can be transferred to real-life situations. But the client is only able to express what becomes evident through *self*-discovery as the consultant does not intervene. In a prescriptive psychodrama the consultant pushes the client into discoveries that might not have otherwise been made. The limiting factor in this approach is that those who stand in for the real characters are not the real characers. For fuller change to occur, the real characters may need to experience the psychodrama just as much as the volunteer client.

Wife-Husband Conflict

In addition to relying heavily on psychodramatic techniques of the sort pioneered by Moreno, Gestalt therapy has as one of its guiding assumptions the central concept of client "wholeness" or "completeness." Lack of completeness is characterized as a personality "hole" produced by an impasse as some point along the way. One purpose of Gestalt therapy is to help the client find the hole and to fill it, thereby identifying and resolving the impasse. This cannot be done as well, according to Perls,[6] by a talking approach (such as psychoanalysis) as it can by an active and directed approach. The impasse must be confronted actively by the client, with the consultant directing the client by keeping him or her focused on the impasse.

Two chairs are used to facilitate this procedure in one version of Gestalt therapy. One, where the client sits, is the "hot seat." The other is empty except when the client shifts over to sit on it while enacting another person or even another part of him- or herself. The consultant may be standing at a podium before the assembled audience.

The Gestalt consultant aims at preventing the client from rationalizing or in other ways escaping from the here-and-now activities. Then, some aspect of a client's personality that has never been completed can move toward closure. In this sense, Gestalt therapy somewhat resembles Frankl's "logotherapy"[7,8] or Wolpe's[9,10] desensitization techniques. Relief results from doing the thing that is feared in fantasy and which, therefore, has been shied away from in reality.

The Gestalt therapy approach parallels psychodrama in such aspects as role reversal. The client enacts his or her own subjective reactions, and then taking the role of his or her adversary (boss, wife, or husband, for example), "answers" by reacting from the adversary's point of view. A series of such reversals provides the client a basis for seeing the way he or she has been projecting ideas and attitudes onto the adversary and, in turn, how he or she experiences the adversary reacting to these projections. Each step along the way is directed in a prescriptive, "Now do this," "Now do that," manner by the consultant who, in addition, may apply pressure on the client to intensify a reaction or to experiment with a different solution to the problem.

Perls illustrates a consultation with a client that demonstrates the prescriptive character of these interventions. For a decade, Carol had been trying to decide whether or not to divorce her [paternalistic] husband. Carol begins in the "hot seat," expressing herself. Then, at the consultant's bidding, she switches over to an empty chair and talks for her husband. This back-and-forth reversal continues, with the client going from being herself to "being" her husband, interrupted only by the consultant.

> *Client:* I'm trying to decide whether to divorce my husband or not, and have been for ten years.
>
> *Consultant:* It's a real impasse, yah! A real unfinished situation. And this is typical of the impasse. We try *everything* to keep the status quo, rather than to get through the impasse. We keep on with our self-torture games, with our bad marriages, with our therapy where we improve, improve, improve, and nothing changes, but our inner conflict is always the same, we maintain the status quo. So talk to your husband. Put him there.
>
> *Client:* Well, I feel like I've been—I've found out some things, Andy, and I found out who you—who you are to me, and I love you in some ways. You know, I didn't love you when I married you, but I love you now, in some ways, but—I feel like I'm not gonna be able to grow up if I stay with you, and I don't want to be a freak.
>
> *Consultant:* Change seats.
>
> *Client* (as husband): That's not fair, Carol, because I love you so much, and we've been together for so long . . . and I want to take care of you . . . I just want you to love me, and—
>
> *Consultant:* I don't understand. First, he says he loves you, and now you say he wants—he needs love.
>
> *Client* (as husband): Yes. I—I really need—I guess I do need love.

Consultant: Is it a trade? A trade agreement—love vs. love? . . .

Client (as husband): I need you.

Consultant: Ah! What do you need Carol for?

Client (as husband): Because you're exciting . . . I feel dead without you.

Client: (herself again): You're a *drag,* Andy. I can't *feel* for *both* of us . . . I'm—I know, I'm scared too, I'm really scared of leaving. I'm scared of leaving, too, but—we're just scared. We both need love. I don't think I can give it to you.

Consultant: Can we start with resentments. Tell him what you resent about him.

Client: Oh, I resent you being such a burden on my back. I resent—every time I leave the house, I have to feel guilty about it. I feel guilty for—

Consultant: Now that's a lie. When you feel guilty, you actually feel resentful. Scratch out the word guilty, and use the word *resentful* instead, each time.

Client: I resent not being able to feel free. I want to move. I want—I resent . . . I resent your nagging at me. . . .

Consultant: Now tell him what you appreciate in him.

Client: All right. I really appreciate—your taking care of me, and your loving me, 'cause I'm—I know nobody else could really love me like you do. I resent you—

Consultant: Now let's scratch out the word "love," and put in the real words instead.

Client: Oh, I resent your smothering me. I resent your keeping me a little girl.[11]

At the end of the session, with Carol still present, the consultant responds to a comment from the audience.

Consultant: . . . I can tell you only this much: It is possible to get through the impasse. If I would say how, I would be "helpful," and it would be of no avail. She has to discover it, all on her own. If she really gets clear, "I'm stuck," she might be willing to do something about it. She is pretty close to realizing it, at least, that she is stuck in the marriage. She doesn't realize yet that she is stuck with her self-torture, in her game. "You should/you should not; you should/you should not; yes/but; but in case this happens/then; why doesn't Prince Charming come/but Prince Charming doesn't exist." All this verbiage, what I call the merry-go-round of the being stuck whirl, the real whirl. I think you got a good example. The only solution is to find a magician with his magic wand. And this doesn't exist. . . .[12]

The consultant has sought, through prescribing in a step-by-step way, to help Carol struggle with her impasse. The prescription here relates more to how the problem should be explored rather than what should be done in resolution, but the latter is also characteristic as she is told she *must* find the solution within herself. In contrast, the manager-accountant example described earlier in this chapter involved *content* prescription as opposed to "process" prescription.

Child-Parent Conflicts

A prescriptive strategy is offered in the following description of behavior modification as an approach that has emerged from the work of Pavlov,[13] Hull et al.,[14] and Skinner.[15] A rationale that applies to behavior modification was stated by E. Stanley Jones some years ago when he said, "It is easier to act yourself into a new way of thinking than to *think* yourself into a new way of acting."[16] Thus the field of behavior modification is premised on the idea that if you can get people to change their behavior, changed attitudes will follow. Other approaches, particularly the acceptant mode of consultation, are based on the opposite: get people to change their attitudes and changes in behavior will follow.

In the behavior-modification approach, the consultant selects the goals to be achieved and intervenes in the client's life to make sure he or she moves in that direction. The purpose of the intervention is to build new skills or strengthen desirable behavior through defining the client's problem in terms of learning needed and specific behavioral goals to be achieved.[17] The client is expected to enter into a mutual agreement, sometimes in terms of a contract between client and consultant. In the contract, the client acknowledges an authority-obedience relationship in which he or she agrees with the regimen designed. The carrying out of such an approach with a particular client can involve a variety of techniques.

An intervention to reduce the frequency of objectionable behavior by a child is described by Zeilberger, Sampen, and Sloane.[18] The approach relies on behavior-modification techniques to structure the child's environment so as to reward behavior that the consultants and/or parents consider desirable and to discourage unwanted behavior.

Rorey, who was nearly five years old, repeatedly screamed and told other children what to do and how to play. He would enforce his demands with punches, kicks, and slaps. The consultant's diagnosis was that these undesirable behaviors were being reinforced by Rorey's mother. In play situations they had seen her giving him excessive attention, as well as not following a consistent pattern of providing discouraging "consequences" for his objectionable behaviors. Instead, she would try to correct Rorey by going into lengthy explanations, giving him attention after each one of his temperamental episodes, without clarifying the connections between the undesirable act and her displeasure.

The consultants prescribed a program to replace what they saw as this mother's self-defeating strategies with Rorey. They suggested she arrange a one-hour play period each afternoon, with neighborhood children present. This daily one-hour session served as a training phase during which the consultants coached and corrected Rorey's mother until she was well practiced in following the instructions below.

1. Immediately after Rorey acts aggressively or disobediently, take him to the time-out (TO) room. One of the family bedrooms was modified for this by having toys and other items of interest to a child removed.

2. As Rorey is taken to the TO room for aggressive behavior, say "You cannot stay here if you fight." As Rorey is taken to the TO room for disobedient behavior, say "You cannot stay here if you do not do what you are told." Make no other comments.

3. Place Rorey in the TO room swiftly and without conversation other than the above. Place him inside and shut and hook the door.

4. Leave Rorey in the TO room for two minutes. If he tantrums or cries, time the two minutes from the end of the last tantrum or cry.

5. When the the time is up take Rorey out of the TO room and back to his regular activities without further comment on the episode, i.e., in a matter-of-fact manner.

6. Do not give Rorey explanations of the program, of what you do, of his behavior, or engage in discussions of these topics with him. If you desire to do this, have such discussions at times when the undesired behaviors have not occurred, such as later in the evening. Keep these brief and at a minimum.

7. Ignore undesirable behavior which does not merit going to the TO room. "Ignore" means you should not comment upon such behavior, nor attend to it by suddenly looking around when it occurs.

8. Ignore aggressive or disobedient behavior which you find out about in retrospect. If you are present, treat disobedient behavior to other adults the same as disobedient behavior to you.

9. Reinforce desirable cooperative play frequently (at least once every 5 min.) without interrupting it. Comments, such as "My, you're all having a good time" are sufficient, although direct praise which does not interrupt the play is acceptable.

10. Always reward Rorey when he obeys.

11. Special treats, such as cold drinks, cookies, or new toys or activities, should be brought out after periods of desirable play. It is always tempting to introduce such activities at times when they will interrupt undesirable play, but in the long run this strengthens the undesired behavior.

12. Follow the program twenty-four hours a day.[19]

The consultants furnish data which make it clear that this regimen had the desired effects of diminishing the frequency of Rorey's disruptive behavior.

Student-Teacher Conflict

Another series of interventions, similar in character but involving a ten-year-old child in a classroom situation, is reported by Whitley and Sulzer.[20] The fourth grader, normal except for being hyperactive, was disrupting class by talking out of turn and leaving his seat. The intervention strategy was for the teacher to use her authority by taking notice of the child only when he was *not* talking and was in his seat. When he met these conditions she was to give him encouragement. When he asked for permission to talk, she was to call on him to speak as soon as possible. If what he then said was to some degree correct, she voiced approval. Furthermore, he was to be responded to when he requested permission to be out of his seat for a good reason, such as to pass books out to others.

When he behaved inappropriately she moved away from his desk, ignored his calls when his hand was not raised, and did *not* respond to any of his behavior that interfered with the desired learning circumstances. The teacher-as-consultant was able in this manner to cause unwanted behavior to become less frequent and desirable behavior to increase.

Aggression in the Classroom

The disruptive effects of disturbed relations with people in positions of authority can be observed in the learning disabilities of even very young children. Prescriptive interventions have had productive effects in terms of shifting unacceptable acting-out behavior to more tolerable classroom conduct.[21] The rationale of the approach was explained in the following way.

To establish a preintervention basis to be used for comparison purposes later, the consultants hired a trained teacher and put her in the classroom with five four-year-old boys who had been carefully selected by psychiatrists and social workers as the cream of the hyperaggressive crop. Her customary techniques of classroom control were futile—the boys were easily able to gain the upper hand by behavior such as refusing to give up Playdoh, turning over chairs and throwing them at her, kicking and spitting at the teacher, or fighting with each other.

> What Miss Sally did not realize is that she had inadvertently structured an exchange where she consistently reinforced aggression. First, as noted, whenever she fought with them, she *always lost.* Second, more subtly, she reinforced their aggressive pattern by giving it serious attention—by looking, talking, scolding, cajoling, becoming angry, even striking back. These boys were playing a teasing game called "Get the Teacher." The more she showed that she was bothered by their behavior, the better they liked it, and the further they went.[22]

Next, the consultants provided the teacher with a mode for rewarding desired behavior: giving the children tokens for attending to lessons, putting up supplies, and so on. These tokens could then be exchanged for desirable activities such as seeing movies, snacks, nature walks, and playing with desired toys. The teacher was also instructed to ignore disruptive behavior. She was helped to do this by being "wired" to observers behind a one-way screen who could inform her as to what was going on and suggest appropriate actions to take.

> First, the teacher had to be instructed in how *not to reinforce* aggression. Contrary to all her experience, she was asked to turn her back on the ag-

gressor, and at the same time to reinforce others' cooperation with tokens. Once we were able to coach her and give her immediate feedback over a wireless-communication system, she structured the exchanges almost perfectly . . . [there was]: a gradual increase in cooperation—from about 56 to about 115 sequences per day, and a corresponding decrease in aggression from 150 to about 60 sequences!

What this meant in terms of changed behavior is illustrated as follows.

Here is an example of their new behavior patterns, taken from a rest period—precisely the time when the most aggressive acts had occurred in the past:

All of the children are sitting around the table drinking their milk; John, as usual, has finished first. Takes his plastic mug and returns it to the table. Miss Martha, the assistant teacher, gives him a token. John goes to cupboard, takes out his mat, spreads it out by the blackboard, and lies down. Miss Martha gives him a token. Meanwhile, Mike, Barry, and Jack have spread their mats on the carpet. Dan is lying on the carpet itself since he hasn't a mat. Each of them gets a token. Mike asks if he can sleep by the wall. Miss Sally says "Yes." John asks if he can put out the light. Miss Sally says to wait until Barry has his mat spread properly. Dan asks Mike if he can share his mat with him. Mike says "No." Dan then asks Jack. Jack says "Yes," but before he can move over, Mike says "Yes." Dan joins Mike. Both Jack and Mike get tokens. Mike and Jack get up to put their tokens in their cans. Return to their mats. Miss Sally asks John to put out the light. John does so. Miss Martha gives him a token. All quiet now. Four minutes later—all quiet. Quiet still, three minutes later. Time: 10:23 A.M. Rest period ends.[23]

Prescriptive interventions based on giving tokens in exchange for desired behavior and withholding reinforcement when unwanted conduct occurred produced a significant reduction in acting-out behavior. Similar applications of token-based interventions with comparable results are reported by the Hamblin team with regard to ghetto and autistic children.

Help in Unexpected Circumstances

Since the consultants and clients involved are unacquainted and are interacting in a remote and anonymous relationship, the value of intervention-by-telephone might be thought to be very limited, particularly with regard to prescriptive interventions. The following example indicates the contrary.

A unique problem, with features common to most emergency calls, occurred recently. A telephone counselor was called at his home, by a girl who reminded him of a call she had made two months previously, when she suspected that she was pregnant. His warm, nonjudgmental attitude at that time, combined with his willingness to be helpful, had stuck in the girl's mind—even though her call had escaped his. The situation was unbelievable. The girl had carried a baby to term without her parents becoming aware of the fact. She was sixteen and had only had intercourse once. At the time of the second call, she was at a friend's house, having just completed a Christmas shopping trip with her mother, who, in turn, was upstairs having coffee with the girlfriend's mother. Meanwhile the pregnant girl had begun to have labor pains; her bag of water had broken. She was crying and feeling helpless, yet neither she nor her friend could summon up the courage to tell her mother.

Rather than expressing cynicism and suspicion, the counselor acted on the face-value statements of the caller, despite their highly unusual nature. He insisted that the girl call her mother to the phone. When the mother answered (still upstairs, while her daughter was downstairs), he explained briefly and to the point who he was and what was happening to her daughter. He concluded with a specific instruction to go downstairs and take her daughter to the hospital. Then the counselor went to the hospital himself. The girl had already been admitted to the delivery room, and the mother wanted to be left alone. However, the counselor discovered that no social worker or psychiatrist in the hospital would be informed of the peculiar situation, and fearing for the girl's emotional difficulties in having to confront intimidating parents (the father put his hand through a wall upon his arrival at the hospital), he called someone himself. After explaining the situation to the head social worker in the hospital—who was grateful that the affair had been brought to his attention—the phone counselor went into the waiting room, where the girlfriend, a fifteen-year-old, was sitting shaking. She had been sent down to wait for her friend's father but had not wanted to tell him exactly what was happening to his daughter. Despite the man's angry and hostile attitude, the girl had ridden the elevator up to the appropriate floor without saying anything. Now she was terrified, uncertain about what would happen to her friend and upset because of her own involvement almost from the beginning. The counselor calmed her down; when the social worker arrived, he left.

The girl telephoned again the next day to tell him she had had a seven-pound, three-ounce boy. Further developments occurred. The counselor found the girl willing to call and talk with him with more honesty and feeling than she was able to bring to contact with the hospital staff or the social workers assigned to her case. He communicated freely with them about the content of her calls, after receiving the girl's permission to do so. Her deep and reassuring trust in him grew out of his quick and decisive intervention. It is doubtful whether any other agency would have ever been called; no family work would ever have been done, and the girl would have continued on without any intervention if it were not for this crisis line. As it was, he continued to give help (always over the phone) to the girl as she dealt with her grief and her unwillingness to give up her baby—issues very important in her life if she is to ever trust relationships with men again.[24]

This prescriptive intervention had an impressive measure of success because the consultant told the client the specific steps necessary to avert tragedy and took immediate concerned responsibility, in a foresighted way, to protect his client and her girlfriend from what might otherwise have been traumatic effects of ungoverned parental "aftershock." The mother's self-isolation and the father's behavior confirm how predictively accurate was the consultant's rapid diagnosis of the impending situation at the hospital. Over the ensuing period, and still without meeting face to face, the client trusted the consultant more than anyone around her. This permitted additional interventions, apparently of a more acceptant character.

Increased Assertiveness

Interventions designed to help clients express themselves more authentically and competently in situations where they ordinarily experience fear of criticism or rejection have been described by several practitioners. Wolpe views this as a sound approach to behavioral change whenever a client is blocked from saying or doing things that would seem reasonable to an unbiased observer. Here is an example.

> *Consultant:* What do you do if you are standing in line for theater tickets and somebody gets in front of you?
>
> *Client:* I don't do anything.
>
> *Consultant:* Well, how do you feel?
>
> *Client:* I feel mad. I boil up inside.
>
> *Consultant:* So, why don't you do anything?
>
> *Client:* I'm afraid of making a scene.
>
> *Consultant:* People are taking advantage of you. Here, this person is taking advantage of you. You cannot allow it. You must say to him, "Will you kindly go to the back of the line?" In doing this, you will be expressing your anger in a way that is appropriate to the situation and socially acceptable.[25]

It is expected that when the client acts in his or her own behalf and is successful, confidence for repeating this behavior in the future will be increased and his or her habitual fear of undesirable consequences will be commensurately reduced.

Summary

Prescriptive interventions in the power/authority area are generally employed for either of two purposes: (1) when the client is abusive of those in positions of power/authority and needs to learn more constructive and compliant behavior; and (2) to aid those who are presently blocked in the exercise of legitimate power to become more effective in using it. Usually this client holds the weaker position in some present relationship. No basis is available for estimating how much transfer of learning occurs from the intervention situation to other parallel circumstances.

GROUP (B-1-2)

When a prescriptive consultant works with a group, he or she most often accepts and works through the existing power/authority system. This may be done in either of two ways: the first way is to tell the group's top official what should be done that is not now being done in order to achieve desired results; the second is to literally step into the top position in the power/authority system and enact the role requirements of that position until a sufficient basis of collaboration permits the consultant to return the formal system to its customary operating mode.

Boss's Withdrawal When Challenged

An example of Gestalt therapy in work groups illustrates how this kind of prescriptive intervention is applied when the focal issue is the top official's faulty use of power/authority. Herman[26] describes the character of a Gestalt-based intervention in the setting of a corporate team. The boss, a high-level manager, had developed a strong commitment to what he called "OD values"—being fair, rational, and helpful. Because this client was a man of great personal forcefulness as well as occasional moodiness—personal characteristics said to be not consistent with "OD values"—he was in conflict with himself. This was made clear by his conduct of staff meetings. For the most part they proceeded satisfactorily, but from time to time the manager would "blow his stack" and pin several of his staff to the wall. His logic was not faulted, but his vehemence led to subordinates' feeling themselves steamrollered. Some defended themselves by presenting counter-logic; one reacted in humor; another felt he had been punished. Regardless of the individual reaction, the boss's response was to "clam up." This in turn led to work issues remaining unresolved.

On a particular occasion the consultant observed the kind of encounter described. A proposal for a policy change had been suggested by one of the team members and received some support from two others. The boss's immediate reaction was negative. He accused the proponents of being unrealistic and, after some discussion, became glum.

How did the consultant deal with this? He could have focused attention in a confronting way on the deadening response the manager's reaction had produced. In a catalytic way he might have encouraged the team to collect and analyze data on steps to take so as to start moving again. Instead, he intervened in a prescriptive way by pushing the manager to follow through, to get it all out. The manager acted on the recommendation, at first clumsily, but, as he warmed up, with gusto. He tore into his subordinates. Those whom he attacked, counterattacked. Soon everyone was shouting back and forth.

At a later time these participants critiqued what had transpired and concluded that these and more recent but similar episodes of explosiveness had resulted in a greater sense of vitality, excitement, and relatedness than had been experienced previously. Subordinates had learned not to buckle under but to stand their ground and fight back. The client had achieved a new respect for both them and himself.

Herman's prescription rested in the Gestalt concept of wholeness. The boss needed to "complete" himself rather than cut himself off half way. By rejecting his typical impulse not to follow through he could further unleash his frustrations. This got others stirred up to the point where they too could respond in ways that made them more "whole."

Suspending Traditional Authority to Increase Creativity

A prescriptive way of reducing the adverse impact on creativity within a group from the exercise of power/authority by the leader is provided by Emshoff.[27] This is another version of the collateral system notion recommended for use in situations where innovation is important. The formal leader remains in charge, but his or her participation is limited to ensuring that the meeting agenda is clear, that realistic time limits are established, and that organization constraints are defined.

To counteract the negative effects of power/authority, the aspect of the chair's ordinary role in leading the meeting is assigned to a neutral facilitator who is responsible for the procedures used and process features of the meeting. The chair may participate as would any other group member. A recorder is also appointed to be responsible for the short-term memory aspects of the meeting.

Other prescriptions in this intervention include "the recorder should be plainly visible . . . a semi-circular meeting arrangement . . . encourages all participants to make eye-contact with colleagues, etc."

This strategy is a prescriptive intervention that sets up a collateral system to get around the conventional power/authority problem. Its origins are in the work of Gordon[28] and of Straus and Doyle.[29]

This intervention disregards the possibility of the leader and others learning how to exercise power/authority in such a way as to stimulate rather than stifle innovation.

Parent Abdication of Responsibility for Teenager

Parents are ordinarily expected to exercise supervision over their children, particularly in the teen years. The notion, if not always the actuality, is that in this way positive growth can be stimulated and traumatic situations either averted or minimized. Sometimes such supervision breaks down, leaving a power vacuum; as a consequence, teenagers may possibly engage in self-destructive behaviors.

Sometimes what first appears to be "the problem" is merely a symptom rather than the problem itself, as illustrated in a situation where the consultants tried to deal with an individual case of heroin addiction. Eventually they recognized that Jim, an intelligent youngster, was using drugs to act out his resentments, particularly against his father who had failed to supply much guidance or to set limits. The consultant decided to intervene upon the family itself, thus redefining the "client" to be both parents and their son.

> Three experienced staff members made an appointment to meet with the family, in their home, one evening shortly after the second episode with heroin. These two men and one woman had not consulted with each other about what they would do beyond thoroughly exploring the family structure and system of interrelationships. They entered the home respected and trusted to an extent, because of our organization's previous work with the family, and because the parents were desperate, afraid, and angry, looking for a kind of help they had never received.

The session began casually, but soon,

> Jim began to rationalize his use of drugs, saying that it was his business. He felt he had a right to do what he wanted, as long as he knew of the possible effects of the drugs. He said he did not know whether he would use drugs again, but there was no attempt to promise. He left the possibility clearly open.

Before long, the consultants had heard and seen sufficient evidence on which to base a diagnosis of Jim's behavior and its consequences within the family group. Jim was displaying

> defensiveness, an irritating disregard for the feelings of his parents, an arrogant self-centeredness, a subtle intellectual game being played of overt reasonableness camouflaging a deep disinterest in anyone but himself. The counselors began to feel more confident about what was going on. An example is sufficient. Jim wore his hair shoulder length, and frizzed out, and he was often mistaken for a girl by his family's friends, to the embarrassment of the parents. They had tried to point out the pain he was causing them (humiliation, embarrassment), and he had listened to them carefully, saying he would take what they had to say into careful consideration; then he let his hair grow even longer. This irritated his parents, but they depended on reason to communicate and to convince. His father was a liberal, who felt that reason was the only appropriate way to deal with the situation. His desperation came from the sinking feelings he got when his son played at being reasonable but continued acting in a selfish way, which hurt his parents deeply.

From this point on the consultants began actively intervening in a prescriptive way.

> As the session focused on the parents' feelings, the counselors began to treat Jim as a four-year-old, interpreting this to both his parents and to him as the only appropriate way to deal with his actions and his defensiveness. He denied he was being defensive, but the counselors cut him off several times, telling him to be quiet, that they were talking to his parents. As his parents talked, their feelings of helplessness were clearly evident. It was

interpreted that Jim seemed to have all the power in the house, able to do whatever he wanted, even if it hurt himself or them. The counselors refused to believe that it had to be that way, pointing out that they did not let Jim control their behavior by either threats or actions.

As the threat to his means of power became clearer, Jim became uncomfortable and attempted to threaten the counselors: "This isn't helping," "I'll probably take drugs just to show you I don't have to do what you say," "Who are you to come in here and do this?" Finally he simply got up and walked out, saying, "I don't have to put up with this bullshit!"

At this point two of the consultants intervened on the parents, telling them that as adults they did not have to accept being abused and manipulated. Also, as the consultants saw it, Jim's father and mother were "allowing him to use drugs." Meanwhile, the third consultant went to bring Jim back by compulsion if necessary. The interventions took effect as

. . . several facts clicked in the father's head. He was the father; he was the one with the power; he could prevent Jim from growing his hair long or from taking drugs; he was the boss. And he surrendered all of this, threatening only to send the boy to where someone else would be powerful and would make him mind. He could also see Jim's incredible anger and resentment, how it was directed at himself through drugs and indirectly at his parents through his hair and his drug abuse. Jim's father got up and went after the counselor and Jim.

For the first time the father used physical force to bring the boy around to doing what the father wanted him to. He realized that, if the boy could not act in a reasonable, adult manner, it was absurd to treat him as an adult. The boy was acting like a four-year-old; so the father tried to pull him back, though he was still indecisive.

The second counselor walked over to where the three were struggling and picked the boy up and carried him back, where he sat quietly. The father then decided that the boy must cut his hair. Immediately the boy protested, saying he must talk to his father alone. The clear implication was that he could control his father, but not them—something the father could not miss. He refused and insisted the boy cut his hair to a respectable length. He said to Jim, "You have been punishing us with your hair, and we are merely stopping you from continuing to do this." After his hair was cut, by himself, with no use of force, Jim ran out of the house. His father ran out after him. He had only walked a block away, to see if he still cared. He returned without a struggle.

Thus, in effect, the focus of power/authority had shifted from son to father. The consultants sum up the results and some subsequent outcomes.

Jim's father had learned that he had to set limits and, more importantly, that he had to enforce them. By being strict with Jim he gave Jim an opportunity to act like a little boy, which Jim needed, expressing anger through swearing, crying, and yelling, instead of shooting heroin. As Jim acted in this new way he was able to relax more, and his personality began to change. He became much more friendly, convincing, open, honest, and stopped playing games. He was a different person.[30]

Although the problem as initially presented appeared to be the problem of an individual, its dynamics involved intense though indirect reactions against a father who had failed to meet his son's unexpressed expectations for close and personally concerned guidance. Recognizing this as they surveyed the family's interaction, the consultants prescribed to Jim's father and boosted his confidence to act in such a way as to give his son the structure and framework needed.

Gang Fights

Consultants who work with juvenile street gangs in a general endeavor to reduce delinquency by encouraging alternative and more constructive activities rarely make use of the prescriptive approach. However, Christie describes one situation where prescriptive methods were employed to resolve a power struggle between two gang members contending for gang leadership.

The consultant was approached on the street by Blackie who said, "Manuel wants to fight me and I hear he's got a gun. I've got a gun too." Christie managed to "park" him at the local Boys' Club director's office before going to locate Manuel. After checking whether Manuel had a gun yet (he hadn't), the consultant invited him to come over to the Boys' Club so that "we [can] all sit down and talk about it." As they talked, the actual cause of these youths' bad feelings toward one another surfaced.

Manuel felt that Blackie, a relatively new member, had challenged his position as the toughest guy in their group. Manuel remarked, "The other guys consider me the bad boy," and when Mr. Simon asked, "What do you mean?" he said, "I'm the toughest guy in the group, and Blackie, being new, plays the role of the tough guy. I've let him push me around in school and other places, but I'm not going to anymore."[31]

This dialogue was intended by the consultant to increase mutual understanding, but it soon became evident that both Blackie and Manuel felt a need to fight it out. So they fought, but with gloves on in a boxing ring. Other members of the Wildcats were spectators as the two slugged at each other wildly, with Blackie getting the edge in the sixth round. Then Manuel wanted to go on fighting, gloves off.

Christie's next intervention was to take Manuel and Blackie in his car, ostensibly to find an alley where they could fight it out according to bare-knuckle tradition, but actually to get a period of time for more talking. He got them to agree to stop for Cokes and then drove them around for another thirty minutes before driving into an alley and parking. The three sat for about five minutes, not saying anything. Then Manuel said, "Fight."

At this point Christie made his prescriptive intervention. He spoke of the "model" they had set for others back at the club by fighting in the ring rather than on the street, thus implying that they could both respect themselves and be respected by others to the degree that they continued to act in terms of this model. He also told them that some gangs get along well enough with two or more equally matched tough guys. If "you two" now fought, there would be a winner-and-loser outcome that could split the club into Manny and Blackie factions.

Neither of these interventions was sufficient. Manuel still wanted to fight, but as the three of them headed for the alley Blackie capitulated. Manuel then insulted Blackie. Christie immediately faced Manuel with what the consultant saw as his real reasons for being antagonistic toward Blackie. Then, acting as angrily as he knew how, Christie—making another prescriptive intervention—ordered them back into the car, slammed the door as he got in, and took off in a hurry. Along the way Manuel and Blackie decided to go home and the threat of a fight ended.

Christie's earlier more or less administrative or supervisory efforts with the two rivals may have set the atmosphere for the final successful outcome. But only after he had dramatized some irritation that he did not actually feel was a successful outcome reached. By prescribing a "forced" action, he successfully broke their will to fight.

Power Vacuum

Crises occur among group members whenever an unexpected event prevents the realization of important objectives. When crises with potentially disastrous results arise they leave those affected with a sense of being powerless to respond; in such cases, prescriptive intervention can provide a basis for restoring the capacity of members to react in a problem-solving way. The consultant, who is not involved in the crisis as a participant, can prescribe by exercising initiatives and direction that group members are unable to exercise upon themselves.

A case study of such a crisis intervention is reported by Thomas, Izmirian, and Harris. For some time they had been working with an organization's training team to help it strengthen its own competency. The training team had recently scheduled its work for the year ahead when it learned that necessary funds for implementing the program would not be forthcoming. Talking with one another the day after the announcement, as well as with others in the organization, had the effect of further blurring whatever facts were available and left team members feeling victimized and hopeless. Under these conditions the consultant's prescriptive interventions were based on the following assumptions:

When the client is	The consultant should
1. The group is unable to provide leadership.	The consultant assumes group leadership.
2. The group is unable to stay with any one task.	The consultant keeps the group on the task.
3. The group assumes it knows less than it really does know.	The consultant provides a method for the group to look at things clearly.

4. The group assumes all power has been taken away.	The consultant provides a method for the group to look at reality.
5. The group therefore doesn't know what it is doing or how to function.	The consultant tells rather than asks the group how to function but not what to function on.
6. Conflict will erupt internally unless movement/success occurs rapidly.	The consultant speeds up the movement.[32]

So the consultants intervened prescriptively to:

1. stop the reactive and self-destructive behavior,
2. lead the evaluation of what the current situation actually was,
3. focus attention on new goals,
4. identify steps—within the "new" circumstances—by which these goals could be reached,
5. "supervise" the step-by-step actions needed for movement,
6. ensure that these steps were taken.

In the situation described, confusion, anger, frustrations, and fear led to emotional contagion, which in turn prevented members from focusing on a task and coalescing around it. The consultants stepped in to impose an agenda topic dealing with how planned and previously scheduled activities would now have to be changed and new goals formulated. With this meaningful and pertinent agenda focus, the consultants were thereafter able to lead a team analysis and evaluation of the situation which permitted members to collect current facts and analyze them in the light of their altered circumstances. With these new findings, it was possible to consider resources available for initiating action and to set concrete priorities for taking necessary steps. With a problem-solving basis restored, the consultant could then return the leadership he had taken to its rightful owner.

Success was largely a result of the timeliness of these interventions, which took place the day after the fund-cut catastrophe occurred while participants were evidently aroused and before despair had set in. Because of its prescriptive character, relying on consultant-based direction and initiative to fill the power vacuum left by the "natural" leadership's demoralization, the group was provided with the power/authority needed to rally its forces.

Summary

The general significance of crisis viewed from the standpoint of inducing change is commented on by Klein and Lindemann.

> Brief work with predicaments has been likened to the situation of exerting a gentle push against someone standing upon one leg. The "disequilibrium" can be maintained only temporarily. The other leg eventually will come down, whether or not one pushes. The opportunities for direct intervention

during the predicament period, as implied in the analogy, are twofold: first, to ensure that the psychological "other leg" comes down on firm ground; second, to exert pressure in such a fashion that the individual is encouraged to move it in a desirable direction as the foot descends and equilibrium is re-established.

The analogy also suggests that in working with a crisis a maximum of change may be possible with a minimum of effort, as compared with intervention in a noncrisis situation when, so to speak, both feet are planted firmly on the ground. At the very least, it may be possible to carry out primary prevention by helping to restore the equilibrium existing prior to the crisis before the situation leads to some form of emotional pathology. Beyond this goal, however, is the opportunity in some cases to foster a more desirable equilibrium between an individual and his immediate human environment than had existed before. It is the second, in many ways more ambitious goal that leads to a form of preventive intervention that can be differentiated from the several brief psychotherapies or ego therapies that have been developed over the past few decades. Preventive intervention shares with such remedial efforts the need to make a careful assessment of the intrapsychic structure and dynamics of personality. However, it extends the assessment to an equally important appraisal of the individual's social role and of the significant role relationships in which he is involved. Hence the weight of emphasis shifts from the individual alone to the individual enmeshed in a social network. The unit of inquiry, planning, and intervention is, therefore, not the individual patient alone but rather the individual and one or more of the social orbits of which he is a member. The essential difference is one of emphasis and focus.[33]

Prescriptive interventions with groups characteristically involve the consultant in substituting his or her personal power/authority for the group's natural leadership. Authority may be turned over to the consultant, as when he or she prescribes group structure or job descriptions; or the consultant may impose himself, as in the Herman and Clark/Jaffe examples, by telling the nominal power/authority person to do something that he or she ordinarily would not do. Stronger degrees of consultant authority helped to solve a gang-leadership power struggle and refocus a group when a crisis had thrown it into confusion. Concentrating as it does on more or less severe situations of authority breakdown, prescriptive consultation is itself a radical approach. Without follow-up interventions of a nonprescriptive character its impact on the group's longer-term capacity for dealing effectively with problems remains questionable.

INTERGROUP (B-1-3)

Prescriptive intergroup interventions are uncommon, probably because both sides need to agree in order to utilize a consultant who "takes over." Since intergroup difficulties needing consultation are usually of the win-lose variety, the needed cooperation is generally lacking. An important exception is the third-party arbitrator in union and management relations. He or she functions to mediate differences, but only when both sides have previously agreed to submit their disagreement to binding arbitration. Two groups—say, management and a union—reach an impasse. The arbitrator, an expert in the subject but a disinterested outsider, hears evidence or otherwise studies the case and renders a decision. This usually takes the form of a prescription that both sides in the dispute are obligated to implement.[34,35]

Thus in intergroup situations the use of prescription exhibits many of the same characteristics identified in prescriptive consultation with a single group. The win-lose power struggle is not solved; rather, power/authority is handed over to a neutral outsider who assists in solving the problem the disputants are incapable of resolving themselves.

When groups are unable to agree on engaging a consultant to prescribe a coordinated "solution," either may decide to base its approach on the formulations of "How-to-negotiate" texts (e.g., Walton and McKersie[36]; Nierenberg[37,38]) or to retain its own consultant for advice on strategy and tactics in what continues to be essentially a win-lose dispute. Such "consulting to win," involving as it usually does an expert "quarterback" calling the plays, frequently takes on the character of prescription. It usually affects the intergroup situation, but its unilateral character can aggravate rather than cure the "disease."

Another example of how a consultant can influence the balance of power in intergroup struggles is provided by Derr.[39] The conflict in this instance was between teachers at different grade levels within an elementary school. One problem was related to establishing a lunch schedule for three different periods. A second scheduling issue was selection of a uniform time of day for teaching math. The third involved reaching agreement on three different periods for using the gym. Three different groups of teachers of grades 1–2, grades 3–4, and grades 5–6 were in disagreement as to preferred schedules for these three activities; each desired solutions favorable to themselves, regardless of the solution's impact on the other groups.

The intervention preserved each group as an entity. It provided for each to bargain with the other two to get their preferred schedules. The consultant set up day-long bargaining sessions with instructions for each group to approach the other two from the standpoint of getting what it wanted. Tactics of negotiation leading to a compromise position with each group forcing capitulation of the others were also suggested. Furthermore, instructions for bargaining authorized group representatives to utilize deception to whatever degree necessary to further their own group's aims.

Bargaining took place at a table where one teacher served as spokesperson for her grade levels. Other teachers from her grades were situated behind her passing her notes, and in other ways seeking to strengthen her bargaining approach.

The grade 5–6 teachers were the most entrenched and historically had dominated the other two. Now an alliance formed between the other two groups who were able to dominate the grade 5–6 teachers to "control the solutions to the rescheduling issue."

This intervention might be judged to have produced a successful outcome in the sense that schedules were put in place. However, the grade 5–6 teachers were "defeated" by the coalition of grades 1–2 and 3–4 teachers who "won." Rather than aiding all grade teachers to define solutions on a schoolwide basis, this outcome can be expected to preserve and strengthen intergroup conflict.

ORGANIZATION (B-1-4)

Prescriptive consultation with organizations dates back to the emergence of the McKinsey consulting firm. A large number of present-day consultants continue to rely primarily on prescription as their mode of assisting organizations to solve problems.

There are three primary areas of organization-based prescriptive consultation. The first is concerned with the organization's power/authority system, where consultation frequently takes the form of recommended changes in organization structure.

Restructuring a Marketing Division

A classical published example of a prescriptive structural intervention involved the Arthur D. Little consulting firm and the top management of Philco. The corporation had engaged A.D.L. to study its organization and to propose needed changes. A several months' study was concluded and reports of findings had been prepared and recommendations were about to be presented to Philco's top man. The prescribed solution involved a needed change in the existing power/authority system. Here's how the crucial intervention was set up to report the consultants' conclusions.

> James M. Skinner, Jr., president of Philco Corp., [arrived] for a momentous meeting that had been six months in the making. Waiting for Skinner in Suite 1808 were the nine somewhat apprehensive men from Arthur D. Little, Inc., the technical consulting firm of Cambridge, Massachusetts.
> . . . Donham spoke first, outlining in general terms what A.D.L. hoped to accomplish with its reorganization plan. What he was proposing, in brief, was a massive reorganization of Philco's marketing setup, which would: make the job of marketing all of Philco's consumer products the responsibility of one division; fix profit responsibilities at precise points in the company; get day-to-day pressure off the backs of men who should be doing long-range planning; and provide much closer support for Philco's independent distributors and dealers.[40]

Rather than reacting submissively, however, Skinner resisted the plan and an intense "battle" between consultants and client followed.

Reducing Bureaucratic Layers

The State Department was actively seeking organizational change via consultant intervention during the late 1960s and early 1970s, and A. J. Marrow was one of its major consultants throughout this era. Though each major intervention is described separately, he has presented them as a coherent whole in *Making Waves in Foggy Bottom.*[41]

One of the most significant interventions resulted in an attempt to convert the State Department into a "Theory Y" organization, using "Theory X" methods. Authority was relied upon to create a more participative problem-solving climate.

In June of 1965, Crockett announced what was called a major reform designed to reduce bureaucratic stratification. It was the formal word of the cutting out of six supervisory layers between Crockett and the operating managers. The announcement signaled the elimination of 125 positions and the transfer of 160 employees to other parts of the Department. Some of the operating units were to be broken up and some relatively powerful unit managers were about to be stripped of some of their former powers. The new program was to follow McGregor's Theory Y managerial approach. Crockett expressed the hope that the reorganization would replace the spirit of authoritarianism in the Department. The announcement was couched in Theory Y concepts—openness, participation, self-management, decentralized responsibility, management by objectives.

Interviews held at a later date with program managers by a research team from the University of Michigan found that the staff perceived the reorganization as an order. They were dismayed at the inconsistency of the preemptory way the reorganization was announced in contrast to the constant references to the new participative management concepts.

It is instructive for the record to see how Crockett outlined the rationale for his proposed changes. In July 1965, Crockett spoke to some 450 managers and employees of the administration area (known as the "O" area). Here is the essence of his remarks.

. . . Our challenge is to find a structure—one which releases people from the obstacles and inhibitions of our highly centralized organization, thus permitting them to feel they are their own managers, with their own operations. Is there a way of organizing ourselves so that each of us can feel that we are a vital part of the whole?

I believe that our present concept of decentralized management by objectives and programs will accomplish these objectives by: decentralizing our management into self-contained, semi-independent, and semi-autonomous programs, each with a manager; eliminating *every* intermediate supervisory level; delegating almost complete authority for daily operations to the program managers; ensuring that each program manager has the resources, the tools, the people, the money, the authority, the regulations, the means, and the conviction for attaining our mutually established goals.

Of course, there are both objections as well as problems that we must face in getting this concept into being. What are some of the objections that have been raised?

1. Existing managers, within the hierarchical structure, will lose part of their operations. (Absolutely true. This is one of the reasons for the new plan.)
2. Many intermediate supervisory jobs will be abolished, and not all of these people like the idea. (Absolutely true. Again, this is one of the basic objectives of the plan.)

3. It is really not decentralization but supercentralization, since all of the managers will report to the top man. (Not true. Each manager will be given almost autonomous operating authority with self-defined policies and mutually agreed-on objectives.)

4. The head man has too long a span of control; he can't supervise so many people. (Not so. Each manager will have his *own* program, and report only as he needs assistance. He will be freed from the usual concept of the old hierarchical control.)

Naturally, there will be some problems. The things you and I must do together are the following:

1. We must define the general purposes and concepts of your program.

2. We must state the general objectives and goals of the program as we see them. What do you think we can achieve next year? What will it take?

3. We must establish what kinds of authority you need to get the job done.

4. We must decide about whom you serve. Is your service really fulfilling your needs?

5. How can I be most helpful. How can you use me to accomplish your purposes and your goals?

Now what do I really expect of each of you managers? These are some of the main things: to achieve the goals we have set; to operate as if you were running your own business; to keep your operations, procedures, and regulatory materials up to date.

And now, what are the things that you can expect from me? This is a two-way street and you'll need assurances and help. The following things come to mind:

1. Full understanding and concurrence with the goals, and the resources and requirements for their attainment.

2. Availability in person or by phone when you need advice or counsel.

3. Support for the things we are agreed that you will need to attain your goals.

However persuasive seemed Crockett's brief for his changes, the old climate of suspicion, fear, and anger was only slightly improved. Grumbling, complaints, and fears were evident among those who had no opportunity to participate in the decisions about the new system. The resistance these people created helped to limit Crockett's original objectives.[42]

The resistance to these changes eventually resulted in their being rescinded and the State Department returning in significant ways to its traditional mode. Change by edict, no matter how well intentioned, is likely to provoke resistances that lead to entrenchment of the status quo.

Strengthening Manufacturing Operations

Another prescriptive intervention, in which Marrow's own organization was the client, involved the Weldon Company. As described by Roberts, his firm, Norris & Elliott, Inc., had been asked to conduct a fact-finding survey of the Weldon

Company and to recommend a program for strengthening cost control and production quality in its manufacturing operations. The survey and analysis identified the need for strong action. Weldon owners and plant staff reviewed the recommendations and authorized the consultants to implement the proposed program, which included changes in incentive rates, production planning, work study methods, and other classical approaches intended to strengthen the "task" side of the organization by centralizing power/authority. Correspondingly, these changes had the effect of breaking up the status quo and reducing the autonomy of managers and supervisors. These new techniques were necessary because, as the consultants commented, the supervisors and their assistants

> . . . lacked . . . an understanding of the principles and methods of controlling work flow and the use of work study in keeping operation performance high. At first, the supervisors reacted to the consulting engineers and their training efforts stoically, as if lining up for an inoculation they did not want or need.[43]

According to Roberts, after a period of resistance, the supervisors came to accept and even to solicit the consulting engineers' assistance. One of the consultants says,

> By the end of 1963 the great majority of employees felt that management wanted them to improve their production and earnings and that they were prepared to provide a great deal of attention and practical aids in getting their earnings up to the level considered favorable in the community. Their morale improved a great deal, and this helped to speed up the later phases of the earnings development program.[44]

Viewing the situation from a behavioral science practitioner's orientation, however, David says that in May of that year, about nine months after the first consultant had begun, another set of interventions was necessary to build cooperation and trust into the Weldon organization. He comments that the progress possible from technical improvements was not being realized because of "hostilities, suspicions, and fears of the Weldon managers and supervisors in their work relations with one another. Not that these had become worse, but just that they had not become better."[45] As a result, acceptant interventions were introduced with beneficial results (see Chapter 28).

Realignment of Power/Authority Structure

Another example of a prescriptive organization intervention is described in step-by-step terms by Levinson, a consultant operating in the psychoanalytic tradition. The consultant gathers data for his own diagnostic use through interviews and questionnaires, by examining financial and performance data, and in other ways. The approach appears to be prescriptive in character, as demonstrated in the following excerpted recommendations. First is a summation of how the consultant sees the present status of the company.

Claypool Furniture and Appliances is now in a tenuous position both financially and psychologically. Profits have fallen steadily during the last 3 years while sales have continued to grow. Because of the falling profits and their aversion to long-term debt, their expansion plans cannot be financed through retained earnings. Their choice is either to forego the plans for expansion or to give up part of the financial control to get the necessary money. The employees have lost confidence (if they had any) in their role in, and impact on, the organization. They see themselves as mere observers of a process that is slowly passing them by. They are angry at the organization and the management for not including them in the plans for growth, either by informing them of the plans or by training them to be an important part of them. They feel that the organization exploits them for its customers. Conversely, management feels that it is losing control of those factors which, in the past, were responsible for the success of the company. The personal relationships with the manufacturers and the other retailers are disappearing. The confidence of the line management is deteriorating because many see themselves as being unable to handle their positions. Robert Claypool and Michael Samson see themselves as being required to assume more of the managerial responsibilities, even though they are already overburdened. Management also feels that it is losing control over the employees. No longer can they manipulate employees freely. As a result, management places more pressure on itself to resolve the apparent conflicts by refusing to delegate responsibility, tightening its control, and increasing its competitive effort.[46]

In the following excerpt a colleague, Spohn, provides the flavor of recommendations included in a Levinsonian diagnostic report. The various recommendations impinge at numerous points on the existing power/authority system and in effect "tell" the Claypool management what the new power/authority system should do to increase its effectiveness.

PERSONNEL PRACTICES
The company should establish descriptions and standards and objectives for all positions. It should develop orientation and training programs to properly prepare people for their jobs and provide appraisal devices by which personnel and their superiors can assess progress and training needs. Positions and training in supervision and management are to be included in this process. A procedure for identifying prospective managerial talent should be evolved. The representative council should be abolished, and it should be replaced by employee task forces appointed to solve specific intraorganizational problems. Such groups, to include stock personnel, would end the isolation of the stock people and contribute to organizational identification and group cohesion.[47]

The prescriptions above assume that executive management is ready to follow the conclusions the consultant has reached, pretty much on an authority-obedience basis. This is seen also in Levinson's feedback strategy: first report conclusions to the top official, then to the next echelon down, and so on to the lowest level involved. The feedback approach seeks to overcome resistance to the report's content.

To feed back his findings and recommendations, the consultant meets with the executive who first retained his services. In setting up an appointment, the consultant asks for two hours for a one-to-one meeting. The executive is asked to listen as the consultant reads the report and to jot down any notes he or she may wish to discuss. The consultant makes clear that, even if the client disagrees the report's substance cannot be changed. Nonetheless, says the consultant, he wants assistance in expressing things in the most advantageous way. The client executive is then given the report and asked to read it overnight and set aside two additional hours for discussion the next morning. The intention is to provide an opportunity for cathartic release of hostility felt toward the report and the consultant—feelings that, unless worked through, could lead to total rejection of both report and consultant.[48] This feedback procedure is repeated with lower-level individuals and groups until the report has been presented to all involved with this aspect of the diagnosis.

At least two features of this approach go beyond the classically prescriptive. One not emphasized here is that individual behavior variables approaching the psychoanalytic level of influence are included in the diagnostic study. The other involves the consultant's effort to work through the feelings and emotions, as well as any rationalizations or projections that such a report arouses, rather than giving a diagnosis and prescription on a "take it or leave it" basis.

Power Reduction

The unsuccessful use of another consultant's strategy to promote organization development via prescriptive intervention is described below by Levinson.

> A major consulting organization undertook to advise on the drastic reorganization of a client firm. The consequence of this drastic reorganization was that many people who had previously held power were successfully emasculated of their power although they retained their positions. The firm traditionally had insisted on and rewarded compliance so these men did not openly complain, but there was widespread depression and anger among them for which the consulting firm assumed no responsibility. In fact, it is doubtful whether their developmental efforts included any recognition of the psychological consequences of what they did.[49]

This strategy, which relies on the consultant's being able to overcome resistance, can be contrasted with Levinson's own approach. His "organization diagnosis" methodology uses prescription but couples it with confrontational methods for working through hostility and other forms of resistance that prescriptions often induce.

Summary _____

Prescriptive interventions at the organization level are premised on the consultant's assuming complete responsibility for defining the problem and recommending solutions to it. Therefore his or her inclination is to present recommendations pretty much as though they were final. As a consequence, the client organization, perhaps unwittingly, is expected to surrender whatever independent initiative it might otherwise have exercised, in accordance with the authority-obedience formula inherent in the relationship.

The use of prescriptive consultation to change an existing power/authority system is fraught with difficulties. Its major limitations seem to be those listed below.

1. The entire system of power/authority relations is shifted by edict. Those who lose power cannot be expected to support changes that weaken their positions.
2. Changes proposed may go against ingrained beliefs and traditions regarding "how things should be done."
3. Insufficient provision is made to assist those who must implement the prescriptions in understanding—even less, agreeing with—the changes they are expected to initiate.

In a sense, the shock wave of change recommendations produces numerous individual, group, and intergroup problem situations that could well use the help of other consultants who are neutral regarding the earlier prescription.

LARGER SOCIAL SYSTEM (B-1-5)

Sometimes the focal issue identified is not only one of power/authority; it may reflect an individual-based problem: incompetence of the top person to perform his or her executive functions effectively. While this misuse of power can have reverberations throughout the entire system and beyond, it is unusual for a top executive to nominate himself or herself as the problem for consultative intervention. Rather, the consultants are more likely to enter the system under some other definition of the issue.

Arbitrary Actions from the Top

A series of prescriptive interventions, initiated as an organization-oriented consultation but resulting in a larger-social-system intervention in the city of Cincinnati, Ohio, are described by Goodstein and Boyer. The Health Department of that city was the initial client, but the "ultimate" client was the mayor. As first defined, the purpose of this consultation was to help the department with its internal management problems as well as in its relationships with certain segments of the community.

Internal Health Department problems had reached the point where unhappy employees were holding meetings to discuss their situation and employee discontent had been communicated to the public at large. Expressed grievances concerned the tone of administration in the department, particularly that of the Commissioner, who was thought to have been arbitrary in some past firings. At about the same time, citizen groups were voicing their concerns regarding the poor quality of health services and were demanding greater involvement in departmental decision making. Newspaper and television coverage of the issues had become extensive.

The Commissioner and others at his level wanted to approach a solution through a leadership and communication workshop and consultants were contacted in connection with this desire. Based on their initial knowledge of the expressed grievances and widespread employee distrust of the Commissioner, and considering the fact that this workshop decision was made by a very few top-level individuals, the consultants rejected the invitation to collaborate with the client within the status quo and according to his felt needs. They felt that a more sound approach would be to engage in their own independent diagnosis and evaluation of the situation without any prior agreement regarding next steps. This led to a sixty-day consulting contract, which was to result in a written report of findings and recommendations.

As they attempted to get started, a high amount of distrust toward them as "lackeys" of the Commissioner and the board made interviewing difficult; they were viewed as pawns or henchmen rather than as credible sources of help through whom complaints could be voiced. Yet by virtue of their listening skills and capacity to paraphrase grievances and tensions—thus "proving" that they understood what they were being told—the consultants slowly earned acceptance and were able to gain access to information, largely through demonstrating their independence of the Commissioner. Thus "acceptant" interventions were used here not as a way of helping one or more individual members of the client's organization (see Dickson and Roethlisberger, 1966, excerpted in Chapter 27), but to gather data for a broader purpose. The consultants made known to interviewees that one of their findings might very well be that ". . . the Commissioner should resign his position."

The prescriptive character of the consultation is revealed in the following.

Through the course of the consultation it became increasingly apparent to the consultants that the Commissioner, because of his management style, had lost his credibility, both in the Department and in the community. This point was made in interviews even by supporters of the Commissioner and it became clear that, regardless of any recommendations which the consultants might make and regardless of the talents the Commissioner had for improving health care, his tenure in office was drawing to a close. Further, the press and other news media had helped create a climate of opinion in the community in which the Commissioner was seen as the one primarily responsible for the current situation.

During the two-week data-collection phase, as this conclusion became even more clear, the consultants met on several different occasions with the Commissioner in order to share this conclusion with him. After several meetings, the Commissioner was convinced that his resignation would be necessary and the question arose concerning the timing of this critical act. The consultants were concerned that his resignation might so defuse the situation that the other issues which were very much part of the current problems would go unexamined in the delight and exultation following the

Commissioner's decision to leave. The consultants worked closely with the Commissioner, the president of the Board, and members of the Board, [with whom a number of feedback sessions were held during the week] in the timing of the announcement of the resignation in order to preserve the impact of their report.[50]

Recognizing that even after the Commissioner left many of the problems would remain, the consultants expanded their concept of responsibility in the following way.

The consulting team had decided that the simple issuance of a final report probably would not have the desired effect of initiating real changes in the Health Department and, further, the consultants had decided that their responsibility in this matter was to the broader community of the City, which was represented officially by the City Council. Therefore, the consultants decided to present their findings to the Council informally, through the Human Resources Committee. The president of the Board of Health was asked and agreed to arrange an informal meeting between the consultants and the Mayor. The consultants' tentative findings were shared with the Mayor and, while he was concerned about the extent and severity of the problem, he was positively impressed with the way in which the report was presented. He recognized that there was a strong data base for the findings and that the recommendations were a natural consequence of the findings. The Mayor was eager to move ahead into the action steps necessitated by the recommendations but first wanted the consultant to share the same feedback with the two other members of the Council's Human Resources Committee.[51]

The remaining Board of Health members also resigned and consequently the department was restaffed and charter amendments were created that altered the administrative structure of the system.

Because of the impasse quality of this situation—i.e., the Commissioner was unable to function because he had lost community confidence, and other members of the organization and wider community were so antagonized that their cooperation was difficult to elicit—a power vacuum existed. Under these circumstances the prescriptive interventions of the consultant were like line-manager decisions which, when approved by the mayor, could become operating decisions.

Goodstein and Boyer[52] reevaluate the impact of the intervention a number of years later and confirm that it was unable to deal with the real problem which persisted even after the original participants had been replaced. Eventually, the conflict was reduced when a new line manager was appointed who apparently was able to grapple with the problem successfully from a managerial as contrasted with an interventional perspective.

The circumstance here is similar to that previously reported in connection with prescriptive interventions in a group[53]—in that situation, crisis had so debilitated the group's capacity to function that the consultants moved in and prescribed actions during the period of impasse in order to restore the group's capacity to function independently.

Health Delivery System

One of the advantages of prescriptive consultation is that an outsider often can recognize what others are unable to see, as clearly demonstrated in a report by Caplan. His conclusion in the following case study is that the problems encountered in the health delivery system in Alaska related to differences in goals between what the Health Department wanted for the villages and what the villages embraced as health objectives for themselves. In his work with the Alaska Native Health Area (A.N.H.A.), which comprised a number of Eskimo and Indian villages, Caplan prepared a final report from which the following excerpts are taken.

PROBLEM 1.1 LOW SALIENCE OF HEALTH ISSUES FOR VILLAGERS AND LEADERS

The outstanding problem in the village is the low importance ascribed to health matters by the villagers and their leaders. This is mirrored in their ignorance of fundamental health issues, their inconsistent and ineffective practice of communal and personal hygiene, and the relatively low prestige and influence of the local representative of the Area Native Health Service, the Health Aide. This person is usually unpaid and is often a woman or a young man, who works at a technician level in relaying information about sick villagers by radio communication to the doctors at the Service Unit and then in dispensing the prescribed medication.

RECOMMENDATION 1.1

I suggested a revolutionary change in the approach of A.N.H.A. to the villages—mainly with the goal of making the promotion of health and the prevention and early treatment of illness a matter of immediate importance to the villagers and their leaders, so that they will actively collaborate with the A.N.H.A. and other professionals in implementing programs in which the improvement of health will be seen as an integral part of total village development; economic, social, educational, cultural, legal, and political.

(a) Generalist Village Workers. As the spearpoint of this new approach I recommended the organization of a network of Village Workers, similar to the community development workers of India, Pakistan, and the Philippines. A Village Worker should be a mature Native man, or occasionally a woman, of prestige and influence in the village. He should continue these occupations to some extent in order to remain identified with the day-to-day life of his neighbors.

His main duties should be broad community development and adult education, within which the promotion of health and the prevention and control of disease would be integrated. As a village leader, he would have special skills derived from his knowledge of local culture, politics, and personalities. In addition he would be given extra knowledge and skills by A.N.H.A. and other interested Federal and State organizations, such as B.I.A., O.E.O., the State Department of Health and Welfare, the Court System, etc., who would wish him to act as their collaborator and agent at the village level. According to the size of the population, he would recruit and supervise full-time or part-time assistants, one of whom might be similar in role to the present Health Aide, and assist him at a technician level to collect and relay information about sick people and to dispense drugs in line with the orders of doctors and public health nurses.

The prescription not only specifies broad directions but also contains detailed recommendations for new norms of collaboration between government-agency professionals and Eskimo and Indian members of the proposed network.

The Village Worker should be treated as a *non-professional collaborator*, and not as a sub-professional agent, by the A.N.H.A. and other Federal and State agencies. He should be given a certain amount of technical orientation by each of them, but his development should mainly arise on the job as he collaborates with representatives of the agencies in his day-to-day operations. Rather than lengthy systematic training in Anchorage or Juneau, he should be involved alongside small groups of Village Workers from neighboring villages in repeated seminars of a few days' duration at Service Units or other regional centers, or in representative villages. These seminars should focus on greater understanding of specific issues and not upon acquiring professional frames of reference and techniques. The community development work of Fred and Carmen Wale in the Division of Adult Education of the Department of Agriculture in Puerto Rico can be used as a model.

The Village Worker should operate under the control of, or within the framework of, the Village Council, or some other accepted representative governing body of the village. In certain villages one of his main tasks would be to revitalize such a Council, so that through its operations the villagers would improve their self-respect and their ability to exercise greater control over their own destinies.[54]

During both the surveying and recommendation-forming stages Caplan believes the consultant should keep in touch as much as possible with the head of the client organization.[55] This strategy has several advantages: (1) the consultant can constantly monitor key persons' preoccupations so as to gauge the acceptability of particular recommendations; (2) he or she can receive guidance from client members, those best able to view their organization as a functioning unit interacting with external systems; (3) the consultant is provided an entree via the top official's influence; and (4) he or she can keep tabs on the executive's responses to consultant recommendations during daily discussions, *before* these are written up. Although the final report is in the format of a prescription, Caplan argues[56] that it is really the product of extensive prior collaboration between himself, client members, and other persons and groups. Accordingly, its acceptance is to some extent preassured.

Delinquency

The way in which individuals are assigned for group living—such as in reformatories, prisons, and other institutions where people are compelled to stay—can either promote greater social health or bring out socially negative, destructive, and pathological behavior. How can assignments to promote social health be accomplished? Assignments according to inmates' choices may amplify the institution's problems by bringing antisocial individuals together. Administrative assignment, on the other hand, may be either (a) *happenstance,* in the sense of refilling dormitories as some inmates leave on release or parole and others arrive to begin their terms of confinement, or (b) *tactical,* in the sense of separating "troublemakers."

There is a possible alternative. By means of sociometric methods, Moreno[57] devised an assignment/reassignment system that can serve comprehensive social health-promoting strategies. In a correctional institution for girls, this involved having inmates record the preferences they currently felt for social proximity to or distance from other girls. Each girl was asked to complete a scale of preference, a "sociometric test," applying to the institution's cottage-residence and work-group arrangements respectively. When this information was tabulated by the consultant, it also indicated the extent to which any individual who had been chosen or rejected by another was reciprocating such degrees of preference. This method also was employed to determine the girls' orders of choice for housemothers and, conversely, the degree to which each of them was chosen by a housemother as a desirable or undesirable resident in her cottage.

From these sets of information the consultant was able to assess the contemporary overall social structure of living and work arrangements within the institution. Thus new living assignments, based on the consultant's integration of sociometric evidence from these several sources, could be made. The objective was to provide each resident favorable circumstances for "mental catharsis" induced through relationships with peers, housemother, and so on. Mental catharsis refers to cumulative effects occurring in the individual during a fairly long period, at least three months and sometimes two years or more, spent within these assigned arrangements. It is not a catharsis brought about directly by the consultant through a brief acceptant intervention.

A still different approach for reducing delinquency rests on in-situation prescriptive interventions rather than in prescriptive grouping. It makes an effort to alter how delinquent boys view and respond to situations in which power/ authority is exercised upon them by engaging them in competition and other game-induced excitements.

At a boys' correctional institution, a specially trained staff executed the prescriptive activities designed by Quay, the consultant. Twenty boys were selected to take part in the program.

> The problem involved a hard core group, *difficult* to manage youths who obviously were not reached positively by the institutional program. A new approach for coping with these offenders was needed as they were not benefiting from rehabilitative efforts being made and their disruptive behavior drew a disproportionate amount of staff time from the rest of the population. Correctional personnel were placed in the position of spending less time with the more amenable inmates in order to cope with the intractable ones.

The base for the research was provided by a theoretical statement by Quay relating extreme acting out (psychopathic) behavior to the need for seeking more varied sensory inputs than the environment usually provides.

The nature of this pathological stimulation seeking also was investigated in experimental studies in which the more psychopathic delinquents were shown to be more susceptible to the effects of boredom, to prefer complexity to simplicity in usual form, and to choose the incongruous over the more everyday type of situation. Thus a program which would provide change, varied activities, and would avoid unfilled time intervals leading to boredom was hypothesized to reduce the necessity for the psychopathic individual to create his own excitement through acting out behavior.[58]

In order to provide excitement and novelty, designed recreations included games and competitive activities among the boys and between them and staff members.

One activity that holds a great deal of interest for most adolescents is auto racing. With points earned in other activities of R.E.A.D.Y., the youths purchased slot car kits which they assembled themselves. Once they had their own cars they were allowed to run them on a slot car track during specified times. This became a very popular activity for most of the boys. In this instance a chaining of positive consequences for appropriate behavior was established. In order to engage in a highly desirable activity a number of preliminary steps were spelled out. This was one attempt to counter the high P's (psychopathic's) conception of his environment as a haphazard world in which everything depends on luck or getting the breaks and has little to do with one's own behavior.

. . . Another type of activity which proved to be popular was competitive endeavor with staff. A team of staff members challenged the youths to a softball game. This was received with much enthusiasm and proved to be very successful (the boys won). Although the students also prided themselves on their basketball ability they were shocked to find the staff won the second kind of sports encounter. It was obvious to most observers that team work was more important than physical condition in this game, because the staff had the former but definitely lacked the latter. The R.E.A.D.Y. boys immediately demanded a rematch which was accepted. In a hard-fought, well-played game the staff again won and everybody seemed pleased.[59]

Staff retained control of the time, sequence, and other aspects of the activities. Games included bingo, basketball, softball, weight lifting, swimming. Other program activities such as psychodrama and movies and debates on topics such as premarital sex, drugs, and so on, were calculated to help the boys in gaining insights into specific problems, but these were not successful. Nonetheless, in comparison with control groups, the subsequent behavior differences of program members seemed on the positive side, though not significantly so.

To the extent that it can be conducted effectively by a single consultant or a number of them working in a coordinated manner, prescriptive intervention in larger social systems (as compared to similar types of intervention with an individual, a group, or an organization) requires relatively greater magnitudes and depths of comprehension. Such insight is needed to identify, span, and interrelate major dimensions of the existing social system and whatever inbuilt inadequacies may be amenable to the mutually strengthening "changes for the better" that the consultant eventually prescribes.

Summary

In prescriptive consultation the subject-matter expertise of the consultant is relied on as an authority/obedience premise for the purpose of solving problems in the power/authority area. The most common application is to assist those *appointed* position-holders of power/authority to exercise it more effectively in their relationships with subordinates. While prescriptive consultation has also been used to aid those in subordinate positions to strengthen their effectiveness in resisting the arbitrary use of power, this is far less frequent. The reason may be that when a "weak" subordinate becomes strong (based upon consultant instructions), his or her strength is perceived by those in a power/authority position to be both out of character and out of line.

Other things equal (i.e., consultant competence), the greater the consultant's degree of control over the situation, the more successful the prescriptive intervention. This tendency is revealed in two different contexts. In behavior modification the client is in no position to resist. The client is not aware of the change and is not prompted to react negatively. Prescriptive consultation is also particularly effective when the client situation is one of total weakness, as in those examples where a hopeless impasse has been reached and the client is prepared to accept whatever recommendations the consultant offers.

Notes

1. C. D. Flory, ed., *Managers for Tomorrow* (New York: The New American Library of World Literature, 1965).
2. A. M. Cohen and R. D. Smith, "The Critical Incident Approach to Leadership Intervention in Training Groups," in W. G. Dyer, ed., *Modern Theory and Method in Group Training* (New York: Litton, 1972), p. 103. © 1972 by Litton Educational Publishing, Inc. Reprinted by permission of Van Nostrand Reinhold Company.
3. J. I. Porras and B. Anderson, "Improving Managerial Effectiveness through Modeling-Based Training," *Organizational Dynamics* (Spring 1981): 60–77.
4. J. L. Moreno, *Who Shall Survive?: A New Approach to the Problem of Human Interrelations* (Washington, D.C.: Nervous and Mental Disease Publishing Co., 1934).
5. A. Fleming, "Psychodrama," *Ingenue* (January 1969): 46–47, 73–74. © 1969 by Dell Publishing Co., Inc. Reprinted by permission.
6. F. S. Perls, *Gestalt Therapy Verbatim* (New York: Bantam Books, 1971). Originally published by Real People Press, Moab, Utah, © 1969. Reprinted by permission.
7. V. E. Frankl, *The Doctor and the Soul* (New York: Bantam Books, 1955).

8. V. E. Frankl, *Psychotherapy and Existentialism* (Harmondsworth, England: Penguin Books, 1967).

9. J. Wolpe, *The Case of Mrs. Schmidt: An Illustration of Behavior Therapy* (Nashville, Tenn.: Counselor Recordings & Tests, 1965).

10. J. Wolpe, *The Practice of Behavior Therapy*, 2nd ed. (New York: Pergamon Press, 1973). Reprinted by permission.

11. Perls, *Gestalt Therapy Verbatim*, pp. 167–68.

12. Ibid., pp. 171–72.

13. I. P. Pavlov, *Conditioned Reflexes* (London: Oxford University Press, 1927).

14. C. L. Hull et al., *Mathematico-Deductive Theory of Rote Learning* (New Haven: Yale University Press, 1940).

15. B. F. Skinner, *The Behavior of Organisms: An Experimental Analysis* (New York: Appleton-Century-Crofts, 1938).

16. E. S. Jones, quoted in O. H. Mowrer, *The New Group Therapy* (New York: Van Nostrand Reinhold Co., Litton Educational Publishing, 1964). (Original source not cited.)

17. J. D. Krumboltz, ed., *Revolution in Counseling: Implications of Behavioral Science* (Boston: Houghton Mifflin, 1966).

18. J. Zeilberger, S. E. Sampen and H. N. Sloane, Jr., "Modification of a Child's Problem Behaviors in the Home with the Mother as Therapist," *Journal of Applied Behavioral Analysis* 1 (1968): 49. © 1968 by the Society for the Experimental Analysis of Behavior, Inc. Reprinted by permission.

19. Ibid., pp. 228–29.

20. A. D. Whitley and B. Sulzer, "Reducing Disruptive Behavior through Consultation," in J. Fischer, comp., *Interpersonal Helping: Emerging Approaches for Social Work Practice* (Springfield, Ill.: Charles C Thomas, 1973), pp. 294–302.

21. R. L. Hamblin, D. Buckholdt, D. Bushell, D. Ellis and D. Ferritor, "Changing the Game from 'Get the Teacher' to 'Learn'." Published by permission of *Transaction* 6, no. 3, copyright © 1969 by Transaction, Inc.

22. Ibid., p. 23.

23. Ibid., pp. 23, 24.

24. T. Clark and D. T. Jaffe, *Toward a Radical Therapy: Alternate Services for Personal and Social Change* (New York: Gordon and Breach, Science Publishers, Inc., 1973), pp. 160–61. Reprinted by permission.

25. Wolpe, *The Practice of Behavior Therapy*, pp. 84–85.

26. S. M. Herman, "A Gestalt Orientation to O.D.," in W. W. Burke, ed., *Contemporary Organization Development: Conceptual Orientations and Interventions* (Washington, D.C.: NTL Institute for Applied Behavioral Science, 1972), pp. 69–86.

27. J. R. Emshoff, *Managerial Breakthroughs: Action Techniques for Strategic Change* (New York: AMACOM, 1980).

28. W. J. Gordon, *Synectics* (New York: Macmillan, 1961).

29. D. Straus and M. Doyle, "Making Board Meetings Work: The Doyle/Straus Interaction Method," *Directors & Boards* (Summer 1978).

30. Clark and Jaffe, *Toward a Radical Therapy*, pp. 194–96.

31. F. W. Christie, as cited in I. Spergel, ed., *Street Gang Work* (Reading, Mass.: Addison-Wesley, 1966), p. 110. Reprinted by permission.

32. A. Thomas, B. Izmirian and J. Harris, "Federal Cutbacks: An External Crisis Intervention Model," *Social Change* 3, no. 2 (1973): 1.

33. D. C. Klein and E. Lindemann, "Preventive Intervention in Individual and Family Crisis Situations," in G. Caplan, ed., *Prevention of Mental Disorders in Children* (New York: Basic Books, 1964), p. 286. Reprinted by permission.

34. S. Lazarus et al., *Resolving Business Disputes: The Potential of Commercial Arbitration* (New York: American Management Association, Inc., 1965).
35. W. R. Linke, "The Complexities of Labor Relations Law," in R. F. Moore, ed., *Law for Executives* (New York: American Management Association, Inc., 1968).
36. R. E. Walton and R. B. McKersie, *A Behavioral Theory of Labor Negotiations* (New York: McGraw-Hill, 1965).
37. G. I. Nierenberg, *The Art of Negotiating: Psychological Strategies for Gaining Advantageous Bargains* (New York: Hawthorn Books, 1968).
38. G. I. Nierenberg, *Creative Business Negotiating: Skills and Successful Strategies* (New York: Hawthorn Books, 1971).
39. C. B. Derr, "Surfacing and Managing Organizational Power," *OD Practitioner* 4, no. 2 (1971): 1–4.
40. E. T. Thompson, "The Upheaval at Philco," *Fortune* 69, no. 2 (1959): 23, 113–14. Reprinted by permission.
41. A. J. Marrow, *Making Waves at Foggy Bottom* (Washington, D.C.: NTL Institute, 1974). Reproduced by special permission.
42. Ibid., pp. 19–22.
43. E. E. Roberts, "The Technical Change Program," in A. J. Marrow, D. C. Bowers and S. E. Seashore, eds., *Management by Participation* (New York: Harper & Row, 1967), pp. 83–84.
44. Ibid., p. 86.
45. G. David, "Building Cooperation and Trust," in A. J. Marrow, D. G. Bowers and S. E. Seashore, eds., *Management by Participation* (New York: Harper & Row, 1967), pp. 95–109.
46. H. Levinson with J. Molinari and A. G. Spohn, *Organization Diagnosis* (Cambridge, Mass.: Harvard University Press, 1972), pp. 485–86.
47. Ibid., p. 491.
48. Ibid., pp. 497–98.
49. H. Levinson, *The Great Jackass Fallacy* (Cambridge, Mass.: Harvard University, 1973), p. 164.
50. L. D. Goodstein and R. K. Boyer, "Crisis Intervention in a Municipal Agency: A Conceptual Case Study," *Journal of Applied Behavioral Science* 8, no. 3 (1972): 333–34. Reprinted by permission.
51. Ibid., pp. 334–35.
52. L. D. Goodstein and R. K. Boyer, "The Cincinnati Department of Health Revisited," in B. Lubin, L. D. Goodstein and A. W. Lubin, eds., *Organizational Change Sourcebook II: Cases in Conflict Management* (San Diego: University Associates, 1979), pp. 157–160.
53. Zeilberger et al., "Modification of a Child's Problem Behaviors in the Home with the Mother as Therapist."
54. G. Caplan, *The Theory and Practice of Mental Health Consultation* (New York: Basic Books, © 1970), pp. 251–52. Reprinted by permission.
55. Ibid., pp. 254–55.
56. Ibid., p. 255.
57. Moreno, *Who Shall Survive?* pp. 304–20.
58. B. Kerish, "Toward a New Phase in Correctional Management," in J. L. Carleton and U. Mahlendorf, eds., *Man for Man: A Multidisciplinary Workshop on Affecting Man's Social and Psychological Nature through Community Action* (Springfield, Ill.: Charles C Thomas, 1973), pp. 163–64. Reprinted by permission.
59. Ibid., pp. 168–69, 169–70.

10

PRESCRIPTIVE INTERVENTIONS

Morale/ Cohesion

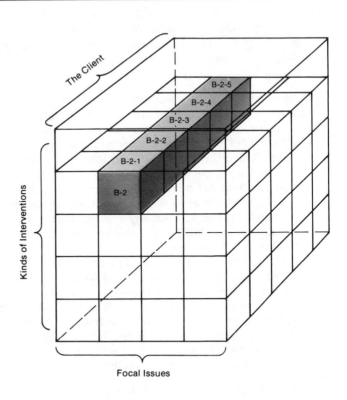

Many times people feel down without being precisely aware of the source of their depression, and if such conditions become chronic, a prescriptive intervention may have a powerful ameliorative effect. Essentially, the consultant pushes some clients to overcome their inertia and begin active steps toward solving the problem(s) associated with the focal issue. With other clients, the key to personal change is blind acceptance of the necessity to carry out recommended actions.

INDIVIDUAL (B-2-1)

Morale or personal cohesion is reduced or may even disintegrate with loss of loved ones, with oversensitivity to events, or in the face of serious challenges to one's self-esteem. An inability to cope with overwhelming difficulties may lead to unwillingness to confront issues and problems. The longer they are neglected, the more serious these issues and problems become.

Low Self-Esteem

Prescriptive consultation is one approach employed to help individuals confront problems that threaten self-esteem. Psychiatric interventions involving short-term therapy often are of this prescriptive character. The consultant first attempts to diagnose the underlying cause of the client's problem and then maps out an action strategy for the client to implement. The thesis is that action, not insight, will clear up the difficulty.

Viscott tells of the following:

> I remember a young woman, Karen Wells, who changed drastically after three weeks. Before therapy she was barely existing in a cold-water flat while her rich, widowed mother was living it up around the world. Dr. McKee, who sometimes supervised me, said after I discussed the initial hours, "Viscott, you go back and tell that girl to cut the crap."
>
> "Tell her to get on the phone and call her mother and ask for some money to help her out. She thinks she has to be in mourning for her father forever. The mother is probably worried about the girl and upset because she can't get her to take any money. This girl is just overdoing her grief reaction for her father. She thinks if she stops grieving that her father's memory will disappear."
>
> "I'll tell her that her father left something more for her than a memory."
>
> "You just do that, Viscott," said McKee. "I'd belt her with the facts."
>
> I did. Karen called her mother the same day and they got together between Karen's second and third visits. They went shopping together and her mother helped furnish Karen's apartment. At the third visit Karen was no longer depressed, no longer felt that her father had left her nothing, and she could believe that her mother had also loved her father and also remembered him. It was an incredible change.[1]

In this instance a poorly functioning client, after being given a prescription, was able to take a decisive step that cleared up her difficulty.

Wife-Husband Conflict

Not all interventions involving prescriptive psychiatry are centered on the type of brief therapy that turned Karen around. Viscott recounts the following advice he gave to Roberta, who had been a client of his for a year or more. She was married to Gary and having an affair with Roy.

> "Roberta, I think it'd be a mistake to base your decision to get a divorce on your feelings about Roy."
>
> "Why?"
>
> "You have to decide whether or not you want to stay married to Gary, independent of your feelings about Roy or anyone else. It's your decision alone and one that Roy really can't help you make. If you decided to get a divorce just because you wanted Roy more than Gary, it would put a terrible burden on Roy, on you, and on the relationship. Roy might feel obligated to love you after all that you gave up for him, and he might even resent you for it. If you want to divorce Gary, you have to divorce him because you don't want to live with him, not because you want to live with someone else. To use Roy as the reason to leave Gary only avoids dealing with the problems that you and Gary have. And that just opens the door for trouble in the new relationship."
>
> "I never thought of that. . . . Maybe you're right, maybe I *am* using Roy to make Gary look worse."[2]

This prescription shed new light on her situation and prevented Roberta from acting on the basis of momentary emotions. After considerable thought, she summed up her new insight.

> "I have to admit to myself what's missing in my marriage and decide if I can get along without it. If I can't, I'll just have to leave."[3]

Depression and Crisis Interventions

Use of prescription in psychiatric treatment for deeply depressed patients has proven to be effective, as illustrated in the following case.[4] The patient, put in a closed ward, spends his waking hours in a drab, sparsely furnished room. He receives a series of assignments that he is compelled to carry out to a high degree of perfection. Activities might include sanding a small block of wood with fine-grain sandpaper. If the client is so severely depressed that he will not even respond to instructions, the consultant may take his hand and guide him. Other monotonous, nongratifying, repetitive tasks include floor mopping, bouncing a ball on a small surface, counting tiny seashells, and so on. Shortcomings in the client's performance are quickly pointed out and conversation is discouraged by telling him he is there "to work, not talk." He is never ridiculed or belittled.

Within three to four days the patient is expected to blow up and refuse any further cooperation. At that point, after he has successfully expressed his hostility, he is shifted to other treatment activities. The prescription has achieved success in the sense that the self-defeating cycle is broken and the client is now reacting rather than maintaining a pattern of passive withdrawal.

A crisis exists whenever someone in serious trouble is unable to manage the situation. Crisis intervention may be calculated primarily to help the client hold himself together while living through the difficult period. The client, rather than worsening to the point of needing hospitalization, weathers the storm and emerges intact or in even better shape than before the crisis hit.

These interventions usually are prescriptive since, in crisis circumstances, the client is unable to be self-directed. Attempted suicide, threatened violence, and psychotic breaks are among the most common of these crisis situations. The strategy is usually to quiet the client by sedation so that the prior life pattern is resumed as quickly as possible. Psychotherapy is *not* relied upon: the client is treated as a *medical,* not psychiatric, patient. Quick recovery and dismissal after a few days or rarely more than two weeks is a part of the basic procedure. Dismissal without complete recovery is often made possible by arranging for the client's family to offer needed posthospitalization support. The rationale underlying crisis intervention is that steps should be taken promptly to arrest what otherwise would be either a process of deterioration or a repression of the traumatic experiences which would subsequently have a negative impact on adjustment.

The following cases deal mostly with crises arising "inside" the person rather than from externally imposed circumstances. The interventions are carried out in medical settings and have been effective with patients who are manic or schizophrenic, acute or chronic, or in drug-induced psychosis. Also involved have been suicidal and homicidal clients, and others exhibiting a wide range of symptoms.

An example of an intervention with a manic patient illustrates a prescriptive approach to alleviating serious symptoms of psychological illness.

Mr. P., a 32-year-old white, Protestant, married father of two children, was admitted from the emergency room where his wife and three neighbors had taken him after he had told her he intended to buy an expensive sports car and drive to the West Coast to close a business deal; the patient was a salesman for a small electronics firm. Ten days prior to admission he had begun to talk animatedly about "a tremendous opportunity for expansion" that only he could negotiate. He told his wife that the consummation of the deal would bring in millions and that he would be able to retire within a few years. He began to stay up all night making elaborate plans for what he intended to do with his riches and reacted to his wife's questions with scorn, jocularity, and occasional outbursts of abusiveness. Mrs. P. recognized that he was in the midst of an exacerbation but was unable to persuade him to go to the emergency room. She was eventually able to enlist the aid of neighbors to bring her husband in for treatment.

On the ward the patient was restless, excitable, and argumentative. This, combined with his rapid shifts in thought, made history-taking impossible. . . . he was totally sleepless the first night despite adequate doses of haloperidol. He was extremely disruptive to the ward partly because the other patients were fascinated by his infectious enthusiasm. The day following admission a medical evaluation for lithium was performed (EKG, serum electrolytes, serum creatinine, blood urea nitrogen, and a urinalysis), and within 48 hours of his admission lithium carbonate therapy was instituted in addition to the haloperidol. The lithium was raised by daily increments to 2.4 gm/day.

By the sixth day he began to sleep more than six hours a night, and his grandiose delusions began to dissolve. He gradually regained a normal mood and by the twelfth day was ready for discharge. Interviews with him and joint meetings with his wife failed to reveal any obvious stress in his recent life to account for the manic break. Both were impressed by the rapid clearing of his symptoms and agreed with the staff that he should remain on lithium indefinitely.

Mr. P. called his employer and his return to work was arranged without any difficulty. He was discharged home to be followed by a nearby clinic which specializes in the administration of lithium to outpatients.

Patients with manic-depressive illness are often free of the major social deterioration characteristic of schizophrenia. It is thus of major value to maintain their social adaptation by attempting to treat them without sending them out of the community to state hospitals. This requires experience with lithium and the ability to handle the patient skillfully while he is on the ward. It is often necessary to make certain adjustments when such patients are on the unit. They should not be over-stimulated and should be allowed to remain out of meetings or alone, if necessary, when they are in an excited phase. The usual gathering of information, social assessments, and interventions characteristic of crisis treatment should be postponed until the patient is able to tolerate them.[5]

Fears

Frankl's concept of *paradoxical intention* is a prescriptive approach to overcoming fears. One feature distinguishing it from similar approaches is the notion of self-detachment.

The patient was a bookkeeper who had been treated by many doctors and in several clinics without any therapeutic success. When he came to my clinic, he was in extreme despair, admitting that he was close to suicide. For some years, he had suffered from a writer's cramp which had recently become so severe that he was in danger of losing his job. Therefore only immediate short-term therapy could alleviate the situation. In starting treatment my associate recommended to the patient that he do just the opposite from what he usually had done; namely, instead of trying to write as neatly and legibly as possible, to write with the worst possible scrawl. He was advised to say to himself, "Now I will show people what a good scribbler I am!" And at that moment in which he deliberately tried to scribble, he was unable to do so. "I tried to scrawl but simply could not do it," he said the next day. Within forty-eight hours the patient was in this way freed from his writer's cramp, and remained free for the observation period after he had been treated. He is a happy man again and fully able to work.*

Frankl points out the importance of humor in interpreting why paradoxical intention is sometimes effective.

> A sound sense of humour is inherent in this logotherapeutic technique called paradoxical intention. This is understandable since we know that humour is a paramount way of putting distance between something and oneself. One might say, as well, that humour helps man rise above his own predicament by allowing him to look at himself in a more detached way. So humour would also have to be located in the noetic dimension.
>   After all, no animals is able to laugh, least of all at himself.†

Thus prescription can be an intervention mode for dealing with specific anxieties and fears that reflect a lack of self-confidence and result in lowered morale. Two further examples follow. The idea underlying both is that a person first does in imagination what he or she fears doing in real life. In the process of experiencing his or her fears imaginatively, the individual is freed from them before actually engaging in the activity.

In the Wolpe approach the client is first taught how to relax. After a degree of relaxation has been achieved he or she is instructed, for example, to imagine some real person whom he or she fears. In the example reported here there were two such real people—Mrs. Benning and Selma. The client feared rejection from both of them but feared more the rejection by Selma. In describing his approach, the consultant first points out the importance of teaching the client how to relax deeply. After practice for fifteen minutes twice per day the client gains the skills necessary for relaxation and is now moved toward dealing with a focal problem.

> *Consultant:* Now, I want you to imagine that you're walking along the side-walk and you see, walking toward you from the other side, Mrs. Benning. Now, as you pass Mrs. Benning, you see she is looking toward you and you get ready to greet her, and she just walks past as though she didn't recognize you. Now, stop imagining that. Now, if imagining that disturbed you even a very small bit, I want you to raise your right index finger now. If it didn't worry you, don't do anything. *(no finger movement)* OK, that's fine, now just keep on relaxing.[6]

The consultant then "increases" the problem in the client's imagination.

> *Consultant:* Now, I want you to imagine again that you're walking on the sidewalk and you see, moving toward you, Selma and you get ready to

---

* V. E. Frankl, *Psychotherapy and Existentialism* (Harmondsworth, England: Penguin Books, 1967), pp. 15–16. Copyright © 1967 by Victor Frankl. Reprinted by permission of Washington Square Press, a Simon & Schuster division of Gulf & Western Corporation.

† Ibid., p. 16.

greet her, and she seems to see you but she walks right on—she doesn't greet you.[7]

After a series of such imaginings, the hypnotic quality of the situation is seen.[7]

Consultant: Now, I'm going to count up to 5 and then you will open your eyes and feel calm and refreshed. 1-2-3-4-5. How do you feel?

Client: I feel like, I wouldn't feel like doing any more work today anymore. The last time when I seen her I just didn't care whether she said hello or not.

Consultant: How did you feel the first time?

Client: I was very mad. At least, the least she could do was to say hello when I live just across the way from her. The last time it was, if she didn't think enough of me to say hello, then let her just go.

Consultant: Very good.[8]

In this series of prescriptive interventions the client had for all practical purposes surrendered her will to the consultant. By permitting him to instruct her in relaxation methods step by step at the beginning of the interview, she relaxed as much as possible in preparation. Then, under the prescriptions assigned, she was able to experience and eventually control situations that she would otherwise have avoided. The Wolpe approach begins with those anxieties and fears that the client reports to be least intense, and moves progressively through a hierarchy of more intense fears until finally the client is imagining the most intense anxiety-arousing experiences without demoralization.

In the strategy applied by Wolpin, another prescriptive consultant also dealing with desensitization, the clients imagine themselves as actually engaged in their most feared activity—from the beginning and without relaxation. While doing this, the client is encouraged and supported by the consultant. A clinical example involves a married woman whose symptoms included a fear of the dark and of being attacked and raped if out at night or even at home alone watching TV. Her goal was to move around outside confidently at night and to feel at ease inside her house. The first four sessions were devoted to interviewing her. During this time she was also given tests and questionnaires to fill out and return. In the following six sessions she was asked to imagine herself in the feared situation. The first session was broken into a series of scenes, each lasting several minutes, during which her prescription was to visualize unsuccessful rape attempts upon herself. In later sessions she imagined herself up late at night watching TV alone, investigating unfamiliar noises in the house and garage, and going outside at night. At a follow-up interview session months later she reported full mastery of the problem, except at times of excessive fatigue.[9]

Severe personal problems involving intense fear or anxiety can sometimes be dealt with by "flooding." The consultant creates a situation where the client must "live through" the situation he or she shuns in real life. Once in the situation the consultant has created for the client, there is no escape; the client literally must go through it. A girl who feared being in a car was subjected to riding in the back seat of a car for four hours, with no way to get out of it. For many, but by no means for all, the dreaded situation may quickly lose its capacity to arouse crippling anxieties in the future, as described in the following example of *agoraphobia,* an intense fear of open spaces.

> *In vivo* flooding is exemplified by the case of Mrs. C., a woman with agora-phobia so severe that she was unable to go on her own more than two blocks by car without anxiety. Attempts at systematic desensitization had failed—apparently because she was unable to imagine scenes realistically. After other measures had also proved ineffective, I decided to persuade her to expose herself to flooding, which had to be *in vivo* because of the demon-strated inadequacy of her imagination. After resisting strenuously for some weeks, she agreed to take the plunge. Plans were made for her husband to place her, unaccompanied, on a commercial aircraft one hour's flight away from the airport where I would await her. When Mrs. C. in due course alighted from the plane, she walked toward me smiling. She had felt in-creasing anxiety for the first fifteen minutes of the flight, and then gradual subsidence of it. During the second half of the journey she had been per-fectly comfortable. She flew home alone the next day without trouble. This single experience resulted in a great increase in her range of comfortable situations away from home. She was now able, without anxiety, to drive her car alone three or four miles from home and to make unaccompanied trips by plane without any anxiety. Plans to build up this improvement by further treatment were foiled by distance plus other practical obstacles.[10]

Explanations are unclear as to why a single exposure to a dreaded situation might produce such constructive results. But the results of flooding, "para-doxical intention,"[11] or systematic desensitization[12] leave little doubt as to the validity of conclusions reached. Dramatic relief from otherwise uncontrollable fears and anxieties has been demonstrated.

Sexual Attractiveness

Other prescriptive approaches to personal problems share common elements with a variety of "pure" approaches, such as Moreno's psychodrama, Perls' Gestalt therapy, Frankl's logotherapy, and Wolpe's desensitization. A clinical example is drawn from a marathon group situation reported by Mintz. Claire had come to the session on the suggestion of her psychotherapist. She told the group that whenever men asked her for dates she did not know how to act. She thought of herself as unfeminine, felt awkward, and was not often asked out a second time. She seemed unaware of her natural attractiveness and made no effort to take advantage of it. The prescriptive approach presumed that Claire needed the directive encouragement and support of a mother-type person. When Eliza-beth Mintz, the marathon leader, suggested that Claire go around the group and speak in a seductive and flirtatious way to each of the men, Claire responded as follows.

> "I couldn't," Claire said.
> "I'll go around with you. Come on."

Claire arose, and I put my arm around her shoulder. She was shaking violently. I stood embracing her while she spoke to the first two men.

"I like your necktie."

"You're getting bald, but that's all right. I like bald men."

Our progress around the circle was slow. After the first two encounters, Claire's trembling diminished. I took my arm away from her shoulder and held her hand as she continued.

"You'd probably be a good dancer."

"You've got such curly hair—I'd like to touch it." She reached out and touched the curly-haired man, and I relinquished her hand. For the next two encounters, I walked beside Claire but did not touch her.

"I know you're married. You have trouble with your wife, you told us, but I'll bet you're one great daddy to your kids."

"I'd love to date you if you weren't from out of town."

I returned to my chair. Claire went on by herself to the last two men in the circle.

"Hi." She touched the face of the man she was greeting. He took her hand, clasped it lightly, and let go.

"Hi to you." She looked at the last of the men in the group, and he reached out his arms, and Claire settled comfortably into his lap. She remained there for a few moments, then arose, her face glowing. She went back to her chair and said, with complete spontaneity and unconscious humor, "Oh, flirting's really fun, it's not so scary!"[13]

The consultant concluded that Claire's problem with men was inhibition. By telling her what to do and by offering support while she did it, the consultant helped Claire become more confident. The prescriptive intervention was sufficient to push Claire into taking actions which she otherwise would have avoided, thus demonstrating to her that her fears were ungrounded. She had been helped in "reality-testing" as the consultant steered her around the circle of men in a "Try it—you'll like it" experiment. Before very long the consultant was able to phase out of the physical steering as Claire became increasingly relaxed.

Another example of shifting feelings regarding sexuality is by Myrick.[14] This intervention involved the consultant working with an effeminate boy's teachers. Effeminacy in a boy may impede the learning of more mature heterosexual behavior. Two teachers, one a classroom teacher and the other a physical education instructor, were directly involved in the intervention. These teachers, in turn, worked with the effeminate boy on a prescriptive basis, sometimes directly, and sometimes indirectly.

The physical education teacher met with the client repeatedly prior to the formal physical education class and taught him the skills of touch football— how to pass the ball to the quarterback from center position, how to throw a pass, and other aspects of the game that were key to the boy's progressively taking on a more central position in the everyday touch football games of his class. On the other hand, the classroom teacher shifted the boy's seating arrangement, putting him beside the most popular boy in the class, who was also a strong athlete. Under these conditions, classroom discussions took place in dyads, with the popular boy and effeminate boy being paired. Shared activities involved participating in class committees, collecting papers and books, carrying materials, arranging chairs, and so on. In addition, on two separate days, the teacher led the class in discussions of (a) friendship, and (b) making new friends. The class talked about personal feelings and ideas, which gave the effeminate boy a chance to express personal fears, concerns, and specific anxieties related to his new experiences with his peers. These classroom arrangements were such that it was possible for the effeminate boy to identify with a model boy as well as to share in emotional experiences related to friendship discussions.

This approach resulted in a number of positive outcomes. For example, in sociometric choices received, the client earned only two before the intervention, but eleven afterward; in terms of rank among the 33 pupils of the class, he shifted from 27th of the 33 prior to the intervention to 8th of 33 afterwards.

This intervention is an example of how a prescriptive approach can provide conditions under which an individual is assisted to change. Even though the boy was unaware of how the teachers were influencing his popularity, the intervention demonstrates how a manipulative strategy may have constructive outcomes.

A significant dynamic underlying successful prescriptive counseling is illustrated in the following telephone counseling situation.

> 4:30 p.m. . . . Girl named Marty called. Hung up about going out with an ex-boyfriend's best friend. She still likes the first boy, but he won't go out with her now for fear of hurting his best friend's feelings. Told her to talk to the present boyfriend and make that relationship more flexible than going steady. Then she could date the boys she wanted to more easily. She'll call back. Phone log July 1970.

Explaining why the advice was accepted and acted upon, the consultants conclude:

> The Ann Landers variety of personal problems is the most common type of a call a center receives. Such calls demand advice, even though giving advice is against standard psychotherapeutic theory and practice. Attempts to engage a caller in conversation often lead to the caller's hanging up angrily at being ignored. After hearing the advice callers commonly hang up quickly, with a sincere but short "Thank you." The suggestions which are most effective coincide with the caller's own inclinations so a counselor is not so much asked to tell the person what to do as to support an unstated but implicitly made choice or to argue effectively against it. To avoid being considered wrong or stupid, the caller states the situation in the form of a question to avoid being held responsible for the decision.[15]

The risk, then, is that the consultant might be induced to "okay" via prescription what the client desires, thus engaging in "felt needs" counseling, which may do little more than confirm the client's injudicious wishes.

Physical Illness Related to Low Morale/Cohesion

That physical illness can have demoralizing mental effects is a well-known and widely accepted truth. There appears to be a developing awareness that the converse of this is also true. We are learning that mental effort can be applied to changing physiological facts.

The several approaches to mind-body correlations share similar properties. One example, "bioenergetics," was developed by Lowen.

> The principles and practices of bioenergetic therapy rest on the functional identity of the mind and the body. This means that any change in a person's thinking and, therefore, in his behavior and feelings, is conditioned on a change in the functioning of the body. The two functions that are most important in this regard are breathing and movement. Both of these functions are disturbed in every person who has an emotional conflict, by chronic muscle tensions that are physical counterparts of psychological conflicts.
>
> In the therapy, the patient is helped to get in touch with his body, with the ground on which he stands and with the air around him—through passive stress positions, active voluntary exercises and by the active intervention of the therapist who places physical pressure on chronically tense muscles to free their blocked energy. This intervention often precipitates dramatic expressions of feelings such as sadness, terror, fear and longing that have long been held back by chronically tensing the musculature. Spontaneous memories and insights often follow these expressions and they can be dealt with psychologically, through verbal interchange.[16]

Lowen describes an intervention using this method.

> . . . I treated a young woman, Lucy, about eighteen years of age, who was markedly retarded in both her emotional and intellectual development. In addition her muscular coordination was severely impaired, a condition that is typical of retarded people. Superficially, Lucy was a very agreeable and pleasant person who made a slight effort to do the exercises and movements I suggested. Her movements, however, were very limited in duration and represented a gesture of cooperation rather than a serious commitment to the activity. She would, for example, kick her legs against the couch several times when saying "No" in a quiet voice that carried no conviction. Then she would stop, after only a few moments of activity, and look at me to see if I approved or disapproved of her. It was obvious that Lucy needed my approval, and I gave it to her at the same time that I encouraged her to let go more fully to these expressions.

Thus the consultant encouraged Lucy to "protest." As he worked with her, some aspects of the "inner" Lucy became apparent.

> During the treatment I would catch an occasional glimpse of an alert intelligence behind her mask of retardation. There were moments when Lucy's eyes would meet mine with a look of understanding. When this happened, her eyes temporarily lost their dullness and became bright and sensitive. I had the impression that she was studying me to see how far she could trust me. On other occasions, when I asked her to open her eyes wide in an

expression of fear, she froze and became completely immobile. Once when I pressed with my thumbs on the muscles alongside the nose that activate the smiling reflex in order to block the smile, her eyeballs rolled up into their sockets and her face became twisted in a gargoylelike expression. She looked like a complete idiot, and I realized that she had cut off her contact with me and had withdrawn into uncomprehension because of some deep inner fear. It was an unusual defense but also a very effective one.

Having now developed a more precise diagnosis, the consultant continued his program of prescriptive interventions.

. . . My treatment of Lucy aimed at strengthening her ego through her asserting opposition and at the development of better muscular coordination. Her kicking became more forceful and sustained, and her no's became louder and stronger. She also hit the bed with a tennis racket repeatedly, saying, "I won't." Bioenergetic exercises were also used to deepen her breathing and loosen her body.

. . . Her ability to express her feelings was blocked by the extreme physical tensions in her body. The muscles at the back of her neck were contracted into hard lumps. The attempt to loosen them by massage was painful, and I always stopped when she became frightened. At each session, however, I could work a little more strongly with her. At first Lucy could not tolerate any stress for more than a few moments. Her tolerance slowly increased as her tensions eased and her breathing became freer and deeper. Initially she moved her arms and legs like a puppet, without rhythm or feeling. As she gained a sense of freedom in expressing herself, her movements became more charged with feelings. She hit and kicked with more vigor, and her voice rose in pitch and intensity as she voiced her no's and "I won'ts." The result was a consistent improvement in her coordination.

Lucy's therapy ended when her family moved to another part of the country. We had worked together once a week for about two years. At the end there were times when a casual observer would have taken Lucy for a normal person. She had made considerable progress, and I hoped that with encouragement and support it would continue.[17]

Other prescriptive mind-body interventions include "Rolfing" and "biofeedback." "Rolfing" was created by Ida Rolf.[18] As is true of bioenergetics, it is a way of attempting to change subjective feeling-states in the direction of morale/cohesion well-being. This is accomplished by first changing the body's muscular tone, posture, or functions such as breathing. By comparison, "biofeedback"[19] is concerned with shifting physiological states that have an effect on morale. Possibilities include decreasing heartbeat rate, decreasing skin temperature, and shifting the frequency of various patterns of brain waves.

ORGANIZATION (B-2-4)

The staff of a government agency was plagued by tensions, mistrust, and strife. A prescriptive intervention by Scholtes was utilized to bring about cooperation and good feelings among the members. This situation of low morale expressed in terms of distrust and distance among organization staff members was focused on directly by a three-step process.

The first phase of the workshop focused on problem identification. In organizationally diverse groups of three or four, participants were given thirty minutes each to discuss problems in working within the organization.

> While the individual shared their experience the other two or three listened and acted as consultants. The instructions given the listener/consultants were: Don't disagree with the speaker's perceptions, don't give advice, don't discount their feelings, don't seek to solve their difficulties, don't share your experience, don't make judgments.[20]

The external consultant prescribed the acceptant listening mode to participants in an attempt to establish trust at this early stage.

Trust was expanded in the next step of problem solving. Actual protagonists of the workshop voluntarily discussed problems on a one-to-one basis. Two hours were provided with similar rules for nonjudgmental acceptance of one another's perceptions. Specific guidelines were also provided for offering and accepting criticism and for working toward resolution of specific issues.

The final engagement aimed at examining and changing the organizational climate through writing of a new contract intended to govern staff relations. The staff was divided into small cross-representative groups of seven or eight members each. They were asked to look at several dimensions at work in their organizations, for example, informal communication, conflict, leadership, and authority. Each group was asked to present two products to the total group: 1) a proposed process or set of activities by which the problems identified in their area of concern would be remedied, and 2) a statement or statements of intent to be considered for incorporation into a contract for organizational change.

The success of any contract for change depends in part on the degree of commitment felt by the parties involved and their willingness to be bound by it. The degree of willingness and commitment is said to be directly proportional to the extent to which participants feel ownership of the final product. While the design called for developing "a process whereby the . . . organization can review, revise, consent to and sign the contract, subscribing to its provisions and agreeing to its follow-up process," it is likely that employees not directly involved in creating the contract feel less allegiance to it.[21]

Though their intervention may have brought forth more constructive attitudes, at least on a short-term basis, the prescriptive limitation is that it bypassed real barriers to behavioral effectiveness. Participants were not aided to learn theory of effective behavior or skills essential for executing it. It is likely that conventional behavior will soon bring about an erosion of the "contracted" attitudes as real problems and conflicts reappear.

Summary

Prescriptive interventions with individuals when the focal issue is morale or cohesion are calculated to correct either lowered or excessive self-confidence, usually the former. They are not of the "buck up" or "pep pill" variety but attempt to push the individual into an action where anticipated fears are unrealized, where rewards are experienced, or where contact replaces withdrawal. Such approaches may be useful when lowered morale is caused by a particular circumstance of crisis or is related to some specific, easily identifiable factor. Manic reactions, involving excessive and unfounded self-confidence, represent the other end of the morale continuum. One strategy involving physical intervention was introduced to suggest how prescriptive interventions may be useful when morale has exceeded the "normal" range on the up side.

Examples of morale/cohesion prescriptive interventions involving a multiperson client are infrequent, perhaps because the depressed feelings in such cases are not usually thought of as the underlying cause of a difficulty but rather as a symptom of some other focal issue. For example, the unilateral exercise of authority in an organization may generate low morale throughout the membership. Yet to concentrate on morale/cohesion would be to work on the wrong problem.

Notes

1. D. S. Viscott, *The Making of a Psychiatrist* (Greenwich, Conn.: Fawcett Publications, 1972), p. 308. Reprinted by permission.
2. Ibid., pp. 244–45.
3. Ibid., p. 247.
4. E. S. Taulbee and H. W. Wright, "Psychosocial-Behavioral Model for Therapeutic Interventions," in C. D. Spielberger, ed., *Current Topics in Clinical and Community Psychology*, vol. 31 (New York: Academic Press, 1971), pp. 53–92.
5. J. Lieb, I. L. Lipsitch and A. E. Slaby, *The Crisis Team: A Handbook for the Mental Health Professional* (Hagerstown, Md.: Harper & Row, 1973), pp. 89–91. Reprinted by permission.
6. J. Wolpe, *The Case of Mrs. Schmidt: An Illustration of Behavior Therapy* (Nashville, Tenn.: Counselor Recordings & Tests, 1965), pp. 7–8.
7. Ibid., p. 8.
8. Ibid., p. 9.
9. M. Wolpin, "Guided Imagining in Reducing Fear and Avoidance Behavior," in California Mental Health Research Symposium No. 2, *Behavior Theory and Therapy*, State of California, Department of Mental Hygiene, Bureau of Research, 1968, pp. 40–41.
10. J. Wolpe, *The Practice of Behavior Therapy*, 2d ed. (New York: Pergamon Press, 1973), pp. 198–99. Reprinted by permission.
11. V. E. Frankl, *The Doctor and the Soul* (New York: Bantam Books, 1955), pp. 178–203. (Originally published 1946.)
12. Wolpe, *The Practice of Behavior Therapy.*
13. E. E. Mintz, "Marathon Groups: Process and People," in L. Blank, G. B.

Gottsegen and M. G. Gottsegen, *Confrontation* (New York: Macmillan, 1971), pp. 20–21. Reprinted by permission.

14. R. D. Myrick, "The Counselor-Consultant and the Effeminate Boy," *Personnel and Guidance Journal* 5 (1970): 355, 361.

15. T. Clark and D. T. Jaffe, *Toward a Radical Therapy: Alternate Services for Personal and Social Change* (New York: Gordon and Breach, Science Publishers, 1973), p. 157. Reprinted by permission.

16. S. Feldman, "Alexander Lowen," *Human Behavior Magazine* (June 1974): 26. Copyright © 1974. Reprinted by permission.

17. A. Lowen, *Pleasure* (New York: Lancer Books, 1970), pp. 173–77. Reprinted by permission of Coward, McCann & Geoghegan, Inc., New York. Copyright © 1970 by Alexander Lowen, reprinted with permission.

18. I. Rolf, "Introductory Lecture-Demonstration of Structural Integration" (San Rafael, Calif.: Big Sur Recordings, 1974).

19. B. B. Brown, *New Mind, New Body* (New York: Harper & Row, 1974).

20. P. R. Scholtes, "Contracting for Change," *Training and Development Journal* (April 1975): 8.

21. Ibid., p. 12.

11

PRESCRIPTIVE INTERVENTIONS

Norms/ Standards

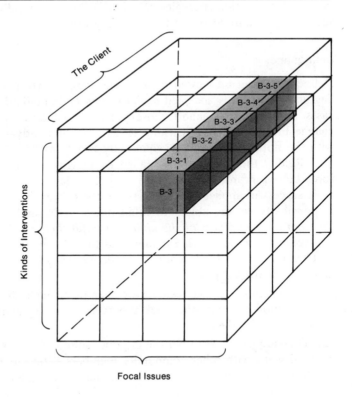

The earliest industrial example of a prescriptive intervention involving norms/standards is reported by Frederick Winslow Taylor. He recounts a particular example where "As soon as a careful study had been made of the time elements entering into one class of work, a single first-class workman was picked out and started on ordinary piece work on this job. His task required him to do between *three and one-half* and *four times* as much work in a day as had been done in the past on an average."[1] Taylor notes that it took about two years to extend this pilot individual intervention to the entire work group. To the unskilled observer who notices that numerous rules, habits, particular work practices, and so on need changing to achieve greater work productivity, it might appear that direct prescriptive interventions focusing on maladaptive norms/standards should be employed from the outset. Actually, the first priority seems to be obtaining the client's acceptance of the need to change and commitment to doing so as opposed to diagnosing the client's situation and devising a needed solution.

INDIVIDUAL (B-3-1)

Client difficulties may result from a disregard or violation of the norms and standards felt to be essential for integration and acceptance in a given community. Intervention strategies calculated to pressure individuals into embracing such norms are discussed in the following examples.

Delinquency

Delinquency can be viewed as a special case of irresponsibility, behavior that flagrantly disregards accepted social norms and standards. Intervention in such cases is intended to enable those presently exhibiting delinquent behavior to change through actively learning to behave differently—that is, in accordance with the norms/standards a community exacts as "dues" for full membership.

"Reality therapy," as it is called by Glasser, is an approach calculated to solve behavior problems by increasing the client's "responsibility." One of its most successful applications has been in the context of delinquency. As defined, responsibility is "the ability to fulfill one's needs, and to do so *in a way that does not deprive others of the ability to fulfill their needs.*"[2] The reality-therapy intervention parallels both Synanon and the Therapeutic Community, described in Chapter 17. Several features of delinquency-directed reality therapy are indicated below.

1. Delinquents are congregated together in an institution (either for daytime education or round-the-clock supervision) where authorities retain physical control over them.

2. They are expected to behave in good, sound, right, valid ways as they study and work with other community members. Consultants have no reluctance to specify what, in concrete terms, constitutes "good, sound, right, or valid behavior."

3. Those not cooperating are segregated into, say, a discipline cottage where they are deprived of membership in the broader community. Return to the broader community results only from improved, more responsible behavior in the discipline cottage; interventions to help the person become more responsible are implemented.

4. Those cooperating become eligible for individual or group therapy sessions.

The consultant, who is ready to pressure the client into acting more responsibly, seeks to involve the client in problem solving. The relationship permits consultant and client to engage in joint planning, with the consultant providing direction and advice if that will produce desired behavior. As clients come to accept and live according to more responsible patterns of personal behavior they become eligible to leave the institution.

Significant in this mode of intervention are the consultant's prescriptions. He or she establishes norms for sound behavior and specifies activities designed to produce that kind of conduct. To a significant degree, this means withholding privileges when norms are violated and stipulating the specific norms and standards that will be judged acceptable and rewarded by restoration of freedom.

Destitution

A variety of circumstances can result in a person's becoming destitute, but whatever the particular "cause," the individual is likely to increasingly disregard the social norms and standards essential for cooperation and collaborative living. Mental-health consultation often helps the destitute person reestablish self-respect and reconnect with the world of work by adherence to established norms and practices. One approach, described by Robinson, relies on prescriptive intervention.

A 35-year-old woman whose 85-year-old father was still working as a mechanic was referred for counseling. Of her two brothers, one held a responsible position; the other was barely making it due to alcoholism. Miss Lee had stopped working and had drifted into heavy drinking and quasi-prostitution. She was living with an unemployed man, whom she had no intention of marrying. Her situation came to the attention of the caseworker through a government official who asked the caseworker to make contact and help her out of her current situation. The consultant shifted the responsibility for making the contact back to Miss Lee through the government official, who then arranged for her to come in for an appointment.

Nine interviews were conducted over a period of several months. During this time the consultant provided financial help that permitted Miss Lee to move to another place where she could fix meals and so on. The caseworker advised Miss Lee to stop drinking and take better physical care of herself, and offered assurance of continued support while she was reestablishing a more healthy way of living. These kinds of directions and support were continued throughout the transitional period until the client was successful in finding employment as a typist.[3]

The success of this prescriptive approach is at least partly due to the situation—i.e., for all practical purposes the client had come to the end of her rope. Her gradual disregard of norms and standards had become so excessive that she could find no foothold to begin a process of reconstruction. For some two years she had been repeating the destitution cycle, and the financial help, advice, and cautions introduced by the consultant provided a sense of direction which she could embrace as a more attractive alternative. Also, she was beginning to experience transference emotions toward the consultant through the strength, protection, and support offered her. No particular insights were suggested by the consultant regarding her "unconscious" motivations and so on. Once the client had regained a mature adult role she was able to adhere to social norms and standards in a way that permitted her to function as a self-sustaining adult.

Disorientation

Whenever a person shows significant signs of *psychotic* ("He's losing contact with reality!") behavior, the classical approach is to arrange for admission to a mental hospital. As a patient, the person is no longer faced with the need for self-responsible functioning in a house/job/community situation. As a patient he or she can be observed, supervised, and treated. In the process, however, the individual is given a diagnostic label whose legal and social significance may hamper future endeavors, no matter how soon he or she is released from the institution. The hospital care offered the client-as-patient can cause a dependency reaction as the client ceases feeling a sense of responsibility for self-help.

A strikingly different definition of the "sickness" and how to resolve it has resulted from viewing the psychotic individual in a somewhat different light. Any episode of disoriented or psychotic behavior is viewed as a crisis reaction to an intolerable situation. Without inferring initial cause-effect connections, this viewpoint acknowledges that other people and accompanying circumstances impact on any person's current situation. Hospitalization constitutes an escape that contributes little or nothing to help the person cope with current realities. However, by *remaining in the "real" situation,* the client may be able to retain or regain an ordinary level of functioning and work with others toward resolving the crisis.[4]

The Family Treatment Unit, which approaches psychotic behavior in this way, includes a psychiatrist, social worker, and nurse. The approach is prescriptive. The client is expected to continue functioning according to previous norms and standards of conduct. For a housewife this means continuing the sustaining routines of housework and family living. Medication may be provided for the individual client and/or family members to help them over the crisis period. After it has passed and the individual client has regained normal functioning, additional help involving counseling, welfare assistance, job retraining, and so on may be provided to increase the likelihood of successful continuance of the normal pattern.

Evaluation data for randomly selected patients treated according to this kind of crisis therapy versus psychiatric hospitalization suggest that prescription crisis therapy helps the patient hold together and return to "normal" functioning more rapidly. From each of the two groups studied an approximately equal number needed subsequent hospitalization for psychotic episodes. However, those who had been hospitalized previously required approximately three times longer in hospital care than did those who had formerly undergone crisis therapy.

In the Soviet Union one intervention for dealing with mental-health problems having a norms/standards focal issue is called "pathogenic psychotherapy." As described by Ziferstein, it is prescriptive in nature.

> This attitude was demonstrated in all five Soviet psychotherapists whose work I observed. They were all very active in giving their patients emotional support and reassurance, advice, and guidance. They vigorously engaged in reeducating their patients and presenting to them values and standards of behavior. And the doctors had no doubts as to what values and standards are realistic, correct (the word *correct* is frequently used), and socially desirable.
>
> These psychotherapists would often intervene quite actively in the patient's reality situation. Where they considered it necessary, they manipulated the patient's environment, his work, occupation, place of work, or residence. One example: the doctor concluded that the patient, a young factory worker, had the capacity to be a good engineer, and that the unchallenging, unfulfilling nature of his present work contributed to his emotional illness. The doctor wrote out a prescription which was addressed to the director of the factory in which the patient worked, requiring that the patient be enrolled in an engineering institute and that the factory pay his full salary during the entire period of his schooling.
>
> The Soviet psychotherapists whom I observed did attempt in their psychotherapeutic work to elucidate the psychogenesis of the patient's symptoms, of disturbed interpersonal relations, of distorted perception of reality, and of pathological character traits. But they took a dim view of the practice of directly interpreting to the patient and bringing to his consciousness his unconscious negative feelings and actions.[5]

The nonconfrontational but prescriptive nature of the approach is illustrated at another point in his description. Ziferstein recounts prescriptive strategies that parallel those of certain Western psychotherapists.

> In the course of my observations of the work of this therapist and of the other therapists, I came to realize that they were often quick to recognize the latent meaning of patients' verbal and nonverbal communications, including dreams. However, they believed that making such unconscious negative material conscious would produce a counter-therapeutic effect. To use their Pavlovian terminology, they maintain that the words of the authority figure, the therapist, serve as powerful stimuli through both the "first signalling system" (nonverbal) and the "second signalling system" (verbal). Negative ideas expressed by the therapist, therefore, reinforce the "unhealthy stereotype" (pathological reaction patterns) already existing in

the patient. The therapist, instead of making the negative unconscious feelings conscious, gives the patient a countervailing suggestion or advice, without verbalizing the latent negative content.[6]

Walled-Off Emotions

A prescriptive approach by Salter to individuals when norms and standards are involved is premised on the notion that personal problems originate from a common cause, namely, an inhibition of emotions. Therefore, the intervention strategy is designed to facilitate free expression of emotions. This approach shares with others the fact that the intervention is not directed at changing thoughts and feelings but rather toward changing the norms and standards of conduct the client adheres to. The proposition is that whenever behavior changes, feelings and thoughts also change in ways that are congruent with and support the new behavior.

Salter[7] suggests six techniques for increasing the expression of emotions. Since the strategy encourages clients to do the six different kinds of things they avoid doing, it parallels other desensitization techniques. These to-be-learned standards and norms of conduct are:

1. *Feeling-talk:* practice in being emotionally outspoken, indicating likes and aversions, annoyances, love, and other feelings. The goal is to tell the emotional truth, expressing emotions as they are experienced.
2. *Facial talk:* deliberate effort to portray one's emotions facially.
3. *Contradict and attack:* learning to disagree with others rather than to feign agreement.
4. *"I"-ness:* using the first person, "I did this . . . I did that . . . ," to learn to identify oneself with activities.
5. *Praise:* if this comes from others, it is to be expressly agreed with. Additionally, one can offer praise of oneself.
6. *Improvisation:* the goal here is to be spontaneously existential; to react out of feeling, without plan or premonition.

The prescriptive character of the intervention is described as follows.

> The therapist uses advice, instruction, suggestion, persuasion, logic, and commands to encourage the client to practice excitation. The client is told: "Don't be so agreeable. Tell people what you think at all times, regardless of whether it's polite or impolite." He is instructed in how to do this in various situations in his life, and is given assignments. He is told that it may seem unnatural, but that "if you do the opposite of what you have been doing all your life, you will probably feel the opposite of the way you feel now. . . ."[8]

Personal Responsibility

A prescriptive intervention in a psychotherapeutic situation consisted of instructing clients in "internalization," i.e., how to take personal responsibility for oneself.[9] Internalization of theories/principles as described in Chapter 2 is a somewhat different concept.

One of the identified characteristics of persons who make progress in psychotherapy is the extent to which the person takes responsibility for his or her own situation as contrasted with accounting for it as due to external factors. The former is called internalization; the latter, externalization. The hypothesis is that the higher the internalization, the greater the progress from psychotherapeutic interventions. This particular intervention was designed to determine the extent to which internalization can be taught. If a person can better learn to internalize, it follows that he or she should gain additional benefits as a result of experiencing psychotherapy.

The intervention was a straightforward discussion between the interventionist and client. In total, eight male and seven female undergraduates took part. Illustrative examples of the client's tendencies toward internalization or externalization were freely discussed during the course of each counseling session. Furthermore, when the client acknowledged that internalization was a better basis for explaining some point involved in the discussion, he or she received reinforcement from the intervener.

The impact of the intervention was determined by taking a three-minute sample from a twenty-minute period of informal discussion prior to the intervention and comparing it with the three-minute sample taken twenty minutes following the intervention.

The first conclusion was that internalization can be taught. The second conclusion reached was that those who came to the intervention with the greatest tendency toward externalization were those who learned most about how to internalize as a result of the intervention.

This study presumes that a precondition for more effective therapy was created as a result of the intervention. However, no additional evidence is provided to demonstrate the impact of training in internalization on actual behavioral outcomes.

This was a prescriptive intervention at the individual level. The focal issue was norms/standards, since the attempt was to shift participants' normative explanations of causation from external to internal.

GROUP (B-3-2)

Prescriptive interventions for solving group problems are less frequent than those directed toward individuals, partly because cooperation among several persons is necessary for the prescription to take effect. While an *absence* of cooperation may already be a deficiency in the group's situation, simply prescribing "cooperation" gives no assurance of attaining it. Several approaches to solving problems of group action through prescriptive consultation are conceivable. Most of them deal with norms/standards as defined by the rules of conduct among group members. Prescriptive group development may focus on content issues or on interaction process, or on both. Formal content matters may include individual job descriptions, the boss's span of control, frequency of meetings, what the agendas of these meetings contain, and so on; process has more to do with such issues as how members interact with one another, how authority is used, and how problems are solved. Most often, the underlying issue is in some way related to how the top person presently is using his or her authority and how better results could be achieved.

From observation or inquiry the consultant may conclude that the team has too few meetings or too many. Deficiencies may be related to "loose" job definitions that result in problems being overlooked, or "tight" ones that pose barriers to needed cooperation. Or the consultant may find a "lack of direction" evidenced by the group's chronic failure to approach problems in a focused fashion. The group may be excessively concerned with triviality, be too constrained by policy, or have insufficient policy guidelines. Beyond these diagnostic areas the consultant may evaluate each member as to individual competence and potential. If the "problems" are of a process character, the consultant will recommend changes in the organization.

Whatever the findings, the prescriptive consultant usually prepares a report for the top person giving both a diagnosis of problem causes and solution prescriptions. He or she may present these conclusions to other members, individually or together, and may recommend specific steps that need to be taken to increase effectiveness. Additionally, the consultant may offer assistance in seeing to it that the recommended plan is executed.

INTERGROUP (B-3-3)

The prescriptive approach to resolving norms/standards or working out rules and procedures for interaction between groups is most frequently a structured one—that is, power/authority is generally addressed as the focal issue. The inherent assumption is that a realignment of power/authority will lead to normative changes in the ways groups relate to one another.

ORGANIZATION (B-3-4)

Japanese Style Management Practices

Increasing attention is being placed upon interventions to bring certain Japanese management practices into use in the United States. This approach is based on classical business school logic. A recommended solution is prescribed to managers with the expectation that thereafter they will implement it. No provision is made for managers to internalize the theory underlying the participation practices (not theory in any rigorous sense but, broadly speaking, a message to "shift away from the 9,1 toward the 9,9 orientation") as described in Chapter 2 or to acquire skills essential for effective application. The premise is "this is the way the Japanese do it and they get good results. To get better results, you ought to do it that way, too." The Pascale and Athos[10] approach to managerial improvement offers no further implementation guidelines. Ouchi's[11] related interventions at best are prescriptive in the sense of a standardized step 1, step 2, and step 3.

In addition, Ouchi's formulation provides a classical paternalistic solution to the conflict problem: conflict resolution by decompression. Decompression requires a collateral system, i.e., managers and those managed leave the job (one system) to socialize (the other system). A party or a dramatic production that engages the principal characters in various forms of accusation, ridicule, buffoonery, and so on allows frustrations to be ventilated indirectly against perpetrators. Then it is "back to work" until tensions build up again. Though presented by Ouchi as a recommended solution to the conflict problem in a Z culture, the readily apparent limitation of conflict resolution by decompression is that it does little or nothing to correct the behavior causing the frustrations in the first place. What is recommended as a solution is little more than an escape valve, an activity that allows for blowing off excessive steam. This cannot be regarded as anything other than tension release. It "hides" the deeper issue of learning to conduct business according to effective relationships, where tensions can be discharged as they arise through confrontation and resolution of differences. Strengthening the relationship and making it a more viable basis for future productivity and creativity hinges on a direct approach to resolving conflict.

It can be expected that a number of organizations will try to shift toward the ingredients of Japanese style management. Some may attempt to achieve participation-by-pronouncement, while others may utilize step-by-step mechanisms to introduce normative changes.[12] The history of organization development strongly suggests that such efforts will be only marginally effective and soon abandoned. There are many reasons for the lack of success inherent in these tactics, including lack of theory and internalization; initiative resting in pockets of interest, not coming directly from the top; top management's merely giving its approval rather than having deep personal involvement; failure to understand or suggest ways of reducing resistance to change; lack of skill for resolving conflicts that increase when there is widespread participation in problem solving, and so on.

Job Enrichment

An intervention dealing with a job enrichment effort was undertaken in four plants of a large, nonunionized clothing pattern manufacturer.[13] The purpose was to increase productivity by adding variety to routine assembly line work. Two forms of job enrichment were used: (1) enlarging employee jobs to include more tasks (job enlargement) in plants one and two, and (2) rotating employees among different jobs (job rotation) in plants three and four. Both had a positive impact on productivity.

In addition, however, managers of plants one and three were told the change would immediately overcome technical and psychological problems arising from over-specialization of jobs and that productivity would be greatly increased; managers of plants two and four were told that the change was simply a "comparative control measure" and increased output was not expected to occur.

These prescriptive interventions by the director of manufacturing were then studied to determine whether expectations that job enrichment should result in higher levels of output would actually influence performance.

The results indicate that the job innovations from which managers were led to expect greater gains showed such gains. Gains in outputs for plants one and three were greater than those for two and four by substantial amounts. In other words, additional improvements in productivity were attributable to managers' expectations of the effects of job enrichment.

"Clearly, what the managers expected and the way they treated their employees, *not the way they organized them,* was the key to higher productivity in plants one and three."[14] Thus expectations played a critical role in the degree of productivity achieved with changes in job designs.

Work Practices

In the following example, a prescriptive consultant listens for the client's symptoms—*without* accepting the client's own conclusions regarding work practices in the company's training division. The episode also reveals how a prescriptive consultant offers a client step-by-step recommendations for solving the problem at hand.

> Dallmeyer talks about one assignment he handled for a Midwest consumer company. The company boasted a hot-shot sales training director. He used every known device—booklets, seminars, training courses—in teaching his men how to push their products, yet profits had stalled. Finally the company's president hired a management consultant. "If there's one thing you won't have to improve," boasted the president, "it's our sales training. We have one of the top men in the country."
>
> It is one of the duties of the management consultant to listen to the suggestions of the client president, but also to ignore his conclusions. Obviously if the client had all the answers before calling the consultant he never would have called him. Dallmeyer spent several weeks scrutinizing the consumer company with the care of an archeologist uncovering lost relics. Finally he made his recommendations.
>
> "Your training director is doing a good job," he said. "In fact, he's doing *too* good a job. You're spending four weeks a year training your salesmen when two weeks should be enough. Get your salesmen out in the field where they can do some good." The consultant also rearranged the sales territories, balanced the work load, and advised pushing certain neglected products. Sales soon increased.[15]

That clients often resist prescriptions offered them is almost too well known to need documentation. The following is typical.

> Even when a sick or dying company obtains accurate advice on how to save itself, it may be unwilling to accept the advice—just as the patient threatened by a possible heart attack refuses to quit smoking or lose weight. I spoke with Carl Devoe, president of Executive House, Inc. As a member of a group of investors, he had purchased control of a once successful auto

supplies manufacturing company whose business had been sliding steadily downhill. The new investors discovered that various management consultants had attempted to advise the company. Gathering dust in its files were two or three extensive reports, any one of which if applied might have arrested the company's decline. The reports had gone unimplemented.

"These reports required such massive doses of treatment," Devoe explained to me, "that the people in the judgment area were overwhelmed. As a result they did nothing." The new investors began to apply the recommendations of the consultants one step at a time. Soon the company began to show a profit again.[16]

When the client refuses the prescription it is reasonable to conclude that the consultant either failed to identify the real causes of inertia or else failed to motivate the client sufficiently to bring about the change.

Behavior Modification

One of the most complete descriptions of behavior-modification methods for improving employee performance on an organization-wide basis is provided by Feeney. His thesis is:

When you try to create a more positive environment where people are supportive, helpful and looking at what you do well, people feel better. Attitudes and all these inner feelings are really caused by consequences. You don't try to change them directly, you change the environmental consequences, which change the feelings so if the consequences are positive for what one does, one feels better.[17]

Emery Air Freight has concentrated on a program of productivity improvement that has four basic sequential steps for each focal application.

1. *Identify the problem.* As Feeney points out, in many situations those who are closest to the problem are unaware that a problem exists. Since outsiders are more likely to notice problem areas, the Emery program uses outside consultants to audit particular individual and group performances. Feeney believes that the highest profit-improvement potential is to be found in areas of performance deficiency. Therefore, rather than helping people to do better what they already do well, efforts should be directed toward correcting major performance shortfalls.

2. *Set standards* for what is acceptable and *measurements* for evaluating actual performance.

3. *Feed back* "how they are doing" to those who produce results.

4. *Reward* satisfactory performance *or* improved performance—no matter how slight the improvement—preferably through personal commendation by the individual's superior. This should be done frequently in the beginning, less often after performance standards are regularly being reached or surpassed.

As described, the Emery program is a prescriptive intervention. Consultants diagnose problems, set up standards, and then devise reinforcement schedules under which people are induced to step up performance. The description does not provide an indication of how—if at all—chronically substandard performance, which cannot be rewarded but which also cannot be ignored, is dealt with by a system that is geared solely to positive reinforcement.

LARGER SOCIAL SYSTEM (B-3-5)

Norms/standards prescriptive interventions in larger social systems generally focus upon various disintegrative processes, such as alcoholism, drug addiction, or delinquency, which occur within or are linked to particular social contexts and circumstances. These maladies are regarded as being induced by the larger social system rather than by individual psychodynamic factors, maladies related to the stresses, strains, and strivings created within the larger social system.

Alcoholics Anonymous can be considered a truncated larger social system; a social system, in other words, which is incomplete because it does not solve or support the solution of food, clothing, and shelter issues. And yet it does support individuals as they seek to cope with alcoholic motivations in specific situations. Thus Alcoholics Anonymous is an "interest group" in the sense of convened meetings where members come together to strengthen one another's individual adherence to sobriety norms/standards. Also, an individual member of Alcoholics Anonymous who is finding it hard to abstain from drinking in social or solo settings away from Alcoholics Anonymous can quickly get supportive help from other members in adhering to AA's norms/standards. While perhaps a majority of the interventions are norms/standards related, a variety of other kinds of interventions are utilized in the total program. There are confrontational aspects to AA in that members may challenge one another in a straightforward way regarding their attitudes, as in the Synanon Game (Chapter 17). Cathartic elements are present in the sense that each member is expected to select someone as a confidant with whom he or she can talk in a very private way about past problems.[18]

Summary

Since behavior that stays within the "normal limits" established by a community ensures an orderly basis for social interaction, it is not surprising that individuals who disregard or reject such norms/standards suffer personal frustrations. The prescriptive solution is to aid individuals to establish or reestablish such norms and standards as guides for their personal conduct. Correspondingly, as Salter's intervention illustrates, behaviors that presently seem too constrained by norms/standards boundaries can be expanded by prescription.

Notes

1. F. W. Taylor, *Scientific Management* (New York: Harper & Brothers Publishers, 1911), pp. 49–51.
2. W. Glasser, *Reality Therapy: A New Approach to Psychiatry* (New York: Harper & Row, 1965), p. 13.
3. V. P. Robinson, "A Discussion of Two Case Records Illustrating Personality Change," in J. Taft, ed., *Family Casework and Counseling: A Functional Approach* (Philadelphia: University of Pennsylvania Press, 1948), pp. 133–50.
4. K. Flomenhaft, D. M. Kaplan and D. G. Langsley, "Avoiding Psychiatric Hospitalization," in J. Fischer, comp., *Interpersonal Helping: Emerging Approaches for Social Work Practice* (Springfield, Ill.: Charles C Thomas, 1973), pp. 253–64.
5. I. Ziferstein, "The Impact of the Socioeconomic Order on the Psychotherapeutic Process in the Soviet Union," in Stanley Lesse, ed., *An Evaluation of the Results of the Psychotherapies* (Springfield, Ill.: Charles C Thomas, 1968), p. 262. Reprinted by permission.
6. Ibid., p. 264.
7. A. Salter, *Conditioned Reflex Therapy* (New York: Creative Age Press, 1949), pp. 97–100.
8. Ibid., p. 61.
9. R. M. Pierce, P. Schauble and A. Farkas, "Teaching Internalization Behavior to Clients," *Psychotherapy: Theory, Research, and Practice* 4 (1977): 217–20.
10. R. T. Pascale and A. Athos, *The Art of Japanese Management* (New York: Simon and Schuster, 1981).
11. W. G. Ouchi, *Theory Z* (Reading, Mass.: Addison-Wesley, 1981).
12. J. Main, "Westinghouse's Cultural Revolution," *Fortune,* June 15, 1981.
13. A. S. King, "Management's Ecstasy and Disparity Over Job Enrichment," *Training and Development Journal* (March 1976): 3–8.
14. Ibid., p. 5.
15. H. Higdon, *The Business Healers* (New York: Random House, 1969), p. 71. Reprinted by permission.
16. Ibid., pp. 47–48.
17. E. J. Feeney, "Performance Audit, Feedback and Positive Reinforcement," reproduced by special permission from *Training and Development Journal* 26, no. 11 (1972): 9.
18. *Alcoholics Anonymous,* new and rev. ed. (New York: AA Publishing, Inc., 1955).

12

PRESCRIPTIVE INTERVENTIONS

Goals/ Objectives

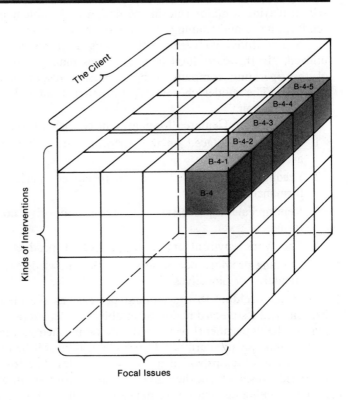

When goals/objectives are the focal issue, prescriptive interventions run the risk of being experienced by the client as an imposition, and therefore may be resisted or rejected. This is most likely to occur when the consultant bypasses the step of ensuring the client's involvement and commitment.

INDIVIDUAL (B-4-1)

Behavioral Reinforcement to Motivate Reaching Goals

An intervention reported by Warren[1] demonstrates success in improving productivity in one unit of a department store owned by Dayton-Hudson Corporation. The purpose was to increase productivity by 20 percent as measured by amount per sale. A men's accessories department, staffed by a number of full- and part-time salespeople and supervised by a department manager, constituted the test site. Selection of this unit as the recipient of an intervention was based on four criteria: (1) the department was fairly autonomous; (2) it was small enough for the program to be easily managed; (3) performance data were relatively easy to track, and (4) the store's general manager supported the choice.

The department manager was briefed on the approach and committed himself to playing a major role in the design and implementation of the feedback, reinforcement, and training elements of the program.

A prescriptive intervention that focused on individual goal achievement was utilized. "In this case, implementation was managed by the personnel executive of the operating company using corporate resources in a consulting capacity. . . . The model chosen, 'Performance Centered Management,' is a five-step application."[2]

Performance Centered Management consists of five conditions:

1. Expectations placed on the performer are known to the performer. They are achievable. . . .
2. Feedback processes . . . compare current performance to expected performance. . . .
3. Reinforcement processes . . . provide positive consequences to the performer. . . .
4. The work environment is supportive of productivity improvement. . . .
5. Training provides performers with the knowledge or skills required to meet standards or objectives.

"After deciding to use amount per sale as the measure of productivity, a baseline and a standard had to be established. An average of current performance [within the department] was arbitrarily established as the baseline. . . . In the same manner, a standard of $23 per sale was established as the objective. . . ."[3]

Feedback was provided in two ways: sales slips for each work period were averaged. Results were then given to the performers in graphic form which permitted tracking current performance for each work period against both baseline and standard. Also, each time a salesperson wrote a sale above the baseline he or she would circle the total. This provided performer-controlled immediate feedback and a quick means for tracking the frequency of above-baseline performances. These feedback mechanisms were chosen because data were available in the work unit and could be obtained and tracked without dependence on administrative systems outside the control of the performers.

Praise by the department manager was given both regularly and randomly; regular praise when average daily sales improved over the prior day. Praise on a random schedule was given to individuals who showed approximation of standard. Recognition was on a regular basis when performance was reviewed with the performers. Performers making progress toward standard were singled out for verbal comment.

Thus the intervention consisted primarily of setting a goal for each sale and reinforcing achievement of it through praise by the department manager. Since selling skills were already present, little training was utilized.

The program was considered to be a successful one. Dollar amount per sale showed an immediate increase. Standard was reached within five weeks and maintained as long as it was tracked.

Three factors were the primary contributors to the increase in productivity reported here. First, expectations were clarified, negotiated, and communicated. They formed the basis for setting specific, time-framed, measurable objectives. Second, feedback was consistently and systematically provided on a timely basis. Finally, improved performance was appropriately rewarded.

Performance Appraisal

Performance appraisal and performance feedback are among the more difficult tasks of management. Organizations rarely provide sufficient support or emphasis to gain maximum benefits from performance appraisal systems.

Tagliaferri[4] reports a major transportation industry company's efforts to appraise employee performance more effectively.

The consultant investigated alternative methods for designing a system which would accomplish the following objectives.

1. Improve communication between the supervisor and the employee.
2. Ensure that employees clearly understand their job responsibilities.
3. Ensure that employees know what their performance standards are and how their supervisors feel they are performing.
4. Obtain employee commitment for personal performance improvement.
5. Develop the full potential of the employee.

A system was recommended that combined elements of MbO and "Work Behavior Methods." The latter involves breaking a job down into its component parts and then using task analysis to identify the key behaviors essential to job success.

This combination was selected with one major added feature. Not only does the supervisor appraise the employee but the employee also appraises him- or herself. Results of the two ratings are then overlaid and compared. Jointly, the employee and supervisor complete the MbO and other developmental portions.

Results of pre-post measurements show marked improvement in supervisory performance in terms of clarification of goals and objectives, encouragement of upward communication, feedback and positive reinforcement, goal pressure, approachability, team building, recognition of employees, job enrichment and enlargement, and rewards for task performance. Employees reported significant satisfaction with the system, indicating that the objectives in terms of communication, understanding of responsibilities, awareness of performance standards and expectations, and commitment to development were met. The importance of performance appraisal and feedback are readily apparent from these positive conclusions.

This intervention centers on goals and objectives. In a prescriptive way, it tells individuals how to conduct a review of performance as an approach to goal setting. This prescription was apparently successful because it enabled supervisors to communicate with employees. At the same time, employees were provided an opportunity to participate actively and to provide input.

School Truancy

In *contracting,* a cycle-breaking mechanism, the consultant specifies a goal of desired behavior and sets up a series of rewards the client will receive for engaging in this behavior. Since the reward can be had only after the desired behavior has been completed, the approach is termed contingency contracting: if A, the desired behavior, occurs, then B, the specified reward, will follow.

Used to help control a truancy problem, contingency contracting had the following results.

> Bill C., a 16-year-old high school junior, had a relatively clear school record. His cumulative folder indicated no behavior problems. His test scores and grades showed that he was above average academically. Things had started to change, however, during the middle of his sophomore year, when his parents separated and Bill remained with his mother and older sister.
>
> Bill started missing school shortly after his parents' separation. His counselor talked to him several times and warned him of the consequences of his behavior. Further, Bill's mother was informed on several occasions that Bill was not attending school, but she was reluctant to accept this fact and took no action to remedy the problem.
>
> Bill became very adept at concealing his truancy. He frequently attended his homeroom period, during which attendance was taken, but missed the rest of the school day. When he did miss a full day, he often wrote his own excuse. He would leave his house at the precise time he would leave were he actually going to school, and he would arrive home at the time he should had he gone to school. As a result, his mother believed he was in attendance and did not wish to accept the counselor's telling her otherwise.

The problem went unchecked until the middle of Bill's junior year. At this time the counselor arranged a conference with Bill and his mother, and the following contingency contract was drawn up:

Problem. Excessive period and full-day truancy.

Background. Bill has consistently missed part or all of his school day for the past year-and-one-quarter. He has been counseled regarding his truancy, his mother has been contacted, and he has been somewhat restricted at home. His mother seemed to be unable to help him because of her working hours.

Behavioral Implementation. (1) Bill will attend all classes he is scheduled for every day. (2) Bill will have his counselor initial his attendance card at the end of each school day. (3) Bill will exchange the completed attendance card with his mother in accordance with the reward schedule stated below. (4) Bill will chart the cumulative frequency of period attendance on a graph in the counselor's office at the end of each school day. (5) Bill will attend a group rap session once each week.

Reward Schedule. Successful completion of the above implementation will be rewarded in the following manner:

1. Bill will exchange the signed attendance card with his mother and will receive ten cents (10¢) for each class attended. This money will be saved for a trip to Disneyland on December 31st. (Note: Bill can hold the money himself or have his mother hold it for him.)

2. Bill will be allowed to go to Disneyland on December 31st for the New Year's Eve party.

When school resumes in January, a conference will be held to determine the need for a new contract.

SIGNATURE AND AGREEMENT STATEMENTS:

I agree to follow the provisions of the contract and to dispense the rewards only if the provisions of the contract are met.

Mrs. C.

I agree to follow the provisions of this contract.

Bill C.

I agree to monitor this contract and to make a verbal progress report to Bill and his mother at the end of each week.

Counselor

Bill did not miss one class for three full weeks, and Mrs. C. followed through on her part of the contract. At the end of the three-week period a conference was held, and Bill decided that he thought he could handle full-time attendance. It was mutually decided by Bill and the counselor that for a three-week period the attendance card previously filled out daily need now be filled out only on Friday to cover the entire school week. Bill felt that his presenting the completed card to his mother was sufficient reward. After three weeks Bill was maintaining full attendance, so his behavior modification program was discontinued.[5]

It should be noted that this approach involves no effort to deal with underlying causes. The assumption is that attitudes follow rather than precede behavior. Change the behavior, in other words, and the attitude change will follow.

Precision teaching is an approach that ensures the client is treated not as a typical or average student, but as an individual with highly specific learning needs. Once these have been identified, interventions to fulfill such individualized needs can be introduced. The following consultant-managed procedures are involved.

1. *Pinpointing the behavior* (both in terms of response class and in terms of response class dimension) to be modified in the classroom.
2. *Recording the behavior* to determine its characteristics in the classroom along dimensions relevant to the curriculum.
3. *Changing something in the classroom* to change the behavior in the direction sought and specified when the behavior was pinpointed. This may include changes in teaching method, curriculum materials, motivational procedures, the classroom environment, or anything else that the teacher believes is useful.
4. *Trying again* when the classroom changes in the first plan do not produce the behavior changes sought.[6]

An example of precision teaching in practice is provided by Johnson.

Jerry, a 14-year-old cerebral palsied child, is enrolled in a special education class. Jerry's oral reading performance is well below that expected for his age group, and he also shows poor performance in reading comprehension. In this pinpointed behavior, his recorded rate of making incorrect responses either equaled or exceeded his recorded rate of making correct responses, depending on the reading level of the test. . . . To change something in the classroom, the teacher decided to introduce a contingency contract in which she agreed to pay Jerry a nickel for every question he answered correctly—a procedure that brought quick results. . . . Following this change in classroom procedure, his rate of correctly answering the question exceeded his rate of incorrectly answering questions, suggestion that the procedure worked. This observation eliminated the last step in precision teaching, namely, trying again.[7]

The advantage of such interventions is their specificity. Through Johnson's methodology a client's difficulties in learning are identified and thus become approachable, rather than remaining so vague that intervention is not deemed feasible.

GROUP (B-4-2)

Prescriptive consultants must often deal with personnel problems that originate at the top of an organization and which crucially affect its capacity for continuity and goal achievement. An example of a breakthrough in a frozen top management group is provided below.

Telling the truth can prove hazardous. Cole tells the story of one president that retained Cole & Associates to do an organization study. Cole noticed that all of that company's top executives had reached their sixties. No younger men had been trained to replace them. Cole walked into the president's office carrying a set of actuarial tables detailing the mortality rates of men in their sixties. He compared the company to a college with all the members of its football team ready to graduate in the spring. Cole suggested that the company make a concentrated effort to hire and promote younger executives. "The president of that company has not talked to me since that day," says Cole. "We hurt his feelings. He followed our advice, but he didn't like it, and I don't blame him for not liking it." Cole paused. "Still, you've got to tell the truth."[8]

The president's acceptance of the conclusion but rejection of the consultant who offered it seems related to the person-centered resentment so often provoked by prescriptive consultants, even when their prescriptions solve the real problems. By implication, the career risks to an organization member undertaking a comparable role in this situation[9] are apparent in this president's adverse reaction to his "outsider" consultant.

INTERGROUP (B-4-3)

An intergroup problem exists when two or more groups in an organization are split on the best route to take. In such cases, a prescriptive consultant may be called on to give an outsider's appraisal of the appropriate goals/objectives to pursue.

In the early sixties a major oil company on the West Coast considered adding food-vending machines in their service stations. The top executives divided down the middle on what soon became a major controversy within the organization. "It was like trying to watch a badminton game from under a net," one executive caught in the middle said. "We decided to call in an outsider. He could be impartial, and perhaps most important, he wouldn't have to live with the losers after it was all over." The outsider called in was the management consulting firm Booz, Allen & Hamilton. In keeping with the high status of the corporation (which ranked in the top twenty-five of *Fortune*'s annual list of the 500 largest U.S. industrial corporations), a Booz, Allen vice-president (who ranked high in seniority with the firm) made the initial contacts and interviewed the key executives. Then he left, leaving the assignment in the hands of an "associate," which on Booz, Allen's three-step pyramid is halfway between the bottom and the top. The associate supervised the work of several "consultants" (the title given to the firm's lowest echelon, their so-called bright young men), who interviewed executives of lesser status and began visiting service stations. They also examined what data they could find related to service station operation in the corporate headquarters.

With the research completed the vice-president returned to present the final report. He commented that most service stations have little surplus parking space. "Food will merely encourage customers to remain in the stations longer," he said. "The result will be congestion. In addition, local restaurant owners, who buy gasoline too, may be offended." The Booz, Allen vice-president recommended a trial in several selected stations. This would permit the oil corporation executives to determine how successful food vending would be before fully committing themselves. It was a polite way of saying, "Don't touch food vending with a ten-foot pole."

The chief executive decided to accept the report. Whether food vending in service stations could have proved profitable may never be fully proved, but the members of the organization—including those who had favored the new lost cause—seemed satisfied with the thoroughness and objectivity of the report. It also showed that good consulting is often more art than science.[10]

In this case the recommendation seemed sufficient to close the breach between the two groups over this goals/objectives issue. Equally or even more often, however, the recommendation is supported by the side of the controversy that "wins" and is blocked by those whose position it defeats.

When objectives of an organizational subcomponent shift away from their initial charter, a prescriptive intervention has been utilized to return the group to its original formulation. Such an intervention is described by Lucas, Roberge, and Thomson[11] concerning a Health Team of the Ottawa Secretariat of the Canadian University Service Overseas (CUSO).

The breakup of colonialism, with its various paternalistic solutions to knowledge transfer among nations, showed how little had been accomplished in this vein and how much remained to be accomplished after World War II. Particularly since the war, knowledge transfer on an international basis has become an increasingly pressing problem.

One approach spawned by the American government is the Peace Corps. Its counterpart in Canada is the Canadian University Service Overseas which, however, is independent of government at this time. CUSO volunteers serve in fifty-two countries in roles related to education, health, and technical and community development.

The goals and objectives in the Health Team of the Human Resources Division of the Ottawa Secretariat of CUSO as they are executed in the field were the basis for this intervention. The shift was intended to bring field work into correspondence with the CUSO Charter; in effect, to make it a prevention-oriented rather than treatment-centered approach.

As an initial intervention intended to bring about change in CUSO health programming, the Health Team, as internal consultants, made a half-day presentation at the annual Inter-Regional Meeting where representatives from each of five major world regions were in attendance. An awareness of health planning issues was created and interest in working more closely with the team was expressed. Health Team members offered to work on site in any overseas program for up to four months helping field staff design and implement their health programs.

Team members initiated direct dialogue with almost all field staff officers and conducted a preliminary field visit. As a result, communication and understanding of different points of view of the team and the overseas regional staff became clear. Most regional staffs did not see much value in having an "outsider" work in their programs. The team at times felt frustration at being seen as more of a nuisance than a help by the overseas representative.

A year after their initial effort, at the 1976 Inter-Regional Meeting, the Health Team presented a proposal designed to foster cooperative efforts to improve health programming. Their recommendation was that a cooperative effort be made to stimulate further development of the Health Programme and that a demonstration project be established in any recommended country with a Health Team member joining the regional staff.

One of the new field staff participated in the pilot project. Activities included involving CUSO workers and host nationals in an evaluation of the country's health needs, placing those needs in the context of CUSO's activities to date, and identifying potential areas for more relevant programming.

The intervention resulted in clearer guidelines for all regions and their health programs. Support staff often find themselves in situations similar to the one reported here. Even though representing a valuable resource, line staff may be threatened by having some support person "interfering" with their operations. Support staff may become frustrated and anxious through under-utilization and attempt to impose changes on line activities. Such a response increases resistance which increases frustration, and a vicious circle results.

This was a prescriptive intervention because the Health Team of the Ottawa Secretariat decided that a change to bring closer alignment of field activities with the CUSO Charter was required. It initiated a series of interventions toward this result, but encountered headquarters/field-related resistance in the process.

The shift to a demonstration project basis may be better understood as a catalytic intervention with the facts yielded by a demonstration having a self-convincing character. However, neither of these interventions seems to have dealt directly with the focal issue of power and authority; by whom and when they are to be exercised, and for what purpose.

ORGANIZATION (B-4-4)

Caplan's[12] description of prescriptive consultation in a government agency provides a clear indication of how a consultant, by imposing his or her own will on a resistant client, may accurately diagnose the problem.

> . . . a consultant was called in by the head of a governmental department to advise on the reorganization of a certain division. On his arrival, after a long airplane flight, he had a short conference with his consultee, who told him that all the technical arrangements for his seven-day stay would be handled by the division chief, who was not available that afternoon but who would meet with him the following day.

The consultation was starting out in the "classical" prescriptive manner; the consultant first met with the head of the government department, the man who had engaged his services. What the consultant had not anticipated, however, was the resistance he was about to encounter from subordinates who were out of sympathy with the entire project. They had engineered a schedule of contacts calculated to ensure that his consultation would never probe the real issues.

> . . . the next morning the consultant was surprised when, instead of the division chief, the latter's secretary came around to his hotel to welcome him. She brought a schedule of his appointments over the next five days that the division chief had prepared for him with exemplary efficiency. This program scheduled him in two-hourly blocks to meet with most of the unit heads of the entire department; but the list included very few of the line workers or even the supervisory staff of the division. The secretary hoped that the schedule would meet his approval and had a car outside to convey him to the head office of the department to begin his program. The consultant asked whether he could first meet with the division chief and discuss the schedule, because at first sight it did not seem to be the best way of utilizing his time. The secretary replied that her chief was busy on some urgent business that morning and would not be available till later that day for such a discussion.

Here is how the consultant viewed the situation he faced.

> . . . this situation presented the consultant with a dilemma. Apparently, the division chief was defensive about his visit and was possibly avoiding him. There was nothing obviously wrong with the schedule except that it filled his time completely and left him little room to maneuver, as well as leading him mainly into the general field of forces in the department rather than into the internal affairs of the division that he had been called in to investigate. And yet it would obviously be rather rude to question the arrangements that had been so efficiently made on his behalf and that were being so obligingly pressed upon him by the charming girl who had been sent to guide him. To accept the arrangements graciously would calm the fears of the division chief, and perhaps there would be time later that day to discuss the program and negotiate its modification. On the other hand, it might be that the absent division chief would persist in being otherwise engaged—his own name did not appear on the interviewing schedule until the fourth day! By then it might be too late to collect enough information about the division to make a valid assessment of its problems. Perhaps the price of being nonthreatening was to accept a role of impotence.

Because the objective of the consultation seemingly was being thwarted, the consultant decided to take the bull by the horns. He shifted to a forceful confrontation mode.

> . . . the consultant asked the secretary where her chief was at the moment. With some reluctance, she divulged that he was chairing a meeting of the unit chief of his division at one of their divisional office buildings on the outskirts of the city, several miles away from the headquarters of the

department where the consultant's scheduled interviewees were awaiting him. The consultant then told her that he was sorry that he could not accept the schedule of interviews and asked her to drive him to the divisional office and then to inform his interviewees at headquarters that he would see them at a later date. He dealt in a friendly but firm manner with her protests, and she took him to the divisional office.

. . . once there, he found out where the meeting was being held and, without more ado, marched into the room. To the consternation of the division chief, he interrupted the meeting; introduced himself to the assembled group; told them about his mission and about his mandate from the head of the department; and said that their meeting provided him with an unexpected and marvelous opportunity to meet immediately with the principal people whose views on the problems confronting the division he was eager to obtain. He then said that if the division chief had no objection, he would like to pre-empt the meeting to discuss these matters, since he had traveled several thousand miles to get there and had very little time available to reach the core of the situation. The division chief was obviously furious but could do nothing but meekly go along with this *fait accompli;* and there followed two hours of explosive and illuminating discussion, which laid bare the fundamental problems of the division that underlay the request of the department head for consultation help.

This dramatic action on the part of the consultant initiated a process of rapid fact finding. He was able to overcome the initial authoritarian impression he had made on most of the staff when they became familiar with his style of conducting individual and group interviews. The division chief, however, not unnaturally, never completely warmed up to him, although by the end of the visit even he began to respect the competence and sincerity of the consultant and to realize that his worst fears about him were ill founded.

Such highhanded and defense-attacking coercive behavior should be an infrequent occurrence in this type of consultation, but a consultant should feel free to make use of it whenever the situation demands. More frequent is the need to influence the staff of an institution to realize that although the latter may perhaps be correctly or incorrectly perceived as authoritarian and coercive, the consultant normally holds his power in reserve and conducts his business on the basis of a free interchange with staff, to whose needs he is sensitive and upon whose personal and professional rights he takes pains not to infringe, within the relatively wide range of latitude that his role usually affords him. Only if there is an obvious attempt to obstruct him or to manipulate him too far off course must he invoke his power.[13]

Given that the consultant possibly did not identify and address the evident cooperation problem between the division chief and the department head, the other interesting aspect of his intervention relates to his zeal in getting these client members back on the track toward the mission's investigative goal. In effect, having been commissioned by the department head to pursue a specific investigation, this consultant, in the final analysis, produced his delegated baton of authority and prescriptively took over the division chief's meeting so as to make the most of his consultation time.

An effort to introduce organization change on a strictly cognitive, intellectual, or philosophical basis without effort to help people acquire the process or behavioral skills essential for translating philosophy into action is reported by Clark.[14] The Tavistock Institute entered into such a change project with a company, utilizing a prescriptive mode of intervention introduced through discussion and give-and-take. The objective of the intervention was to write a document jointly with the management to reflect the management philosophy that was to be implemented by the organization. The prescriptive aspect is seen in the statement of philosophy that resulted from this collaboration. It is almost a behavioral science manifesto.

This intervention failed; a later evaluation by Clark[15] presumes the failure to have been due to an insufficient process for earning top down support for the document. This explanation is not too likely. Greater insight into the failure is in recognizing that by ignoring the translation of thought into action, this intervention violated one of the basic precepts of change: the necessity for feedback and critique for internalizing and for learning what the concepts mean in practice. Acquiring skills essential for managing an operation according to new and different customs and approaches requires competencies that cannot be presumed to exist without a specific instructional program designed to bring them into use.

LARGER SOCIAL SYSTEM (B-4-5)

No published examples of larger social system prescriptive interventions are available. If any have been implemented, it is understandable that few clients of this magnitude would publicize the fact that they had required assistance in setting basic goals. In less fundamental yet more technical areas, nonetheless, there are a number of examples of prescriptive interventions in larger social systems. Consultants may be brought in, for example, to evaluate telephone rates or to offer solutions to problems of public utilities, transportation networks, hospital services, and so on. In most of these cases the consultant's intervention is premised on expert knowledge and the client has opted for outside consultant services (versus developing autonomous competence) as an economical way of enlisting short- or medium-term technical advice, much of which relates to goals/objectives. Alternatively, consultants are drawn in, with the expectation that their conclusion will be reinforced and justify the course of action already preferred. These kinds of consultation, while in the prescriptive mode, are more akin to contracting for the delivery of a service and are not further dealt with here.

Summary

Goals and objectives introduced via behavior modification strategies seem to have been more successful than other ways of utilizing prescription to achieve desired outcomes. At a deeper level, however, prescriptive interventions are most appropriate when a problem exists for which a solution is needed, but where the client is immobilized, without direction, and unable to cope.

Notes

1. M. W. Warren, "Using Behavioral Technology to Improve Sales Performance," *Training and Development Journal* (July 1978): 54–56.
2. Ibid., p. 54.
3. Ibid., p. 56.
4. L. E. Tagliafferi, "How Performance Appraisal Can Improve the Appraiser's Performance," *Training and Development Journal* (March 1978): 37–39.
5. B. David Brooks, "Contingency Contracts with Truants," *American Personnel and Guidance Journal* 52, no. 5 (1974): 318–19. Copyright 1974 American Personnel and Guidance Association. Reprinted with permission.
6. N. J. A. Johnson, "Precision Teaching: A Key to the Future," in R. Karen, *An Introduction to Behavior Theory and Its Applications* (New York: Harper & Row, 1974), p. 418. Reprinted by permission.
7. Ibid., pp. 418–19.
8. H. Higdon, *The Business Healers* (New York: Random House, 1969), p. 76. Reprinted by permission.
9. I. Janis, *Victims of Groupthink: A Psychological Study of Foreign-Policy Decisions and Fiascoes* (Boston: Houghton Mifflin, 1972), pp. 148, 216.
10. Higdon, *The Business Healers,* pp. 41–42.
11. J. Lucas, J. Roberge and M. Thomson, "CUSO: Collaboration for International Development," *The Journal of Applied Behavioral Science* 13, no. 3 (1977): 400–410.
12. G. Caplan, *The Theory and Practice of Mental Health Consultation* (New York: Basic Books, 1970). Copyright © 1970 by Basic Books, Inc., Publishers, New York. Reprinted by permission of Basic Books and Tavistock Publications Ltd., London.
13. Ibid., pp. 229–30.
14. A. W. Clark, "Sanction: A Critical Element in Action Research," *Journal of Applied Behavioral Science* 8, no. 6 (1972): 713–31.
15. A. W. Clark, "Update on 'Sanction: A Critical Element in Action Research,'" in B. Lubin, L. D. Goodstein and A. W. Lubin, eds., *Organizational Change Sourcebook II: Cases in Conflict Management* (San Diego: University Associates, 1979), pp. 178–79.

13

PRESCRIPTIVE INTERVENTIONS

Summary and Implications

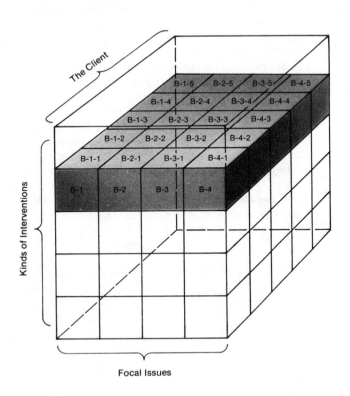

Prescription is an intervention strategy in which the consultant explicitly tells the client what to do to solve the problem at hand. Collaboration between consultant and client is based on the assumptions inherent in the authority-obedience model: the consultant exercises authority and the client is expected to comply with the recommendations given. Some prescriptive approaches include built-in arrangements to eliminate or at least reduce the likelihood of client noncompliance. One such arrangement is a strict adherence to confidentiality, more stringent than simply rendering anonymity as in a catalytic approach.

Prescriptive approaches appear to be most commonly employed in connection with behavior problems involving self-doubt and lost confidence. They are also used to resolve situations that are not presently being addressed by the client (or cannot be, given the technical and other resources available to the client). Other applications include crisis situations, and instances when the client is at "wit's end" and has thrown up his or her hands in despair.

Jacques has identified certain weaknesses more or less inherent in the prescriptive approach.

> The very nature of the therapeutic role, however, often makes real collaboration difficult. The situation is often encountered where the social scientist is called in and given a complete mandate to "set things right." Too frequently, such a mandate may represent an unconscious defeatist attitude on the part of the group concerned, with an underlying and understandable desire to evade, if possible, the responsibility for facing up to a complex and unpleasant situation. Because the solution of the problem may seem relatively simple there is a great temptation for the social scientist to jump in and take the responsibility "just for a short time." Having taken full responsibility on his shoulders, however, he will to a greater or lesser degree have precluded the possibility of the group itself developing new roles which would allow them to cope with their own problems by themselves. Thus, although he may clear up the problem, any thanks he receives may be given rather grudgingly, for he will presumably have exposed the inadequacies of the persons concerned without helping them towards new insights and self-reliance. Under these conditions further work is unlikely, and the project may suddenly come to a halt. On the other hand, he may fail with the task, in which case he will likely be left with the blame on his own shoulders for all the previous mistakes and results of mismanagement, and ill effects of which may be displaced and projected in his direction.[1]

For an illustration of the pertinence of Jacques' statement the reader may refer to the example in Chapter 12 of a corporate president's "accepting the solution but rejecting the consultant." Such reactions to prescriptive consultation have led many consultants to seek a basis of collaboration with their clients. However, the most common alternative—the catalytic approach—may "solve" the rejection problem but create others.

An analysis and summation of some of the implications of the prescriptive approach with individual clients in an industrial context is provided by Steele in the following. His conclusions are probably applicable to clinical and other situations as well.

> I think the role of "expert" is a quite seductive one for the consultant—all the more so in behavioral science since the variables and their relationships are often quite fuzzy and complex. It can be quite personally gratifying to have others see me as someone who really "knows" what is going on or what should be done in a given situation. Besides personal gratification on the part of the consultant, another factor pushes him toward the stance of expert: The client's wish to see himself safely in the hands of an expert who is wise and able so that anxiety over present or future difficulties can be reduced.

Steele has here identified the core dynamics underlying the use of the authority-obedience model in prescriptive consulting. He continues:

> Both the consultant's and the client's needs, then, may propel the consultant toward exclusive occupancy of the role of expert in their relationship. This may have some benefits such as making it more likely that the consultant will be listened to, but it may also have some costs. One that is usually mentioned is the potential price paid in terms of increased dependency of the client on the consultant—a dependency that may keep the client from developing his own strengths and competencies for diagnosis and problem solving. A second cost—one that is less often considered—is that a focus on the consultant as the exclusive expert may often lead to inadequate decisions. The client often has great wisdom (intuitive if not systematic) about many aspects of his own situation, and an overweighting of the consultant's knowledge-value may indeed cause poorer choices to be made than if there were a more balanced view of that which each can contribute to the situation.[2]

Granted these limitations, there appear to be many kinds of client situations that are helped significantly by prescriptive consultation, especially those situations in which the client is unable to act in his or her own behalf. In other instances, structure and reward are introduced into a situation in order to induce purposeful behavior—even if the envisaged goal for the moment goes no further than the next nickel. The consultant-envisaged goal, of course, is individual improvement, an objective that in time might be internalized by the client.

The success of a prescriptive intervention is dependent not only on the degree to which the client is helped to solve the immediate problem, but also on the client's ability to incorporate and maintain the pertinent improvements introduced during the period of consultation. Failure to maintain improvements illustrates the disadvantages associated with "behavioral doctoring"—i.e., clients do not necessarily become more effective in their own right simply by having answers handed to them. They are not learning how to solve problems; they are only acting under problem-solving instructions. They may become even less sure of themselves than before. A dependency situation is created when a client surrenders his or her self-will and accepts that of a consultant; he or she may turn to the consultant whenever stumped or whenever there is disagreement between the client and colleagues as to the soundness of any given course of action. The "cure" could, over the long term, be more damaging than the ailment it was intended to correct.

Notes

1. E. Jacques, "Social Therapy: Technocracy or Collaboration?" in W. G. Bennis, K. D. Benne and R. Chin, eds., *The Planning of Change* (New York: Holt, Rinehart and Winston, 1961), pp. 163–64. Copyright © 1947 by *The Journal of Social Issues*. Reprinted by permission.
2. F. I. Steele, "Consultants and Detectives," reproduced by special permission from *Journal of Applied Behavioral Science* 5, no. 2 (1969): 193–94.

Part III

CONFRONTATIONAL INTERVENTIONS

14

CONFRONTATIONAL INTERVENTIONS

Confrontational Interventions: An Introduction

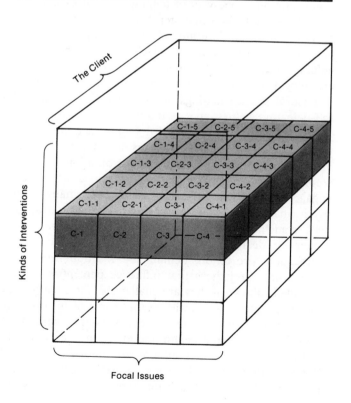

Values underlie how people think and feel and what they regard as important and what as trivial. Sometimes guidance from a particular set of values is sound—things go smoothly, results are good. Sometimes values cause problems—they are inappropriate, invalid, or unjustified under the circumstances. Often people who must work in concert hold different values; failure to achieve agreement in such situations results in antagonisms, disorder, or outright chaos.

Many deeply held values are related to *authority/power* dynamics: "Rank has its privileges," "It's not what you know, but who you know that gets you ahead," "The boss is always right," are but a few examples. *Morale/cohesion* focal issues between individuals and among groups, organizations, and larger social systems often relate to unreconciled differences in basic values. For example, loyalty to a national ideal or to an historical image may form the basis of an older generation's morale but have no relevance for a younger generation. With regard to *norms/standards,* individual values fuse into group or organization-wide enforced norms—whether "official" or not—that define "right" and "wrong." Those who subscribe to them are in good standing; those who do not are ostracized.

To successfully break out of self-defeating cycles, the individual must first explicitly identify and understand the values he or she currently embraces. Confrontation is one way of helping a client explore the consequences of value-related behaviors as a first step toward implementing change. A consultant who operates in a confrontational mode pinpoints for the client inappropriate, invalid, or unjustified values which the client has historically denied or rejected holding. The confrontational consultant seeks to create awareness of a discrepancy between generally accepted values—either validated in the light of behavioral science findings or in terms of a sound philosophy of life—and the self-defeating values and assumptions actually operating within the situation.

Many values that undergird human activities are deeply embedded, often constituting second-nature truisms not subject to introspection. Nevertheless, value scrutiny is the goal of a confrontational intervention. Initially it could seem a poor choice of intervention, since when "confronted," people often engage in defensive practices. Defense mechanisms of the kind described in psychoanalytic literature are best understood as stratagems for protecting deeply held, sometimes unconscious values, often those related to maintaining self-esteem or decreasing feelings of weakness and inadequacy. Rationalization, justification, projection, denial, and reaction formation are examples of such mechanisms. Prejudices that influence perceptions have the same character as embedded values—if they are challenged, the client ordinarily adopts a defensive posture, unable to acknowledge that some of his or her deeply held beliefs may be unjustified. By the same token, of course, certain personal values are fully consistent with mental health and effective interpersonal functioning.

Confrontational interventions are among the most effective in reducing the efficacy of defense mechanisms. A well-designed confrontation literally forces the client to face a contradiction between his or her stated values and those—as yet unrecognized by the client but evident to the consultant—on which his or her behavior *actually* is founded. Once the contradiction becomes apparent, the client is better prepared to explore the consequences of failing to manifest his or her professed values. Usually such consequences are less desirable than the consequences of behaving in terms of values already preferred at the cognitive level, and so the client may decide to shift his or her behavior accordingly. The following summary of confrontational intervention ground rules is useful in understanding what the confrontational consultant seeks to do as he or she intervenes with individuals, groups, and so on.

A confrontational consultant's strategy takes into account the likelihood that the client will rationalize and justify his or her present behavior as consonant with professed values, thereby explaining away difficulties rather than facing them squarely. The underlying assumption is that the client can be helped to see his or her actual values in a more objective manner if challenged to explain the "whys" of present behavior.

The consultant avoids, however, telling the client in a prescriptive way what he or she has inferred these underlying values to be. Rather, the consultant asks questions that encourage the client to recognize them independently, and then points out inconsistencies the client may have missed. For example, "You said you expect candor from your subordinates, but how can you expect that when you are not even being open and honest with me?" If the client responds defensively rather than giving thought to the question, the consultant picks this up as further evidence of reality-avoiding attitudes that need attention. The impact of a confrontation is increased when the behavior or attitude it identifies is occurring at the moment, rather than when it is an historical reconstruction of past events. The client is unlikely to be able to reconstruct the feelings accurately that propelled him or her into some previous action or attitude. Thus, when dealing with the past, it becomes much more difficult for the client to sense the contradiction that the confrontation seeks to identify and resolve.

A confrontational consultant might proceed in the following manner. He or she:

1. Takes nothing for granted as the client describes the situation. In answering questions, the client either does or does not show understanding of the situation. Until understanding is evidenced, the consultant keeps asking questions that direct the client toward awareness and honesty.

2. Presents facts, counterarguments, and logic to help a client test his or her objectivity.

3. Challenges the client's thinking regarding different courses of action, once the client understands his or her actual values and assumptions.

4. Probes for reasons, motives, and causes that will give the client a clear and possibly different perspective on the present situation.

5. Gives the client his or her own thinking in such a way that the client doesn't feel personally attacked or demeaned.

A confrontational consultant deals with individuals in a somewhat different way than he or she deals with larger social units, such as teams or organizations. In working with an individual, the consultant necessarily has less input on which to base judgments and therefore is often slower to pinpoint the real issues. Also, when working with teams or larger units, a consultant may find collusion—i.e., several members unwittingly working together to deny the possibility that they might be operating on the basis of unjustifiable values. As these client members reinforce one another, they create additional difficulties. At the same time, they provide the consultant with richer data to use in formulating a confrontation strategy.

The "richer" the data, however, the more complex the situation—and therefore the more difficult to unravel. In addition to reinforcing one another's shared but inappropriate values, group members are likely to be motivated by unique values, more privately held. Thus it becomes more difficult for the consultant to frame confrontational interventions that are not subject to rejection by some members as being "unfair criticism" or as "your misperception of what's really going on in our situation." Eventually, however, the group's value pattern may become clear to the consultant, and from that point on he or she is prepared to intervene with a jolt.

15

CONFRONTATIONAL INTERVENTIONS

Power/ Authority

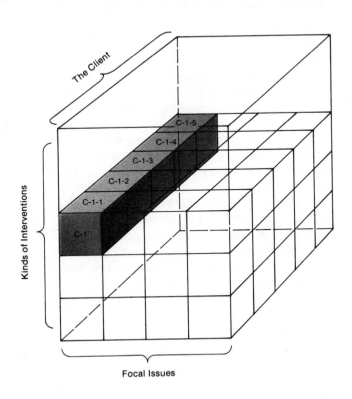

Confrontations that deal with behavior or attitudes in the power/authority area are themselves based upon the power/authority relationship between the consultant and the client. If the consultant can be regarded by the client as junior to him or her in age or experience, or comes through as weaker—say, by signs of reluctance to stand by the confrontations and "force" the client to give them self-analytical consideration—then the client may reject, more or less out of hand, what the consultant has to say. While dynamics such as these are likely to weaken any intervention regardless of the focal issue, confrontation in the power/authority area is most susceptible to failure.

INDIVIDUAL (C-1-1)

Confrontations related to power/authority issues can aid an individual client to understand the assumptions presently underlying his or her own conduct. As mentioned before, these assumptions often arise from deeply embedded personal values and the client may strongly resist facing and evaluating them.

Authority-Obedience as Boss's Managerial Style

Argyris[1] describes a confrontational intervention with the chief executive of a large company. The chief executive was interested in getting his top forty executives, who were stationed throughout the world, involved in a Management-by-Objectives (MbO) program and wanted the consultant to attend a one-day meeting to help him sell them on the idea. His underlying value was that the boss-subordinate relationship is one of authority and obedience. However, he saw the impending situation as one in which he needed to bolster his authority to push the program through and was anxious to enlist the consultant's independent "authority" in support. The consultant responded by indicating that success for any such program results from personal commitment rather than the knuckled-under compliance of those who must carry it forward. The necessary commitment could hardly be generated during a one-day meeting. He pointed out, too, that MbO has its own value system and that unless the operating values present in the broader organizaional context are congruent with and supportive of the MbO value system, the strain of contradiction will cause the effort to crumble. He also remarked that one aspect of an MbO program is performance appraisal, and that in his experience many performance review sessions are inconsistent with and sometimes antagonistic to the objective of helping executive development.

These points having been made, the conversation continued.

> *Client:* I know there are these problems and that is why we need you to be
> there. I am sure that you can sell the executives on the importance of
> interpersonal relationships and dealing with people.

The client has not yet sensed that the consultant's reaction is based on a difference in value orientation.

Consultant: Even if I were effective in selling such programs to top management, little internal commitment would be generated. The initial enthusiasm soon would become a vivid memory while behavioral change, or even a modest increase in sensitivity, on the part of the executives would not emerge. Therefore I appreciate the invitation, but I best not accept, for your sake and for mine.

That the consultant had not yet been successful in getting the client to face his power/authority values is seen in the latter's rejoinder.

Client: But this meeting is important. I think that you have much to offer us. Many of our officers have heard of you. Surely there must be something useful you can do in a day.[2]

The consultant had challenged the value orientation of the client by pointing to discrepancies between the value system espoused in the Management-by-Objectives program and the authority-obedience values inherent in this client's leadership of the organization. An extended discussion followed and some conclusions were reached. The consultant indicated that a positive basis for his participation with the top forty executives would be in helping them diagnose the potential problems they saw in the MbO program and in identifying and evaluating factors that would help or hinder their effectiveness in implementing it. He suggested he could confront them with the possibility that certain leadership styles currently being employed were adverse to, or at least not congruent with, the value system essential for an effective Management-by-Objectives program. Such a meeting did occur; it is commented on in the Group section of this chapter.

Combining research procedures with interventional practices has led Argyris to formulate a change strategy actually developed for management but pertinent to interventions in professional education. Concentrating on the uses and misuses of power, his contention is that most current hierarchical situations are premised on setting goals unilaterally. This leads to win/lose situations, which create defensiveness and the need to "be rational," which results in closed, growth-stultifying relationships. He calls this Model I behavior (some other features are involved).

Psychoanalytic conceptions of power/authority applied in the work setting have been used to equate the work group (where a male has the dominant leadership position and a female the subordinate role) with the historical version of the conventional nuclear family. This Bayes and Newton[3] version of the psychoanalytic model served as the framework for interventions in a situation where they concluded that sex role stereotypes were being violated by virtue of a woman's having been assigned as leader of a mental health unit. The intervention, extending over a period of two years, involved two primary activities:

the consultant first attended meetings with the principal work group, and second, held one-on-one meetings with the female leader.

Though the specifics of the intervention are not described, the presumption is that the sex role model served as the basis for the consultant's thinking about the situation rather than as a shared cognitive model of human relationships. Drawing attention to discrepancies and contradictions between typical reactions to a male leader and actual reactions to the current female leader defines the intervention. Such an intervention extended awareness of how exercising power as males did in the conventional nuclear family may have accounted for the difficulties this woman encountered as the leader in a work group.

This was an intervention focused on power/authority and distortions in its use produced when a woman operates under circumstances where the nurturant, supportive role identified as historically appropriate for women is replaced with the exercise of power/authority in a manner conventionally reserved for men. The analysis presents only two ways of exercising leadership—control, mastery, and domination, characteristic of a 9,1 orientation or the nurturing, caring, and supportive character of the 1,9 orientation. The possibility that the client moved from a 1,9 orientation to a 9,1 orientation is implied, but the option she might have exercised in experimenting with the 9,9 orientation is given no attention. This intervention has been criticized by other women professionals for its narrow reliance on the psychoanalytic version of the nuclear family and its failure to recognize the utility of other models.

Overcontrol by Boss

Kuriloff and Atkins' report of an in-company T Group, described later in Chapter 27, also has a confrontational aspect. Kuriloff had recently become vice-president and general manager of a manufacturing organization. Participants were involved in a team-building session, with Atkins as the consultant. Helen, the office manager, had said some things about her deteriorated work relationship with Bob, her former boss, and an acceptant intervention had induced cathartic release on her part. Soon afterwards, the consultant confronted Bob about his underlying power/authority attitudes as evidenced during participation in the ongoing discussion.

> I asked Bob why he felt so responsible for everyone—Helen, the men in the field, production, engineering. Giving my further impression, I said to Bob that it appeared to me that he had a strong fear of failure and shouldered responsibility that was not rightfully his. "Why do you try to make everything perfect?" I asked.
>
> "That's enough, laddie. I've said my piece," Bob concluded with finality. "No more. I have to leave for school in a few minutes and now I'm all upset."[4]

This value-oriented intervention had pointed out that Bob appeared to exercise too much control and shouldered excessive personal responsibility for whatever happened. The consultant made an interpretative linking to what might be one of Bob's basic values, in the comment about his seeming to have "a strong fear of failure"—the other side of an "I-highly-value-being-a-winner" orientation. Adding a confrontational point, "Why do you try to make everything perfect?" brought the issue to a head. Bob did not accept the consultant's reality-testing challenge. The consultant "backed off" (a retreat strategy), assuming that Bob was resisting hearing an accurate portrayal of his approach and its value-based rationale. The confrontational intervention had failed to penetrate existing defenses sufficiently to open two-way discussion of the pros and cons of alternative values.

Less-than-Frank Clients

Uses of survey research, primarily in a catalytic frame of reference, are described in a later chapter. If a survey topic is relatively noncontroversial, little difficulty is encountered in obtaining clients' cooperation in furnishing requested data. However, if the area being evaluated through survey-research techniques is personally significant to the client, or embarrassing to him or her, or in other ways constitutes a topic that motivates or stimulates defensiveness, then either the catalytic consultation fails or the consultant shifts the approach to confrontation. Confrontation is calculated to cut through the client's defenses in order to make it possible to gather the needed data, which in turn will be treated in the catalytic manner.

The use of confrontation by survey interviewers is demonstrated in the following.

> In instances where lack of cooperation was felt to be of [the] spoofing kind, good-humored bluff-calling tended to create a release of tension and subsequent cooperation. For example, one woman stoutly insisted she had no partners other than her present one. The interviewer put down her notebook and, with a broad grin, said "Get off it honey. I'm not that innocent!" The respondent laughed and gave a detailed history.[5]

Still other techniques were used by these interviewers to encourage participation, often with boomerang effects. Efforts to manipulate, such as through compliments, appear to be less effective in getting to the heart of the matter than is readiness of a consultant to confront the behavior or attitudes of the client and thereby relieve him or her of the defensiveness presently blocking candor and cooperation.

Authority Exercised by Parents

Power/authority is basic in parent-child relationships. One approach for strengthening family ties involves a process through which adults learn to be more effective parents by "hearing themselves talk." It is described by Gordon[6] as a component of Parent Effectiveness Training (PET). One of the many facets involved deals with the kind of "message" the parent communicates, particularly when some tension-producing situation has arisen with the child.

Of the many messages parents communicate to children, two are of particular importance. An "I-Message" is authentic and does not cause a child to feel that parents are rejecting him or her. When a mother or father communicates the feeling being experienced, the parent is sending an authentic message. For example, "I'm very tired!" is a *statement of fact*. A "You-Message" is an inaccurate expression of a parent's momentary frustrations. By contrast a "You-Message" says to the child, "You're a pest!"

"You're a pest" and other "You-Messages" are likely to be received by the child as an *evaluation* from a person with power/authority, which to the child means "I am bad." The "I-Message," on the other hand, simply conveys "Dad is tired," thereby enabling the child to gain a fuller perspective and deeper understanding of the momentary situation, and to adjust his or her behavior accordingly.

Interventions during PET sessions offer a way for parents to study what their unexamined power/authority values are, how these are conveyed to their children, and what are the consequences for the child. In the following episode, mother and daughter had agreed that the latter would return home from a movie date no later than midnight. However, the daughter came in at 1:30. Mother had missed sleep while worrying that something awful might have happened. The mother and another person enact the incident.

> *Mother:* I'm angry at you.
> *Daughter:* I know I'm late.
> *Mother:* I'm really upset at you for keeping me awake.
> *Daughter:* Why couldn't you sleep? I wish you'd go to sleep and not worry.
> *Mother:* How could I? I was mad at you and worried sick that you might have been in an accident. I'm really disappointed in you that you didn't stick to our agreement.

While most "You-Messages" are saturated with power/authority attitudes, not all "I-Messages" are devoid of power/authority value assumptions. For example, at this point the consultant interrupts to confront this mother, saying something like, "Not bad—you sent some pretty good 'I-Messages,' but only the negative ones. How did you actually feel when Linda walked in the front door? What was your first feeling?" The mother answered, "I felt terribly relieved that Linda was home safe. I wanted to hug her and tell her how glad I was to see her in one piece."

The consultant then asked this mother to repeat the incident.

> *Mother:* Oh, Linda, thank God you're home safe. I'm so glad to see you. What a relief. (Hugs the instructor) I was afraid you'd been in an accident.
> *Daughter:* Gosh, you *are* glad to see me, aren't you.[7]

The replay differed significantly from the mother's actual handling of the incident. This second set of messages was more expressive of true person-to-person feelings of intimacy, and in the power/authority sense less evaluative, judgmental, and rejecting.

Authority Exercised by Teachers

Classroom problems between teacher and student may "belong" to the student, causing no one else difficulty;[8] on the other hand, the problem may impede the teacher or interfere with classroom learning. In such cases the appropriate intervention relies on confrontation with I-Messages that show the client the consequences of his or her behavior for others, rather than You-Messages that make him or her feel wrong and guilty. In the following example the teacher is the consultant. The intervention begins with a confrontation and quickly shifts to an acceptant basis.

Teacher: Allan, you being late to class is causing me a problem. When you come in late I have to stop whatever I'm doing. It's distracting to me and I'm frustrated.

Student: Yeah. Well, I've had a lot to do lately and sometimes I just can't get here on time.

Teacher: I see. You're having some new problems of your own lately. (Active listening)

Student: Right. Mr. Sellers asked me to help in the chem lab after third period—you know, setting up for fourth period. It's a good deal.

Teacher: You're really pleased he asked you. (Active listening)

Student: Right on! I can probably get to be the lab assistant next year and I could sure use the job.

Teacher: There may be a good payoff for you and that's pretty important. (Active listening)

Student: Yeah. I know you're upset about me being late. I didn't think it would be such a problem. You know, I've tried to sort of slip in quietly.

Teacher: You're a little surprised that it's such a problem to me even when you try to be quiet. (Active listening)

Student: Well, not really. I can see your point. You do have to stop and change the attendance record and stuff. Mostly I'm late because Mr. Sellers and I get to talking too long. I'll tell him it's a problem for you and I'll just split a few minutes earlier, okay?

Teacher: That would sure help me. Thanks, Allan.

Student: No sweat.[9]

By shifting to a different consulting mode, in this case an acceptant one, the consultant can help the client take responsibility for solving the problem.

Summary

These interventions demonstrate how deeply held and difficult to bring into the focus of attention personal assumptions about power/authority may be. The hidden aspect of authority seems to involve feeling "responsible" for someone else. The person with the power/authority knows "what *they* need," or "what *they* should do." Confrontations may bring these assumptions to the surface, but confrontation per se may be insufficient to change them.

GROUP (C-1-2)

One of the central issues of modern society relates to authority and its uses. In boss-subordinate relationships, an authority-obedience value orientation demands group loyalty and compliance, without regard for understanding; denies the pertinence of participation, involvement, and commitment for effective problem solving; and assumes that compliance based upon obedience is sufficient for putting into effect the boss's wishes. These and many other facets are significant for understanding the role of a confrontational consultant in the power/authority area. It is his or her purpose to bring clients face-to-face with the impact that power/authority assumptions are having on their effectiveness in resolving problem issues and on personal satisfaction.

The consultant is more likely than his or her clients to embrace values congruent with behavioral science research findings, a value system premised on involvement, participation, and commitment. In terms of these values, leader-member relationships are most sound when work problems are identified and solutions are sought in such a way that everyone involved actively participates. Shared "ownership" of the problem can lead to team-wide commitment to implementing effective solutions.

Authority Unilaterally Exercised by Boss

An example described by Argyris and reported earlier illustrates how a confrontational consultant resisted accepting the power/authority assumptions under which a chief executive was inviting him to help sell a Management-by-Objectives program. By confronting the resistance, the consultant shifted the chief executive and some forty key executives toward an examination of the value orientations underlying their behavior. The consultant requested a meeting of all top executives to provide an opportunity for them to question and confront their boss, as well as for the consultant to confront them all.

An initial hour-and-a-half meeting was held with twelve of the officers present. The agenda focused on what they wanted to accomplish with regard to the introduction of a Management-by-Objectives program and what their reactions were to the interventionist's views on the matter. Following this meeting the officers met without the consultant to decide whether he should be invited to the later meeting. Their session on this matter was taped and sent to the consultant for evaluation.

Then a third meeting was held to discuss whatever conclusions the consultant had reached from the tapes in regard to the values and assumptions revealed in that second meeting.

> *Consultant:* I listened to the tape and found it fascinating and helpful. I should like to attempt to accomplish two objectives during this meeting. One is to answer some substantive questions raised about the proposed session. The other is to develop a better understanding of my relationship with you. I should like to start with this objective first, unless someone prefers differently. *(pause)*
>
> I heard on the tape such comments as, "The benefit will come when he criticizes us publicly;" "He may say, 'your attitude is wrong'." Are we ready to take criticisms publicly, to have someone get to the nerve?"
>
> I should like to ask a question. What did I do or say that led you to believe that I would make such comments?[10]

Since in the subsequent discussion no one in the client group could identify the source of such an impression beyond "Just looking at you!", Argyris was able to demonstrate that at least one assumption used as a judgmental basis was somewhat less than reliable.

Argyris provides another example of a confrontational intervention in which he observed here-and-now events occurring within a group. Authority-obedience dynamics operating in structuring boss-subordinate relationships are demonstrated.

The consultant had asked the marketing vice-president, "Is there anything you do that may make it more difficult for marketing people?" Before he could reply, the president cut in and said, "I'm sure that A [the marketing vice-president] can answer that better than anyone, but let me try." The consultant listened. When the president had finished, the marketing vice-president partially agreed, then the president and he explored their differences. The event was over, but not for the consultant.

> *Consultant:* "May I ask why you felt that you had to answer for A even though you stated A could answer it better than anyone else?"
>
> *President:* "I don't know. That's a good question. I do it an awful lot with A."
>
> *A:* "Yes, you do."
>
> *Consultant:* "How did you feel when he answered for you?"

The marketing vice-president recounted how he had felt and concluded that he was angry at himself whenever this happened. The president asked if this was dominating behavior and went on to say:

President: "I wonder if others feel that way. No, I don't think so because they know me well and would say so."

Interventionist: "I can't confirm or disconfirm your view. Perhaps you can check your view some day by asking them directly."[11]

This episode is useful for understanding confrontational interventions. The president was acting on an authority-obedience premise: his value-based, probably implicit, assumption was that it was his prerogative to cut off any subordinate by whom the question might best have been answered in order to answer it himself. Not only was this one of his hierarchical "rights"; he undoubtedly thought that important questions got answered quicker and—despite his compliment to A—answered better that way. Furthermore, the president's presumption of prerogative is matched by subordinates' presumption of obedience: one lets himself be cut off. One of the costs, though, was the anger and lack of creative involvement felt by A, and probably by other subordinates as well. But the president seemed unaware of this until the consultant intervened to produce some evidence.

Later in the meeting the consultant asked the president how he felt.

President: "Exhausted, but I have a lot to think over."

Consultant: "Do you feel the spotlight has been on you?"

President: "Hell, yes!"

Consultant: "How do you feel about that? For example, do you feel ganged up on? Are you wondering if A, B, C, and D maybe got together and planned this session?"

President: "Well, as a matter of fact, I felt that way during the meeting."[12]

The discussion continued. One issue considered was how people may become defensive when they feel others are out to "get" them; another was concerned with how trust, as well as some ground rules, can be developed among group members so that the probability of subordinates ganging up against the boss would be reduced.

Not all client-held values are equally susceptible to confrontational interventions. Among the most resistant to change are attitudes of paternalism on the part of the client in which the authority/obedience value is one component of the orientation and the other is warm feelings toward "good" (i.e., outwardly respectful and obedient) subordinates and kindly treatment of them. Confrontational interventions that focus the client's attention on paternalistic behavior and attitudes are likely to be rejected because the client emphasizes in his or her own thinking the "good things" that he or she does for people. Accordingly, he or she expects recipients of these favors to be grateful and compliant and tends to be insensitive to those coercive actions and attitudes on his/her part that likely promote subordinate frustration and anger. If this is the case, the consultant's intervention does little more than provoke righteous indignation—which itself is another defensive way for the client to avoid facing the consequences of the consultant's confrontation.

Paternalism

An example of team-based confrontation that proved unsuccessful in dealing with paternalism is described by Levinson.

> A rigid, authoritarian company president, who built his organization into international prominence, was disappointed by the fact that he could not seem to retain a corps of young managers who had top management executive potential. While he hired many, they left after two or three years with the organization, usually moving up into higher level roles in other companies. He himself attributed this loss to an inadequate management development program and sought the help of a social scientist well versed in the concept of confrontation. Certain that the problem was the president himself, and equally certain that he would profit by attack from his subordinates, the social scientist arranged an organization development program whose first steps included just that kind of confrontation. In the course of the experience, the president became livid with frustrated rage, angry that his paternalism was unappreciated, and abandoned his efforts to develop the company further. In impulsive anger, he sold it, a fact that ultimately cost him dearly and enmeshed his management in the adaptive problems of a merger which made his company merely an appendage of a larger organization.[13]

The strategy of confrontation did not break through the authority-obedience-love basis of paternalism, but instead provoked greater resistance and anger on the part of the president, who could not understand why his subordinates would want to bite the hand that had fed them so well.

Therapist as Focus of Power/Authority Attitudes

Possibly as important as any approach for analyzing the exercise of power/authority, viewed within the psychiatric context, is the post–World War II research at the Tavistock Clinic by Bion,[14] Ezriel,[15] and others and the operational use of these understandings for inducing consultant-assisted change by the A. K. Rice Institute, as described by Klein.[16]

Freud probably concentrated more attention on the systematic examination of this aspect of individual behavior and institutional functioning than anyone prior to his work. Analyses by Freud of the exercise of power/authority in the military and Catholic Church remain classics in the field.[17]

The conceptual link between Freud and Bion is one that permits a logical extension of individual psychology into group relations. The linking notion is that of the "unconscious group assumption."

Central to the approach is the idea of confronting unconscious group assumptions in order to bring them into deliberate focus in such a way as to permit those who are embracing these assumptions to learn more about them, to study what has brought these assumptions into prominence, and in their thinking to explore ways by which the unbridled reign of such assumptions can be curbed or eliminated.

Confrontations are basic in psychoanalytic group therapy. However, the rationale of the psychoanalytically oriented consultant needs to be understood in order to appreciate what he or she concentrates interventions on and what he or she ignores as of no importance. This may be seen in a medical sense; that is, authority-obedience as a sickness-producing rather than health-giving set of value assumptions.

The following selection is from Ezriel, a psychoanalyst whose confrontational interventions deal with people in groups. The thesis is that each participant brings his or her own tensions to the meetings, tensions that may cause the person to react to other participants in something less than objective terms. These tensions may exist subconsciously and in that sense are uncontrolled by the client. Ezriel's view is that each person tries to move others into roles that will relieve his or her unique unconscious tensions.

Initially, most group members accept, without question, the authority of the consultant under an authority-obedience convention. They have come to obtain his or her expert advice. If, instead, the consultant acts passively, a "Rorschach card" situation results where each person's reactions to the consultant's not giving the expected advice tells something of that person's underlying tensions toward authority. By eventually identifying these reactions, participants come to comprehend their tensions about authority, and thenceforth to get control over them.

When the consultant acts passively, the group is thrown on its own resources and must find something to talk about. Whatever the content of discussion turns out to be, an underlying problem develops that is shared by all in varying degrees. Ezriel refers to this as an "unconscious group tension." Confrontations are intended to make clear to participants what their unconscious group tensions are, and to help them understand how they are affecting each person's characteristic way of dealing with the dilemma.

This conception of group behavior is illustrated in the following recounting of a group's first session.[18] It occurred after the consultant had introduced group members to one another and had stated that the purpose of the group was: "for people to find out the causes of their difficulties." He indicated also that no topic was barred from discussion. A silence of three minutes was ended by:

F2[19]: I suppose we are all waiting for somebody to say something.

M4: What do you want us to do? Do you want us to get everything off our chest, explain our own problems, our own difficulties, or should we not do that? If so, as a first thing, one of my problems is to be able to speak to a lot of people, to lecture. Do you want us to explain our difficulties, or are you already familiar with them? Does anybody else experience difficulty in speaking in front of a number of people?

M2: I think it is fairly common in most people—you don't like to push yourself forward.

M2 had come up with a value proposition, whether or not this was an accurate commentary about "most people" or was more in the nature of a personal norm of his own.

M4: But you must admit it is a very bad thing. For certain jobs you have to master it somehow or else you don't get very far.

M2: Is there not a difference between talking about a technical subject and talking to people personally?

M4: I don't think the subject matters, as long as you know what you are talking about. If you don't know what you are talking about, it is more difficult. A person who is inclined to be a bit nervous in front of people does not really think of what he is saying. He is inclined to get a little bit confused—as I am doing now.

At this point, one of the group's members seems to feel that M4 needs help from an authoritative source.

M2: Is your part, Dr. Ezriel, passive, or are we allowed to draw you in?

Dr. E: What do you think M2? I think it would be a good idea if you acted as a reference point. Then if we come to blows we can get you to arbitrate.

M4: It might ease the situation.

F2: I don't think he wants to. I think that if there are going to be any blows, he wants us to fight it out among ourselves.

(Somebody): Why should there be blows? This is the Peace Conference.

M2: I take it that in this group no subject is barred. Therefore we are likely to talk on subjects people don't normally discuss—subjects in which you are likely to get more disagreement. (*short silence*)

Here is a second value proposition coming from M2. It is quite consonant with the first one, and the two may be seen from the outside as facets of a particular value system. Again, M2 has phrased it as what "people" don't do—but others in the group will have had their experiences of what people do, and perhaps they believe otherwise. Indeed, M2 could be a minority of one.

M2: I'm sorry. I have turned the discussion off.

M4: No, it all leads on, I presume.

M2: I don't want to alter it from the point of the difficulty of talking. I still think it makes a difference what one is talking about.

F5: No. Because you don't really think about what you are talking about. You are thinking about yourself all the time, then you come home and think of all the things you should have said.

(Somebody): A sort of inferiority complex.

M2: Can we ask Dr. Ezriel what an inferiority complex is?

Dr. E: What do you think?[20]

As participants continue jockeying to find an acceptable basis for the discussions with one another and for their relationships to the consultant, even greater focus is placed on the role of the person who "should" be in authority. Different reactions and attitudes toward the consultant, ranging from working to please him to being resentful of his nonresponsiveness, come to the fore. The consultant can then confront any participant with that person's particular way of dealing with the common group tension.

Dr. E: (By refusing to answer the questions put to me and referring them back to the questioner I had prevented the group from pushing me into a role which they wanted me to play, i.e., that of a person in authority.)

I pointed out to the group that they apparently wanted the presence of such a person who would take responsibility for what happened, since they feared that without such a safe guard the free expression of their problems might lead to dangerous quarrels in the group. I added that they resented my not playing the part of this controlling figure. I then pinpointed M2 who seemed to fear the consequences of his hostile impulses even more than the rest of the group.[21]

The confrontation identified a common group tension related to authority and obedience: the members of the group were expecting the consultant to act as an authority—as arbitrator, information giver, and so on—and when he resisted doing so, tension built up. The confrontation focused attention on what had been happening and each participant's particular reaction to it.

A parallel use of confrontation strategies based on Bion's and Ezriel's psychoanalytic formulation but applied in the context of "businessmen as students" is described by Rice. Its character is revealed in the following excerpts from the first meeting of such a study group. Someone said, "Let us introduce ourselves." But after the introductions an embarrassed silence fell on the group. While Rice was pondering what to say, one member commented, "Well, we didn't learn much from that—in fact I've forgotten most of the names already. I seldom pick them up the first time." This remark stimulated another round robin of mutual introductions which ended again in embarrassed silence. Someone slapped his hand on the table and exclaimed, "Well, that's cleared the decks."

In the nautical spirit of the moment, Rice weighed anchor and sailed in with a confrontational intervention, referring first to the "clearing of the decks." He commented that the decks may have been cleared for a fight directed against him for not giving the kind of leadership expected. He pointed to their hostility to others who had tried to take a lead, shown by lack of support. The members individually and collectively denied they had any such feelings:

"I don't feel hostile, but I do feel afraid of what is going to happen. If only we had a clear purpose."

"We need to establish formalities to enable us to discuss."

"We're trying to find a common denominator. This is an unnatural situation. The trouble is that nothing is happening. There is nothing to study. We're not competing for a job or anything . . . (*a pause, in which tension in the groups could be felt to mount*). We all look at Mr. Rice . . . (*then another pause*). For God's sake somebody else talk!"

And then the tension was broken by laughter.[22]

Rice's intervention focused attention on his nontraditional leadership behavior. He indicated that in his view his "refusal" to engage in the typical implicit rules of cooperation had put members on the spot, and they reacted with hostile feelings toward him. This is the same reaction subordinates have to a boss whose unfamiliar "leadership through delegation" leaves them nonplussed. Rather than critical fingers being pointed inward, they tend to be pointed at the boss as cause of their trouble.

Rice comments upon aspects of his role as a confrontational consultant working with a group.

> The consultant's job is to confront the group, without affronting its members; to draw attention to group behavior and not to individual behavior; to point out how the group uses individuals to express its own emotions, how it exploits some members so that others can absolve themselves from the responsibility for such expression.
>
> As a group fails to get its consultant to occupy the more traditional roles [authority-obedience relationship] of teacher, seminar leader, or therapist, it will redouble its efforts until in desperation it will disown him and seek other leaders. When they too fail, they too will be disowned, often brutally. The group will then use its own brutality to try to get the consultant to change his task by eliciting his sympathy and care for those it has handled so roughly. If this manoeuvre fails, and it never completely fails, the group will tend to throw up other leaders to express its concern for its members and project its brutality onto the consultant. As rival leaders emerge it is the job of the consultant, so far as he is able, to identify what the group is trying to do and to explain it. His leadership is in task performance, and the task is to understand what the group is doing "now" and to explain why it is doing it. Drawing attention to interesting phenomena without explanation is seldom used.[23]

In the above example, the psychiatric model of confrontation was "transferred" to the industrial context in order to create a learning situation for business people. More recent developments have occurred at A. K. Rice Institute, an organizational mechanism through which these notions are concentrated on and enriched for operational use in change projects.[24]

Confrontational interventions can be made with the object of helping business, government, and other leaders study the extent to which values and assumptions regarding authority-obedience are embedded in their group behavior. Such examination, in turn, often points toward alternative possibilities—e.g., supervision based on participation, commitment, and involvement.

Summary _____

These confrontational interventions provide insight regarding the depth and pervasiveness of power/authority-related assumptions in group life. Confrontation is likely to be successful when the consultant can mobilize sufficient indications of the client's unrecognized behavior or unexpressed attitudes to counteract denial. In addition, consultants may be able to focus attention on issues of unexamined behavior or unexpressed attitudes by *themselves* serving as a model of certain behavior and attitudes opposite to those that the consultation seeks to intervene upon. This is possible, for example, when the client's values are carefully hidden but the consultant counters with openness and spontaneity. Such interventions also give an indication of existing defenses—sources of resistance to change that prevent present assumptions from undergoing significant alteration.

One of the easiest ways for a consultant to reduce intervention effectiveness is to allow the client to provoke him or her into win-lose attitudes of argument. Such attitudes are relatively easy for the confrontational consultant to fall into, and once this has happened the ability to force a reexamination on the part of the client is greatly reduced. Indeed, the core problem the client may need to reexamine is a readiness to create win-lose situations. Thus if the client is successful in maneuvering the consultant into such behavior, the very attitudes involved become, from that moment, unavailable to identification because each person—client and consultant—is unwittingly acting them out in his or her own interactions.

INTERGROUP (C-1-3)

Confrontational interventions may be necessary when an intergroup relationship has become set or frozen in ways that make needed cooperation difficult. This is particularly true when the frozen state is characterized by hostility, antagonisms, and mutual disrespect. If the frozen state is one of indifference, it is unlikely that consultative assistance will be sought as there is little motivation to change.

Student-and-faculty relations involving power/authority tensions were approached by confrontational intervention in a New Jersey high school workshop. The confrontation was based on the assumption that each group—students and faculty—had its own motivations and, in addition, might have been seen by the other quite differently than either group saw itself. Clarifying these values and assumptions about one another while preserving the integrity of both sides was basic to the intervention.

Volunteer students and teachers were separated into their respective groups and were each asked to develop a list of ways they saw the other. Here are some of the results.

HOW STUDENTS PERCEIVE TEACHERS
Unaware, think they are correct because they are older, putting on a big show, some making honest effort, think they are more mature because they are older, less outspoken, passive when the principal is there, take things personally, don't really listen, are prejudiced, some willing to listen even when they don't agree, curious about students' views.

HOW TEACHERS PERCEIVE STUDENTS
Cherish individuality, hopelessness, confusion, self-confidence, frustration, sensitivity, eagerness, resistance to seeing both sides of the question, clannish, irresponsible, candid, bored, angry at inequities, powerless, flexible, racially polarized.

The students and teachers then exchanged basic attitudes toward one another and tried to explore the meanings behind them. Subjective aspects of these descriptions were emphasized on the presumption that resolving mutual misunderstandings is a prerequisite if realistic problem-solving collaboration is to replace authority-obedience.

The initial response was positive. As the school year wore on, however, collaborative efforts ended for reasons that are not explained except that separation pressures were greater than the bond of cooperation developed during the confrontation sessions. This may have been because neither students nor faculty involved their constituencies to any significant degree, with the result that participating teachers might have been seen by their colleagues as "soft," and participating students as "traitors" by their peers.[25] If so, this would indicate the significance of the intergroup nature of the client system. Because only a representative portion of the total population was included and no efforts were made to spread the strategy throughout the respective student and faculty populations, the former reference-group norm was sufficiently strong to reestablish authority-obedience relations and dissolve the desired basis of collaboration.

ORGANIZATION (C-1-4)

The use of power/authority throughout an organizational system is most likely to be experienced by members lower in the organization as a reflection of signals received from the top. Unless the top leadership is interested in changing, it is unlikely that major shifts in the use of power/authority will be initiated at lower levels.

Under these circumstances, when the real key to change, from the consultant's perspective, is to confront power/authority as the focal issue, his or her natural inclination is to start with the top person or group. This may have been the circumstance of the Argyris interventions described earlier. Unless successful at the pinnacle, a consultant is seldom provided opportunities to set up situations of confrontation throughout an organization.

LARGER SOCIAL SYSTEM (C-1-5)

Power/authority differences among segments within larger social systems may result from real or presumed inequality. Sometimes frictions arise when people are not satisfied with the status quo situation and attempt to shift in a direction more favorable to their self-interests. Consultant interventions with a final objective of a mutually satisfactory resolution to power/authority conflicts are described in this section.

Border Disputes between Nations

Confrontational interventions have been attempted as the basis for dealing with border disputes between nations. One such intervention, described by Walton,[26] involved Ethiopians, Kenyans, and Somalis. The handful of participants in this workshop were checked out and "green-lighted" by their respective governments, but were not empowered to act as official representatives. They met on neutral territory.

After an initial period of developing contacts among members and practicing teamwork skills in crisscross groups, national groups were assembled as units to list "key grievances or disputes your people have with each of the other countries. . . ." On a second sheet they listed their predictions of the grievances or disputes the other two countries would come up with. This intended confrontation was not successful, possibly because the consultant compromised when resistances appeared rather than assisting clients to gain insight into their reservations about moving forward. Two of the three national groups resisted using the intervention design as structured by the consultants. Unable to reach agreement as to what the issues were, the workshop made no progress in gaining consensus regarding proposed solutions. Nonetheless the approach is suggestive of an alternative which might be more effective than conventional win-lose bargaining approaches or "shuttle diplomacy."

Police-Community Relations

In the following example, confrontational techniques were used to reduce the perceived arbitrary exercise of power by a stronger group. The intervention, described by Bell et al.[27] involved a police-community intervention in Houston, Texas, in which 1400 members of the police force participated. Police officers met with community members in six different sessions spanning a six-week period. Each week, subgroups of twenty or so officers were scheduled into three-hour sessions with an equivalent number of community members. Police participants were required to attend; citizens attended voluntarily and most citizen participants did not successively attend all six sessions. Invitations for citizen attendance were aimed at ensuring participation by a cross-section of the community, but especially by representatives from (1) minority groups, (2) poverty groups, and (3) dissidents. Consultants provided leadership.

During initial sessions, police and community groups first met separately to develop images of themselves and of the other group. Then the two groups convened in a general session where images were compared and discussed. During subsequent sessions efforts were made to diagnose causes of disagreements, correct distortions, identify key issues, and devise better methods of conflict resolution. The flavor of what was accomplished is provided in a consolidation of image elements, summarizing the key factors of many similar sessions.

POLICE SELF-IMAGE

"As officers we are ethical, honest, physically clean and neat in appearance, dedicated to our job, with a strong sense of duty. Some officers are prejudiced, but they are in the minority, and officers are aware of their prejudice and lean over backwards to be fair. We are a close knit, suspicious group, distrustful of outsiders. We put on a professional front; hard, calloused, and indifferent, but underneath we have feelings. We treat others as nicely as they will let us. We are clannish, ostracized by the community, used as scapegoats, and under scrutiny even when off duty trying to enjoy ourselves. We are the blue minority."

COMMUNITY IMAGE OF POLICE

"Some police abuse their authority, act as judge, jury, and prosecutor, and assume a person is guilty until proven innocent. They are too often psychologically and physically abusive, name-calling, handle people rough, and discriminate against blacks in applying the law. Police are cold and mechanical in performance of their duties. We expect them to be perfect, to make no mistakes and to set the standard for behavior. The police see the world only through their squad car windshield and are walled off from the community. Our initial reaction when we see an officer is 'blue'."

SELF-IMAGE OF CITIZENS AS MEMBERS OF THE COMMUNITY

"We lack knowledge about proper police procedures and do not know our rights, obligations, and duties in regard to the law. There is a lack of communication among social, geographical, racial, and economic segments of the community. We do not involve ourselves in civic affairs as we should, and we have a guilty conscience about the little crimes (traffic violations) we get away with, but are resentful when caught. We relate to the police as authority figures, and we feel uncomfortable around them. The black community feels itself second class in relation to the police. The majority of the community is law-abiding, hard working, pays taxes, is honest and reliable."

POLICE IMAGE OF COMMUNITY

"Basically the public is cooperative and law-abiding, but uninformed about the duties, procedures, and responsibility of the police officer. The upper class, the rich, support the police, but feel immune to the law and use their money and influence to avoid police action against themselves and their children. The middle class support the police and are more civic-minded than upper or lower classes. The major share of police contact with the middle class is through traffic violations. The lower class has the most frequent contact with the police and usually are uncooperative as witnesses or in reporting crime. They have a different sense of values, live only for today and do not plan for tomorrow. As police officers we see the Houston Negro in two groups, (1) Negro—industrious, productive, moral, law-abiding, and not prone to violence; (2) 'nigger'—lazy, immoral, dishonest, unreliable, and prone to violence."[28]

Assessment of the effectiveness of this intervention is difficult but indications point in a positive direction. It is reported that the Houston police characterized the summer that followed these interventions as a "cool" summer in contrast with 1967. Another positive sign was the 70-percent drop in citizen complaints about police behavior for the seven-month period following the program. The consultants saw this kind of a confrontation as the beginning of a development endeavor rather than as an intervention capable of removing the effects of years of rancor and distrust.[29]

School Administration versus Community Residents

In Chapter 24 a mental health consultant's catalytic approach to a worsening relationship between residents of a black community and their school system is presented. That intervention was insufficient to bring the outstanding issues of controversy into focus and, as a result, problems were not resolved. Tensions increased further during and after the period when the consultant was participating in discussions with the school authorities. At the beginning of the next year, these heightened tensions resurfaced and the consultant was brought back. This time the approach was confrontational.

> On the first day of school, there had been some disorder in the school yard, sparked by black community leaders and parents who had come unannounced to confront the principal and who were apparently not seen by him. The police had been called to remove "unauthorized persons" from the school building. The following day, a group of community organizers descended on the school and marched most of the students, together with some of their teachers, to a nearby community recreational building, where they set up a "Freedom School." The sponsors of this overt act of rebellion were the parents' committee, aided by a number of black community militant organizations.[30]

Even though the mental-health center's previous school consultation had been inadequate, a new opportunity was created when five professional community workers called upon the center director.

> . . . They gave him a more detailed story of what was happening, and they emphasized the dangers of a serious community conflagration if the impasse were not quickly resolved. They felt that the main problem revolved around the school authorities' refusal to meet with the parents and to discuss their legitimate demands; and they placed particular blame on the new school principal, who was making matters worse by his highhanded authoritarian approach to the parents. They said that the parents' committee represented the moderate leadership of the ghetto community, which wanted to resolve the conflict peaceably and were interested only in improving a very bad school. They also said that the black community contained a group of extremist militant leaders who intended to use this situation to wrest power from the moderates and to provoke a bloody confrontation with white authorities, particularly the police, whose brutality they wished to expose publicly. Press, radio, and television reporters were continually on the scene, and the stage was set for a major battle.
>
> The group of community professionals, which included both white and black workers, said they had come to ask the center staff to intervene in this situation because the center's consultation contract with the school system gave it direct access to the superintendent. The center must use its influence to persuade him of the absolute necessity of reinstituting communication with the black parents so that the problems might be handled quietly and rationally. Otherwise, they would become a cause of racial strife, in which people would be injured and possibly killed and property would be damaged.[31]

An interesting episode from the standpoint of how colleagues from another discipline saw the felt-needs aspect of earlier catalytic consultation came about when

> . . . the director gave a brief report on their consultation activities in the school and said that they had not yet begun their program for the new school year. The visitor [a black professional] asked somewhat aggressively, "How can you justify this passivity and slow routinized style of operations, when people's lives are at stake?"
>
> The director replied with some heat that he saw no need for them to justify their style of consultation on these grounds; their program with the school system was in its early stages and the beginning relationships had to be developed gently lest the school staff feel that the center was infringing on their internal domain. It was center policy that no moves should be made into new problem areas until the school board staff asked the mental health workers to help them. This meant that inevitably the consultation program would develop slowly and at a rate dictated by the consultee institution. The alternative could easily be the disintegration of the center program and their ejection from the school system—a fate that had befallen many other mental health workers in the past, who had come in with missionary zeal to reform that institution.
>
> The community organizer was not convinced. He apologized for his vehemence but said he was concerned about the immediate dangers to his community and to the school system. He accused the center of "fiddling while Rome burned." He admitted that the center approach to its consultation program was in keeping with the latest and best theories of mental health consultation, but he asked whether the center had no concern for basic issues of community life that had clear implications for the mental health of wide sections of the population. He urged that such concern should convince the director to set aside, at least temporarily and as an emergency measure, his slow, deliberate professionalized style of operations. He also questioned the wisdom of the center's decision several months earlier to retire from the community action approach in the ghetto school.[32]

This confrontation by the community organizer was sufficient to break through the catalytic assumptions on which the center previously had been working and to bring a new set of forces into play.

> The next day the center director and some of his staff had an emergency meeting at school headquarters with the deputy superintendent and the district superintendent. The director described his discussion with the community workers and offered his help in resolving the communication impasse with the parents of the ghetto school.
>
> At first the superintendents were rather surprised to discover the center's interest in this matter. The deputy superintendent said he could not see what this administrative issue had to do with problems of emotionally disturbed or subnormal children, which he thought was the center's area of interest.
>
> The director replied that his center was concerned with all community issues that might affect the sense of well-being of children and their families and that might be conducive to mental health or mental disorder. He felt

that racial tensions and lack of consonance between parents and educators must inevitably affect the feelings of security of many families, and might have a deleterious effect on the emotional stability of schoolchildren. Moreover, problems of communication between individuals and groups were a topic of special interest to mental health specialists and one in which they had developed some expert knowledge.

He also told the superintendent that his visitors had predicted a more dangerous community upheaval if the local problem between the ghetto school and the parents' group was not quickly resolved. He said that the center staff, like all citizens, had a fundamental interest in preserving public order and preventing damage to public property and lives, such as had recently occurred in other cities as a consequence of similar racial conflicts in the schools.

The superintendents' immediate response was very positive. They freely admitted to being at their wit's end and warmly welcomed this offer of help. They then gave a detailed account of their problems in dealing with the parents of the ghetto school. The parents were making a series of outrageous demands, most of which could not be dealt with in practical terms. For example, they wanted complete community control over the school, with power to hire and fire its personnel. They demanded a black principal. They wanted several of their number to be put on the school payroll as "guardians of discipline" in the school.[33]

Center personnel now proceeded to make their resources available in the context of this deep-seated community tension.

The center staff offered two types of assistance. First, they promised to consult with the district superintendent, whenever he felt the need, about the day-to-day tactical problems of managing the crisis. He accepted this offer with alacrity and set up the first consultation appointment for that afternoon. Second, they offered to make informal contacts with leaders of the black community to explore how and where the two sides could get together for a behind-the-scenes discussion outside the orbit of the public.[34]

What transpired next is complicated by a variety of secondary issues. Eventually meetings were arranged that were attended by high-ranking school authorities and by three or four members of the parents' committee as well as a black leader. The center director was able to act as chairman. The meeting ran smoothly until, close to its end, one of the parents' committeemen drew from his pocket and read a provocative written statement that had been composed by several parents. Of particular interest is how the consultant intervened.

The amicable atmosphere immediately gave way to tense hostility. The school administrators showed signs of barely suppressed anger, and the parents began to speak provocatively and with raised voices. The center director broke into this discussion and pointed out that the meeting had been progressing well until the inflammatory words "local control" had been used. He felt that such "fighting words" should be ruled out of order, because they probably meant completely different things to each side and because they were more like battle cries than attempts to convey information. He called on all participants to return to the spirit of cooperation which had brought them together.[35]

A further series of meetings was held. Though characterized by numerous ups and downs, it is reported that eventually the inflammatory situation cooled and basic problem-solving relationships were restored.

This was an instance of a confrontational intervention complicated by the interplay of ever-widening community variables. The example is imperfect in many respects, yet it offers an indication of how confrontational methods can be employed in defining, confronting, and resolving community-based disputes. It also demonstrates the difficulties encountered by the community organizer as he tried to confront the real issues needing attention. By trying to go against the established collusion among the administration and the conventional mental-health approach to following the felt needs of clients, he was eventually successful in surmounting seemingly impregnable barriers.

Should the Social Worker Confront on Behalf of the Client?

Social-work practice is geared to helping clients, usually individuals and families, solve problems they are unable to resolve independently. Many times the fundamental problem needing solution is not amenable to the social worker's direct efforts. Either the solution is available within the existing society ("the establishment") which may be unresponsive, or the solution is contingent upon changing the establishment.

To deal with the client's problem, the social worker may feel personally committed to intervene on the client's behalf within the agencies and systems of the establishment itself. Such interventions often challenge the power/authority system, and in effect say, "This is what the agency should do." This kind of unsought consultation is likely to be interpreted as insubordination because the consultant/social worker is also an employee. Such interventions often take on the character of advocacy and the employee may be seen as a "traitor" to the establishment.

Dilemmas often arise for the social worker who undertakes confrontational advocacy for his or her client vis-à-vis institutions of the establishment. Even though they are not a direct employer, they come within the same family of governmental or other agencies that does employ the social worker. This is a situation where establishment representatives stand against institutions of the establishment. For example, a social worker's voice carries little weight unless his or her skills of confrontation are particularly effective, or the issue happens to be one the establishment is disposed to resolve goodnaturedly with perhaps the initial response, "Now, let's not get all heated up about this. . . ." Then the social worker may gain a resolution without creating antagonism.

However, this result is by no means assured. As far as the establishment is concerned, the social worker who intervenes in a confronting way may polarize into a win-lose orientation one or more issues that previously had been "sleeping dogs." To curb such confrontations, the establishment may threaten or take reprisal measures against the social worker's agency, thus reverse-confronting the agency with risk to its continued capacity to function. Next, to remain acceptable to the establishment, the agency itself might apply counterpressures against all social workers. As a self-protective response, the social workers might then organize in protest, possibly through professional associations, so the area of conflict would widen. Even though issues and areas of professional integrity may receive better definition as an outcome of the controversy, this does nothing to solve the client's problem.

This dilemma of confrontational intervention has been studied by the National Association of Social Workers' Ad Hoc Committee on Advocacy. The committee's report[36] and a subsequent paper[37] have described difficulties encountered from attempted intervention, both in terms of dealing with the establishment and from the standpoint of providing needed reforms through legislation.

Summary

Confrontational interventions ranging from the individual to the societal level share a significant feature when the focal issue is power/authority: the consultant usually takes a stand that challenges unilateral or arbitrary use of power/authority. He or she may, for example, lend outside support to the weaker of those represented.

However, there is a high probability that the consultant will be seen by those on the stronger side as biased and opinionated in favor of the weaker, thus reducing the likelihood that his or her interventions will be effective. If the consultant enters the situation on the stronger side, success in bringing about a confrontation of power differences is far more likely. But the stronger side may not see the need for such an intervention, since the difficulties it experiences are viewed as difficulties of the weaker component, unrelated to its own behavior.

One of the most basic issues of confrontational consultation in the power/ authority area is the power ration in the client/consultant relationship. If the consultant is "weaker" than the client, he or she is unlikely to be listened to, no matter how valid his or her interventions may be. If his or her own power/authority is equal to that of the client, then a successful basis of intervention may be established. However, if the consultant is significantly "stronger" than the client, interventions are likely to be responded to as though they were prescriptions and taken at a level of absoluteness that they in fact do not deserve.

Notes

1. C. Argyris, *Management and Organization Development: The Path from XA to YB* (New York: McGraw-Hill, 1971). Reprinted by permission.

2. Ibid., p. 28.

3. M. Bayes and P. M. Newton, "Women in Authority: A Socio-psychological Analysis," *Journal of Applied Behavioral Science* 14, no. 1 (1978): 7–20.

4. A. H. Kuriloff and S. Atkins, "T Group for Work Team," reproduced by special permission from *Journal of Applied Behavioral Science* 2, no. 1 (1966): 63–93.

5. K. W. Back and J. M. Stycos, "The Survey under Unusual Conditions: Methodological Facets of the Jamaica Human Fertility Investigation," in D. P. Warwick and S. Osherson, eds., *Comparative Research Methods* (Englewood Cliffs, N.J.: Prentice-Hall, 1973), pp. 248–67. Reproduced by special permission of the Society for Applied Anthropology, monograph no. 1, 1959.

6. T. Gordon, *Parent Effectiveness Training* (New York: David McKay, 1970).

7. Reprinted with permission from the book *Parent Effectiveness Training* by Thomas Gordon, copyright 1970. Published by David McKay Co., Ltd., p. 123.

8. T. Gordon, *T.E.T.: Teacher Effectiveness Training* (New York: Peter H. Wyden, 1974).

9. Ibid., pp. 146–47.

10. Argyris, *Management and Organization Development*, p. 39.

11. C. Argyris, *Intervention Theory and Method*, © 1970. Addison-Wesley, Reading, Mass., p. 168. Reprinted with permission.

12. Ibid., p. 169.

13. H. Levinson, *The Great Jackass Fallacy* (Cambridge, Mass.: Harvard University Press, 1973).

14. W. R. Bion, *Experiences in Groups* (London: Tavistock Publication Ltd., 1959), pp. 1–183.

15. H. Ezriel, "A Psycho-Analytic Approach to Group Treatment," *British Journal of Medical Psychology* (1950): 23, 59–74. Reprinted by permission.

16. E. B. Klein, "An Overview of Recent Tavistock Work in the United States," in C. L. Cooper and C. Alderfer, eds., *Advances in Experiential Social Processes,* vol. I (New York: John Wiley, 1978), pp. 181–202.

17. S. Freud, "Group Psychology and the Analysis of the Ego," 1921, in *Complete Psychological Works of Sigmund Freud* (London: Hogarth Press, 1950).

18. Ezriel, "A Psycho-Analytic Approach."

19. F and M are female and male respectively; 1, 2, 3, and 4 indicate different group members.

20. Ezriel, "A Psycho-Analytic Approach," pp. 64–65.

21. Ibid., p. 65.

22. A. K. Rice, *Learning for Leadership* (London: Tavistock Publications, 1965). Reprinted by permission.

23. Ibid., pp. 65–66.

24. A. D. Colman and W. H. Bexton, eds., *Group Relations Reader* (Sausalito, Calif.: GREX, 1975), pp. 1–70.

25. M. A. Chesler and J. E. Lohman, "Changing Schools through Student Advocacy," in R. A. Schmuck and M. B. Miles, *Organization Development in Schools* (Palo Alto, Calif.: National Press Books, 1971), pp. 185–212.

26. R. E. Walton, "A Problem-Solving Workshop on Border Conflicts in Eastern Africa," *Journal of Applied Behavioral Science* 6, no. 4 (1970): 453–89.

27. R. R. Bell, S. E. Cleveland, P. Hanson, and W. E. O'Connell, "Small Group Dialogue and Discussion: An Approach to Police-Community Relationships," *Journal of Criminal Law, Criminology and Police Science* 60, no. 2 (1969):

242–46. Reprinted by special permission of the *Journal of Criminal Law, Criminology and Police Science,* © 1969 by Northwestern University School of Law.

28. Ibid., pp. 242–46.
29. Ibid., p. 246.
30. G. Caplan, *The Theory and Practice of Mental Health Consultation* (New York: Basic Books, 1970). © 1970, reprinted by permission.
31. Ibid., p. 363.
32. Ibid., p. 364.
33. Ibid., pp. 364–65.
34. Ibid., p. 366.
35. Ibid., p. 370.
36. NASW Ad Hoc Committee on Advocacy. "The Social Worker as Advocate: Champion of Social Victims," *Social Work* 14, no. 2 (1969): 16–22.
37. R. Sunley, "Family Advocacy: From Case to Cause," *Social Casework* 51 (1970): 347–57.

16

CONFRONTATIONAL INTERVENTIONS

Morale/ Cohesion

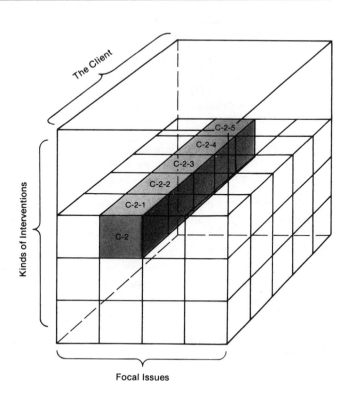

There are few examples of the use of confrontational interventions when the focal issue is morale/cohesion. One reason is that a consultant is more likely to adopt an acceptant orientation to promote the expression and discharge of unpleasant feelings and tensions than to challenge or confront whatever underlying values he or she discerns as associated with the present state of low morale/cohesion. Another is that when morale/cohesion is on the positive side, even to an excessive degree, it is rare for a client to request consultation of the sort that will test the validity of these feelings in real-world terms.

GROUP

An example of a confrontational intervention by a consultant in premarital counseling is seen in the work of Meadows and Taplin. One explanation of the rising divorce rate is that couples enter marriage without sufficiently extended or deep enough understanding of one another to make sound marital decisions. Differences appear after marriage and the couple's inability to deal with them results in increased divorce rates. Given this explanation, the question is, "How might such shared understanding be increased prior to decisions about marriage?"

The intervention involved triads consisting of a couple considering marriage and a counselor. Meetings of the triad followed prior meetings in which the counselor had discussions with each partner singly.

In describing their counseling goal, Meadows and Taplin indicated

The approach stressed a) the need for each partner in the premarital relationship to possess a deep understanding of the personality and emotional life of himself [or herself] and the intended marriage partner, b) the importance of the perception held concerning the appropriate marital role of each marriage partner, c) the importance of communication skills in marital adjustment, and d) the necessity to develop problem-solving skills in order to resolve the inevitable areas of conflict that arise in both the engagement period and marriage. Values were considered to be especially important dimensions in potential marriage adjustments.[1]

The points enumerated above encompass each of the focal issues of the Consulcube. Power/authority is seen in the analysis of the intended role of each partner and morale/cohesion in the emotional and support needs. Norms and standards in terms of shared/distinct values are considered to be important to the partners. Goals and objectives are less clearly focused, but even here we see that emphasis on communication and problem-solving skills was considered essential for goal attainment.

The intervention itself was confrontational.

The counseling method was somewhat directive and cognitive. An attempt was made to have each couple confront together certain key issues that have been held to be important in marital adjustments. They included such questions as the following: What means of expressing affection do we consider appropriate during the engagement period? How do we feel about the management of financial affairs? How shall we relate to in-laws? How do we feel about the exercise of authority in our married lives?[2]

Couples participated in one to three triad counseling sessions.

Results evaluated by questionnaire showed that the majority of participants found the experience very or somewhat helpful. Presence of the third person (the counselor) was helpful because, through his or her neutral position, premarital members were confronted with basic issues that were not being faced and the likelihood was increased that they would be openly and objectively discussed.

Supporting the notion that the intervention primarily focused around cohesion, it was the conclusion of the majority of participants that the primary problem area was "adjustment to fianceé with respect to emotions, values, and interests."[3]

Another group example, this time a confrontation between subordinates and their bosses, was arranged by a consultant to follow laboratory training designed to promote greater openness and trust.

The idea was that traditional communication patterns that often tend toward dishonesty, lack of caring, and manipulation were subject to interventional change and could be shifted through recognition and reward toward openness, caring, honesty, and nonmanipulation. Golembiewski and Carrigan report on use of a laboratory teaching method followed by organizational testing of learned values, attitudes, and behaviors that reinforced more positive patterns of behavior and helped bring about openness and trust.

This design has three basic elements. First, members of small organization units are provided with an off-site learning experience that centers around values, attitudes, and behavioral skills . . . [utilizing] "sensitivity training" or "T-groupings" in small groups composed of peers who work together.[4]

Second, the learning was extended into the organization by permitting participants to confront their hierarchical superiors as a test of the values, attitudes, and behavioral skills reinforced or developed in the initial training.

Third, the learning design calls for a "reinforcement experience" some 9-12 months after the initiation of the program of change. The intention is to provide a kind of "booster shot" for the values, attitudes and behavioral skills that were developed or reinforced in the two earlier training phases.[5]

The reinforcement experience is not described.

The intervention was tested with two populations of marketing managers, one population of fifteen and the other of nearly fifty managers.

There were eight experimental units altogether . . . in two separate areas of the same large firm. Each [learning] unit was composed of six to ten managers, with two units being Growth-Oriented and six being Stability-Oriented. The two batches of units each comprised a broader organization unit. . . .[6]

Change was measured by self-reports on the Likert Profile of Organization Characteristics which taps six basic organizational processes including leadership, motivation, communication, decisions, control, and goals. System 4 is consistent with the values of the laboratory approach. The theory was not utilized in the interventions, but rather the measurements were used to evaluate the results.

The pattern was one of overwhelming change toward System 4. The initial training experience had the intended effects. The preponderance of evidence implied the efficacy of the training design in inducing marked and persisting changes in the style of interpersonal and intergroup relations.[7]

Many organization members have been involved in planned change efforts designed to move them toward what were thought to be productive patterns of organizational behavior. This successful intervention at the individual level is congruent with organizational objectives of increased productivity and improved morale as well as with individual objectives of greater job satisfaction. However, no external criteria were used to evaluate whether such results were borne out in operational terms.

Summary

Confrontation may be indicated in a morale/cohesion situation when a client has the capacity to solve a problem, but is unwilling to face those people in positions of power/authority who are responsible for the situation. Under these conditions, a confrontational intervention can have sufficient "arousal impact" to push the client into actions that can lead to resolution of problems associated with his or her lowered morale/cohesion. Such a confrontation, in other words, has a trigger value for activating a person to approach, rather than avoid, problems.

In addition, confrontational interventions can be of use when low morale/cohesion is related to failure. In principle, it would seem appropriate to challenge the client for having a perceived lack of goals; for setting objectively unattainable goals; or for not reaching them due to morale/cohesion-related deficiencies along the way. These three situations, as well as others that are conceivable, were probably caused by earlier states of low morale/cohesion. Another causative possibility is that current circumstances may exist that are adversely affecting a client's well-being.

However, many problematic situations can be conceived wherein a current state of lowered morale/cohesion is not the real cause of the client's difficulties, but rather the result of difficulties occurring in some other focal area.

Notes

1. M. E. Meadows and J. F. Taplin, "Premarital Counseling with College Students: A Promising Triad," *Journal of Counseling Psychology* 17, no. 6 (1970): 516–17.
2. Ibid., p. 517.
3. Ibid., p. 517, Table 2.
4. R. T. Golembiewski and S. B. Carrigan, "Planned Change through Laboratory Methods," *Training and Development Journal* (March 1973): 18–27.
5. Ibid., p. 21.
6. Ibid., p. 22.
7. Ibid., pp. 24–26.

17

CONFRONTATIONAL INTERVENTIONS

Norms/ Standards

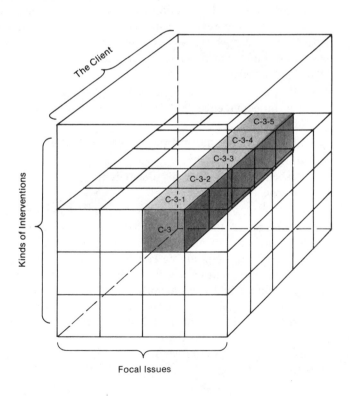

Norms/standards can operate so subtly that those whose behavior is affected by them are unaware of the impact on their actions. Thus outsiders may be in a better position than insiders to discern how norms/standards are influencing behavior. In addition, to the degree that norms/standards are relevant and central to a membership unit, those who might challenge their appropriateness are subject to conformity pressures and the risk of various sanctions, including rejection. These considerations suggest that an external consultant who is intervening in a confrontational way may have less to lose than an internal consultant, should the interventions prove unsuccessful.

INDIVIDUAL (C-3-1)

Use of a confrontational approach to aid a physically mature adult break out of continued welfare dependency and achieve a norm of autonomy and self-reliance is presented in a casework study by Robinson.[1] Joseph Marks, an unemployed thirty-two-year-old at the time consultation began, was being provided financial support and a variety of reassurances that had the effect of causing him to jump from one job to another without really trying to be successful at any one. After two and one-half years of this pattern, circumstances caused a change of consultants handling his case. Rather than picking up and continuing what had become regular support procedure, the new consultant studied the pattern and saw Marks as "leaning on the agency." In a variety of ways the new consultant confronted Marks with this possibility. These confrontations included the following tactics:

1. The consultant questioned whether the agency was of any worth since there was little evidence that in two and one-half years it had been of help to Marks.
2. Challenged his motivation to put forth the effort to work at a job on a continuing basis.
3. Pushed him to face his dependent outlook and habitual need for reassurance and support.

As a result, Marks began to face up to the prospects of constructing his own reality rather than merely reacting to the external reality created by others. He accepted a job to prove that he could take initiative and stick with the effort and succeeded in maintaining constructive work relationships.

These interventions focused Marks's attention on the weak, dependent crutches that he had been leaning on to get by. Being able to reject them made it possible for him to act in terms of increased self-reliance and he was eventually able to terminate the consultation since it no longer offered him anything he could not provide on his own.

Ellis[2] presents a confrontational approach to personal growth based on the idea that people make problems both "for" and "of" themselves when they embrace norms that are irrational, superstitious, or senseless—that inevitably lead to personal difficulties. The solution is to "unlearn" these invalid norms and standards, and to replace them with others that provide a more realistic basis for living. Ellis indicates that each of the following norms for self-evaluation are inculcated in Western societies but are unjustified by fact.

1. It is a dire necessity for an adult human being to be loved or approved by virtually every significant other person in his or her community.
2. One should be thoroughly competent, adequate, and achieving in all possible respects if one is to consider oneself worthwhile.
3. Certain people are bad, wicked, or villainous and should be severely blamed and punished for their villainy.
4. It is awful and catastrophic when things are not the way one would very much like them to be.
5. Human unhappiness is externally caused and . . . people have little or no ability to control their sorrows and disturbances.
6. If something is or may be dangerous or fearsome one should be terribly concerned about it and should keep dwelling on the possibility of its occurring.
7. It is easier to avoid than to face certain life difficulties and self-responsibilities.
8. One should be dependent on others and needs someone stronger than oneself on whom to rely.
9. One's past history is an all-important determiner of one's present behavior and that because something once strongly affected one's life, it should indefinitely have a similar effect.
10. One should become quite upset over other people's problems and disturbances.
11. There is invariably a right, precise, and perfect solution to human problems and that it is catastrophic if this perfect solution is not found.[3]

Knowing and rejecting these absolute norm-based statements in a cognitive way is one thing; seeing their application to one's own behavior is another. The consultation technique described by Ellis involved confrontation to bring this about.

The effective therapist should continually keep unmasking his patient's past and, especially, his present illogical thinking or self-defeating verbalizations by (a) bringing them forcefully to his attention or consciousness; (b) showing him how they are causing and maintaining his disturbance and unhappiness, (c) demonstrating exactly what the illogical links in his internalized sentences are, and (d) teaching him how to re-think, challenge, contradict, and re-verbalize these (and other similar sentences) so that his internalized thoughts become more logical and efficient.[4]

Ellis's confrontation strategy makes a concerted attack on the client's illogical norms and standards in two main ways: The consultant

(1) . . . serves as a frank counter-propagandist who directly contradicts and denies the self-defeating propaganda and superstitions which the patient has originally learned and which he is now self-instilling.

(2) . . . encourages, persuades, cajoles, and occasionally even insists that the patient engage in some activity (such as his doing something he is afraid of doing) which itself will serve as a forceful counter-propaganda agency against the nonsense he believes.[5]

In this particular approach, the consultant has a well worked out alternative set of norms/standards that "make sense" on rational grounds. Through being confronted with rational alternatives time and again, individuals can be persuaded that it is in their own best interest to calibrate their thinking according to more rational standards.

Cognitive therapy is based on two simple and straightforward notions: 1) people create mental problems for themselves based on faulty thinking and logic, 2) if the faulty thinking and logic are corrected, the mental problem will disappear.

Beck[6] describes the concepts of cognitive therapy and provides examples of their use to aid individuals in resolving personal problems. This kind of intervention is confrontational and centers on personal norms and standards that guide thinking. The norms/standards that are involved are those that guide an individual on what to say and what not to say. Beck calls them rules. The rule within a patient's thinking about him- or herself, as in the following example, is, "It would be awful for someone to form a low opinion of me." Until that rule changes, it controls the client's behavior. We see here how the therapist proceeded to help the client change an evaluative behavioral rule.

Patient: I have to give a talk before my class tomorrow and I'm scared stiff.

Therapist: What are you afraid of?

Patient: I think I'll make a fool of myself.

Therapist: Suppose you do . . . make a fool of yourself. . . . Why is that so bad?

Patient: I'll never live it down.

Therapist: "Never" is a long time. . . . Now look here, suppose they decide you're the worst public speaker that ever lived. . . . Will this ruin your future career?

Patient: No. . . . But it would be nice if I could be a good speaker.

Therapist: Sure it would be nice. But if you flubbed it, would your parents or your wife disown you?

Patient: No. . . . They're very sympathetic.

Therapist: Well, what would be so awful about it?

Patient: I would feel pretty bad.

Therapist: For how long?

Patient: For about a day or two.

Therapist: And then what?

Patient: Then I'd be O.K.

Therapist: So you're scaring yourself just as though your fate hangs in the balance.

Patient: That's right. It does feel as though my whole future is at stake.

Therapist: Now somewhere along the line, your thinking got fouled up . . . and you tend to regard any failure as though it's the end of the world. . . . What you have to do is get your failures labeled correctly—as failure to reach a goal, not as disaster. You have to start to challenge your wrong premises.

In the next appointment, after the patient had given his talk—which, as he predicted, was somewhat disorganized because of his fears—we reviewed his notions about his failure.

Therapist: How do you feel now?

Patient: I feel better . . . but I was down in the dumps for a few days.

Therapist: What do you think now about your notion that giving a fumbling talk is a catastrophe?

Patient: Of course, it isn't a catastrophe.

Therapist: What is it then?

Patient: It's unpleasant, but I will survive.

The patient was coached in changing his notion that a failure is a catastrophe. He found that he had much less anticipatory anxiety prior to his next talk a week later, and felt more comfortable during the talk. At the next session, he completely agreed that he had attached too much importance to what the reactions of his classmates might be. The following interchange occurred:

Patient: I felt much better during my last speech. . . . I guess it's a matter of experience.

Therapist: Did you get some glimmer of the notion that it really isn't vital for the most part what people think of you?

Patient: If I'm going to be a doctor, I've got to make a good impression on my patients.

Therapist: Whether you're a good doctor depends on how well you diagnose and treat your patients, not how good you are at public speaking.

Patient: Well, I know I'm good with patients—and I guess that's what counts.

The rest of the therapy was devoted to challenging his maladaptive attitudes that produced discomfort in other situations. The patient articulated the new attitude he was acquiring when he said: "I really can see now how ridiculous it is to be concerned about perfect strangers. I will never see them again. So what difference does it make what they will think of me?"[7]

The conversation was confrontational because the consultant focused the client's attention on the discrepancy between the client's anticipation of what would happen were he to break the rule and what actually occurred.

GROUP (C-3-2)

Groups whose memberships are relatively stable quickly develop norms/standards to regulate members' conduct. These norms/standards have been looked at from the point of view of a work group, yet there are other more intimate groups where faulty norms/standards are the core issue. One such unit is the family—either the husband-wife pair or the more extended family.

Communication

Valid communication among members is critical to effective family functioning. When communication is free and open, members are able to understand each other's intentions and expectations, and family goals of intimacy and love and personal development for each member can be pursued with greater confidence and prospects of success. One aspect of therapy aids families in replacing invalid communication norms with sound ones.

Satir[8] presents an approach that treats family-wide problems, or problems of any one member, as group-centered communication problems. One or more sessions are conducted with the several family members present.

Here is an example of how the consultant confronts the communication processes of interaction within a family:[9]

Consultant: (to husband) I notice your brow is wrinkled, Ralph. Does that mean you are angry at this moment?

H: I did not know that my brow was wrinkled.

Consultant: Sometimes a person looks or sounds in a way of which he is not aware. As far as you can tell, what were you thinking and feeling just now?

H: I was thinking over what she [his wife] said.

Consultant: What thing that she said were you thinking about?

H: When she said that when she was talking so loud, she wished I would tell her.

Consultant: What were you thinking about that?

H: I never thought about telling her. I thought she would get mad.

Consultant: Ah, then maybe that wrinkle meant you were puzzled because your wife was hoping you would do something and you did not know she had this hope. Do you suppose that by your wrinkled brow you were signalling that you were puzzled?

H: Yeh, I guess so.

Consultant: As far as you know, have you ever been in that same spot before, that is, where you were puzzled by something Alice said or did?

H: Hell, yes, lots of times.

Consultant: Have you ever told Alice you were puzzled when you were?

W: He never says anything.

Consultant: (smiling to Alice) Just a minute, Alice, let me hear what Ralph's idea is of what he does. Ralph, how do you think you have let Alice know when you were puzzled?

H: I think she knows.

Consultant: Well, let's see. Suppose you ask Alice if she knows.

H: This is silly.

These questions confront the husband with the need to explain his personal communication norms and standards. His answers to these questions suggest he and his wife do not have a shared norm of understanding. The consultant continues.

Consultant: (smiling) I suppose it might seem so in this situation, because Alice is right here and certainly has heard what your question is. She knows what it is. I have the suspicion, though, that neither you nor Alice are very sure about what the other expects, and I think you have not developed ways to find out. Alice, let's go back to when I commented on Ralph's wrinkled brow. Did you happen to notice it, too?

W: (complaining) Yes, he always looks like that.

Consultant: What kind of message did you get from that wrinkled brow?

W: He don't want to be here. He don't care. He never talks. Just looks at television or he isn't home.

Consultant: I'm curious. Do you mean that when Ralph has a wrinkled brow that you take this as Ralph's way of saying, "I don't love you, Alice. I don't care about you, Alice"?

W: (exasperated and tearfully) I don't know.

Consultant: Well, maybe the two of you have not yet worked out crystal-clear ways of giving your love and value messages to each other. Everyone needs crystal-clear ways of giving their value messages.

The consultant has summarized for the couple the fact that they do not have shared norms and standards for communication. She has also emphasized the importance of having such norms and standards within the family if mutual understanding and intimacy are to prevail. Next, she checks out the son's communication norms as these apply in communicating with his parents.

Consultant: (to son) What do you know, Jim, about how you give your value messages to your parents?

S: I don't know what you mean.

Consultant: Well, how do you let your mother, for instance, know that you like her, when you are feeling that way? Everyone feels different ways at different times. When you are feeling glad your mother is around, how do you let her know?

S: I do what she tells me to do. Work and stuff.

Consultant: I see, so when you do your work at home, you mean this for a message to your mother that you're glad she is around.

S: Not exactly.

Consultant: You mean you are giving a different message then. Well, Alice, did you take this message from Jim to be a love message? *(to Jim)* What do you do to give your father a message that you like him?

S: (after a pause) I can't think of nothin'.

Consultant: Let me put it another way. What do you know crystal-clear that you could do that would bring a smile to your father's face?

S: I could get better grades in school.

Here the consultant confronts the mother to check out what the son's communications sound like to her.

Consultant: Let's check this out and see if you are perceiving clearly. Do you, Alice, get a loving message from Jim when he works around the house?

W: I s'pose—he doesn't do very much.

Consultant: So from where you sit, Alice, you don't get many love messages from Jim. Tell me, Alice, does Jim have any other ways that he might not now be thinking about that he has that say to you that he is glad you are around?

W: (softly) The other day he told me I looked nice.

Consultant: What about you, Ralph, does Jim perceive correctly that if he got better grades you would smile?

H: I don't imagine I will be smiling for some time.

Consultant: I hear that you don't think he is getting good grades, but would you smile if he did?

H: Sure, hell, I would be glad.

Consultant: As you think about it, how do you suppose you would show it?

W: You never know if you ever please him.

Consultant: We have already discovered that you and Ralph have not yet developed crystal-clear ways of showing value feelings towards one another. Maybe you, Alice, are now observing this between Jim and Ralph. What do you think, Ralph? Do you suppose it would be hard for Jim to find out when he has pleased you?[10]

Numerous consultant-induced confrontations occurred between members of the family as they attempted to explain to one another what each was thinking and feeling, and the discrepancies between what they had intended to communicate and what the receiver actually "got." In addition, the consultant set up confrontations between family members in the interest of testing understandings and clarifying intentions and values. The common denominator of the consultant's interventions was the act of challenging family members' communication norms and standards, which came through as incomplete, provocative, or distorted, and therefore inappropriate for problem solving. In this way, unrecognized distortions were brought into view.

Sexual Inadequacy

Consultant interventions to solve sexual-inadequacy problems of married couples as a unit were expanded in the 1960s through the work of Masters and Johnson. Their working hypothesis was that, regardless of which member of a pair has the major problem, a sexual difficulty is couple-based and can be resolved most successfully by dealing with the couple-as-group rather than with either member separately.

This usually two-week, rapid-treatment intervention takes place in a medical setting under the supervision of a man and a woman as coconsultants. Four steps are involved. One is routine physical examinations. Another involves case-history taking, with the male consultant interviewing the husband, and the female the wife. The third and fourth intervention steps are unique features of the Masters and Johnson approach, and therefore are described here in more detail.

The third step, often lasting several hours, is called Roundtable, and is attended by both consultants and husband and wife. Using primarily case-history data, the purpose of the Roundtable is to compare the client pair by holding up a "professional mirror" in such a way that the pair can see their respective sex-pertinent norms and standards—spoken of as attitudes, values, myths, misunderstandings, and so on—through the consultant's eyes. This is approached in a manner that permits discrepancies between soundly based medical knowledge about sexual norms and standards and personally held or couple-shared beliefs to be recognized for what they are. Since these confrontations are carried out in an objective, nonjudgmental manner, the Roundtable makes it possible for couples to face their actual situation in a more reality-oriented way. Weaknesses and vulnerabilities, when brought to awareness, can be talked about; needed but previously unavailable facts can be presented; accompanying behavioral problems can be resolved in a way that puts the couple on a sounder conceptual footing about sex. According to Masters and Johnson this is a necessary but not sufficient basis for achieving sexual adequacy.

The fourth step is prescriptive in character. The couple is provided with guided "skill practice" in how to become more sexually effective. Though the sequence of skill-practice experience varies with the couple, it (1) advances from undemanding, mildly erotic interactions to more consummatory sexual activity; (2) concentrates first on the husband and next on the wife; (3) shifts from mechanical exercises to functional performance.

Major differences exist between this approach and other strategies for solving sex problems in marriage. Among the more significant are that it (1) is brief; (2) involves nonpsychoanalytic and nonpsychiatric confrontations regarding the sexual norms and standards held by either partner or shared by both; and (3) engages the couple in concrete exercises for the purpose of aiding a husband to gain adequacy, and the wife to become more spontaneously responsive and pleasure seeking. Other problems that hinder sexual adequacy are also dealt with, but the aforementioned are the more central.[11]

INTERGROUP (C-3-3)

In an intergroup situation, confrontational interventions are likely to be successful when the component groups holding different norms/standards share some degree of common organization membership. These conditions are present in many industrial and government situations.

Union-Management

In the following union-management situation conflicting norms and standards had created a perpetual win-lose battle. After the consultant helped management become more aware of its own underlying antagonisms toward the union, he challenged them to shift fundamental attitudes from a win-lose to a problem-solving basis. That confrontation led senior managers to arrange a conference with the international union's business agent to propose a "union-management laboratory," to be conducted by behavioral science consultants. The union officers eventually agreed but actually felt that management's intent in proposing this approach was to "get them," one way or another. So the question remained, "How could such a meeting be of any real merit?"

On the agreed-upon day, the nine most senior union officers and nine ranking managers met with the two consultants. The union group included the international union's business agent, the local's president and vice-president, secretary, and others; the nine management representatives included the general manager, the head of administrative services, the employee relations manager, and others, down to first-line supervisors. At the outset, management and the union got together for a brief general orientation. Consultants outlined the purpose, the ground rules, and the background of the approach. One consultant began by saying, "During these next two days, we wish to explore the problems that are blocking your relationship, to identify them and, if possible, to plan constructive steps for their elimination. Therefore, we are not concerned with issues of bargaining, problems of grievance handling, or attitudes about problems now being arbitrated. Nor are we concerned with personalities. The key concern is with the *character* of the relationship between your two groups and with the shifting away from the unproductive strategies which have characterized relations between the two of you in the past."

One consultant worked with management, the other with the union. At certain times the groups met separately. During these periods the consultants' interventions were primarily designed to challenge the power/authority assumptions each held toward the other, as well as to aid each group to see its own win-lose posture. Meeting separately, each group prepared a description of how it saw its relationship with the other group and developed an image of how it saw the other group's behavior toward itself. These images were written on newsprint for use when the two groups reconvened in a general session.

The union got off to a false start. They were unable to distinguish between the process of behavior as characterized by actions, feelings, and attitudes and the content of problems they were arguing about on a day-by-day basis; consequently, they began discussing issues that had been in controversy at a recently completed bargaining session. After several minutes the consultant intervened to redefine their task. "The present task is to describe the *character,* the quality, of the relationship; that is, typical behavior and attitudes. The task is *not* to debate technical, legal, or operational issues."

The union local's secretary, addressing the business agent, said, "I think we should caucus before we go further."

The consultant immediately commented, "Look, if this cannot be discussed in my presence, then there is little hope that anything can be achieved in the next two days."

There was silence for some moments. Union members exchanged glances, but no one spoke. Finally the business agent began again. Gradually, tediously, the discussion shifted toward a detailed picturing of the union's behavior and attitudes relative to their relationships with management. Participation gradually spread to include all members.

Meeting in a separate room, management launched into the first task with greater assurance, confident that they could quickly put their finger on the real problems. Examining "process" didn't come easy for them either, but from prior training they had grasped the basic concept and were able to develop a strategy of work and move into the task. Then they, too, ran into trouble. Their relationship with the union was so antagonistic that discussion of their own attitudes repeatedly slipped into a discussion of union personalities. The consultant intervened, "As I understand it, you plan to develop your own image first, and then to develop your picture of the union. You are having difficulty doing this. Your own image is repeatedly forgotten and union behavior and personalities keep coming into the picture. Everyone wants to get something off his chest." The consultant recognized the need for an emotional unloading and said, "Let me suggest that you might table your own image for the time being and begin on that of the union. If this moves easier, then stay with it. Having done this, you may find it easier to talk about your own behavior. Alternatively, you might work on both images simultaneously as thoughts about either occur to you, or when parallel behavior is seen by both groups."

This intervention caused management to examine how it was working. "Let's admit it. They are no angels, but neither are we. Let's get a mirror up here where we can see ourselves, and put down what we see, whether we like it or not." Eventually both groups managed to complete this initial "image" task. The results are shown below.

Management

Image of Itself	Image Created by the Union
1. Concern with running the business effectively.	1. (an issue not considered)
2. We show equal concern for production and people.	2. Management is concerned only with production.

3. Autonomous decentralized decision-making body.

3. They follow all headquarters' policies and dictates.

4. Want to learn to work better with international.

4. Opposed to all organized labor.

5. Prefer to deal with independent unions.

5. Prefer to deal with independent unions.

6. Strive continually to upgrade super-vision.

6. . . . .

7. Goal is to establish problem-solving relationship with the international.

7. Their goal is to drive us out of the plant.

8. Maintain flexibility in areas concerning our "rights to manage."

8. Management wants power and control over every aspect of a worker's life—they are "fatherly dictators."

9. We are inconsistent in how we treat independents and the international.

9. They treat the independents one way and us another.

10. Honest and above-board in our dealings.

10. They are underhanded and lie.

The Union

Image Created by Management	Image of Itself
1. Little concern shown for the profit picture of the company.	1. Concerned primarily with *people*.
2. They are skillful and have intense pride.	2. Proud of our craft and skills.
3. Controlled by a scheming professional leader and a minority clique.	3. We are governed by the will of the total membership.
4. Legalistic and rigid in interpreting contract.	4. Approach problems and contract with open mind.
5. The union pushes every grievance to the point of arbitration. When they want to establish a precedent, they want to arbitrate.	5. Do not want to have to arbitrate every grievance; we want to work these out with management.
6. They want to prove they can "win"— they don't care what, just so it is something.	6. We want good relations and to solve our problems with management.
7. They want to co-manage. They want a say in every decision we make.	7. We want a voice in those areas that directly concern us.
8. The union wants the training of their people back under their control.	8. We want joint control of the training and apprenticeship program.
9. The union does not communicate internally. Their people don't know what is going on.	9. Our people always know what is going on and what important union business is coming up.
10. Union is concerned only with seniority and job security. They are not concerned with our problems.	10. We want greater consideration for our skills and what we can contribute to the plant.

Many hours were spent working from these two sets of images toward a diagnosis and understanding of (1) basic attitudes and (2) the discrepancies existing between them. The consultants intervened frequently to challenge participants' readiness to find explanations based upon feelings of hostility and tension rather than to search for understanding based upon a more objective view of the situation.[12] Eventually these confrontations produced a "controlled" explosion, after which a problem-solving basis of cooperation was possible.

Headquarters-Field Interrelationships

A second example of confrontation, also at the intergroup level, involved a company headquarters division of manufacturing and those responsible for running one of its major plants located thirty miles away. The headquarters division was headed by a vice-president; a general manager ran the plant. These two had gotten increasingly out of "tune" with each other over the years until they had reached a nearly total impasse. The problem of their relationship might mistakenly have been seen as a power/authority standoff. Their differences arose from two quite distinct ways of life, two sets of norms and standards for guiding action. The headquarters "culture" valued efficiency, modernization, youth-in-management, and competitive spirit while the plant "culture" rested on tradition, seniority with loyalty, compliance, and discipline based on a deeply rooted organizational paternalism, with managers expected to pursue a lifelong plant career rather than using it as a ladder into headquarters management.

The vice-president of manufacturing and the ten headquarters people who reported to him, and the plant's general manager and the twelve who reported to him convened for a three-day period at a neutral location to study their relationship. The first task was for each group to describe what a "really good" relationship between headquarters and the plant would be like. After recording their thoughts on newsprint, the groups reconvened and posted their results on the wall. The two descriptions of a sound relationship were quite similar; differences were discussed and resolved.

Thereafter, each group described what the relationship was *really* like as seen from its particular vantage point. Newsprint sheets were again posted. The relationship described as viewed from headquarters was "totally" different from the relationship pictured from the plant's point of view. These dramatic divergences stimulated heated exchanges. The consultants, one working with each group, had to intervene constantly in confrontational terms to focus issues and to identify rationalizations, justifications, denials, and projections. The consultants created a "controlled" explosion by keeping the discussion focused on issues rather than personalities. Only by working through these defense stratagems was it possible to puncture the status quo and unfreeze the relationship sufficiently to create a shift toward mutual problem solving. A more accurate picture of the present relationship gradually emerged that permitted both groups to identify the many problems that constituted barriers to cooperation and progress.[13] Task forces and other arrangements were set in motion to concentrate effort on solving identified issues.

ORGANIZATION (C-3-4)

Personnel Practices

An organization development intervention that is targeted to shifting organization norms from their current level of operation to a new, expected level of operation is provided by Jamison.[14]

The background for understanding this approach is the premise that inequitable treatment is so widespread in present-day American institutions that two basic modes of discrimination are uniformly present. Black/white minority discrimination and male/female discrimination continue to pose problems for individuals and organizations. A high degree of motivation is inherent in solving these problems by virtue of legal requirements as well as considerations of fairness and equity. These two sources of discrepancy between what is and what should be are utilized as focal concerns for initiating a total organization change effort.

The change strategy is seen in a series of axiomatic statements that depict the longitudinal sequence of effort underlying this approach.

1. External consultants working with organizational personnel carry out a tentative or provisional diagnosis of circumstances prevailing in the organization with regard to black/white and male/female issues of equal treatment. This is through interviewing people at all organization levels.

2. Key executives at the presidential or vice-presidential level are initially involved during the consultant's second or third visit when interview findings as to black/white and male/female issues are reviewed with them and discrepancies between what is and what should be are brought to their attention.

3. During this discussion, the concept of a five-year effort to bring needed changes from what is to what should be is introduced and the broad strategy for bringing the shift about is reviewed.

4. Step 3 is repeated with operational heads; other ways of getting information distributed are utilized so that the project is understood throughout the organization.

5. Since the discrepancies between what is and what should be cannot be presumed to be within the awareness of organization members, a period of awareness training is essential for bringing these discrepancies into bolder relief. Participation is sufficiently large to reach a critical mass for the purpose of movement and change.

    Awareness training is in 20 hours of participation focused first on woman/man issues. An additional 20 hours is applied to black/white issues, making for a total of 40 hours of contact training for purposes of developing insights as to the discrepancies that prevail.

6. A research and study group is formed as an organizational diagonal slice. This group might be made up of a senior vice-president, the EEO manager,

the head of personnel, line managers, women and men, minorities, and clerical employees. The research and study group develops expertise in identifying, in precise detail, the actual situation as it currently prevails, particularly with regard to departures between stated policy and actual practice as well as creating conditions under which it is competent to make recommendations along with carefully constructed rationales of what prevails when the planning group completes a five-year plan. It is responsible for research and study on all policies and practices where discrimination can be expected to be present: recruitment and selection, training and development, promotion and transfer, organization structure, performance evaluation, career planning, mentoring, external affairs, salary administration, and affirmative action.

7. The Planning Group is composed of key executives whose authorization is required for the development and approval of policies with regard to all organizational practices that impact on these two discrimination issues.

8. Because essentially all issues of personnel practice are impacted by these two types of discrimination, it is virtually assured that no human practice of significance will be left untouched once the policy positions to be achieved have been identified.

9. Once identified, it is essential for an education phase to be included so that those who implement policy-in-practice can do so with efficiency and skill.

10. Monitoring of the shift from one set of norms to another during the anticipated five-year period is prearranged on a quarterly basis the first year and at six-month intervals thereafter.

The approach entails organization development. It is centered upon organization norms as these are reflected in policies and practices that are more or less uniform ways of doing things. It is confrontational because the status quo is brought under challenge by demonstrating that practices, as they prevail, are discrepant from legal requirements and even from policies that are espoused but not followed.

The limitations of this kind of intervention are found in the fact that it takes personnel practices as its primary concern and touches on operational aspects only insofar as they directly influence the personnel function. In other words, there are many operational problems that may remain unaffected by this approach. For example, an organization may be confronted with an early-quitting problem, a safety problem, a quality-control problem, or a waste-management problem. These are all important issues that, to a significant degree, are only indirectly related to male/female or black/white discrimination. The discrimination problems can be resolved, but other serious and sometimes debilitating problems will remain.

Another limitation of this approach is that it provides no direct or systematic training related to the theory and skill for executing effective relationships. While the above report mentions that problematic behaviors are identified and alternatives taught, it does not follow that the newly learned behaviors are necessarily consistent with sound behavioral science principles of human effectiveness.

Organization Myths

Ill-founded and untested mythical beliefs influence organizational behavior just as do any other organization-based norms and standards. They may have detrimental effects on an individual's, as well as on an organization's, functioning unless they are identified and rejected as inappropriate and counterproductive.

Bradford and Harvey present several examples of organization myths and outline a kind of discrepancy intervention useful in eliminating them. The following is an example of a belief that later was proven to be a myth:

> *Consultant:* What are some things that block you from getting your job done?
>
> *Client:* Well, for one thing, it's no use trying anything new here, because somebody would block it. It's just not allowed.
>
> *Consultant:* Is this what others think? Have you talked to other people about this belief?
>
> *Client:* I'm sure everybody thinks the same thing. I've never talked to anybody about it because it's so obvious that everybody thinks the same way.
>
> *Consultant:* What makes it obvious?
>
> *Client:* Well, you don't see many new things tried here.
>
> *Consultant:* Have you tried something different, or have you seen someone else try something new?
>
> *Client:* Well, yes. So and so installed a whole new process of working in her department.
>
> *Consultant:* Did it work and was it allowed?
>
> *Client:* Yes, it did. But I'm sure that was an exception.[15]

Other examples include challenging the client who embraces organization myths regarding the presumed high risk of asking questions, the dangers of being wrong, and so on.

The authors recommend the use of external consultants to help identify myths, or of insiders who are sufficiently skeptical not to accept myths without questioning their veracity. The external or internal consultant's particular usefulness is in being able to identify myths through an open-ended interview survey, carried out through several successive organizational levels. Such interviews involve two steps: (1) questions designed to aid individuals in describing positive and negative aspects of the organization, and (2) questions to check out whether what has been reported as true can be objectively verified.

Once in hand, interview findings that point to the existence of a myth are returned to small groups of interviewees, preferably in boss-subordinate family groupings. The myths can then be discussed either with those who presently accept them or by those who dispute their validity. For example, the proposition

"Bosses don't want to be asked questions" can be directly tested when subordinates who believe this are grouped with the bosses who can prove, if they have the evidence, that this is a myth. If the myth is convincingly shown to be false, this is one kind of success. If, however, the "myth" is shown to be true, a problem is identified to those who are in a position to begin solving it.

LARGER SOCIAL SYSTEM (C-3-5)

The norms and standards that people adhere to can be a cause of maladaptive behavior. Our first example occurred in an organized work setting in which forces from the larger society were key in confronting internal problems. The studies that follow show how such norms of conduct can be changed via "temporary" communities, in which individuals reveal their norms and standards through interactions with others and then learn to live by new, more satisfactory norms.

Remedying Poor Service

Confrontational interventions have been employed in the community-building processes of Albania: elected representatives of consumers are allowed to confront those responsible for the delivery of services to them. Confrontations focus upon shortcomings that have occurred and corrective actions that should be taken.

The selection below involves some machine-shop mechanics who were assigned in a consultant capacity to investigate and rectify unsatisfactory service at the local hospital that machine-shop personnel and their families use as needed.

> The workers of Hospital No. 2 in Tirana, which was our first objective, extended a good reception to our group and did their best to create all the necessary facilities for us to discharge the task we were charged with. We had not come here to find anyone at fault but to help make the service towards patients as good as possible. Since the work in the hospital has a specific of its own, we were helped by the workers in carrying out our control. This was, in fact, a joint control. This helped us to take up key problems and draw valuable conclusions both as regards serving the patients as well as behaving in a cultured way towards them. We discussed our tasks and conclusions with all the workers employed by the hospital. They expressed many valuable opinions and helped us delve deeper into the causes of the shortcomings we had observed. Together with the collective of the hospital we drew up a very detailed program of work with dates and names of persons who would carry out these tasks. On this occasion, the group of worker control drew up a number of suggestions and remarks for the Health Sector of the Executive Committee of the Regional People's Council and for the Public Health Department of the Ministry of Public Health and Sanitation.
>
> All tasks left behind by the worker control team are binding to the administration of the institution which has been controlled. Therefore, at the

end of the time limit set, another group of worker control went to the hospital again to verify how the tasks left behind by the first group have been carried out.[16]

The authors also describe how they and other group members intervened in a catering supplies enterprise and a creche, both of which had been performing below par in servicing their plant and the wider community. As in the hospital, their approach here was basically confrontational in focusing the attention of administrators and others on problems producing inconvenience to consumers. While the mode was confrontational, there are also prescriptive elements in Albania's control mechanisms to ensure that "recommendations" are in fact put into operation.

Drug Addiction

Synanon, a live-in community approach for dealing with drug addiction, is an intervention strategy designed to further personal growth and social effectiveness, thus making dependence on drugs unnecessary. Part of the reason that Synanon works is because of its insistence on self-responsibility as an important aspect of change. The program is based on two different sets of norms and standards: one set applies when participating in the "game"; the other applies in doing the work expected of all members.

The Synanon Game's confrontational character and its basic assumptions are illustrated in the following. Imagine several people coming together for the game. While the game takes place in a group setting as part of a broader institutional culture, what is studied is the distinctive reactions of each individual.

> The position of the game seems to be that anything a person already knows about himself is probably false and irrelevant and is certainly misused to maintain his narrow, unchallenging and less than completely satisfying life. . . . Any valid self-knowledge will survive the acid bath of doubt the game will put him through. We want to shake his assumption about life and himself, to test and question, not justify and excuse. The usual manipulations just won't work. . . .

The game's norm is "take nothing for granted; challenge anything and everything a person does or says." This norm violates many customary social-convention norms, such as "be polite, friendly, and keep your distance," behind which members may be hiding. Breaking through protective self-deceptions is a basic feature of the game.

> We want people in the game to examine what they actually *do* in their lives, not what they think they do, and examine the *values they actually live by,* not the ones they mouth. Rationalizations, cover-ups, "I forgot" are spotted as lies by the world's greatest experts in lying and are probed and examined until the person is forced to see what he is really doing. . . .[17]

Enright describes how the game operates. Ten to fifteen members from the larger Synanon community meet for up to three and one-half hours. The membership is rarely the same in any two sessions. Two ground rules are employed: (1) no physical violence, and (2) no drugs. Players are expected to try to tell the truth about themselves and others. Attempts are made to strip away every mask that is put on, to clear away self-deception, and, in a sense, to drive a person out of every less-than-authentic position he or she assumes. Even friendships that a person might use to find support are left at the door.

Compared with the game's direct confrontation of personal and group norms, the broader Synanon community operates in accordance with different norms and standards. As a community person each Synanon member is expected to be cooperative, civil, responsible, constructive, positive, and self-controlled. He or she is expected to act in a mature manner at all times; in other words, the community norms are "ideal." Thus the game and the community pull in opposite directions, both of which support growth and development.

Although Synanon started as a strategy for coping with problems of drug addiction, it is important to realize that its game sessions are sometimes attended by people for whom participation involves self-learning for its own sake, rather than learning for help with a drug problem. The game's mental health value is seen in the following:

> From this point of view, the game is to emotional life what exercise is to physical life; a place to challenge and push myself beyond the relatively low demands of life. Because I jog or play tennis regularly I feel better in normal daily physical activity and have an extra reserve of stamina available for emergencies such as running for a bus. If I play the game weekly, hold my own against its spirited and exaggerated attack, and give as good as I get, I am readier for the emotional emergencies of life, and the usual emotional demands are child's play.[18]

The power of the game is in assisting an individual to recognize his or her own values and assumptions as to rules for living.

Alternative Culture Norms/Standards

The term *alternate culture* generally describes a culture that is destined—or so its proponents believe—to replace the established culture. Values within the two cultural systems are quite different, and at many critical points are incompatible.

Radical therapy denotes a consultation approach calculated to bring about a shift from establishment to alternate culture. Radical therapy groups are found in various cities and maintain a loose association with one another.

At any given time, client problems in this form of therapy occur in three main areas: need for legal help in dealing within the established culture, help with drug problems, and issues relating to sex. The underlying thesis of radical therapy is that these problems arise from faults inherent in the establishment culture. Only by changing the prevailing culture can such problems eventually be overcome.

. . . The old culture relies on drug use, confinement, coercion, and punitive conditioning to force people out of deviance, drug use, depression, or confusion. Thus, when a person in transition comes under the control of a conventional therapy center, the results are apt to be brutalizing and to aggravate the initial anger and confusion as a result of the conflict of values and goals between the individual and the treatment center. Alternate services are needed because support for personal growth, temporary shelter, and alternative living and working arrangements are a means of avoiding such dehumanizing treatment.

The collective for alternative service, crisis intervention, or radical therapy is important not only to the people who come for help. The structure and process of the alternate group also act as a laboratory for the basic issues of how a new culture deals with its day-to-day business of working and living. Staff members can use their personal sensitivity and experience of crises to help in defining and establishing guidelines for relationships within a new culture. The social change movement received its earliest lessons in the structure of our society and government by confronting them directly, and now we have turned some of our energies to defining and practicing fair and human relationships among ourselves. Psychedelics and new therapies have led to a new psychological sophistication, to go with the movement's economic and structural critique of our culture. Communes, group marriages, consciousness-raising groups, extended family living, and great mobility under extreme pressure have also exposed problems, even created some new ones, as well as building new methods as for dealing with them as they arise. Intimacy and openness elicit fears and conflicts which traditional families rarely experience, and our upbringing in such families has given us few tools with which to face these situations. Radical therapists are called on to help communities learn to incorporate such experiences into their lives.

Although radical therapists may only be a half a step ahead of their brothers and sisters, that half-step may be crucial to a new community racked with personal pain. The role of a radical therapist or alternate service is thus to be both explorer and educator, seeker and helper.[19]

Some aspects of the alternate culture's value system and how it would change the fabric of the larger social system are indicated below.

The myth of one love, for example, forms the basis for such monogamous systems as marriage and going steady. It is also a metaphor for the basic independent relationship, where appropriate behavior by one leads to the fulfillment of all needs by the other. To question this myth, to assert that there can be many loves, or at least a few, perhaps even simultaneously, and that a dependent relationship is unnecessary and ultimately frustrating, implies that marriages are unnecessary, even undesirable. Living with someone, or living alone, even the raising of children by one parent instead of two or in a small communal situation, all become viable alternatives. Whatever the counter-culture is, it is a discussion of the moral issues of our time, and the search for new alternative modalities for self-expression.

As the individual examines the social obstacles to moral growth, the relationship between personal and social changes become evident. Young people are close to the truth. To question the dependence assumption, to challenge the internalized authority-parent figures, to violate the social authority of the family and school in an attempt to survive—these actions threaten the viability of the entire social system at its roots. Economics, the political structure, attempts to remove moral examination of the self and to institutionalize morality through laws and the legal system are all extensions of the basic structure of the society, the family.

Why interventions help in bringing about this form of escape from the establishment culture is suggested by the following.

The usefulness of therapy to young people must come through its ability to assist in their struggles for liberation. When therapists accept young people as their clients, they are making a political move. To view their problems from the fragmented and incoherent perspective of the society— that is, as problems of the individual, who must have some basic deficiency or inadequacy—is to do them an injustice. Granted, young people's behavior strategies may be self-defeating and destructive, and the first step may be to help the youth regain some sense of self and personal power and responsibility; this is no more than helping him regain what the society is trying to take away. But if therapy stops with the attempt to help a person adjust his behavior to his social situation as it is, then the root of the problem will persist, and more young people will appear with "problems." Eventually this minimal treatment will fail of its own impoverishment. Young people will find it meaningless and irrelevant, just as they have many other forms of mystification and obfuscation. Therapy must make radical social changes, as well as radical personal ones. Support groups must be developed, consciousness raising processes for the young must be started, alternative institutions must be examined carefully and thoughtfully for their potential contributions and detractions to the gradual development of political and economic bases for young people.

Effective therapy will move the individual beyond the narrow confines of his own internalizations toward new alternatives in his life style and new possibilities in the social institutions he will help to form. The internalization of the family and dependency assumptions will be the two issues confronting psychotherapists working with adolescents. The demystification of love, sexuality, and aggression will only come about when the internalized punishment-and-reward system is destructured; otherwise the individual will not "understand" what is meant. Avoiding the tendency to atomize adolescents and their problems will make the therapist aware that, as with members of other politically oppressed groups in therapy, successful change implies radical social change as a necessary outcome, and that the problems of young people are indeed the unresolved moral questions of the entire society—the questions of what is right, and what is wrong.[20]

Delinquency

In contrast, the underlying strategy of an experimental intervention calculated to reduce what is legally defined as "delinquency" is described below. The setting is Provo, Utah.

. . . Although a "bad" home may have been instrumental at some early phase in the genesis of a boy's delinquency, it must be recognized that it is now other delinquent boys, not his parents, who are current sources of support and identification. Any attempts to change him, therefore, would have to view him as more than an unstable isolate without a meaningful reference group. And, instead of concentrating on changing his parental relationships, they would have to recognize the intrinsic nature of his membership in the delinquent system and direct treatment to him as a part of that system.[21]

Fourteen- to eighteen-year-old boys who had repeatedly been offenders lived at home but became members of a reformation project in preference to incarceration. The program relied on complex strategy features, several aspects of which are unique. Under the supervision of an adult leader, boys met in ten-person discussion groups once a day and on weekends. A premise underlying the use of peer-based discussion groups is described as follows.

A treatment system will be most effective if the delinquent peer group is used as the means of perpetuating the norms and imposing the sanctions of the system. The peer group should be seen by delinquents as the primary source of help and support. The traditional psychotherapeutic emphasis on transference relationships is not considered the most vital factor in effecting change.[22]

The core of the intervention methodology involved the peer group in defining norms and setting standards which, when adhered to, led away from self-defeating cycles of delinquency toward nondelinquent behavior.

. . . A successful program must be viewed by delinquents as possessing four important characteristics: (1) a social climate in which delinquents are given the opportunity to examine and experience alternatives related to a realistic choice between delinquent or nondelinquent behavior; (2) the opportunity to declare publicly to peers and authorities a belief or disbelief that they can benefit from a change in values; (3) a type of social structure which will permit them to examine the role and legitimacy (for their purposes) of authorities in the treatment system; and (4) a type of treatment interaction which, because it places major responsibilities on peer group decision-making, grants status, and recognition to individuals, not only for their own successful participation in the treatment interaction, but for their willingness to involve others.[23]

Adherence to nondelinquent norms was reinforced in several significant ways. One was that boys were expected to live by the wider society's norms and standards and function as responsible community members.

. . . During the winter, those boys who were still in school continued to attend. Those who were not in school were employed in a paid city work program. On Saturdays, all boys worked. Late in the afternoon of each day boys left school or work, came to Pinehill, and attended a group meeting.

After the meetings were completed, they returned to their own homes. During the summer every boy attended an all-day program which involved work and group discussions. On rare occasions a boy might work apart from the others if he had a full-time job.[24]

Another major reinforcement mechanism was that a program member who resisted the reformation group norms was rejected by either his peers or the staff, depending on the severity of the resistance. Rejection was through extra work, detention over weekends, or being exported from the program to a reform school. Power/authority constituted an important backup to ensure the development of new norms and standards as a method of cycle breaking.

The consultant strategy in the Pinehill meetings was to provide a model for members to confront each other regarding their problem behavior. When they were doing this effectively, the consultant would not comment but remained ready to do so at any pertinent moment. This is demonstrated in the following.

Sam: Mr. G [group leader] pisses me off. I keep askin' him what I should do an' he won't tell me.

George: Isn't that what your mother does—always front for you? You want him to do that?

Phil: Yeah, that's somethin' Sam has to decide.

Sam: What do you mean?

George: Can't you see that you don't think for yourself?

Sam: (shouts) Well, fuck! If you want me to do something different you got to tell me what to do. If I don't know how, how the fuck can I change?

Leader: You want me to be your mama? I'm trying to tell you that you're somebody and should learn to think like somebody.

Phil: You're Sam, not some punk that everybody tells how to live.

Even thought the exchange was painful to Sam, it revealed attention to him as a person and respect for his individuality—responses he had obviously not had in the past. His remarks, even though emotional, may also have revealed a desire to learn more about himself. The responses of the other boys, in turn, indicated a respect for that desire.[25]

The significance of peers engaging in constructive learning from one another is revealed in the following comments from boys who were interviewed concerning crucial aspects of the reformation program. One sentiment expressed repeatedly was that peers were of greater help than staff.

"Boys know more about themselves than grownups do. The first couple of months don't do any good. Then you find out that the meetin' knows you better than you know yourself. They can tell when you're lyin'. They can tell you things about yourself, an' find out what your problems are."

"What can the group leader do that helps the most?"

"To shut up an' let the boys figure things out."

"Mr. ——— suggested a lot of things that helped, like we should check each other out when we're workin'! An' he made an overall summary so that you got the main thing of what the meetin' was about. But I jus' don't like to listen to adults lecturing . . . it is boring as hell."

"All the help I got, I got from other guys in the meetin'—nine other guys instead of one stupid adult talkin' to you. I felt they done the same things I done, an' know exactly how I feel, an' why I do them things."[26]

The following observations are key to understanding the Provo intervention.

1. Prior to delinquency most individuals have learned socially responsible norms as a basis for self-conduct.

2. Once delinquent acts appear, the person is unlikely to think of himself as delinquent.

3. Through reformation-group confrontation discussions, the person is "forced" to recognize his antisocial assumptions.

4. Such discussions also provide positive alternative models for socially responsible normative behavior that can help the person avoid future delinquency.

5. Reformation-group sanctions reinforce the readiness to achieve according to prosociety norms.

6. Being successful in work or school reinforces personal effectiveness in meeting legitimate social expectations.

Unlike a classroom type of learning situation or a clinical treatment situation, the Provo program enabled the boys to identify and reject their old self-defeating patterns of behavior as well as to acquire insight and skill in practicing and internalizing new behavior patterns. The consultants point out that, for many, progress was made toward socially effective behavior, although the program was not universally successful.

An experiment similar to the Provo experiment is reported by Stephenson and Scarpitti.[27] The strategies of this intervention had been unfolding since 1951, although the particular version described occurred in the early 1960s. Delinquents, sixteen to seventeen years old, living at home, were placed on probation, predicated on their taking part in the Essexfields Program. They engaged in "total" work and group-discussion activity. Since all worked together in a yard maintenance project, work behavior was relevant for examination in the daily ninety-minute discussions. These discussions were each centered on a particular boy—either self-nominated or nominated by others—who became the agreed topic.

A new boy would be introduced to the group meeting by reviewing his personal delinquency history. Other boys would question, cross-examine, and probe to uncover the unvarnished truth. The thrust of the meetings was to create the kind of environment that would lead each boy to give up his antisocial ways and accept the norms of established society. When evidence was available that he was doing this, as well as helping other boys do the same, he became a candidate for release from the program. A fundamental characteristic in this intervention as well as in the Provo experiment was the deliberate decision by those in charge not to rely directly on their own power/authority as the means of enforcing obedience to established norms. In place of it, the power/authority to exercise initiative and to enforce norms and standards was in the hands of the boys themselves. Staff interventions of an authority-obedience character were rarely needed. Occasionally graduates of the program returned as consultants to the group either as catalytic facilitators or for confrontation or prescription.

Mental Illness

In the "therapeutic community" described by Jones[28] for treating individuals severely disturbed by anxiety, patients are subjected not only to catalytic interventions but also to significant confrontational and acceptant interventions. Members of the entire hospital community: psychiatrists, social workers, nurses, occupational instructors, and resettlement counselors, as well as other persons who have been admitted for therapy, participate in the treatment process. Such interventions are intended to facilitate a shift from norms that project weakness drawn from disabling anxiety toward norms promoting a self-reliant capacity for work and family-oriented relationships. As at Synanon, one norm of the therapeutic community is that everyone works. Each participant's attitudes toward work, supervision, and other members of the community are commented on in a discussion group.

In addition, participants may choose to prepare a written psychodrama that is later acted out with the help of others. Psychodramatic activity is more in the direction of cathartic tension releasing to improve morale/cohesion than for uncovering and working through unexamined norms and standards.

Confrontations may be initiated by the consultant or, based on the consultant as role model, by any participant. For example,

> Dr. Baker now asked the new patients in the group to stand up and introduce themselves. All six had arrived the day before and had been shown around the workshops and had met their doctors for an initial interview. One of these new patients was asked to take the place of Mr. S. Mr. W., a patient with a long record of unemployment, did so. Dr. Baker now turned to the patients and asked what sort of questions he should put to Mr. W. Having been briefed he asked Mr. W. what his last job had been. Mr. W. said he had done heavy work in the engineering trade but had had to give it up.

Was the "why" of his giving up on heavy work related to being physically incapacitated or not?

> "Why did you find it difficult?" asked the doctor. Mr. W. replied that it had been dull and boring so he had tried other work but it had always been the same story.

So it was a value-related reason. The consultant and other members of the group began gathering data from this "area" of Mr. W. and relating his responses to possibilities they saw for placing him as a working member.

Dr. Baker asked again, "Well, what would you like to do here?" Mr. W. replied, "I don't want to do anything." Dr. Baker then turned to the patients one of whom suggested that Mr. W. should be allowed to wander around the workshops where he would probably settle down in one. Another, however, pointed out that Mr. W. had been around once, and if after further wandering he still did not settle, we had the same problem. Another suggested that the community should find out what his interests were because maybe he wanted a job where he could use his brain as well as his hands. So Dr. Baker put these questions to Mr. W. who replied, "Yes, I've been a fur dresser and I liked that." "And why did you give that up?" asked Dr. Baker. Mr. W. replied, "Because I liked night work and when that ended I did not like the same job on the day shift, I don't like mixing with people."

By now Mr. W. had expressed what presently was of key personal value to him. This value might be summarized as "Touch Me Not." As group members discussed further how Mr. W. might fit into the therapeutic community, *their* contrasting value—which, as a norm, might be expressed as "People who live and work together should mix together"—emerged.

A patient then suggested that we should place him in one of the workshops in the morning and send him to the local Government training center at Waddon in the afternoon where he could be tried out in a trade. Dr. Baker remarked, "But we don't yet know if he is suited for a trade." A patient now stated, "We don't usually send new patients to Waddon—he might not be suited for it temperamentally." Another patient suggested that physical training was the best activity we had. Dr. Baker asked Mr. W. about physical training but the latter replied that he would not last an hour at this. Dr. Baker then asked another patient, Mr. C., who had been in the hospital for some time, to come out and explain the work therapy to Mr. W. The latter was told that he ought to mix more with other people at work. Mr. W. replied, "But I don't want to mix with other people." Mr. C. answered this with, "You meet people at the local, don't you?" "Don't go to pubs," said Mr. W. bluntly. Mr. C. responded with, "Well, I suggest that you go and look at the occupation shops for a week." "I always keep myself to myself," Mr. W. stubbornly replied. Mr. C. said in explanation, "That's part of your neurosis. You must give things a trial and try to change, for after all you can keep yourself to yourself even in the workshops." Dr. Baker thanked Mr. C. who returned to his seat in the audience.

Other members of the group, who did not share Mr. W.'s "Touch Me Not" value, discussed its rationale and certain of its consequences with him in a way that pointed up the contrasts between their norms and the ones he was trying to "import" into the community. Even though Mr. W., at this moment, may have been a long way from adopting the norms and standards he was hearing, the confrontation at least set up a comparison basis for what until then had been his private world of personal values.

A patient now queried, "Does he want to mix with people?" Mr. W. replied, "I'll mix but I won't talk, but if an argument starts then I'll join in." A patient questioned, "Is he afraid of talking in case he makes a fool of himself?" Dr. Baker suggested, "Well, go ahead and ask him." Mr. W. agreed that there might be something in this. "Perhaps he's learnt he gets people's backs up when he talks," suggested another patient. Dr. Baker agreed that the discussion related Mr. W.'s work difficulties to his personality defects and that if these could be remedied it would be much easier for Mr. W. to find satisfactory employment. He went on to point out that Mr. W. had already taken an active part in the community life of the Unit by his performance, that he had been given an opportunity to talk without being misunderstood or being laughed at, and that perhaps he would go on improving.

The hospital consultant, addressing the group as a whole, made his own concluding points. While this was a calculated prescriptive intervention, Mr. W. might "hear" part of it, particularly if these general comments connected, for example, to what he was able to remember experiencing as a child.

In conclusion Dr. Baker pointed out that there was general agreement that no one liked the idea of being compelled to work. Indeed, many patients were over-sensitive to any suggestions of compulsion. This was related to experiences in their early lives when compelled to do things to please an aggressive father or over-anxious mother. The patients were encouraged to review their past work history and their patterns of behaviour which had led to failure, and then to use our workshop facilities to try and create new and healthier patterns.[29]

To illustrate the pertinence of Dr. Baker's comment on patients' earlier life experiences, here is an instance of an "aggressive father" and an "over-anxious mother" reacting in contradictory fashion to an action by their young son. The incident is described by a group-therapy client in another setting. The client is now aged twenty-four and the incident that he recalls is said to have occurred when he was of preschool age.

Consultant: Spell it out.

Henry: It's like . . . everything Mother says is irrelevant . . . and most of what Father says is frightening. So where are you?

I was playing with some matches once. I set some leaves on fire in the backyard. Father said the police would come and take me away. He said they would take me to Juvenile Hall. Then Mother came out and put her arms around me and told me I was her darling angel. Then Father began yelling. I think he got mad at her and forgot all about me. I remember, later that evening, he gave me a present. I never understood it. He was smiling and cheerful like what happened earlier had never happened.

But I couldn't stand all the shouting in the house. There was always shouting, and my mother was always afraid, always crying and talking about heaven and Jesus and hugging me and looking off into space and not even knowing she was holding me.

Consultant: You must have felt terribly frustrated.

Henry: Frustrated, yes. And afraid. I felt afraid of people. I've always been very shy.[30]

Jones's strategy of creating a community in which all members, professionals and participants alike, accept responsibility for intervening confrontationally is to help client-members recognize and reject norms and standards of conduct that run counter to health. Group-norm pressures coexist with the supportive character of the community when an individual reveals his or her "real" problems, whether in discussion groups or in psychodrama.

Summary

For a confrontational intervention to have a significant impact, it is insufficient merely to challenge existing norms and standards that serve to regulate actions between groups. Even though two groups may agree that they have an unsatisfactory relationship, change is unlikely to occur unless current behaviors are replaced by more cooperative ones. Thus it is important to suggest "new" norms/standards as possible replacements for the old ones.

The family-as-unit is likely to be the focus of many emotionally charged experiences. Unfulfilled expectations can result in unhappiness, frustration, and anxiety. Interventions to aid family members in examining their norms/standards and in replacing them when invalid are likely to be confrontational in character, particularly when the norms/standards have become frozen and habitual, so that people are unable to shift them merely by talking with each other.

The Synanon game, radical therapy, the residential approaches to delinquency, and the therapeutic-community strategies appear to be based on similar approaches for inducing change. The underlying proposition is that change is unlikely to occur unless the norms and standards upon which personal behavior rests are brought sharply into focus and invalid aspects of one's orientations are modified or replaced by new norms and standards that permit more productive living. In each of these approaches, confrontation is the tool used to help the client identify these invalid aspects and explore alternative systems and their possible consequences.

Notes

1. V. P. Robinson, "A Discussion of Two Case Records Illustrating Personality Change," in J. Taft, ed., *Family Casework and Counseling: A Functional Approach* (Philadelphia: University of Pennsylvania Press, 1948), pp. 150–64.

2. A. Ellis, *Reason and Emotion in Psychotherapy* (New York: Lyle Stuart, 1962). Reprinted by permission.

3. Ibid., pp. 61–87.

4. Ibid., pp. 58–59.

5. Ibid., p. 95.

6. A. T. Beck, M.D., *Cognitive Therapy and the Emotional Disorders* (New York: New American Library, 1976), pp. 250–56.

7. Ibid., pp. 250–52.
8. V. M. Satir, *Conjoint Family Therapy*, rev. ed. (Palo Alto, Calif.: Science and Behavior Books, Inc., 1967). Reprinted by permission of the author and publisher.
9. The client family members are (H) husband, (W) wife, and (S) son.
10. Satir, *Conjoint Family Therapy*, pp. 97–100.
11. W. H. Masters and V. E. Johnson, *Human Sexual Inadequacy* (Boston: Little, Brown & Co., Inc., 1970).
12. R. R. Blake, J. S. Mouton, and R. L. Sloma, "The Union-Management Intergroup Laboratory: Strategies for Resolving Intergroup Conflict," *Journal of Applied Behavioral Science* 1, no. 1 (1965): 25–27.
13. R. R. Blake, H. A. Shepard, and J. S. Mouton, *Managing Intergroup Conflict in Industry* (Houston: Gulf Publishing Co., 1964).
14. K. Jamison, "Affirmative Action Program—Springboard for a Total Organizational Change Effort," *OD Practitioner* 10, no. 4 (1978): 1–8.
15. L. P. Bradford and J. B. Harvey, "Dealing with Dsyfunctional Organization Myths," reproduced by special permission from *Training and Development Journal* 24, no. 9 (1970): 2. Copyright by the American Society for Training and Development, Inc.
16. D. Lalmi, T. Romana, and N. Hoxha, "Worker Control," *New Albania* 27, no. 2 (1973): 22.
17. J. B. Enright, "On the Playing Fields of Synanon," in L. Blank, G. B. Gottsegen, and M. G. Gottsegen, *Confrontation: Encounters in Self and Interpersonal Awareness* (New York: Macmillan, 1971), p. 164. Reprinted by permission.
18. Ibid., p. 165.
19. T. Clark and D. T. Jaffe, *Toward a Radical Therapy: Alternate Services for Personal and Social Change* (New York: Gordon and Breach, Science Publishers, 1973), p. 4. Reprinted by permission.
20. Ibid., pp. 24–25.
21. L. T. Empey and M. L. Erickson, *The Provo Experiment: Evaluating Community Control of Delinquency* (Lexington, Mass.: D. C. Heath, 1972), p. 4. Reprinted by permission of the publisher.
22. Ibid., p. 6.
23. Ibid., p. 7.
24. Ibid., p. 9.
25. Ibid., pp. 114–15.
26. Ibid., pp. 58, 61.
27. R. M. Stephenson and F. R. Scarpitti, *Group Interaction as Therapy: The Use of the Small Group in Corrections* (Westport, Conn.: Greenwood Press, 1974).
28. M. Jones, A. Baker, T. Freeman, J. Merry, B. Pomryn, J. Sandler, J. Tuxford, *The Therapeutic Community: A New Treatment in Psychiatry* (New York: Basic Books, 1953), chap. 4. Copyright © 1953 by Basic Books, Inc. Reprinted by permission.
29. Ibid., pp. 61–63.
30. N. Branden, *Breaking Free* (Los Angeles: Nash Publishing, 1970), p. 21. Reprinted by permission.

18

CONFRONTATIONAL INTERVENTIONS

Goals/ Objectives

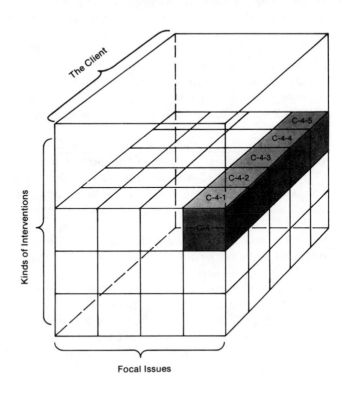

Few accounts of confrontational interventions calculated to solve goals/objectives problems have appeared, and the paucity of such identifiable examples needs to be accounted for. In many settings conduct as perceived "from the outside" often seems controlled more by norms/standards than by goals/objectives. Whether or not this is actually the case in specific circumstances, the consultant encounters difficulty in determining whether the situation is best evaluated as a norms/standards or as a goals/objectives focal issue. For practical intervention purposes, especially when the client is more than one person, addressing the situation as a norms/standards issue provides a readier entrance into problem areas susceptible to some degree of quick-action resolution.

An example of the difficulty can be drawn from the Alcoholics Anonymous approach to the problem of alcoholism (Chapter 1). As a norms/standard, the rule of abstinence constitutes a means of aiding an individual to regulate what otherwise would be an uncontrolled drift into downward-spiral behavior. The social-support system of Alcoholics Anonymous in itself reinforces the abstinence norm, and the extended-group aspect of being able to call upon other members of Alcoholics Anonymous under trying circumstances provides further norm strengthening.

Looked at in another way, the pursuit of abstinence is a goal/objective that an individual member of Alcoholics Anonymous commits to seeking. Viewed as a goals/objectives issue, however, it is more difficult to see how actual interventions of Alcoholics Anonymous might work as compared to the efficiency of those interventions premised on a norm/standard of abstinence. In time, despite possible setbacks, everyday compliance with that norm can become habitual. In any event, the norm/standard intervention focuses the issue on "making a beginning *right now* by not taking the next drink." Given adherence to that norm, the clock-and-calendar goal of sobriety is or is not achieved from one day to the next.

There are circumstances where the most practical intervention might be a goals/objectives confrontation. Even here, however, the entry consultation is likely to be concerned with confronting the client to examine his or her current norms/standards. Once he or she has done so and found them wanting, then the consultation may proceed in the direction of identifying alternate goals and objectives to be pursued. The confrontational aspect is in challenging the client to recognize and become committed to the attainment of goals/objectives that otherwise might not be attempted or even recognized.

The above remarks are no less valid for analyzing situations confronting groups, organizations, or even larger social systems. A group or an organization may, at its point of formation, have clear-cut goals/objectives; but soon, behavior in pursuit of such goals becomes repetitive and mechanical, coded into a bureaucratic set of formal rules that regulate what individuals do and how they interact with one another. When organizations take on such a ritualized character, the problem of change is initially and centrally a problem of challenging existing norms/standards. Eventually, the client system can be challenged to examine the goals and objectives it *should* be striving for. Even here, although the client system may become aware of its problems from a norms/standards point of view, it is likely that if the focal issue shifts to one of goals/objectives the intervention will take on a prescriptive rather than confrontational character. The closeness of a confrontational approach to a prescriptive intervention is seen in the following.

ORGANIZATION GOALS DISCREPANCY ANALYSIS

A major difficulty in the planning and management of the public sector revolves around conflicting and unclear messages communicated by the various constituency groups to which public agencies are responsible. At the state level, for example, an agency is barraged by community expectations, client needs, state legislative mandates, and federal rules and regulations. In some agencies external provider groups add another layer of complexity. Being responsible and responsive to such a diverse public requires flexibility, but the degree of flexibility provided agencies has historically been limited by strict legal and administrative constraints at federal and state levels. Role clarification, goal and objective setting, and long-range planning become especially difficult tasks.

Moore reports an intervention designed to provide a state government department with a data base to assist in the areas outlined above.

The methodology is an "action research" approach. Semistructured interventions are used to establish a within-organization data base.

> The first interview task is to discover the goals and objectives of the respondent. . . . Priorities among objectives are also identified. . . . The second part of the interview repeats the process focusing on the respondent's subordinates. . . . The third section . . . is attenuated considerably by asking the respondent to name only joint projects and shared responsibility areas with specific other managers. . . . The fourth section . . . refocuses on the respondent's job. . . . For each objective, the respondent is asked about the obstacles to achieving quality performance. . . . Other sections of the interview are designed to relate to unique needs of the organization. . . . Often a group undergoing such a detailed assessment prefers that respondents and the consultant maintain absolute confidentiality.[1]

The respondents in this case were twenty-three managers representing the top three levels in the organization.

> The products of the study included an extensive data-based 'white paper,' prepared sets of goals and objectives for the 23 respondents, and individual and combined data summaries regarding superior-subordinate agreement levels and joint planning data. All respondents received copies of all reports and data summaries. In addition, presentations of the study data . . . were made at meetings of the participants. . . . It was recommended that each

group hold meetings with the optional presence of the consultant to re-assess the data implications and obtain a shared view of reality. . . .[2]

This is a confrontational intervention dealing with goals and objectives at the organization level. The confrontational aspect comes from discrepancy analysis, highlighting differences in expectations between boss and subordinate and providing a basis for clarifying goals and objectives that should be jointly established as opposed to goals and objectives that are unilateral and unshared.

Notes

1. M. L. Moore, "Assessing Organizational Planning and Teamwork: An Action Research Methodology," *Journal of Applied Behavioral Science* 14, no. 4 (1978): 480–81.
2. Ibid., p. 489.

19

CONFRONTATIONAL INTERVENTIONS

Summary and Implications

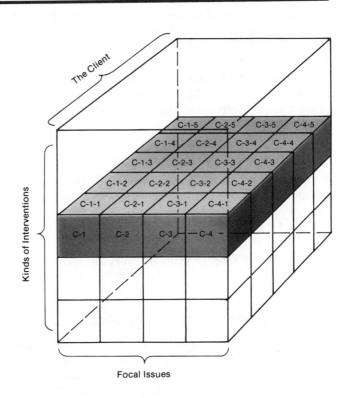

Some values and assumptions lead to self-defeating cycles of behavior. By becoming aware of these, a client has the possibility of reorienting his or her behavior in more valid and justifiable terms and thus escaping unproductive behavior patterns. The strongest confrontation presents the client with facts that reveal his or her values and assumptions in ways that are undeniable and indisputable. This kind of feedback brings into focus a contradiction between expressed beliefs and operational values: a company president may say he or she respects the rights of others, but then ignore their rights by using rank to interrupt; management may claim to respect the union, but the union may be able to identify endless examples of disrespect that management cannot dispute. The client is faced with either changing behavior to be congruent with more valid values or continuing it in the face of recognized inconsistency.

WHAT THE CONSULTANT DOES

The confrontational consultant does not take the problem situation at face value, nor does he or she respond to the client's felt needs. Rather, it is the consultant's objective to highlight the client's underlying value system in such a way as to enable the client to become forcefully aware of how present value orientations control present behavior. At the same time the consultant may assist the client in examining alternative values that are more legitimate or justified in the light of existing circumstances. Under ideal conditions, this value reexamination is achieved by directing the client's attention to here-and-now behavior rather than previous events that can only be indirectly observed by the consultant through the client's reports. The client finds it more difficult to rationalize and thereby explain away the implications of value-based behaviors observed in his or her contemporary situation.

LIMITATIONS

A major limitation of this approach is the possibility of client resistance to participating in the kinds of interactions described. Many clients sense that confrontational interventions may reduce their ability to "control" a situation and thus feel it safer not to throw open Pandora's box. In addition, it is a common tendency for a challenge, even if stated in the form of a question, to be perceived as criticism and thus to generate win-lose arguments regarding the facts themselves.

WHY CONFRONTATION CAN BE HELPFUL

One of the main benefits to be derived from confrontational modes of intervention is that the client is enabled to examine aspects of behavior that might otherwise go unrecognized. These aspects have uncontrolled influence on his or her conduct; therefore, a confrontational intervention can make a consciousness-raising contribution.

When the client is composed of a group, team, or organization, challenging less-than-valid values becomes even more crucial and more difficult—the values may be hidden or may be well known and held in common, in which case they are not subject to challenge within the membership itself. Shared values produce norms and conformity, and a person transgressing the norm or even speaking against it must be willing to oppose values the entire group holds. This opens up the unwelcome possibility of rejection.

As an individual, the reader may readily do a role play, imagining himself or herself as the recipient of a confrontational intervention coming from an unfamiliar "outside" source—a consultant. An "outsider" may be defined as anyone who, in everyday life, is assumed to have no legitimate reason to be interested—far less, interfere—in what you are feeling, thinking, and doing. So in everyday life situations, if and when someone is confronted by an outsider who makes a comment that zeroes in on the most sensitive nub of whatever you hold dear—your present values—your immediate reaction might be a dramatic and colorful expression of indignation. At the other extreme, you might retreat and say nothing. Either way, it is probable that you would feel hurt.

But what is hurting? A variety of intervention situations have been illustrated, all intended to improve the everyday life of some particular client. In each of these situations, then, the outsider does have a legitimate interest in confronting "you," however painful for the moment, in areas where you are sensitive. In each case, "what's really hurting" is more likely to be obvious to the detached consultant than to the client or member of the client group.

Value-based assumptions are as basic to understanding behavior of groups, teams, committees, or families as they are for comprehending patterns of individual behavior. While an almost endless variety of values related to power/authority, morale/cohesion, norms/standards, and goals/objectives can be identified in an individual, a more limited range underlies the behavior of people in groups. Other episodes in Chapters 14 to 18 demonstrate that confrontational interventions at the intergroup level can be useful when norms and standards of one group clash with those of another and produce rationalizations, defensiveness, justification, projection, and a number of other deep-seated defense mechanisms. The aggregate effect of these mechanisms at the intergroup relationship level is to preserve self-defeating cycles of interaction. A consultant usually employs two different points of interventions, both important to success. The first is to intervene by identifying assumptions regarding the character of the relationship; the second is to get each group to identify the stereotypes it has both of itself and of the other group and then to challenge the self/other stereotypes if perceived as "inaccurate." Each group justifies its posture of win-lose, withdrawal, apathy, and so on, by "protecting" the stereotype it has of the other. It can only break out of its own defensiveness by reexamining and discarding implicit and possibly destructive values and attitudes. Through awareness, possibilities open up for each group's membership to seek a more objective basis of interaction.

Consultants can intervene with a total organization in a confrontational manner by challenging assumptions that are hampering organization effectiveness.

Two general considerations underlie the large variety of confrontational organization interventions: one deals with the specifics involved in making an intervention; the other has to do with how a confrontational consultant builds his or her relationship with the organization. Blake and Mouton[1] have identified nine specific approaches to confrontational interventions that are used in here-and-now problem solving within an organizational framework for issues of power/authority, morale/cohesion, norms/standards, and goals/objectives.

1. *Discrepancy.* This intervention calls attention to a contradiction in action or attitudes and is useful for keeping the organization on a new course rather than allowing it to shift unwittingly into old and less satisfactory behavior patterns in response to momentary pressures.

2. *Theory.* A type of intervention in which confrontation draws on behavioral science concepts and theory to throw into bold relief the connection between underlying assumptions and present behavior.

3. *Procedural.* A challenge of various steps in problem-solving efforts that may not in fact lead to the most effective action.

4. *Relationship.* This kind of intervention focuses the attention of participants on issues that arise between people, by virtue of different value orientations, as they work together.

5. *Experimentation.* An intervention that involves introducing experimentation as the basis of testing and comparing two or more courses of action before a final decision is made, particularly when the way to proceed has become institutionalized or tradition-bound.

6. *Dilemma.* A dilemma intervention aids in accurately identifying a choice point in managerial actions. It often can help members reexamine outworn assumptions and search for alternatives other than those under consideration.

7. *Perspective.* Many times in the intensity of the effort applied in production settings, it seems almost inevitable that individuals or teams will lose their sense of direction. A prescriptive intervention permits present actions to be challenged by providing a background of broader historical orientation.

8. *Organization structure.* The fabric of the organization itself can prevent communication, decision making, and the application of effort from being as effective as they might be under different organizational arrangements. An organizational intervention focuses on issues that confront the total organization membership or its various subcomponents.

9. *Cultural.* A cultural intervention challenges traditions, precedents, and established practices that constitute properties of the organizational fabric itself. Challenging the appropriateness of organization culture is difficult because culture permeates actions in such a silent way. The intervention that lifts up culture for examination may indeed be one of the most critical.

Not all confrontational consultants utilize all of these to focus attention on implicit values and attitudes. Probably the most common are *discrepancy, procedural,* and *relationship* interventions.

Jaques's approach to work in organizations parallels, in certain respects, that of psychoanalysis with individuals or groups. He calls it "social analysis," but the mode of intervention is based on confrontational assumptions. His account is noteworthy because he has been specific about what a consultant should and should not do as he or she intervenes in organizations. According to Jacques, the consultant should steadfastly avoid developing social relations with any member of the client organization. He stays away from off-the-job contacts that might conceivably be interpreted as a "special relationship" with any one of the organization's individuals or groups. Under this ground rule, he refuses invitations to go to members' homes, to "have a drink with us," and so on. This rule is to ensure that the consultant's capacity for intervention is in no way compromised.

Other rules aimed at preserving this necessary independence include:

1. Complete confidentiality of the consultant-client relationship.
2. Participation in the analysis of problems without entering into recommendations that would cause the consultant to "share" responsibility.
3. Remaining free to accept other consultation opportunities, thus avoiding dependence on any one source of livelihood.
4. An understanding that his participation in the analysis of problems must be initiated by the client.[2]

These contractual arrangements with an organization-as-client do not prevent Jacques's participation from being confrontational. He concentrates on assisting organization members who seek his help to go deeply into organization questions, to get behind facades, to discard behavioral clichés, and to seek reality-based solutions, even though these may require dramatic shifts away from current modes of thought or operational practices.

The substantive issues that organization members of the "client" bring to the consultant cover a wide range of concerns, including structure, policy, pay, products, personnel practices, training, and even fundamental matters of finance. The consultant confronts the particular client with whatever assumptions underlie the latter's convictions, assumptions ranging from the most empirical to the most philosophically abstract.

Block's[3] how-to-do-it book on consultation is a guide for the confrontational mode of intervention. This is based on Block's recognition of the distinction between the client's felt needs and real needs that must be solved if progress is to result. His insistence is that the client should be confronted with such differences when felt needs are not the real problem. Because the approach concentrates on behavioral issues it says little as to technical/business problems and how to solve them. The book, therefore, is likely to be most useful for the would-be consultant who has already acquired knowledge about the administrative/technical/business side of organizations and who wishes to develop an understanding of interaction processes and ways of bringing these processes into awareness as a precondition for change.

Because of the barriers of client defensiveness and the implicit risks involved, confrontation is a more difficult intervention mode for the internal consultant than for an external consultant. Given that a client may be provoked to "lash back" under confrontation, catalytic interventions are inherently safer.

Confrontational interpretations can introduce insights that result in resolution of a problem, but positive results are seldom predictable. In contrast, the theory-oriented mode of intervention is less likely to provoke dependency or hostility reactions toward the consultant. Thus, under that mode of consultation, it is unnecessary to deal with such reactions except as they are the cause of blockages within client-system relationships.

Notes

1. R. R. Blake and J. S. Mouton, *The Managerial Grid* (Houston: Gulf Publishing Co., 1964), pp. 282–83.
2. E. Jaques, *The Changing Culture of a Factory* (London: Tavistock Publications, 1951), pp. 11–16.
3. P. Block, *Flawless Consulting—A Guide to Getting Your Expertise Used* (San Diego, Calif.: University Associates, Inc., 1981).

Part IV

CATALYTIC INTERVENTIONS

20

CATALYTIC
INTERVENTIONS

Catalytic Interventions: An Introduction

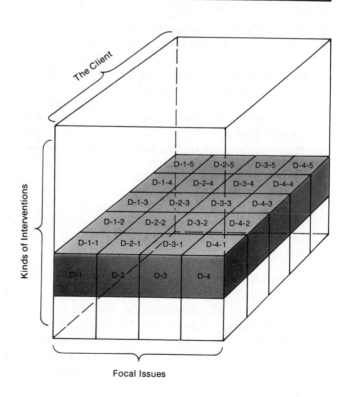

A client is often hampered by limited or incorrect perceptions about social reality. Though emotions may be involved, the underlying cause is lack of data. Problems of social perception indicate a need for greater awareness, and catalytic interventions are often relied on in these circumstances. They help the client bring his or her view of the situation closer to reality and bridge the gap between what is known and what is needed to be known by providing information or by verifying existing data.

Catalysis is a concept employed in chemistry to describe a certain kind of reaction. A catalytic agent, when added to certain other substances, brings about a change in speed of reaction. The change would not have occurred at the same rate had this agent not been introduced.

In intervention, a catalytic consultant is the agent. He or she enters a situation with the intention of increasing the rate at which a process of change is occurring. The goal is to assist those within the status quo to do what they are doing in an improved way.

The consultant may employ a number of approaches to gain cooperation from the client in order to help with the problem. He or she tries to get inside the client's frame of reference, see the situation from the client's point of view. In this way, the consultant can collaborate with the client in a catalytic manner.

Caplan offers a consultant's point of view of a catalytic intervention used in a mental-health setting.

> First, he has accepted no coercive authority from the director, and so collaboration of the staff, although authorized, must be freely volunteered by them and is more likely in regard to certain issues than others. Second, the consultant is continually aware that while he is collecting information he is also building relationships that will form the vehicle for eventual consultation intervention. In fact, his intervention usually starts at the moment of his first contact with his potential consultees, who may from the beginning be watching such things as his way of asking questions and the areas of his major interest, as part of the process of identification with him that is one of the major ways in which they are influenced. Third, although the area of his inquiry has not been predetermined by a request to deal with a particular administrative predicament, and so is apparently wide open to include any or every aspect of the organization, the consultant realizes that the resources at his disposal are necessarily limited. He must therefore narrow his focus to those issues that the consultees feel to be currently most pressing, and which they are thus likely to want to discuss.[1]

"Deal[ing] with . . . those issues that the consultees feel to be currently most pressing . . ."—this is the meaning of "getting inside the client's frame of reference. . . ." The advantage is that the client's interest in being helped is aroused. However, it could be that the problem definition formulated by the client, based on his or her feelings, is wide of the mark. If so, consultant and client would be collaborating on solving the wrong problem.

Rather than relying on pedestrian step-by-step diagnosis as the basis for planning strategy, intuition is the consultant's tool for finding out about the client's problem. How the consultant goes about this is revealed below.

> The special skill which consultants develop with increasing experience, and which is similar to the "intuition" of a clinician in following productive leads in psychotherapy, is that of superficially scanning the entire field of the life of the organization and then making quick judgments of the "hot-test" areas for deepening his inquiries—that is, choosing those topics that provide leverage points in regard to salience and feasibility for the consultees. An ongoing systematic examination of such statistics as staff turnover in different departments, patient, client, or product movement, or staff absenteeism, or sickness rates should form the background of his data collection and may suggest leads for further exploration. But the consultant's main method of scanning will probably be that of moving about as a participant observer within the life space of the organization and chatting with as many people as possible at different administrative levels, so as to find evidence of unusual behavior or preoccupation that may indicate administrative difficulty.[2]

The way this works in practice is suggested in the following passage, depicting how the consultant proceeds to test for "felt needs."

> If the consultee appeared interested, the discussion would progress. If not, some other topic would be discussed. The plan, if any, that emerged would be that of the staff member or group involved, and not that of the consultant, who would guide the unfolding of the process only by his choice of contacts, which would determine the area of the social system and the levels of the administrative hierarchy involved. In addition, the consultant would catalyze and facilitate a rational investigation of the issue and the development of an effective remedial plan by supporting his consultees in confronting the problems and by helping them overcome emotional or cognitive obstacles in their reactions.[3]

A dilemma of consultation is related to felt needs versus real needs and how the consultant should deal with the client when the felt need as expressed by him or her is different than the real need the consultant judges to be the cause of the problem. The two lists below are an example of this discrepancy. One list is stated in terms of the client's expressed needs, and the second in terms of the consultant's sense of the real needs existing beneath the surface.

Felt Needs

Poor profits, low productivity, inadequate sales, poor product quality, extensive equipment down time, high inventories, late deliveries, rising costs, and noncompetitive prices.

Real Needs

Managerial skills, unmotivated employees, poor employee relations, and poor interdepartmental relations.

Bolster[4] recommends that the consultant accept the client's definition of the problem as real whether it is in fact a felt need or the true definition of the problem that must eventually be solved. In doing so, the consultant should join hands with line managers and/or technical specialists to find solutions to problems as defined. The underlying real problems involving human relations issues of communication, power, decision making, and intergroup frictions are then likely to come to the surface and can be dealt with as they become evident. When they do emerge, underlying problems are resolved in the context of explicit operational issues rather than implicit managerial concerns. Theoretically, the approach to these underlying problems is also catalytic but this is an inferred conclusion.

There are several alternatives to this approach. One is to distinguish between felt and real needs at the first point where the client can derive meaningful insights as to the implications of the difference. Another approach, predicated on the client's understanding of deeper issues of differences between felt and real needs, is to teach theory-based diagnostic skills so that the client learns to make the distinction.

The consultant is faced with the dilemma of staying at the felt-needs level until something else develops or pursuing a more direct approach. Often credibility is lost by reliance on the former approach. Often, the client is aware of the underlying problem(s) and may consider the consultant naive if he or she does not identify and make explicit the real need.

When issues have been identified that the consultant and client agree need attention, the consultant may intervene based on several related but additional assumptions characteristic of the catalytic approach. One assumption is that more information about the problem will have a significant impact on changing the perception of the situation. This means that whatever is preventing progress can be dealt with by utilizing available information that is not now being applied to resolving the problem. Secondly, the data-gathering methodology is less important than the content and quality of the information obtained. Methodologies may involve revelatory tests and measurements, encouraging several people to talk about their work as a group, intergroup contacts, organization activities, or even activities within larger social systems in a free and open style. *Procedural* suggestions by the consultant can help the client system gather information that sheds new light on the situation. Although these procedures usually are immediately understandable to participants, insufficient importance was attached to them before the consultant suggested their use.

The consultant either assists clients as they gather impressions to illuminate their situation or gathers the data directly. Often the client is not skilled in the gathering and analysis of pertinent information, and through observation, interviews, or research the consultant is able to fill this gap. Information, often called "data" in a loose sense, need *not* be physical-reality facts or mathematical relations—often data consists of "social facts," or a summary of the existing state of the client's attitudes and emotions. The presumption here is that feelings are information. Once recognized, allowances can be made for them in the search for solutions. Thus feelings and emotions can be presented informationally, without the need for direct confrontation or other immediate response.

An example of this approach is provided by Crockett, who at the time was Deputy Secretary of State for Administration. He describes a State Department project in group development. The consultants, Ferguson and Seashore, initiated the approach by interviewing all twelve staff members to probe subsurface reactions. Anonymity was promised to each respondent.

With participants seated in a large circle, the first session was started by Ferguson. He reviewed the agenda and procedures to be employed during the next two days, indicating that he would present summarized interview-based information regarding each respective group member. Each participant could then react to the summaries, with others joining the discussion to whatever degree they wished.

The interview-gathered information on each participant was displayed on a large board. In order to reduce hostility or embarrassment, the summaries were presented in anonymous fashion and categorized so that the frequency of each distinctive description of an individual was indicated. As an example, these are the reactions posted to describe Crockett.

> For example: "He doesn't delegate properly." "He gives contradictory instructions to different people so that there are binds within the group." "He makes unilateral decisions relating to our responsibilities without first talking them over with us." "He takes action in our areas without telling us." "We are not generally informed about what's happening in the whole group." "We are kept ignorant about one another's activities." "He doesn't like confrontation and conflict." "He can't make tough (people) decisions." "We can't get in to see him." "He sees the wrong people." "He doesn't give us his attention when we do see him." "He has too many irons in the fire at one time." "He confuses us about priorities." "He is manipulative."[5]

Then participants discussed with one another the meanings which came through from the posted information.

> But here again the consultants tried to give us an understanding of the deep difference between a cold, hard, objective, critical "appraisal" by the boss on the one hand and a legitimate (even if critical) "feedback" that is given in a climate of trust and warmth and caring, on the other. We discussed the obligations which were imposed upon all who opted into such a group; specifically, we were reminded of the obligation of "caring" for other group members. Members who "cared" had obligations both individually and collectively to help the others to understand how they "came through" and "were seen," how they were "felt" and "perceived," how they were helpful or were hurtful in their communications. Each had an obligation to give and to receive feedback, and to give coaching to the others.[6]

How it worked out in practice is seen in the following session with Crockett.

For example, where one had said I did not delegate, I denied it by saying "I am the best delegator in the Department. You all have authority. You have responsibilities in your area. And it is up to you to get them done." And then the anonymity would disappear because the person who had put this item on the list would come in hard to justify his stand. And so with illustration of time and place and circumstance he would prove when I had not delegated properly or how I would fall back after I had given them authority, or how I had made a decision unknown to them or how, before evidence had come in, I had changed their decision, and so on. This kind of confrontation only started the conversation. Chuck would not let any of us off so easily. He probed deeply. How did my action make them feel? How did they see me? What were my motives? How did this affect the group's work together? This and many more questions that he asked would give me the opportunity to reply, "Yes, but you don't realize the pressure I am under from the White House . . . or from the Congress . . . or from the Secretary. . . ." And the whole complexity of relationships, the pressures upon me, and explanations for my seemingly erratic behavior would come out. From such explanations and probings came understanding and a sense of sharing that had never before existed in the group.[7]

This kind of "feelings about relationships-as-facts" approach not only reduced pluralistic ignorance within the group regarding how each reacted to the others, it also aided some members to overcome individual blind spots.

Many group leaders are plagued by doubts concerning the real state of affairs existing between themselves and those who report to them. Should they ask these people point-blank, "How are things going between us?" The answer may be little more relevant than are many diplomatic remarks. If they don't ask, the real situation remains obscured. They can listen to rumor and scuttlebutt, but the validity of such sources cannot be taken at face value.

Another formulation of the catalytic model is provided by Cash and Minter.

Process-Consultation Model—Assumptions

- The client and consultant jointly diagnose the problem.
- The consultant's role is to train the client in using diagnostic and problem-solving techniques.
- The client has the major responsibility to develop his/her own solution and action plan to the problem.
- Problem solving is more effective when the client identifies what processes need to be improved (e.g., reporting relationship, reward system, organizational structure).
- The client has more knowledge and insight about what will work in the organization than does consultant.
- The client has more of a commitment for implementing the action plan if involved in the entire diagnostic problem-solving phases.[8]

Catalytic assumptions are basic to this formulation, which offers no solution to getting the intervention beyond the felt-needs level.

With this initial background, further technical understanding of catalytic interventions can be gained by studying examples of the various types of methodologies employed in different situations. Some may be used solely with an individual or a group; others, although the format will vary, occur in situations where the unit of change may range from an individual to a larger social system. Thus a general description of the more widely used methodologies is presented first in order to avoid duplication of material throughout the various applications.

PROCESS CONSULTATION

Knowing something about aspects of behavior dynamics, a catalytic consultant recognizes that interaction skills are difficult to acquire on a teacher-tell basis. An alternative is intervening in a group, intergroup, or organization setting using the client's problems as case material. The consultant may act as a "mirror" to individuals, although this is rare. Through pertinent questions, information can be produced for study and insights derived as to what is going on. The goal is to focus members' attention on evaluating and understanding their own situation so they are in a better position to perpetuate aspects that are desirable and to change what is unwanted. The consultant may limit participation to inviting group members to "look at" their interventions in order to stimulate information gathering and informational feedback. He or she may exercise more initiative by suggesting alternative approaches or possibilities that permit the gathering— whether through interview, survey methods, questionnaires, or other means—of information that is not readily available from here-and-now behavior, but is needed. In using the client's "felt needs" to govern the intervention, a catalytic consultant is likely to offer suggestions that are little more than a step away from what people are prepared to do on their own initiative. By formulating tentative possibilities that participants can accept more or less as a restatement of their own ideas, the consultant ensures that responsibility for the consequences remains with the client.

Another consideration that makes this possible is the consultant's special role vis-à-vis the client. First of all, he or she is *invited* in because help is wanted. Yet because they are not group members, consultants do not share the everyday pressures members may feel, and thus can more easily focus their attention on procedures, processes, and relationships. Since he or she is not a "carrier" of group history, the consultant probably will not have the same commitment to consistency with the past, nor the same blindness to new possibilities. Although the past may no longer be pertinent to the here and now, the group may unwittingly be acting out of habit. A catalytic consultant can comprehend the group situation more fully than members do and work indirectly to fill vacuums in their awareness. By contrast, a confrontational consultant would forthrightly state perceived discrepancies between consultant and client comprehensions.

This reticence to deal with issues directly tends to preserve another consultant advantage: he or she is not likely to be party to participant-centered frictions, antagonisms, and cliques. Beyond that, the consultant is relatively free from the pressure and discipline that members often feel when they are part of a power structure created by formal authority relationships. Consultants, by virtue of their interventionist role, are membership free. They can be accepted for the help they offer, without regard for hidden purposes or vested interests. The same holds true for an internal consultant who is not a member of the unit with whom he or she is consulting.

An example of catalytic process consultation within a group setting is provided by Culbert. By proposing two kinds of interventions, Culbert sums up several of the issues trainers must deal with in conducting a T Group. The first intervention involves *phase-shifting*—assisting a group to shift from the initial and often shallow search for commonalities to a more here-and-now perception-exchanging basis of interaction. While the examples offered are from a T-Group setting, the same approach can be employed in organizational "family-group" development. Progress can be stimulated by exploration of one another's immediate thoughts and feelings. This brings about a new phase of summary, recapitulation, and closure. The following exemplifies a phase-shifting intervention calculated to move the group into the last-mentioned phase.

> I'd like to state my understanding of what we have been doing so far as a group. We began by agreeing that important personal learning could be had by exploring interpersonal differences. When we began our small-group discussion, however, we were confronted with trust issues. It was as if we really couldn't expose our differences until we found out more about one another; and we proceeded to talk at a low-risk level about things we have in common. At least, this is my understanding of why we have been so much in agreement. It's as though the implicit task in what we have been working on is to find out that we are enough alike to risk revealing some of the ways in which we might be different. Soon I expect that some of you will begin risking more by making personal statements which will express your differences from the others in the group.[9]

A second example, also seeking to bring about a shift from one phase to another, follows.

> We began the group by acknowledging the learning value to be gained from exploring personal differences. However, when the group began, we were confronted with the work that needed to be accomplished in creating a climate of trust. As a group, we tried to get to know one another without risking disagreement. We now seem to have come to a point where sufficient trust has been developed to allow some of you to take risks through making personal statements which expose your "differences." The trust question still appears to be with us, for most of the self statements being made sound fairly encapsulated to me. It seems that we are still more involved in finding out how others will react to our differences than we are in possibly learning from their reactions. My last statement is based on the "yes, but" character I hear in reactions to attempts by others to give feedback. It seems to me that as the trust level increases we shall begin to be more open to the com-

ments of others and begin to interact more. In this way I think we'll become more effective resources for one another's learning.[10]

The other kind of intervention, termed *phase-relevant,* is intended to enable whatever is presently going on to continue in a better or deeper way. Both phase-shifting and phase-relevant interventions appear to be catalytic in intent. Though Culbert utilizes his own personal map of progression to guide clients from one development phase to another, this map is not taught to participants or in other ways internalized by them. The opposite happens. When the consultant determines the group is ready, his or her other interventions crystallize what is anticipated to become a felt need for the group. Public expression is given by the consultant to what members are privately sensing. The intervention tips the scales and a new activity gets under way.

In addition to here-and-now, direct-process consultations, so many different strategies and tactics are involved in catalytic interventions that on the surface each may appear unique. For example, many exercises and instruments are available, almost on a recipe basis, and are used by consultants to assist participants in experiencing one or another of the many phenomena involved in team behavior. For the most part, they are premised on small group activities carried out in a data-gathering manner, with the consultant facilitating the experience and feedback in a catalytic manner.[11] When examined from the standpoint of what the consultant's assumptions are and what is done, however, it turns out that they really are adapions of a basic methodology engineered to fit local circumstances. Since the catalytic consultant relies on information that can be fed back in a summarized but nonevaluative way, various additional interventions for information gathering and feedback can be categorized according to how the information is gathered and used.

MODELING

Another belief widely shared among catalytic consultants relates to modeling— i.e., the consultant does not make the issue the basis for a prescriptive intervention but nonetheless envisages his or her own behavior as exemplifying how others ought also to behave. By identifying with the consultant, the client may change by imitation, following the consultant's example in such matters as personal openness, giving feedback, and caring. This aspect of change may never be explicitly pointed out, as the mechanism may work best when it is not deliberate and calculated. Consultants emphasizing the importance of modeling include Ferguson,[12] Bennis,[13] and Golden,[14] among others.

A combination of process consultation with an individual, which invites modeling, is summarized by Caplan in the following selection.

In addition to such personally idiosyncratic distortions, mental health consultants often identify misperceptions and stereotyped expectations among administrators based upon cultural prejudices, such as those that relate to

rejected ethnic, religious, or racial groups or to members of other professions or occupations which are believed to be inferior. One way of handling
this, in addition to acting as a mediator to bring the parties together so that
they can meet each other as people rather than as stereotypes, is for the
consultant to ask his consultee for a factual account of the professional
behavior of the person who is being stereotyped and then to discuss this in
such a way that the realities of the situation begin to shine through. In this
conversation, the consultant temporarily lends his perceptual apparatus, as
it were, to his consultee. He gives him specific ego support by using the
leverage of the consultation relationship to enable the consultee to identify
with him and to stand back for the moment from his preconceptions and,
along with the consultant, take a fresh look at the other person. The consultant will usually have to begin by pointing out some specific details of
his own perceptions or inferences about the case, and then he can start to
involve the consultee in the joint task of adding items to the list.

Another method, which can be used on its own or to supplement the
above, is for the consultant to recount an anecdote from his memory or
his imagination about his own experience with a person of the category
under discussion. He indicates his respect for this person by his tone of
voice and by the admiration with which he talks about him, and perhaps
drives the message home by telling of the surprise he felt when he discovered how effectively the hero of his parable operated, and how much he
himself had learned from that encounter.[15]

Confrontational consultants, particularly those in the psychoanalytic tradition, would see this kind of identification with the consultant as positive transference, and frown upon its use in inducing change. They would view the tendency to model through imitation as something the client should be assisted to
understand, and only to engage in as a deliberate, conscious decision, based on
rational consideration.

GATHERING INFORMATION THROUGH INTERVIEWING

A catalytic consultant usually prefers having some understanding of the client's
problem and situation before an actual meeting. When the client is a larger unit
than an individual, one approach to information gathering is interviewing members separately with regard to a number of more or less standard topics. For
example, members may be asked about openness, trust, frictions, operational
procedures, and so on. Broader, more open-ended questions may be used, e.g.:

"How are things going around here?"
"What changes would you like to see?"
"How do you think this organization could be more effective? What do you
feel it does best? Does poorly?"

The interviewer may also ask about managerial behavior.

"How would you describe the management style of Mr. X? How do you think
he could be more effective?"

The consultant may introduce a question or two calculated to stimulate the person being interviewed, but thereafter keep the discussions open-ended. He or she can follow the client's lead as to what topics are pertinent, and thereby keep closely in touch with the felt needs of the system. At the same time the consultant avoids introducing private, personal thoughts about what he or she considers the more important or more trivial topics.

Questions may also be asked about relationships with other parts of the organization.

> "Whom do you like to work with most? Least?"
> "Who is most influential in your organization?"

And about relationships with other organizations and units:

> "When there are problems with other organizations, what can you do about them?"
> "Can you give examples of unresolved issues with other organizations?"
> "Do you think you could give them advice that would help them do a better job?"[16]

As indicated by these lines of inquiry, interviewing is an approach for gaining access to private views and feelings on a wide range of topics. The consultant then studies the replies and attempts to summarize them into a number of functional categories. These often furnish the principal basis for a catalytic intervention.

In followup meetings that take place after the individual interviews, discussion is likely to be initiated by the consultant. He or she feeds back the summarized findings, being careful not to reveal the identity of particular interviewees. Anonymity offers the consultant a detour around the candor problem because participants are usually prepared to be frank when their identities are concealed. In addition, personal exposure of thoughts, feelings, and convictions that could result in face-to-face acrimony among members is avoided. Anonymity is maintained by grouping reactions from different members into categories so that in most cases more than one person will have made the same or similar point. A view held by one person only is not likely to be reported.

When feeding back information about members' behavior, the consultant usually avoids specifically reporting to the group verbatim reactions to such questions as, "How would you describe the management style of Mr. X? How do you think he could be more effective?" This would expose Mr. X to data he would be compelled to react to without knowing its source.

Interview-based information gathering with feedback, and with the consultant helping in processing the information, is the most common catalytic version of group development. Members' participation in planning development sessions and in determining how to handle meetings is sought in order to get support for carrying this activity to its conclusion. Participation may involve such issues as, "Who gets the feedback first?, How will followup decisions be made?, Will the findings be published and if so, who will see them?, Should we have night sessions?"

An extensive use of interview-based information gathering with group-development feedback is described by Davis.

> We have also conducted more than 85 team development efforts. These vary in format, but a typical one involves interviews with each of the members of the team (a job family consisting of a supervisor and his immediate subordinates) and then perhaps a three-day off-site meeting where the interview data are fed back for the groups to work with. The team ends the meeting with explicit action items. Follow-up to the off-site meeting involves implementing the many action items.[17]

Through interviewing, the consultant becomes the information-gathering instrument as well as a resource for helping the group respond to the data revealed. His or her direct group-development contributions include offering procedural suggestions, inviting alternative explanations, asking pertinent questions, and so on.

SCALES AND INSTRUMENTS

An approach different from direct interviewing but calculated to serve the same purpose involves the use of tests, questionnaires, and scales. The gathered reactions can then be utilized to formulate the agenda for developmental discussions.

One advantage to using a set of scales is that the consultant, by selection of the items included in it, can ask participants to deal with issues they might not have previously recognized as important. For example, questions concerned with mutual trust and mutual support, communications, listening, objectives, conflict, use of member resources, how control is exercised, and group climate can be included. While these are known professionally to be significant barriers to effectiveness, most of them are not issues that managers spontaneously raise in day-to-day work meetings, even though they are in fact latent needs that become felt needs as soon as the scales are introduced. These particular questions are not the only ones that might be asked—indeed, group members could be invited to "invent" the scales to be used by their group.

In an intergroup setting, Mangham[18] provides an example of a questionnaire that, according to him, is based on Blake and Mouton instruments. The instructions invite groups to evaluate their own teamwork. Categories such as "objectives" and "conflict" are provided, as are multiple-choice options from which participants can select the answer most descriptive of their situation.

In a company where the questionnaire approach was utilized, one department of eight employees ranged in background from Ph.D. with long experience to a recently hired process trainee. The development meetings were held at the work place. Prior to the first meeting, each member filled out the questionnaire and added whatever comments seemed pertinent. This information was collected so that it could be summarized and fed back anonymously, all in accordance with the supportive, nonconfrontational nature of Mangham's intended catalytic interventions. However, members felt little would be gained through anonymity and, therefore, they identified their own scores. This he agreed with, given the ground rule that people who did not want to do so would not be pressured to conform.

When participants began to see the collated data, they noticed many discrepancies between their individual answers to identical questions. This came as a surprise. Presumably, they had taken for granted that every other person would see the group's mode of operation in the same way. The consultant noted that the most penetrating item—in the sense of the intensity of reactions it produced —was "conflict." The scores indicated that participants preferred to "let sleeping dogs lie" in their work situations.

A catalytic intervention ensued when the consultant tried to help the group use these data. First, he asked members to throw out ideas of what conflict meant to them by speaking the first words that came to mind in connection with it. The list of associations included "violence," "destruction," "vicious," "cruel," "hurt," "smash," "batter," "war," "fight," "bitter struggle," "immature squabble," and so on. The significance of these associations was discussed and a brief paper on conflict was distributed. The consultant then pointed out that (1) conflict can be positive, and (2) it can be worked through and resolved. Other catalytic interventions took place later. For example, Mangham asked, "What does this discussion mean for the [group] here and now? What conflicts do we envisage in talking about the problems we have in working together?" Open-ended questions such as these focus attention on an issue, but permit the consultant to avoid showing his or her hand.

SURVEY RESEARCH

The term survey research refers to the technique of having a large number of people complete the same questionnaire. Mann provides a summary of its use as an organization intervention and reviews those strategies that seem likely to produce successful outcomes. Central to each of these seven statements is a reliance on client participation.

1. *Concern for superiors*—and particularly those at the top of the organization. Where superiors took a genuine interest in the findings, studied them and tried to apply them, the data were discussed more adequately and used more constructively in working out action steps than in those units where superiors showed no such interest.

2. *A high degree of participation and personnel involvement.* Where superiors and subordinates were involved to a high degree in the research planning and particularly in the analysis and interpretation of the findings the results were better understood, emotionally accepted, and utilized in making changes than where a high degree of participation was not achieved.

3. *Participation in the form of self-analysis.* Analyses and interpretations of data and their relevance for change were more likely to be followed by change

if the relevant individuals or members of a group made these analyses rather than an outsider.

4. *Objective survey data about one's own organization.* Quantitative summaries about the attitudes and perceptions of subordinates and associates facilitate critical self-evaluations.

5. *Timing and pacing.* It was preferable to let those who were to change set the pace at which the change process went. Too fast a rate for intellectual and emotional acceptance resulted in little or no change; too slow a rate resulted in dissipation of motivation.

6. *Group forces.* Group discussions leading to group decisions about action steps were found to facilitate attitude and behavioral changes in human relations under most circumstances. Decisions concerning changes were carried through when made by all members of the group because of the reciprocally binding nature of such decisions. In a few instances it appeared that objective information identifying the strengths and weaknesses of particular sub-units should not be presented simultaneously to all of the members of an organizational family unless the group had already had some experience in working together as a team towards the solution of human relations problems.

7. *Membership character of the change agent.* Line superiors were able to exert more force toward change than members of either the company personnel staff or of the university research team.[19]

These points were drawn from early work, yet they continue to reflect pivotal issues in effective survey research.

A refinement of the survey-research model calculated to avoid weaknesses of earlier approaches is reported by Bowers and Taylor.[20] They point out that survey results, fed back conventionally, are likely to be received in any of three ways, none of which is likely to have positive organizational impact. Instead, the data will be:

1. Set aside for considerations at some undesignated future date.
2. Handed to subordinates with a general recommendation to "do something with them."
3. Used to serve partisan ends, e.g., to bolster or justify performance of certain managers.

Bowers and Taylor's interventions have attempted to reduce these weaknesses by strengthening the participatory basis of both information-gathering and feedback steps. Rather than tailoring interviews or questionnaires to the individual client, a standardized questionnaire assessing four basic areas of organization has been developed. These are "leadership," "organizational climate," "group process," and "satisfaction." This is not a morale survey, but rather a descriptive survey of organizational conditions and practices. Two-thirds of the questions are perception based; the remainder deal with reactions, feelings, desires, and satisfactions. The answers are read electronically and can be stored on magnetic tape for future reference or used in longitudinal analyses of progress.

Bowers and Taylor indicate that while the instrument can spot strengths and weaknesses, organization executives and others often "prefer not to hear bad news." This suggests that data feedback is insufficient to bring about desired results. Catalytic consultants must also intervene in the power/authority system. Unless feedback is provided with this requirement in mind, the information will probably not have the intended impact.

The devised catalytic solution to defensiveness or resistance is to use a resource person trained to provide each supervisor and his or her immediate work group with a set of findings, an explanation of the information, and suggestions concerning its interpretation and use. Private counseling of supervisors on how to use findings with their own subordinate groups is also provided. Since the approach, which advocates participative management, does not rely on training the managers themselves in skills of effective participation and does not formally teach a theory of participation, its benefit lies in the catalyzing effects of the information, reinforced by consultation regarding this information's interpretation.

While Bowers and Taylor emphasize the consultant's role in the above description, one of the first examples of action research, by J. R. P. French, Jr., emphasizes the importance of client participation.

About three years after opening its new Virginia plant, Harwood experienced problems in developing an expanded work force. World War II had created a manpower shortage, and Harwood was confronted with changing the traditional aversion of its supervisors toward employing "older" workers. Growing labor shortages made it necessary to employ older people; yet such hiring was resisted. At the time this was a critical issue to the company, and it is a problem that illustrates how Harwood has learned some things about management.

Dr. John R. P. French, Jr. was then director of personnel research for the company. He cited scientific proof that older people did have the kinds of skills and aptitudes required for the jobs in this plant, but the staff attitude remained unchanged. Dr. French realized that merely telling the staff that their attitude was contrary to the facts would not persuade them. It would have been easy to impose a new hiring policy, but it was felt that this approach would be self-defeating. He concluded that it was necessary for the staff to unlearn their mistaken beliefs and that this would occur only if they would seek out the facts for themselves. Only then could they recognize the discrepancy between facts and belief.

Accordingly, Dr. French sought to involve the staff members in research of their own. A modest project was suggested to them. If older workers were inefficient, it would be advisable to determine how much money the company was losing by continuing the employment of those older women who were already in the plant. There were a number of such women, those who had several years of service, or who had been taken on more recently as a favor to the community—a widow, possibly, or a hardship case.

Full responsibility for designing the project was placed, not with the research director, but with the members of the management staff. They were to determine the best methods of collecting data. The project was theirs, not his, and so would be the credit. They could come up with something which was of their own devising.

The findings were in sharp contrast to the staff's expectations. Not age, but other factors, determined success or failure on the job. But the analysis being their own, the staff trusted it. Thus being enabled to re-examine their beliefs through first-hand exploration, they were helped to new understanding. In the process, they "unlearned" some of the beliefs they had been convinced were true and were now ready to affirm quite different ones. They also learned something about the value of research applied to organizational problems.[21]

This experiment is a good example of the kind of action research that Lewin advocated and that Harwood used when feasible. It points up that when members of a group take part in a fact-finding inquiry of this sort, the very circumstance that the findings are their own inspires them to change their attitude and subsequent behavior. As Lewin put it, "This result occurs because the facts become really their facts (as against other people's facts). An individual will believe facts he himself has discovered in the same way that he believes in himself." When the findings are their own, people cannot challenge them as inadequate, or impute any bias to the fact-finders. They then recognize they must have been mistaken before.[22]

In contrast to action research (examined in the next section of this chapter), then, survey-research techniques are information-gathering and feedback devices that have evolved from an academic tradition of research. Survey research often deals with such issues as employee satisfaction; individual and group concerns about particular problems such as morale and productivity; the character of leadership and supervision; or how grievances are handled. These data are not reflective of current realities. Typically they describe some ideal *end condition*— satisfaction, morale, and productivity—instead of a process (e.g., trust, openness, etc.) for achieving the desired end and often do not address the interpersonal variables, such as win-lose competitiveness, which may be causing them.

Generally, an outside survey-research consultant and organization participants collaborate from the beginning, first in perfecting the instrument by identifying features that should be engineered into it. Analyzing and interpreting collected information also are joint activities. However, the survey-research instrument may be taken without much change from any of the classical versions. One of the most inclusive is presented by Likert.[23] When standardized versions are used and instruments are completed by participants in more than one segment of the organization, it is often convenient to summarize the information through computer analysis. Decisions as to who is to receive information, and when, are collaboratively arrived at by survey-research consultants and organization representatives. In reaching such decisions, the survey-research consultant may offer procedural suggestions as to desirable courses of action and introduce alternatives that participants may not previously have considered. Then summaries, correlations between various questions, and cross-department comparisons on a group-by-group basis can be made available to each participating group for its own study, interpretation, and evaluation. Information typically is fed back to the respondents and possibly to others at higher levels. Though usually not pointed out by the consultant, anonymity, which bypasses the openness issue, is a characteristic feature.

A closer glimpse at survey research is afforded by examining a sample survey-research instrument prepared by Likert. Data regarding group meetings were generated by posing the following kinds of questions to managerial personnel:

> Are there any *group meetings* in which the non-supervisory people in your department can discuss things with the supervisors? (Check one.)
> ____Yes, and they are always worthwhile.
> ____Yes, and they are usually worthwhile.
> ____Yes, but usually nothing much is accomplished.
> ____Yes, but they are just a waste of time.
> ____No, we never have such group meetings.[24]

Miles, Calder, Hornstein, Callahan, and Schiavo explain how survey-research information used for group development may be handled. The example is a useful one for showing how traditional status-quo values set the boundary limits for consultant interventions in the catalytic mode.

> Often, though not always, the data are shown first to the "head" of the family group, at which point his presentation of the data to the rest of the group may be discussed or rehearsed. Then the data are presented to the rest of the group, who are, in fact, "heads" of other family groups. Subsequently, they will examine the data with their groups. Thus, the survey feedback takes place through an interlocking set of conferences. Typically, outside staff members are present at each of the conferences.
> Ordinarily, examination of the data leads to action planning in response to problems made salient by the data. Consequently, these feedback conferences provide activities in the presence of outside staff members who attempt to use their training skills to help members of the group improve their work relationships.[25]

It is now possible to summarize standardized features of survey research as a catalytic intervention. A three-step sequence of activities usually is involved. First, information-gathering instruments are created or prefabricated instruments are utilized and information is gathered. Second, various groups—actual groups one level above where the information was gathered or the head of the family group itself—have meetings with the consultant to discuss this information and plan its use. Finally, if the procedure is carried to its natural conclusion, the survey-research consultant may work with the client groups on problems the survey information identified. The client groups themselves are supported as they analyze and interpret their own interactions in live information sharing. The consultant facilitates the group's interpersonal interactions, identification of norms, and evaluation of their problem-solving procedures. His or her comments make it legitimate to focus group study on such here-and-now phenomena.

The consultant may then recommend that participants attempt to relate this personal feedback to their own actual behavior, by trying to act according to the feedback given them rather than according to habit. This, in turn, can become a stimulus producing further information about personal reactions. The desired effect is that client effectiveness will be enhanced.

ACTION RESEARCH

Lewin[26] first introduced the concept of action research. Ideally, in terms of the Bradford-Gibb-Benne definition,[27] this approach "is an application of scientific methodology in the clarification and solution of practical problems . . . also a process of planned personal and social change." In essence it is a method of empirical data gathering for action planning. Extensive collaboration between a consultant and client is involved regarding concrete uses to be made of data, including how to gather it, discussion of its meanings and implications, and explicit planning of action as a consequence of data-based findings. Evaluation of an action taken in one cycle becomes the data for a second cycle, and so on. While descriptions of the steps and the sequence vary in detail, the actual steps are essentially the same. The main steps are described by W. French[28] as follows.

1. *Diagnosis.* As an initial step, usually the most senior-ranking member of the client system and the consultant reach a joint assessment. As an additional substep, subordinates may be interviewed to procure supplemental data. Questionnaires and survey feedback may be used to round out the diagnosis. French points to the importance of working with the client's "expressed needs" by indicating the importance of postponing or going slow, rather than confronting consultant-client differences in problem perception. The client is never "caused" to recognize his or her problem as different from what he or she previously felt it to be.

2. *Information gathering.* After initial problem-definition is agreed upon by consultant and client, interviews are relied on to get at the facts in more specific and concrete terms, but questionnaires or survey-research procedures may also be developed.

3. *Feedback.* Feedback sessions to report the findings from the data-gathering procedures are arranged, most typically in the form of group-development sessions. The consultant summarizes common problems and participates by process observations that commonly result in a T-Group-type experience.

4. *Action planning.* This step culminates the cycle of action research, involving further data gathering and team-building sessions with lower-level teams. French is not specific in commenting on how this takes place or what the intervention of the consultant might be.

The action-research approach constitutes a catalytic intervention in much the same way as does the approach initiated by interviews, or by questionnaires and scales, or by survey research. All share the basic proposition that information collection and feedback are necessary and sufficient conditions for bringing about change. The major difference in action research is that the sequence might be thought of as the consultant's *planned* approach.

The key assumption behind action research is that the only thing participants require is access to information. Since its diagnoses are always kept within the client's framework of expressed needs, the consultant automatically accepts the status quo as given, not subject to challenge or confrontation. An accompanying assumption is that change will not be resisted when the facts of a situation are brought to the attention of participants in the manner indicated. However, it is known that traditions, precedents, and past practices are forces that may operate on participants in silent and therefore unrecognized ways. The readiness of participants to reject information through rationalization, or to distort its meaning through defensiveness, projection, and so on, is a blind spot in the action-research approach. Further learning of theory, techniques, or skill as a basis for comprehending dynamics underlying behavior is not a component of the action-research approach.

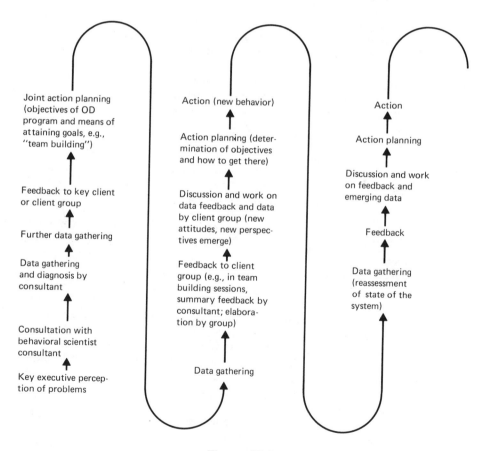

Figure 20.1

Source: W. French, "Organization Development: Objectives, Assumptions and Strategies," *California Management Review* 12, no. 2 (1969), p. 26. © 1969 by The Regents of the University of California. Reprinted by permission.

A CATALYTIC MODEL

The catalytic approach to consultation is so typical that it is now possible to describe a classical model.

The model moves from "Entry" and the issues that are involved in it, into "Data Collection," followed by "Feedback and Discussion of Priorities and Alternatives" and concluding with "Follow-up—Implementation and Evaluation."

The assumption that operational functioning can be improved by better development and distribution of information is inherent in this approach. A version of the approach as used in an academic setting is amplified below.

ACTION RESEARCH PROCESS WITH ACADEMIC DEPARTMENTS

1. *Entry—Consultant's Relationship to the Organization*
   - Faculty Research Center approached by department head
   - Begin developing trust and role expectations
   - Establish ground rule that data will not be shared with central administration but will be public within department
   - Determine the initial willingness of the department chairperson to entertain changes which may alter his/her role or behavior
   - Begin a process of leadership education

2. *Data Collection*
   - Meet with department faculty to review discussions from (1) above and entertain questions about the consultation process
   - Establish ground rules that before any data is collected faculty must agree to meet for three hours to discuss the results and action implications
   - Faculty vote to proceed or not on the consulting relationship
   - Identify issues about which the department wishes more information
   - Modify standard Department Analysis Questionnaire and interview schedule to fit the department's needs
   - Conduct 1½-hour individual interviews (est. 10–20 per dept.)
   - Request completion of questionnaire (20–25 min. per individual)
   - Prepare summary report of results without interpretations and conclusions

3. *Feedback and Discussion of Priorities and Alternatives*
   - Distribute departmental report to all faculty and the department chairperson
   - Meet with the department chairperson to continue process of leadership education begun at entry, to facilitate thinking about the results and the department, and to plan agenda for the faculty meeting
   - Meet faculty (3 hours) to help the faculty validate the results and to test what the department wants to do
   - Facilitate the setting of priorities and preparation for action

4. *Follow-up—Implementation and Evaluation*
   - Implementation depends on the issues and the priorities assigned by the department.
     Some typical examples are:
     —work with department chairperson on improving leadership
     —assist in improving departmental meetings

—assist in the revision of the undergraduate curriculum

—conduct teaching effectiveness workshops

—consult on developing new means of involving graduate students in departmental teaching research activities

—assist department committees in developing policy statements and processes regarding by-laws, promotion and tenure, and program requirements

—assist in the design of studies of market needs for students from a particular discipline

—consult on long-range planning

—help develop new programs in career planning and development for faculty

— Evaluation of follow-up activities is made mutually by the client and consultant. There is periodic review of the consulting relationship.[29]

Summary

The ground rules for the way a catalytic consultant operates include the following. He or she:

1. Starts an intervention with informal conversation to create an easy-going nonauthoritarian atmosphere, an informal give-and-take situation. "How are things?"

2. Invites the client to describe his or her situation, and accepts the needs described by the client as the only legitimate frame of reference to work within. As the consultant listens, he or she tries to formulate suggestions for gathering new information that may illuminate some aspect of the subject the client seems interested in pursuing.

3. Suggests procedures that might be followed to gather more information. These may range from, "Why not just freewheel about your situation. No need to outline, just tell it as it comes out," to using action-research or survey-research methodologies.

4. Gives encouragement whenever possible by supporting the client's efforts at defining or redefining the problem at hand.

5. Avoids giving specific suggestions. Even suggestions re procedures for data gathering are offered in a *very* tentative way. The consultant seeks to stay within the limits established by the client even when it is readily apparent that the client is not "facing up." For the consultant to impose his or her will on the situation or to challenge the client's self-deception would possibly promote resistance, which in turn might shift responsibility for solving the problem from client to consultant. To ensure that the client feels and knows that he or she retains control over the situation the consultant does not overstep these bounds. "How about this possibility?", "Do you think this would work?" are as far as the consultant is willing to go.

6. Encourages the client to make his or her own decisions. The consultant is graceful about it, but will *not* make them for the client, tip the balance one

way or another, or confront the client whose definition of the situation is blocking progress. Consequently, the client feels that whatever action comes about is of his or her own choosing.

While catalytic interventions are calculated to alter the rate of change occurring within the status-quo system, there is no assurance that client reactions will provide added impetus to this rate, or that change will occur in positive directions. The catalytic approach, probably more than any other, can stimulate reactions whose characteristics are difficult to predict. The most common miscalculations result in either (1) the client rejecting the entire approach, or (2) confrontations between participants which become win-lose struggles.

Notes

1. G. Caplan, *The Theory and Practice of Mental Health Consultation* (New York: Basic Books, 1970), p. 276. Reprinted by permission.

2. Ibid., pp. 276–77.

3. Ibid., p. 280.

4. C. Bolster, "Using the Manager's Problems as OD Interventions," *OD Practitioner* 8, no. 2 (1976): 12–13.

5. W. J. Crockett, "Team Building—One Approach to Organizational Development," reproduced by special permission from *Journal of Applied Behavioral Science* 6, no. 3 (1970): 297.

6. Ibid., p. 299.

7. Ibid., p. 300.

8. W. B. Cash and R. L. Minter, "Consulting Approaches: Two Basic Styles," *Training and Development Journal* 33, no. 9 (1979): 26. Reprinted with permission.

9. S. A. Culbert, "Accelerating Laboratory Learning through a Phase Progression Model for Trainer Intervention," reproduced by special permission from *Journal of Applied Behavioral Science* 6, no. 1 (1970): 26.

10. Ibid., p. 27.

11. R. A. Schmuck, P. J. Runkel, J. H. Arends, and R. I. Arends, *The Second Handbook of Organization Development in Schools* (Palo Alto, Calif.: Mayfield Publishing Co., 1977).

12. C. K. Ferguson, "Concerning the Nature of Human Systems and the Consultant's Role," *Journal of Applied Behavioral Science* 4, no. 2 (1968): 179–93.

13. W. G. Bennis, "Theory and Method in Applying Behavioral Science to Planned Organization Change," *Journal of Applied Behavioral Science* 1, no. 4 (1965): 337–60.

14. W. P. Golden, Jr., "On Becoming a Trainer," in W. G. Dyer, ed., *Modern Theory and Method in Group Training* (New York: Van Nostrand Reinhold, 1972), pp. 3–29.

15. Caplan, *Theory and Practice,* p. 289.

16. J. K. Fordyce and R. Weil, *Managing with People* (Reading, Mass.: Addison-Wesley, 1971), pp. 140–41. Reprinted by permission.

17. S. A. Davis, "An Organic Problem-Solving Method of Organizational Change."

Reproduced by special permission from *Journal of Applied Behavioral Science* 3, no. 1 (1967): 292.

18. I. Mangham, "Building an Effective Work Team," in M. Berger and P. Berger, eds., *Group Training Techniques* (Epping, England: Gower Press, 1972), pp. 69–82.

19. F. C. Mann, "Changing Superior-Subordinate Relationships," *Journal of Social Issues* 7, no. 3 (1951): 58–59. Reprinted by permission.

20. D. G. Bowers and J. Taylor, "Survey of Organizations," as reported in University of Michigan Institute for Social Research *Newsletter* 3, no. 6 (1973).

21. A. J. Marrow and J. R. P. French, Jr., "Changing a Stereotype in Industry," *Journal of Social Issues* 12 (1945): 33–37.

22. A. J. Marrow, D. G. Bowers, and S. E. Seashore, *Management by Participation* (New York: Harper & Row, 1967), pp. 24–26. Reprinted by permission.

23. R. Likert, *The Human Organization: Its Management and Value* (New York: McGraw-Hill, 1967).

24. R. Likert, *New Patterns of Management* (New York: McGraw-Hill, 1961), p. 123. Reprinted by permission.

25. M. B. Miles, P. H. Calder, H. A. Hornstein, D. M. Callahan, and R. S. Schiavo, "Data Feedback and Organizational Change," in R. T. Golembiewski and A. Blumberg, eds., *Sensitivity Training and the Laboratory Approach* (Itasca, Ill.: F. B. Peacock, 1970), p. 357. Reprinted by permission.

26. K. Lewin, "Action Research and Minority Problems," *Journal of Social Issues* 2 (1946): 34–46.

27. L. P. Bradford, J. R. Gibb, and K. D. Benne, eds., *T-Group Theory and Laboratory Methods: Innovation in Re-Education* (New York: Wiley, 1964), p. 33.

28. W. French, "Organization Development: Objectives, Assumptions and Strategies," *California Management Review* 12, no. 2 (1969): 26. © 1969 by the Regents of the University of California. Reprinted by permission of the Regents.

29. R. K. Boyer and A. F. Grasha, "Theoretical Issues and Practical Strategies for Administrative Development," in J. A. Shtogren, ed., *Administrative Development in Higher Education* (Richmond, Va.: Higher Education, Leadership, and Management Society, Inc., 1978), p. 39.

21

CATALYTIC INTERVENTIONS

Power/ Authority

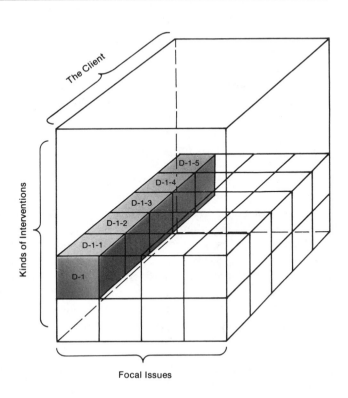

When power/authority is the focal problem, the catalytic consultant intervenes to bring this issue more into the client's field of awareness. Usually some methodology is employed that does not involve direct consultant participation in diagnosing the problem and recommending solutions. Instead, the client is helped to collect pertinent information which he or she can then interpret and act on.

INDIVIDUAL (D-1-1)

Performance Appraisal

The appraisal of performance is fraught with difficulty stemming from the inevitability of power/authority embedded in the boss-subordinate relationship. The result is that subordinates inherently feel vulnerable to being judged and found wanting. As a consequence, subordinates tend to be anxious and reserved and many investigators have found performance appraisal to be a severely limited process for inducing personal development and growth.

Approaches to the mechanical aspects of performance appraisal abound and Bass[1] utilizes a methodology that is based on survey and feedback techniques. It is aimed at identifying differences in perception between superiors and subordinates. The methodology relies on the Bass-Valenzi Profile, a survey instrument that gives individualized feedback on similarities and differences in the way that managers and subordinates view the work situation and their relationship with each other. The premise is based on nonpsychological logic: if boss and subordinate know where they differ, then they can solve the difference. No training in process or dynamics is necessary, only shared information is needed. Questionnaires completed by both the superior and subordinates measure perceptions of such factors as organization, task, work groups, and managerial style. Once completed, a computerized profile is prepared for the individual manager that reflects the manager's own score as well as the mean score and range for subordinates.

Profiles are shared during individual or small group sessions, and a series of questions to stimulate managerial thinking and planning for constructive change are then answered individually and possibly discussed in group settings.

Effectiveness in producing positive behavioral change is reported for twenty-one library directors and ninety-four of their subordinates who were interviewed approximately six months after participating in the Profile intervention. Two-thirds of directors and one-third of subordinates felt the Profile experience had some positive impact, but other changes reported by superiors were not noted by the subordinates. Performance criteria outside of participants' reports were not used to evaluate validity of the approach.

Changing the Principal

A catalyzing strategy often employed in consultation is creating a distinction between what is actual and what is wanted, rather than letting the gap remain on an implicit level. An intervention-based experiment involving several hundred elementary school principals and their teachers, intended to bring about change in the principal's behavior-as-boss, is reported by Daw and Gage. The teachers described their *actual* principal and their *ideal* principal in regard to the following twelve criteria.[2] The ideal principal

1. Encourages teachers with a friendly remark or smile.
2. Gives enough credit to teachers for their contributions.
3. Does not force opinions on teachers.
4. Enforces rules consistently.
5. Criticizes without disparaging the efforts of teachers.
6. Informs teachers of decisions or actions which affect their work.
7. Gives concrete suggestions for improving classroom instruction.
8. Enlists sufficient participation by teachers in making decisions.
9. Demonstrates interest in pupil progress.
10. Interrupts the classroom infrequently.
11. Displays much interest in teachers' ideas.
12. Acts promptly in fulfilling teacher requests.

Some of the principals were told how their teachers had rated them in comparison with an ideal principal; others, who had also been rated, were not given this feedback. Thus it was possible to evaluate the effect of "pure" information feedback on reducing the size of the real/ideal gap. The feedback did effect positive changes in the principals' behavior.

Shifting Supervisory Practices

A catalytic intervention intended to aid a person to be more effective on the job is described by Bavelas and Strauss.[3] Their client was a foreman responsible for an assembly-line operation. He was in trouble. Workers were complaining about pay, speed, heat, and so on. The consultant worked with the foreman to assist him in altering his style of supervision—use of power/authority—when dealing with the complaints.

> The consultant who was brought into this picture worked entirely with and through the foreman. After many conversations with him, the foreman felt that the first step should be to get the girls together for a general discussion of the working conditions—something, incidentally, which was far from his mind originally and which in his own words would only have been "begging for trouble." He took this step with some hesitation, but he took it on his own volition.
>
> The first meeting held . . . was attended by eight girls. They voiced the same complaints again . . . [emphasizing physical] ventilation. . . . The foreman promised to discuss the problem of ventilation and temperature with the engineers, and he scheduled a second meeting to report back to the girls. . . . (He did so, but could get no cooperation from the engineers or his boss.)

This first meeting probably had cathartic components, but it is also likely that the facts of poor ventilation and high temperatures, which had previously been interpreted as gripes, were now seen as real problems to be resolved. The character of the intervention strategy is revealed in the following.

> The foreman came to the second meeting with some apprehensions. The girls . . . had a proposal of their own to make. They felt that if several large fans were set up so as to circulate the air around their feet, they would be much more comfortable. After some discussion the foreman agreed that the idea might be tried out. (Immediately after the meeting, he confided to the consultant that he probably shouldn't have committed himself to this expense on his own initiative; also he felt that the fans wouldn't help much anyway.) The foreman and the consultant discussed the question of the fans with the superintendent, and three large propeller type fans were purchased.

One after another, the complaints were handled by a similar procedure. Information gathering through discussion focusing on the real problems and possible alternatives brought many solutions to the fore. Approval for implementation was secured from the foreman's boss, the engineer, and the superintendent.

Against this background of success the final problem identified related to the women's dislike of the constant speed of the endless chain of hooks that carried objects in and out of their spray-painting booths.

> The group's leader frankly explained that the point wasn't that they couldn't work fast enough to keep up with the hooks, but that they couldn't work at that pace all day long. The foreman explored the point. The girls were unanimous in their opinion that they could keep up with the belt for short periods if they wanted to. But they didn't want to because if they showed that they could do this for short periods they would be expected to do it all day long. The meeting ended with an unprecedented request: "Let us adjust the speed of the belt faster or slower depending on how we feel." The foreman, understandably startled, agreed to discuss this with the superintendent and the engineers.

The consultant's catalytic influence had by now helped focus the power/ authority issue as an interesting contrast between the operator's viewpoint and that of industrial engineering.

> The engineers' reaction naturally was that the girls' suggestion was heresy. Only after several meetings was it granted grudgingly that there was in reality some latitude within which variations in the speed of the hooks would not affect the finished product. After considerable argument and many dire prophesies by the engineers, it was agreed to try out the girls' idea.
> With great misgivings, the foreman had a control with a dial marked, "low, medium, fast" installed at the booth of the group leader; she could now adjust the speed of the belt anywhere between the lower and upper limits that the engineers had set. The girls were delighted, and spent many lunch hours deciding how the speed of the belt should be varied from hour to hour throughout the day.

Production increased, and within three weeks (some two months before the scheduled ending of the learning bonus) the girls were operating at 30 to 50 percent above the level that had been expected under the original arrangement. Naturally the girls' earnings were correspondingly higher than anticipated.

But the solution of one set of problems created another set of problems that had not been anticipated.

The girls were earning more now than many skilled workers in other parts of the plant. Management was besieged by demands that this inequity be taken care of. With growing irritation between superintendent and foreman, engineers and foreman, superintendent and engineers, the situation came to a head when the superintendent without consultation arbitrarily revoked the learning bonus and returned the painting operation to its original status. The hooks moved again at their constant, time-studied designated speed, production dropped again, and within a month all but two of the eight girls had quit. The foreman himself stayed on for several months, but, feeling aggrieved, then left for another job.[4]

Relying on a catalytic approach, the consultant had aided the foreman to view the group-dynamics issue facing him and to get more worker involvement as he sought to deal with difficulties existing among these paint-room operators. By shifting the supervisor's use of power/authority to one that promoted information gathering through discussion, the supervisor was able to see not only how to solve gripes but how to improve productivity as well.

His efforts failed, however, because the status quo itself came under scrutiny. Eventually the assembly-line operation was brought back to where it had been in the beginning. The failure seems to have been caused by the consultant working with the supervisor *as an individual* when he should have been working as an organization consultant, involving all those who must support change: the foreman, the foreman's boss, the superintendent, the engineers, and the women as well. Because this was not done, new resistances related to challenged authority arose, which neither the foreman nor the consultant could resolve.

The consultant's objective in this example was to help the client gather and interpret data regarding his situation, and to offer procedural suggestions (for example, "Why not ask the girls?"), yet to avoid taking part in the client's final decisions. This remained the complete responsibility of the client. The failure should not be taken as a limitation of the character of the intervention; it simply reflects the kind of problem that can arise when the consultant intervenes with the "wrong" client.

GROUP (D-1-2)

Misperceptions regarding the use of power/authority are particularly pertinent as focal issues in group functioning. The boss views his or her behavior one way, many times in terms of "good intentions." Each subordinate, however, is likely to have a different perspective of the boss's behavior, especially as this impinges on the subordinate's own job responsibilities and status in the group. Catalytic interventions within groups can aid members to share their perceptions, pool information, clear up misunderstandings, and thereby increase the likelihood that more valid problem solving can take place.

Where should team building be introduced into an organization? The answer given by catalytically oriented consultants such as Shepard[5] is that it is best to start where there is a pocket of constructive interest, regardless of the level. "The first persons to be invited should be those who consistently turn all their experiences into constructive learning. Similarly, in introducing team development processes into a system, [one should] begin with the best functioning team."

The approach recommended by Shepard is catalytic, the low-risk point of entry is with the team which is most ready and whose expectations the catalytic mode is likely to meet.

It is doubtful that this advice is a sound strategy for gaining the organization-wide benefits of team development. Evidence supports the conclusion that team pride prevents other teams from following the lead of the first teams engaged in development. Spread is not spontaneous. The more likely reaction is "if it is good for them, they are to be commended for doing something about their problems, but certainly our situation is different. Therefore, we will decline the invitation to do the same thing as they have done, and possibly identify some other thing that would be more pertinent to the uniqueness of our situation."

The felt-needs/real-needs issue is nicely put by Shepard, who counsels consultants to start where the system is. That is, to respond to felt needs. "The change agent needs to understand how the client sees himself in a situation and needs to understand the culture of the system. . . ." Shepard justifies dealing with felt rather than real needs as being both ethically and technically virtuous, and implies that it is essential to do so in order to gain needed access for diagnosing and later developing a sound strategy.

How the team-building consultant breaks out of the client's felt-need system in order to bring the real issues of team ineffectiveness into focus is not explained. The likelihood that this transition will be difficult is reinforced by another admonition he provides. "Individuals and groups, locked in destructive kinds of conflict, focus on their differences. The change agent's job is to help them discover and build on their commonalities, so that they will have a foundation of respect and trust which will permit them to use their differences as a source of creativity. . . ." This suggests, however, that the consultant will find him- or herself sealed into the felt-needs system, and unable to escape from it. Promoting harmony through congeniality and turning away from the real problem by concentrating on areas where few or no problems exist may be enjoyable, but is not likely to be productive.

Team building as described by Dyer[6] is close to pure catalytic in its underlying assumptions, which include (1) felt-need diagnosis, (2) data gathering by interview or questionnaire prior to team building, (3) facilitation of team building by internal or external consultants, and (4) action planning for implementation of needed change. Instruments useful for data gathering are illustrated in the text.

The New Boss

A description of a catalytic consultant specializing in process consultation is depicted by what took place in a small manufacturing organization. The intervention involved a "family" group composed of heads of different departments with their new general manager, Kuriloff. These group-building meetings were being held with Atkins as the consultant to identify and to resolve interpersonal difficulties and to study factors that had been slowing the solution of economic problems. Power/authority was frequently the central issue. The following dialogues took place during the first session.

Participants understood they had convened to study how they worked with one another and how they might work together more effectively. The general manager called the meeting to order. Finally someone asked Jack, one of the consultants: "What are we supposed to do?" The consultant started things off with procedural suggestions of the catalytic kind: suggestive but tentative, direction-giving but not demanding.

> Jack . . . explained that the purpose of our getting together was to explore our feelings and relationships. . . . "It's important to express feelings about one another, including us trainers. No holds are barred. . . . However, everyone should also feel free *not* to respond if it becomes too difficult or too uncomfortable. Openness is valued, but so is the right of privacy."
> After a slow beginning, something happened.
> Jim . . . voiced concern about his relationship with Rod. . . . "What's happened to us? Lately we can't seem to get anywhere on design problems."
> "Strange," Rod replied, "I've noticed it, too."[7]

Rod went on to say that once Jim was no longer subordinate to him, Jim's whole philosophy of management seemed to change; this came through to Rod as "dishonest." Jim and Rod tried to clarify this misunderstanding. Other participants stepped in from time to time to assist this process.

The consultant had been successful in getting these two members of the group involved in critique and feedback.

> "If you had only let me know how you felt," Jim implored, "we could have straightened this out long ago."
> "Well, I got the message that you didn't much care what I thought," Rod countered. "When you invited the engineering people to come to your house for that barbeque, you didn't invite me. I assumed you wanted the opportunity to solidify your position with your new people."[8]

Jim explained that no slight was intended—Rod hadn't been invited because Jim understood Rod would be out of town. Soon afterward a cathartic by-product of the mutual feedback emerged.

> The first session ended, and during the coffee break Rod and Jim stood in the hall, drinking coffee and talking busily. Excited, Rod said, "I'm sure glad we could clear the air! I feel a lot better now that I got it out in the open. I think I can sit down and work with you now. My feelings won't be standing between us." Rod extended his hand. He did not smile.[9]

This kind of communication about "feelings-as-data" gives each person the additional information essential for interpersonal problem solving. In this instance, feelings associated with changes in status were in the forefront. By sharing emotions and respective interpretations of events, perceptual clarification was increased.

The consultant's behavior in this situation is primarily facilitative in the sense of hastening the process. However, as an outsider, he can see and point out for particular attention what insiders have accepted without second thought.

> Finally, the trainers employ their skill in pointing out the group's processes, that is, when they are evading important issues or avoiding expressions of feelings. They also lend support and protection to those who find it difficult to function in a group.[10]

This latter function is particularly relevant where there are real or perceived differences in the use of power/authority within the group.

Levinson describes the consultant-as-intermediary intervention as an appropriate strategy when members of a team are so emotionally involved that direct or face-to-face consultant interventions would lead, not to constructive outcomes, but to destructive results. Feelings and emotions may be too deep-lying to be channeled constructively. Under these conditions an intervention approach that moderates tensions and provides a way for nonconfrontational awareness building can offer the possibility of useful though not necessarily dramatic progress. Levinson reports such an explosive situation and how it was dealt with.

> A president with a good managerial history was brought in to head a scientific company whose key men neither understood nor wanted to be subject to professional management. When they threatened to resign, and some did, urgent consultation was requested. Diagnosis of this situation took into account organization history and scientific values, desertion by the company's founders, exploitation by a previous president, cohesion of the in-group, and the need to retain adaptive profitability. On the basis of a comprehensive assessment, it was decided to hear the men out in individual interviews, then summarize those interviews and present them simultaneously to the interviewees and the president. This procedure produced problems and issues to be dealt with, without subjecting the group to the possible exploitation of the president, whom they feared, and without running the risk of their destroying him under confrontation attack. The consultant became, in effect, an intermediary. On the one hand, his job was to help the president understand the nature of the complaints and the kinds of people he was dealing with as well as certain basic psychological principles. On the other hand, his task was to help the group recognize its need for a professional manager and to offer these men more constructive ways of giving the president support and guidance. After the initial contact of three, three-day sessions, the consultant maintained a distance from the group so that he would not be seen as "running the company." Many of the key managers individually took part in executive seminars to learn more

about the psychology of management, and the consultant was available to all of them as individuals by phone or personal contact. This enabled the president and his key figures to develop a working relationship in which all could count on the distant but supportive influence of the consultant and the new and consistent pattern of leadership the president established.

This case example is one where power/authority is at the core of the problem, yet significant issues of morale/cohesion need attention also.

Once general comfort was attained in these relationships and the men could come to trust the president (in part because the consultant drew off some of their hostility toward him), they decided that it would be wise to get together as a group at monthly intervals in order to open up avenues of communication, which they knew needed opening but which would have been destructively explosive had they been opened before. The group continues to function effectively together, now more closely than ever. However, this process of carefully differentiated steps extended over a three-year period.[11]

This intermediary kind of role—almost one of keeping protagonists separated—is a way of preventing a status-quo explosion. By offering suggestions as to ways to proceed and through preserving the anonymity of interviewees, the consultant aided the president on the one hand, and his subordinates on the other, to enlarge and objectify their mutual perceptions. Eventually the clients did improve their communications, but they did so without being taught to be more open and candid in face-to-face interactions.

Boss Inaccessibility

Frequently bosses think they have open-door policies; that is, subordinates are free to approach the boss whenever they need to. Often subordinates hear the *words,* but, for whatever reason, still see the boss as inaccessible. This can create a power vacuum, which may be unrecognized by either boss or subordinates. In effect, there are "invisible seals" within the system, keeping two or more individuals' perceptions and information separate and preventing shared insights into power/authority problems and their resolution.

Harvey and Boettger[12] identified and intervened in this kind of situation. The consultation involved a corporate services group, including a vice-president and fifteen division directors, referred to as COSCOM (Corporate Services Committee on Operations Management). The members met periodically to exchange information, discuss problems, and find and evaluate solutions. Most COSCOM members had already engaged in an "unfreezing" experience involving T-Group participation. Because of this they expressed interest in applying laboratory method to improving COSCOM functioning. The consultants then interviewed the boss and division directors concerning their views of problems, including problems facing the total company, those in their own divisions, those involved in how they worked with other divisions, and the concerns each had as to his or her own work in the company. Each interview lasted approximately an hour.

Interview findings were summarized and a variety of problems identified. One set of issues concerned difficulties division directors had in communicating with their boss, the COSCOM vice-president: "The vice-president is inaccessible"; "The vice-president has too many people reporting to him for me to have the time that I need to talk with him"; "The vice-president does not seem to want to know what I think." All of these point to a power/authority focal issue. A particular facet of the problem was that interviewees experienced some personal frustrations from being required to reply to memoranda from their boss.

> "It seems as if every morning when I show up for work my desk is loaded with a bunch of memos."
> "I spend half of my time around here trying to answer those ————— memos the vice president sends me, and my staff spends half of their time getting me enough information to answer them."
> "I have a hard time getting my work done. I am always busy fielding his 'rockets'."

Such reactions to memoranda suggested an important communication problem. Complaints about the frequency of memos led the consultants to extend their data gathering by finding out how many memos actually were transmitted over a six-month period. Three hundred sixty-seven memos had been sent to fifteen subordinates. Interview information was then fed back to the COSCOM members as a team.

In the joint-action planning phase, the following information-gathering strategy was designed.

1. Each participant would provide the consultant with the most inappropriate (confusing, irrelevant or unessential) memo the vice-president had sent him.
2. The vice-president would do something similar, except he would be providing the consultants with replies he had received.
3. After memos had been projected on the screen, for all to see, each person wrote:
   a. What he thought the memo said to do.
   b. What action he would take in response to the memo.
   c. What priority he would give work on the memo—high, medium, or low.
4. Each participant, other than the actual instigator and recipient, read aloud the conclusions reached under (3) to the total COSCOM group.
5. The recipient of this missive reported how he had understood it and what action he had to take, and the priority given it.
6. The vice-president did the same in regard to his intention when he had composed the memo.
7. The next day entailed diagnosis of "communication" problems between the vice-president and memo recipients. Recommendations for action were also developed.[13]

After some discussion of the information, participants developed a cooperative spirit and set higher goals of achievement. The project was reported to have had a successful outcome.

Viewed from the perspective of an action-research strategy, the key executives of this organization perceived the possibility that problems existed. Consultants were invited to apply the "laboratory method" with which these executives already had some familiarity. Initial exploratory information gathering and diagnosis by the consultants took place and then a second round was conducted to test the objectivity of the group perceptions (of memo frequency). Feedback was provided followed by action planning as a means of obtaining desirable goals. This action-research strategy provides a sequence of interventions that can have a catalyzing effect, quickening the readiness to solve problems sensed on a felt-needs basis but not previously recognized with enough clarity for their negative impact to be fully appreciated.

Retirement Home Residents' Problems with Home Authority

Many individuals face a painful and difficult period of adjustment upon retirement, which may be accompanied by loss of self-esteem, feelings of worthlessness and rejection, periods of loneliness and isolation. These symptoms may be exaggerated and compounded when the retirement-aged person has not developed interests and acquaintances outside the job. Some employers are offering counseling sessions in the preventative mode to help retirees plan their retirements just as they may have planned their careers.

An intervention with working-class citizens by Heap[14] describes an attempt to ease the initial transition to retirement and provide ongoing support once adjustment to retirement is made.

The Centre in this example offers members a steadily expanding range of activities, including discussion groups. Some are of short duration and deal with specific and well-defined subjects for those with particular interests. Other discussion groups have a much longer life and give an opportunity for ventilating and considering some general recurrent problems experienced by retired people in modern industrial societies. These groups are led by social workers. They meet weekly for about one and a half hours, and have a duration of two to three months. Most members of the Centre had at some stage—usually early in their membership—participated in such a group.

A detailed account of one such group session, attended by eight members, focuses on issues of autonomy and independence. Using a catalytic approach of summarizing and clarifying information as members discussed and gave feedback on an egalitarian basis, the social worker provided support and encouragement for members to share experiences and feelings about their own autonomy and independence.

A central power/authority theme often emerged. Group members indicated a degree of resentment and hostility over being "bossed" by Centre volunteers. The social worker provides the following description of an intense conflict in a group discussion that focused on the appropriate role of Centre volunteers.

After some active discussion and exemplification, which I structured rather more than usual, it became clear that the displeasure with the volunteers was partly quite realistic and partly an expression of the members' sensitivity around the crucial issues of dependency and self-manifestation. I acknowledged the importance of the issue raised; . . . I proposed that we should work towards an extraordinary general meeting—where the agenda was to be planned and prepared by a sub-committee of members and volunteers—where grievances were to be specified and remedies proposed. (I foresee both a stormy time and—possibly—a further increase in . . . control and autonomy [by members].[15])

The elderly clients in this group setting are probably typical of most in wanting to be the "masters of their own fates and captains of their own souls." Power/authority issues are similar to those encountered by any group that perceives itself to be in a low-power position.

Simultaneous Hierarchy and Equality

Widespread recognition of the problems that can result from unilaterally exercised power/authority within an hierarchical structure has led to the formulation of various *structural* solutions regarding how to gain the benefits of equality while preserving the official hierarchy that itself connotes inequality.

Collateral system is a structural intervention that preserves the power/authority status quo, while creating an alternative to it. Several authors have actively intervened in an organization to bring about power/authority "splits," while others have commented on possibilities that might prove feasible.

One example is provided by Zand.[16] The rationale of this collateral-system intervention rests on the following. The functioning of a work group is strengthened to the degree it can shift its operating style to accommodate change and diversity. This may mean, for example, that one particular problem situation calls for authority to be highly focused in a single individual with several others implementing solutions he or she alone has devised. Another type of problem may be better addressed by widely shared solution-seeking participation, with contributions based on personal capabilities rather than on rank. These two contrasting styles of exercising authority by no means exhaust the possibilities, but they are the two systems concentrated on in collateral-system interventions.

The idea that problems are of two types—well-structured and ill-structured— is the second premise of this approach. Well-structured problems, according to Zand, are suited to resolution through organized routines and close supervision. In contrast, ill-structured problems are complex—hard to define and to solve under established procedures and tight or close supervision. Work supervised under tight control is more effective when dealing with well-structured problems than with those in the ill-structured category. More general supervision, with free give-and-take, is better suited to the solution of complex, difficult-to-define problems.

Given the premise that hierarchical work groups are inflexible, the only alternative is to form a second or *collateral organization*. Although the same individuals may be involved, they are expected to see themselves in a different light and act accordingly when operating in the collateral mode.

This intervention encourages the work group to use the collateral organization whenever a manager becomes aware that he or she is faced with an ill-structured problem or opportunity. In the collateral organization, hierarchy-based relationships and attitudes are set aside to facilitate creative problem solving.

An example involves the vice-president of a bank. Mr. Brady wanted to increase his department's competence to meet competition in the worldwide market. While the goal itself was clear, many ill-structured issues needed to be identified and resolved in a coordinated way.

In daily work, this vice-president interacted routinely in an authority-production mode. Mr. Brady was in the habit of masterminding solutions to daily operations problems, and his subordinates were largely implementers of these solutions. Thus, as the vice-president began discussing strategy issues with several key subordinates, he found them unable to contribute in an effective manner. Each subordinate seemed to view the "whole" from a position close to his own sphere of responsibility.

Zand's intervention approached the situation in a catalytic manner. First he interviewed Mr. Brady and his subordinates, in addition to observing their daily work and decision making. He apparently concurred that the subordinates would have great difficulty dealing productively with broad strategy matters even though, as individuals, they were competent. Each had the international-banking knowledge essential for identifying valid solutions to ill-structured problems. The consultant concluded that a departure from the usual pattern of power/authority production-centered work was necessary.

> The OD specialist explained the need for a collateral organization to Mr. Brady and his group. He proposed an initial three-day meeting, at which strategy and operating issues would be discussed, analyzed, and if possible, resolved. (The men were so busy they insisted it be from Friday afternoon to Sunday evening.) Aware that collateral organizations frequently fail because managers may have unrealistic expectations and cannot foresee the difficulties of a collateral mode, the specialist stressed setting limited, attainable goals. He suggested that the group try to identify key issues but discuss only two or three priority issues in detail. Since there would be many unanswered questions after the meeting, they would also have to approve some structure which would be used to work on finding answers after they returned to work. Finally they should discuss how they could organize to solve ill-structured problems more effectively in the future.
>
> Ten days before the meeting, the OD specialist interviewed each manager, gathering information for the meeting and answering questions about format. Each manager described the issues he most wanted discussed, the outcomes that would make him feel the meeting was worthwhile, and the difficulties that might interfere with managers being reasonably open about important issues. The interview process itself stimulated managers to think about norms that departed from those of the primary mode.[17]

The consultant introduced the following considerations in a general session presentation that served as a preamble to this outside meeting.

> The power difference in the formal organization would still exist when the managers returned to work. Mr. Brady, the vice president, was the group's superior, and this was his meeting, not the consultant's. The group or its members could make recommendations, but Mr. Brady would have to approve any proposal before it could be implemented. Regardless of formal position, managers usually have valuable insights and proposals that cut across many different areas. It would be the responsibility of the high managers to facilitate expression and use of these views. The OD specialist would suggest procedures and ask questions to help the group's problem solving.[18]

This summary illustrates the consultant's two-headed theme of "preserve the formal structure for well-structured problems, but switch out of it for solving nonroutine problems." Operating in a catalytic mode,

> the specialist then reported a summary of the issues managers wanted to discuss. At first, the group operated in an authority/production mode. Managers frequently proposed solutions before a problem had been clearly defined. The specialist made process observations to alter these norms. Discussion was brought back to managers whose views had not been heard adequately. There was regular testing to ensure that any problem was understood by all before solutions were discussed in depth. Regardless of status, managers began contributing important information and insights. This helped the senior managers see how the open channels of the collateral mode improved problem solving.
>
> On the second day, the managers agreed to experiment with a collateral mode after they returned to work. They would set aside "unstructured" time (multichannels, free questioning, and so on) to study several ill-structured problems. Based on their new experience, they also adopted a special norm for their collateral mode: incomplete ideas, although not thoroughly reasoned and defendable, were welcomed. This was a deliberate and significant departure from behavior in their primary organization. It was intended to stimulate search and creativity. They reiterated, however, that in the hierarchical (primary) organization, a recommendation would still have to be supported by thorough reasoning and documentation. They had grasped the distinction between primary and collateral modes without falling into the trap of insisting that one had to displace the other.[19]

Upon completing this intervention on operating as a collateral organization, members returned to their everyday assignments. While continuing to operate the business in a formal mode, they dealt with several sticky problems on a one-morning-per-week basis over the next six weeks in the collateral mode. This helped to stabilize their skills, yet preserved the sharp demarcation between power/authority and catalytic modes of problem solving.

An update on collateral organization is provided by Zand showing its use in aiding a group of foremen shift from supervision based on craft specialization to multicraft supervision. Foremen discussed and shared information on some of the difficulties in supervision, particularly dealing with such issues as overtime, inexpensive purchases, guarantees for workers' effectiveness, and scheduling. When joined by their managers, all agreed to recommend steps to resolve some of these barriers. Some of their recommendations were implemented.

This is a clear example of utilizing a collateral participative mode to solve problems that seem intractable within the authority system of the hierarchy. The major change is the mechanical suspension of the hierarchy in order for people to share information. Greater insight and skill in using hierarchy in such a way as to avoid the emergence of such problems is not seen as an appropriate approach to strengthening organization effectiveness.[20]

Another alternative structure involves a *temporary system* as discussed by Miles[21] and elaborated on by Bennis and Slater.[22] A temporary system is an association of two or more people for some specific purpose, with shared understanding that it is temporary, i.e., has a limited duration and will dissolve when the objective for organizing it has been met or when individual members' current interests are no longer meaningfully served.

By comparison, a collateral organization is likely to dissolve for at least two reasons. One is when the unique problems the collateral organization is capable of solving cease to exist. Another is that the formal organization may "internalize" the particular power/authority mode of the collateral organization, making formal distinctions between these and traditional modes unnecessary. In other words, needs for switching back and forth from formal to collateral organization no longer exist. In a team-building sense, the needed flexibility to deal with both well-structured and ill-structured problems has been achieved.

A parallel use of the collateral organization basis for intervention is described by Weisbord, Lamb, and Drexler. The client in this case is the police department of Urban City, where authority-obedience was suspended to permit problem diagnosis and solution recommending.

> First, data about the bureau was gathered by interviewing and observing the police officers in their daily activities. From this data emerged a strategy to be used to build a more effective middle management. All supervisors would be given an opportunity to name the most pressing problems, trained in group problem-solving techniques and then immediately given a chance to use their new skills in special task forces which would be organized to solve the problems they had named.[23]

One aspect of the collateral organization rests on the use of diagonal slices of the organization to define problems.

> These task forces would cut across the lines of rank and divisions to include those with authority over the problem, those with the skill to solve it, and those most affected by it. The task forces would be "collateral" or parallel to the formal organization. That is, they would include the same men as the formal organization, but in new relationships, working under special ground rules, whose task would be to solve problems not easily handled in a formal

way. The task forces would supplement the usual decision-making process, not replace it; they would have the power only to recommend solutions to the commissioner and chief. Underlying the use of task forces are the assumptions that several people of varying backgrounds together can solve joint problems more creatively than by working alone, and that people are more committed to carrying out decisions they have had a part in making.

Sessions were scheduled at various times so that all men could attend, regardless of shifts worked. The program involved half a dozen formal meetings, varying in length from two hours to one and a half days, plus several informal meetings arranged by the men themselves.

In the first session, each of the four groups, which were mixed by rank, made a list of the problems they saw in the bureau. The lists were then combined and the problems sorted into long- and short-range designations and assigned priorities by the officers working in peer groups by rank. Then the resulting lists were merged according to the priorities assigned.[24]

Task force assignments of the same personnel were then made.

From this came a task force assignment list, with each task force centered around a specific problem the officers had named, such as vehicle maintenance, discipline, the reporting system, and the promotional system. The men were then given training in group problem solving, including theory, a personal style questionnaire, observation of groups at work, and a training problem (interference at crime scenes) for all the men to work through together.[25]

The close resemblance of collateral organization to the confrontation meeting (actually catalytic in character) is revealed in the following.

The men were asked to select the task force they preferred. Each task force thoroughly investigated its assigned problem and made recommendations in an oral presentation and written report to the chief and the commissioner. Some answers were given by the chief and the commissioner on the spot, and some further assignments were made; then the recommendations, responses, and actions taken were summarized in a memo from the commissioner and the chief to all the men. In addition, some new task forces were created as a result of questions raised by the first groups. This necessitated a second round of task force work and the same kind of reporting sessions and memo back to the officers as in the first round.

Most of the men found the training sessions useful, particularly the aspect of being able to discuss mutual problems in groups. Many also said that the training seemed to improve their communication and problem-solving skills (on all levels) in their daily work.[26]

Even though based on subjective data, an evaluation of impact was attempted from which the following conclusions were drawn.

As for changes made to correct the problems facing the bureau, in a survey comparing the bureau before and after the sessions, the officers felt that 15 out of 18 items in the questionnaire had improved after the training and task forces. As further proof, the survey was also given to patrolmen, who were not directly involved in the training but certainly would be able to see its effects. They, too, reported improvement in most of the critical problems facing the Bureau of Police. In addition, interviews with senior officers a year later indicated that task force problem solving had become standard operating procedure for difficult, non-routine problems. In short, the "collateral organization" had become a new administrative tool as intended.[27]

All of these examples are interesting commentaries on the ability of people in groups to shift with the rules of the game. In a way, though, the focal issue is how to distribute power/authority in the first place rather than having to develop a second organization to grapple with problems created by but that appear to be unmanageable in the first.

Assisting Teachers to Learn More About Authority in the Classroom

A developing conviction is that if teachers understood themselves more fully—particularly their own use of power/authority—they could replace actions that provoke classroom difficulties with others that preclude difficulties. The consultant focus, then, shifts from child behavior per se to helping teacher-as-client. Sometimes this process is facilitated by working with teachers in groups instead of in one-to-one consultations.

An example of such an approach is offered by Dinkmeyer and Carlson.[28] In the following excerpt, the consultant works with a group of classroom teachers, and through his interventions, focuses issues and assists teachers to share their experiences with one another.

Teacher 3: I think he is fighting her. Whatever she says, he is going to do the opposite.

Consultant: You believe it is his need to be in control?

Teacher 3: Yes, some think they are in charge.

Consultant: You feel challenged by these students?

Teacher 3: Right. I can't let them get by with anything.

Consultant: What do some of you think about that?

Teacher 4: I recognize I have the same problem about wanting to be in control.

Consultant: If it's important for you to have the power, what do you think the child experiences?

Teacher 1: I imagine our real problem is getting involved in fighting with them.

Teacher 2: I've found things go better when I refuse to become involved in power contests.

Consultant: Let's look at this in another way. What if you're busy writing and somebody comes by and says, "That's really good work. Now I hope you keep that up."

Teacher 4: No, I don't think I would like that. . . .

Teacher 5: You're not satisfied with it. *(laughter)*

Consultant: Yes, what is the implication?

Teacher 4: Well, I don't expect you to really finish.

Teacher 1: . . . that he won't cooperate.

Teacher 4: It's like a backhand slap.

Teacher 1: That's really true, because I don't expect him to finish and I gave him the clue.

Teacher 2: I can do that with the brighter children and say "Oh, that sounds like a good story," or "Oh, that sounds like it's going to be exciting; go on and finish it." That excites them to want to go on. With the slower children, or the child who needs discipline, why should it work in a reverse order?

By this open-ended inquiry the consultant successfully keeps teachers focused on their own behavior, which comes to be seen as involving a communications problem. An alternative issue could be how teachers use their classroom authority to control students.

Teacher 4: We have to learn to be more aware of our communication and the messages we send.

Consultant: It seems difficult to understand, but our communication does affect the child's motivation.

Teacher 2: It really has to be a habit, where you have to be able to do it unconsciously, always positive.

Consultant: And I think that you are right about a habit. It takes a long time to get to that because you're so used to doing it the other way.

Teacher 4: One thing, I don't know whether I mentioned it here, but I have found it is a tremendous help if I really take some time out when the children come in and call five or six of them out in the hall and say to each, "Robert, I'm so thrilled that you are here because you were such a good boy this morning and it was so nice to have you in my room." I suppose it would be like the boss coming along and saying to you he's proud of your work. I reflect on that and my afternoons go ten times better!

Teacher 2: I have got to try that. Thats sounds good.

Teacher 4: But a lot of times I come in and begin yelling and say, "Sit down, be quiet." This is like throwing the monkey wrench into the machinery.

Consultant: Or, when you come in you could say something like, "I noticed that you were really working at that math this morning." . . . just some little encouragement.[29]

Beyond functioning as a discussion rallying point, the consultant's contribution is mainly in asking "What if. . . ?" kinds of questions that aid participants in expressing their thoughts and feelings. Through this sharing, common-sense wisdom can be marshalled and made available to the teacher. The limitation is that the issue may, as seems to be true in this case, be defined as a communication and reward problem, when the underlying dynamics actually concern misuses of authority and obedience as a means of control.

Academic Warfare

In this case, a small academic department was split into factions or camps on major issues. The usual interpersonal tension problems, such as mutual distrust, accusations of boss-manipulation for personal benefit, and so on, were evident. This department became the client for two different catalytic change strategies: an unsuccessful intervention by an external consultant followed by a more successful internal-consultant intervention. The report is by Varney and Lasher.[30]

Within the department, indications of increasing ineffectiveness were becoming evident. In response, a one-day team-building session was arranged. It was led by an outside process consultant and initially appeared to have been successful in identifying the causes of manifest problems which could thereafter be dealt with more openly. However, two or three faculty members were outspoken in questioning the need for "some outsider to come in and help us solve department problems." These attitudes had a veto effect and the consultation fell victim to the cleavage it was intended to bridge. Furthermore, efforts by colleagues to reduce divisiveness were not accepted either.

The next step was initiated by an insider, an administrative officer of the university who also held a faculty appointment. Along with the two authors, he joined a group of interested students and requested permission of the department faculty to conduct a survey. The survey data, organized on an "as is" versus "ought to be" basis, would be summarized and fed back to them as clients for reflection and diagnosis. Agreement to do this was reached.

Data were fed back at two departmental meetings attended by all faculty. Real issues were identified and articulated. Action plans included the preparation of working papers as a means of thinking through and sharing points of view. Sharing of feelings also became more apparent, cooperation improved, and pride in organization was indicated by wanting to bring about "changes geared toward making the department the most effective in the college."

Summary

In each of the examples above, power/authority was centralized when the intervention began and more or less equally distributed at its completion. An egalitarian value system seems to underlie many catalytic consultants' actions.

INTERGROUP (D-1-3)

Catalytic interventions have been used to help solve intergroup problems. Gathering empirical information and feeding it back is the fundamental strategy, whether the problem is between vertical hierarchical levels or lateral groups.

Tensions Between Vertical Levels

A four-year change project was undertaken in a metropolitan law enforcement agency[31] where a new sheriff took over the agency and introduced a departmental staff of young educated and dedicated law enforcement officers. Within the next year, however, interpersonal differences, competition, and hostility among subordinates emerged. The sheriff, who had encouraged an open-door policy, directed that all departmental communications, including those of his top administrative staff, be channeled through the under-sheriff. The sheriff would be involved only if a matter could not be settled at the lower level. Within the next few months, however, tensions began to mount and at this point the sheriff called in a consultant.

The consultant recommended top team participation in a six-day training session. The intervention began with consultant interviews of the total administrative staff. Included were such questions as: "What are the most critical issues facing the department?"; "What are the critical issues between divisions?"; "What does the sheriff do that bothers you?"; "What could the sheriff do more of?"; and "If you could make five changes in the department what would they be?"

The problems that surfaced during the interview sessions included disapproval of the managerial style of the under-sheriff, frustration and hostility created by the sheriff's inaccessibility, extremely high turnover in the department, absence of the sheriff from the department, arbitrary decisions made by the sheriff and announced by memo, and financial mismanagement. All of these added up to very low trust and high suspicion. Four of the five division heads were considering resigning and the sheriff had decided not to run for reelection.

The six-day session began with an exercise concerned with decision making. Although hypothetical, the exercise was filled with typical types of chaotic process and conflict that characterize many actual decision-making groups. This served to lift the lid on conflict present in the group. Thereafter an image exchange design was used to clear the air between the two top staff and the rest of the five administrative staff members. The following three questions were answered in the image exchange by the administrative group. "How do you see yourself in relation to the staff?"; "How do you see the staff?" and "How do you think the staff sees you?" The questions were also answered by the five staff members. The following are the results from this image design.[32]

How Administration Sees Themselves	*How the Staff Sees Administration*
intelligent	fiercely dedicated
dedicated	somewhat lonely
experienced	unyielding
fast to react	hardworking
opinionated	aloof
stubborn	attitude of superiority
put in long hours	politically motivated (in a

"rooting" (sticking your nose
in our business)

negative way)
impossible to please
insensitivity
unwilling to give credit where due
lack of administrative skills
caught up by their power
overreaction oriented
good cops "rooting"

How the Staff Sees Themselves

professional
diligent
worthy of respect and
consideration
competent
untiring
unyielding
super cops
dedicated
intelligent
humorous

How Administration Sees Staff

good cops
hardworking
together-clique
backbiting
hard to work for
stubborn
closed minds
unconcerned about political
pressure

A period was spent after the lists were exchanged to review them and to give participants a sense of mutual acceptance by confirming their shared perceptions. During this activity the responses to the preconference interviews also were summarized and acknowledged by individuals on a voluntary basis. Communications were restricted to clarifying and giving examples in a nonjudgmental manner, with each participant being encouraged to ask questions pertaining to himself.

The next step was problem solving through interpersonal contracting to ensure actions on the issues raised. Thus, each member answered the question: "What will I do to help the organization function more effectively? What will the rest of the group do to help me?" Individuals made commitments to change and the group committed itself to support the individual's efforts. Resolving problems associated with organizational and independent departmental communication was the final step.

This intervention dealt primarily with the way in which power and authority were being exercised and the impact of this on decision-making processes.

Impact was measured in two ways. One was in terms of a trust scale, which showed that the average score on a 10-point scale moved from 1.5 at the beginning of the team-building session, increased to 5.8 by midweek, and to 9.5 at the end. A second prepost measure drew comparisons with similar law enforcement agencies in the same cultural geographic and political environment. It showed positive changes on five of the six categories.

While catalytic interventions have for the most part proved unsuccessful (because sharing of information is not sufficient), this one appears to have had positive results. One way of explaining this is that this top team effort served to initiate a series of organizational restructuring efforts that included interventions up and down the organization, such as off-site training sessions, management training for supervisors, process consultation, survey feedback, third party consultation, technological interventions, policy formulation, and so on. This variety of interventions over a period of four years resulted in statistically significant improvements. Turnover decreased, prison walkaways and escapes were reduced, the movement toward unionization was discontinued, and the sheriff was returned to office for two additional terms because of demonstrated effectiveness. The cumulative impact was probably responsible for the effective outcome.

Intervention in a "Frozen" Warfare Situation

Problems in bureaucratic organizations often involve and are compounded by multiple hierarchical levels. When vertical conflicts develop, persons at each level may "side" with one or another of the principals who are directly involved in the controversy. What may have begun as a personal disagreement or personality clash between two persons can escalate into full-scale organizational "war."

Sebring and Duffee[33] describe such a situation. They were invited into a Pennsylvania correctional institution as organizational consultants. Their charge came from the regional educational director who had authority to more than double the prison's vocational education budget. Reluctance to commit more money to this particular facility arose from reports of conflict in the institution's vocational educational program. The regional education director asked the consultants "to obtain more information about what was going on inside the prison" and to, as he put it, "see if he was getting his money's worth."

Initially, the consultants gathered information on the conflict and attempted to identify underlying causes. They concluded that what apparently had begun as a philosophical difference between the prison's education director and a member of her teaching staff ultimately divided the institution staff into two warring groups. Sebring and Duffee describe the situational dynamics in these terms: "Repeated clashes occurred between the two. As confrontations increased in number each contestant developed a loyal cadre of supporters. . . ."

Some staff members recognized the organizational damage inherent in these conditions. As the consultants report, "we could easily see that the prison staff were worried, frustrated, insecure and depressed. They all wanted things to change, but they were frozen into . . . paranoid patterns of behavior."

They describe their approach to this problem as process consultation. Their effort was to hold a series of meetings with key players at different levels in an effort to "actively involve the staff members themselves in the early planning, data-gathering, assessment and diagnosis, and goal-setting stages." Ideally, this participation should enhance commitment to both the process and the eventual solution.

At the third in a series of such meetings, correctional institution staff were asked to participate in an assessment of the current situation.

For the next three days, one-hour in-depth interviews were conducted with thirty persons, including all educational staff members, the home economics instructor, the educational director, and others. The questions focused on the following areas:

1. The problems facing the organization.
2. The kinds of things causing the problems.
3. The perceived organizational strengths that could help solve the problems.[34]

Results from the interviews were fed back to key executives individually. Next, a group feedback session was held to discuss with staff the "hot" organizational issues, the issues that had to be resolved immediately. After answering questions about the data, the consultants divided the participants into three problem-solving groups to discuss the findings and to identify steps to be taken to improve the situation. After an hour, each group reported back to the larger group.

Denials and refusal to accept responsibility were the prevailing responses to this catalytic intervention with no viable suggestions for improvement offered. The consultants reported that their attempts to develop mutual conflict resolution motivation had apparently failed.

A series of retrospective suggestions that might have contributed to a more successful outcome are included with the authors' account of this intervention. Such "20–20" hindsight clarifies the importance of planning and managing an intervention, rather than following "felt need" and just "letting it happen." Typically, consultants are hired for their expertise in organizational theory and behavioral science principles. Application of this expertise to the selection of intervention tactics and strategies is critical to eventual success.

This catalytic intervention in a real conflict situation was of little or no value because the underlying feelings of antagonism were only indirectly related to "facts, data, and logic." The use of a "facts, data, and logic" approach, therefore, is unlikely to get to the root of a conflict that is centered in antagonistic feelings and emotions.

Unclear Power Relations Between Faculty and Staff

One of the difficulties encountered by interdependent groups is inappropriate or unclear power relations. When each group suffers from pluralistic ignorance as to what the power relationship is or should be, needed coordination can hardly follow.

This line of reasoning led Alderfer[35] to view the classroom relationship between faculty and students in the following manner. The consultant observed that students often talked to one another about courses, but that similarly pertinent discussions between students and teachers, where the data generated could have had potent change effects for all participants, were rare. Since it was even more rare for faculty members to discuss their teaching practices on a colleague-to-colleague basis, neither did they influence one another to any significant degree.

The intervention design did not entail communication between already intact groups. Instead, a faculty committee concerned with teaching and learning convened a sample group of faculty members—three each from humanities, social sciences, and natural sciences—for an evening of discussion with a representative group of their students. One student was randomly chosen from courses taught by each attending faculty member. After introduction, two separate groups, one of faculty and one of students, were formed for an hour-long discussion of, "How the student-teacher relationship affects teaching and learning." Consultants sat with each group. Faculty members are reported to have had greater difficulty in discussing the topic than did the students.

Points on which two or more participants agreed were recorded. Then two new groups were formed, this time with a crisscross composition, each group half faculty, half student. The agenda for this one-hour discussion was to identify similarities and differences between the faculty and student lists produced during the previous hour.

The four hours of discussion were video-recorded and then edited to a one-hour summation that was shown to the original discussion participants. A summary of findings follows.

Students' View of Faculty	*Faculty View of Itself*
Faculty should be more available for discussion and clarification	
Initiative in evaluating course progress rests with teacher	Feedback from discussion sections useful in assessing progress
Teachers' enthusiasm for subjects and students very important	
Faculty should be prepared and well organized in their presentations	Scanning audience useful to see if the lecture is making sense
Professor should establish his right to teach and should earn the respect of his students	
Primary responsibility for lecture course rests with teachers	Lecture format creates an enormous distance between faculty and students[36]

Student perceptions of the faculty had little in common with faculty's perceptions of themselves. This kind of intergroup design can be useful to those who participate in it, but since the individuals in this situation were not participating as members of an intact group, nor even as chosen representatives of their respective membership groups, the intervention was not likely to have any significant effect in terms of generally shifting such power/authority aspects as one-way communication, responsibility, and initiative taking.

ORGANIZATION (D-1-4)

Organization problems may be solved through altering the power balance. The examples that follow all have in common the use of catalytic methods of data gathering, feedback, and process consultation to involve lower levels of the hierarchy in decision making.

Involving All Levels of a School System in Decision Making

Numerous mechanical changes that are routinely introduced into the operation of a school system, as between the Board, superintendent, staff, as well as various principals, teachers, and specialists, are well known. What is less well understood is how to bring about a more coherent, operational school system.

The situation is seen differently by different experts. One sector of observers advises establishing a philosophy of education around which all groups can cohere. Another suggests an organizational structure creating a clear management committee, comprised so as to ensure that all major points of view and vested interests are represented among its members. A third approach entails achieving a sharp separation between Board responsibilities for setting policy, and school administrator responsibilities for policy implementation.

The acting superintendent of a school system employing 100 teachers (and with 2500 students attending one high school, one junior high school, and eight elementary schools) requested consultative help in finding a sound basis of coherence.

> Mackey [the superintendent] wanted to change the administrators' job responsibilities and their relationships to one another and to him in order to increase sharing of information and participation in the system-wide decision making. The School Board . . . supported Mackey and his wishes for reorganization. Our objective was to develop processes and structures to support them that would help the system to achieve its objectives and would facilitate change in response to new needs as they arose.
>   . . . The Board wanted "an organization chart." More than any particular style of leadership, they wanted formal and explicit plans. . . . We persuaded the Board to let the explicit plan emerge from the process of our intervention.[37]

The consultant's first step was to interview the twelve Board members and twenty-three administrators. The information was fed back, anonymously and uncensored, at a meeting of all Board members and administrators. Interview responses reflected tension, jealousy, "backbiting" and fear of power.

> Though feedback was uncensored, we influenced it by assembling data in categories that seemed obvious and important. . . . We worked long hours with Mackey to help him develop alternative styles of interaction [around the survey results]; these sessions included theory, feedback, illustrations, role playing, coaching, and modeling, to encourage openness, the sharing

of feelings, more direct identification of differences, and confrontation over them.[38]

In terms of structural redesign, a management committee was established to discuss system-wide issues and to assist the superintendent in making important decisions about the system. Participative management and collaborative problem solving were to be the end results of this structural change. Workshops were held with the management committee to reinforce these changes. The consultants acted as facilitators in the first workshop where "many management team members experienced considerable anxiety generated by the more open climate, by potential changes ahead of them, and by increasing pressure from us to confront their differences." During the second workshop "defensiveness gave way to enthusiasm" and real progress was made.

This system-wide intervention was focused on power/authority as a way of developing norms and standards of participative sharing of information, decision making, and problem solving throughout the system. The mechanism for doing so involved setting up and staffing a management committee and aiding it to function more effectively through team building. The intervention is judged successful because the participative process continues in existence after a two-year period.

Involving Students in Decision Making

School systems have historically served as one avenue for imparting societal values, and democracy is one value that receives considerable emphasis and attention in American public schools. Though the merits of democratic processes are repeatedly conveyed to students, the administration of public schools often is typified by use of undemocratic practices. This is particularly so for relationships between administrators and students. Teachers and principals represent ultimate authority and students are expected to obey and comply. Since what is practiced often conflicts with what is preached, students predictably react negatively, sometimes to the point of rebellion.

A case study is reported by Alschuler et al. that represents a long-term (six-year) intervention. It is designed to provide students with direct exposure to "collaborative problem solving and democratic decision making" in the school. Three external consultants, members of the University of Massachusetts School of Education, worked primarily with the principal and teachers of a junior high school to instill Freire's values and practices of shared participation in the Springfield, Massachusetts, school system. Based on their report of this intervention, the authors were guided by Freire's theories but these were not learned by the people operating the school system for their own use in designing solutions. Thus the intervention appears to be catalytic in character, with consultants facilitating the change process in conventional terms.

The consultant's initial efforts were to gather information useful in identifying the central conflict affecting the system.

We tried to see the school system from the participants' perspective by talking with students, faculty, administrators, and parents in classrooms, hallways, washrooms, cafeterias, bus stops, athletic fields, and guidance offices. We spent several weeks sitting in the front office observing activities in this organizational nerve center, and several days following students from class to class through the day, as well as remaining in one classroom while different classes passed in and out. Finally, Irons examined all referrals to the front office during the Fall semesters of 1971 and 1972 to seek clues to important patterns of conflict. Throughout these first two years we conducted several workshops and held weekly discussions with members of the social studies department.

As a result of several thousand hours of informal study and reflection, consultants identified "the battle for students' attention" as the central conflict. We decided that the best "name" for this continuing battle for students' attention is the "discipline problem. . . ." We attempted to analyze the causes of the discipline problems from a system-blaming rather than a person-blaming perspective.[39]

The notion was that students "collaborated" to defeat the system and that teachers and administrators leaned on discipline to prevent students from defeating the system.

After the core problem had been identified, analyzed, and clarified through discussions, solutions were sought via teacher support groups, cadres of from four to thirty teachers in a school who met weekly to do collaborative problem solving.

The solutions that emerged from the support groups are as varied as the problems posed, but most are related to the battle for students' attention. Numerous teachers have developed classroom rules collaboratively with students rather than dictating rules to students and then policing, judging, and executing sentences. At present, sixteen teachers have used a "survey" feedback process in their classroom that 1) collects base-rate data on attention time, student level of participation, students liking of the teacher, and more; 2) presents these data to the class as a potential problem to be solved; 3) collaboratively devises solutions to problems of mutual interest; 4) collects follow-up data to see if the solutions are working.

In all of these specific solutions we have stressed that the values and processes are ultimately more important than the immediate solutions.[40]

At the time of this report, the authors had not completed the evaluation and assessment component of their intervention. In terms of the process, however, the intervention had indicated that participation and collaborative problem-solving efforts are both possible and potentially productive in the public school setting. This intervention actually shifted the power/authority structure by involving students in decision making. Once this shift occurred, it made possible an intervention into the norms/standards operating in the system in terms of the rules of the school and practices in the classroom.

Involving Nonmanagers in Decision Making

Organization interventions most frequently have as their impetus management's felt need to solve a problem or to bring about improvements in productivity, morale, job satisfaction, and so on. Nonmanagement staff are seldom involved in strategizing or decision making about whether or not the intervention is necessary or appropriate and if so, by whom the effort should be undertaken.

Gavin and McPhail report an intervention in which power was shared by involving two levels in the solution of organization problems. After negotiations with both management and nonmanagement staff, members of an eight-person consultant team approached an organization and initiated participation in a change effort. The agreed-upon contract called for an exchange of consultant services, without charge, for the opportunity to conduct research. The client, an Admissions and Records (AR) Department of a large midwestern university, was a nonacademic, service-oriented organization comprised of fifty-four employees. Thirteen of the department's employees were in first-line, middle- or upper-level management positions (PS or "professional staff") while the remaining forty-one were in nonmanagement or "state classified" positions (SC).

> Having received consent from both the PS and SC, our activities progressed to the design of diagnostic measures. Diagnostic data were to be obtained from three major sources: anonymous interviews, questionnaires, and unobtrusive observations. . . . 1-hour structured interviews with all AR personnel were conducted. At the beginning of the second month, a 20-part research and diagnostic questionnaire was administered. On-site unobtrusive observations along with the interview data were used in developing the questionnaire.[41]

To this point, the intervention was catalytic. Gathering and analyzing information to yield insights into the organization was the initial task upon which later approaches were to be built. The second phase focused on the provision of data feedback and served to create organizational consciousness of problems and issues.

"The third month began with feedback sessions based on profiles we had developed. The presentation of findings to the entire department had a dramatic impact. Identified problems were fed back to a sometimes startled and embarrassed audience." The effect of this intervention appeared to be far more than simply "unfreezing"; the open portrayal of problems brought the situation virtually to a boiling point. The feedback phase fell short of being confrontational. The catalytic character was apparently maintained by focusing on the problems and issues the data reflected rather than on underlying causes or shifting to deal with emotions evoked by newly revealed information.

During the third phase, problem-solving and team development sessions were held with SC staff. While the interventionists provide only a sketchy description, it appears that the sessions were data-based discussions. The time invested in team development meetings varied, ranging from a minimum of eight to a maximum of thirty-two hours. The sessions focused on problem identification, brainstorming solutions, and behavioral goal setting, following the feedback reports.

Positive results cited include perceptions that more accurate, more valuable and useful information was being shared, with increases in job freedom and feelings of responsibility and commitment to the job, and changes in perceived power distribution. The changes in feelings of power over time showed that every power base except coercive power showed highly significant changes over time, in the direction of a general power increase in the organization.

Involving Field Personnel in Decision Making Within a State Organization

Agencies with state-wide programs and responsibilities have traditionally operated from a central headquarters where decision-making authority and organizational power are lodged. Yet increasing organizational diversity and complexity coupled with the emergence of local advocates and constituency groups reveal obvious limitations in this kind of centralized management approach. As a result, many agencies have regionalized their operations to more adequately meet local needs. However, changes in customary power/authority relationships arise from the imposition of more decentralized organizational structures which often generate conflict, distrust, and misunderstandings between headquarters and regional managements.

An intervention by Carew et al. describes a major organizational shift from centralization toward decentralization in the New York State Division for Youth.[42] As an external team, the consultants proposed a collaborative problem-solving approach to the organization's difficulties being experienced with inadequate communication, poor morale, fragmentation of services and lack of clear purpose/direction.

The intervention consisted of several identifiable aspects. It began when the newly appointed Deputy Director for Rehabilitative Services approached the consultants for "assistance in working with the Rehab unit's central office staff around four major issues: 1) administrative organization, 2) the community-based alternative programs grant, 3) training in the division, and 4) various administrative issues."

A three-day workshop for over fifty central office staff was the initial intervention. The workshop examined the existing structure of the Rehabilitative Services unit and problems or gaps within that structure; it developed and examined proposals for alternative structures; and it chose the one best suited to the unit at that time. Regionalization was again proposed as a way to organize and make sense of the Division's structure.

Subsequent workshops were held in different regions. Their focus was on using the ideal strategic model, by looking at current systems, designing an ideal system, and then planning and problem solving to bring actuality closer to the agreed upon ideal. Other sessions focused on utilization of cooperative problem solving to facilitate implementation of new directions and approaches.

Two days of follow-up meetings were held with forty-five middle managers, central office staff, and regional representatives to determine what had happened since the initiation of the effort, to examine what was going well and what was not going well, and to determine needed changes. The evidence generated, both from survey instruments and discussions, indicated that the organizational climate of the Division had changed significantly in a positive direction. The system was perceived as more alert, professional, trustful, flexible, facing problems, sharing decisions, cooperative, experimental, and participative.

This catalytic intervention dealt with organizational norms and standards for leadership and decision making as these become embedded within organizational structure. The interaction encountered little opposition and generated considerable support. One explanation is that, independently of one another, regional groups repeatedly reached the same conclusions about structure. The shift, in other words, was "in the cards." It needed little or no exploration and development. This suggests that the changes that were involved might have been equally acceptable without the workshops and other consultation.

Temporarily Suspending the Conventional Power/Authority Systems to Solve Problems

Supplementing the exercise of power/authority rather than strengthening its use can be accomplished by the consultant *acting in behalf* of those in authority to stimulate organization problem solving. The consultant convenes various lower-level groups for problem diagnosis. Anonymity is promised. Information generated at these sessions is grouped into categories and fed back by the consultant to senior authorities for their reactions, recommendations, or decisions. The facts made available by this approach may be quite different from the "facts" available to authority levels through reliance on the line organization's report. But neither the recipients nor the providers of the information have been subject to a change intervention. When new problems that cannot be solved by conventional line procedures arise, it can be predicted that a repetition of this same procedure will be called for.

Creating openness and candor in identifying problems existing within an organization is a first step toward change in Jacques's approach to organization intervention. Its distinctive feature is that, after initial discussions, Jacques synthesizes his conclusions in a written report that is then widely circulated.

Jaques describes approaching the diagnosis and solution of problems through a number of diagonal-slice groups, structured so that major contemporary tensions from the larger organization are represented within each subgroup. A group is free to discuss any matter. Gripes tend to dominate early discussions.

> There is very rapid fire discussion, which gradually takes on the character of a grouse session. There seems to be nothing good in the company. The executive feels the workers are lazy and junior management inadequate; the

supervisors feel they can get no cooperation from above and are a target for nothing but abuse from below; the workers feel that they are getting a raw deal generally and that they cannot trust anybody. The picture grows worse and worse, until suddenly someone suggests they have been overelaborating difficulties caused by other people, and should perhaps have a look at their own behaviour. There is a silence. Then others begin to agree, and from that point the discussion veers round to a more constructive tone.

In a nonthreatening way the consultant encourages members to proceed.

There seems more to the initial grousing than just the group "getting things off its chest." We suggest to the group that it has been seeing whether we were prepared to face any difficulties, reasonable or not, without taking sides or passing moral judgments. There is a bit of rather tense laughter, followed by relaxation and agreement that perhaps this may have been the case.

This interpretation seems to have produced considerable reassurance about us. The group begins to get down to considering its own differences. We suggest that these reflect here-and-now some of the differences between various sections of the community, and suggest it might be useful to examine them together. The group then begins to make a discovery for itself. It finds that while it is easy to criticise and scapegoat members of other sub-groups in their absence, some of the criticisms seem less reasonable in their presence. There is not time to pursue this further, however, because the next group is waiting and we find that we have already carried over our time. Previous experience, however, leaves us assured that the discussion will be continued outside, both during and after working hours.[43]

Common themes expressed in such discussions suggest a diagnosis of tensions within the organization, and a written report based on this diagnosis receives the widest possible circulation. Thereafter, additional diagonal-slice groups convene to follow up on the report's conclusion. In such discussions

it is commented that the problem has been more thoroughly aired, with a different orientation, than has previously been the case. Issues which have been lying around unexpressed have come out openly for the first time. It is agreed to stop at this point, and to meet again after there has been a chance to think matters over further.

This discussion is followed by others with the same and with other groups. There is a general pattern of talking round problems in such a way that a broader perspective about intergroup difficulties is obtained, on the basis of which executive action is eventually taken.

This catalytic approach generates an initial unloading which is at least quasicathartic, interspersed with encouragements calculated to make participants aware of their own attempts to escape from painful frankness. Tentatively and in a manner inviting friendliness, the consultant draws attention to various defensive strategies and unwitting collusions. In the following example the consultant brings a contradiction into focus.

Our suggestion seems to be overlooked, however, since the discussion turns to complaints about wasting time talking, and the desire is expressed that the executive should decide what should be done and take action without consulting anyone. We point out that there is some inconsistency between such desires and previously expressed resentment about being dominated by those above, and ask whether this can be related to the wish to get away from a painful situation. If this is so, it appears easier to recommend more democracy and opportunity for participation for other people in the firm, than to cope with the difficulties and complex issues which arise when given the opportunity to participate yourself.[44]

This kind of intervention keeps consultant suggestions on a clue level—he or she is not forced to reveal his or her actual opinion and thereby induce a confrontation. Though it permits escape, it also provides organization members the opportunity to deal with problems that previously had been beyond their reach.

One of the earliest interventions relying on survey research as the basis for feedback is by Baumgartel.[45] Survey instruments were completed by members of six accounting departments in various operating components of a large insurance company. These instruments focused on three aspects: the work itself, human relations, and the organization. Sixty supervisors and 640 nonsupervisory employees in six departments participated. All six departments completed evaluation instruments both before and after the survey-research instruments were administered, regardless of whether or not they received feedback. Then four of the six departments received data feedback—which they discussed over a twelve-month period. Two control departments did not get the feedback. This strategy provided an answer to the question, "Did the feedback of survey-research data provide any change in regard to the power/authority focal issue?" Responding to a second survey two years after the first one, relatively more members of departments that received feedback and discussed it felt their supervisors were: (1) better at "handling" people, (2) better "leaders," and (3) more "likable." The consultant concluded,

The results of this study suggest that the creative use of new information for conferences and meetings at all levels of departmental organization may be one of the best and most dynamic avenues to management development and organizational growth.[46]

The so-called confrontation meeting is a catalytic way of gathering data about an organization in order to feed it back to key executives in the authority system. It also is a procedure that temporarily suspends the traditional power/authority structure of the organization. Its title word, "confrontation," is a misnomer; more appropriately it is another example of a temporary collateral system. This intervention is led by an outsider or by a staff member, and relies on the participatory activity of those in attendance. Several echelons of a department that have a common boss are present. Often, though not always, the boss and the key people who report directly to him or her are not involved in the study of the problems. Once the problems have been identified by lower echelons, an arrangement is created whereby the information is fed to the top person and his or her group. Management is expected to listen and, to the degree that they interact with lower levels, limit their participation to queries for clarification.

A typical confrontation meeting schedule follows:

 9:30 to 10:00 Introduction
10:00 to 11:00 Data collection—problem generation
11:00 to 12:00 Information sharing and categorization
 1:30 to 2:45 Priority setting and action planning
 2:45 to 4:30 Confrontation and implementation

Providing an indication of the character of information that is gathered, one group listed the following.[47]

- Meetings like this should start on time. "Minor irritants," like postponed meetings, are rarely communicated to people.
- The authority structure is unclear. Who's my boss: Who judges my work?
- Until recently, there has been little cross-fertilization.
- The Director is inaccessible. Members of the power structure are very accessible to some, but Dr. X (Associate Director) doesn't return my calls. As a result, the number of memos has increased.
- There is no system of setting priorities on distribution of materials. Does a policy exist? Is it possible to have one?
- It is a problem for newcomers to discover who does what in the organization.
- There are too many people employed and then not permitted to exercise the skills they were hired for.
- Too many meetings are held without a specific agenda.
- How do information and decisions that come out of these meetings get communicated?
- Taking over responsibility as acting project director has taken me away from my primary interest—this is irritating and annoying.
- Difficult to get a sure assessment of people's strengths and weaknesses.
- Who makes decisions around here?
- Funding is chaotic. Whom do we go to for funds?

This kind of information, generated by strategies that bypass ordinary reporting channels, is calculated to have a catalyzing effect on the upper-level group to whom it is addressed. Corrective actions on many of the issues identified are not difficult to set in motion, for most lower-level suggestions tend to accept the status quo and seek to bring about improvements in how it operates. The catalytic interventionist's contribution is primarily in helping introduce the participatory norm. Though Beckhard calls this approach a confrontation meeting, it is an identifiable kit of catalytic strategies. First, it involves a one-day activity, designed to suspend established lines of communcation and decision making and make it possible to bring together widely diverse segments of the organization for diagnosis, priority setting, and action recommendations. As described here, a confrontation meeting does not involve confrontation. Rather, anonymous, more or less off-the-cuff feedback is forwarded to higher-level group from lower-level personnel. The meeting is designed according to catalytic assumptions and focuses on exploiting participation.

Two conditions are particularly amenable to this kind of meeting. One is when the organization is under unusual stress: new top management, loss of a customer, a launch of a new product. The second is when top management is a cohesive unit but a culture/communication barrier exists between it and lower echelons. The purpose is to bridge the gap in a quick mobilization of the entire organization toward change and improvement.

Following is a description of how the confrontation intervention works, reconstructed from Beckhard's experience in one organization. From the top person to front-line supervision, the management comprises about eighty people, all of whom take part. The time allocated is two sessions, perhaps three hours one afternoon or night session, followed by three hours the next morning. The intervention begins with the management head or the consultant giving an introduction that clarifies the meeting's purpose and encourages participants to express themselves fully and freely. Assurances that anonymity will be respected and no one punished are included.

The participants then subdivide into five- or six-person subgroups on a diagonal-slice basis, so that no boss is in a group with his or her subordinates. Same-level colleagues also are split up. Top management meets together, except for the highest-level executive.

> The groups are assigned the following task: "Thinking of yourself as a person with needs and goals in this organization, and also thinking of the total organization, what are the behaviors, procedures, ways of work, attitudes, etc., that should be different so that life would be better around here?" Each group is asked to make a list of its items. They have about an hour for this task.[48]

Subgroups then reconvene in a general session, where their prepared lists are posted and categories of common problems identified.

The second session starts with a meeting where individual items are placed in the categories developed during the first session. New group alignments are formed on a functional basis, each guided by one of those who report to the top boss. For example, manufacturing gets together under the leadership of its own boss, marketing with its boss, and so on.

Instructions for each functional group are as follows:

1. Go through the entire list and select three or four items which most affect you or your group. Determine what action your group will take on those and the timetable for beginning work on the problems. Be prepared to report this out to the total group.

2. Go through the list again and select those items to which you think top management should be giving highest priority. (Criteria for inclusion on this list is that your group can't deal with it.)

3. Since this is a large meeting, and all of us are off the job, develop a tactical plan for communicating what happened at this meeting to those who are not here.[49]

Later, another general session is held in which each functional group indicates its three or four top-priority items and its plans for dealing with them. Beyond this, each functional group puts forward, for top management to consider, action problems that require higher-level handling. The top boss is expected to offer some commitment to respond to these suggestions.

A follow-up program is built in before the session begins. Beckhard recommends a two-hour general meeting five or six weeks hence, in which each manager reports progress on the items on his or her list.

A third example also provided by Beckhard[50] indicates that his strategy relied on participatory gathering, feedback, and action planning as the basic steps of change. One- to two-hour interviews, nondirective in character and ranging over a wide variety of topics, were conducted by the consultant with all general managers and central-staff department heads, and with a sample of lower-ranking personnel. Interviewees were informed as to why they were being interviewed, and what uses would be made of the information. They were assured that their anonymity would be preserved in findings or conclusions reached.

Findings from interviews were arranged under a series of headings.

1. Communications between president and line (or staff).
2. Line-staff communications.
3. Location of decision making.
4. Role of clarification or confusion.
5. Communications procedures.

The interview results were then listed under these categories and color-coded to identify the category of respondent (i.e., general manager, staff head, staff assistant, and so on).[51]

An off-site, three-day meeting attended by the president, general managers, and central-staff heads was opened by the consultant reviewing these interview findings. Some ninety items that needed attention had been identified. The group as a whole then spent most of the first day arranging items into a priority listing. Solutions for most problems, it was felt, must come from the group itself. As a change in pace and to provide alternate perspectives on some of their problems, the consultant introduced some ideas about organization communication the first night.

During the next two days, problem causes were diagnosed by tracing their origins to history, structure, personality, or the nature of the business. Practices, procedures, and attitudes that constituted barriers to progress were identified. Beyond the procedural steps the consultants had introduced, they also offered the group *process consultation.*

During the discussions, the consultants' contributions pinpointed how the group was functioning, guidelines for working on a problem, bringing conflict to the surface where it could be worked on, and systematic diagnosis of the causes of some of the problems that were identified.[52]

Since only a start had been made, a second session was scheduled for a month later. During the intervening period the group lost ground in terms of being able to work effectively together, and it was necessary to spend a few hours reestablishing the earlier climate of trust. The manner in which this was accomplished is not indicated.

A major outcome was top management's increased awareness of the concerns of subordinate levels of management, and greater readiness to pay attention to these. A series of meetings similarly designed—information gathering, feedback and discussion, and action planning—was set up for two different sets of subordinate managers. An additional feature, however, was to bypass several layers of management and arrange for the president to receive feedback from the subordinate managers during the last half-day of the conference. The ground rule was that the president should indicate his position regarding each issue presented.

Building such meetings into an organization's regular practices is one way to avoid the regressions that occur when people refocus on day-to-day operating problems. It also is a way of increasing the likelihood that further progress will be made:

> These meetings have proved to be continually effective and are held today on a semiannual or annual basis in all of the hotels. They have become a "way of life" for identifying current concerns, organizing work to deal with them, and planning action. The consultants' role has become that of "sponge" (collecting their data), "water faucet" (giving the information back to them), and "catalyst" (bringing all elements of management together).[53]

Such a participatory basis momentarily takes problems out of the power/authority hierarchy, and then puts them back in at the point where authorization and approval for needed change are available.

Fordyce and Weil describe a catalytic mode of organization intervention for information gathering which also bypasses power/authority systems in a manner similar to the confrontation meeting. The arrangements are suitable for forty to a hundred representatives from large organizations and require a two-day meeting period. As in many such approaches, the consultant begins the sessions with a plea for candor. Additional steps proceed as follows:

1. Participants are divided into subgroups of five or six individuals from different parts of the organization. The top group, however, remains intact, except for the absence of its top man.

2. An hour is provided each group to list changes in any area of functioning—objectives, procedures, policies, and so on—that would be organizationally and personally beneficial if they were to be brought about.

3. Using chart pads, each subgroup reports its list to the total group. Commentary for clarification is permitted but debate is discouraged.

4. The consultant studies the lists and identifies general categories that information fits into.

5. Each participant receives a copy of all item lists and of the categories. Then, in general session, all take part in classifying proposed changes into categories.

6. New subgroups, each led by a key manager and attended by those participants who are from his organization, meet for three purposes:

   ■ To select the three or four items most important to them, and determine what action they will take and when they will start.

   ■ To select the items to which they believe top management should assign highest priority.

   ■ To plan for communicating the meeting results to others in the organization who are not in attendance.

7. Each subgroup reports its conclusions in general session with time for discussion provided. The top man now enters the situation and makes decisions, though possibly only in a preliminary or tentative way, regarding each item referred to him. Follow-up planning ends the meeting.[54]

This kind of development activity runs the risk of superficiality because (1) time is insufficient for deep analysis; (2) if participants have process problems in reaching agreement they are unable to get issues into the open for broader examination; and (3) the compulsion to compromise is high and can diffuse accountability so broadly that no one feels responsible for seeing to it that results are achieved. Accordingly, people become excited in the group sessions but later on feel let down because changes they expected have not occurred.

A somewhat more formal intervention for organization diagnosis, referred to by Fordyce and Weil as a "manager's diagnostic team meeting series," provides for continuing efforts toward assessing effectiveness as contrasted with focusing on a particular problem needing change. The composition of the team includes:

■ The top manager or a principal assistant.

■ A consultant from outside the organization.

■ A staff assistant or assistants with organization-wide responsibility, such as the personnel manager and the administrative or business manager.

This group may be enlarged from time to time, and it may bring in a needed specialist for particular purposes. Basically, however, it meets to pool information on organizational health and to recommend changes. Information gathering is by sensing, interviewing, questionnaires, and instruments. Findings from these sources lead to recommendations for action. The team may become the steering committee for a more extended development effort and thus become a more formal piece of apparatus in the power/authority system.[55]

Culbert[56] describes a "pocket of interest" approach to OD which is intended not so much to help an organization be more productive as to help employees be more mature, complete, and fulfilled as individuals. It seeks to redress the imbalance of power/authority between the unresponsive organization that has power and employees who have needs for greater self-realization but who lack the strength to bring it about. This catalytic intervention is consciousness raising for organization liberation in a manner comparable with consciousness raising for women's liberation.

The strategy is directed toward middle and lower layers of management and proceeds through a succession of five stages geared to help participants learn to express their personal needs more fully. Initial stages assist participants, who interact in support groups with other employees of like-minded interests, to convert vague feelings of uneasiness into an awareness of the discrepancies causing them. Generally a divergence between what would best serve the employees' self-interests and what the organization expects of them is recognized as the underlying problem.

Later stages involve formulating operational recommendations for how individuals might correct perceived injustices created by the power/authority imbalance. This step may move in a confrontational direction. While power/authority is the focal issue, the formation of individuals into a support system, particularly to analytically explore causes, effects, and possible alternatives for change, is effective in increasing morale/cohesion for participants.

While acceptant and confrontational interventions are a part of the multistage approach, the underlying assumptions are mostly catalytic in character. As Culbert[57] noted, "The basic problem in catalyzing self-management within the middle and lower levels lies in getting people the information they need to build a more comprehensive picture of reality and the support they need to act on it." While emotional aspects may be and are present, particularly in stage one, here again we see emphasis on empirical-rational data gathering as the essential condition for bringing about change.

Reorganization

Argyris[58] describes the application of a catalytic model in the context of corporate reorganization. He initially questioned how executive management might reduce resistance to structural changes. Could this be done by direct involvement of management employees in the reorganization design and execution? A reorganization intervention was begun by involving managers from all levels in a diagnosis of the organization's existing problems. Groups composed of representatives from various functions but of about equal rank were assembled, with each group meeting twice for several hours. Brainstorming was used to identify problems, although solutions were not requested.

Information from these meetings was fed to a steering committee composed of all managerial ranks. Blind spots or inconsistencies in the findings were pinpointed and major questions that needed to be answered before the overall diagnosis could be considered valid were identified. Smaller task forces consisting of personnel with relevant functional knowledge dealt with these questions. Based on task-force answers, the steering committee attempted to formulate a new organizational structure. Since vested-interest resistances to the reallocation of power/

authority began to be encountered within the steering committee itself, an educational course was designed that helped members deal with intergroup rivalries, emotionality in groups, and hidden agendas.

Thereafter it was possible to prepare a final reorganization plan that was discussed fully with top executives and then with key representatives of all departments. Alternative suggestions were invited and given serious consideration. Further data gathering followed, using a questionnaire to critique the plan. New suggestions resulted. A final plan received top-management approval along with an implementation time schedule extending over the next seventeen months. Success is reported.[59]

This approach is based on felt needs and therefore does not consider possibilities outside participants' vision or experience at a given point in time. It accepts the organization's present products, people, and processes existing within established traditions, precedents, and past practices. Catalyzing change within the boundaries of the here-and-now status quo apparently was an acceptable definition of the problem. Its major difference from the past was that it introduced a new *participatory* norm that reduced resistance to change.

Another organization-restructuring intervention is described by Bourn. It took place in a welfare organization in Great Britain.

> As with other Health Departments, the range and scope of the services provided by this Department had grown away from the historical conception of preventive medicine as concerned mainly with improving environmental hygiene, through inspection and regulation. It had moved toward a broader conception of preventive medicine which included the fostering of community health by the provision of a wide range of personal and social services, in such fields as school and child health, subnormality, mental health, nursing, midwifery, health visiting, speech therapy and child guidance.[60]

Allaway and Bourn were asked to lead problem-solving discussions using "Exploration Groups."

> The purpose of these Exploration Groups was to provide an opportunity for the staff of the Health Department to participate in an unstructured review of its aims, functions and organisation. The Exploration Groups were not expected to produce actual blueprints for change, but rather to consider whether change was needed and, if so, the broad outlines for a new system.[61]

A series of steps premised upon catalytic assumptions followed. Two Exploration Groups, composed exclusively of senior professional and administrative staff members, examined how best to restructure the organization to meet its present requirements. They were not asked to come up with detailed plans for organization.

The consultants accepted the status quo premise that emerging solutions could not threaten the historical status and position of either the professional or the administrative groups, and worked to prevent any intergroup or interpersonal confrontation of these vested interests.

The opening sessions of the Groups were slow and hesitant, the members feeling rather apprehensive about the whole idea of open and unstructured discussion of such potentially sensitive issues. However, this anxiety did lead participants to question some of the hitherto accepted attitudes common in the Department.

. . . At first, when no-one could foresee the outcome of the review, the discussion was more concerned with protecting the established positions than with trying to envisage fresh approaches to the work of the Department.

. . . The majority difficulty was that, for any alternative form of organisation to be accepted, not only did it have to promise increased Departmental efficiency, but it also had to preserve the essential interests of all the major sections and groupings represented in the Exploration Groups. This explains why, as the ideas behind the Divisional Structure emerged from the discussion, the atmosphere changed from being negative and defensive to being positive and even enthusiastic.

. . . This change of heart seemed to be due to the changing balance of anticipated advantages accruing to the various sections of the staff. As their initial fears were allayed about the way in which the reorganisation was likely to affect their own interests, so the climate of the discussions changed from resisting to supporting change.[62]

Eventually a reorganization was brought about which improved functioning without threatening rupture of existing relationships.

Of all groups in the Department, the Senior Medical Officers and the Deputy Medical Officer of Health gained the most from the reorganisation. The increased emphasis in the Department's work on the provision of an integrated range of professional, social and medical services for the community, strengthened the professional basis of the authority of the senior medical staff, whilst their co-ordinating role in the new divisional structure increased the importance of their administrative work. Because they had previously felt unsure of their role as medical administrators, the senior medical staff were at first anxious about the idea of unstructured discussion. As they saw a new and enlarged role emerging for themselves, however, they began to favour the proposals for reorganisation.[63]

Significant limitations arising from this approach to organizational change involved hidden personal maneuvering beneath the cloak of "What's good for the Department had better be good for us."

In the case being reported here, each section and level of the staff contributed to the pool of information on which the ultimate decisions were based and almost all the staff who participated in the change programme were strongly committed in the proposed re-organisation. At the same time, the form of the re-organisation was influenced by sectional and group pressure. However, as staff co-operation was the key to making the Department more flexible in its response to community needs, the anxieties of the staff could not simply have been overridden or ignored. They had to be taken seriously, and carefully worked through in the Exploration Groups. However, because the Exploration Groups contained senior staff in a service organisation, the process of inter-group adjustment was not conducted explicitly. The only legitimate subject on the agenda was the effectiveness of the Department and its services; to have openly avowed sectional interests would have been unacceptable to the proclaimed sentiments of the members of the Groups, especially the members of the Professional Staff Group. At this senior level it was only considered legitimate to argue a case on whether or not it would advance the Department's interests. This meant that, because the true reasons for opposing change often could not be revealed, many of the arguments put forward were of a rather tangential and masked kind. Therefore, the process of adjustment and accommodation to sectional interests in the Department was disguised, a latent function hidden behind a discussion which, on the surface, appeared to be solely concerned with ways of improving the effectiveness of the Department.[64]

The rationale for using this kind of catalytic intervention, where the methodology of unstructured discussions is employed, is explained by the consultants in the following passage.

I would conclude that such unstructured discussion can ease the process of organisational change provided that (a) there is a minimum level of commitment to organisation goals, (b) the divisions of interests within the organisation are not so sharp that they cannot be resolved without recourse to sanctions, and (c) the discussion is not used merely to rubber-stamp decisions already taken at the top. If these conditions are satisfied, methods of this kind can make a genuine contribution to unfreezing bureaucratic structures and engendering a new spirit of commitment and cooperation.[65]

Beyond the elitist aspects of this approach, which limited the planning of change to the organization's top echelons and resulted in a strengthening of their power/authority, no efforts were made to

1. Work through and resolve vested interests on the basis of insight.
2. Involve those lower in the hierarchy so they could contribute their insights as well as derive increased convictions for implementing the change.
3. Design an ideal model unencumbered by tradition, precedent, or past practice for what the organization could become as an effective health-delivery system.

A third example of a reorganizational intervention relates to resolving problems created by a "classical" merger of several school boards into a single school system. The so-called organization that resulted

had all the classic behaviors and attitudes of any large-scale merger: mutual suspicion, cries for autonomy, generalized hostility to the head office, competition for resources, and a collection of principals who were clustered in groups that were somewhat isolated from each other and from the total system.

In this situation, the basic problem was, "How can we create an organic entity out of this collection of discrepancies?"[66]

The intervention was begun with interview-based problem perception. Once the problem had been identified, functional work groups of eight to ten participants were convened to study it and to design various possible solutions. Each recommendation was tried out in a role-playing session so that consequences could be dramatically versus literally experienced and evaluated. During the role play, consultants focused participant awareness on their strategies of decision making, approaches to conflict resolution, communication barriers, trust levels, and so on. Sometimes the solutions that had been pretested during the learning phase were such that goals could be set for future "culture building." Suggested administrative and operational decisions were arrived at, or at the least, policies for follow-up or specific action proposals for problem solving were agreed upon.

The intervention is reported to have been successful. Since the problem involved a merger situation characterized by mutual suspicions, hostile feelings toward the head office, competition for resources, and so on, such an approach could help participants develop patterns of collaboration where none had previously existed. Reduction of mutual ignorance produced by lack of a shared history can bring about the cooperation needed to strengthen organization effectiveness. The new processes of information gathering and decision making may become embedded in the emerging system and increase its future efficacy.

Another set of interventions that also resulted in power/authority reorganization was premised on introducing wider participation to supplement the conventional exercise of power/authority. The intention was to quicken the rate of change. It took place in the State Department and is described by Levinson.[67] He recommended that a number of task forces be formed to look into various aspects of State Department functioning. The assumptions guiding this recommendation were as follows:

1. Organization members want to manage themselves in a better manner.
2. Top management can promote internal progress but cannot create it.
3. Task forces, formed mostly on a diagonal-slice basis, can identify needed changes.
4. Once authorized by top management, these changes can be implemented.

These task forces are reported to have worked well. As seems necessary in most catalytic approaches, participants had to be assured from time to time that openness was okay, they would not be punished, their findings would be paid attention to, and so on. Eventually the reports of thirteen task forces were integrated into a final report prepared for the top decision maker. Nearly all the findings were given approval. Then specific recommendations were grouped according to priority: (1) those to be implemented immediately; (2) and (3), those to be implemented within 90 to 180 days respectively; and (4) those needing further study. Results were unavailable when this approach was reported but progress was encouraging.

Questionable though it is, Levinson's description indicates that it is not necessary to (1) intervene in an educational way, i.e., help people see things differently or more clearly; or (2) aid managers in developing skills of teamwork, conflict management, or communications. Culture, as evidenced in traditions, precedents, and long-established practices, is deemed to be relatively insignificant in impeding change; and so, under that assumption, can be ignored. By contrast, the needed element provided by the intervention was widespread support through introduction of a participatory norm, making it legitimate for many members to offer suggestions for change.

Collateral Organization

Collateral organization as developed by Zand or Weisbord involves the same organization members engaging in two distinct problem-solving systems. A different kind of collateral organization, intended to produce organization change results, is employed by the Institute of Social Research at the University of Michigan.

The strategy was to identify one work unit from among many, or to create a synthetic group from representatives of others, and then set its operation up in a way that permitted it to function independently of the "old" culture. Thereafter, it was helped to develop more effective problem-solving techniques, unhampered by the traditions, precedents, and practices of the past. It was collateral since it operated "alongside" other similar groups who remained free to continue their conventional practices. These similar groups might themselves incorporate changes they observed in the collateral group, or be "broken out" of conventional practices for similar change purposes at a later time.

> One of these experiments has already shown promising results in the area of employee performance. Late in 1973, the Rushton Mining Company in Rushton, Pennsylvania, established a joint steering committee composed of representatives from both labor (United Mine Workers) and management. With the help of a consultant, Professor Eric Trist of the University of Pennsylvania, the members of this committee formulated a plan for an experimental work group with 27 volunteers from among the regular work force, 9 on each shift. All of the workers were put on top pay, and all were trained so that they could rotate to any job in the team. Each shift foreman has sole responsibility for the safety of his crew, and all responsibility for the production of coal rests with the crew itself. Grievances were also agreed to be the responsibility of the crew, and during the experiment workers have no recourse to either a foreman or the mine's grievance committee.
>
> Although it is too early to draw definitive conclusions, the researchers report, there are hints that exciting changes are taking place in this experiment. As the men in the experimental work crews describe it, the incentives for working hard are very low in the rest of the mine. Most employees cannot wait to leave at the end of the day, and they are glad when the machinery breaks down so that they can get free time.

"WE MATTERED"

But in the experimental group: "Suddenly we felt that we mattered to somebody. Somebody trusted us. . . . When a machine busts down nowadays, most of the time we don't bother to call a maintenance man. We fix it ourselves, because, like I said, we feel it's as much ours as our car at home." Often the men linger around the locker room past quitting time to resolve any problems that have come up during the day and to discuss the next day's work.

In short, the mine is saving money in this area, even though the pay is higher. The experimental group of mine workers boasts lower supply costs, higher production rates, lower absenteeism, lower turnover, a record low accident rate, and the lowest number of safety violations in the mine's history. The ISR researchers caution that as yet they have no proof either that the system can be implemented in the rest of the mine or that these improvements will become stabilized over time. The staff will continue to monitor the experiment and collect and analyze data on all aspects of it in order to determine the full implications of these preliminary findings.[68]

How the "Hawthorne" effect dilemma is handled once the project is over is not indicated, nor is the anticipated spread effect resulting from the creation of these demonstration models described.

Renovation of Existing Organization Practices

Derr[69] provides a case study of an organization intervention premised on consultant information-gathering interviews followed by feedback and process consultation. Though the project was unsuccessful, the report is instructive, for the project's failure is related to the same survey-research weakness reported by Bowers and Taylor.[70] In both cases, the data tended to be dispersed by being (1) tabled or filed, (2) handed to subordinates with instructions to "Do something," or (3) used in a partisan manner.

The client organization consisted of fourteen special-service departments in a big-city school system. Consultants were to suggest reorganization alternatives that would enhance school system effectiveness. Getting started was a problem. The school system was defensive about outsiders coming in at all, as evidenced by a two-month delay before an exploratory meeting between consultants and school officials took place. Finally information gathering, through twenty-four interviews, each from thirty to ninety minutes in length, got under way with interviewees representing a diagonal slice of the organization. Senior school officials had no active participation in or understanding of the consultants' intervention methods, and consultants were committed to confidentiality of interview sources.

This approach identified four perceived problem areas: (1) poor coordination, (2) inadequate communication, (3) poor adaptation, and (4) destructive power struggles. Information feedback sessions with department heads were held to verify the diagnosis and to achieve consensus about ways of improving the system, but certain key members declined to attend these feedback sessions. Instead, they requested that the consultant team prepare a written report. This was submitted and administrative action restructuring took place, but it was outside the intent or recommendations of the consultants.

Original interviewees were reinterviewed a year later. Findings were that feedback sessions had been a useless exercise, since no change in capacity to exert upward influence occurred. The original problem remained unsolved.

Another intervention combining survey research and feedback, along with a catalytic version of process consultation, is reported by McElvaney and Miles[71] in a change project also within a school setting. The interventions focused on two issues:

1. The ease and accuracy with which information flows throughout the organization.

2. The character of problem solving within boss-subordinate relations, whether based on authority-obedience or collaboration, or to what degree it is based on each.

Information gathered from participants was intended to serve as a mirror in which they might see themselves more objectively and, with improved perception, be better able to determine what self-correcting actions were needed.

The school involved first became interested in a change project when asked to provide survey information as a control unit in an experiment where other schools were the experimental units. The administration inquired as to the possibility of getting its own information back in summarized but uninterpreted form, so that school personnel could evaluate the information's meanings.

The first feedback session was attended by eleven participants from the district, including the supervisory principal, his associate, three secondary and four elementary principals, and the district's business manager. Selected anonymous interview responses provided a wealth of information that was dealt with as follows.

1. Examination and review of the information: analyzed initially item by item, then for themes, then broken down so that building-by-building comparisons could be made.

2. Problem identification by subgroups, leading to a number of agenda categories, such as district philosophy, communication issues, role confusion, quality of staff meetings, and so on.

3. Short lectures on pertinent concepts such as trust, decision making, and group operations.

4. Process critique—i.e., examination of problem-solving effectiveness among participants and their reactions to the session.

5. Assignment of particular problems to specific task forces for recommendations and improvement steps.

6. Next-step planning for future meetings, additional feedback of information to teachers on a building-by-building basis.

The catalytic character of the interventions related to process consultation can clearly be seen in the following participant description of one of the two consultants. His procedural contributions are emphasized:

> He's observant; he steps in and quizzes us on what we mean. He gets things straight. He's a catalyst between the administrators and the principals. . . . He's made his presence necessary for progress' sake. He's done a fine job of directing and redirecting the group's thinking toward specific goals.[72]

As reported by the consultants, top administrators made progress in operating more effectively together: facing negative feelings promoted greater openness among them; intergroup suspicions were reduced; some improvement in communication was noted; policy clarification resulted. The authors' final conclusion provides a basis for assessing impact.

> Although constructive change has often seemed to be painfully slow, the authors feel it highly probable that basic methods of functioning have changed for the better and that the health of the district will continue to improve.[73]

LARGER SOCIAL SYSTEM (D-1-5)

Many larger-social-system interventions involve citizen-clients near or below the poverty line. The assistance provided often entails the consultant serving as a rallying point for group formation. Working at the level of felt needs, participants are helped to make progress within their status quo expectations. In addition to the more routine methods of catalytic consulting, the consultant frequently introduces social mechanisms that provide participants with new competency-building experiences.

Problems cropping up within larger social systems are frequently associated with lack of opportunity or lack of skills for exercising power/authority over matters most citizens expect to control. Several examples of catalytic interventions in the focal-issue area of power/authority reveal different aspects of the problem, and indicate how community structures can be designed to provide people, who themselves are unskilled or inexperienced in exercising authority, with access to the skills essential for doing so.

Urban Community Action

Zurcher's[74] description of an intervention permits evaluation of the catalytic assumptions underlying certain activities of the Topeka Office of Economic Opportunity. A city-wide committee, formed to design a community-action program, eventually incorporated as "The Economic Opportunity Board of Shawnee County, Kansas, Inc." Its charter provided that at least one-third of the board's membership would include elected representatives of the poor, themselves selected from chairmen and vice-chairmen of a larger number of local Target Neighborhood Committees. While on the one hand this particular structure was used to implement the Economic Opportunity Act, it was also designed to provide an "experience in social process" for poverty-neighborhood participants. Zurcher points out that the design required the board and its other components to engage in "equal status" pursuit of mutual goals. It was intended to break down stereotypes, encourage communication and broader understanding, and facilitate social change.[75] By participating as board members, neighborhood representatives could expand their social roles and skills, and thereby acquire more capacity for influencing community decisions affecting their lives.

Agricultural Community Action

Rural farming communities of the underdeveloped parts of the world have been the target of change efforts primarily emphasizing the technical aspects of farming rather than training in how to organize and engage in organization building activities basic to exploiting technology. This next intervention dealt with the latter aspect and aided community leaders to exert more influence than they had exerted previously.[76]

A voluntary agency in India recruited poor farmers from twenty-five contiguous villages to be trained as village peer group leaders. This training consisted of three different aspects. Of primary importance was the farmers' awareness of their situation. Many of these illiterate peer members had no basis for evaluating their own situation in comparison with something else that they understood and therefore were not in a position to see how their circumstances might be improved. Awareness training or consciousness raising, in other words, was the first and most critical aspect of the intervention. Farmer information and skills for influencing the situation were the secondary emphasis. This involved information as to possibilities as well as influence-exerting skills (e.g., taking initiative on a planned basis rather than simply responding to the "as is" situation). The third interaction was intended to provide farmers the skills necessary for organizing themselves as groups in order to exert influence from a collective point of view rather than as individuals each acting one-by-one and on his own personal responsibility.

The interventions took place with two groups from among the sample of groups available. These two groups were matched for literacy, age, size of farm tracts, and other characteristics.

How the interventions were carried out is not made explicit but based on the above it can be presumed that they involved participative discussion, with focused questions and exercises calculated to aid participants in acquiring some of the skills essential for exerting influence. During this three-day training period the person responsible for the intervention lived with the farmers. Common activities involving preparing food and maintaining other living arrangements were shared. In this way the consultant quickly came to be accepted by the farmers, not so much as an expert, but as a person acting in a helpful and supportive role.

The evaluation data, basic to the analysis of impact of these behavioral interventions, were related to separate technical training intervention given all twenty-five peer-group leaders in 1975. During this intervention each participant agreed to keep a diary of daily activities that would be available to the voluntary agency staff. The two experimental groups who received the behavioral interventions were available for systematic analysis of what they had done in comparison with what had been done by others who were not recipients of the three-day training but who constituted a control group that had been recipients of technical training.

The two experimental groups were significantly more active in exercising initiative than they had been prior to receiving the organization-building experiences. They were also more active in exercising initiative than were the untrained groups with which they were matched. The difference, furthermore, stands out when the exercising influence is group based. The experimental group emerged as conspicuously more effective. The same is true when the target of influence is the village, with both the experimental groups being far more active in exerting influence at the village level than the control groups.[77]

This catalytic intervention focused on strengthening the exercise of power/authority at the larger-social-system level.

Therapeutic Community

Mental hospitals constitute a residential and treatment social structure that differs from many public institutions, particularly in terms of the diagnosed sicknesses of the inmates. Jones[78] conceived the idea that a mental hospital could nonetheless be transformed from a doctor-oriented social system into a community of "members." The hospital-as-community would thereby be made more therapeutic because the basic shift in power/authority between staff and patients would demand more mature and reality-oriented behavior on the part of the latter. Certain responsibilities for the hospital's functioning were to be placed on patients' shoulders—not completely, but to a significantly larger degree than in traditional mental hospitals.

Jones reviews the underlying strategy of this kind of intervention:

> The social structure of a therapeutic community is characteristically different from the more traditional hospital ward or decentralized unit. The whole extended community of staff, patients, and their relatives is involved, in varying degrees, in treatment and administration. The extent to which this is practicable or desirable of course depends on many things, for example, the attitude of the leader and the other staff, the type of patients being treated, and the sanctions afforded by higher authority. The emphasis on free communication both within and between staff and patient groups and on permissive attitudes which encourage free expression of feeling implies a democratic, egalitarian rather than a traditional hierarchical social organization.
>
> In a therapeutic community, staff and patient roles and role-relationships are the subject of a frequent examination and discussion. The aim of this is

to increase the effectiveness of roles and sharpen the community's perception of them. For example, it may be felt that a nurse's role is more effective if it is made less formal, and if she therefore ceases to wear uniform. It may take many hours of discussion to decide that, say, a nurse only feels secure enough to discard uniform when she has been on the ward for an average of four months. To share this discussion with the patients is to increase their awareness of the difficulties of the nurse's role and may in time modify their relationship to her. The aim is to achieve sufficient flexibility of role behaviour so that at any one time it can reflect the expectations and needs of both staff and patients collectively.

An essential feature of the organization of a therapeutic community is the daily community meeting. By a community meeting, we mean a meeting of the entire patient and staff population of a particular unit or section. We have found it practicable to hold meetings of this kind with as many as 80 patients and up to 30 staff; we think that the upper limit for the establishment of a therapeutic community in the sense that the term is used here is around 100 patients. . . .[79]

The above comments depict a catalytic strategy for increasing perceptual objectivity through improved information gathering and interpretation, based primarily on critique and feedback of ongoing happenings to the entire community.

The next selection, also from Jones, describes an increase in the extent of patient participation through an even more radical shift in traditional power/authority relationships. Though the approach remains catalytic, albeit with a readiness to shift to a prescriptive mode when required, it places patients in potential "confronting" kinds of relationships with one another and with staff as well.

Another approach which has been widely tried is that of patient government or patient councils. The function of these ward councils varies considerably from hospital to hospital, but in the main they are limited to the handling of practical ward details, such as privileges, arrangements for ward cleaning, rosters, and so on. Nevertheless, through time they tend to take on increasing responsibilities. In our opinion, they should not assume too much responsibility unaided and should be supervised by staff and the content of their discussions fed back to the community meetings. Much good can come from the development of patient responsibility skillfully supervised, but it would be foolish to assume that this kind of development can occur without considerable conflict. . . .

This principle of expanding the role of patient to include that of therapist is, I think, a fundamental one in community treatment procedure. It can of course be mistakenly seen as the handing over of ultimate responsibility to the patients, which, in my opinion, is neither practicable nor desirable. What one wishes to do is to give patients that degree of responsibility which is compatible with their capacity at any one time. In no sense do the staff or the doctor in charge relinquish their ultimate authority, which merely remains latent and can be invoked when necessary. The application of this more flexible principle calls for considerable experience and skill. As an example, a community may be functioning fairly smoothly and effectively and the patients may be carrying a considerable amount of responsibility. Then, on a particular day, four or five of the most responsible and successfully treated members leave to be replaced by four or five new patients who may be in a state of considerable disorganization. The loss of patient leadership within the ward and the effect of the disturbed newcomers may be such that the ward functioning is materially altered for the worse, and at this point, the staff have to step in and play a more active and controlling role than they were previously doing. This is fundamentally similar to what happens in individual or group treatment sessions when ego strength fails or anxiety level rises and the therapist feels it necessary to be largely supportive for a time.

The sort of patient responsibility I am considering here is of a higher order than one usually understands by the term "patient government." Patient government is usually restricted to decisions on relatively minor matters of ward organization and activities. What I have in mind is the sharing of fairly major decisions with the staff, involving such matters as interpersonal problems, difficulties in staff-patient relationships, the handling of acting-out behaviour, the discharge of patients, or their transfer to other wards, and the choice of disciplinary action when deviant behaviour occurs. This sharing of serious responsibility with the staff is one of the most effective ways of overcoming the lack of confidence, the low self-estimate and the over-dependency which all too frequently characterizes the patient in the psychiatric hospital. The fostering of responsibility can also be extended to the patients' work roles, and if the hospital can undertake productive work for the community the range and scope of such roles is greatly enhanced: one can have patient foremen, timekeepers, etc.[80]

The possibility of effecting such a shift in the power/authority balance is limited by the readiness of hospital staff to share responsibility for the care of the patient population, and so on. This is analogous in some respects to the situation described by Zurcher[81] in which a "poverty warrior" consultant intervened to promote information and power-sharing among city, business, and neighborhood leaders during the process of community development.

Dilemmas of Industrial Philosophy

The creation of social awareness through drama is not limited to psychodrama or other improvisation techniques. Formal drama also has been used for catalytic intervention purposes.

An example of this is provided by Dvoretsky, a Russian playwright whose *Calling in an Outsider* focused widespread attention on a basic dilemma of modern Soviet society. The play explores the assumption that concern for production and concern for people necessarily conflict in modern technological society.

The central character of the play, Cheshkov, is a manager called in to improve the productivity of a factory department. Its present unsatisfactory state is largely due to "people who are living in the traditions of their former reputation, which has imperceptibly developed into complacency and indulgency in their working relations."[82] Cheshkov uses an authority-obedience managerial style in his attempt to turn the pleasant, easygoing factory culture around. He enforces rigid discipline, demands fulfillment of production plans, and creates conflicts and tensions by trying to shift tradition in this arbitrary manner. Although Cheshkov "wins" in the end, his victory follows a climax in which most of his engineer and foreman subordinates resign.

The play, a smash hit in several of the Soviet Union's main cities, by its nature invites members of the audience to identify either with Cheshkov or with the engineers and foremen—that is, to respond either to efficiency values or to cherished traditions. Lvova[83] reports that *Calling in an Outsider* has been the subject of numerous conferences of theatergoers, with factory workers, engineers and students actively participating. Thus it is having a catalyzing effect on Soviet society by facilitating a widespread dialogue regarding alternative ways of achieving production through people.

Inter-Nation Problem Solving

While he has not described his intervention strategies in any detail, evidence at hand suggests that Henry Kissinger's Middle East efforts, seeking to resolve differences between Egypt and other Arabian states on the one hand, and Israel on the other, at least up to the breakdown in the discussions that occurred in March 1975, were almost entirely *catalytic* in character.

His basic strategy involved assisting each side in clarifying its positions and options and then serving as a personal go-between, helping the other side digest the data reported and then recycling. Seeking to resolve problems in this step-by-step way, he tried to find areas of agreement on the easiest items first, hoping the nations would be able to grapple with the more difficult issues thereafter.

That prescriptions were not involved is demonstrated in the postbreakdown fears of Israel's Foreign Minister, Yigal Allon, who cautioned the United States against offering its own peace plan. "Such a prescription," he said on June 19, 1975, "would create a pressure-cooker atmosphere that could destroy progress."[84]

The absence of confrontational interventions is demonstrated by the fact that the parties to the disagreements were never in direct face-to-face contact, and, beyond that, the parties themselves have indicated that Kissinger served each side as a reliable reporter when meeting with the other. There are no indications that his approach involved theory-based interventions. While there may have been acceptant kinds of active listening, these certainly were of a secondary character.

Many believe that these catalytic interventions have proven too weak to dislodge either side from fixed positions. The result is a step-up of pressure on both sides to face one another in a Geneva type of confrontation peace conference. Stepped-up progress premised on third-party prescriptions and other power pressure tactics also is in the wind.

We know in technical terms how the Camp David interventions were carried out. The evidence in hand suggests that the *peace process,* words made famous by President Jimmy Carter at Camp David in discussions between Prime Minister Menachem Begin and President Anwar Sadat, did not involve *process* intervention as understood in the field of consultation. As reported by Sarchar, Carter's interactions are best characterized as negotiation practices or persuasive communications rather than as consultation.[85]

The several reports by Doob,[86] one of which is commented upon by Walton,[87] involve efforts to promote information exchange between representatives of contending factors within countries such as Ireland, or between countries such as Somalia, Ethiopia, and Kenya and cannot be regarded as examples of consultation. The reason is that in these cases the clients, i.e., the participants in the workshops, are better viewed as spectators because they are not in a decision-making capacity nor are they authorized to make any changes.

Summary

In each of the larger-social-system examples, the intervention's success depended on shifting perceptions concerning *who* held power/authority as well as toward how created awareness about power/authority could be used. Catalytic interventions assist people in resolving and coping with power/authority problems.

In a laboratory or industrial chemical process the effect of some particular catalytic agent is predetermined by laws that without exception govern the interaction between catalyst and units of change. In human affairs, however, simple cause-effect deterministic processes, if they operate at all, are not readily discernible to the catalytic consultant as he or she interacts with a client—hence the almost infinitely greater possibility of unpredicted and/or unknown effects of consultant interventions. Given this situation, it is understandable that the catalytic consultant does not employ power/authority as a mode of operating, but instead tries to work within the client's power/authority system so as to aid it to change itself.

A typically low-key way of achieving this change is the creation of conditions in which previously unrecognized aspects of the power/authority focal issue are brought to light. Most often awareness is accomplished by assembling and presenting pertinent information—as when subordinates who have been unwilling to confront their boss directly regarding the use of power/authority are enabled to deliver this information by means of an anonymous-response survey tabulation, no longer restrained by fear of reprisals.

Notes

1. B. M. Bass, "A Systems Survey Research Feedback for Management and Organizational Development," *The Journal of Applied Behavioral Science* 12, no. 2 (1976): 215–29.

2. R. W. Daw and N. L. Gage, "Effect of Feedback from Teachers to Principals," *Journal of Educational Psychology* 58, no. 3 (1967): 181–88.

3. A. Bavelas and A. Strauss, "Group Dynamics and Intergroup Relations," abridged from W. F. Whyte et al., *Money and Motivation* (New York: Harper & Row, 1955), pp. 91–94. Copyright © 1955 by Harper & Row, Publishers, Inc. By permission of the publishers.

4. Ibid., abridged from pp. 91–94.

5. H. A. Shepard, "Rules of Thumb for Change Agents," *The OD Practitioner* 7, no. 3 (1975): 1–4.

6. W. G. Dyer, *Team Building: Issues and Alternatives* (Reading, Mass.: Addison-Wesley, 1977).

7. A. H. Kuriloff and S. Atkins, "T-Group for a Work Team," reproduced by special permission from *Journal of Applied Behavioral Science* 2, no. 1 (1966): 70–71.

8. Ibid., p. 72.

9. Ibid., p. 73.

10. Ibid., pp. 89–90.

11. H. Levinson, *The Great Jackass Fallacy* (Cambridge, Mass.: Harvard University Press, 1973), pp. 165–66.

12. J. B. Harvey and C. R. Boettger, "Improving Communication within a Managerial Workgroup," *Journal of Applied Behavioral Science* 7, no. 2 (1971): 164–79. Reprinted by permission.

13. Ibid., p. 164.

14. K. Heap, *Process and Action in Work with Groups: The Preconditions for Treatment and Growth* (Oxford, England: Pergamon Press, 1979).

15. Ibid., pp. 118–19.

16. D. E. Zand, "Collateral Organization: A New Change Strategy," reproduced by special permission from *Journal of Applied Behavioral Science* 10, no. 1 (1974): 63–89.

17. Ibid., p. 73.

18. Ibid., pp. 73–74.

19. Ibid., p. 74.

20. D. Zand, *Information, Organization, and Power* (New York: McGraw-Hill, 1981).

21. M. B. Miles, "On Temporary Systems," in M. B. Miles, ed., *Innovation in Education* (New York: Columbia University, 1964), pp. 437–92.

22. W. G. Bennis and P. E. Slater, *The Temporary Society* (New York: Harper & Row, 1968).

23. M. R. Weisbord, H. Lamb, and A. Drexler, *Improving Police Department Management through Problem-Solving Task Forces: A Case Study in Organization Development* (Reading, Mass.: Addison-Wesley, 1974), pp. 4–5. Reprinted by permission.

24. Ibid., p. 5.

25. Ibid., p. 5.

26. Ibid., p. 5.

27. Ibid., p. 5.

28. D. Dinkmeyer and J. Carlson, *Consulting: Facilitating Human Potential and Change Processes* (Columbus, Ohio: Merrill, 1973). Reprinted by permission.

29. Ibid., pp. 229–30.

30. G. H. Varney and J. Lasher, "Surveys and Feedback as a Means of Organization Diagnosis and Change," in Thomas H. Patten, Jr., ed., *OD—Emerging Dimen-*

sions and Concepts (Washington, D.C.: American Society for Training and Development, 1973), pp. 75–82.

31. R. W. Boss, "It Dosen't Matter if You Win or Lose, Unless You're Losing: Organizational Change in a Law Enforcement Agency," *The Journal of Applied Behavioral Science* 15, no. 2 (1979): 198–220.

32. Ibid., p. 204.

33. R. H. Sebring and D. Duffee, "Who Are the Real Prisoners: A Case of Win-Lose Conflict in a State Correctional Institution," *The Journal of Applied Behavioral Science* 13, no. 1 (1977): 23–40.

34. Ibid., p. 33.

35. C. P. Alderfer, "A Video Assist to Student-Faculty Dialogue on Teaching and Learning," *Social Change* 3, no. 2 (1973): 6–8.

36. Ibid., pp. 6–8.

37. A. R. Cohen and H. Gadon, "Changing the Management Culture in a Public School System," *The Journal of Applied Behavioral Science* 14, no. 1 (1978): 62, 63.

38. Ibid., p. 65.

39. A. Alschuler, S. Atkins, R. B. Irons, R. McMullen, and N. Santiago-Wolpow, "Collaborative Problem Solving as an Aim of Education in a Democracy: The Social Literacy Project," *Journal of Applied Behavioral Science* 13, no. 3 (1977): 315–27.

40. Ibid.

41. J. F. Gavin and S. M. McPhail, "Intervention and Evaluation: A Proactive Team Approach to OD," *The Journal of Applied Behavioral Science* 14, no. 2 (1978): 177–78.

42. D. K. Carew, S. I. Carter, J. M. Gamache, R. Hardiman, B. W. Jackson, III, and E. M. Parisi, "New York State Division for Youth: A Collaborative Approach to the Implementation of Structural Change in a Public Bureaucracy," *The Journal of Applied Behavioral Science* 13, no. 3 (1977): 327–40.

43. E. Jaques, "Interpretive Group Discussion as a Method of Facilitating Social Change: A Progress Report on the Use of Group Methods in the Investigation and Resolution of Social Problems," *Human Relations* 1, no. 4 (1948): 544.

44. Ibid., p. 547.

45. H. Baumgartel, "Using Employee Questionnaire Results for Improving Organizations," *Kansas Business Review* 12, no. 12 (1959): 2–6.

46. Ibid., p. 6.

47. W. G. Bennis, *Organization Development: Its Nature, Origins, and Prospects,* © 1969. Addison-Wesley, Reading, MA, pp. 6–8. Reprinted with permission.

48. R. Beckhard, *Organization Development: Strategies and Models* (Reading, Mass.: Addison-Wesley, 1969), p. 39. Reprinted by permission.

49. Ibid., p. 39.

50. R. Beckhard, "An Organization Improvement Program in a Decentralized Organization," reproduced by special permission from *Journal of Applied Behavioral Science* 2, no. 1 (1966).

51. Ibid., p. 9.

52. Beckhard, *Organization Development,* p. 10.

53. Beckhard, "Organization Improvement Program," p. 14.

54. J. K. Fordyce and R. Weil, *Managing with People,* 2nd Edition (Reading, Mass.: Addison-Wesley, 1979), pp. 104–107. Reprinted by permission.

55. Ibid., pp. 91–92.
56. S. A. Culbert, *The Organization Trap and How to Get Out of It* (New York: Basic Books, 1974).
57. Ibid.
58. C. Argyris, "Today's Problems with Tomorrow's Organizations," *Journal of Management Studies* 4, no. 1 (1967): 31–55.
59. Ibid., pp. 52–55.
60. C. J. Bourn, "Planned Change in Welfare Organisation," *Human Relations* 26, no. 1 (1973): 114. Reprinted by permission of Plenum Publishing Co., London, England.
61. Ibid., p. 113.
62. Ibid., pp. 120–21.
63. Ibid., p. 122.
64. Ibid., p. 123.
65. Ibid., p. 125.
66. R. Duffin, A. Falusi, P. Lawrence, and R. Morton, "Increasing Organizational Effectiveness," reproduced by special permission from *Training and Development Journal* 27, no. 4 (1973): 37. Copyright 1973 by the American Society for Training and Development, Inc.
67. Levinson, *The Great Jackass Fallacy,* pp. 148–58.
68. E. Lawler and S. Seashore, "Joint Planning Teams Improve Management," as reported in *ISR Newsletter* 3, no. 3 (1975): 2, 6.
69. C. B. Derr, "Organization Development in One Large Urban School System," *Education and Urban Society* 4 (1972): 403–19.
70. G. Bowers and J. Taylor, "Survey of Organizations," as reported in University of Michigan Institute for Social Research *Newsletter* (Spring-Summer 1973): 3, 6.
71. C. T. McElvaney and M. B. Miles, "Using Survey Feedback and Consultation," in R. A. Schmuck and M. B. Miles, eds., *Organization Development in Schools* (Palo Alto, Cal.: National Press Books, 1971), pp. 113–38.
72. Ibid., p. 132.
73. Ibid., p. 137.
74. L. A. Zurcher, *Poverty Warriors: A Human Experience of Planned Social Intervention* (Austin, Texas: The University of Texas Press, 1970).
75. Ibid., pp. 17–19.
76. R. Tandon and L. D. Brown, "Organization-Building for Rural Development: An Experiment in India," *The Journal of Applied Behavioral Science* 17, no. 2 (1981): 172–89.
77. Ibid.
78. M. Jones, *Social Psychiatry: A Study of Therapeutic Communities* (London: Tavistock, 1952).
79. M. Jones, "The Therapeutic Community," in G. and B. Stanford, eds., *Strangers to Themselves* (New York: Bantam Pathfinder Editions, 1973), pp. 263–64. Reprinted by permission.
80. Ibid., pp. 267–68.
81. Zucher, *Poverty Warriors.*
82. G. Lvova, "The Human Element in the Scientific and Technical Revolution," *Social Sciences* 42, no. 12 (1973): 171.
83. Ibid., p. 172.

84. "Allon Warns U.S. Not to Offer a Peace Plan for Negotiations," *The International Herald Tribune,* 19 June 1975.

85. H. Sarchar, *Egypt and Israel* (New York: Richard Marek, 1981).

86. L. W. Doob and W. J. Foltz, "The Belfast Workshop: An Application of Group Techniques to a Destructive Conflict," *Journal of Conflict Resolution* 17, no. 3 (1973): 489–512.

87. R. E. Walton, "A Problem-Solving Workshop in Border Conflicts in Eastern Africa," *The Journal of Applied Behavioral Science* 6, no. 4 (1970): 453–89.

22

CATALYTIC INTERVENTIONS

Morale/
Cohesion

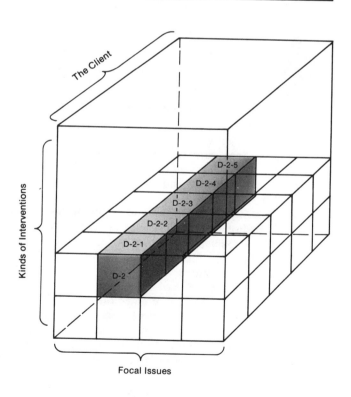

The Client

Kinds of Interventions

D-2-5
D-2-4
D-2-3
D-2-2
D-2-1
D-2

Focal Issues

Problems of morale and cohesion can be approached from the perspective of catalytic interventions, but this focal issue is addressed less often in this way than are the other focal issues.

INDIVIDUAL (D-2-1)

A common theme among most self-help therapies and other-directed helping relationships is the importance of a positive self-image. Thinking positively about oneself can be a life-changing, individually transforming influence. Early work on the extent to which our self-perceptions are dependent on others' perceptions of us demonstrated the significance of positive expectations on work and school performance. When teachers, employers, parents, and others expect an individual to succeed, it is likely that he or she will be more successful than when these others expect poor performance or failure. Negative expectations are just as likely to breed failure as positive expectations are to breed success.

Developing Positive Expectations

Crawford et al., describe an intervention founded on the Pygmalion principle of positive expectations. The client was a San Diego–based combatant ship with a crew of approximately 230. The commanding officer (CO) requested assistance for improving the productivity of several low-performing sailors. The CO made his crew available to participate in three mutually supportive tracks consisting of: (1) supervisory training, (2) mentor/counseling training for selected supervisors, and (3) low performer's growth workshops. Supervisory training

> consisted of a 1½-day motivation and leadership workshop for all supervisory personnel in the command. . . . In essence, the consultants attempted to change supervisor attitudes toward their subordinates in the areas of (1) acceptance and support, (2) rewards for demonstrating acceptable behaviors, and (3) expectations for subordinates not biased by past events. . . . As the workshops progressed, this initial reluctance gave way to guarded optimism and later to enthusiasm concerning the impact that they might have as supervisors. The consultants felt that this shift [in attitudes] was due in part to the training segment that consisted of teaching the principles of behavior modification and then brainstorming actions that would constitute positive reinforcers in the eyes of the low performers. The supervisors were thus given some specific tools to back up their newly acquired positive expectations.
>
>   . . . [Mentor training] consisted of selecting and training senior enlisted supervisors to serve as counselors and role models for the target sailors. . . . Training for the mentors consisted of a one-day workshop in counseling and guidance skills. Active listening[1] was stressed as an important technique for enhancing both the self-concept and expectations of the counselee by allowing him to assume responsibility for his own problems and to develop appropriate solutions.
>
>   . . . Twelve individuals reported for the workshops. . . . Initially, all

twelve low performers (LP's) were interviewed by the consultants. . . . Both the interviews and personal history data yielded one significant finding— virtually all of the LP's had low expectations of success and were not disposed to setting goals or developing plans.

Training and workshops consisted of two separate, three-day packages. . . . The workshops focused on making LP's aware that they alone were responsible for what happened in their lives and that they also had the power to determine what happened in the future. . . . In essence, the workshop borrowed heavily from the reality therapy approach developed by Glasser[2]. . . . The final event of the three-day concentrated effort was the introduction of the LP's to their counselors/mentors.

Three additional days of follow-up workshops (one day per week for three weeks) focused on topics specifically requested by the LP's.

In summary, the overall intervention dealt with the expressed lack of power felt by both the LP's and their supervisors. By giving the low performers as well as their supervisors a feeling of power, including some actual techniques and practice, positive expectations were created that we hoped would break the existing negative attitude-behavior cycle.[3]

This three-phased approach proved successful in altering the expectations of both supervisors and supervisees, in improving work performance, and in reducing disciplinary problems. Beyond setting new norms/standards, each phase of the intervention provided reinforcement. Positive results were again demonstrated as the supervisors altered their behaviors and attitudes toward the low performers, and the low performers altered their perceptions of themselves and attitudes toward their supervisors in terms of Navy rules and regulations.

Improving Morale on the Job

The catalytic mode of intervening with individual clients is described in the next example in which the consultant helps the client gather her own information and teaches the client to observe herself as she goes about her work. Consultant and client then discuss the client's self-observations, with the consultant aiding the client in crystalling her perceptions and generalizing from them as to how she might alter her behavior.

The intervention involved Miss Jones, a ward nurse. After a period of absence from the job, Miss Jones returned to her duties eager to get back to work and discovered that the regular charge nurse was away. In her absence the "disturbed" ward of the hospital had been supervised by a substitute. During that time Miss Jones thought patients had become much more "difficult" than before and that other ward staff members had become tired and discouraged so that they were less effective than usual in coordinating procedures and dealing with patient needs. Miss Jones herself became tired and frustrated.

Discussions of a cathartic character (described later in Chapter 28) helped bolster Miss Jones' morale, and she gained relief from her tensions and frustrations by talking out her feelings. The consultant then shifted to a catalytic mode: he proposed that she step up her information gathering by being more observant of what was going on as she participated in ward activities.

> Instead of focusing only on your failures, your difficulty in functioning, your poor relations with patients and staff, and your discomfort on the ward, you might be able to take a little different approach. In addition to participating on the ward with low morale, you might also become an observer of this low morale and see how it works.[4]

Miss Jones at first had difficulty in becoming a participant observer of her own activities. As the consultant raised questions about the experiences she related to him, though, she gradually came to have less intense feelings about her low morale. She started to see, reflect upon, and examine the connections between her low morale, the ward situation, and her relations with patients. The catalytic tone of the intervention suggested that she might adopt an *attitude of inquiry* toward herself and her relations with others through gathering information about what actually was taking place in a given situation. In this way Miss Jones might be able to reduce her subjective reactions and respond more objectively to events.

Additional aspects of the discussions were devoted to helping the client develop a new outlook on the dynamics of her interpersonal relationships. Consultant and client-nurse deeply explored interactions with patients and colleagues and sought to identify alternative action possibilities that might prove more constructive. In line with the earlier cathartic interventions, open expression of feelings about ward situations was encouraged.

This example demonstrates the use of more than one type of intervention in the same consultation. Cathartic interventions (to be described in Chapter 26) paved the way for catalytic interventions by first dealing with emotional blockages—cathartic intervention *alone* might not have been sufficient to bring about the changes that were eventually achieved. The authors sum up their conclusions as to the effect of these catalytic interventions on Miss Jones.

> She had been preoccupied, on the one hand, with escaping from the situation of low morale and, on the other hand, with altering it by pulling herself up by her bootstraps. Failing to do either, she continued to feel she was a failure. In the discussion, she changed her goals to that of learning about the ways in which her low morale developed and of understanding the interpersonal processes constituting it. With this new perspective she focused less of her attention on her failure in the ward situation and more on the possibility of deriving something positive from a situation which up to this point had appeared to her as exclusively negative.[5]

A strength of the participant-observer approach to information gathering is that it helps the client concentrate on situational "facts" and on examination and evaluation of behaviors that may have previously gone unnoticed. The consultant remains detached from the client's problem, but the catalytic intervention sets up a basis for here-and-now self-consultation. Responsibility for diagnosis is retained by the client.

On-the-job perceptions of one's own behavior are inescapably limited by biases and distortions, but these are more likely to go unchecked by a catalytic intervention than by, for example, a confrontational approach. Therefore, gains that could be made if such distortions were eliminated probably will not be fully realized under catalytic interventions unless increased self-knowledge is objective and reality based.

Reducing Despair from Termination

Terminating employees has never been a pleasant activity. A recent trend has been to employ consultants to carry out this task. Outplacement, as practiced by some consultants, however, is more than announcing a termination because one of the genuine problems of termination is the depression and sometimes despair experienced by the terminated person. This can immobilize him or her and make job hunting that much more difficult. Outplacement engages the person in constructively thinking through his or her situation and gives support in taking positive steps, all of which reduce despair and may even provide a boost to morale. It has come to include aiding those who are terminated to identify their marketable skills and develop competence in writing job inquiries and conducting employment interviews. Sometimes the consultant supports the client until he or she has been successful in finding a new job.

Expert guidance is available to help the terminated person sort out objectives, formulate a "marketing" plan, and implement it. He or she can find new employment in less time than the conventional severance allowance contemplates because of the training offered in "how to do it."

> [We have] been engaged in this specialized service for many years and [have] put thousands of displaced executives through the program. Each individual was sponsored by the company releasing him and each one [was] coached on an individual basis until he made it across the gap to his next career. . . . [When] an individual applies himself diligently to the program and is receptive to coaching, these are some of the results:
>
> 1. Approximately 80 percent are placed within 60 to 180 days of their start on the program.
> 2. Most find new employment at salaries equal to or better than [those] . . . in their former positions . . . .[6]

The remaining 20 percent find employment even though it takes longer. Not all want to continue work. Some, having vested pension rights or other resources, take early retirement. Some go into business for themselves. The expense of outplacement counseling is usually borne by the ex-employee's company, making it possible for the terminated person to benefit from consultation to the fullest extent possible.

GROUP (B-2-2)

When a group loses its sense of esprit de corps, its members usually begin dispersing until the group collapses. An exception is when the group is part of a larger entity and is held together by virtue of common organization membership, with replacement members being recruited as others leave. Prevention may include interventions designed to address issues of morale/cohesion directly.

Human emotions surface which may, if not dealt with, result in tension, conflict, and lack of cooperation in achieving critical objectives. Recognizing the importance of positive human relations to military efficiency and productivity, the Israel Defense Forces established the "Military Psychology Unit of the Manpower Wing."

Greenbaum, et al., describe the Psychology Unit's role in the following terms:

> . . . to act as a consulting body to corps commanders and the General Staff. It provides periodic reports on morale, organizational climate, leadership effectiveness, and performance of different corps at the IDF. Field Psychologists are assigned to training bases and field units in order to work as consultants to unit commanders at different levels on issues related to human relations and performance.[7]

A multiphase consultation mode, basically catalytic in character, was developed and applied to various active duty and reserve military groups. First, the unit commander and consultant negotiate a working agreement that defines the parameters of the interventions. Secondly, information from all unit levels is gathered, summarized, and analyzed to assist the consultant in diagnosing the unit's primary problems and concerns. Plans for addressing identified issues are formulated and recommended by the consultant during the third phase of the intervention. The fourth phase allows for systematic presentation of feedback at appropriate levels of results derived in stages one through three. Finally, follow-up measures employed include subsequent meetings and discussions, officer training on human relations issues, and evaluation of the intervention's effects.

This systematic and comprehensive approach was used and refined during and after the 1973 Yom Kippur War. Following an immediate post-battle period, an infantry brigade comprised of 18- and 19-year-old men was identified for work by the Psychology Unit. Using the approach outlined above, the consultants worked with the soldiers and their commanders to address the brigade's specific concerns. Major issues identified through the interview process included recent heavy losses in the officer ranks, appointment of and attitudes toward new commanders, morale, and physical fatigue.

Open discussion of these identified issues among the officers provided the opportunity and impetus for both group and individual problem solving. Meetings were also held with the soldiers where interview perceptions were validated through completion of a written questionnaire. According to Greenbaum's account of the intervention, at this stage information from the interviews, meetings, and questionnaires described above were shared at each authority level. Problems and concerns raised in the feedback session were discussed in terms of specific feasible solutions.

Results of the case study presented here are not discussed in the original work. Generally, it is assumed that such an intensive intervention should have a positive impact on morale/cohesion in the client group. No comparative evaluation was completed, but the need for such hard data to support the assumption of effectiveness was recognized. This model can be applied to any focal issue. A similar model is in use in the U.S. Army.[8]

INTERGROUP (B-2-3)

When groups that must interact feel positively toward one another, mutual support and needed cooperation are evidenced; but when feelings are antagonistic, each group is likely to feel threatened by the other and may withhold the support needed to get the job done.

Headquarters versus Field

One example provided by Golembiewski and Blumberg[9] involved a divisional management's efforts to bring about operational improvements—in particular, to reduce or even eliminate "we-they" anticohesion feelings between the headquarters organization and the field sales force. Forty-six participants from a large drug company took part in three days of intervention meetings.

A "cafeteria" selection procedure was used for identifying the two sides in any existing intergroup problem relationship. Perception exchanges between groups were arranged on a "taxi dance" basis; for example, if Group A wanted to have an exchange with Group B, Group A was to get Group B's agreement to do so. Their exchange was subsequently scheduled if a ninety-minute time slot was available.

The consultants attempted to provide periods for intergroup representatives of any two groups who shared some degree of interdependence in their relationship to come together for discussions. Before meeting the other side, each group privately created the images it wanted to exchange. Although an exchange period of up to ninety minutes may not be sufficient for exploring the historical background or feelings associated with a problem in any significant depth, or for planning developmental steps, it may be enough time to communicate a certain amount of data and give participants a sense of the issues.

The strategy used to deal with the core issues identified during the first two days of intergroup image exchanges, as exemplified in Table 22.1, was to have participants design implementing steps for solving their recurrent problems.[10] Using a self-selecting or cafeteria basis for organizing the effort, participants signed up to be members of whichever core group they felt themselves most interested in or concerned about. An intervention such as this can be expected to loosen up previously clogged communication channels as well as to pinpoint a

Table 22.1 A sample 3-D image by one regional aggregate* with *promotion* as the relevant other

---

A. How members of regional aggregate see themselves in relation to promotion department.

1. Circumvented
2. Manipulated
3. Receiving benefits of their efforts
4. Nonparticipating (relatively)
5. Defensive
6. Used
7. Production
8. Instrument of their success
9. Have never taken us into their confidence in admitting that a promotion "bombed"
10. The field would like to help, but it must be a two-way street

B. How members of regional aggregate feel promotion department sees them.

1. Insensitive to corporate needs
2. Noncommunicative upwards, as holding back ideas and suggestions
3. Productive in field saleswork
4. Naive about the promotion side of business
5. Unappreciative of promotion efforts
6. As lacking understanding about their sales objectives
7. Belligerent
8. Overly independent operators
9. Not qualified to evaluate the promotions sent to us
10. Honest in opinions

C. How members of regional aggregate characterize promotion department.

1. Autocratic
2. Productive
3. Unappreciative of field efforts
4. Competent with "things" but not "people"
5. Industrious
6. Inflexible
7. Unrealistic
8. Naive
9. Progressive in promotion philosophy and programs
10. Overly competitive within own department
11. Plagiarists who take field ideas but do not always give credit

---

* One of three field-division-manager groups formed for learning purposes during the three-day experience.

few problems that participants can solve on their own initiative. It is unlikely, however, that the underlying causes of intergroup problems embedded within the status quo system itself will be affected.

Characteristic of the catalytic approach is the fact that global statements rather than operationally descriptive comments were formulated in the images each group drew up. A rationale for being general rather than specific follows.

> In general, restraints against communicating "dangerous materials" still are powerful. And the very writing-up of a global 3-D Image tends to encourage less defensiveness than, for example, a verbal and necessarily linear statement of the same content.[11]

In comparison with a confrontational approach, where the objective is to provide opportunities for defensiveness to surface in order to study and work through underlying causes, the catalytic approach facilitates communication within the status quo. This is evidenced by the parallel character of consultant-originated strategies for conducting these intergroup sessions:

■ A cafeteria-selection basis so that those whose intergroup situations are "ruptured," and who may not wish to come to terms with their problems, can avoid doing so.

■ A short duration, such as ninety minutes, which may be enough to get "big" images presented, but not nearly enough to work through their meanings in any detail, and certainly insufficient for operational problem solving.

■ Core groups for problem analysis, again composed on a cafeteria basis of self-selection, rather than intact real-life groups, composed of *all* those who have a vested interest in the outcome of such deliberations.

The consultants called the procedure used a "confrontation" meeting, but "confrontation" translates to "catalytic" when a closer examination is made of the intervention strategies employed. Nonetheless, according to the clinical description of what transpired, an unforeseen "confrontation in reverse" did occur when the client challenged the consultants to explain or justify the values and assumptions underlying their interventions. These "wrong way" confrontations were prompted by the managers' feelings of having been offended by the consultants. They confronted the consultants spontaneously in a way that was not a calculated feature of the design.

Administration versus Staff

Another consultant-suggested intergroup image exchange for perceptual clarification, also premised on the catalytic intervention mode, is provided by Argyris and Bennis. The intended effect of the exchange was to reduce distrust rather than solve problem issues. Bennis provides a background of the State Department in the 1960s at the time this intervention was carried out.[12]

> Among the recent problems facing the U.S. Department of State was unproductive divisiveness between the Foreign Service officers, sometimes referred to as "the club" or "the guild" and the administrative staff of State. The stereotyping and mutual distrust, if not downright hostility, blocked communication and reduced effectiveness enormously, for each "side" perceived the other as more threatening than a realistic overseas enemy.

A representative sample of top echelon officials from the administration and foreign service was divided into two subgroups. Separate rooms were assigned in which each subgroup developed words and phrases that would summarize their answers to the following three questions.

1. What qualities best describe our group?
2. What qualities best describe the other group?
3. What qualities do we predict the other group would assign to us?

Partial results are listed below. "Prediction of the others' perceptions of us" lists are omitted.

The Foreign Service Officers saw themselves as:

1. Reflective
2. Qualitative
3. Humanistic, subjective
4. Cultural, broad interests
5. Generalizers
6. Intercultural sensitivity
7. Detached from personal conflicts

The Administrative Officers saw the Foreign Service Officers as:

1. Masked, isolated
2. Resourceful, serious
3. Respected
4. Inclined to stability
5. Dedicated to job
6. Necessary
7. Externally oriented
8. Cautious
9. Rational
10. Surrounded by mystique
11. Manipulative
12. Defensive

The Administrative Officers saw themselves as:

1. Decisive, guts
2. Resourceful, adaptive
3. Pragmatic
4. Service-oriented
5. Able to get along
6. Receptive to change
7. Dedicated to job
8. Misunderstood
9. Useful
10. Modest! [added by the individual doing the presenting][13]

The Foreign Service Officers saw the Administrative Officers as:

1. Doers and implementers
2. Quantitative
3. Decisive and forceful
4. Noncultural
5. Limited goals
6. Jealous of us
7. Interested in form more than substance
8. Wave of the future! [Exclamation mark theirs]

After these lists were exchanged the groups discussed them, each questioning the other with respect to what had been "seen." The discussion was intense, high-pitched, noisy, argumentative, good-humored, and finally, several hours later, thoughtful. The consultants concluded that "each side moved to a position where they at least understood the other side's point of view."[14]

Many of the features of the Golembiewski-Blumberg example are duplicated in the Bennis exchange. This intergroup image exchange is of the catalytic character for several reasons. First, the participants were *representative* rather than intact or *organic* groups. As such they were in no position to authorize change, even if they had wanted to do so. Then, too, the instructions called for each group to indicate qualities rather than to formulate line-and-verse operational statements. Participants produced their images in private, thus ensuring the anonymity of individual contributions. As mentioned earlier, global, abstract generalizations instead of specific statements were formulated. A period was provided for each group to be questioned by the other group with respect to reported perceptions, producing accusations and counteraccusations of a win-lose polarized sort. Discussions apparently involved some confrontational attack-counterattack in the sense that they were high-pitched and argumentative. But resolutions of the sort that a truly confrontational intergroup experience might be expected to produce could not have occurred given the description provided. Since neither side was an intact group, no resolution of differences in any practical sense could be achieved.

Summary

The image-exchange approach for resolving morale/cohesion issues is a catalytic intervention designed to help groups better understand each other and clarify and share existing information. If the differences are sharp or the feelings keenly antagonistic, it can prove difficult if not impossible to move via this procedure into a problem-solving approach.

ORGANIZATION (B-2-4)

When morale/cohesion difficulties permeate an entire organization, more massive, long-term intervention strategies are sometimes called for.

Changing the Arrangements of Work

The introduction of change by edict, though sometimes justified by advancing technology, can have a demoralizing effect on organization members because it breaks up long-established patterns of work, brings an end to friendships, and so on. A consultant-based approach for improving working group arrangements while strengthening productivity in conjunction with the introduction of complex machinery, referred to as a *socio-technical system intervention,* is reported by Trist and Bamforth.[15]

Besides finding that the complex system was ineffective in terms of the technology designers' expectations, Trist and Bamforth concluded that an unintegrated three-shift system of work had shattered cohesion and mutual support among workers and was inducing unnecessary emotional strain. Through their study of the work itself—a coal-mining operation—and the social relations among workers that the machinery "created," the consultants were influential in bringing about alternative combinations of technical and social arrangements that increased productivity while facilitating cohesion and esprit de corps.

Data gathering and analysis took place over a two-year period. During the information-gathering phase, repeated discussions and interviews were conducted with twenty or so key informants who represented a cross-section of occupational roles and had wide and varied experience in the industry. Similar discussions were conducted with management, including all grades of supervisors and managers up to the area level. Other informants included three psychiatrists acquainted with miners' physical and emotional health problems. The work of Trist and Bamforth appears to have been of a catalytic character in that a consensus as to what constitutes a "better socio-technical system" gradually emerged as the detailed information analysis took shape. There is no evidence in the report of personal interventions in the workplace by Trist and Bamforth. Their report itself *was* the intervention, bringing the morale/cohesion issue to the awareness of mine managers and engineers whose previous focus had more or less concentrated exclusively on maintaining the technical system's status quo. Management had been unaware of the focal sources of ineffectiveness and "poisoned" morale inherent in the social organization accompanying the longwall method. In their conclusions Trist and Bamforth[16] comment briefly on the first changes being tried in the direction of developing better morale/cohesion through revised shift arrangements, mechanization alternatives that stressed the value of the strongly knit primary work group, and so on.

Reducing Tensions among Members of a Religious Order

Taking place in the setting of religious communities, a catalytic intervention, focused on enhancing morale and cohesion, sought to reduce tensions between older and younger members of a religious order.[17] Encounter weekends were the catalytic intervention, and survey research the evaluation mechanism.

The intervention failed to achieve the purpose for which it was intended. Change toward improved morale and cohesion did not occur, but rather the opposite happened. This is seen particularly in younger people's leaving the religious order.

The research revealed that the stated or felt problem, morale and cohesion, was not the real problem. The real problem was ideological in character and involved embracing or rejecting the obligations and requirements of living and relating placed on its members by this Catholic order. The weekend sensitivity intervention did bring the issue into focus, and because it was unsuccessfully handled, the impact was that of the defection mentioned above.

Sensitivity and encounter are not useful ways of dealing with antagonisms, conflicts, hostilities, and tensions that are rooted in history and ideology. This situation probably called for the standard intergroup confrontation design[18] in which older and younger members of the order would have developed images of themselves and the other, exchanged them, and worked through the emotionally saturated differences toward some basis of resolution that might have reduced the ideological chasm or at least brought it into focus where its longer-term consequences could be seen more clearly.

LARGER SOCIAL SYSTEM (B-2-5)

One of the more serious problems within larger social systems is the lack of community—morale/cohesion is at a low ebb, and citizens often seem unwilling or unable to make the contacts essential for producing neighborhood life. Several different kinds of catalytic interventions are used to establish or restore community identification among those living in the same area. These are "enabling" interventions based on the recognition that community participation can only arise when people want to take part on a voluntary basis—coercion has no place here in inducing change.

Community Involvement in the School System

Ability to see and appreciate different points of view is basic to community relations, particularly when a community is strife-ridden. The circumstances related to this intervention included the fact that a strike affecting a community had created three sets of protagonists. One was the United Federation of Teachers; a second subgroup was comprised of parents and children; and the third, the School Board.[19] The intervention did not focus on the strike itself and had no effect on the ultimate resolution of the disagreement. It did focus on issues of concern about schools and how they should function in the best interest of utilizing teachers and in teaching students.

Participants in an assembly meeting, which was of one night's duration, were divided into instrumented learning teams[20] in such a way as to ensure maximum differences between participants in terms of the original positions taken on a variety of issues.

Each team was then to develop a "platform" on its assigned issue. It was also to elect a representative who would present his or her team's point of view in the General Assembly. Discussion of a given topic by persons who stood for different positions on it aroused differences but also seemed to stimulate group solidarity and had a "cooling off" effect on tensions aroused by the strike itself. When group members were asked to choose among the different representatives, i.e., the representative from their own group and other groups, they did so by selecting to a significant degree their own representative over the others. This conclusion validates laboratory research showing that group loyalty dominates over initial convictions on an issue in determining attitudes toward members.

This is a catalytic intervention. Facilitators were used to initiate the discussion, topics at the felt needs level were suggested for discussion, and a heterogeneous sample of the larger social system engaged in the project on a mechanical basis.

Those responsible for the intervention conclude that the intergroup model has been used repeatedly in years since this intervention was introduced in order to grapple with community-wide conflict.

Community Development

"Spontaneous" community development, particularly involving people with minimal education and little economic security, has been slow starting and not particularly successful in the few attempts reported. Robbins[21] reports one such intervention that proved an effective approach to the problem as indicated by the enthusiasm it generated.

The assumptions underlying this intervention are that it must

1. Be based on felt needs of participants.
2. Readily shift from concentrating on a planned content to dealing with an immediately sensed need that had previously not been recognized.
3. Be done in an informal, give-and-take way that reduced the social distance between experts and students.
4. Be characterized by friendly relations supported and maintained by informal social contacts, such as home visiting by the consultant to dine and socialize with participants, and so on.

On this basis, an intervention that began with extensive interviews, particularly with opinion leaders to identify what participants wanted, led to the following list of community problems.

1. A feeling of isolation and despair.
2. Poorly organized community; ineffective leadership.
3. Poor communication among the people; a lack of trust and much conflict.
4. Little confidence in their ability to influence the community at large.
5. A negative and unrealistic self-concept.

In response to these data, the consultant drew up a list of "desired outcomes" of a leadership training program he was requested to design and conduct. Included was the need within the community for its members to

1. Have more self-confidence.
2. Have a more realistic self-concept.
3. Develop and use leadership skills.
4. Be effective communicators, both in formal and informal settings.
5. Function effectively in organizational structures.[22]

Rather than establish a rigid course structure, the consultants decided to have a number of prepared activities available for presentation at any one session. Whenever participants mentioned a particular problem, relating to some aspect of community leadership presently causing them difficulty, the consultants could introduce an appropriate training activity to which that day's session would be devoted. The activities were designed to give participants an improved basis of confidence in approaching community leaders. Since the consultants had to fly weekly from another city to conduct the sessions and had a long wait for their return plane in the evenings, the custom developed of their having a meal and discussions in participants' homes. Since each "host for the week" would usually invite fellow client members also, long-standing Black-Chicano-Anglo barriers were tentatively broken. Subsequently, as the consultants continued to work with the community, they saw these kinds of interactions increasing, suggesting improved community cohesion.

Community Repair after Despair

Communities sometimes go downhill, unable to solve their problems of living and growth. Lawrence, Kansas appeared to be in such a self-defeating cycle that collaboration between community groups had broken down to such an extent that

> this community has in recent years experienced open conflict between blacks and whites, arson, student violence and death. The town is large enough to harbor several communities with their own way of life. It is small enough for every citizen to feel the impact of colliding values. The people I met looked at events through the lens of their own personal experience and defined truth by what they saw. So fiercely had each adherent sworn loyalty to his part of the whole, that the idea of community—of a place where people exist competitively without malice—would be hard to repair.[23]

Several steps toward resolving these problems were undertaken. In one approach, the Menninger Foundation provided consultation services to a number of workshop groups composed of community members. The groups convened outside Lawrence, with consultant interventions to facilitate problem diagnosis and recommendations for change.

> The workshops produced about 80 suggestions to improve community relations. These included allowing citizens to ride as observers in police cars, continuing the workshop programs, establishing a day care center and increasing the staff in the human relations department. There were recommendations for improved police-community relations, for more involvement in the schools and their problems, for more job opportunities and in particular better relations between blacks and whites.[24]

This catalytic mode of community intervention sought to break the self-defeating cycle generating community malaise. Its operational outcomes were not evaluated at the time the report was published.

Shifting of Traditional Roles by Community Agents: The Police

Homes are sometimes the settings for violent acts, often in the midst of disputes that represent a breakdown in morale/cohesion due to power relations among husband and wife, parents and children, various other family members, and erstwhile friends and visitors. Even preceding physical violence, the dispute may have been noisy enough to attract outside attention. Police are likely to arrive, either of their own accord or in response to a call.

Necessarily, such police interventions often occur "after the fact" of injury or death and are made in terms of whatever laws have been broken. Nonetheless, many severe family disputes can or might be kept from violence by more timely interventions that deal with the mental-health aspects of the problem and in this way steer the situation toward resolution. The intervention can ease violence-inducing tensions or, at the least, can forestall acts of violence.

Police officers have been trained not only in the prescriptive interventions of law enforcement, but also in catalytic types of mental-health interventions involving efforts to aid protagonists in relieving tensions and restoring home-centered morale/cohesion. Although found to produce successful outcomes, these interventions may also create legalistic dilemmas. In the United States, for example, even a foresighted catalytic intervention with a family in a situation where no violence or other law violations have yet occurred can be interpreted as unconstitutional in the sense of violating privacy. Yet, without the intervention, the conflict may culminate in physical violence. At that point, action can only be taken legally in terms of arrests, sentencings, court orders, and other law-enforcement agency/judicial-branch options and determinations. This suggests that very difficult problems are to be anticipated where a "prescriptive role person," such as a police officer, is expected also to assume a catalytic role such as is characteristic of some community casework.[25] Tensions between police and the poor community often result because poverty seems to generate a sense of powerlessness—a belief that "others," luck, or fate control one's destiny. Law enforcement efforts are targeted to poor neighborhoods, leading in a self-perpetuating cycle to increased arrests, more frequent patrols, and so on. Police are often seen in the role of exercising authority and are often resented for the power they represent. Events since 1964 have shown that the tensions and conflicts resulting from mutual distrust and misunderstanding can escalate into widespread violence.

Efforts in Syracuse, New York, were made to break this cycle of resentment and hostility through a human relations training program designed to improve police/community relations.[26] Police officers and Model City residents, mostly black and poor, participated in week-long sessions that provided for the practical application of human relations training. The training groups were designed to have equal numbers of police and community participants attending as equals in a learning experience. This involved each group working separately in identifying things that irritated them about the other group. These lists were shared with the other group and served as the basis for discussion, diagnosis, and planning for better relations. The trainers helped participants develop skills by setting up situations that enabled them to discuss or act out (role play) the problem at hand, and by helping the group to see that stereotypes and prejudices create unnecessary barriers to effective communications.

Participants worked together on mechanisms to improve police/community relations toward the end of the week-long training. These took the form of recommendations presented to city, police, and Model Cities officials.

Evaluation data from a variety of sources indicate positive change in an eight-month period. This project helped Syracuse take a major step forward in improving police/community relations.

To the degree that personal attitudes are anchored in larger group attitudes, change efforts that concentrate on individuals-in-isolation are found to be of limited value.

Minister: From Prescriptive to Catalytic

Changing the function of already established institutions is another aspect of community change. A shift in the character of the relationship between a minister and the church membership is described in the following example. The shift is from "minister as prescriptive agent of outside power" to "minister as community consultant."

Conventionally, church-centered traditions and rituals such as the sermon, the passive role of members, and choral and community singing are reinforcement mechanisms helpful in maintaining the surrender of self-will to a higher authority. The minister, likewise, is the agent of this prescriptive format. How one church changed the character of such an established institution is described below.

> The University Church of Goleta workshop service has emphasized movement and action in all parts of the workshop. There are no pews, thus seating and movement has open-ended possibilities. People are provided opportunities to participate in all aspects of the service. During the singing, everybody sings; during the sacramental celebration itself, everybody is given the opportunity to move around and participate, even to dance if the person so desires. During the sermon opportunities for involvement are provided. Instead of one man talking, everybody participates and all persons are given the task of putting content into the worship experience.
>
> . . . In the communal service, people participate in the experiencing of ideas and create the sermon for themselves. The minister becomes a catalyst for group activity and participation. During the communal sermon persons interact with other persons in groups of six or eight. They play with blocks, color with crayons, or use some other simple tool of expression in order to wrestle with theological ideas and to experience them in relation to other persons. They function in a context that encourages them to take themselves seriously.
>
> The communal sermon as a catalyst to encounter rather than a package of truth, can open the possibility of discovering the individual self as incomplete, perhaps absurd, and human. This self-view can bring about a recovery of authentic dealing with a person's secret feelings of guilt and shame.[27]

The minister's role is one of introducing procedures and of providing process facilitation rather than that of extolling expert prescriptions. By avoiding advocacy, the resolution of problems is left open ended, with each member free to reach his or her own conclusions as to how personal responsibility should be interpreted under higher authority.

Destitute Social Conditions

Hallowitz,[28] in describing a neighborhood service center (NSC), indicates different contributions its paraconsultants are able to make to the client. One possibility is to expedite assistance for clients who require professional help but who are so overwhelmed with the problems of everyday living that they have little energy to invest in problem solving. For example, a request for assistance was referred to the center by a guidance counselor in a local elementary school. Johnny, a boy of nine, had been showing symptoms of behavior problems since the start of school in the fall, and his schoolwork had dropped off markedly. Over the previous two months, the school counselor had worked with Johnny's mother, Mrs. Jones, on a week-by-week basis with the intention of having facilitating discussions with her about Johnny. However, each time this client met with the school counselor, her primary concerns related to troubles she was having with the Welfare Department. She needed to find better housing, there was a lack of heat and hot water, she repeatedly had to go to court when her husband failed to provide support payments, and so on. Such difficulties were even more salient to her than the concerns she had earlier expressed about her son.

The NSC undertook to assist Mrs. Jones. One of its paraconsultants went to the school to meet with her in the presence of the guidance counselor, who first explained to Mrs. Jones why this aide had been invited. The NSC worker then described the kind of services the neighborhood center was able to contribute. Before leaving, she said, "I'd like to see you soon. I can do it this afternoon or tomorrow morning; and if you like, I can come visit you at home." Mrs. Jones was surprised, but pleased, that the aide would take the trouble to visit her.

Issues of misunderstanding about how the Welfare Department operates were clarified and requests for winter clothing, additional bedding, and household items were expedited as the paraconsultant worked with Mrs. Jones. The probation officer at the court arranged for her support payments to be made on a full-allowance basis rather than a supplementary one so that she would not have to suffer in the event of her husband's defaulting. Finally, with the paraconsultant's assistance, Mrs. Jones contacted her neighbors in the building, with the result that a multiple-building-violations complaint was filed and a rent reduction obtained. The consultant was giving procedural assistance and at the same time, through a strategy of process consultation, was helping Mrs. Jones learn how to make her needs known, how to assert herself, and how to work through the complexities of gaining the assistance welfare agencies are capable of providing.[29]

Another catalytic intervention by paraconsultants operating out of the neighborhood service center involves *sociotherapy*. This is initiated when the mental-health paraconsultant decides that an important part of the client's developmental needs is to become active in community affairs. Three purposes underlie this decision. One is that an increase in socialization—the process of entering the culture of the larger social system—will reduce the client's present feelings of isolation. A second purpose is to provide constructive channels for working through aggressive tensions. A third is to offer each participant an opportunity to contribute through helping others, in itself an important source of self-esteem.

Mental-health consultants find it feasible to involve clients in such activities as organizing welfare recipients and escorting clients to health facilities, organizing tenant councils, conducting voter registration drives, and sometimes assisting with clerical chores. As the consultants work alongside their clients, they have the opportunity of observing their strengths and weaknesses in their everyday contacts with other people. These observations can in turn be fed back to the expert-consultant to further clarify the diagnostic picture, enabling him or her to be more precise in thinking through treatment plans and desirable interventions.

A third kind of catalytic intervention made possible by the neighborhood service center involves part-time supervised work within the center itself, an arrangement particularly helpful for referred patients who have not used their skills for a long period of time. The client is able to be tested out at the center in a quasi-protected environment, gradually increasing the number of hours worked per week. While the client is supervised at work, he or she is still being seen occasionally by the clinic's professional consultants, so there is the opportunity to discuss and evaluate the work experience. Such an arrangement permits discussion of poor work habits, attitudes, and behavior, which would be self-defeating drawbacks on a regular job. The client often comes to recognize what behavior must be phased out in order for him or her to compete effectively in the open job market.

New Communities

Under certain circumstances, urban redevelopment for example, families are uprooted from their existing homes and moved to newly constructed neighborhoods. Such enforced relocation can have a destructive effect on what was previously a community by fragmenting it and placing the individual families in new surroundings where they feel both ill at ease and isolated. Increased geographical mobility, made possible by greater access to transportation and job opportunities, has further dissolved a sense of community in many areas.

Friendly, supportive, social and project-related activities with neighbors can be significant positive elements in the improvement and maintenance of social relations. Community mental-health consultants feel these activities are needed if positive morale/cohesion is to emerge among those who live together in a shared geographical space. The proposition is that, "people grow to their full stature when they are associated with others in warm, enjoyable fellowship, not based on artificial emotion but on intimate common interest in some aspect of being and doing."[30]

These kinds of needs often are not considered by those planning new residential areas. Because of this, the negative effects associated with mobility generally work against the establishment of social relationships in the new neighborhood. Consultant-based interventions may be needed to initiate and strengthen community cohesion.

Based on experiences of the social project team in Bristol, England, the following suggestions are offered as to how a community organizer can stimulate the development of community-building relationships. Though these suggestions apply particularly to new communities, they have value for already existing communities and are not necessarily limited to relatively poor, ill-educated, or problem-plagued citizens.

The first suggestion is for the consultant to engage in cohesion building between community authority and citizens.

(a) To act as a link between authority (especially the local authority) and the people—explaining and representing *both ways,* and in the process affecting the attitudes of both parties. There is a tendency for those with authority to think that, because they understand what they are doing and why, therefore this must be clear to the citizenry. In fact, this is not so; the process of explanation is an intimate one and needs continuous attention if "they" are to be felt to remain within human reach. Equally, citizen aspiration often gets lost because it has no way of making itself perceptible to those with power, usually because it does not know how to formulate its objectives. This is where the function of interpretation could contribute to the establishment and preservation of a sense of human relationship between authority and those for whose benefit authority is established.

A second contribution to community cohesion is for the consultant to be available as a rallying point through whom initial contacts between citizens with common interests can be made.

(b) The community organizer should help people to bring to fruition constructive group intentions: that is to say where people want to get a society going for the study of railway-lore or to discuss pigeon breeding; to start a cycling club or to push for a better local clinic or library. The community organizer should be a person to whom they know they can go, not to do the job, but to tell them how to go about it, whom to contact, where to look for a room, what forms to fill in, who might help them to keep the accounts. Middle-class organizers, active political leaders, and people used to business negotiations tend to have no idea how difficult it is for average citizens with limited contacts and experience to get started on putting ideas into practice if they range beyond the family circle.

A third aspect is for the community consultant to identify and provide for the expression of "latent" needs so they will be "felt."

(c) The third function of the community organizer is to try to generate social groups of one sort or another where he sees promise which does not look as if it would mature by itself. This, of course, is often done at present by specialists, particularly in the field of adult and further education. Its very success in these fields is a good reason for considering whether it could not be developed in the purely recreational and informal club field, through which some people grow in stature just as much as do others through activities which have higher educational status.[31]

Interventions (a) and (b) are facilitative in nature and are responses to felt needs. Intervention (c) is not in that category. After identifying latent needs, the interventionist takes steps toward creating local situations in which such needs will be recognized and fulfilled by the residents themselves.

Families under Tension

Stresses and strains are felt within most families regardless of their socioeconomic standing. Among the poorer and otherwise problem-ridden members of the community, the impact of tensions and strains can be most overwhelming, since in many such families there is little solidarity or cohesion. Members are not sufficiently integrated to cope, and interventions are needed to help the family remain intact. Sometimes the identity of these "families in trouble" is obvious and the requisite support and assistance can be provided; sometimes the need for help to arrest a deteriorating situation is totally unrecognized. How might a community consultant arrange an early-warning system to detect emerging family crises?

Based on his experience with the Bristol Social Project, Wilson[32] suggests three community sources that are useful under such circumstances. One is the rent collector or facility manager. He or she is likely to know of particular clients who are having serious financial problems and is familiar also with the personalities and concerns of these tenants. A second source consists of teachers plus the school welfare service of counselors, attendance officers, and so on. These personnel keep informed about "unusual" behavior, such as truancy on the part of a family's children, or deeply hostile attitudes toward school and teachers that may reflect stress within the home. A third source is the general medical practitioner. He or she comes into contact with family members from time to time, and if he or she has more than a physical health concept in mind, useful information as to problems needing attention can be passed on to a community organizer. By becoming aware at an early state of emerging family crises via these unobtrusive information sources, the community organizer is able to intervene in ways that contribute to the management and resolution of such crises.

A community of any size is likely to include women whose self-confidence has fallen so low that they are unable or unwilling to mix and make friends. When facilities exist for fostering improved mental health through group or club activities, such women can break out of their loneliness by gradually permitting themselves to gain some of the benefits of mutual help offered by friends and neighbors. In the Bristol Social Project,

> activities included sewing and cookery, the care of the feet, darning and shoe repairing, the making of lampshades, the care of the hands, and sex instruction for girls. The children played together in an adjoining room.

Competitions in the making of simple articles were held most weeks and prizes given for the best work. There were several talks from outside speakers, a councillor, a health visitor, and a marriage guidance counsellor.

It is never easy to assess precise results, but this experiment in home-making undoubtedly fulfilled in part a real need for advice and friendship on the part of a group of mothers who did not feel able to join the established women's organization at Upfield. There is little doubt that the scope for the organization of groups of this kind is very wide, particularly among mothers whose family involvements give them little opportunity for companionship outside the home.[33]

As noted before, the role of the community consultant is to provide a rallying point for group formation, while preparing the group to be able to continue its activities and maintain its identity.

Rumor Control

Rumors that disturb people can have a negative effect on morale/cohesion. Rumor Control Centers sprang up in the United States during the turbulence of the 1960s. Their purpose was to fill a need felt by people who wanted to "know the score."

After hearing a rumor, these centers first check out the facts and then establish standard answers based on the best judgment possible in light of these facts. Disseminated in response to telephone inquiries or by other means, these answers serve a perception-building function. For example, they may provide an inquirer with access to social realities that otherwise might be unavailable. They serve a morale/cohesion need by helping the inquirer deal with his or her fears and anxieties by determining whether they are real or imaginary.[34]

Integration of Mental Patients into the Community

A two-step application of the basic idea of an intermediate living situation between mental hospital and open community is described by Fairweather, Sanders, and Tornatzky. It started as a training program designed to assist mental patients in acquiring social skills and rapidly expanded into patient government. Research evaluation demonstrated that patients in such a program improved more rapidly than would be expected under standard conditions. However, they were unable to maintain the gain when released. The rate of return to hospitalization was comparable in both groups.

The extension of in-hospital, more or less autonomous problem-solving group training involved the creation of lodges in the community where groups of patients would continue to live and collaborate after hospital discharge. Training during hospitalization to solve problems after discharge was provided and lodge administration was patient-based, with nominal administrative representation or support provided by live-in hospital staff. The consultants describe lodge life as follows.

A lodge is a special kind of social organization in the community for ex-mental patients with features that make it different from any other kind of place for such patients, whether it be a family home, a boarding house, other forms of transitional residence such as a half-way house, or whatever. The essential characteristics are:

A. *The lodge depends on lodge members themselves to keep their members in the community rather than upon the support of hospital personnel.* Three basic practices help create this distinguishing feature.

    1. *No live-in staff.* Unlike most other community facilities for ex-mental patients, staff persons are kept to a minimum. No staff persons reside on the lodge premises under any circumstances. Typically, only a single person or a few hospital personnel will have contact with the lodge during any eight-hour work day, and this contact will exist only because he or they have been specifically designated by hospital authorities as the staff for the lodge organization.

    2. *Only lodge staff on call.* Unlike most other community facilities, the lodge staff are the medium through which lodge members contact the hospital. Only these designated staff members should be used by the members when they feel the need for assistance. The staff is available to lodge members for all 24-hours of a day, not for a "shift" or "8-hour work day." The resultant minimized contact with the hospital staff should decrease the lodge members' dependence upon hospital staff persons for direction and guidance in everyday life in the community. . . .[35]

Summary

In these examples of catalytic interventions, the focal point has been either the individual-within-society or the development of a larger sense of community. Alternate forms of existing institutions as well as new and more vital ways of working within existing organizations appear to be needed to achieve higher and more sustained levels of morale/cohesion.

In interventions with individual clients, it is noteworthy that the catalytic consultant takes care not to provoke defensiveness. If he or she finds defensiveness present or can diagnose its latency in the client, the consultant attempts to dissolve this barrier rather than confront it directly. The approach may or may not be successful, but in either case the specific effect of a particular catalytic intervention is not readily observable. By contrast, a confrontational intervention is much more likely to draw forth a discernible reaction from the individual or group client.

When the client system is at a group to larger-social-system level, a catalytic consultant may find additional possibilities for interventions directed toward improvement of the *contexts* of members' circumstances as an indirect means of heightening morale/cohesion. The Trist/Bamforth, Wilson, and Fairweather et al., reports contain evidence of this approach. Trist/Bamforth is a "pure" example of a detailed—and, at the time, novel—analysis and report that *itself* catalyzed the client system by indicating that its technical and social subsystems were out of joint. The Wilson and Fairweather et al., consultations show "context" interventions taking place in conjunction with more directly focused catalytic interventions.

Notes

1. R. R. Carkhuff, *Helping and Human Relations*, 2 vols. (New York: Holt, Rinehart & Winston, 1969).

2. W. Glasser, *Reality Therapy* (New York: Harper, 1965).

3. K. S. Crawford, E. D. Thomas, and J. J. Fink, "Pygmalion at Sea: Improving the Work Effectiveness of Low Performers," *Journal of Applied Behavioral Science* 16, no. 4 (1980): 482–505.

4. M. S. Schwartz and G. T. Will, "Intervention and Change in a Mental Hospital Ward," in W. G. Bennis, K. D. Benne, and R. Chin, eds., *The Planning of Change* (New York: Holt, Rinehart and Winston, 1961), p. 578. Reprinted by permission.

5. Ibid., pp. 478–79.

6. C. H. Driessnack, APD, "Outplacement: A Benefit for Both Employee and Company," *The Personnel Administrator* (January 1978): 26.

7. C. W. Greenbaum, I. Rogovsky, and B. Shalit, "The Military Psychologist During Wartime: A Model Based on Action Research and Crisis Interventions," *Journal of Applied Behavioral Science* 13, no. 1 (1977): 8.

8. "Organization Development in the United States Army: An Interview with Lt. Col. Ramon A. Nadal," *Journal of Applied Behavioral Science* 14, no. 4 (1978): 523–36.

9. R. T. Golembiewski and A. Blumberg, "Confrontation as a Training Design in Complex Organizations: Attitudinal Changes in a Diversified Population of Managers," reproduced by special permission from *Journal of Applied Behavioral Science* 3, no. 4 (1967): 525–47.

10. Ibid., p. 534.

11. Ibid., p. 545.

12. W. G. Bennis, *Organization Development: Its Nature, Origins, and Prospects*, © 1969. Addison-Wesley, Reading, MA, p. 4. Reprinted with permission.

13. Ibid., pp. 4–5.

14. Ibid., pp. 4–6.

15. E. L. Trist and K. W. Bamforth, "Some Social and Psychological Consequences of the Longwall Method of Coal-Getting," *Human Relations* 4, no. 1 (1951): 3–38.

16. Ibid., pp. 37–38.

17. S. A. Culbert, "Using Research to Guide an Organization Development Project," *Journal of Applied Behavioral Science* 8, no. 2 (1972): 203–36. S. A. Culbert, "1978 Reflections on 'Using Research to Guide an Organization Development Project,'" in B. Lubin, L. D. Goodstein, and A. W. Lubin, eds., *Organizational Change Sourcebook I: Cases in Organization Development* (San Diego: University Associates, 1979), pp. 96–99.

18. R. R. Blake, J. S. Mouton, and R. L. Sloma, "The Union-Management Intergroup Laboratory: Strategy for Resolving Intergroup Conflict," *Journal of Applied Behavioral Science* 1 (1965): 25–57.

19. G. Levin and D. D. Stein, "System Intervention in a School-Community Conflict," *Journal of Applied Behavioral Science* 6, no. 3 (1970): 337–52. G. Levin and D. D. Stein, "Update on 'System Intervention in a School-Community Conflict,'" in B. Lubin, L. D. Goodstein, and A. W. Lubin, eds., *Organizational Change Sourcebook II: Cases in Conflict Management* (San Diego: University Associates, 1979), pp. 21–23.

20. J. S. Mouton and R. R. Blake, *Synergogy: An Instrumented Team Learning Approach* (Austin, Texas: Scientific Methods, Inc., 1981).

21. J. G. Robbins, "Using Trainer Participation in a Community Development Program," reproduced by special permission from the *Training and Development Journal* 27, no. 10 (1973): 14–19. Copyright 1973 by the American Society for Training and Development, Inc.

22. Ibid., p. 16.

23. W. Moyers, *Listening to America* (New York: Harper's Magazine Press, 1971), p. 122. Copyright © 1971 by Bill Moyers. All rights reserved.

24. A. Auerback, "The Psychological Health of the City Today," in J. L. Carleton and U. Mahlendorf, eds., *Man for Man: A Multidisciplinary Workshop on Affecting Man's Social and Psychological Nature through Community Action* (Springfield, Ill.: Charles C Thomas, 1973), p. 288. Reprinted by permission.

25. M. Bard and J. Zacker, "Dilemmas of Community Intervention," *Journal of Marriage and the Family* 26, no. 3 (1961): 677–82.

26. G. M. Parker, "Human Relations Training," *Training and Development Journal* (October 1974): 7–12.

27. D. R. Kennedy, "The Church as a Therapeutic Community," in J. L. Carleton and U. Mahlendorf, eds., *Man for Man: A Multidisciplinary Workshop on Affecting Man's Social and Psychological Nature through Community Action* (Springfield, Ill.: Charles C Thomas, 1973), pp. 104–5. Reprinted by permission.

28. E. Hallowitz, "The Expanding Role of the Neighborhood Service Center," in F. Riessman and H. R. Popper, eds., *Up from Poverty: New Career Ladders for Nonprofessionals* (New York: Harper & Row, 1968), pp. 92–105.

29. Ibid., pp. 94–95.

30. R. Wilson, "Difficult Housing Estates," *Human Relations* 16, no. 1 (1963): 23–24. Reprinted by permission.

31. Ibid., p. 24.

32. Ibid., pp. 28–29.

33. Ibid., p. 36.

34. J. R. Ponting, "Rumor Control Centers," *American Behavioral Scientist* 16, no. 3 (1973): 391–401.

35. G. W. Fairweather, D. H. Sanders, and L. G. Tornatzky, *Creating Change in Mental Health Organizations* (New York: Pergamon Press, 1974), p. 108. Reprinted by permission.

23

CATALYTIC INTERVENTIONS

Norms/ Standards

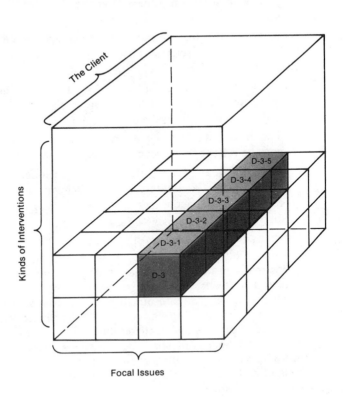

Norms involve shared perceptions, and the catalytic methodology appears suited to dealing with norms/standards as a focal issue, particularly when norms/standards do not involve deeply held values. Catalytic awareness interventions can help the client see what norms/standards are guiding behavior. As the client becomes cognizant of these latent behavioral influences, he or she may be able to replace them when more valid alternatives are called for.

INDIVIDUAL (D-3-1)

Counseling that deals with a client's emotions-as-facts can be carried out through catalytic interventions relating to personal norms and standards. Although an individual may be aware of these norms/standards, he or she may not always adhere to them. Instances where personal norms and standards have been violated may become the focal issue of consultation. Two prominent practitioners of this approach are Mowrer[1] and Jourard.[2] The rationale is based on several considerations introduced by Mowrer.

1. Many emotional difficulties arise because people feel guilty about some past misdeed—that is, an instance in which they violated a norm or standard—and try to hide it from others. Yet the memory remains clear to the client. The incident has not been buried.

2. By admitting the norm violation to the consultant and to the more significant of these "others," such as husband or wife, tensions associated with norm violations are reduced or eliminated.

3. The consultant can assist the client in disclosing a personal norm or standard and how it has been transgressed. This can be done by "setting a model" of such disclosure. For example:

   a. The consultant first reveals to the client his or her own past difficulties and the relief experienced from past and continuing self-disclosures.

   b. The consultant writes out a similar episode, offering the client a case study that sets a standard of self-disclosure together with an explanatory rationale and encourages the client to engage in his or her own self-disclosure.

Mowrer provides the following example of this process.

Recently I have been seeing a talented young woman whose life situation raises many of the same issues in a little different way. The presenting picture was that she had been drinking much more than was good for her, "imposing upon" (as she put it) and embarrassing her friends when intoxicated, and not meeting her responsibilities in connection with her work. In her sober moments she realized that if this trend continued, it would be only a matter of time until she would lose her very responsible and attractive position. She was, in fact, scheduled for an important promotion soon; and instead of feeling pleased and zestful about it, she was acutely apprehensive.

During our first interview this young woman reported an accident in which she had been involved a few months ago and implied that this was what had unnerved her; but when I said it seemed to me that her symptoms bespoke a deeper source of disturbance, she acknowledged that there *"was* something," which in our second interview she courageously reported. Some three years earlier she had permitted herself to become involved homosexually with an older woman she very much admired and liked. Although this was decidedly against her "better judgment"—she said the excitement and enthrallment "clouded out everything else," until after the affair came to an end and she was left with only ashes and remorse. She felt she did not deserve the trust people were inclined to put in her or the preferment which her very real abilities and good work had won for her in her profession; she therefore began to drink excessively, disillusion her friends, neglect her work, and to feel, as she put it, that she was fighting for her very "survival" psychologically.

As she rose from her chair at the end of the second interview, this woman remarked that she already felt "much better"; and she was now able, simply at my request, to leave off the drinking forthwith. She settled into her work again, and she manifested an active and sincere desire, in our ensuing talks, to find a way of further restoring her self-respect and social integrity. I explained to her my feeling that in situations of this kind "treatment" may begin with a specialized "therapist," but that full recovery is achieved only in restoration to community in the ordinary, common sense of that term. Obviously, in entering into the homosexual venture, this young woman had isolated, alienated herself from the "significant others" in her life and had created what Donald Cressey, in a different context, has called an "unsharable problem." She said that for a long time she had felt that she could "work this thing out" herself; but she had come to realize that this was an illusion, that she must have "help"; and she was now not too resistant to the idea that such help cannot come entirely from just one other person.[3]

By adhering to the standard of disclosure and revealing her past, the client was released from her burden of guilt. The consultant served as listener. Thus far, it was an instance of catharsis—the consultant's *catalytic* intervention came in his information-sharing suggestions about "reconciliation."

One criterion of mental health is that a well-functioning person is able to interact freely and spontaneously. The healthy individual does not feel compelled to hide or deny past deeds in the interest of maintaining acceptance. When such burdens exist, they reduce freedom and spontaneity and probably diminish the individual's energy to pursue daily objectives.

Mowrer's catalytic yet emotion-based counseling approach deals with these issues in a double-norm way. He says:

I find myself, more and more, guiding neurotic individuals into a two-fold strategy which involves (a) confession of past misdeeds and (b) *concealment* of present and future "good works." Instead of advising disturbed persons to continue to pay fees to a professional counselor, I urge them to take advantage of the opportunities which are always freely available for becoming honest and open with respect to past mistakes and then to take the equivalent of a fee (in time or money) and devote it to "charity by stealth."

A case example is offered in the following:

A bright young man with a history of adolescent delinquency and debauchery, had, when I first saw him, already been attracted to and joined a religious group and had undergone a conversion of sorts; but he continued to be ruminative, moody, unpredictable in his interpersonal responses, and never quite certain when he might revert to his old mode of life. At the suggestion of a mutual friend, he came to see me; and we moved quickly and with surprisingly little resistance toward the decision to make a clean breast of his past to two trusted members of this group, and from this step the new policy of openness was extended to "significant others."

The relief experienced by this young man and the personal change noted in him by his friends were very striking; and we were soon able to start thinking about the more positive aspects of the program. At this juncture I began introducing him to Clive Randolph's "secret." The lad was much interested, and presently I saw his face contort into a sort of scowl, his eyes light up, and with some difficulty he succeeded in re-stating the idea in a way which, to me at least, was both clarifying and novel. I am sorry I do not have a record of his exact words; but they went something like this: "What you seem to be saying is that when we tell or brag about some accomplishment or favor we've done someone, we exchange the "credit" for immediate satisfaction, that is, we 'spend' it. And in the same way, when we confess an *evil,* something we feel *guilty* about, we likewise get rid of it, dissipate it . . . like those things I did and thought I wasn't ashamed of but was. Now that I have admitted them, they aren't really a part of me anymore—they just don't seem very important. By admitting these things, I have 'spent' my guilt. And now the same principle seems to work also the other way 'round. Just as the wrong kind of 'credit,' if accumulated, will eventually destroy you, so will good 'credit,' if *not used up,* give you strength and inner confidence. The net effect is that you *are,* in any case what you keep back, *save:* strong and self-accepting if what you hide and keep back is good and weak and self-hating if what you keep and hide is bad."[4]

The Clive Randolph's "secret" referred to above consists of the following consultant-distilled double-norm rationale from a literary source: Lloyd Douglas' *Magnificent Obsession.*[5]

Most of us live *depleted* existences: weak, zestless, apprehensive, pessimistic, "neurotic." And the reason is that when we perform a *good* deed, we advertise it, display it—and thus collect and enjoy the credit then and there. But when we do something cheap and mean, we carefully hide and deny it (if we can), with the result that the "credit" for acts of *this* kind remains with us and "accumulates." A person who follows such a life style is chronically bankrupt in the moral and spiritual sense. If, at any given moment, his life were "required of him," he would be found *wanting,* could not pay out, settle up; for his "net worth" is less than nothing, negative. Small wonder, then, that a person of this kind has no confidence or zest and lacks creativity. He is too busy pretending, too "insecure," too afraid of being "found out."

So what is the alternative, the remedy for a person who had already fallen into, or wishes to avoid, such a miserable and meaningless existence? It is, quite simply, to reverse this whole strategy: admit and thus divest oneself of one's weaknesses, errors, follies, and *hide* one's charities, good deeds, virtues. This, Randolph tells Dr. Hudson, is the secret of "that mysterious power I mentioned. By following these instructions to the letter, you can have anything you want, do anything you wish to do, be whatever you would like to be. I have tried it. It works. It worked for me. It will work for you!"[6]

Norms/standards catalytic interventions supplement the client's information system so that his or her situation can be seen in a broader, and therefore possibly more valid, context. As the client seeks to release withheld information with the consultant's help, the likelihood is increased that a person will view his or her situation in a richer, more objective, and more problem-solving manner.

Summary

Catalytic interventions centering on the individual-as-client are pertinent in any situation where (1) the client is involved but is not so emotionally upset that thinking is impractical; (2) the client is burdened by being the sole possessor of guilt-laden information regarding his or her past. Given the client's uncertainty as to what to do, he or she is interested in exploring an acceptable course of action. The consultant facilitates these processes by "modeling" for the client "how to confess," thus helping the client release hidden information and be freed from its negative effects.

GROUP (D-3-2)

In the catalytic consultant's search for a helpful group intervention, he or she frequently looks at norms and standards as the force holding members in an unexamined status quo position. If a group is operating according to dysfunctional norms/standards, the consultant tries to help members examine alternative norms/standards that might be more appropriate to their situation. This is a difficult feat for a group to accomplish alone, since individual members are open to rejection if they challenge the status quo. A consultant, by comparison, can ask an "innocent" question regarding almost any topic, such as "Why is *this* done *that* way?—and be a hero for voicing the unspoken criticisms.

Staff Meetings

Meetings demand significant expenditures of time, resources, and energy, often without any identifiable product or tangible results. Considering the number of elements involved in any group discussion—content, context, interactions, etc.— it is clear that meetings are exceedingly complex activities, the effectiveness of which is usually taken for granted.

Koehler, Lehner, and Fisher[7] describe how two external consultants to the Milwaukee Personnel Department joined with an internal consultant to focus on increasing the effectiveness of staff meetings.

This was a two-day intervention. The first day involved information gathering and feedback. The second day included sessions in which staff groups analyzed their own effectiveness and designed plans for improvement. In the first day each conducted a regular staff meeting while consultants observed. This was an opportunity for the consultants to obtain through direct observation an understanding of substantive issues that the meetings discussed, a flavor of the processes by which the meetings were conducted, how participants interacted, and so forth. Information and impressions gathered served as a background for providing a general description of how each team worked and for aiding groups in planning and implementing the activities for the following day.

Participants from each of the four departments met for team development during the second day. The morning began with introductory comments and an overview of the processes of team development. Then each of the four teams made a chart listing factors that might increase team effectiveness at meetings. Various questions were raised about how each group had worked as a team. This led to examination of each team's mode of functioning. The next task was for each team to select a key concern, issue, or recommendation and to develop a course of action for implementing a desired change. To increase the likelihood that these team-building activities would subsequently result in more effective meetings, each of the four teams also explored relevant follow-up activities.

With consultant assistance, the participants gained limited understanding of team building and clinical experience with applying those processes when dealing with a work-related problem. Transfer of learning under such limited conditions is to be expected. Deeper issues of effectiveness were not concentrated upon in this abbreviated experience. For example, issues of conflict, its causes, and approaches to its effective resolution cannot be learned in such a brief experience. Self-deception as to one's personal effectiveness is also beyond the reach of such a design.

Preparing for, conducting, and attending meetings probably occupy more of a manager's time than any other single activity. Managers often complain that the meetings they conduct or attend are unproductive or even counterproductive. Consideration of how costly in terms of time and money an unproductive meeting can be is sufficient impetus for limiting the number of meetings held and maximizing productivity in meetings that are truly necessary.

An intervention to solve the problem of unproductive meetings at Chesapeake and Potomac Telephone is described by Steelman[8] from his perspective as an internal consultant. A workshop intended to result in increased organizational effectiveness in conducting meetings was prepared and delivered to company managers.

The workshop was designed to accomplish a high degree of commitment, involvement, and ownership through front-end analysis. ". . . Go to the people who want the workshop and find out . . . what they want included in it; how they want it presented; what their ideas are. . . ."[9]

A questionnaire to guide the workshop planning interviews was designed to get managers' spontaneous feelings on various questions. With this so-called front-end analysis, the format and process of the workshop fell right in place. Managers wanted a highly participative workshop, not a "tell" session as to procedures for conducting an effective meeting. As part of the workshop, participants practiced conducting a meeting and received feedback from the other conferees as well as the trainer. This was an ongoing process. As different phases of the workshop were covered, emphasis was placed on how each phase could be used when conducting their own meeting. The practice meeting, incidentally, was included as a result of the front-end analysis. It was one of the suggestions most frequently requested.

Though the workshop's impact on the quality of organizations' meetings was not measured, the consultant reports that participants were highly satisfied with the experience because it met identified needs and was congruent with their expectations.

Agenda Determination

The following intervention by Schein[10] facilitated group functioning by focusing attention on how the agenda for meetings was determined. The consultant reports being a participant observer of barriers to effectiveness among group members who were contending with work problems.

> In the Apex company I sat in for several months on the weekly executive-committee meeting, which included the president and his key subordinates. I quickly became aware that the group was very loose in its manner of operation; people spoke when they felt like it, issues were explored fully, conflict was fairly openly confronted, and members felt free to contribute.

Nonetheless, as he listened, the consultant began to identify a repetitive cycle that constituted a growing problem.

> This kind of climate seemed constructive, but it created a major difficulty for the group. No matter how few items were put on the agenda, the group was never able to finish its work. The list of backlog items grew longer and the frustration of group members intensified in proportion to this backlog.

Part of the problem was that members were responding in a "more and more of what we did before" fashion.

> The group responded by trying to work harder. They scheduled more meetings and attempted to get more done at each meeting, but with little success. Remarks about the ineffectiveness of groups, too many meetings, and so on, became more and more frequent.

The consultant could see the problem pattern more clearly.

> My diagnosis was that the group was overloaded. Their agenda was too large, they tried to process too many items at any given meeting, and the

agenda was a mixture of operational and policy issues without recognition by the group that such items required different allocations of time.

Consequently, he introduced a procedural suggestion but did not attempt to sell the group on it. Rather, he left it to the members for debate and decision.

I suggested to the group that they seemed overloaded and should discuss how to develop their agenda for their meetings. The suggestion was adopted after a half-hour or so of shared feelings.

His later facilitations came in response to the eventual group-agreed decision.

It was then decided, with my help, to sort the agenda items into several categories, and to devote some meetings entirely to operational issues while others would be exclusively policy meetings. The operations meetings would be run more tightly in order to process these items efficiently. The policy questions would be dealt with in depth.[11]

Thus the intervention dealt almost exclusively with procedures involved in the work discussions of this particular group.

Policy

The Open Space Board of Trustees of Boulder, Colorado, is an organization concerned with rendering decisions about acquiring land in behalf of the city. Boulder's City Council had charged the Open Space Board with formulating a policy for the acquisition of "open space land."[12] Such decisions are difficult, partly because there are no systematic criteria for making them, and partly because such decisions touch on vested interests which create new pressures in the form of lobbies, etc. Consultation services were volunteered with the goal in mind of increasing the explicitness and objectivity behind such decisions. The Board members agreed to the consultant's suggested methodology.

Each step of the procedure is described in detail.

Members discussed and agreed upon the salient factors that influenced their judgments about the desirability of parcels of land for open space.

Each Board member made judgments about the desirability of forty hypothetical parcels of land. Individual judgments were analyzed by computer.

The participants received individual feedback that provided insight into qualitative and quantitative facets influencing their own decisions. The result was that each individual's decision-making policy became more explicit.

The level of group agreement/disagreement was assessed and a "Compromise Policy" was proposed and demonstrated to the group.

Each member compared his or her decision policy with other group members' decision policies. A final Compromise Policy was obtained by taking the means of revised individual judgments.

Thirty-one actual parcels of land were "judged" by the group in terms of the agreed-upon approach.

Group rankings resulted in a priority listing of the lands under consideration.

The priority list, plus a description of the Procurement Policy showed how information on seven significant factors produced the list. This information was submitted to the Open Space Board of Trustees. The report was accepted by the Board and was entered into its minutes as the official statement of its land acquisition policy.

Computer technology represents a catalytic intervention because the product in this example was used to make information about norms/standards more explicit. Computer assistance in decision making lends a considerable degree of logic and objectivity to an often emotional and subjective process. Conceivably, the application of computer technology to decision making may improve the quality of group decisions while minimizing group conflict and dissatisfaction. However, this intervention is not judged to have been successful because the policy was quickly replaced. One reason given is that follow-up consultation was not provided. An alternative explanation is that members did not wish to have their decision making brought under such explicit control and influence. This explanation implies that underlying conflicts as to values, vested interests, and so on resulted because members had not committed themselves to a set of superordinate goals. As a result, the approach was abandoned as "too rigid," "mechanical," etc. The limitation in the consultation is found in the absence of a process orientation that might have brought personal goals and objectives of members into the open where they might have been confronted and resolved.

Levels of Productivity and Morale

A multiplicity of interventions, all of the catalytic variety, were shown by Christian and Gross[13] to shift norms of productivity and satisfaction.

The setting for this intervention is the city of San Diego. This project in improving city government was intended to increase productivity and morale without allowing either goal to interfere with achievement of the other. One branch of the city government, the communications and electrical division, was the experimental unit. Other branches of the same city's government were used as control for evaluating the impact of the one-year organization development project. This suggests that the authors conceive of productivity and morale as being two independent goals rather than two dimensions of one basic process. Baseline data were collected to indicate levels of productivity and job satisfaction.

The interventions involved five different approaches: interviews, team building, counseling, process consultation, and management skills training.

Interviews and surveys were conducted with all individuals in the C&E division to discover employee perceptions of the organization's climate. These interviews were open ended. They included such questions as, "What makes cooperation between work groups difficult?" Likert answers on a scale from one to five provided the insights as to why.

Interviews were followed by team-building workshops from the top management group down. Workshops included the following: 1) training in communication and management skills, 2) a briefing on the overall results of the earlier data gathering from interviews and employee attitude surveys, and 3) a role clarification exercise in which each member had the opportunity to identify the duties of his or her position and to verify role perceptions with the division superintendent and 4) a formal exercise designed to identify specific organization problems and plan solutions to them.

In the top group, the superintendent was the focal point for role clarification, and in each subordinate group the leader served in the same manner. Important results from this step involved the identification of organization problems and development of plans to solve them.

The counseling focused primarily on strategies for implementing the OD effort. Content of the counseling effort also involved offering practicing managers additional options and alternatives that the counselors had learned through other experiences.

Consultants provided participants with insights and feedback concerning decision making, problem solving, and communication within the group. Consultant activities focused on facilitating group process with only minor contributions to the contents of the conference.

A series of two-hour training events on topics supervisors had previously identified included: 1) City Manager expectations for supervisors, 2) methods of conducting effective meetings, 3) stress reduction, 4) effective discipline, 5) leadership style, 6) employee motivation, 7) performance evaluation, 8) solving organization problems, 9) effective time management, and 10) the city's Memorandum of Understanding with employee labor unions.

Evaluation entailed comparison with the buildings division of the City of San Diego and the Long Beach Communication and Electrical Workers, another directly comparable group in terms of productivity and job satisfaction measures.

Productivity was evaluated by tabulating a number of specific tasks completed by two sections of the communication and electrical division for the year preceding and the year following these interventions. These tasks included the number of street lights relamped, number of outages repaired, and total number of preventative maintenances performed. Other measures involved efficiency indicators, including the ratio of productive work hours and so on. The intervention was successful. With respect to productivity, the C&E group increased the amount of work done for four of five specific tasks. Less time was required to complete four of eight tasks that could be assessed. Of two cost measures, one increased at less than the rate of inflation where the other fell by a significant amount.

Improvements in satisfaction were associated with these increments of productivity. Both verbal responses and unobtrusive measures indicate improvement in morale for this group that already had relatively well-satisfied employees.

This group-level effort involved a multiplicity of interventions, all of which appear to have been catalytic in character. Norms and standards were the focus since changes in *rates* of productivity and level of morale were the indicators of results.

Creating Patient-Oriented Norms/Standards

Daily involvement with suffering can sometimes lead to callous, even hostile, attitudes toward patients on the part of service providers. Processes and procedures focused on reporting and recording of services are given priority in order to satisfy multiple accountability systems. Rather than providing a means of delivering services, they often become "ends" in themselves, with patient needs and preferences receiving low priority.

An intervention designed to move health care provision toward more "patient-oriented" norms/standards is described by Harris. Patient orientation refers to the degree to which a health care organization demonstrates concern for and responsiveness to the patient as a person.

> The demonstration project was carried out at two U.S. Naval Regional Medical Centers. . . . Four ambulatory care clinics participated at each site. . . . Short questionnaires to be completed prior to leaving the clinic asked patients about their satisfaction with the clinic's service.[14]

The intervention proceeded in five well-defined stages: 1) top-level management commitment and cooperation were obtained at the level of commanding officer and chief of ambulatory services levels, 2) efforts of the intervention team and staff focused on determining salient informational items that staff indicated would be helpful in providing better patient care, 3) questionnaires were designed to elicit the desired information with computer analysis programs developed and implementation procedures outlined, 4) a one-month pilot test was conducted to determine the appropriateness of approach, and 5) project evaluation was completed.

Using a random sample of 100 patients per week, satisfaction or dissatisfaction levels were determined by patients' questionnaire responses and fed back to treatment personnel.

> Staff who were involved in the selection of questions and/or staff who reviewed the data felt that the patient satisfaction data had positive value and usefulness. Staff in all clinics perceived post-project levels of satisfaction to be high. In general . . . the clinic staff's perceptions were fairly consistent with patients' reported satisfaction.[15]

These findings are subject to a number of interpretations. The administration of the questionnaire itself could have significantly impacted both staff attitudes and behaviors as well as patient satisfaction with services. Control groups were not established to determine whether the information gained from the questionnaire was the key factor or whether the major influence was the questionnaire itself and processes that surrounded its development, administration, and utilization.

Behind this approach lies the assumption, challenged elsewhere, that clinic staff have the requisite skills, desires, and systems of coordination to meet patient needs. The value of feedback is limited by such deficiencies. For example, if

various specialists have no coordinating mechanisms, and furthermore, if significant hostilities exist among them, feedback that implies poor coordination is
unlikely to bring about a solution to the problem.

Work Practices

An intervention by Rice involving a textile weaving factory in India is of a
socio-technical genre similar to that reported by Trist and Bamforth, but is more
illustrative of consultant-client collaboration in performing an analysis of socio-
technical interrelationships inherent in the factory's weaving process. It was
carried out, however, not to solve a cohesion problem but as an issue of
norms/standards.

> The analysis was made in collaboration with a development group in which
> the author worked with the Chairman, the Mill Manager, and Works Man-
> ager of the Company. (The Works Manager was the direct executive subor-
> dinate of the Mill Manager, who reported directly to the Chairman. The
> Works Manager also acted, however, as Technical Staff Officer to the
> Chairman.) The members of this group and the author collaborated closely,
> working as a group, in pairs or singly as the situation demanded, until each
> was satisfied, from his own point of view, of the validity of the analysis.
> They reported as a group to the other members of senior management at
> all stages. The decision to initiate the reorganization was taken by the
> Chairman at a meeting which was attended by all Senior Managers. At that
> meeting the Weaving Master of the mill concerned was called. He listened
> with evident enthusiasm to the proposals and began at once to produce
> from his own experience arguments in their favour. The Works Manager,
> as the senior executive responsible for the experimental loom shed, then
> discussed the proposals with the Top Supervisor of the shed. Thereafter
> the supervisors and workers in the loom shed took over the proposals as
> their own; and within a few hours, to the surprise of management, the work-
> ers had organized their own working groups. The Chairman, the Mill Man-
> ager, the Works Manager, and the author did not attend any of the discus-
> sions with supervisors or workers, nor did they visit the loom shed again
> until the reorganization had been implemented.[16]

Rice[17] described the group pattern identified by initial socio-technical analysis as "an aggregate of individuals with confused task and worker relationships
and with no discernible internal group structure." Even so, the focal issue was
evidently not one of morale/cohesion (as in the case of Trist/Bamforth coal-
mine study), since relationships among supervisors and workers were already
quite positive. The norms/standards focal issue was traditional status quo assumptions about "who *should* do what" that were still operating within a highly
automated plant. Interestingly, these were not traditional Indian assumptions but
had been imported at earlier stages of industrialization and, in effect, had been
sanctified by task-by-task industrial engineering practices.
    The first significant norm shift occurred when higher management decided

to *discuss with* lower-level managers and workers an experimental reorganization, with an associated piecework pay offer. Taking full advantage of the newly
legitimized participation/involvement opportunity, supervisors and workers re-
organized their own work arrangements. Rice reports[18] that after an initial
adjustment period productivity stabilized at a higher level than before.

Providing employees the opportunity to set their own working time within
preset limits is a management work practice that has enjoyed some popularity
in the last few years. Ground rules used for implementing such an approach in
one company included the following.

Responsibility downward for establishing the specific flexible work hours
program resides with the division's general manager, to be redelegated downward. The first line managers made the various scheduling decisions based on
the type of operation or function performed. The first line manager is responsible
for maximizing employee's work time preferences without productivity loss. A
checklist given to division and line managers outlined the following guidelines
for authority delegation, handling infractions, control measures, monitoring
devices, goal establishment, and lunch hour definition.

- Allow a minimum of ten days for detailed planning prior to implementing
  a flexible hours schedule.
- Anticipate what will happen in each department based on the mode of
  flexible work hours chosen.
- Restrict the choice of flexible hour mode where technological constraints
  are present (e.g., manufacturing).
- Start the program by overcontrolling. It is easier to remove controls than
  to add them.
- Restrict the flexibility initially. Employees can be rewarded with increased
  flexibility, but there will be adverse effects if flexibility is restricted later.
- Meet with employees to receive feedback prior to finalizing the operational
  program. This will eliminate unnecessary future administrative changes and
  increase the program's acceptability.
- Maintain proper controls at all times.
- Don't exclude given groups of employees from flexible hours program
  participation without considerable discussion and thought. This can lead to
  feelings of inequality and jealousy.
- Don't expect this to be a cure-all program; it isn't.
- Don't expect 100 percent manager and employee program acceptance. Some
  individuals are reluctant to change.[19]

Four implementation methodologies encompass most of the tactics for
implementing flexitime under varying organization conditions. These are:

1. *Individual flexibility.* . . . All individuals within a unit are allowed to vary
   their daily start and finish times with no change in the total hours worked in
   a day or week. This mode was utilized by 85 percent of the managers,
   affecting 850 employees (58 percent of the total).

2. *Staggered hours.* . . . Individuals may choose one of [any designated] options . . . and work those hours daily for one week. This mode was utilized by 39 percent of the managers, affecting 518 employees (36 percent of the total).

3. *Group flexibility.* All employees within a department or work group may . . . change their hours concurrently . . . working the same hours daily. . . . This mode was utilized by 17 percent of the managers, affecting 26 employees (2 percent of the total).

4. *Summer hours.* Work hours are only changed in the spring and fall . . . due to various operational restrictions within specific departments. This mode was utilized by 17 percent of the managers, affecting 59 employees (4 percent of the total).[20]

This catalytic intervention is centered on norms/standards within the given organizational system. It is catalytic because facts and data are made available to individuals who are then aided to sort out the options available to them and to choose the work schedule preferred.

After three years of flexitime experience, a questionnaire completed by 286 nonexempt employees yielded the results shown in Table 23.1.

The most important impact is found in better morale, with increases reported by 85 percent of those who experienced flexitime. This shows that morale/cohesion is strengthened by norms/standards that are better suited to the needs of individuals. Beyond this, 51 percent of managers concluded that productivity had increased and only 3 percent felt that flexitime was associated with a decrease in productivity. However, the injection of morale associated with flexitime can be expected to wear off as flexitime becomes accepted as routine. In this sense, it is a hygienic motivator.[21]

Office Work Practices

Office technology is rapidly changing by virtue of automated equipment, computerized typewriters, and so on. These mechanizations have greatly enlarged capacities for performing office functions by replacing outdated, outmoded equipment and historical uses of secretarial and clerical personnel.

Most organizations fail to attend to the socio-technical implications of new equipment. As a result the new equipment is placed into the old social system involving manager-secretary relations or manager-secretary (typist) couplings. A newer trend resolves the problem by concentrating this equipment in a word processing center, thereby decoupling manager and secretary (typist). This may elicit adverse reactions in organizations where people previously had closer interpersonal relations. A second adverse consequence of this new trend is that support previously given the manager by the secretary may now be reduced causing the manager to absorb additional functions that previously were performed at the secretarial level.

Important normative changes are involved in the effective utilization of office technology and consultant interventions may be helpful for bringing this about.[22]

Table 23.1 Summary of nonexempt employees' reactions to flexible work hours program (N = 286)

	Increased %	Unaffected %	Decreased %
• Driving time	24	19	57
• Pressures and frustrations of trying to get to work on scheduled time	13	14	73
• Need to leave work before quitting time	13	27	60
• Leisure time	59	22	19
• Morale	85	10	5
• Attitudes toward the company	65	18	17
• Productivity	66	23	11
• Need to supervise employees (control)	30	24	46
• Cooperation and coordination between departments	41	35	24
• Cooperation and coordination between shifts	49	38	13
• Abuses	21	13	66

The intervention reported here involved external consultants in interviewing and administering questionnaires to determine how work was characteristically carried out and to gain indications of readiness versus resistance to change. This was followed by the development of a steering committee and study teams who took the data as the basis for considering alternative ways of designing new systems that might achieve the benefits potentially available from effective socio-technical integration. The involvement and participation of those who are to implement the changeover is an essential condition for renovating the strategies of work as they relate on the one side to effective utilization of automated equipment and on the other to provision of support between manager and secretary.

In catalytic interventions of this sort the consultant limits participation to the gathering and feedback of data and to aiding teams and study groups in examining the implications of the data as they consider alternative forms of organization that might be more suitable to the situation. This is a norm-focused intervention because it is intended to shift the practices of work from what they have been to another basis more acceptable to those whose performance is impacted by the introduction of automated word processing equipment. It is best characterized as a team level intervention because it brings together people who work in the same situation for problem diagnosis and problem solving. In other words, the teams involved may be permanent, but they may also be temporary teams assembled for the purpose of collaboration and achieving an integrated solution. During implementation of the solution the team is dissolved and individuals rejoin the system to perform its functions in the newly designed manner.

Management Development

Managers occupy a key role in determining the degree of motivation and commitment employees exhibit. Increasing awareness of this fact has led many organizations to initiate or expand management training and development efforts. Some have approached these efforts haphazardly, adopting the latest management fad or fashion and viewing it as a cure-all for ills. Zeira[23] reports an unsuccessful attempt to design a systematic management development program based on current management theory and specific organizational applications. Instead of system-wide change, individual change was the result.

The chief executive established a new management training department whose head decided to organize an experimental training course according to the systems approach and deliver it to the top management team in one of the divisions. The objectives were jointly defined by the division head and the training department. The goal was to enable the division's top managers to overcome their specific managerial problems and adapt the division to its new environmental demands.

Management theories were presented by the trainers and jointly analyzed by the trainers and trainees. This knowledge was compared with existing patterns of managerial behavior in the division. As a second activity on the basis of analyses and comparisons, changes to be initiated were identified and implementation plans were designed.

The major achievement was to help the majority of the trainees perceive the need for planned change. The course succeeded in changing certain attitudes and increasing the satisfaction of affiliation and ego needs. However, the group did not develop a formal plan for organizational change. All changes implemented by certain trainees as a result of the course were both individual and voluntary in nature.

If planned, consistent, and systematic change is the desired end, top management must clearly state this expectation and then reward and reinforce positive performance. To do less is to court confusion, organizational disparity of treatment, and a host of concomitant problems. Management viewed the intervention as a success. The intervention staff did not share this enthusiasm. From their perspective, the intervention fell short of its mark. A firm organizational mandate for change was lacking. Managers acted on their own discretion for implementing the theories and principles presented.

Team Norms within the Larger Society

In correctional and other settings, such as high schools, Vorrath and Brendtro[24] offer an intervention termed "Positive Peer Culture." This is a carefully designed influencing sequence of passive, active, and "mood changing" steps along with other initiatives undertaken by an adult who continuously sits in with a group during its regularly scheduled meetings. Basically the Vorrath/Brendtro methodology involves having the adult leader monitor the informal interactions among teenagers during the beginnings of the group process. The leader exerts influence in a variety of ways ranging from overt confrontation to ostensibly passive withdrawal. His or her "behavior kaleidoscope" is chosen according to momentary readings of process events during the four successive stages of guided group process delineated by Vorrath/Brendtro:[25] "Casing," "Limit Testing," "Polarization of Values," and "A Positive Peer Culture." The last-mentioned stage constitutes effective functioning.

In effect, the adult leader-interventionist acts as a leavening agent that, when added to the teenage group's own process, serves to convert that process to the production and enforcement of what the larger adult society views as positive norms of behavior. For this reason, the long-term, overall intervention can be described validly as catalytic, even though various other interventions may be used on a moment-by-moment basis.

Family Norms of Parent/Youngster Interaction

An intervention concerned with norms/standards is reported by Gordon. Designed to help parents and youngsters resolve impasse situations, the process is termed the divided-sheet method of "no-lose" problem solving. In the following description, parents learn the methodology and implement it with their children; in similar circumstances and with some rephrasing, Gordon-trained children might initiate the approach with their parents. Success is possible only when both parents and children "buy" the procedure.

> . . . We designed a surprisingly simple method for overcoming the resistance and distrust that kids bring to a problem-solving session. All parents need is a pen and a sheet of paper divided into two columns by a line drawn down the middle. The parent can start the session by saying something like:
>
> "I've brought a sheet of paper divided down the middle. We'll list our problems and conflicts on this sheet as they are brought up by any of us. In the left column I'll write those conflicts we've had about behavior of you kids that really does not tangibly or concretely affect us, even though it might have bothered us. One I can think of immediately is your homework. In the right column I'll write down those conflicts we've had about behavior of you kids that really does affect us, things you do that interfere directly with our lives. An example would be your not carrying out the trash.
>
> "When we've completed our list, then we'll promise not to hassle or nag you about any of the problems in the left column. We'll simply throw those problems away—no more bugging you. Take the homework, for example. We agree never to mention it—it will be up to you when you do it, or whether you do it. You are capable of taking care of this yourself.
>
> "But all the problems in the right column will have to be worked out some way so that we come up with a solution for each that is acceptable to all of us—no one loses. Any questions about how we're going to operate here? [After answering questions] Okay, let's start listing the problems—anyone can bring up a problem. Then we'll take each one that's brought up and decide whether it goes in the right column or the left."[26]

Table 23.2

Problems agreed to be child's responsibility (no mutual problem solving)	Problems that must be problem solved
1. His school work—how much he studies, when he studies, where he studies.	1. How much he contributes to the work required around the house.
2. How he wears his hair.	2. The problem of allowance and what parents buy and child buys.
3. When he goes to sleep.	
4. What he eats.	3. The problem of parents not being told when child will or will not be home for dinner.
5. What clothes he wears to school.	
6. His choice of friends.	4. The problem of the use of the family car.
7. How often he takes a bath.	
8. How he decorates his room.	5. The problem of the child not cleaning up his mess in the family room.
9. Where he goes when he goes out.	
10. How he spends his allowance.	

By adopting this newly suggested norm, parents can convert power/authority impasses into a joint search for agreement. Table 23.2 shows the sheet of problems one family came up with. In this family, as in most, there were far more problems in the left column than in the right. Gordon[27] recommends this intervention for use "in families where parents have been authoritarian, that is, have been hassling and nagging their kids a lot about behavior that does not tangibly and concretely affect them, the parents." He does not indicate at what age levels this approach is most suitable, or what happens to the left side when solutions to problems on the right-hand side cannot be found. Neither does he deal in detail with how parents help their children solve problems that do not affect the parent but which, if ignored, may adversely affect the child's very basic growth needs. Presumably the expression of felt needs followed by problem-solving discussions are expected to resolve these issues.

Therapeutic Norms for Interaction

One of the factors in psychotherapy presumed to be a deterrent to progress is related to the client's defensiveness. Until negative emotions are brought to the surface, analyzed, discussed, and dealt with, the likelihood of progress is reduced. Defensiveness means maintenance of social protocol, particularly with regard to denying negative emotions. Defensiveness, therefore, is self-defeating to development and change. One technique thought to have value in enabling clients to more fully reveal their negative emotions is related to marathon groups in comparison with traditional group therapy.[28]

A marathon group meets for a much longer time period, say 24 to 36 hours, with only very brief interruptions. A typical group therapy session often meets for two hours or less.

The participants in one marathon were hospitalized patients in an institution dealing with mental health problems. This intervention involved one group that met for six hours for each of three days in comparison with the control group which received the same 18 hours of treatment over a three-week period in three two-hour sessions per week.

Through this arrangement of meeting times and durations, it is possible to evaluate the question, "Are defenses against expressing negative emotions reduced by more extended or concentrated therapy sessions in comparison with traditionally timed sessions, or is there no difference?"

The intervention is probably catalytic, but, based on the report, it is difficult to specify accurately. The objective was to reduce the frequency level in terms of which protocol, i.e., social norms and standards, restricts the expression of negative emotions.

Under each condition the impact was measured through an adjective check-list which gave individuals an opportunity to check emotional words revealing self-feelings that were both positive and negative. Results show that the marathon group elicited significantly more expression of negative feelings than was characteristic of the control group.

Another measure of outcome was the impact of different schedules of meetings on group cohesion; cohesion being defined as the number of members who continued to attend group sessions. Cohesion was more prevalent in the extended meeting groups than in the traditional groups.

INTERGROUP (D-3-3)

Norm clarification is an approach used in tense intergroup situations that result because (1) neither group is able to recognize the norms and standards that characterize the other's approach, or (2) the norms/standards in operation are recognized but not accepted as legitimate. The solution is to identify existing norms/standards and help the interacting groups to institute norms of collaboration and cooperation.

Pure versus Applied Research Department

Lorsch and Lawrence[29] premise their interventions on a rationale that is explained to managers of both groups prior to intergroup problem analysis. The following are its main points.

1. Any complex social system, such as a company, is composed of differentiated parts.
2. These differentiated parts must be integrated into a unified effort to accomplish corporate purpose.
3. Any part, because of the tasks it performs, develops at least four distinctive attributes: (a) time orientation, (b) interpersonal orientation, (c) internal formal structure, and (d) goal orientation.

The more unlike one another any two interdependent groups are in terms of the four attributes, the greater the likelihood of difficulties in achieving an effective integration between them. Through questionnaires and interviews, consultants seek to understand how the two interdependent groups differ in regard to each of the four attributes. Top managers of both groups are then convened as intact units to receive feedback of interview-based data. Managers have the opportunity to test feedback from the other group for congruence with their own understanding of intergroup difficulties of integration. Problem solving to reduce or eliminate the barriers to integration (by shifting the intergroup norms in one or more of the four attributes) is the final step.

One intervention example involved integrating two research subunits within the same organization. One subunit was supposed to be engaged in fundamental, long-range research; the other was to be involved with applied research of shorter range significance. The consultants collected data by interviews and questionnaires and concluded that extremely poor integration was characteristic of the intergroup relationship. Also, while their internal characteristics were highly differentiated in structure and interpersonal attitudes, both laboratories were trying to perform the same kinds of tasks and had similar time orientations. A further finding was that members of one laboratory saw the members of the other laboratory as competitors.

The consultants convened meetings of top managers, and this information was fed back as the basis for presenting the following conclusions.

> We explained that the high differentiation in interpersonal and structural attributes was related to the problems of achieving integration, but that the fact the units were occupying the same task and time space seemed to be intensifying the difficulties in achieving collaboration. In this discussion the managers recognized that two things were needed; first, a clearer differentiation of the role of the laboratories and second the development of improved integrative devices.[30]

The consultants comment that this information supported the laboratory managers' intuitive hunches and clarified underlying norms and standards. Discussion followed, moving in the direction of redefining operating norms and standards for each laboratory as a first step toward better integration between the two.

Staff versus Line

A variation on this theme is referred to as the *organization mirror*. This technique answers the question posed by a group inside an organization. How do outsiders see us? The problem is to get information from the outsiders transferred to the inside group so that insiders can see themselves more objectively and take needed corrective actions. An example of this kind of one-sided intergroup intervention is reported by Fordyce and Weil. A seven-person staff organization had been working to improve its effectiveness for about a year, yet still experienced either friction or indifference from the various line groups it was supposed to aid.[31] Something in these relationships was out of balance, and the consultants hoped a catalytic intervention would help the group see its own performance in a "mirror" provided by others in the organization who were actual or potential users of its services. The mirror is composed of data: feelings, attitudes, and reactions the "consumer" groups held toward this staff group. The consultant began by interviewing to learn something about the problem as these outside individuals, singly or in groups, saw it.

The following steps suggest how a consultant intervenes to enhance the flow of data from outsiders. In the above example, he first reviewed interview findings. Then the outsiders, an aggregate rather than intact group, composed of two prospective "consumers" from each of the line organizations invited by the central staff group, met among themselves. They discussed and interpreted the interview data while the seven-person staff group listened as the audience.[32]

This cycle completed, the staff group met to discuss what its members had heard outsiders say and to identify issues requiring further clarification. After a general session that focused on reviewing progress and specifying next steps, task groups were created. These were made up of members from the staff group and from among the outsiders. Working on the same tasks but independently of one another, each identified the most important changes needed to improve the effectiveness of the staff group. Findings were reported in a general session, and a single priority list of items to be addressed was then created. Agreed-upon priorities served as the basis for each task force reconvening to develop plans and/or specific action steps for change with regard to each item. The remainder of the period was for summary purposes. Conclusions and assignments for further work after the meeting's close were also discussed. The following schedule outlines an organization "mirror" meeting.

Meeting Schedule

8:30– 9:00	Introduction by staff director.
9:00– 9:30	Review of interview data by third party.
9:30–10:15	Outsiders discuss among themselves to try to interpret the data while insiders listen to them and take notes on what they heard to use in the next step.
10:15–11:00	Insiders discuss what they heard outsiders say and identify issues needing clarification while the outsiders observe the discussion.
11:00–12:00	General discussion to summarize what has happened thus far (group rule: don't start working on problems).
12:00– 1:00	Break for lunch.
1:00– 1:30	Four task subgroups, each comprising both outsiders and insiders, identify the five most important changes needed to improve the effectiveness of the organization.

1:30– 2:00	Reports from subgroups.
2:00– 2:30	Total group synthesizes lists.
2:30– 4:30	The four task subgroups develop a plan and specific action items for change.
4:30– 5:00	Meeting summary—each task group reports plans, action items, person responsible, and reporting dates.
5:00– 5:30	Staff director concludes meeting by reviewing day's work and assigning remaining action items.[33]

The intervention is implemented through a consultant-as-interlocutor. The interventions are facilitative in that they provide a procedural framework involving a sequence of steps, while interview-based interventions produce information that can be helpful to the group in viewing itself more objectively.

All this is predicated on the assumption that because it has been "asked for," the information will be received openly and nondefensively. Under the "rational man" assumptions of this catalytic approach, there is no mechanism for confronting the staff group's underlying motivations or for working through the fundamental internal or intergroup antagonisms that often are present but unrecognized, or that surface during such periods of self-discovery.

The situation is prone to conflict when an organization is built on subsystems, with each performing a unique task but with each task indispensable to overall performance. The situation is prone to conflict, and the management and resolution of conflict under such conditions constitutes a major managerial task.

Technical and Professional Staff

Organizational distinctions between technical and professional staff often generate interpersonal conflict based on perceived discrepancies in status, power, flexibility, etc. Typically, professional staff are better educated, better compensated, and higher in the organizational hierarchy than are their technically oriented counterparts. An organization's technicians may resent working "just as hard or harder" than professional staff while reaping fewer organizational rewards. Where such tensions exist, attaining organizational objectives may be jeopardized unless the conflict between these groups is resolved so that effective communication and necessary coordination occur.

A government research and development organization experienced conflict between a group of science and engineering professionals involved in experimental design work and technicians who were members of a test support division. In the role of an internal consultant, Stumpf[34] assisted through identifying five areas of conflict between the two groups. Thereafter, an employee attitude survey with anonymous responses was summarized by organization and by division levels and reported. The survey confirmed the consultant's initial identification of conflict areas between the professionals and technicians.

Faced with evidence of the need for better coordination, management explored different approaches for bringing this about, but neither the professional nor technical managers supported their suggestions as workable alternatives. Open meetings were held to solicit ideas and identify the problem more clearly. An engineer suggested using nonsupervisory professionals as integrators—the role to be primarily that of coordinator. Activities of professionals and technicians were to be funneled through this central point to ensure communication, necessary planning, and to maximize use of available resources. The decision to use the integrator concept was determined by management, not by the consultant.

Predetermined performance measures permitted an evaluation of the success of the intervention by comparing the cooperation of control groups where an integrator had not been used to that of experimental groups where an integrator had been installed. A two-year comparison of the total number of published and internal reports and the total number of approved and funded projects was scored as productivity criteria. The experimental groups demonstrated significantly better results.

The catalytic character of this intervention can be seen in the consultant's reliance on data gathering and feedback techniques to assist in defining the problem. No attempt was made to influence the reduction of conflict directly. Instead, supportive documentation highlighted the presence of organization conflict and the need for an intervention. The solution relied on a nonsupervisor being assigned responsibility for strengthening needed cooperation.

The intervention deals with intergroup conflict—approaching a solution by providing individuals whose job descriptions as integrators put them into the communication network. Integrators can contribute to the coordination that the prevailing line management system has been unsuccessful in providing. The focal issue is norms/standards of cooperation, but the solution eventually reached left the formal system intact and "solved" the problem by asking a person without formal power/authority to induce the needed cooperation.

Upper versus Lower Levels of Management

Another use of organization mirrors providing an example of an intervention that was inappropriate relative to the problem to be solved is provided by Culbert and McDonough.[35] It used a version of the mirror in an intergroup setting. All groups within a department staffed by 100 engineers identified the groups with which they dealt. They indicated what "they" did or didn't do that hindered or helped the execution of work. In a mass feedback session, all supervisors met with other groups with whom they collaborated to report the specific actions needed from the other to increase cooperation. All supervisors had an opportunity to clarify what they were being told. The four key leaders of the department received the same input. One key restructuring action at the department level took place and little more. Even this change was derided.

What went wrong?

A number of limitations in such an intervention might be emphasized. One is that it was a catalytic "data sharing" intervention without any reported theory-based intervention to prepare the group for openness, confrontation, and conflict resolution. The intervention resulted in each group telling "them" what "they" should do. Furthermore, the development of concrete superordinate intergroup goals that would progress toward mutually shared benefits was disregarded. Without such a step participants "unloaded" in unconstructive terms. Little change can be expected under such conditions.

This is an example of an inappropriate intervention. Relying on a catalytic approach to generate and communicate information based on logic disregarded the presence of antagonisms and hostilities. The mass feedback session was an opportunity for each supervisor to unload frustrations, but in such a way as to antagonize. The situation called for an intergroup confrontation design, and exploded when provided with a catalytic sharing design.

Union and Management

Truskie reports a union-management intergroup intervention designed to generate increased mutual understanding. During ongoing negotiations, union and corporation representatives had become cognizant of the need to improve relations between their respective groups and had negotiated an agreement to arrange a joint human relations program. This agreement became part of the overall three-year contract.

In the resulting human relations program, which used a university extension instructor as moderator,

> a total of 125 foremen, general foreman, union stewards, negotiators, and grievance committeemen participated in the program which began February 27, 1972 and lasted for eighteen consecutive weeks. The eighteen sessions were divided so that six were devoted to communications, six to human relations, and six to grievance handling. Membership in each subgroup consisted of 18–23 participants. The union-management ratio of the total group—41% union and 59% management. The groups met on company time and on company premises.
>
> Mr. Kirby was the moderator for each group throughout the entire program. His role was one of advising, motivating, and guiding. He provided the participants with the knowledge base, training aids, and discussion leadership. The participants were encouraged to interact freely on a give-and-take basis. Random observations of the groups indicated minimal group interaction during the first few sessions, but as the program progressed, interaction within the groups increased significantly.
>
> An interesting aspect of the program was the formation of a steering committee which met biweekly during the eighteen weeks to evaluate the progress and over-all direction of the program. In some cases, slight program modifications were made upon suggestions of the steering committee. The committee consisted of the moderator, the University representative

(the writer), two management representatives, and two union representatives.[36]

At the program's final session, all participants were asked to complete evaluation questionnaires. Truskie reports that responses to survey questions were highly favorable regarding the program's value and essentiality in improving management-union and company-union relations, in gaining better outlooks on intergroup problems, and in promoting proper conduct between representatives. In modified form it was continued the following year. Acknowledging that these evaluation methods cannot be taken as firm evidence that union-management relations were improving, Truskie concludes:

> The important point of this case study lies in the realization that union and management personnel can join in an extensive learning encounter to discuss substantive, job-related issues and problems—to the mutual benefit of both groups. Union-management relations in the future will improve only to the extent that both are willing to learn and appreciate each other's role. The above approach appears to be a logical step in that direction.[37]

Summary

When the focal issue between groups is norms/standards, catalytic procedures can more precisely pinpoint where differences lie than when power/authority, for example, is the focal issue. This could be because the particular units studied had more or less equal power and therefore were less threatening and more open, both to each other and to the consultants.

ORGANIZATION (D-3-4)

Flexitime working hours are an organization practice at the normative level. The time-honored notion that all employees work in an eight-hour fixed sequence, day-in and day-out, year after year, without regard for personal needs or preferences is an historical example of corporate domination of the individual. This has begun to change, with the shift referred to as flexitive. Flexitive means the individual elects when to arrive and when to leave, within a framework of core time when everyone is present. This break away from fixed routine is only possible in some kinds of work, but the issues are, "how is it brought into use?" and "when applied what are the results?"

Golembiewski, et al. describe a catalytic intervention that provides employees some flexibility in the traditionally rigid area of work hours. The particular brand of flexitime implemented by Sun Oil evolved from the consultants' discussions with officials representing the Personnel and R&D functions. Other supervisors and managers provided input through opportunities for participation and involvement.

Golembiewski describes flexible work hours as a simple concept, with somewhat complex application to specific work sites. Complexities arise when such
variables as hourly vs. salaried payment, departmental work requirements, supervisory preferences, etc., are taken into consideration.

In describing this particular intervention, the following information is
provided: "an individual may start work at any time . . . an employee may
work 5 hours in any one day, the core day of 9:15 A.M. to 3 P.M."[38]

Reports of the results of this "pilot" intervention reflect positive employee
perceptions of the approach. The consultants indicate "The first 6 months of
Flexi-Time contributed significantly to improvements in many features describing
the quality of the work environment." Managerial reactions are summarized in
this way: "As employees, supervisors are definitely positive about Flexi-Time;
as managers, however, supervisors seem to be responding to a range of interests
and concerns that are answered only in part by Flexi-Time."[39]

Hiring and Promotion Practices

Another example of organization norms includes practices surrounding the
hiring and promotional system of a company. While career planning and employee development have been used extensively in business and industry, their
application to the public sector has been more recent. With pressure from equal
employment opportunity and affirmative action requirements, public agencies
have begun to evaluate new ways of recruiting, hiring, and retaining qualified
women and minorities, particularly at managerial levels. This approach to equal
opportunity development is by Jackson,[40] who served as internal consultant to
implement a comprehensive upward mobility program. The state's Workers
Compensation Department piloted the approach under the direction of the
Executive Department Personnel Division, Staff Development and Training Unit.

This pilot program consisted of five phases. In Phase I, the agency's upward
mobility policy was evaluated through a comprehensive process of data collection
and analysis. The agency also was asked to anticipate its manpower needs over
the next two years. The Education Committee, which reviewed training requests
and developed agency training policy, served as a link between the agency and
the personnel division training unit. It became a vital component in implementing
the upward mobility project.

In Phase II statistical data were gathered on all employees, and the employee's career interests and goals were determined through a comprehensive
questionnaire to help interested upward mobility candidates begin thinking about
their career goals, aspirations, interests, and skills.

During Phase III, briefings and progress reports were presented to managers
at all levels. Interested supervisors also provided follow-up activities for their
employees. The interventions during this period were primarily catalytic and
consisted of data collection, summary and feedback regarding the actual
methods, and progress relative to upward mobility. Training sessions for individual self-assessment and goal setting also followed this same pattern and
provided strengthening experiences for individuals.

In Phase IV an external consultant examined the personnel system and made recommendations for changes essential for implementing an effective upward mobility program. This intervention was prescriptive relative to needed systems changes.

During Phase V, participants evaluated each phase of the project, and a final evaluation form was distributed to all candidates. Over 75 percent of the respondents felt that the project had met or exceeded their expectations. The Workers Compensation Department concluded that upward mobility would be an ongoing program.

A systematic intervention utilizing survey research was employed through a sample of both black and white and male and female management to shift hiring and promotion practices.[41] The four authors were joined by a twelve-person advisory team composed of six blacks and six whites, counterbalanced as six males and six female members, presumably to demonstrate that those responsible for the effort were themselves not acting out of bias.

The survey research instrument dealt with how members of various subgroups experienced the character of race relations in the company and developed a picture of discrimination as it prevailed in the company. They also indicated how they saw hiring practices being applied, issues of advancement as related to race, as well as issues of firing, etc. Actions for change were evaluated, and reactions to the study itself were assessed. As the basis for the evaluation of next steps, these data were treated statistically and fed back to senior management.

The only significant resistance encountered in the process came from legal department personnel who felt that the findings of the survey could provide a basis for future legal action in terms of EEO considerations. Management committed itself to data feedback taking place throughout the organization and to their own readiness to implement the requisite next steps called for by the findings of the survey.

This study demonstrates the use of a diagnostic instrument for evaluative purposes. The description of this intervention stops at the level where top management commits itself to taking additional steps. It does not describe the specific interventions that followed or impacts derived from their application.

This is an organizational-level intervention that clarifies discrepancies between legal requirements for treatment and other standards of equitable treatments in comparison with what actually is occurring. The information produced seems to have been sufficient to result in the needed changes.

Organization Culture

Employees are continually searching for ways to meet higher order needs (e.g. achievement, self-actualization, etc.) through their jobs. Organizations, whether public or private, can maximize employee potential by providing an organizational climate that is receptive to and supportive of productive, motivated, committed employees regardless of equal employment legislation or affirmative action requirements.

Mann provides a clinical example of the survey-research interaction in which eight thousand employees engaged in a company-wide data-gathering effort to determine attitudes and opinions. Three sets of data were produced.

(1) Information on the attitudes and perceptions of 8,000 nonsupervisory employees toward their work, promotion opportunities, supervision, fellow employees, etc.; (2) first- and second-line supervisors' feelings about the various aspects of their jobs and supervisory beliefs; and (3) information from intermediate and top levels of management about their supervisory philosophies, roles in policy formation, problems of organizational integration, etc.[42]

These attitudes and perceptions covered several significant issues but appeared to concentrate on norms and standards. A chain of interlocking conferences, beginning with a report of major findings to the president and senior officers and then repeated down through organization "families," permitted each boss and his or her subordinates to participate in examining the data. Data made available to particular groups came either from their own group or from subordinate groups for which they were responsible. Each group interpreted the data and then decided what further analyses were needed for administrative action. Finally, they planned how feedback of data to the next lower level should be carried out.

Consultants took part in helping line officers prepare for these meetings according to the following:

Usually a member of the Survey Research Center and the company's personnel staff assisted the line officer in preparing for these meetings, but attended the meetings only as resource people who could be called upon for information about the feasibility of additional analyses . . . .

Mann's evaluation of this survey led him to conclude that:

Our observations of the feedback procedure as it developed suggested that it was a powerful process for creating and supporting changes within an organization. However, there was no quantitative proof of this, for our work up to this point has been exploratory and developmental.[43]

Another effort at changing organization-wide norms as a means of increasing effectiveness is described by Allen and Pilnick.[44] Realizing that norms/standards constitute one manifestation of organization culture, their approach seeks to change norms/standards either by discussing and comparing current norms with ideal norms, thereby pointing up an ideal/real gap and generating a desire to close it, or by participants' completing a norms profile that permits a similar discovery of norm discrepancies.

The norms profile is a sixty-item questionnaire organized into ten areas, such as (1) organization pride, (2) performance excellence, (3) teamwork, and so on. Each respondent indicates not what his or her own personal norms are, but rather, his or her "estimation of what most other employees would do when confronted with that behavior by another employee." The instrument can then be scored in two ways. One is how participants perceive the actual culture of their organization or division, department, etc. Each participant can compare his or her attributed perceptions with statistical averages of attributed perceptions. The alternative, made possible by the fact that each scale has a good and bad end, is to compare perception of the actual with what would be ideal: the wider the gap, the greater the need for improvement.

The authors provide an example of how this norms/standards approach is used to bring change about—pilferage among employees and customers was involved. The actual norm was perceived to be: ". . . pilferage is not my problem. It is the responsibility of security alone." A positive answer does not mean the respondent holds this attitude; rather, it is his or her perception of attitudes held by others. Allen and Pilnick do not report how it was achieved, but a shift toward greater responsibility for reducing pilferage was brought about. Presumably discussions led to widespread support of a new norm of shared and individual responsibility for reducing pilferage. However, it is reported that observed pilferage was now confronted, whereas previously it had not been, and that individual and group success in reducing theft levels was positively rewarded.

The authors suggest that ten conditions, actually ten norms, must be embraced throughout an organization for this approach to achieve significant impact. These include top-management commitment to the norms-change program; top management's modeling the behavior it desires to see others embrace by adhering to these norms themselves; feedback to indicate whether norms are changing or not; reward of norm-consistent behavior; etc.

Sears, Roebuck & Company initially implemented an anonymous survey among its managerial staff in 1971. It was repeated in 1974. Smith, an internal consultant, and Porter, an external consultant, describe both phases of the intervention and highlight some of the organizational changes that resulted.[45]

The executive survey focused on known problems, and it also attempted to assess reactions to several actual and planned organizational changes that were to affect management people at all levels.

A core group of attitude scales that had been used to measure job satisfaction at the hourly employee level for more than ten years was included in the questionnaire, which also contained wide-ranging questions tapping perceptions of what we might call the organizational climate.

The questionnaire took three hours to complete, and post-survey interviews indicated that because the questionnaires explored critical concepts and issues, they proved to be thought-provoking and challenging. Over 95 percent of the questionnaires were returned in both the 1971 and 1974 surveys. Extensive feedback to the Board, and subsequently to each management level, took place.

All functional officers used the survey data as a point of departure. They carried out discussions of their functions with their department managers. Department managers conducted individual feedback sessions with the particular department or function. The process provided many managers with insight into their own leadership roles and their impact on organizational growth and effectiveness.

By focusing on the executive level staff, managers evidenced an understanding of the importance of managerial attitudes, leadership styles, and behavior. By virtue of their role, managers are powerful models. Mangers have significant influence over the degree of motivation and commitment their employees demonstrate in meeting organizational goals and objectives. Employees are likely to emulate their boss in an effort to gain his or her favor and to enhance their own status in the organization. The broader a manager's sphere of influence, the more important it is that he or she exhibit organizationally constructive patterns of behavior.

This catalytic intervention dealt with norms and standards as perceived by individuals as members of groups. It served to facilitate communication and to strengthen relationships on a boss-subordinate basis, such as those involved in performance review, as well as to impact policies of relocation practices, executive compensation, etc.

An intervention with a plant as a whole that involved a multiplicity of development interventions is reported by Beer and Huse.[46] This intervention rejected many of the emerging notions as to what constitutes effective OD at the time when it was undertaken. It is particularly worthwhile as a special study project because Beer recounts the almost complete failure of the intervention as evaluated a number of years after it had been completed.

The interventions in the plant were based on the following:

1. Eclectic OD is preferable to systematic OD. Systematic OD refers to the use of a coherent set of principles and strategies employed in a step-wise way to produce cumulative impact. Eclectic OD involves a number of essentially independent interventions that have no inherent connection with one another, although sequencing and input in the whole may be a consideration.

2. It is preferable to concentrate attention at the entry point on the problems at hand rather than to involve managers in learning theories or in acquiring social skills. The notion is that if the consultant helps the manager grapple successfully with some vexing problem, and success is realized in its resolution, this is far more motivating than taking a manager away from the work situation in order to learn theories and the conditions for their effective application as a prior step. Education on theories and principles came as a later step.

3. Organization development initiated by personnel staff and guided by external and internal consultants can be as effective as line manager leadership. Behind this generalization is the idea that it really does not matter too much where or how organization development starts nor the manner in which it is guided over time. What does matter is that it starts and that it does benefit from guidance.

4. Starting with a felt need in a unit that has sufficient autonomy to grapple with the felt need is a logical point of introduction.

These propositions reject points of view that were emerging when this intervention was undertaken from 1966 to 1968.

The intervention was multi-faceted, but an important underlying assumption guiding each phase was the exercise of catalytic influences on the organization. Included among the various aspects of the intervention were counseling on the job, job enrichment, communication meetings, survey feedback, seminars for cognitive inputs, and face-to-face analysis of differences.

Assessment of short-term results led Beer and Huse to conclude that considerable improvements resulted from their interventions. Communication was more open, workers felt well informed, jobs were experienced as interesting and challenging, and goals were being set and achieved on a mutual basis.

Beer reexamined the impact of this intervention a decade after it had been completed. The negative conclusions as to its impact are significantly different than were the short-term positive assessments. Included are:

1. Significant regression is evident in communication mechanisms of the kind that were installed during the intervention itself. Communication meetings had either been greatly reduced or discontinued entirely, and production employees who at the end of the intervention felt well informed saw themselves as receiving the least attention in the post-ten-year period.

2. Motivation has shifted from the kind of intrinsic reward associated with completing meaningful and challenging tasks to extrinsic rewards for compliance based on money.

3. There has been a rotation of several plant managers in relatively rapid succession, further causing discontinuity in the emerging culture of the plant and indicating that headquarters management saw no reason to select plant managers who might be expected to further the OD effort.

4. A deficiency was working with the plant in isolation without corporate-level commitment or support. A decade later it is realized that OD within one unit is unlikely to be successful in the long run unless the approach is also applied to the organization above it.

5. The single conclusion as to positive impact is with regard to job enrichment. When jobs were shifted to make them more complex and challenging, and when this became the standard way of work, this has persisted over time. In other words, there has been no discernible shift or regression toward simplifying jobs, making them less meaningful, etc.

   The following might be added to these conclusions drawn by persons responsible for the interventions themselves.

6. The project was started and led by the personnel function, and this may account for the lack of involvement and continuity of the plant manager and other managerial levels.

7. The first plant manager was only mildly interested in the idea. Rather than giving it wholehearted support, he simply allowed it to happen.

The importance of these two divergent descriptions, i.e. of the original interventions and a decade later of the longer term measurement of their impact tells us to be wary of short-term evaluation. The interventions themselves could be described as unsuccessful. The challenge is to explain why.

There are two possibilities. One is that the catalytic methodology of intervention is not sufficiently strong to cause permanent change. The other, and more probably the correct, explanation is in the violation of the tenets for successful OD interventions, i.e., the need for corporate support and committed top-level leadership within the plant, line responsibility, and a theory base to produce enduring and cumulative impact was more or less disregarded. Add to this the eclectic quality of the approach and the effort simply did not add up to something that had coherence and sufficient character to justify its continuance.

Collateral Organization

An intervention by Alderfer designed to strengthen the flow of information throughout the system is based on the premise that organizational changes can result from targeting a small but representative communications group as the focal point for change in the division. Twelve managerial and nonmanagerial employees were selected as representatives of 250 employees within one division of a corporation. Established as a microcosm of the larger population, improvements in communications and relationships among members of this group were expected to diffuse and to result in similar changes between other divisional subgroups. This is another example that typifies the basic notion of using a collateral system to implement activities that the line organization is not carrying out in a satisfactory manner.

Alderfer describes his role as the external consultant and details the developmental processes and procedures by which the microcosm group was formed and taught to function. He and an internal consultant comprised the consulting team.

The intervention began when the division manager and his immediate subordinates established procedures for selecting diagonal slice members of the communication group. After membership had been determined, interviews were completed with all the members plus the division manager. Rapport was established, resulting in high mutuality between members of the consulting team and people in the division. Members of the communications group nominated six other divisional members whose views were considered crucial to understanding communication problems.

> The initial interviews provided the consulting team with the information and relationships to help continue the process of psychologically establishing the group for its members and for the division as a whole. An entire workday was set for the next step in this process: establishing a formal charter for the group.[47]

During this meeting, the consultants facilitated a group process in which management and nonmanagement identified their hopes for the communication group and their fears concerning it. Considerable similarity between these two factions formed the basis for group consensus and more clearly defined the group's role.

Once the charter was in place and group officers elected, this information was communicated throughout the division. Nonmembers were invited to share in communication group activities by suggesting issues to be resolved or by attending group meetings. An attitude survey administered to all members of the division reflected that "judgments about the group were quite positive."

In the short run, this intervention apparently had some positive effects, most especially on those directly involved in the communication group itself. Obviously, many group members' higher level needs were being met by the status and acceptability afforded them as "representatives" of the larger organization. Viewed from a different perspective, however, it is possible that this collateral system had the effect of weakening the line manager's feelings of responsibility for strengthening the system of communication.[48]

Changing Supervisory Roles

Luke, et al.[49] describe an intervention in a grocery chain in which the norms and standards reflected in organization structure were shifted. Through the use of consultant-trainers, close supervision and tight control were shifted toward store leadership intended to aid store operators to be more effective on a collaborative basis. The shift-over was accomplished based on redesigning the organization structure in such a way as to accommodate the consultant-trainer role within the role definition of an architect—one who makes him- or herself familiar with the client's problems and needs and works with the client to meet the need, but leaves the final acceptance decision to the client. Luke does make reference to the extent to which power and authority were disregarded in the initial undertaking. By inference, we can conclude that deficiencies of impact resulted from this. It is interesting to note that those responsible for the intervention were apparently unaware of the extent to which they exercised power and authority in the process of implementing the consultant-trainer role. This suggests that the intervention may also have been prescriptive in character.

LARGER SOCIAL SYSTEM (D-3-5)

Community action to solve social and other problems often cannot be taken because no basis exists for identifying the problems, determining their real depth, or assessing the amount of concern they generate. Action is blocked in the absence of shared norms or standards for perceiving the issues that need attention.

Closing a Plant

Large-scale crises (a hurricane, tornado, flood, large fire, etc.) may disrupt the functioning of entire communities. Though not so dramatic, a plant closing where hundreds of persons simultaneously join the ranks of the unemployed also constitutes a crisis. These dramatic events require that a wide range of community resources be brought to bear to alleviate suffering and restore community functioning. A coordinated approach to human service delivery is needed.

In the absence of a coordinated approach, people who need help are confronted with a maze of human service agencies delivering specialized services without benefit of communication or the needed coordination. Needs of people are addressed in fragmented, piecemeal fashion with each agency responding only to a small part of the client's total problem or situation. Referrals to other appropriate services may or may not be made, depending on the worker's knowledge of other services and perceptions of their availability.

Such a crisis in one Michigan community prompted an intervention designed to increase human service agency communication and coordination in providing services to a specific target population. Taber, et al. discuss a plant closing that resulted in the discharge of 850 hourly and salaried employees previously involved in producing automotive components and trim for new cars.

Plant representatives contacted the Institute for Social Research (ISR) to obtain help in providing their former employees with the resources and coping skills needed to deal with impending job losses.

> ISR recommended that . . . former employees could best be assisted by establishing, in cooperation with the United Auto Workers and relevant social service agencies, a "community action team" for dealing with unemployment. The program which eventually was implemented consisted of two major components to increase cooperation among community agencies and to ensure that the services were fully used.
>
> First, an organization was developed to coordinate those community agencies which could offer services or resources to the unemployed. Second, an in-plant counseling program was established to help the workers define their problems and contact the appropriate helping agencies.
>
> As change agents, we assisted through a rational change style, in implementing the community action strategy and the in-plant counseling program and served as consultants to the Community Services Council by providing advice, information, and training to all leaders of the Council.[50]

Three phases were identified in the report of the Community Action Team's development. Efforts in the initial phase were to secure community acceptance and support of the project concept. In the second phase, the focus was on establishing the Community Services Council, a group of organizations (e.g. CETA, United Way, Michigan Employment Security Commission, etc.) committed to assisting the plant's unemployed in a coordinated and interdependent way.

> During this phase of development, the [consultants'] action steps consisted of four primary activities: First, we provided the channel of communication by serving as official minutes keepers of all meetings. Second, we made process interventions during the meetings. Third, we used our research skills to gather and systematically feed back accurate information about the type and extent of problems being faced by the unemployed. We then provided direct consultation (to each of the five committees) in problem-solving

techniques. Fourth, we consulted with the leaders of the Council concerning organizational structure issues.[51]

In phase three, the Community Services Council began to explore a broader goal of developing coordinated programs for the entire community with community leadership and support.

> It became clear that a structural intervention was necessary to bring the structure and functioning of the Council into line with its newly evolving goals. ISR proposed, therefore, that a temporary planning group be formed. Our predominant consulting role during this period was oriented at showing the Planning Committee the locus of its current structural problems, and making suggestions for new alternative structures.[52]

The account does not indicate whether or not the Community Services Council remained a viable organization or if its broad goals were achieved. However, a foundation for cooperation and communication among several autonomous agencies had been created when the intervention was terminated. Ideally, the community built on that foundation, demonstrated the effectiveness of a cooperative effort, and communicated their experiences and results to other communities. A network of cohesive human service agencies involved in a holistic approach to individual and family needs might eventually result from development of similar programs in other communities.

This is a larger social system intervention because the problem to be solved is at the community level. The focal issue is in developing norms and standards for coordination of community services. It is catalytic because the consultants provided a rallying mechanism; data and process interventions were calculated to help the coordinating group become more viable. To whatever degree advice was offered, it apparently was tendered in a tentative rather than prescriptive fashion.

Democratization of Industry

Movements toward democratizing industry spread throughout Europe in the aftermath of World War II. They took many forms: joint consultation; labor representation on corporate boards; and other forms of employee participation including the redesign of work, autonomous group efforts, and so on. This intervention, which took place in Norway, is an illustration of the redesign of work.

In the early 1960s, Norway instituted the Industrial Democracy Project. This joint venture of government, employers, and unions was intended to stimulate employee participation in the workplace with more democratic, less hierarchical and less authoritarian organizational forms. Internally initiated change, planned and undertaken by the employees who are directly impacted, is the foundation of the democratic process and was emerging in Norway's organizations.

The intervention by Thorsrud is a workshop for identified and invited companies that has as its objective the establishment of a learning situation for company members engaged in organizational redesign. Workshop staff select participant companies on the basis of their willingness to participate and degree of commitment to planned organizational change. Each company selects a four- to six-member team from different organizational levels (including managers, workers, and a union representative) to attend the four-day workshop.

Workshops were designed and conducted according to an established pattern. The first afternoon's activities consisted of the following.

> A presentation by each firm of its markets and technology, and its organizational problems and preliminary ideas for solutions, is given by one of the team members.
>
> An outline of future changes in the industrial environment is given by one of the researchers at the end of the first day. A discussion indicates which changes are most important for different firms.[53]

A brief theoretical introduction (more akin to philosophy of work than behavioral science theory of shared participation) to democratic organizational design begins the second day of the session.

> The theoretical introduction usually ends by a review of objectives and constraints of development projects in different forms. The workshop staff take pains to make explicit the values behind the theory they present.
>
> Analysis of work situations in each firm is undertaken by each company group during the second day of the workshop. The analysis includes a number of jobs which are likely to be changed in the near future. In most cases a change is foreseen in which some segmented jobs are reorganized into autonomous work groups. The staff of the workshop play a rather passive role during this phase.
>
> After a plenary meeting where the groups present their findings, some questions are usually raised about basic conditions for group work. Conditions for group autonomy are stated in brief lecture in the middle of the second day.
>
> Two groups work together during the second part of the second day. One group presents the analysis of a specific department or plant and the plans for change; the other group raises questions and criticizes the plans. They then shift roles. When the summaries of these intergroup discussions are presented in a plenary meeting, a number of common problems or themes are identified. These themes represent conditions for moving in the direction of a nonhierarchical type of organization. They are dealt with the following day.
>
> Reconsideration of project development for the next two to four months is done by each company group during the fourth day of the workshop. A number of strategic questions are raised. The summing up of the workshop gives each design group a chance to prepare for returning home. Different groups usually agree to keep in touch, and they commit themselves to joint action and mutual support.
>
> Follow-up of the workshop is arranged by the staff, which is available for visits in the companies. A follow-up meeting takes place usually after three month's time, when the design groups have faced specific problems

in the first phase of their projects. Again the groups work through their own problems and seek advice from other groups and from staff. New themes are identified for exploration, and reference is made to other companies or professional groups with relevant experience. A network is growing.[54]

The extent to which Norway's efforts in the area of industrial democracy may be facilitated by the intervention reported here remains to be determined.

Training in participative skills of goal setting, conflict solving, and open communication was not regarded to be of importance. Attention is focused on reducing formal aspects of hierarchical structure by changing procedures, job redesign, and establishing autonomous work groups. In the absence of a boss, these groups assume shared responsibilities for establishing direction, assigning work, coordinating effort, and so on. Displaced supervisors may become members of these autonomous groups; they may become a central group to solve extraordinary problems, or may perform intergroup linking functions.

The intervention is at the larger social system level and is focused on shifting norms and standards so as to move away from formal, hierarchical authoritarianism toward a lateral, participative, and more autonomous approach. The approach is catalytic, with team facilitation provided by the researcher/specialists.

Relationships Between Various Ethnic Groups

The community self-survey is an intervention calculated to enable a community to arrive at shared norms and standards for social perception and actions. Its use to investigate tensions between the established ethnic majority in a community called Northtown and two minority groups—blacks and Jews—is reported by Wormser.[55] The survey was carried out during the 1940s and was expected to reveal discrimination in employment, housing, education, public facilities and services, and community organizations. An objective was to use the survey data to increase the clarity with which community members perceived social facts to which they may not ordinarily have been exposed. Thus the survey itself became a mode of community intervention.

The survey was premised on several propositions, including:

1. The importance of focusing on felt needs of community members, as exemplified by creating a broad-based community committee of actively interested persons to "steer" the project.

2. That such a committee should review each survey question and either confirm or change it according to whether the members felt it evaluated an important issue.

3. That interviews should be carried out by local citizens.

4. That interpretation of information summaries and report writing should be carried out by representative citizens.

5. That feedback sessions with community action groups should be undertaken by those responsible for information summary and interpretation.

This approach is catalytic because its main aim is perception building, with identified issues focusing almost entirely on felt needs or points of tension. The information, once summarized and interpreted, is assumed to be sufficient to bring about desired changes in tense relationships.

Opinion Polling

Another type of catalytic intervention, quite well known to the public, involves empirical information gathering and feedback by such professionals as Gallup, Roper,[56] and Harris.[57] When operating as consultants, each starts out with interviews designed to determine what it is their client wants to know. They then formulate opinion sampling, usually structured interviews or questionnaires, and administer these to a representative sample of the total community. Through newspapers, TV, books, and other media, reports of their findings are fed back to the community with interpretive suggestions provided through breakdowns by political party, sex, age, and so on. Assessment of long-term trends is also possible when the same questions are used periodically.

Alternatively, a particular client, such as the Republican or Democratic party, can commission opinion studies and use the results for action planning and program implementation. In another application, exemplified by Dichter and other motivational researchers, opinion-sampling techniques are employed for analyzing attitudes within the larger society toward commercial products of any variety. Such data can be analyzed by economic group, geographic region, and so on, and a profile created of probable markets for a new product. This can shorten the trial-and-error phases of new-product launchings.[58]

Police versus Minority Groups

Information used to broaden perception can also have the catalyzing effect of reducing rather than increasing the likelihood of a particular outcome, as shown during police and minority-group confrontations in the mid-1960s. On-the-street encounters appear to have been significantly modified by a previously held police training session.[59] This intervention took the form of a six-hour seminar spread over a one-week period, undertaken in the context of a crash training program whose major activities involved drill, antiriot measures, uses of special equipment, and so on. The seminar, attended by forty-five uniformed policemen, began with lectures on the civil rights movement. The origins and composition of the rights march, which was imminent, were dealt with.

The presentation of this kind of historical and legal perspective produced much private conversation among the police. The intervention created a common intellectual framework, replaced ignorance and prejudice with factual information, and promoted an exchange of points of view. As discussion continued, shared norms began to emerge concerning the genuine responsibilities of a police organization in the civil rights field. The intervention bolstered "the professional image of officers called upon to enforce a social change not necessarily in line with their sympathies or sentiments."[60]

Summary

When the client is the larger social system, survey methods in particular can have an impact on reducing pluralistic ignorance. The very fact of "knowing where people stand," particularly if they are near agreement, can have a powerful motivating effect on behavior change.

Norms/standards function forcefully to hold behavior "in place" by promoting socially shared perceptions that discourage deviance or change. What is surprising is the apparent lack of attention to this focal issue when change is desired. There are several possible explanations. The most obvious is that the consultant is likely to share the same norms/standards and therefore "sees" them no more clearly than does the client. Or, the consultant might intuitively sense that an examination of norms/standards would promote immediate defensiveness on the part of the client.

Notes

1. O. H. Mowrer, *The New Group Therapy* (New York: Van Nostrand Reinhold, 1964). Reprinted by permission.
2. S. M. Jourard, *The Transparent Self,* rev. ed. (New York: Van Nostrand Reinhold, 1971).
3. Mowrer, *The New Group Therapy,* pp. 50–51.
4. Ibid., pp. 69–70.
5. L. Douglas, *The Magnificent Obsession* (New York: Grosset & Dunlap, 1929).
6. Mowrer, *The New Group Therapy,* pp. 66–67.
7. W. R. Koehler, G. Lehner, and F. E. Fisher, "Team Effectiveness Training," *Training and Development Journal* (October 1974): 3–6.
8. S. H. Steelman, Jr., "Using a Front-End Analysis at C&P Telephone," *Training and Development Journal* (June 1978): 48–51.
9. Ibid., p. 48.
10. E. H. Schein, *Process Consultation,* © 1969. Addison-Wesley, Reading, MA, p. 106. Reprinted with permission.
11. Ibid.
12. D. O. Steinmann, T. H. Smith, L. G. Jurdem, and K. R. Hammond, "Application of Social Judgment Theory in Policy Formulation: An Example," *Journal of Applied Behavioral Science* 13, no. 1 (1977): 69–88.
13. F. P. Christian and A. C. Gross, "Increasing Productivity and Morale in a Municipality: Effects of Organization Development," *Journal of Applied Behavioral Science* 17, no. 1 (1981): 59–78.
14. R. T. Harris, "Improving Patient Satisfaction," *Journal of Applied Behavioral Science* 14, no. 3 (1978): 382–99.
15. Ibid., p. 389.

16. A. K. Rice, "Productivity and Social Organization in an Indian Weaving Shed," *Human Relations* 6, no. 4 (1953): 298. Reprinted by permission. See also E. Trist, "The Evolution of Socio-technical Systems: A Conceptual Framework and an Action Research Program." In *Issues in the Quality of Working Life: A Series of Occasional Papers*, no. 2, June 1981. Toronto: Ontario Ministry of Labor, Ontario Quality of Working Life Centre.

17. Rice, "Productivity and Social Organization," p. 327.

18. Ibid., p. 328.

19. L. R. Gomez-Mejia, M. A. Hopp, and C. R. Sommerstad, "Implementation and Evaluation of Flexible Work Hours: A Case Study," *Personnel Administrator* 23, no. 1 (1978): 39–41.

20. Ibid., pp. 39–41.

21. F. Herzberg, *Work and the Nature of Man* (Cleveland: World Publishing Co., 1966).

22. T. N. Lodahl and L. K. Williams, "An Opportunity for OD: The Office Revolution," *OD Practitioner* 10, no. 4 (1978): 9–11.

23. Y. Zeira, "Training the Top-Management Team for Planned Change," *Training and Development Journal* (June 1974): 30–35.

24. H. H. Vorrath and L. K. Brendtro, *Positive Peer Culture* (Chicago: Aldine, 1974).

25. Ibid., p. 52.

26. T. Gordon, *Parent Effectiveness Training* (New York: David McKay, 1970).

27. Ibid., p. 280.

28. H. L. Myerhoff, A. Jacobs, and F. Stoller, "Emotionality in Marathon and Traditional Psychotherapy Groups," *Psychotherapy: Theory, Research, and Practice* 7, no. 1 (1970): 133–36.

29. J. W. Lorsch, and P. R. Lawrence, "The Diagnosis of Organizational Problems," in N. Margulies and A. P. Raia, eds., *Organizational Development: Values, Process, and Technology* (New York: McGraw-Hill, 1972), pp. 218–28. Reprinted by permission.

30. Ibid., p. 223.

31. J. K. Fordyce and R. Weil, *Managing with People*, 2d ed. (Reading, Mass.: Addison-Wesley, 1979). Reprinted by permission.

32. Ibid., pp. 165–67.

33. Ibid., pp. 101–3.

34. S. A. Stumpf, "Using Integrators to Manage Conflict in a Research Organization," *Journal of Applied Behavioral Science* 13, no. 4 (1977): 507–17.

35. S. A. Culbert and J. J. McDonough, "Collaboration vs. Personal Alignment: An Experiment That Went Awry," *Journal of Applied Behavioral Science* 13, no. 3 (1977): 351–59.

36. S. D. Truskie, "A Case Study of a Union-Management Learning Encounter in Industry," *Personnel Journal* 53, no. 4 (1974): 278. Reprinted by permission.

37. Ibid., p. 279.

38. R. T. Golembiewski, "A Longitudinal Study of Flexi-Time Effects: Some Consequences of an OD Structural Intervention," *Journal of Applied Behavioral Science* 10, no. 4 (1974): 503–32.

39. Ibid., p. 523.

40. C. Jackson, "Upward Mobility in State Government," *Training and Development Journal* (April 1979): 39–43.

41. C. Alderfer, C. P. Alderfer, L. Tucker, and R. Tucker, "Diagnosing Race Relations in Management," *Journal of Applied Behavioral Science* 16, no. 2 (1980): 135–65.

42. F. C. Mann, "Studying and Creating Change," in W. G. Bennis, K. D. Benne, and R. Chin, eds., *The Planning of Change* (New York: Holt, Rinehart and Winston, 1961), p. 609. (Originally appeared in *Research in Industrial Human Relations,* Industrial Relations Research Association, Publication no. 17 (1957): 146–67. Reprinted by permission.

43. Ibid., p. 610.

44. F. A. Allen and S. Pilnick, "Confronting the Shadow Organization: How to Detect and Defeat Negative Norms," *Organizational Dynamics* 1, no. 4 (1973): 3–18.

45. F. J. Smith and L. W. Porter, "What Do Executives Really Think About Their Organizations?" *Organizational Dynamics* (Autumn 1977): 68–79.

46. M. Beer and E. F. Huse, "A Systems Approach to Organization Development," *Journal of Applied Behavioral Science* 8, no. 1 (1972): 79–101. M. Beer, "The Longevity of a Systems Approach to OD," in B. Lubin, L. D. Goodstein, and A. W. Lubin, eds., *Organizational Change Sourcebook 1: Cases in Organization Development* (San Diego: University Associates, 1979), pp. 62–65.

47. C. P. Alderfer, "Improving Organizational Communication Through Long-Term Intergroup Intervention," *Journal of Applied Behavioral Science* 13, no. 2 (1977): 193–210.

48. Ibid., p. 208.

49. R. A. Luke, Jr., P. Block, J. M. Davey, and V. R. Averch, "A Structural Approach to Organizational Change," *Journal of Applied Behavioral Science* 9, no. 5 (1973): 611–35. R. A. Luke, Jr., "Reflections on 'A Structural Approach to Organizational Change,'" in B. Lubin, L. D. Goodstein, and A. W. Lubin, eds., *Organizational Change Sourcebook 1: Cases in Organization Development* (San Diego: University Associates, 1979), pp. 148–49.

50. T. D. Taber, J. T. Walsh, and R. A. Cooke, "Developing a Community-Based Program for Reducing the Social Impact of a Plant Closing," *Journal of Applied Behavioral Science* 15, no. 2 (1979): 133–55.

51. Ibid., pp. 145–47.

52. Ibid., pp. 148–49.

53. E. Thorsrud, "Democracy at Work: Norwegian Experiences with Non-Bureaucratic Forms of Organization," *Journal of Applied Behavioral Science* 13, no. 3 (1977): 413.

54. Ibid., pp. 414–418.

55. M. H. Wormser, "The Northtown Self-Survey: A Case Study," *Journal of Social Issues* 5, no. 2 (1959): 5–20.

56. E. Roper, *You and Your Leaders: Their Actions and Your Reactions* (New York: Morrow, 1975).

57. L. Harris and B. E. Swanson, *Black-Jewish Relations in New York City* (New York: Praeger, 1970). L. Harris, *Is There a Republican Majority?: Political Trends, 1952–1956* (New York: Harper and Brothers, 1954).

58. E. Dichter, *The Strategy of Desire* (New York: Doubleday, 1960).

59. R. Shellow, "Reinforcing Police Neutrality in Civil Rights Confrontation," *Journal of Applied Behavioral Science* 1, no. 3 (1965): 243–53.

60. Ibid., p. 252.

24

CATALYTIC INTERVENTIONS

Goals/
Objectives

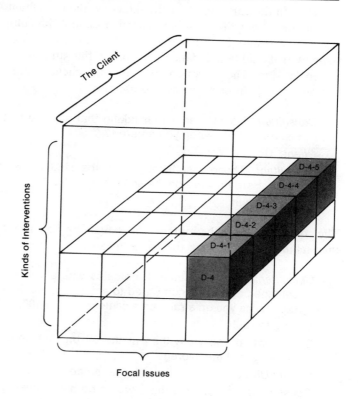

INDIVIDUAL (D-4-1)

The catalytic consultant may find it particularly difficult to penetrate a client's real problem when the focal issue is goals/objectives. The exception—a unit of change in which helpful goals/objectives catalytic interventions are made—appears to be when the client is an individual. Major shifts in a person's goals/objectives often occur as part and parcel of age, education, or work-related changes.

Career decisions may be difficult because of insufficient knowledge of available opportunities, or even of one's own talents and abilities. Interventions in this area range from assisting school and college students who are trying to "find themselves," to aiding middle-aged managers who may be questioning their own career histories and searching for more rewarding kinds of assignments, to preretirement or retirement counseling.

Career Planning with a College Student

A college student seeking to improve his unsatisfactory academic performance profited from a catalytic intervention in career planning. A teacher had suggested that he go to the University Counseling Bureau for further discussions of his situation. In the early phase of the interview the consultant gathered background information about the client's repeated in-school difficulties and then suggested a review of results from a series of tests administered earlier. This intervention assumes that additional data might assist the student to reach a more viable career decision. The scores could enable the client to see his current career objectives in the light of his measured abilities.

> *Consultant:* Do you remember taking that science test and the algebra test last September when you entered?
>
> *Client:* Uh-huh. Yes, I do . . .
>
> *Consultant:* Those results might be the kind of things that we're talking about. Here they are on the sheet here . . .
>
> *Client:* Uh-huh.

The consultant takes the initiative by explaining *how* to interpret the data rather than telling the client *what* the scores mean.

> *Consultant:* In this column it indicates where you ranked . . . on the percentage basis . . . compared to entering agriculture freshman. This number places you on a rank on a scale from 1 to 100.
>
> *Client:* Uh-huh.
>
> *Consultant:* If you were then at the 50 on that, that would mean that you were right at the average.
>
> *Client:* Uh-huh . . . So I'm below average . . .
>
> *Consultant:* The ranking there would be below average. Those tests, by the way, have been given to quite a few students over the years in that

college and they have an idea of how you might be able to handle the work in that college from how you do on these tests.

Client: Uh-huh.

Consultant: Scores . . . uh . . . like this would be the kind of scores . . . that persons make who have difficulty in making a satisfactory record . . . in that college.

Now the client begins to see possible implications of the information.

Client: The answer, I mean, I always did have a hard time and it was through my high school and . . .

Consultant: Uh-huh. Do you find that you have that same sort of trouble in your college chemistry?

Client: Yes, I think I do.

Consultant: Uh, huh. It's the same thing there . . .

Client: Uh, huh. Uh . . . do you think that's because of the background . . . that I didn't have too uh . . . good a background in those subjects?

The consultant presents a previously explored alternative to the client.

Consultant: Well, yes. Either that or you didn't master it well . . .

Client: Uh-huh.

At this point he refocuses the discussion.

Consultant: There are those two possibilities. You know there are all kinds of abilities and academic ability is just one kind of ability. It might be that you don't stand too well in that kind of ability. It may be that there are others for you. What sort of things do you think that you can do well?

Client: You mean in subjects?

Consultant: Or anything.

Client: Well, I don't know . . . I don't believe I understand what you mean.

Consultant: That's kind of a hard question to answer. What I mean is are there other things that you like to do better than school work or that you feel that you do better than school work?

Client: Well, I mean there isn't much else . . . I mean, there's . . . I've lived on the farm all the time . . .[1]

The catalytic nature of the consultant's approach is clear in several ways. He avoided expressing any personal convictions about the appropriateness of this student's college program and career interests. What did he do? Through *procedural* suggestions he aided the student to gather and to interpret information pertinent to understanding his own performance. The consultant undoubtedly appreciated that test scores can take on unmerited importance in the client's mind and thereby inhibit self-analysis and decision making. Scores may be interpreted as absolutes, having a prescriptive character rather than being used as indicators or "clues" of limited validity. Thus the consultant serves as a sounding board to help the student clarify whether or not his current academic and career objectives are realistic.

Identifying and measuring a person's general pattern of interests and feeding back this information, with predictions as to how his or her interests will "fit" each of several vocations, is a well-known and time-honored way of assisting a client in selecting a career.[2] The client fills in a standard vocational-interest blank, and his or her responses are then evaluated in the light of answers given to the same questions by successful people in each of several lines of work. An additional use of such an interest questionnaire is to ask the client to answer the same questions again, but to do so according to his or her "ideal self." In this way discrepancies between "the way I am" and "the way I would like to be" become clearer, and the consultant can aid the client in exploring implications for vocational decision making.[3]

Job Transfer

In this situation a young man has requested a job transfer and is being interviewed as to the reason for the request. The consultant is helping him review and clarify his own self-development plans and aspirations. While the client's aspirations seem rather grandiose, the consultant does *not* brush them aside. He focuses the client on examining information as one basis for aiding him to reach his own conclusions as to what his career goals are or should be.

> *Client:* Goal? I guess I'd like to hold an important position in the company.
> *Consultant:* What level in the organization do you have in mind when you refer to an important position?
> *Client:* Well, chairman of the board or president, I guess.

Now the consultant suggests a procedural strategy for information gathering.

> *Consultant:* We could try to set down all the skills and experience we feel the president should have and evaluate just how much you'd need to do to get to that level of expertise. You could then decide whether you'd commit yourself to that kind of effort and try to estimate how successful you might be in carrying it off. But we'd also have to take a look at your competition, so let's examine that angle first. Assuming the next president will come from within the company, how many people do you figure you'd be competing with?
> *Client:* I'm not sure.
> *Consultant:* What thoughts do you have about the kind of person who would be more likely to be promoted? Do you feel that the next president could be someone upgraded from the wage ranks?

The client is now examining "facts" he believes to be true but that he had previously not evaluated.

> *Client:* Oh no, the job will require a professional background.
> *Consultant:* Then your competition will number, say, some four hundred or more people. What we have to do now is to identify what *you* have, that they *don't* have, which gives you an edge in achieving the presidency of the company.

Client: (no response)

Consultant: In view of our type of operations, how significant do you feel the level of technical or professional proficiency, broadly speaking, would be in the selection?

Client: I'd say that it would be very important.

Consultant: Well, then, how do you see yourself in this regard as compared to the four hundred people we're looking at?

Client: Smarter than some, not as capable as others.

Consultant: About in the middle?

Client: Yes.

The consultant narrows the search further. Questions aid the client to collect more information and thus view his situation from a different perspective. It is important to notice that the consultant resists judging the man's career plans; decisions reached are the client's alone.

Consultant: If this kind of proficiency were the prime consideration, then we might say that the competition has been narrowed to two hundred. Now what advantage do you see yourself as having over these two hundred?

Client: (no response)

Consultant: Well, to what extent would you work harder than they would, to get there?

Client: I don't think I could say I'd work harder. I'm sure they'd all make as much effort.

Consultant: How about desire? How much more do you feel you want the position than they do?

Client: I couldn't truly say that I'd want it more. I really hadn't thought out very carefully what I said about the presidency. I guess that the goal isn't a realistic one for me at this stage of the game. Perhaps an intermediate goal is what I should establish.[4]

The interview continued, but focused on lesser, more attainable goals. The client came to appreciate that there was little *realistic* possibility, at least in terms of any present evidence of progress or in his personal efforts at self-preparation, of his achieving the presidency. Accordingly, he scaled his career plans to more limited but possibly attainable objectives.

Obsolescence

The rate of technological change in the last three decades has made it increasingly difficult for people to maintain currency in their chosen field. Once individuals complete formal education, their training may be obsolete within five to ten years. In many organizations this problem is recognized by conducting internal continuing education programs or encouraging, and sometimes sponsoring, employee participation in external training and development experiences.

Miller[5] reports an intervention which describes how IBM (San Jose) meets its responsibilities in the context of knowledge obsolescence. The author served as internal consultant in facilitating the intervention.

Growth and vitality are key needs, and work should contribute to their development and maintenance. By focusing on these as prime purposes of work (not on other goals such as product output or morale), improved motivation, satisfaction, and quality of working life are likely to result.

Recognizing this need, IBM established a series of committees. These committees served two purposes: first, they gained management understanding and involvement; and second, they elicited specific action proposals.

Each committee made specific recommendations that received top management approval and were subsequently implemented and eventually institutionalized. During this first step of a four-step process, the emphasis was on actions that would primarily impact values and attitudes. One example of such an action is a one-day convocation called "Challenge of Change" for professionals, managers, and nonmanagers.

> The purpose was to dramatically demonstrate the need for growth and learning, to build confidence in the future, and to communicate management's interest and philosophy.
>
> Step 2 consists primarily of substantive changes in what is done and how it is done. One of the ad hoc committees proposed several approaches to job rotation. Another positive step . . . the Professional Development School, a one-week program for non-management professionals, concentrates on enhancing their understanding of the organization and their ability to influence their own careers.[6]

Organizations have traditionally experienced considerable difficulty in defining and objectively measuring the output of professional staff. Step 3 involved improving the organization's understanding of professional productivity. Feedback is generally more difficult to provide when the output is nebulous and its impact is unclear. These issues were addressed in Stage 3, but the author reports only limited progress in this particular area.

The fourth and final step involved experimenting with a variety of ways to improve self-understanding and build self-confidence. Educational programs and self-administered analytical devices were made available and the process of improving discussions between managers and employees related to individual development and self-understanding was underway.

Perhaps the most salient feature of this intervention is in the expressed and demonstrated commitment to meshing individual and organizational needs for growth and development. Today's employees expect more out of work than an annual income. If employees cannot meet their higher order needs in the organizational climate as it exists, attempts to influence the climate in more supportive and positive directions are one option.

Mid-Career Changes

A career direction, once established, tends to perpetuate itself from its own momentum. Yet early- or mid-career shifts into other activities may result in more gratifying and rewarding work. Retirement similarly offers another opportunity for a person to sort out his or her thinking and plan future activities, often unrelated to previous responsibilities.

The initial job a person accepts in industry or government is generally related to academic preparation, at least to some extent. He or she is considered for promotion as vacancies arise for which his or her qualifications are suitable. Under these conditions, there may be a poor fit between personal interests and goals on the one hand and organizational needs on the other. If maturing talents and interests could be identified relatively soon after beginning employment, when a wide range of options is still open but long enough after a person has absorbed initial and reality-producing work experiences, his or her career might take a different direction.

A career-planning approach intended to be helpful in the early years of managerial employment is described by Marsh.[7] The entire strategy rests on aiding participants to periodically retest and reset their career goals. It is accomplished through:

1. Participants' completing information-gathering instruments prior to exercises that permit feedback. They work in self-selected trios whose members provide one another feedback regarding formal as well as informal aspects of behavior. In effect, the trio members are data sources for each participating individual.

2. Clarifying and testing self-perceptions of their strengths, weaknesses, skills, and interpersonal effectiveness.

3. Increasing their understandings of the contents of those jobs to which they might aspire.

4. Identifying gaps between present competencies and what would be required for success in particular future positions.

5. Preparing and implementing their personal plans for acquiring the skills essential for success in qualifying for and moving into one or more targeted positions.

During a week-long workshop, self-selected participants engage in a number of activities aimed at accomplishing these purposes. Consultant assistance during the information-gathering sequence includes facilitating:

1. Questionnaires that are completed as prework by each participant and by his or her acquaintances to provide information that will enable the person to contrast self-perceptions with the perceptions held by others.

2. A "first impressions" exercise in which participants exchange initial reactions to other group members.

3. Each participant studying his or her own past experiences with a view to identifying those work themes in which he or she has been most successful and those that have been most satisfying.

4. Each participant studying the performance requirements of higher-level jobs. In this way, he or she is enabled to appreciate the knowledge, attitude, and skill requirements essential for success in more advanced job assignments.

All of these activities share in common a catalytic character: they provide the participant with empirically derived perceptions calculated to increase his or her goal clarity. Although a theory basis of self-diagnosis using the Transactional Analysis model is introduced, it is employed as a perceptual "test" for feedback rather than as a central strategy for career planning.

An organization-simulation exercise is followed by decision-making tasks in which participants alternate between participating as managers and as observer-advisors. On the fourth day, the focus turns to the compilation of career development plans. Trio participants study and discuss upper-level job requirements in the corporate structure and relate these to each person's self-perceptions and past experience. Personal obstacles to achievement are identified.

On the final day, after a briefing on criteria for setting and writing goals, participants work individually to formulate their own career development programs. After trios critique these, participants form teams to role play career development discussions of the kind individuals will soon be having with their supervisors. Each team's role playing is videotaped for subsequent comparative analysis.

After the workshop, the company's facilitator gets in touch with each participant's supervisor to smooth the way by giving advance notice of the request for a career discussion. The facilitator continues to monitor and provide background support as all or part of the plans are put into effect following the supervisor-subordinate discussions. Participants convene six months later to write a commentary on progress toward their career goals. Thereafter, annual reviews and updates of the plans are made.[8]

A somewhat comparable approach to career consultation is offered by Haldane. It attempts to help the individual identify those elements and activities in his or her past life that have provided success and/or enjoyment, array and compare various jobs that include some or all of these features, and evaluate the desirability of change from a present assignment to one identified as more rewarding.

> Take, for instance, the case of a brilliant man of 35, the controller of a large corporation. He had a good salary and had worked his way up to his present position after getting his master's degree in accounting. But he was very frustrated and his anxieties were at a point where psychiatric counseling was essential. The doctor referred him to us for career counseling.

The counselor asked him to recall experiences from which he had derived satisfaction. He mentioned several.

1. Raising funds for a Boy Scout drive.
2. Selling magazines.
3. Developing a printing business.
4. Selling photographs.
5. Operating concessions in college.

Although he had followed his father's advice and pursued a college education and had a successful professional career, his heart was not in his job.

> In his free time he had volunteered for every community activity that involved selling or promotion of any type. He had sold tickets, he had organized groups to sell tickets. He had raised funds, he had organized groups to raise funds for many community activities. He had worked for community betterment projects and organized groups to promote them, then lobbied successfully to have them accepted by the city council.
>
> And, all this time, he had been becoming increasingly job-frustrated. While often commended for his controller work, he had always been glad when the week ended, somewhat resentful at having to go to work in the mornings. Because he had seen many other executives suffer the same feelings, he thought frustration was normal. Only when his home life had deteriorated substantially did he bow to his wife's insistence and discuss his problems with a psychiatrist.
>
> After he was referred for career counseling it was soon apparent that at least some of his frustrations were due to his being in a figures-and-paperwork job rather than in a selling and people-persuading job.
>
> Counseling helped him think through how he could swing within his company to an activity in the sales department where his accounting skills would be useful. He, on his own, suggested some private studies in marketing techniques and strategy. A program developed for him led to his becoming regional sales manager for the company within two years. The company had lost a man who was about to become a disaster in his controllership but gained a man who proved to be happy and highly productive in sales management.[9]

The Haldane intervention recognizes and centers on the possibility that the talents an individual has and the satisfaction derived from using them may not be applicable in his or her present job assignment. Trying to assist the client to find greater gratification *within* that assignment, such as by helping the person see how significantly his or her work contributes to organizational effectiveness, would miss the point. The career-planning objective is for the client to recognize those talents from which he or she can derive greater gratification and then to set job goals within which they can find expression. This may be within his or her present career ladder, or far removed.

A similar use of catalytic intervention, but at a different and usually later point in a person's career, is designed to help the individual develop "life plans."[10] The information-gathering method was pioneered by Shepard and makes use of a number of self-study and group activities. In broad outline, it involves each individual's:

1. Reviewing past experiences that were rewarding and finding the main patterns or themes that run through them.
2. Sharing one's findings with several others engaged in the same activities to obtain helpful reactions and suggestions.
3. Based on conclusions reached, designing developmental goals that the par-

ticular individual can work toward so as to develop requisite competencies or find situations that permit more frequent involvement in rewarding activities.

An application of this general approach within corporate situations is described by Fordyce and Weil[11] in the setting of a "Life/Career Planning Laboratory." This technique can be used at any critical career point, such as when a person is considering a new job opportunity, or shifting from a technical into a managerial assignment, or accepting early retirement.

These various interventions on the part of the consultant are of a catalytic character. They supply participants with procedures that permit them to explore their self-information, gather new information, and interpret its meaning. The consultant's participation hastens a process of self-discovery that could have gone on anyway but probably at a slower rate and possibly on a more superficial level. He or she ensures that each member gets a "proper" share of attention and aids participants in identifying options that may never have occurred to them. Wishful thinking is separated from realistic prospects, and the person may find that the cause of his or her present situation is not the organization, the boss, or fate, but is within the individual.

Retirement Counseling

At the other end of the employment cycle is retirement. Since retirement presents a different set of problems, it also has become an important area of counseling.[12] The range of new problems calling for innovative adjustments at retirement is unusually large: less income; an end to the everyday workplace relationships within which many long-term personal friendships may have been formed and sustained; the search for new activities to replace those of several previous decades; the consequences, for some, of spending most days at home; and, usually, the prospect of diminishing physical activity.

Pre-retirement as well as post-retirement counseling may be conducted either with individuals on an interview-by-interview basis or in group settings. Whichever the case, its *educational* aim is to aid those facing termination of their careers to understand the retirement benefits their companies offer and to know more about Social Security. Its *counseling* aim is to aid retirees to anticipate and become adjusted to their new situations by selecting from the goals open to them those best suited to their needs. This kind of retirement counseling rests on a catalytic approach for problem definition, broadening perception, and making goal choices.

Summary

There are still other applications of the catalytic approach to counseling individuals. For the most part, however, they differ by subject and situation rather than involving basic shifts at the strategic or career-goals level. Included are rehabilitation, special disabilities, marriage, divorce, and so on, where the approach adopted depends to a substantial degree on whether an individual, a couple, a group, etc., can be aided best by procedural assistance, face-to-face information gathering, or through survey or aptitude and interest devices.

GROUP (D-4-2)

Nonexistent or unclear goals may be the factor causing things to be less satisfactory than they could be. Given that the client group feels the problem is in the goals area, the catalytic consultant may be able to make a constructive contribution to the situation.

Setting Objectives in Industrial Situations

Management by objectives has gained cornerstone status as a management tool. With its dozens of variations, MBO is used in countless public and private organizations. Varying degrees of success are reported from its use.

Ivancevich et al.[13] describe an MBO-type intervention used in Tenneco, Incorporated, a large, diversified, multi-industry company. Tenneco's version, called Program Planning & Evaluation (PP&E), attempts to relate achievement of organization objectives to developmental goals that provide employees with a personal sense of satisfaction and achievement for individual contributions. The PP&E system is designed for improving work performance and management development for managerial and professional-level employees in all corporate staff groups and divisional companies. The preparatory steps were completed by company representatives. A task force that represented each divisional company was appointed by the president, and each company had at least one representative. The task force developed scenarios of crucial problems to avoid in implementing a goal-setting system.

Several sequential steps are entailed in using the system. First, the job and situation are diagnosed and the employee states his or her responsibilities and objectives for the year. After one year, the employee's actual performance is measured against stated objectives and priorities. The subordinate is told how well he or she is doing, and specific developmental plans are made.

A survey methodology was used by external organization researchers to evaluate the effort. Attitudes about goal-setting activities, job characteristics, organization climate, and what it is like to set PP&E plans with a superior were evaluated.

The intervention is not described in concrete terms, but it appears to have involved providing the task force with extensive literature related to goal setting and explanations for successes or failures. The intervention also involved development of one seminar for conceptual understanding and skill practice in conducting goal-setting sessions and another to aid managers of managers in evaluating performance, coaching, and counseling.

Another example of how a catalytic intervention occurs with boss and subordinates as they engage in management by objectives is provided by Humble. In the introduction of MBO in an organization, a third party consults with boss and subordinate to facilitate the program. In Humble's terminology, these third-party consultants are "company advisers."

> Company Advisers must be selected and trained to a highly professional standard in the various [MbO] techniques. An Adviser is a source of professional advice on the whole programme. He develops suitable techniques and methods with managers; counsels each individual manager in the Key Results Analysis preparation; is present at first Reviews; helps to analyze training plans. He is an "educator" and "catalyst," *not* a man who states what the standards should be, nor what the priorities are and how the problems should be solved. That is management's task.[14]

Humble sees the consultant's role in a catalytic way when he maintains that this role is to "stay out" of the issues, limiting participation to what Schein (Chapter 23) would probably refer to as "process consultation."

Redefinition of Objectives in Nursing Services

A catalytic intervention intended to provide a basis for management by objectives within a hospital department is described by Pearsall and Kern.[15] Although the final solution was actually not the one planned, its development offers useful insight into the catalytic process.

The hospital had opened nearly a year earlier and, as its first anniversary approached, the director of nursing services was becoming increasingly concerned about discrepancies she sensed between her department's stated goals and some of its actual practices. She formulated a proposal to make the anniversary a target date for evaluating and recharting departmental policy and practice. The administrative staff of the hospital endorsed this proposal. When the nursing director raised the question of objectivity, it was agreed that she was much too personally involved to provide objective leadership for this analytic undertaking. Instead, they decided to tap the resources of their affiliated college of medicine's department of behavioral science by asking for a "skilled discussion leader."

The nursing director put this initial request to an anthropologist in a college department, who commented that discussion leadership seemed an inadequate way of providing the nursing director with detailed feedback about staff functioning. Instead, she proposed and the director agreed to undertake a limited observational study. Accordingly, the anthropologist interviewed the nursing organization, observed and took notes at departmental meetings, and so on, maintaining a friendly, though still rather distant, demeanor. Trust and other indications of acceptance were accorded her by the nurses who would later be recipients of her findings.

The thrust of the intervention was to assemble, on the basis of the anthropologist's findings, hypothetical organization charts to mirror *actual* behavior. In this form, the findings were readily comparable with the hospital department's present organization chart and job descriptions.

In her intervention some weeks later, the anthropologist, rather than describing her findings in conventional organization-theory terms, used simple and picturesque allegories such as "tribal territories," contrasts between "emerging into an open mountain meadow" and staying within organizational "neat and bounded woods," and so on. The audience of nurses listened with interest but remained passive.

The nursing director and the anthropologist had no prior arrangement as to who would lead the discussion after the report. On the spur of the moment, the director seized the initiative. She "translated" the report's generalizations into detailed and specific nursing-service language. Thus, before she knew it, *she* had become discussion leader rather than turning that job over to the anthropologist, as the hospital administration had advised. At the same time, the objectivity issue had been resolved by the director's acting as translator and illustrator of the anthropologist's report.

In effect, the two principals had found their way to a consultant-client relationship rather than, as had been the case initially, the nursing director needing to "pass the torch of leadership" temporarily to an outside person. Pearsall and Kern indicate that this series of evaluation meetings evolved into lively policy making and planning staff meetings, with the anthropologist as "sideline resource person." In this way the consultant took a more catalytic rather than directive role in the goals/objectives-setting process.

Clarifying Goals in an Educational Agency

An illustration of the risks faced when consultants orient their interventions around felt needs, rather than real needs, is provided by Milstein and Smith.[16]

The real need in this situation was for an intervention to enable the organization to confront and resolve ideological conflicts arising from deep-lying value differences as to the purpose of education. The client's felt need was for help to improve goal clarification, communication, and decision making.

Over time the "work" at the felt needs level seemed only to intensify the deeper conflicts that erupted in the form of a muted mutiny. A second intervention, calculated to bring forth underlying conflicts in a catalytic way, also failed to bring a basis of resolution.

The client, a Board of Cooperative Educational Services (BOCES), was one of more than forty BOCES systems in New York State. School districts contract collectively with a particular BOCES for a variety of services (e.g., planning, survey research, special education, etc.) that none of the districts can afford to provide individually.

The superintendent of one BOCES contacted the consultants for assistance in working with his administrative staff to clarify and to update their educational goals and coordinate these goals across programs.

> We agreed to work on the project, but only after we interviewed all staff members to ascertain their perceptions of the situation. At a staff meeting we shared our diagnosis and sought group agreement regarding whether an intervention would be justified. Interviews and observations during the entry period indicated that felt needs existed in the areas of goals clarification, communication, decision making and change.
>
> On the basis of that diagnosis, the staff agreed that an intervention was justified. A half-day session was held to introduce the staff to the intervention process.
>
> During the workshop, BOCES staff experienced simulations, discussions, and action planning sessions. Evaluations of the sessions ranged from 75% to 87% effective.
>
> During the last session of the workshop, BOCES members were asked to identify the three most pressing intraorganizational issues and to develop some action strategies for dealing with them. Plans formulated during this session included clarification and prioritization of goals, a workshop to identify further skill and trust needs, and planning of MbO in-service work. All of these actions were subsequently carried out as planned.[17]

A few months later, the consulting team was contacted again to help resolve conflict and communication problems that had intensified after the first intervention. Interviews were held with each staff member, and the data collected became the basis for a second workshop proposed by the consultants. The initial day of this three-day workshop was devoted to discussion of the interview data in an effort to isolate the group's primary problems. On the second day, an imaging exercise was used to provide insight into the group's perceptions of themselves and of one another.

> The two groups (upper and middle management) did come to recognize their contributions to intraorganizational problems. In some cases, there was even commitment to modify unsatisfactory behaviors.[18]

This is a catalytic intervention focused on goals and objectives at the organizational level, whereas the real need was for a confrontational intervention dealing with power and authority. The catalytic approach to interviewing and data gathering took respondent answers at face value and led the consultants to propose an intervention at the least hazardous, or process analysis, level in order to bring forth identifiable problems (not necessarily important ones) and to stay at this level rather than to grapple with deeper-lying issues.

Unclear Goals in a Community Agency

Grambs and Axelrod describe an intervention with a professional staff of a community center that typifies the catalytic mode in several respects. In this example, the intervention was unsuccessful. The consultant failed to aid the group to reformulate its goals/objectives in such a way as to make progress; another failure was not dealing with the existing power/authority structure in order to grapple with the problems presented by it. Both are representative of difficulties faced when the consultant seeks to work *within* the status quo situation.

> For example, the consultant presided at the first two meetings. He tried to find out about the center's program and problems, and the staff tried to explain what the center was really trying to do for its members. In these discussions, they began to see that the key factors in the kind of program that would lead to these goals were volunteer leaders.
>
> Before the end of the second meeting they reached the seemingly inescapable conclusion that the supervisors themselves were responsible for recruiting and training, guiding and helping the volunteers—who actually carried on the program.
>
> In an outburst of self-confession the staff members admitted that they had been more concerned with materials, membership drives, the appearance of the building, and recruiting more volunteers—than they had been in doing their best with the volunteer leaders.
>
> In fact, they admitted, only a minimum of attention was being given to those aspects of the volunteer's job most closely connected with what the center was trying to give its members.
>
> The group felt good following this self-revelation of shortcomings. The director thanked the consultant for not having criticized the admitted inadequacies of the staff. She ended by hoping that the future training sessions would be "a shot in the arm."[19]

The approach helped participants redefine their development goal, and this in turn resulted in a review of past deeds as "emotional" facts and "misdeeds." How a consultant may "cooperate" with the status quo problem-solving atmosphere rather than challenge it is evidenced in the following.

> The consultant chatted informally with those who were there until the director and the last staff member arrived, 15 minutes late. Then it was discovered that arrangements for the coffee-break had been forgotten, so two staff members rushed out to handle this detail. As the meeting was called to order, the director leaned across to the consultant and said, "Well, so far we've been having fun—but today, maybe we can get down to work."
>
> The consultant had planned to ask one of the staff members to summarize the agreements reached at the end of the last meeting and restate the problem that was to be explored. But pressed "to get down to work," he felt he had better do it himself.[20]

Just as the third session was ending the following happened.

> Suddenly, as the members were moving toward the door, the director called out, "I forgot to tell you that I will be obliged to miss our next training meeting since I must be at the state AASW conference. I'm sorry, because it promises to be an interesting one. We've got the ball rolling now. We've got it rolling."[21]

Rather than the consultant directly raising certain identifiable issues of its operating effectiveness, the fourth session reveals the same basic acceptance of the group's status quo and the effort to work within it. Other aspects of the consultant's efforts to catalyze change without challenge are revealed in the study's final summary.

> The consultant's behavior points up some interesting aspects of the training leader's role in leadership training. For instance, when the members started listing desirable qualities of volunteer leaders on the blackboard in the third session, he probably could have predicted a letdown when they realized they didn't know and hadn't planned what, if anything, to do with their list. He could have anticipated this and perhaps prevented it by urging them to carry out some other activity (and this might have helped make that session run more smoothly and accomplish more tangible results). But this is a program to help them learn to be better leaders. How much should he protect them from making their own mistakes? If they can learn more about leadership from making mistakes and evaluating the results than they can from following his directions, he should probably let them venture. This may be an acceptable principle to govern the leader's judgment. But the actual judgment is never an easy one for any training leader to make.[22]

Each of these episodes exemplifies the meaning of "cooperating" with the status quo, one of the key features of the catalytic mode of intervention. What *may* change as a result of the consultant's interventions are those aspects of group functioning that relate to their felt needs. Other matters, even though they may be barriers to effectiveness in the consultant's eyes, are deemed inappropriate for examination. By not questioning the felt-needs aspects of the staff group's definition of goals/objectives, the consultant appears to have lessened the prospects of change.

INTERGROUP (D-4-3)

The lack of examples available in this category is probably attributable to the fact that rarely do two groups perceive their problems as goals/objectives issues— each tends to view the other's distinctive goals with disapproval, and both generally ignore similar or superordinate goals that might be achieved by cooperation.

Intergroup strains in a Consortium group composed of representatives from member schools were studied by Brown, Aram, and Bachner[23] as they attempted to improve communication and understanding of representatives of each other's goals and objectives in an effort to improve the overall functioning of the larger group. The client consisted of a seven-school consortium as represented by a policy-making Plenary Council that met three times a year. The consortium had been in existence for four years, and its major goals were to maximize use of resources and develop new programs and opportunities for the represented schools.

A consultant group of four faculty members and students from a university management school's department of organizational behavior was asked to assist this group in problem definition, goals/objectives setting and action planning. A long-term project with three objectives was recommended by the consultants. The objectives were: "a) increased understanding of the advantages and disadvantages of Consortium membership, b) clarification of the priorities, problems, and opportunities of Consortium membership, and c) work on the developmental priorities that were identified."

As a first step in approaching their assignment, the consultants conducted interviews with Plenary Council members. Four major problems surfaced. These became the focus of a diagnostic questionnaire. Responses to this instrument were solicited from council members and other school members. Then a Management Skills Workshop based on identified needs was constructed and conducted. Six of the seven schools participated.

"The workshop included activities that focused on four sequential phases: 1) development of the climate and skills for open and direct communication, 2) clarification and communication of each school's needs in the Consortium, 3) identification and communication of each school's problems with the Consortium, and 4) development of action steps."

Comparing questionnaire responses given both before and after the intervention, the consultants assessed the effectiveness of their efforts. Results suggest only marginal success in terms of identifying problems, reaching consensus on objectives, and developing action plans. Information sharing was shown to have occurred in that the schools learned more about one another, but this newly acquired knowledge was not directed toward problem solving or positive action.

Some obvious shortcomings of the approach used here are cited by the consultants. "The *time perspective* of this project was the result of compromise between the researcher-consultants and the client. The researcher-consultants would have preferred a longer workshop with extensive follow-up activities, and the clients wanted a workshop with little pre- or post-work. In retrospect, trying to deal with such complex and difficult issues in such a limited period was unrealistic."

The clients' lack of commitment to both the process and objectives was clearly demonstrated by their lack of interest and reluctant participation in the Managerial Skills Workshop. The deeper issues are related to the fact that Consortium members are in fact group representatives. As such, the problems of cooperation are probably only resolvable by bringing vested interests into the open and resolving them and then having the Consortium set superordinate goals that members could more fully commit themselves to achieving.

ORGANIZATION (D-4-4)

More and more organizations are beginning to question their traditional goals/objectives, particularly when faced with external economic or social threats. Thus an entry issue is likely to be formulated in goals/objectives terms.

Improving Psychological Health and Productivity

Effecting change in large, decentralized organizations presents an interesting challenge. Each autonomous organizational unit has its own unique characteristics and, hence, sets of problems and needs may exist that are unique also. It may be that an approach that has a positive impact on one organizational unit may have no impact on another, or even an adverse impact on some other unit.

Porras and Wilkins[24] evaluated the work of an internal consulting group in a national food service company comprised of 400 relatively small autonomous food service units (FSUs) scattered throughout the United States. The interventions were intended to improve both the psychological health and the productivity of the organization by improving the way people worked together in each food service unit. The authors did not plan or execute the interventions. Their role was to assess objectively the impact of interventions developed and implemented from within the organization itself.

Team building for the first-level employees was designed and implemented as a continuing response to the need for change sensed by the executive officers. The intervention was based on the assessment of typical food service unit dynamics and the desired organizational relationships and functions at that level. From this comparison of actual dynamics and desired outcomes, the internal OD staff formulated a strategy for intervention and change of the typical FSU.

The OD staff designed a series of three separate interventions to be implemented by four consultants. The first and second intervention activities involved the entire FSU, all managers and staff, while the third centered on managers only.

The first formal intervention consisted of an educational activity in which behavioral concepts (e.g., participation in decision making, trust and candid communication, conflict management and motivation) as well as basic corporate principles were described and discussed for background appreciation. The second consisted of activities designed to support and illustrate the material presented in the first part. The third part dealt with direct identification of barriers to the effective functioning of the individual staff members, with action plans developed for removing barriers and solving problems.

The second formal intervention took place approximately six months later. The technique in this phase was a day-long team building session that first built team relationships and then brought out key organizational problems to be dealt with. Attitudes and perceptions about the problems were discussed and solutions agreed upon with accompanying schedules for action.

The third formal intervention was conducted about six months after the second. It was directed solely at the unit managers, and productivity was the theme of the meeting. An analytical model for improving productivity was presented providing a framework through which managers could identify human, structural, and technical obstacles to unit productivity and choose methods for overcoming them. Managers discussed performance problems and developed plans to resolve them by using data from their own units.

The authors selected two general types of research variables in assessing the intervention's impact. Their hypothesis was that, over time, the intervention would have limited but positive effects on both "human process" variables and organizational output variables. "Human process variables consisted of participant's perceptions of organizational climate, leader attributes and behavior, group processes and individual satisfaction, and self actualization."

Generally speaking, the three interventions negatively affected the attitudes and perceptions of both managers and unit staff. Managers believed that the quality of supervision had worsened as a result of the interventions. Staff developed a more negative attitude toward work. All of these changes were counter to the intent of the intervention.

> While managers were becoming less satisfied, the staff were becoming more self-actualized, yet neither perceived any changes in the effectiveness of the unit. These results showed a slight tendency for the processes of the organization to change in a negative direction, while the outcomes [as measured objectively by food-costs-per-meal] became slightly more positive. This finding was not only counter to prediction, but also counter to a fundamental perspective in organizational change theory that process drives outcome.[25]

Results reported in this study provide few answers as to what could or should have been done differently but raise many questions about whether anything should have been done at all. Perhaps a key to the failure of this effort can be found in the preparation stages. It must be remembered that the approach was designed for the "typical" unit. Medicine prescribed for the "typical" person without regard for the individual's unique needs or physical attributes could actually do more harm than good. Likewise, unless the individual unit needs a particular intervention, it might be better left alone.

Goal Setting for Increasing Performance Effectiveness

When an organization invites its employees to critique current practices and recommend changes in direction, it must be prepared either to implement recommended changes or explain why the change cannot or will not be made. Attitudinal and related surveys raise employee expectations that their opinions make a difference. Unless organizational follow-up is evident, both productivity and morale are likely to suffer.

An employee attitude survey was used to obtain employee feedback and stimulate organizational change in the City of Phoenix.[26] A report from external consultants covered in detail the rationale behind the survey, its design, the methodology, a profile of respondents and city-wide findings, as well as each department's responses. An executive summary provided a condensation of the rationale and the city-wide findings.

The intervention was conducted by external consultants who designed the questionnaire, tabulated the responses, and made recommendations based on the results.

The city-wide data were analyzed by a city-wide OD steering committee. The steering committee was comprised of executives, middle managers, and supervisors representing many city departments. Departmental data were assigned for evaluation to individual department OD planning teams that varied in size from six to twenty members, including management and supervisory levels. Larger departments appointed several teams.

To better identify reasons for responses received and to plan action to improve the situation, each issue was studied by these OD teams through a variety of processes. Over 400 improvement actions were identified.

Commitment by the city manager to using the data for organization change demonstrates awareness of two important insights. First, those who do the actual work are in a position to recommend work-related improvements; second, employees take such opportunities for input seriously and expect that needed improvements will be implemented.

This catalytic intervention apparently identified many goal-setting opportunities for decision making and problem solving, at least on a short-term basis. Long-term evaluation of permanent impact is not available in this report.

Organization Integration through Goal Clarification

The recently appointed president of a community college, familiar with behavioral science theories of effective behavior, wished to bring new strength to the campus but seemed unable to do so by his own direct efforts. As a result, two consultants were engaged to assist the president in achieving these aims.[27]

This intervention began with the president, and it eventually involved all eighteen administrators. It commenced with interviews and clarification with the president and continued with interview-based data gathering throughout the administration. These findings were shared with the president and two deans, who planned a session for the full administration, but this threesome was threatened by what was revealed. Only after a fortunate episode of one dean revealing a frustration he experienced in dealing with the president did the air clear sufficiently that the larger meeting could be held. The data were fed back anonymously at a three-day, off-site session where progress was reported to have been made in setting goals, clarifying roles, and in examining group processes. Such matters as bringing high-level abstractions to more concrete statements, talking back and forth in a crisp and straightforward way, focusing conflict, exploring its causes, and bringing conflict resolution about based on understanding and agreement were positively addressed.

Following this, each administrator spent an extended period of time developing goals and objectives for his or her segment of the college with the help of process-related consultative assistance. These goals and objectives were then forwarded to the president and served as the basis for discussion and review of college activities and programs. Additionally, team building with the president and the three deans (one added) took place as did additional consultation with departmental chairs, etc.

From the standpoint of its formal aspects, this organization development effort terminated at the end of two years, but it continued from the point of view of the use of the strategies that had been acquired during the active period.

This is a catalytic intervention (with episodes of confrontation) that involved bringing into use what seemed natural and sound, including management by objectives, candid communication, conflict resolution, etc. Since there was no reliance on learning theories of behavior essential for bringing these and other deeper-lying values into use, the report is difficult to interpret as a clear success.

The case study of this intervention suggests that the extensive catalytic aproaches were essentially beside the point and that the unintended confrontational intervention was what made the difference.

Redefining Organization Mission

As their reason for being becomes less important through environmental and climactic changes, some organizations experience the phenomena of declining organizational relevancy. This intervention concerns the process of change by which out-moded organization definitions may be replaced by newer ones that are more fitting to the needs of the organization and of its environment.

Historical examples are numerous and include, for example, the shifting from horsepower to combustion engine technology. Another example is organizations' concerns with maintenance of law shifting over from the imprisonment of criminals to the development of adjudicated individuals through rehabilitation.

The intervention that brings about these shifts in organizational focus is called "Paradigm Reframing."[28] Clarifying the emerging shiftover and aiding those responsible for the resolution of related organizational problems to address issues in a fuller and more deliberate manner comprises the primary intervention activities.

The paradigm reframing process can be described by picturing how new ideas flow into an organization in an unplanned manner. The steps involved are:

Stage 1—Fertile Voids: The Birth of New Perspectives. This is where new ideas take place usually on the periphery and are initiated by individuals or small groups on the periphery of the system.

Stage 2—Crisis. This is a disruptive event that threatens the organization and usually takes place outside of the organization itself.

Stage 3—Diffusion. This is spreading the idea throughout the organization and having it embraced by a large number of people.

Stage 4—The Struggle for Legitimacy. A new concept becomes a significant one when it is the basis for influencing policy, determination, or allocating money.

Stage 5—The Politics of Acceptance. This takes place when a champion, defender, or a person in leadership picks up the new idea and forwards its acceptance through giving it his or her personal support.

Stage 6—Legitimization. This process is culminated when the new ideas are embedded in the organization culture and become an aspect of its new traditions, precedents, and past practices.

The consultant who is aware of the shifting nature of organization objectives as described can hasten the process in two ways. One is by stopping unproductive work on the system that is becoming antiquated, and the second is to support the organization by focusing attention on the new, emerging ideas. The consultant does this at each point in the six-step sequence of new idea inflow as pictured above.

This is an organization intervention because it involves the basic reasons for the organization's existence. It is concerned with goals and objectives because prior activities that were legitimate under old goals are replaced by newly defined goals and shifted activities congruent with their accomplishment. It is catalytic because the consultant orientation is to facilitate by data gathering, by giving focus and emphasis to emerging trends, and by aiding those needing to be involved in engaging themselves in the examination essential for the change to occur.

LARGER SOCIAL SYSTEM (D-4-5)

Community problems abound, often because citizens who might join together to solve them don't know how to get started. Unable to get together, they can't identify goals they might reach in concert. Often the community consultant initiates and supports group formation in order to move into goal achievement through community problem solving. The first two examples are of this character; the third involves community residents' antagonistic feelings toward their school. The latter was approached in a catalytic manner, since feelings by residents were sufficiently crystallized to enable them to take confronting actions on their own initiative.

Community Action Groups

Creating an urban *block organization* for community action is a development-oriented program dating back to at least World War II. The idea is most pertinent in socially and economically deprived neighborhoods plagued by untenable conditions requiring united action. The social-worker approach for stimulating group formation and action usually is catalytic, but the resultant organization may later come to rely on political confrontation as a way of forcing change. One method of group formation involves finding "indigenous" leaders, around whom other residents can mobilize. Suggested leader criteria include:

1. The ability to articulate community needs.
2. Some degree of stability as evidenced in family, marital, or employment relations.
3. Some previous demonstration of activity on his or her own behalf.
4. An awareness of the potential value of group action.

5. An ability to look at reality with a degree of objectivity.
6. An ability to understand cause and affect in relation to immediate problems.
7. Some evidence of a degree of independence of thought and action from people in positions of authority.
8. Evidence of physical and mental health.
9. A genuine feeling for, and interest in, people.
10. Evidence of willingness to assume some concrete responsibility.[29]

The second approach involves interventions with individuals who have shown interest in forming a group but lack the knack of getting together on their own initiative. The following describes a typical early meeting and shows how the consultant adopts a catalytic role.

The group was busily engaged in perusing literature and pictures from other blocks. It was suggested that 8:30 P.M. would be a more convenient meeting time since Mrs. Ring had left home without eating; Mrs. Blake had had to return home to put the children to bed.

The consultant initiates discussion by putting before them a task-oriented goal.

I told the group I had discarded a letter I had prepared to go to all block members at such time as we decided to hold our general meeting since I felt this was something we might all work on together. They agreed. After several unsuccessful attempts at wording by Mr. Feld and Mrs. Ring, Mrs. Bough's suggestion that we make a leaflet instead was picked up eagerly by the group.

I wondered how we wanted to word it. They felt the heading should be something striking, compelling. Mr. Feld suggested, "Look." This seemed acceptable. Mrs. Bough asked for pencil and pad: "I can write better than I can talk." I asked how we wanted to continue. Mrs. Mack suggested, "Dear Neighbor, We are trying to get something done for the betterment of the neighborhood." Mrs. Ring suggested, "To the people of Fifth Street, we are trying to get together to better the conditions of our homes and neighborhood." This was a combination of Mrs. Mack's and her own contributions and was accepted by the group.

Mrs. Bough suggested "Calling Fifth Street" instead of "Look" as a headline. This was agreed upon with enthusiasm. Mrs. Ring continued, "We are calling a meeting to discuss clean halls, hot water, plumbing, rat holes, steam heat, ceiling plaster, etc."

Mrs. Bough: "Don't forget painting." *Mrs. Fox:* "All who are interested, and we are sure you are . . ." *Mrs. McGirk:* ". . . come to the meeting to discuss these problems." *Mrs. Fox:* "United we stand, divided we stand!" Some wondered when we fell. All laughed, and the correction was made.

I read the completed leaflet, adding that this was their own creation, made by their own efforts.

A discussion followed about the next meeting. Mrs. Rubin felt it should be a general one of the block. Mrs. Ring cautioned, "We are getting the cart before the ox. This group must plan for the next big meeting." I gave her support here. It was agreed to meet the following Thursday.

I felt we might want to consider everything that would go into getting out our leaflet. The Center could do the mimeographing but would need assistance in delivering. Mr. Feld volunteered to handle the distribution in 309 and 311. Mr. Blake, Mrs. Bough, and Mrs. Fox would take 303 and 305; Mrs. McGirk, 301.

Earlier, Mrs. Fox volunteered to act as temporary chairman and Mr. Feld, temporary secretary.[30]

The social-work rationale for such intervention is summarized as follows.

1. Encourage voluntary and self-developing interaction of members toward the group by using the common interest (project or program) as a catalytic agent.
2. Permit the release of hostilities and aggressions without damaging the group process.
3. Meet the dependency needs of members while enabling them to move toward more independent action.
4. Offer constructive opportunities for sublimation.
5. Enable individual members of the group to function better inside the group and their block.
6. Lead the group through the natural leader toward a successful achievement of their project.

It is not possible to delineate all the basic group work principles used. Some are implicit in the foregoing material. Four other principles enunciated were:

1. The necessity of choosing as a project one that will unite all members of a group rather than identify with a subgroup.
2. The necessity of keeping the leadership group geared to the larger block group and to develop a program after the organization is ready for it.
3. The necessity of doing things with people, not for people, in order to develop independence.
4. The necessity of having programmed clearly the means, not the end, in order to enable individuals to grow within and toward one another.[31]

Often the action sought by the block organization involves confrontation of elements in the larger community. An example is their request for additional police protection. After a meeting on the subject, the group went to the precinct station, with Mrs. Hink leading the delegation and with the consultant present as backup spokesperson.

Mrs. Hink served ably as spokesman. She told who we were, where we were from, and our purpose in being there. We spoke to Captain Merrill, who seemed duly impressed with the number of people and the vigor of their statements. Mrs. Hink said that we had come before with no results and now wanted action.

Everyone participated. They told how many windows were broken and in which apartments, the dangers of flying glass and missiles. They listed the names of boys they had seen on the roof. Mrs. Ring said, "We're human beings, not dogs. We pay taxes for protection and want it."

I told the captain this was our second visit. We had seen no policemen on the block; this was our last trip. If we got no action, we would go to the Police Commissioner. The Captain winced; he would see that we got action; he knew nothing of our previous visit; he would send plainclothesmen to the block. He spoke of the man shortage. Mrs. Hink felt this was the Captain's problem; all indicated approval. The Captain flushed, cleared his throat, and said we would get action this week. He rose, shook hands—the conference was over.

All filed out with a dignified air of importance. They had accomplished something together. Participation was well distributed. This positive experience of concrete accomplishment will serve as encouragement for further forthright action on the other issues.[32]

A negative aspect of this catalytic approach to community development is found in a gradual tendency toward reacceptance of the status quo situation, with diminishing hope of improving it, if the consultant is no longer available to act as a catalyzing agent.

The group seemed disappointed when I reminded them that I was leaving. When they said, "We'll have no worker of our own," I told them that the Director would be available whenever they needed him. They said, "But we'll have to go to him. He won't be able to come to us."

Mrs. Ring said that this was really their organization and they would have to prove that they could run it themselves. The worker would hear that things had not fallen apart.

The consensus was that there should be no meeting during the summer. They would meet again during the fall to determine what path their organization should take.

After the worker left, leadership could not be provided by the Center. Actually, the people never met again as a group. Some members remained quite active by joining Blocks United. However, this group's activity was truncated by the termination of the project.[33]

An approach to community action useful in dealing with any existing problem and relying almost solely on the use of a catalytic facilitator is offered by Strauss and Stowe. Examples of its application include community problem census and community growth goal setting that cut across the conventional power structure, solving parent and youth problems, finding jobs for the hardcore unemployed, and establishing effective communication between the local community and state legislators.

The catalytic agent is a facilitator who can

1. Help the participants explore a problem and improve their understanding of it.

2. Help them integrate their thinking and work together to reach a decision on which they can agree and which they will carry out with zeal.

3. Help them plan and organize the process for carrying it out, including the assignment of responsibilities to individuals.

4. Help them plan evaluation of progress, review the findings, and replan and reassign responsibilities as necessary.[34]

This approach goes beyond reliance on the professional consultant by training local community leaders to acquire catalytic-oriented discussion skills. This training is completed in three two-and-one-half-hour training sessions throughout one day or evening. Central to this training is discussion of the elements quoted below, the requisite skills of an effective discussant.

HOW GOOD A DISCUSSANT ARE YOU?

HOW OFTEN DO YOU—

To Facilitate Progress of the Discussion:
1. Question what a statement means.
2. Ask about an overlooked viewpoint.
3. Question the course of the discussion.
4. Summarize.
5. Test for consensus.

To Make Discussion More Penetrating:
6. Ask a pertinent question.
7. Initiate thinking.
8. Use logic in attempting to find a solution.
9. Try to separate facts from opinions and assumptions.
10. Try to integrate separate ideas.

To Improve Both Discussion and Group Solidarity:
11. Listen.
12. Draw others into the discussion.
13. Build on others' contributions.
14. Bring discussion out of chaos.
15. Support others, give others recognition.
16. Change position when clarification is made.
17. Under tension make conflict reducing remarks.
18. State your thoughts or opinion for clarification.
19. Give needed information.
20. Seek clues to acceptable solutions.

To Improve Group Solidarity:
21. Show approval by gestures, posture, or facial expression.
22. Show politeness or friendliness.
23. State your feelings about others usefully.

To Satisfy Your Personal Needs:
24. State your feelings destructively.

25. Ask non-pertinent questions.
26. Attempt to sell your viewpoints, regardless.
27. Interrupt unnecessarily.
28. Talk excessively, reminisce, tell stories, talk with neighbors.
29. Try to impress others.
30. Repeat yourself or others.
31. Backtrack when opposed.
32. Become antagonistic.
33. Read.
34. Be apathetic, preoccupied, withdrawn, hurt.
35. Show boredom or tension by doodling, nail-biting, shifting in chair, etc.[35]

Considerable success from using this mode of intervention for community development is reported.

School and Community Goal Discrepancies

Goals embraced by one group may be at variance with those favored by another group that is serviced by the first. Resolution of resultant conflict is possible through goal clarification. However, when a catalytic approach leads toward goal clarification but mutual agreement as to shared goals is not reached, the effort may lead nowhere and the situation may deteriorate. Caplan presents an example of such an episode in which the consultant sought, by catalytic interventions, to help a school system during an intense school/community cleavage. The consultant, whose contractual duties involved being available at the school one half-day per week for mental-health problem solving with individual students, was discussing related matters with the school's principal when a deputation of black parents came into the principal's office.

> They told the principal that they were not satisfied with the way in which the school was being run, and they complained aggressively about the quality of education their children were getting, as well as about the deplorable conditions of the school building, with its broken windows, inadequate heating, peeling paint work, and unsanitary toilet facilities. They said they had been complaining individually about these things for years without results. Now they had banded together into a committee and were demanding immediate action.[36]

The principal was shaken by this unanticipated challenge.

> The consultant supported him during the ensuing discussion; and after the parents had temporarily withdrawn into the outer office, he helped him review their demands and work out a reasonable reaction. The principal discussed the problem over the telephone with his district superintendent. He then called the deputation back into his office and informed them that their grievances would be brought to the attention of the school administration and that something concrete would be done about the matter.[37]

The consultant helped the principal to discern the legitimacy of certain of the goals-for-change that had been placed before him and to recognize that it was actually the hostile manner in which they were presented that caused the principal's initial upset. Furthermore, the consultant offered to serve as a "resource person" at a parent-teacher meeting scheduled two weeks hence.

The consultant made this offer, which was accepted, prior to discussing its implications with the director of the mental-health center where he was a staff member. When he did mention it, the director pointed out that this mode of intervention brought the center into a new area altogether: intergroup tensions between school and residents. Furthermore, it could cause residents to see the consultant as the school's ally or even as one of its staff members. However, it was decided that this principal did need support; and, coincidentally, that the center itself needed to learn more about racial tensions within the community. This situation afforded an opportunity for the center to serve both interests, the client's and its own. But it was also decided that the consultant should as far as possible avoid taking an active role in the meeting; rather, his interventions could well be limited to post-meeting consultation with the principal.

When the meeting took place—the first time that such an interchange had occurred between parents and teachers in many years—it was well attended by both groups. The principal led off by stating that the parents' demands had been passed up to higher levels of the school system and that certain building repairs had already been authorized, while other demands, particularly those involving additional budget, were deferred because actions could not be taken on them until they had been reviewed by the city board of education. As they were expecting specific and concrete actions and had little use for promises, several of the parents were angered by his remarks.

At this point, nonparent militants began speaking in hostile and insulting terms, and by attacking the principal and his staff succeeded in stirring up audience support. The principal and two teachers tried to rebut the accusations with logical counterarguments but were shouted down. The meeting ended in disorder.

The consultant did not get directly involved in the confrontation and tumult, but in a post-meeting session he intervened with the principal and some of the teachers to help them recover their composure and gain some understanding of what had happened. As the consultant saw it, the parents' proper concerns for the school's effectiveness and the well-being of their children were being pushed out of focus by the more diffuse racial tensions existing within and outside the neighborhood. Militants were exploiting the circumstances, with a view to publicizing and perhaps amplifying black/white conflict. He suggested also that since the situation's scope extended beyond the school's immediate jurisdiction, it would be appropriate to refer the matter to the school system's higher levels and offered the center's assistance as a specialized resource for dealing with these larger issues. Caplan describes the events that followed.

On the consultant's return to the center, the director concurred with his position and offered to attend a meeting with the district superintendent and perhaps to try to bring in some of the local black leaders for a behind-the-scenes discussion. The consultant phoned the principal and conveyed the director's offer, and the principal said he would discuss the matter with his district superintendent.

The following week, the principal reported to the consultant that the district superintendent did not wish to open up this matter in the manner suggested by the center and that while he appreciated their offer, he would not accept it at this time. If he felt the need for the center's help, he would get in touch with the director.[38]

Thus community tensions were approached catalytically by aiding the school group's representatives to clarify goals and by offering procedural suggestions. When this proved insufficient for bringing group protagonists into any sort of problem-solving harmony, contacts between the consultant and the school were discontinued. By the beginning of the next school year tensions had worsened to a significant degree. Then a confrontational approach was attempted by the consultant, as discussed previously in Chapter 15.

Peacekeeping Between Nations

Peacekeeping activities by the United Nations initiated during the Hammarskjöld era appear to have been premised on catalytic assumptions. This catalytic approach was implemented in several situations where (1) vital interests of leading Security Council members were *not* at stake, and where, therefore, the Secretary-General could exercise his good offices according to personal discretion; and (2) both sides in the controversy gave their explicit consent that the UN peacekeepers could employ measures short of armed force to dampen local violence, to reduce the likelihood of escalation, and to create a climate conducive to negotiations.[39] Such initial consensus between the contending factions was prerequisite to intervening in this manner. Additionally, as a means of defusing hostility, the UN took no actions of a sort that would specify one party or the other as guilty of aggression: far less, use force against one or more states. Finally, it made no attempt to sketch or explore potential areas of political settlement.

Inferentially at least, the Hammarskjöld-directed UN interventions were geared to produce information that would aid both parties in seeing the problems existing between them and in finding the means to improve mutual understanding of national interests, particularly as these bore upon issues that were or were not open to future negotiation. As a third party, the UN representatives stepped away from confrontation or arbitration in preference to providing catalytic consultation, helping protagonists identify both nonnegotiable and negotiable goals.

Summary

Catalytic interventions with goals/objectives as the focal issue are increasing in their frequency and use for improving the effectiveness of teams and organizations. One of the limitations in the cases reported appears to be that attempts to clarify or shift goals/objectives may be impeded if issues of power/authority are not dealt with also.

Power/authority issues are particularly pertinent in efforts to induce change through management by objectives programs or by setting changes in motion that call for commitment of those involved in the activities. If the supervisory or managerial style characteristic of the organization is contradictory to the participatory techniques utilized in the catalytic approach to redefine, reformulate, or set goals for change, then it is likely that results several years after the intervention will be reported as less satisfactory than had been expected.

Notes

1. E. G. Williamson, *Counseling Adolescents* (New York: McGraw-Hill, 1950), pp. 513–14. Reprinted by permission.
2. E. K. Strong, *Vocational Interests of Men and Women* (Stanford, Calif.: Stanford University Press, 1943).
3. B. Beit-Hallahmi, "Counseling with the SVIB: The 'Ideal Self,' " *Personnel and Guidance Journal* 52, no. 4 (1973): 256–61.
4. M. I. Gould, "Counseling for Self-Development," *Personnel Journal* 49, no. 3 (1970): 22–28.
5. D. B. Miller, "How to Improve the Performance and Productivity of the Knowledge Worker," *Organizational Dynamics* (Winter 1977): 62–79.
6. Ibid., pp. 67, 68, 69.
7. P. J. Marsh, "The Career Development Workshop," *Training and Development Journal* 27, no. 7 (1973): 38–45.
8. Ibid., pp. 38–45.
9. Reprinted by permission of the publisher from *Career Satisfaction and Success* by Bernard Haldane. © 1974 by AMACOM, a division of American Management Associations, pp. 4–6.
10. G. L. Lippitt, "Developing Life Plans: A New Concept and Design for Training and Development," *Training and Development* 24, no. 5 (1970): 2–7.
11. J. K. Fordyce and R. Weil, *Managing with People: A Manager's Handbook of Organizational Development Methods,* 2d ed. (Reading, Mass.: Addison-Wesley, 1979), pp. 138–40.
12. R. A. Beaumont and J. W. Tower, *Executive Retirement and Effective Management,* Industrial Relations Counselors, Inc., Industrial Relations Monograph no. 20 (New York: 1961); M. R. Greene, H. C. Pyron, V. V. Manion, and H. Winklevoss, *Preretirement Counseling, Retirement & Adjustment, and the Older Employee: An Experimental Study Measuring the Interrelationship of Factors Affecting Retirement Adjustment, Resistance to Retirement, and the Effectiveness of the Older Employee* (Eugene, Oreg.: Graduate School of Management and Business, College of Business Administration, University of Oregon, 1969); D. Pellicano, "Retirement Counseling," *Personnel Journal* 52, no. 7 (1973): 614–18; H. C. Pyron, "Preparing Employees for Retirement," *Personnel Journal* 48, no. 9 (1969): 722–27.
13. J. M. Ivancevich, J. T. McMahon, J. W. Streidl, and A. D. Szilagyi, Jr., "Goal Setting: The Tenneco Approach to Personnel Development and Management Effectiveness," *Organizational Dynamics* (Winter 1978): 58–79.
14. J. W. Humble, *Improving Business Results* (Maidenhead, Berks.: McGraw-Hill, 1967), p. 60. Reprinted by permission.

15. M. Pearsall and M. S. Kern, "Behavioral Science, Nursing Services, and the Collaborative Process: A Case Study," *The Journal of Applied Behavioral Science* 3, no. 2 (1967): 243–66.

16. M. M. Milstein and D. Smith, "The Shifting Nature of OD Contracts: A Case Study," *The Journal of Applied Behavioral Science* 15, no. 2 (1979): 179–91.

17. Ibid., pp. 181, 182.

18. Ibid., p. 185.

19. J. D. Grambs and J. Axelrod, "Time Out for Training: A Record of Staff Training in a Community Center," *Adult Leadership* 2, no. 2 (1953): 17. Reprinted by permission.

20. Ibid., pp. 17–18.

21. Ibid., p. 18.

22. Ibid., p. 20.

23. L. D. Brown, J. D. Aram, and D. J. Bachner, "Interorganizational Information Sharing: A Successful Intervention That Failed," *The Journal of Applied Behavioral Science* 10, no. 4 (1974): 533–54.

24. J. I. Porras and A. Wilkins, "Organization Development in a Large System: An Empirical Assessment," *The Journal of Applied Behavioral Science* 16, no. 4 (1980): 506–34.

25. Ibid., pp. 520–21.

26. L. G. Verheyen, "Change Through Employee Feedback," *Training and Development Journal* (September 1979): 40–43.

27. R. J. Dunsing, "A Community College in a Self-Change Process," in J. A. Shtogren, ed., *Administrative Development In Higher Education—The State of the Art: Volume I* (Richmond, Va.: Dietz Press Inc., 1978).

28. D. Nicoll, "Exploring a Subterranean Organizational Process," *OD Practitioner* 11, no. 4 (1979): 1–7.

29. M. G. Bowens, "The Neighborhood Center for Block Organization: An Experiment in Self-Help at the Neighborhood Level," in C. E. Murrey, M. G. Bowens, and R. Hogrefe, eds., *Group Work in Community Life* (New York: Association Press, 1954), pp. 19–20. Reprinted by permission.

30. Ibid., pp. 30–31.

31. Ibid., pp. 22–23.

32. Ibid., p. 37.

33. Ibid., p. 48.

34. B. Strauss and M. E. Stowe, *How to Get Things Changed* (Garden City, NJ: Doubleday, © 1974), p. 193. Reprinted with permission of the authors.

35. Ibid., p. 216.

36. G. Caplan, *The Theory and Practice of Mental Health Consultation* (New York: Basic Books, Inc., © 1970), p. 359. Reprinted by permission.

37. Ibid., pp. 359–60.

38. Ibid., p. 361.

39. L. L. Fabian, *Soldiers without Enemies: Preparing the United Nations for Peacekeeping* (Washington, D.C.: The Brookings Institution, 1971).

25

CATALYTIC
INTERVENTIONS

Summary and Implications

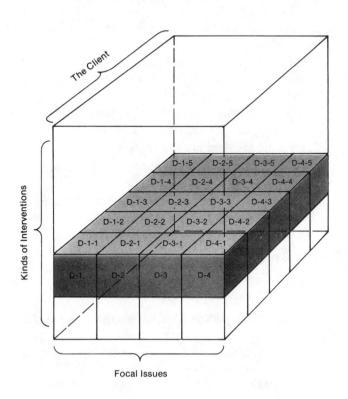

Catalytic interventions, whether the client is an individual, a group, two or more groups in an intergroup situation, an entire organization, or a larger social system, have recognizable common features. First, and most important, are the three basic assumptions on which the approach rests. The consultant can offer help in dealing with each of these.

1. Deficiencies of information are a significant cause of malfunctioning. The "solution" is to strengthen perception of problems through improving the flow of information.
2. Barriers to improved information flow include inadequate procedures and processes used by the client.
3. Mutual isolation of member components within the client system prevents them from coming together. This may be observably true of clients consisting of two or more individuals. For the individual as single client, it may be inferred that an analogous "separatedness" is associated with his present lack of integrated awareness of a focal issue.

TECHNIQUES

Techniques of catalytic consultation include:

1. Working within the status quo by accepting as given the felt needs of those who operate it.
2. Serving as a rallying point that enables members of the client system to get together.
3. Offering (a) procedural suggestions for steps that might be taken in seeking to satisfy those felt needs, and (b) "process" observations to help people see how to be more effective.
4. Gathering data, either through interviews, survey research, group meetings, instruments—or aiding the client to do so.
5. Feeding the data back to those who are in a position to take action.
6. Helping in the design of implementation steps through which resolutions are possible.
7. Building into the client's mechanisms a repetition pattern so that regression can be avoided and the possibility of further progress increased.

Client Readiness

A test of client readiness for catalytic consultation consists of affirmative answers for most of the questions shown below.

PROCESS CONSULTATION—CLIENT "READINESS" CRITERIA

	Yes	No
1. The client has appropriate problem solving skills required for joint diagnosis with the consultant and others.	___	___
2. The client perceives the need for improvement.	___	___

Yes   No

3. The client is problem solving oriented (rather than solutions oriented). ____ ____

4. The client is willing to learn from the consultant and work group by going through diagnostic problem solving phases. ____ ____

5. The client wants to help in solving the problem. ____ ____

6. The client is interested in an "original" rather than a prescriptive solution. ____ ____

7. The client will permit the consultant to learn about the work climate through on location observation, discussions with employees, review of confidential files, etc. ____ ____

8. The client and consultant are able to interact effectively at the interpersonal level. ____ ____

9. The client and consultant agree that the problem is worth solving. ____ ____

10. The problem has high priority with the client. ____ ____

11. The client desires to be actively involved in diagnostic phases of the problem solving process. ____ ____

12. The client is willing to commit additional resources (within reason) to aid the consultant in the fact-gathering and diagnostic stages. ____ ____

13. The client is trainable (i.e., the consultant feels that the client can, wants to, and has the time to be trained) in using diagnostic problem solving tools. ____ ____

14. The client is open to innovative problem solving approaches. ____ ____

15. The client is willing to work with feedback survey data (such as interview data, or questionnaire data) collected by the consultant. ____ ____

16. The client has a high risk orientation relative to identifying and solving problems through the utilization of participative techniques with his/her work force. ____ ____

17. The client is supportive of vertical team building approaches. ____ ____

18. The client is willing to implement mutually agreed upon solutions and action plans. ____ ____

19. The solutions are not obvious to the consultant based on past experiences with other clients. Diagnostic work is necessary. ____ ____

20. The client and consultant will not be violating professional ethics, laws or morals.* ____ ____

---

* W. B. Cash and R. L. Minter, "Consulting Approaches: Two Basic Styles," *Training and Development Journal* 33, no. 9 (1979): 26–28. Copyright 1979, Training and Development Journal, American Society for Training and Development. Reprinted with permission. All rights reserved.

LIMITATIONS

To consultant and client alike, felt needs may seem close to or even identical to the definition of the problem. Consonant with the "rational man" approach, they may presume that information will strengthen perception and that clear perception is the key to solving many if not all problems. A major weakness of the catalytic approach is that information deficiency is more likely to be a symptom than a cause of problems. A pertinent question is, *why* is "available" information unattainable? The consultant may ponder this question, but he or she does not raise it with the client. A certain kind of institutionalization can occur when reliance is placed on consultants operating within the broad ambience of a catalytic orientation.

> In TRW Systems, we are now moving in a number of directions, some of which I would like to describe. We are now moving more toward day-to-day coaching—on-the-job feedback, if you will—with or without consultants and without calling special meetings, but just as we work together. We are paying continuing attention to process as a way of doing business. We are moving more and more toward using third-party facilitation as a standard operating procedure.[1]

A risk is that, given heavy reliance on "third-party facilitators," this may become "standard operating procedure." The need for an organization to have effective managers who can solve problems without "artificial" help is disregarded.

When the consultant is permitted free access to all parts of the organization certain problems can arise in determining which issues are worked on, when, and by whom. Caplan pinpoints the consultant's difficulty as follows.

> The consultant may intervene at an individual, or organization level. His interventions are of a time-limited, circumscribed nature; and whether or not they are prompted by his own awareness of an issue or initiated in response to a feeling of need for consultation by a member of the organization's administrative staff, they must be limited by the boundaries of what the consultees feel are salient current predicaments. This means that although the consultant may be visiting the organization on a regular weekly basis for several years, and having continuing contacts with particular individuals and groups with whom he develops stable relationships of a gradually evolving character, his consultation interventions continue to be of an *ad hoc* type focused on temporary intercurrent episodes. This is so even though the consultant may recognize in his own mind that certain repetitive issues are linked to major continuing difficulties in the organizational structure. From time to time he may choose an opportunity for focusing discussion on these major problems; but on the whole, his strategy is to help the consultees handle them piecemeal in relation to the crisis and social system disequilibria they produce.[2]

The catalytic consultant's task, then, is subject to a fundamental dilemma. As he or she relies on the client to voice felt needs, to move toward defining the problem, and to become an active participant in its resolution, the consultant can lose his or her own perspective. Yet to the degree the consultant retains responsibility for definition and resolution, he or she is likely to meet with client resistance to imposed views. Carried further, the latter course would become prescriptive intervention, the consultant assuming full responsibility for the project.

APPLICATIONS

When the client's current problems appear to be related mainly to power/authority, the consultant attempts in a low-key manner to bring the client to an awareness of this as the focal issue. He or she is careful not to intervene in ways that would suggest to the client that "consultant power/authority" was being employed.

If the issue, however, is one of morale/cohesion, the consultant may suggest at least the rudiments of some procedure by which the client can initiate activity to "dissolve away" the present problem and its prevailing effects. The consultant may be able to select any one or more of a number of options for intervening in the problem-related context, thus helping indirectly to improve the client's morale/cohesion.

If norms/standards constitute the focal issue, a catalytic intervention may be more precise in the sense of instituting procedures whereby related problems of pluralistic ignorance can be resolved. Survey research is a prime example of such a technique.

The catalytic approach to a goals/objectives focal issue seems particularly helpful with individual clients; it is seldom applicable to problems at the group, intergroup, organization, and larger social system levels except to the extent that some external threat to such a unit of change is already facilitating the formation of interest groups that, in turn, can be aided in their goal-setting processes by this mode of intervention.

Notes

1. S. A. Davis, "An Organic Problem-Solving Method of Organizational Change," *The Journal of Applied Behavioral Science* 3, no. 1 (1967): 18–19. Reprinted by permission.
2. G. Caplan, *The Theory and Practice of Mental Health Consultation* (New York: Basic Books, © 1970), p. 283. Reprinted by permission.

Part V

ACCEPTANT INTERVENTIONS

26

**ACCEPTANT
INTERVENTIONS**

Acceptant
Interventions:
An Introduction

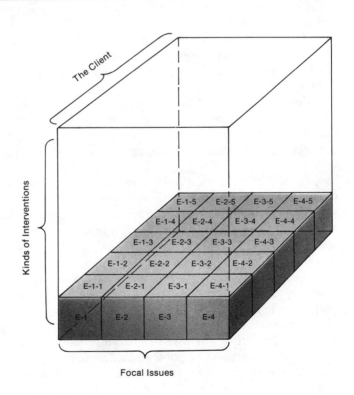

Invariably, human existence is punctuated by emotionally charged experiences. Many are uninvited and unwanted, upsetting and disturbing. Sometimes emotions produced by these experiences fade with no apparent aftermath. If they persist, the person might be able to turn his or her thoughts inward and to identify the emotions blocking normal functioning. Introspection is a means of bringing negative emotions under control by viewing the disturbing influence from a calmer perspective—hopefully, one is then able to resume activities. Sometimes, however, negative feelings continue to be burdensome, making it difficult or impossible to carry on normal activities.[1] Though a client may exclude intense emotional reactions from conscious awareness, behavior may still be influenced at an unconscious level. The technical term describing this phenomenon is *repression*.

For practical purposes, one who is able to be objective is not under the influence of disabling emotions. The ability to take an objective view of a situation, or of oneself, or of both, is an essential first step toward correcting many self-defeating cycles. Emotionally charged attitudes about one's boss, for example, may so hinder a person that he or she loses effectiveness. This is a power/authority issue. By comparison, a morale/cohesion problem may exist when a person's feelings of self-worth are so low that a sense of helplessness impedes corrective actions.

Problems may develop around norms and standards as well. This issue arises, for example, whenever a person is rejected by his or her colleagues for being a "rate-buster" or a "goldbrick." In both cases an individual is violating group norms by working either too much or too little. Goals/objectives may be the focal issue when a person continuously "fails" because he or she sets out to achieve unrealistic goals.

Problems in any of these four areas can be made even more difficult than the situation warrants when emotions contribute to faulty thinking in the interpretation of what is going on. Frustrations, anger, anxiety, even vague feelings that something is wrong can block constructive problem solving. When a person—or several in a group, or numbers of them in larger social units—is emotionally off balance, a consultant may help relieve the situation by indicating ways of dealing with emotional disturbances.

This relief involves *catharsis* and can be induced by acceptant interventions. Catharsis, a technical term, refers to a process of "cleansing" that brings about a release from tensions. When a client can express and work through the emotions hampering performance or impacting behavior in negative ways, it becomes more likely that the situation can be approached in an objective, problem-solving fashion. In other words, cathartic release permits the client to free his or her thinking from disabling emotions.

Acceptant consultation aids a client through sympathetic listening and empathic support. It might seem that any good friend can do this just as well—but some clients have no good friends and, in any case, the consultant avoids certain actions that friends might take. For example, the consultant does not adopt a partisan point of view and help the person justify the reasonableness of his or her own positions and feelings, thus perpetuating the situation. The client's behavior cycle must be broken, not perpetuated. The kind of acceptance and support offered by the consultant, who is neutral in regard to interpersonal aspects of the focal issue, helps the client relax his or her defenses, confront disabling emotional reactions, and study better ways of dealing with the situation.

Sometimes a person does not talk about how he or she feels but simply opens up in the presence of another person. The sense of being accepted gives a feeling of "safety" not experienced with nonconsultants or when alone. "Letting it all out" reduces emotional pressure and opens avenues to thought.

The following are some ground rules a consultant might establish when working with a client as an acceptant interventionist. He or she:

1. Tries to understand the client's situation from the client's own point of view, without necessarily accepting it as valid for problem solving. This may mean vicarious sharing in the sense that the client becomes aware the consultant "feels" the problem.

2. Practices active listening. Encourages the client to talk more, that is, looks him or her in the eye, smiles, nods acceptance of what is being said, says, "Uh-huh." The consultant may let the client know he or she is listening by responding, "This is what I hear you saying. . . ."

3. Helps the client talk about how he or she sees the situation. Encourages with "tell me more" expressions.

4. Helps the client *clarify* his or her feelings and *accepts* their existence. Says, for example, "You've described the situation. How do you *feel* about it?"

5. Might restate this last remark, if the client falls silent, in a way that lets him or her know the consultant fully understands and accepts—without judgment—what has been said.

6. Stays *out* of participation in the *content* of the client's problem. Neither agrees nor disagrees with what the client says and takes no sides.

7. Might say, "What do you think the problem is? What ways are open for dealing with it?" It is seen as preferable that all diagnosis comes from the client.

8. Expects the client will make progress by this acceptant approach in defining his or her *real* problem and successfully solving it. The presenting problem is unlikely to be the client's real problem. As the client builds skill and confidence in dealing with his or her own frustration, anger, or low self-esteem, the real problem unfolds.

The following example illustrates an acceptant intervention and demonstrates the power of acceptance alone. As reported by Calia and Corsini,[2] the consultant never spoke except to greet the client at the beginning of the session and ask her at the session's end if she wanted to return. Thus there was neither spoken communication of the sort where the consultant listened to what the client had to say and then acknowledged understanding, nor any other overt effort to "help." Rather, acceptance and support, implicit in the consultant's silent presence, constituted the only intervention during the four sessions, at the end of which the client's feelings of depression had lifted and she was able to resume her normal activities.

> In a manner of speaking the incident was nothing, for the girl said nothing when she came in. I mean this literally. She knocked on the door, and I went to open it, and greeted her pleasantly. At my invitation she sat down, and we looked at each other. I waited for her to say something, to explain, complain, or ask questions. I looked at her trying to be as pleasant and as accepting as I could. Her eyes filled with tears and the tears rolled down her face, but she said nothing. I wondered what I should do. The simplest and most natural thing might have been to say, "What is bothering you?" But it must be remembered that I had been trained precisely not to ask questions or to give advice, and so, feeling quite foolish, I just kept looking at the girl. For half an hour, nothing happened. I then said to her, "It is time to end our session. Would you like to see me again?" Somewhat to my surprise and relief, she nodded, and when I suggested another appointment at the same time next week, she nodded again, and went out without having said a single word.
>
> The following session was a repeat of the first one. We looked at each other, she cried silently, I waited, and then she once again accepted my invitation for another session without a word being said. Not to weary the reader, we had two more sessions and they were all exact duplicates of the first two, though several times I thought that the student was about to talk. At the end of the fourth session, when I again asked if she wanted to have another session, she shook her head, and walked out.

The client, a high school student, returned at a later time and reported the following:

> "I want to thank you very much for what you did for me, Mrs. ———."
> "But I did nothing!" I impulsively cried out. "I wanted to so much help you, but I just did nothing but look at you."
> "You did a great deal. You changed my whole personality. That you had the kindness and love to wait for me to talk, to just be there, and not to ask me questions, or try to make me talk, that you were willing to just be there, and not be critical, and not complain that I was wasting your time was the best and most wonderful thing. While we were looking at each other I was thinking how wonderful the silence was, how good it was for you to understand me, and make me feel good and important. I felt you were loving and comforting. I just couldn't talk, and if I had it would have been banalities. Because you valued me so much, that you just were willing to be with me, I realized that my crazy thoughts that no one loved me or cared for me, were wrong. You loved me and you cared for me and you were patient and kind and understanding and warm, and you didn't put any pressure on me or try to get me to talk or to manipulate me. I felt so comfortable with you, and the relationship was so real. No, you did a great deal for me, and as a result I decided I was worthwhile and I was a good person and I was one to be respected, and I was able to solve my problems which I had sorely exaggerated."[3]

This is the acceptant method in an almost "pure" form. The client reveals that the consultant was giving her complete acceptance without reservation or qualification. Within this relationship, she was able to "let go" and to benefit, perhaps permanently, from the release of tensions associated with her feelings of unworthiness. The consultant's acceptance provided a basis for the client to reestablish her own self-confidence and to become more objective and problem solving.

Another client—also an adolescent girl—gives her evaluation of longer-term interaction with an acceptant consultant.

> I've been thinking about what you are to me. It's as though you were myself —a part of me. You're a balance wheel; you're not a person. It's almost as if I were talking to myself, but with someone listening and trying to think on it. I'm not getting rid of anything but a lot of stored up feeling. I don't come for advice. No, sometimes I do. But then I'm conscious that I want advice. It really bothers me when you become a person. What you do is let a person talk and put in comments that keep it going instead of stewing in a circle. That's why I say that you're a balance wheel. It's different now. When I first met you, you were a person. I disliked you because you were touching sore spots. Now I know you'll be a person when I need you to be. Other times you're someone to blow off steam to and to talk to so I can make up my mind.[4]

This client's reaction adds another facet to understanding how the acceptant consultant intervenes. The clue comes from the client's indication that the consultant's active and sympathetic listening and supportive ways of intervening do make a positive contribution beyond simply creating a secure climate where the client feels free to explore personal quandaries. Climate is of undoubted importance, but the point here is that the consultant introduces specific comments to aid the client in moving forward in her thinking rather than moving in circles.

By general attitudes, nods of agreement, positive comments, and by empathic sharing through nonevaluative acceptance of whatever is expressed, the consultant supports the client so that the latter can unload tensions, anxieties, frustrations, and hostilities in a one-to-one situation; or can share such feelings with others in the client membership if several people are involved. The consultant gives no advice and offers no suggestions. It is the consultant's basic assumption that, if done well, the client will be helped to diagnose the situation in a more objective manner, to see what is causing it to be as it is, and to figure out how to improve matters.

Notes

1. J. R. Gibb, *Trust: A New View of Personal and Organizational Development* (Los Angeles: The Guild of Tutors Press, 1978).
2. V. F. Calia and R. J. Corsini, eds., *Critical Incidents in School Counseling* (Englewood Cliffs, N.J.: Prentice-Hall, 1973). Reprinted by permission.
3. Ibid., pp. 7–8.
4. V. W. Lewis, "Intensive Treatment with Adolescent Girls," *Journal of Consulting Psychology* 4, no. 5 (1940): 184.

27

ACCEPTANT
INTERVENTIONS

Power/
Authority

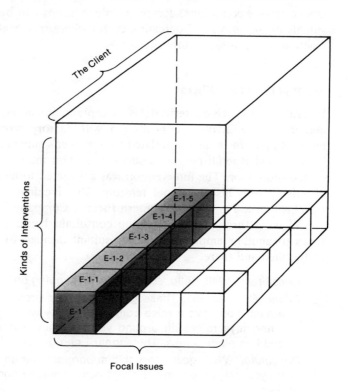

Power/authority is a particularly prevalent source of significant difficulties in modern society. General power/authority problems are two-way in nature. Some persons with power/authority exercise it ineffectively. Other people, who know they are subject to power/authority, have trouble accepting that fact, whether or not the power/authority is presently being exercised upon them and regardless of the manner in which that power/authority is exercised. How people react to power/authority can be a factor in increasing or decreasing their effectiveness, creativity, and personal satisfaction. When attitudes toward authority in general or toward a specific person in authority arouse antagonisms or the sense of being threatened, the subordinate becomes less objectively competent in dealing with his or her situation. Thinking may become distorted, and self-defeating cycles of behavior may result. When these kinds of distortions in thinking and feeling occur, the consultant's task is to intervene in such a way as to release the client from these unproductive reaction cycles. This is so whether the authority is an abstract concept such as "The Establishment," or specific individuals, such as a boss, a parent, a teacher, the police, and so on.

INDIVIDUAL (E-1-1)

Under certain conditions, acceptant interventions can be useful in helping individuals break out of self-defeating cycles where the focal issue is emotion-laden reactions to persons in authority.

Anger at Boss and Others

Several reports characterized as acceptant interventions focus on power/authority. One involves consultation with factory workers. Inside a factory, tensions that are frequently related to a worker's supervisor arise spontaneously. Dickson and Roethlisberger[1] describe acceptant interventions with an employee on the shop floor. The intervention was calculated to help the worker deal more effectively with his emotional tensions. The incident cited here took place in the Hawthorne Plant of the Western Electric Company.

Walking through the plant, the consultant heard Joe talking in emotional tones to another employee. The consultant decided to make himself available to Joe then and there.

Consultant: Well, hello, Joe. What's been going on?

Client: Oh, hell, Bill. These goddam bosses around here, they aren't worth a dam. You have a raise coming and they won't give it to you. They give other guys raises all around you and they won't give you a raise. This goddam place stinks. The sooner I can get out of here the better I'll feel.

Consultant: Well, gosh, Joe, this apparently has got you pretty upset. What do you say we go upstairs and have a smoke and talk it over till quitting time.

The consultant avoided "polarizing" by siding with the boss and getting a rebuff from Joe. Instead, he expressed sympathetic interest and invited Joe to talk. Objectivity was maintained by his not taking Joe's side either.

> *Client:* Well, I'll tell you, Bill. I heard that some of the boys around here got a merit increase in their pay so I simply went up asking for a raise and he tells me that getting a raise around here is matter of luck. Boy, that burns me up. I am working for the Western Electric Company, I'm working, not gambling. If this goddam thing is a gamble, I don't want any of it—I don't want to gamble. I can go across the street here in these dives and gamble my money. I came here to work, I didn't come here to gamble. If it is all a matter of luck, I don't want any of it. I want to get a job where I can work and get ahead on my merit.

A sympathetic attitude coupled with readiness to listen and to "accept" his feelings are all it took to get Joe started toward breaking out of his repetitive cycle by "unloading." The need for recognition based on merit is expressed, even though Joe's anger may be clouding his perceptions of his own (and others') performances.

Joe continues to vent his feelings.

> *Client:* Yeah, it seemed to me as if I had a reasonable squawk why I should get a raise. I simply asked the department chief for a raise and boy, he just flew all over me. A guy that talks like that to me . . . why I haven't any use for him . . . I won't work for him at all. I told him too that he wasn't the Western Electric Company, that he was only a representative of the Western Electric Company, and that I wasn't working for him, but by God, if I can't convince a man like that that I deserve a merit increase, why how in the hell am I ever going to get ahead? He tells me that I am at the top of Grade 34 and I can't get any higher, that's as far as I can go.

The conversation continues in this general tenor for some time. Joe rambles from one complaint to another. Later he begins talking about learning as a means of advancement. This topic leads to expressions of resentment toward the "machine setters."

> *Client:* Why hell, Bill, we don't learn anything—they won't explain anything, they shove you out of the way, they do everything they can to keep you from learning anything, and it is a hell of a hard racket. You know how those machine setters are, especially screw machine men, they won't tell you anything.

The consultant has been actively listening, but often he does little more than reflect his sympathetic understanding of what is being said by repeating it in a way that shows he accepts what he's been told. No "good" or "bad" labels are placed on any of Joe's observations or feelings. At this point, the consultant offers a comment and gauges Joe's reaction.

> *Consultant:* I see. They seem to be pretty selfish about their knowledge of screw machines.

Client: Selfish isn't the right word. They are absolutely tight. They won't tell you anything. As a matter of fact, if you try to learn anything, they try to hide it from you. Take for example, when I got in there, I wanted to get some books on this subject. Now, there is another case too, if the department chief had been on the up and up he could have gotten me some books on that stuff, so I could learn, but no, he sits you down there and leaves you cold. He never would make any attempt to get you to study. The only way I got my books was that another department chief that I used to work for came through our place one day, and he stopped me and he said, "Oh, so you are working on screw machines now." I said, "Yes," and I said, "I would like to have some books so I could read."[2]

Joe's reaction comes through loud and clear. His emotional tensions lead him to gripe about one thing after another. From the consultant's view, this venting of anger is necessary. Joe can't think straight until these immediate pressures have been relieved. Slowly the conversation gets away from gripes, and Joe's energies shift toward problem solving. The consultant still does not offer suggestions. He prefers to help Joe by supportive listening, clarifying, and empathic sharing.

With these tensions off his chest Joe's mind turns to constructive actions he might take. He reaches the independent conclusion that it would be worth his while to have a talk with his department chief. Now he is able to do so more calmly and probably more effectively than if he had tackled this supervisor while under the influence of the emotions that now have been discharged. Afterwards Joe decided to stay on his present job. The consultant contacted Joe several times subsequently, and Joe seemed to be satisfied with the decision he had reached.[3]

This consultant's interactions with Joe were acceptant in nature. He encouraged Joe to talk about his problems yet avoided participating directly in their solution. He neither recommended alternatives nor prescribed actions, but his approach encouraged Joe to think through his situation and reach his own conclusions. Thus Joe retained "ownership" of the problem at all times, and the sense of being personally responsible is an important part of the effort toward change.

Anger at a Teacher

Ginott, a consultant especially concerned with the parent-child relationship, emphasizes the importance of parent interventions of the supportive and accepting kind. By encouraging catharsis, the parent can help reduce the child's frustration and promote a problem-solving attitude.

In this example, a mother is following a recommended intervention, interacting as a professional consultant with her son. Ten-year-old Harold came home from school cranky and complaining.

Harold: What a miserable life! The teacher called me a liar, just because I told her that I forgot the homework. And she yelled. My goodness, did she yell! She said she'll write you a note.

Mother: You had a very rough day.

Harold: You can say that again.

Mother: It must have been terribly embarrassing to be called a liar in front of the whole class.

Harold: It sure was.

Mother: I bet inside yourself you wished a few things!

Harold: Oh, yes! But how did you know?

Mother: That's what we usually do when someone hurts us.

Harold: That's a relief.[4]

Once the child experiences the security inherent in the parent's nonjudgmental *acceptance,* he then opens up. This permits the parent to ascertain the child's true feelings and guide the child toward understanding his frustrations. The acceptant intervention helped free Harold and increase the possibility of his moving forward on his own.

Frustrations toward Parents

Emotional tensions can be so severe as to disorient the child who is too young to cope. Moustakas[5] seeks to intervene in an acceptant way in these circumstances by being passive and supportive while providing a play therapy situation for the young client. This approach appears to encourage the client to talk by creating a situation where children can express themselves in actions as well as words.

A variety of playroom materials such as sand, water, paint, and clay as well as items such as toy guns, knives, and swords are available in the consultation area. Dolls, puppets, and other representations of human figures are often provided for the child to use in whatever way he or she wishes. These props function in much the same way as do auxiliary doubles, alter egos, and so on, in psychodrama. The Axline and Moustakas approach described below, as well as psychodrama, help the client express in words or actions the emotions and feelings causing his or her subjective difficulties. When representations rather than real people are interacted with, the client usually feels very free to respond to them as his or her emotions direct. There are no "others," apart from the consultant, who might get hurt, or would seem to have some capacity for retaliation. A child can stomp on a doll that, for him, is his "real" bossy brother, or plead for affection from "mother" or express fear toward "father," with or without words. The consultant helps the child to release tense, pent-up feelings most likely produced by antagonisms toward authority figures and to experience his or her own insecurities in ways that can restore a capacity for problem solving.

At the beginning of the third session Richard's hostility reached a climax as he screamed out at the therapist: "I'll drill the whole place full of lead! Do you hear me? I'm gonna dirty this place up so far that I don't think you'll be able to clean this stuff up with all the water in the world. I'm gonna really fix this stuff, I'm telling you. I'm gonna mess this room up like a coyote. And then I'll take this jackknife and cut everything up. Then I'll try it on you next!"[6]

The consultant abstains from evaluation. His contribution is in "reflecting" phrases that enable the child to express aggressive feelings. As this progresses, differentiation is often noticeable from the child's initially diffused or indirect expressions to a more focused, direct expression of negative and positive feelings.

Dibs was a five-year-old boy who, for two years, had rarely spoken to other children in his nursery school and acted in such a way as to be classified as mentally defective. The focal nature of the power/authority issue is revealed in Dibs' acting out frustration and fears engendered by punitive parental chastisements at an earlier time. Axline describes how emotions were blocking Dibs' capacity to relate not only to adults but to children as well. The acceptant character of her work with Dibs is shown in the following play-therapy incident that occurred after several months of once-a-week sessions.

Dibs had arranged a tea party on a small table by filling nine plastic cups with water. In one sense Dibs was talking to himself. In another he was talking to his consultant.

"We will use our good tea set, today." His tone of voice changed. It became restrained, a little on edge. He imitated perfectly the precise inflection and expression of his mother's voice. "If there is to be a tea party we will do it properly," he said. "Yes. There will be tea, a little tea in each cup, then fill it up with milk. That is too much tea. I said a *little* tea in each cup, then fill it up with milk. If you want more water, that will be all right. But no more tea. And no arguments." He spooned water into each cup. "Cup six has too much tea," he said, with a note of severity in his voice. "Please remove some of the tea from cup six and follow my instructions more accurately. And that is enough sugar for children. *Enough sugar.* It should not be necessary to repeat everything I say. If you want to have a tea party you will sit down quietly at this table and you will wait until everyone is served. You may have a piece of cinnamon toast with your tea. You do not speak with food in your mouth."

Dibs set the table. He drew a chair up to the table. His manner became meek, subdued, quiet as he drank his tea in the little cup.

He continued in this way until:

he reached across for the toast and upset one of the cups. He sprang up from the table, a frightened expression on his face.

"No more party," he cried. "The party is over. I spilled the tea!" Quickly he emptied the cups and returned them to the shelf.

"The party ended because you spilled the tea?" I asked.

"Stupid! Stupid! Stupid!" he cried.

"It was an accident," I said.

"Stupid people make accidents!" he shouted. There were tears in his eyes. "The party is over. The children are all gone! There is no more party."

His voice chocked on the tears. This had been a very real experience to him. "It *was* an accident," he told me. "But the party is over."

"It frightened you and made you unhappy," I said. "The accident of spilling the tea ended the party. Did the boy who upset the tea get sent to his room?"

Dibs paced around the playroom, wringing his hands. "He did. Yes. Yes. He should have been careful. It was very stupid of him to be so clumsy." He kicked over a chair. He swept the cups from the shelf. "I didn't want a party," he shouted. "I didn't want any other children around!"

"It makes you angry and unhappy when something like that happens," I said.

Then Dibs wanted to get out of the playroom and they went out together. Later, after a long time spent in silence, he began to talk again.

"I'm sorry."

"Sorry? Why are you sorry?" I asked.

"Because I spilled the tea," he said. "I was careless. I shouldn't have been."

"You think you should have been more careful?" I asked.

"Yes," Dibs said, "I should have been more careful, but I am not stupid."

"You were careless, perhaps, but not stupid?"

"That's right," said Dibs. There was a smile on his face.

Dibs had successfully weathered this storm. He had discovered a strength within himself to cope with his hurt feelings.[7]

By not acting as an authority figure, the consultant was able to release emotions and attitudes that probably would have remained hidden and unresolved. In summarizing her work, Axline describes the strategy she used for this and other acceptant interventions.

I attempted to keep my comments in line with his activity, trying not to say anything that would indicate any desire on my part that he do any particular thing, but rather to communicate, understandingly and simply, recognition in line with his frame of reference. I wanted him to lead the way. I would follow. I wanted to let him know from the beginning that he would set the pace in that room and that I would recognize his efforts at two-way communication with some concrete reality basis of a shared experience between the two of us.[8]

Social Withdrawal

Acceptant interventions may produce beneficial effects even with young children who are so seriously disturbed that they are treated in a live-in school devoted to their rehabilitation. Bettelheim describes a treatment strategy that promotes cathartic release through acceptance, yet has significant catalytic elements. Children are attended by counselors, who react to their behaviors in nonjudgmental and supportive ways. For example, they are given full opportunity to vent their hostilities on the counselor, even though these feelings originated prior to their entering school. While such feelings might have arisen first with parents, they often have come to apply to all adults in general.

Bettelheim draws an implicit distinction between criteria for using acceptant and catalytic approaches. His view is that when an expression of hostility can be diagnosed as having some specific cause, it should be answered with a catalytic response. When hostility seems to be of the indiscriminate type, the counselor should be accepting so as to let it flow out.

> If the child's hostility is due to some discomfort that the counselor can relieve either through talking or realistic assurance, the counselor should make an effort to work through the child's hostility and help him with the underlying problem that gave rise to it. But if the child's aggression toward the counselor is more the outward expression of an internal battle between the child's efforts at control and his asocial drives, then it is best if the counselor suffers the child's aggression quietly and submits—as far as he can realistically do—to the child's hostile whims.[9]

Not only hostile, but also fear-related behavior can be addressed through consultant acceptance. These emotions may be most prominent with children as they are waking up. Bettelheim remarks that "All therapeutic functions of the counselor are greatly in focus during the awakening period; it is perhaps the time of day when the child needs his counselor most."[10] An example of this is Walter, aged ten, who is being helped to start a new day.

> Walter seemed to withdraw during the night even more deeply than the others. When he fell asleep at night only his body was covered, but every morning he was all covered up, even his head. His counselor would pat lightly on his blanket and talk softly to him until somewhere from beneath the covers a hand would appear. If the counselor took it and held it quietly for a few minutes, Walter would finally poke his head out. But even after such contact he was still too removed from reality to meet it, and pretended he had gone back to sleep. Repeatedly she would come back to his bed and talk to him for a minute; each time he would again pretend to have fallen asleep, but each time he was in better contact than before. The conversation would increase from a soft "hello," to comments about how he felt and what he might like to wear. Then he would slowly let her help him get dressed, though he was still not quite in this world. She had to help him in orienting himself by letting him find out certain things for himself. He was usually pleased when he had figured out for himself which day of the week it was, and what activities would be going on that day. By then he was ready to get up and start to play, but this process took an average of forty-five minutes.[11]

The approach in this school, then, is for the consultant to help the child perceive the nonthreatening reality aspects of his or her current surroundings more clearly. The child is in control. He or she can "test" the adult-consultant in his or her own way and speed, thereby concluding what is "safe" behavior. This confidence-building support assists the child in reestablishing an internal definition of appropriate behavior. Thus feelings of powerlessness and submission to "powerful others" give way to self-control and self-direction.

GROUP (E-1-2)

The Kuriloff and Atkins[12] study introduced in Chapter 21 with examples of catalytic interventions also contains examples of acceptant interventions that helped release emotional tensions within a management group. Kuriloff had recently become vice-president and general manager of a manufacturing organization, so this group was comprised of his subordinates. Participants were involved in a group session with Atkins as the consultant when the following incident took place.

Helen, the office manager, was talking with Bob, the distribution manager. He had once been her boss, and at that time they had had a good relationship. Helen didn't understand why her relationship with Bob had deteriorated. The unknown trouble between them disturbed her.

> "Bob, I give up," Helen said, painfully and with deep puzzlement. "What do you want from me?" she begged. Bob did not respond. Perhaps the group had shut him up. Perhaps he could not answer. He listened. Her voice shaking, Helen explained that they had gotten along well when they both started with the company a year ago, when she worked for him. What had happened?

Describing his work situation as a never-ending cycle of burdensome responsibilities, Bob responded to Helen, "Every time I get someone trained to help me, they're taken away."

On hearing this, Helen, who was on the verge of tears, was addressed by the consultant, "I have the feeling that you've been wanting to cry."

> "I wish I could," she mumbled. "I'm afraid I'll look foolish."
> "We won't laugh," the consultant promised.
> She began to weep. The group was quiet, apprehensive.
> We waited.
> She stopped.
> Then softly, as she wiped her eyes, she said, "I feel much better. Thank you for being so patient."[13]

The Helen-Bob story doesn't end here, of course, yet progress had been made because a recurring cycle of repeated misunderstandings was brought into the open. After additional interventions, the mutual understanding begun here developed further. If Helen had not expressed the feelings she had been holding back and Bob revealed the frustration he felt, it is unlikely that much constructive progress would have occurred.

Resentment

When the boss of a work team is too "strong," i.e., exercises a high degree of direction and control, frustration and resentment are likely to be generated among subordinates who are afraid to "talk back." Sometimes tight control is on a one-to-one basis rather than on a one-to-all basis, creating suspicion and distrust among team members. An intervention discussed by Margulies and Raia[14] illustrates such a situation.

They describe a catalytic intervention in a utility firm with a client group of clerical personnel and their supervisors. An acceptant incident described below cleared the air and paved the way for increasing effectiveness of the work group. The initial "felt need," a turnover problem, that led to the consultants being invited in by a member of management was *not* the problem they eventually helped with. As they interviewed employees, the consultants found that people in the employment office preferred to talk about their *immediate* problems. The intense reactions provoked by the interviews served as the beginning of the acceptant intervention process.

Having conducted the interviews, Margulies and Raia summarized them and fed back their findings. In this way they were able to focus attention on the stresses arising from a climate of low trust. The consultant's report evoked a sense of despair among participants for it portrayed a situation worse than they had perceived. As often happens, it also generated motivation to do something about this lack of trust. The result was a plan for four meetings over a period of several weeks. Here is what happened in the first session:

> There appeared to be a good deal of anxiety and nervousness in the group. The participants, seated in a circle, clustered in small sub-groups. Barbara, Joann, and Judy, all of whom had come to the employment office less than six months ago, sat next to each other. A second sub-group included Louise, Lorraine, and Pauline. These were "old-timers" who had worked in the office for a number of years. Jerry and Sandy, who had come to the employment office from another department, seemed to be uncommitted to any sub-group and resisted overtures from the other participants. Mary, the selection supervisor, sat tapping a pencil on the notebook on her lap and seemed generally unconcerned. Nick, her boss, the Employment Manager, was also present.
>
> Most of the session was spent struggling with ways to express feelings toward the supervisor.
>
> "Mary," Judy said at one point, "I wish I could tell you how difficult you make it for me around here. And I know that some of the others feel the way I do, but just won't say it."
>
> "O.K.," Mary replied, "Go ahead and say what you want to, all of you. It's your meeting."
>
> "Well, it's *that* kind of comment and the way you look right now that makes it awfully hard for me to say how I feel," said a somewhat flushed Judy. Suddenly she cried to the rest of the group, "Where are the rest of you in this! Doesn't anyone else care about what goes on around here?"
>
> Barbara offered some support. Hesitantly, she said, "Yes, Judy, I do feel the way you do about Mary's behavior. I just wonder if it's worth exposing myself. But I'm willing to try if it will do any good." Several others, in a very detached way, shared some of their impressions of the supervisor's behavior.

Judy's catharis started a process among the women of expressing and sharing their tensions and emotions.

> With some help from the trainers, a few of the participants were able to explore their relationships with the supervisor. Much of the discussion centered around the feelings of frustration and dependency, aroused in the newer girls by what appeared to them to be Mary's persistent need to know everything and to control everyone. Barbara told of how she had cried at home the night before after being "scolded" by the supervisor earlier in the day.
>
> "I only stopped in to ask Judy a question about the interview form," she said to her supervisor, "I was only in there a couple of minutes when you came in and chewed me out."
>
> "Our job is to process those applicants," Mary replied. "If you have any questions, if you want to know something, you should come to me. That's what I'm here for."
>
> Throughout the meeting Nick remained silent. At times, particularly during some of the emotional exchanges between Mary and the younger girls, he seemed uncomfortable. Although Mary appeared to be composed during most of these exchanges, she was visibly shaken at the end of the session.[15]

The authority-obedience assumptions characteristic of Mary's supervision had long prevented the women from giving her any meaningful feedback. Once it started, Mary "heard" attitudes that either she previously had been deaf to, or that perhaps had been hidden from her by the women for fear of consequences. For Mary, such emotional expressions from her subordinates had an "insight" effect. They provided her with information that altered her self-perception. "I didn't know they felt this way," she said to one of the trainers, "I didn't know I was such a terrible supervisor."[16]

Significant changes in Mary's supervision resulted. Morale improved after the clearing-the-air sessions, as did productivity and work satisfaction. With the subordinates less fearful of punitive consequences, it eventually became possible to focus on and successfully solve significant work problems.

Weakness on the Part of the Boss

Fordyce and Weil[17] describe a situation in which subordinates were frustrated because they perceived their boss as too "weak" rather than too "strong." Unprofitable business practices were allowed to continue because the boss took no action to correct them.

A consultant-initiated group activity involved opening communication through cathartic release of emotions. The consultants interviewed members individually, in an acceptant way, about the changes each wanted and how the various team members currently interacted with the top man. These interviews provided an x-ray of feelings and tensions existing within the section and indicated that team members needed the freedom and opportunity to share their anxieties and misunderstandings directly with one another and with the boss.

When the top boss invited subordinates to air their complaints, three major concerns surfaced. First, subordinates felt weak because the boss didn't give them the backing they wanted. Second, they felt blocked when he wouldn't take decisive action to stop what they identified as unprofitable activities. Third, they felt impotent when he failed to follow through on their recommendations to fire incompetent managers. Fordyce and Weil call this airing of feelings a "garbage out" process that helps clear the air.

The consultants contributed (1) by encouraging participants to express their feelings in an unfiltered, authentic way, and (2) by ensuring that participants listened to one another understandingly and appreciatively to hear what was really being said. As participants did this, they began supporting one another in expressing their various feelings and emotions. For example, had the boss in the instance above "answered" complaints or justified them by "explaining" them, his subordinates' frustrations would probably have been increased rather than reduced. The consultants reinforced the free expression of feelings by the nondefensiveness in their own behavior.

Loss of Control

Many times a need for action is recognized, yet group members are hampered by vague fears as to the possible consequences of their actions. Frequently they believe they will lose their present positions, prestige, or control unless they can clearly see how action will maintain or enhance their power. Fear of the unknown has a "better-not-risk-it" effect. Releasing participants from ill-defined fear may be a first step toward progress.

Gibb[18] describes a pertinent situation that illustrates this point. Team building was about to get started in an organization, but there was resistance to participation. This was diagnosed as "fear" by the consultant. He explained the advantage of dealing with fear rather than brushing it aside, for failure to resolve such feelings can result in "foot-dragging," absenteeism from team-building sessions, or taking part with minimal interest and involvement.

Several top managers who were to participate in the team-building sessions came together in a preview session, and the consultant provided them the opportunity to explore as many of their fears about team building as they were able to ventilate. In an acceptant way, the consultant helped participants to share freely their doubts and reservations. For example, managers initially feared that team building could reduce their power to deal with subordinates. These managers were accustomed to boss-determined decisions and one-to-one implementation. They felt that if they began to permit subordinates to have more involvement and participation, poorer decisions might result. After exploration of such feelings, participants began to discover that some of their fears were imaginary. A number of constraints and barriers that might have doomed the team-building program were thus removed, and other more realistic fears were identified and faced as potential risks.

INTERGROUP (E-1-3)

Power/authority dynamics operate between two or more groups just as they do between two or more individuals. Awareness of differentiated degrees of power/authority can produce antagonism on the part of the weaker group. Polarized disagreements or a readiness to defer rather than confront can result. Given this kind of situation, some or most of the associated emotions stay bottled up. Hurt feelings can fester and produce chronic demoralization. When these feelings are prevalent among group members, it becomes necessary to treat the problem in group-dynamic terms. Though it might be possible under one-to-one acceptant consultation to relieve an individual's feelings, he or she is likely to feel alienated from other members upon returning to the group. Former emotions dealt with individually may be reactivated through interaction with these others. The two examples to be presented involve emotions arising between groups of unequal power/authority. In the first example, a union is the weaker party; in the second, a headquarters is clearly the stronger group.

Union-Management Antagonisms

Union-management relationships are susceptible to the kinds of emotional disturbances that provocative win-lose position taking can produce. Frequently, in order for each group to gain something—to win—the other must "give," and giving is often equated with losing. Each new contract-bargaining round begins in the shadow of past embittered contests. Bickering, mutual suspiciousness, exaggerated demands, accusations and counteraccusations have become standard reactions. The true reasons for such emotions and frustrations are rarely even approached in ongoing bargaining.

In the following example, contract bargaining is underway. The situation is more or less hopeless and going nowhere. The management and union representative groups voice their frustrations by griping about one another, yet these expressions give little relief—they are mere wisps of steam escaping from two overpressured vessels. A consultant suggests that both groups take a fresh look by getting away from the bargaining table and sitting down in a special no-bargaining conference. The underlying purpose is to explore, express, and, hopefully, heal the negative feelings obstructing collective action. Union and management agree to give it a try.

Two acceptant-oriented consultants help a cathartic process to take place. One works with the union throughout, joining in both private meetings and face-to-face interactions with management. The other works with management under similar circumstances. Realizing the importance of airing emotions before trying to grapple with operational problems, one consultant focuses the union members' attention on their feelings toward management. He suggests that, "If the relationship with management is as tight and rigid as you report it to be, it is important to start out by examining your own feelings, whatever they may happen to be right now." His open-ended query is, "What are your complaints?"

He goes on, "As you identify your feelings, they can be written on this flip chart. After examining them later you may decide some are repetitious, or that, while true, they are not really pertinent."

As remarks are made, the consultant helps participants enlarge upon their statements by reflecting or restating in different words what he hears being said. In this way feelings and reactions are accurately described. This help is often necessary as members try to express themselves on topics about which they feel tense and blocked. The other consultant follows similar procedures with management.

Having completed this study on an each-group-by-itself basis, they convene in a joint session. To increase acceptance of what is being said, each group "speaks" to the other via its respective selected spokesperson. This arrangement reduces confusion and increases the responsibility for being accurate and for avoiding tension-increasing accusations. Because consultants are not *partisan,* and because they accept each group as sincere, they create a climate of openness and trust even while pointing up emotionally generated aspects of the intergroup tensions. They help reduce the defensiveness that has routinely made it difficult for either group to listen objectively to the other.

During three intense days of union-management catharsis, the "real" problem in communication and negotiation emerged. Union members' distrust of management stemmed from their "fantasy" version of an actual incident that had occurred thirty years earlier.

> "In 1933," the union said to management, "you S.O.B.'s had us down and out because of the depression. And what did you do? You cut everybody's pay in half, and, having done so, then you turned us out into the yard to dig up all the pipe and repack it. How do you expect us to bargain with a bunch of cutthroats that would do that to human beings who are down?"

The managers did a retake. They said, "Oh, but that wasn't us; that was five dynasties ago!" But this disclaimer did nothing to mollify the union. It was a "logical" answer to emotion-based attitudes that had resulted from the story being told and retold for thirty years.

Later, the 1963 management walked the 1963 union back through time in an attempt to reconstitute the thinking that had characterized 1933 management.

> "We shouldn't let people go home with no jobs; we have a responsibility to keep them going somehow, despite hard times. We can't employ them full time because we don't have that much production scheduled—market demand is way down. Rather than laying off people wholesale, the human thing to do is keep people productively occupied somehow. With operational activities currently at such low levels, the only thing we can do that has long-term usefulness is to dig up the yard pipe and repack it for maintenance purposes."

The 1933 management's intentions were probably well-meant, even though clouded by overtones of paternalism. The union's legend regarding those intentions, endlessly repeated, portrayed them as malicious and exploitative.

Eventually the 1963 union, after reconsidering the management's dilemma in that past era, agreed that the prior management had taken a responsible attitude toward employees. Slowly the old legend dissolved.

The emotions and feelings discharged in those three days were intense, deep-rooted, and both potentially and actually destructive. But fantasies of misdeeds from the past finally were unloaded. This cathartic freeing up permitted the bargainers to break their cycle of mutually antagonistic interactions and get back to their deliberations in a more problem-solving way. Only by getting those kinds of emotionally colored misunderstandings into the open, and worked through, was it possible for union and management to restore a businesslike basis of working toward a contract.[19]

Plant Management Embarrassment with Headquarters

Ill feelings and tensions are sometimes characteristic of groups in a hierarchical relationship, one having power over the other. The subordinate group is likely to keep negative feelings hidden for fear of the consequences that might result. The stronger group, of course, is likely to be impatient with and reject what it interprets as criticism of itself.

A hierarchical situation that was improved by acceptant intervention involved a headquarters and a plant. In accordance with a long-term practice that had become tradition, the president and three vice-presidents journeyed to each of the plants on a more or less regularly scheduled basis. The key plant managers convened to work with the visiting "brass." Occasionally these sessions were productive, but over time they had become more a matter of protocol. Agendas were made up on the spot and limited to topics that were *not* likely to touch on sensitive issues. However, this particular year, rather than starting the discussion in the customary way, a consultant (one of the authors) suggested that each group meet separately to review their feelings about the other. The consultant's reason for making this suggestion was to enable participants to clear the air so that when the session moved to an examination of operational problems, they might be discussed in a more open and straightforward manner than in recent years.

Headquarters representatives concluded that although the plant's problems were real and quite serious, their own feelings toward the plant's leadership were on the positive side. They found little to communicate to them on a "feelings" plane. But they said they were prepared to listen.

Not so with the plant's managers, however. Given the opportunity to ventilate, they expressed their feelings in the following way.

> "When you four visit, you embarrass us because you don't act in a business-like manner. You [the President] show up in a sports coat, open shirt, wearing a cap. You other three are comparably informal. This embarrasses us with our own people, for although they work hard, they don't see you taking us seriously. We notice that you don't dress this way in your own office. Many comments are heard about the Acapulco playboys from headquarters.

Not only do others in our own organization feel as we indicate, but we do too. It gives us the feeling that you don't come to visit us for serious business but, rather, as an interlude when you can relax. Our real concern is not with the way you dress as much as with our feelings that the way you dress indicates how you feel."[20]

This catharsis resulted in headquarters management seeing the effect their behavior had upon the plant managers' attitudes toward them. They shifted to a problem-solving basis and developed agreement with the plant's leadership on the importance of increasing the purposefulness of their visits and of dealing with significant matters.

ORGANIZATION (E-1-4)

Many consultant interventions are concerned with power/authority as a focal issue. This is especially understandable in the context of organizations since their operations are usually accomplished through the exercise of direction and control within boss-subordinate relationships.

When the use of power/authority hinders organizational effectiveness, it may become essential to deal with the problem. Unless some action is taken, the potential for synergistic effort toward successful overall results remains impaired. However, the acceptant mode of intervention is rarely utilized by consultants within an organization.

Nonetheless, there have been occasions when this mode has proved useful. Paternalistic organization leadership can stir organization-wide emotions and yet prevent expression of them. By relieving these tensions, energy for constructive action can be released, particularly when new management enters after a departing paternalistic management. This often occurs when a family-owned company is taken over by a publicly owned corporation.

Bartlett describes such a catharsis-inducing experience, implemented through a dramatic acceptant intervention in a company where there had been an influx of new people. The new employees were being assigned by a paternalistic president to take over a number of responsibilities that had been handled poorly in the past.

As Epsilon grew, the Vice President (VP), a fine line supervisor, had gradually been drawn in on managerial problems and policies so far over his head that he began to avoid decisions. As a result, the formal process of decision making had broken down except on a "management-by-crisis" basis. This left each department head to operate like a feudal baron: equal in power, independent, and in direct competition with all others.[21]

In response to the ensuing difficulties, the president had begun importing new personnel to assume various elements of the vice-president's responsibilities. At lower organizational levels, supervisors and foremen had chosen up sides as supporters of the vice-president or the general manager. The general manager had been methods/personnel director before being promoted to his recently created position. Currently the vice-president was reporting to him.

Throughout the organization both open and hidden resentments, as well as procedural confusion made worse by sabotage, were rife. A series of interventions were utilized to reach many levels of the organization membership.

1. Lower-level members expressed their true feelings of frustration to one another on a mutual sharing basis.
2. With anonymity preserved through voice-disguised tape recordings, these expressions of frustrations by lower-level members were fed back to the executive level.
3. An acceptant consultant helped the executive level to "believe" the existence of such feelings and to express their own emotional and other reactions to the expressed lower-level frustrations.
4. The executives were encouraged to ask the lower-level members to continue this process of openness, but on a face-to-face basis.
5. Intermediate hierarchy levels were included to help executive levels become more responsive and to explore and express their own feelings.

This organization-wide catharsis led to a search for reasons why these pent-up emotions had developed in the first place. Solution-seeking proposals to improve operations and relationships followed.

This illustrates in principle that the pent-up and often hostile emotions felt toward people at higher levels who exercise their power/authority in a paternalistic manner can be successfully reduced. Through acceptant interventions, a more constructive basis of relationship can be established, and those who have felt frustrations receive an unprecedented opportunity to ventilate their feelings in a nonthreatening environment.

LARGER SOCIAL SYSTEM (E-1-5)

There are two ways of viewing interventions that deal with larger social systems. The first views a given larger social system as a set of arrangements established to provide members with food, clothing, shelter, and safety. By this concept of larger social system, a community has such properties, as does a nation. A hospital is a special case of a larger social system in that, in addition to providing these basic requirements, it is organized to aid clients to solve mental or physical problems. A residential college or university also qualifies as a larger social system.

Alternatively, larger social systems may be viewed in terms of the numerous individual problems created and perpetuated by the system's existing conditions. This being the case, fundamental resolutions call for system-wide changes. Examples are such current and critical social problems as alcoholism and other forms of drug addiction, delinquency, or underachievement.

Several of the approaches to solving individual problems such as these, which in aggregate are symptoms of difficulties in the larger social system, involve creating special simulated or truncated social systems within which individual members are provided special opportunities and support for breaking out of self-defeating behavior patterns.

Educational Underachievement

Underachievement in high school is a chronic problem facing contemporary American education. Academic failure by students who had demonstrated at least the potential to succeed eliminates their chance of going to college and later entering professional careers. With rare exceptions it means that the under-achiever will be less effective later in life than if the causes of his or her present underachievement could be identified and removed, or significantly reduced.

One focal issue that may be a widespread source of underachievement is negative attitudes held by youth toward authority. An example illustrating this point begins with about a hundred ninth- and tenth-grade students being selected for participation in a summer campus residential program, Upward Bound.

> The students came from poor socioeconomic backgrounds (their parents' incomes all met the Office of Economic Opportunity's poverty criteria), had low educational aspirations, and in spite of their good scholastic potential, most experienced failure in school. A high percentage (22 percent) of the students came from fatherless homes and 45 percent of the families were welfare recipients. Thus, these students suffered not only monetary but also psychological deprivation.[22]

Their attitudes toward authority were either withdrawing or hostile in nature.

> It became apparent from contact with some students that their distrust and fear of authority brought about either total compliance or overt and aggres-sive acting out. Consequently, the students were either timid, submissive, and withdrawn or hostile, defiant, and aggressive. The feelings toward authority manifest in these two types of behavior do not permit the students to function effectively in the public schools, which they reject. The public school system is a middle-class institution. Its classroom size and inflexible curriculum tend to make it highly structured and authoritarian. Therefore, it increases the students' feelings of alienation so that they remain on the periphery, almost completely cut off from the school culture.[23]

In this live-in setting, several features of the social system were utilized as part of the intervention process. One, acceptant in character, involved student government, organized in such a way that the staff could only convey under-standing and acceptance of the students' actions.

> The idea of self-government was presented to the students early in the program but it was adopted only after positive student reaction became evident. There were no preconceived plans or rigid guidelines. The students were allowed to assume the responsibility for their own student council and the staff merely responded to their initiative. The responsibility, powers, and duties of the student council were established through the students' frank discussion with the administration. In general, they were given the authority to exercise broad power in almost every area of the program, except the strictly academic. Mutual involvement was encouraged by which both the administration and student body could raise issues of mutual concern. How-ever, the students after evaluating the staff's opinions were free to make the final decision themselves.

But the students' acceptance of the student council's authority did not evolve easily. Initially, they were resentful of accepting discipline from peers. As one student said, "I resent the fact that I have to be judged by my friends." However, when the student body observed that the staff was supporting the council's opinions and backing its decisions, they began to accept the idea of student authority. The staff's expression of full confidence in the council's decisions greatly increased the council's prestige.[24]

Within this framework of acceptance, group counseling occurred four times a week. It was led by staff members who aided students in expressing feelings about their educational experiences. They could discuss any problems of current personal concern to them.

Another purpose of group counseling was to provide a setting in which the students could express their feelings of alienation from school and their attitudes toward authority and so work through their problems. The group's permissive atmosphere encouraged this. The group counselor as an authority figure was perceived by the students to be representative of society—the teacher, school system, or parent. The group served as an arena in which transference relationships with the group counselor, resident counselor, or other group members were formed. Furthermore, the group counselor could deal with a hostile group without becoming angry, could handle strong feelings without being threatened, and could control the group without punishment. For all the students this was probably a unique experience. The students seemed to be asking the counselors: "Are we backward?" "Are we really hopeless?" The counselors' acceptance of their feelings gave the students reassurance that they were not backward and that staff attached much worth and importance to them and their feelings.[25]

One objective of the summer program was to help participants prepare for entering college. Its emphasis was future-oriented rather than an attempt to rebuild attitudes toward the home environments and public schools. Nonetheless, it was recognized that "looking back in anger," however justifiably, at unfortunate situations of the past can significantly affect one's approach in the present and future. Attitudes can color perception so as to make learning experiences in general seem unattractive. Acceptant interventions can aid the client to see his or her past in a more purposeful way and the now-and-future situation in a more positive light. This appears to be particularly true when the causes of negativism are traceable to disturbed relations between the client and those previously in authority over him or her. The opportunity to experience nonjudgmental, supportive adults in a nonthreatening atmosphere can enable the client to review and reject past-influenced antagonistic attitudes and replace them with more constructive orientations toward authority figures encountered in future situations.

Authority-related issues are also viewed as contributing to delinquent behavior among adolescents. One explanation, applied particularly to youngsters who have never known a self-respecting relationship with grown-ups, is that they are acting out resentments against authority. Peer groups develop which likewise resent what they see as the hypocrisy of grown-ups. Externally imposed authority is accepted by them only in the presence of those able to exert it. As soon as the authority is absent, the youngsters are ready to vent their hostilities in antisocial and sometimes violent ways.

Given this concept of delinquency, what kind of interventions might be expected to decrease readiness to engage in delinquent behavior? Wilson discusses delinquency in a community in Great Britain and suggests how social workers might approach a resolution through acceptant interventions.

> The only possible approach is "permissiveness," out of which may come a measure of self-understanding. But the first effect may appear to be worse, as the youngsters test out the professed goodwill of the worker. This means that the worker must be prepared to bear the most tremendous tensions—from the youngsters testing the worker out, and from the neighbourhood wondering why the worker does not apply "discipline" and resenting more fiercely than ever the appalling behaviour of the gang.[26]

By the consultant's giving warm, empathic, and acceptant understanding, youngsters are provided the opportunity, through catharsis, to ventilate and work through their hostilities. During the initial period, when they are testing the adult's credibility prior to ventilation, the delinquent behavior may appear to worsen. Yet they are simultaneously learning to trust adults who can help them. Wilson points out, however, that citizens of the community, particularly those in positions of authority, are likely to repudiate the "testing" behavior and believe the acceptant interventions are making the situation worse. For this concept of coping with delinquency to have any chance of success, the consultant must be prepared to accept this kind of testing, and members of the community must also be aware of the fact that increased antisocial and destructive behavior may be a prerequisite for establishing the kind of contact that can eventually reduce the severity of delinquent behavior.

The kinds of behaviors that appear in individuals, but that have their origins in malfunctionings of the larger social system, are not likely to be resolved in an effective way solely through acceptant interventions. When such problems become chronic, different kinds of interventions are needed than the sort that releases tensions through modes of emotional expressiveness, talking out, and acting out.

Summary

Rejection by someone who is personally significant to oneself and who possesses power or authority—like a parent, boss, teacher, or older brother or sister—is certainly a distressing occurrence. Why do *they* do it? From the standpoint of the person having authority or power, a refusal or put-down, given without explanation, can quickly eliminate disagreement, reestablish control, and permit "progress" on the authority person's terms. From the angle of the rejected person, elimination of disagreement in this way amounts to suppression, pure and simple. When taken seriously by the rejected person, the message conveyed is interpreted as personal unworthiness, ineptitude, or "wrongness." People find the message implicit in rejection difficult to take. An immediate reaction is to become antagonistic toward the authority person. Often the rejected individual will start fighting back or griping with a bitter sense of personal "rightness." Others may simply walk out, removing themselves from the authority person's field of power and influence, although in situations of childhood and adult dependency this might be a practical impossibility. Still others, accepting the authority of the rejector, seem to conclude that yes, they *are* unworthy. They may buckle under and follow commands, but somehow they are not the same from then on.

Whatever the reaction to being rejected through suppression, strong emotions are involved. Feelings such as resentment, hostility, frustration, or self-rejection in the belief that "I am a worthless person," can lead to unhealthy, unproductive, and even self-destructive behavior.

Intervention by a consultant who is acceptant, particularly when this consultant is also viewed as an expert authority, communicates the very opposite. The intervention says, "Accept yourself and value yourself as a worthy person," a theme that helps the client express and come to terms with feelings provoked by rejection and suppression by authority.

Disruptive emotions can occur whenever one person imposes his or her will on others in a manner that pushes them to do things differently than in the past, and/or in ways they do not fully understand, and/or without perceived opportunities to voice reservations and doubts. In adult life this kind of imposition of will usually comes from one's boss, though it appears that if children could seek out help, they would report similar feelings.

Three kinds of group situations where the focal issue is one of power/authority seem to be helped by acceptant interventions. The first involves tensions in here-and-now relations based on present or former subordinate-boss relationships, as was the case between Helen and Bob. The next two examples illustrated situations in which a common group tension shared by every team member is focused upon the boss. In the utility firm report by Fordyce and Weil, the boss was considered too weak. In the third situation, tensions are shared among equal-rank colleagues engaged in a designated activity. The Gibb example described the use of acceptant interventions to bring out the feelings of managers *prior* to a training activity that they perceived as potentially threatening to their authority.

All three kinds of situations share a common element: the individuals involved have "bottled up" their emotions and have been "blocked" from sharing. Such feelings prevent members from finding immediate solutions and must be worked through before real progress can occur.

The existence of undisclosed feelings often can be accounted for by one of the two interacting groups being and feeling weaker than the other, and/or dependent on the other for its security. The weaker group then avoids open criticism or other overt rejections of the stronger group and hides feelings that might provoke negative reactions. In a similar manner, since the stronger group does not receive emotional feedback, it is likely to come on stronger, sometimes to the point of arrogance. These two basic features of a relationship can result in increased misunderstandings and reduced capacity for problem solving as time goes on.

Acceptant interventions that create a sufficient degree of security for the weaker group to unveil its emotions for the stronger to understand and appreciate can be a sufficient basis for reestablishing mutuality and a problem-solving approach.

Power/authority can evoke strong emotions in persons on whom it is exercised. Reactions include experiencing feelings of self-doubt, fear, alienation, hurt, and even more severe responses that lean in the direction of autistic behavior.

Acceptant interventions may be useful when such emotions are bottled up or otherwise hidden. As we have seen, it is possible for the person experiencing such emotions not to be consciously aware of them; he or she may even deny their existence. Though the acceptant intervention process is often slow and tedious, the client's experience of the consultant and intervention circumstances as acceptant, nonjudgmental, and supportive, offers the security that permits the client to formulate and express his or her feelings. Next, the client may begin to differentiate fantasy-induced emotions from those that might better correspond to "arousal factors" in his or her objective circumstances. When fears and anxieties are not rejected and when the client can express them in a non-self-rejecting way, he or she has taken the first major step toward dealing with power/authority in an objective manner.

Notes

1. W. J. Dickson and F. J. Roethlisberger, *Counseling in an Organization: A Sequel to the Hawthorne Researches* (Boston: Division of Research, Graduate School of Business Administration, Harvard University, 1966), pp. 280–82. Reprinted by permission.
2. Ibid., pp. 280–81, 282.
3. Ibid., p. 287.
4. H. G. Ginott, *Between Parent and Child* (New York: Macmillan, 1965), pp. 27–28. Reprinted by permission.
5. C. E. Moustakas, *Psychotherapy with Children* (New York: Ballantine Books, 1970). (Originally published by Harper & Row, 1959.) Reprinted by permission. C. E. Moustakas, "Psychotherapy with Children," in G. Stanford and B. Stanford, eds., *Strangers to Themselves* (New York: Bantam Pathfinder Editions, 1973), pp. 218–31.
6. Ibid., pp. 35–36.
7. V. M. Axline, *Dibs in Search of Self* (New York: Ballantine Books, 1964), pp. 132–34. Reprinted by permission.
8. Ibid., p. 44.
9. B. Bettelheim, *Love Is Not Enough* (New York: Avon Books, 1978), p. 105. (Originally published by The Free Press, 1950.) Reprinted by permission.
10. Ibid., p. 107.
11. Ibid., p. 111.
12. A. H. Kuriloff and S. Atkins, "T-Group for a Work Team," reproduced by

special permission from *The Journal of Applied Behavioral Science* 2, no. 1 (1966) : 63–93.

13. Ibid., pp. 77–78.
14. N. P. Margulies and A. P. Raia, "People in Organizations: A Case for Team Training," *Training and Development Journal* 22, no. 8 (1968) : 2–11. Reprinted by permission.
15. Ibid., pp. 5–6.
16. Ibid., p. 6.
17. J. K. Fordyce and R. Weil, *Managing with People: A Manager's Handbook of Organization Development Methods,* 2d ed. (Reading, Mass.: Addison-Wesley, 1979), pp. 29–35.
18. J. R. Gibb, "TORI Theory: Consultantless Team-Building," *Journal of Contemporary Business* 1, no. 3 (1972) : 33–41. See also, J. R. Gibb, *Trust: A New View of Personal and Organizational Development* (Los Angeles: The Guild of Tutors Press, 1978).
19. R. R. Blake and J. S. Mouton, "The D/D Matrix," in J. D. Adams, ed., *Theory and Method in Organization Development: An Evolutionary Process* (Washington, D.C.: NTL Institute for Applied Behavioral Science, 1974), pp. 3–36. (Originally published Austin, Texas: Scientific Methods, Inc., 1972.)
20. Ibid.
21. A. C. Bartlett, "Changing Behavior as a Means to Increased Efficiency," reproduced by special permission from *Journal of Applied Behavioral Science* 3, no. 3 (1967) : 383.
22. Y. Bakal, W. Madaus, and A. C. Winder, "A Motivational Approach to Compensatory Education," *Social Work* 13, no. 2 (1968) : 17. Reprinted with permission of the National Association of Social Workers.
23. Ibid., p. 18.
24. Ibid., pp. 19–20.
25. Ibid., pp. 21–22.
26. R. Wilson, "Difficult Housing Estates," *Human Relations* 16, no. 1 (1963) : 33–34. Reprinted by permission.

28

ACCEPTANT
INTERVENTIONS

Morale/
Cohesion

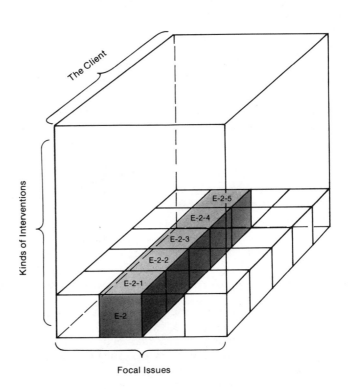

When correlated with objective circumstances, feelings and emotions associated with a sense of well-being or with attitudes of despair can lead to irrational behavior. On one end of the scale, the euphoria of "cloud nine" well-being can lead to mania. The opposite end point—the despair of depression—can result in loss of identity, self-rejection, and personal disintegration. These behavioral extremes and many points between are related to problems of morale/cohesion. Nonadaptive behavior derived from morale/ cohesion issues may characterize individuals, groups, organizations, and even larger social systems.

INDIVIDUAL (E-2-1)

Certain dilemmas people face are associated with low morale. Discouragement on the job, indecisiveness in career choice, demotion, fear of failure, loneliness, and despair are just a few examples. Lowered morale can diminish the capacity to cope with the ordinary stresses and strains of everyday life. It is not surprising, therefore, to find that acceptant interventions are useful in aiding clients to overcome the apathy and uncertainty produced by disabling emotional reactions.

Work Discouragement

Schwartz and Will describe how a nurse was helped to correct a low-morale problem. Miss Jones, after being away from the job for a period of time, returned to her duties eager to get back to work and discovered that the regular charge nurse was away. In her absence, the "disturbed" ward of the hospital was being supervised by a substitute. The ward was overcrowded. There was a shortage of personnel. Preestablished treatment plans were not being fulfilled. The patients themselves were uneasy about the disorganized conditions. Miss Jones thought they had become much more "difficult" than before. Other ward staff members had become tired and discouraged and so were less effective than usual in coordinating procedures and dealing with patient needs.

Miss Jones thought things would settle down in a few days and that she and the staff could improve the functioning and climate of the ward. However, conditions did not improve. Instead, Miss Jones herself gradually became discouraged. By the end of the week she was having the same feelings and attitudes as other staff members. Her functioning was similarly ineffective. She reports,

> I began to be more and more unsuccessful in my relationship with patients. My hostility toward them was most disturbing. I actually began to visualize them as irritating, demanding people. This was sensed by them as they seemed to withdraw from me. Aggressive patients began to snarl at me. Miss F's remarks about my being ineffectual were more frequent and my anger was personal and intense. Disparaging remarks from other patients would upset me and I would keep away from them.[1]

During the second week, she started talking with one of the consultants. During these discussions, the consultant's general approach to Miss Jones was, "If you're able to find out something about the *content* of your low morale, how it developed and what it's related to, you might be able to help yourself and other nurses prevent it in the future." At first Miss Jones found it difficult to express herself. After the first few discussions she was talking more frankly and in detail about her work experiences and the feelings that had accompanied them.

The following provides an example of the consultant's method of intervention during this period. Previously he had observed an incident between this nurse and a patient.

> Breakfast trays were served. Miss Jones brought in Miss Q's tray: "Ready to eat breakfast?" Miss Q did not reply. The tray was placed beside her. Miss Jones started fixing the egg, but did not sit down.
>
> She soon left and went to the office, returning about five minutes later. "You haven't started to eat. Don't you want your breakfast?" No reply. Miss Jones picked up a spoonful of egg and started to feed the patient. Miss Q scooped the egg off the spoon and smeared it on her bathrobe. "Really, Miss Q, you can do better than that." Miss Q started muttering and holding on to her dish of eggs. "Damn it, damn it." The next several spoonfuls she refused. Miss Jones walked away, saying, "I'll check back in thirty minutes for your tray." However in about five minutes she returned with some hot coffee. "I brought you some more coffee." Miss Q was still sputtering and as Miss Jones approached her, Miss Q threw the tray of food on the floor.

Later, in terms of the approach he had suggested, he asked the nurse how she had experienced the incident. She replied,

> It had a lot to do with how I was feeling, I think. I certainly didn't approach her as I had before. I got sort of tired of her messing around, I guess. As I cleaned up the food, I was not really angry. I felt I didn't care if she ate her food or threw it at me, and I didn't speak to her or offer to get her more breakfast.
>
> I didn't report this incident or put it in the patient's record, partly because I felt I had failed and partly because I felt no one else would care, or read the notes. Also I felt rather isolated from the rest of the personnel and didn't want to discuss the problem with them or seek their advice.[2]

The opportunity to ventilate her feelings was a source of relief in itself, for up to this point the client had concealed her anger and resentment. In the course of her "talking out" experience, she noticed that the consultant voiced no criticism; consequently she had no need to feel defensive. She felt increasingly comfortable in exploring her own feelings, and found they did not seem as "terrible" as she had previously thought. This in turn made it easier for her to share with another person her sense of personal failure.

After several discussions, both consultant and client noticed some positive changes. Participation with other staff members and patients improved significantly. As the discussions continued, freedom to fully express feelings continued to be reflected in positive behavioral change. After a couple of weeks, performance reached previous levels of effectiveness. By intervening in a nonjudgmental, supportive way, the consultant was able to help Miss Jones free pent-up emotions and regain a positive outlook on her work situation. How the consultant helped Miss Jones alter her work-related behavior through a catalytic mode is described in Chapter 22.

Indecisiveness

Indecisiveness, as it relates to a career choice, may cause low morale and indicate deeper uncertainties about one's own competence. Feelings of failure "before the event" may result in a person's continuing to drift through life rather than attempting to shape his or her future. Vocational counseling can sometimes aid a client in making a career choice, but this is not always so. The following example occurs during an interview in which the topic being discussed by the student is the grades he is making in his college work. The conversation's wider context, however, regards study habits, attitudes toward school, and choice of a career. Another acceptant intervention approach to a focal issue of low morale is illustrated by the following.

> *Consultant:* Sometimes you feel that way about your courses, and sometimes you don't.
>
> *Client:* Yeah, that's right. Sometimes it looks like everything is against you and other times everything is pulling for you, but I like all of my studies this quarter, so that should be in my behalf or something.
>
> *Consultant:* Perhaps that makes it a little easier to put off the problems you'll meet at the end of the quarter.
>
> *Client:* Yeah. I believe it would. *(Pause and laugh.)* At the end of the quarter I'm going to have the problem of what to take next quarter and all that.
>
> *Consultant:* You don't like to think about that, though, do you?
>
> *Client:* No, boy! *(Laugh.)* I don't like to think about that until I come to it. Oh, I've been thinking, when I had some free time, trying to figure out what to take next quarter and all that, but oh, I don't know, it's a kind of material you want to put off.
>
> *Consultant:* You want to put it off if you can?
>
> *Client:* That's right.
>
> *Consultant:* That's one of the things that—
>
> *Client:* You shouldn't do, I know.
>
> *Consultant:* No; well, you feel that people would disapprove of it. That's one of the reasons why you feel two ways about coming in for an appointment like this, because here there's always a risk you might get to thinking about some of those problems that you'd rather put off.
>
> *Client:* Well, that might be, I doubt it.
>
> *Consultant:* It is a lot more comfortable to put them off, isn't it?
>
> *Client:* Yeah, that's right. But people—*(pause)* and it would be better for you if you wouldn't put them off, that's one sure thing.

Consultant: But it takes a lot of courage sometimes, to really think them through ahead of time. *(Very long pause.)*

Client: About this question of studying, do you think—ah, what do you think is the best way to study for a midterm? Do you think you ought to make an outline of the material you've had and then go through that outline and the parts you don't know, or . . . *(He continues in this vein.)*[3]

This episode exemplifies the use of an acceptant mode to help solve a dilemma that has been reducing morale. The "lead" in defining the content to be discussed remains with the student. The consultant's contribution is active listening and restating and reaffirming what the student has said. Carried out empathically, this approach is sufficient to give the client a lift in morale and permit him or her to face the real issues in the situation.

Demotion

Promotion often produces a sense of elation and joy because it signals to a person that he or she is well regarded by those in supervisory positions. Demotion, unanticipated early retirement, or firing can arouse feelings of rejection and self-doubt. Even though the demotion or separation may be unrelated to the individual's competence or abilities, adverse personal actions are generally interpreted as implying that one is neither valued nor appreciated.

Golembiewski, Carrigan, Mead, Munzenrider, and Blumberg[4] describe a situation in which people were offered a demotion as an option to early retirement or separation. The consultants discuss what they did when the reality of the situation brought individuals face-to-face with doubts about their personal adequacy, worth, and value to the organization. The intervention proved useful in fostering the readjustments that demotion required.

The first step toward helping those demoted to adopt a more realistic attitude toward their new jobs was to assist them in expressing and working through the tensions, frustrations, and hostilities aroused by the implication of rejection. That step was followed by further cohesion-building through direct contact with the employee's new boss. The initial supervisory/employee meeting was conducted in such a way that harmonious, even warm, feelings arose. Those affected came to appreciate receiving helpful support from their new bosses, who were compassionate and sympathetic rather than criticizing and pressuring during the transitional period. The general method, rather than a sink-or-swim approach, was to help employees deal with emotions engendered by self-doubt. By actively planning with their supervisors, the employees found ways to remove potential barriers to future success. This action-planning component of the intervention was catalytic in character, as will be described in a later chapter.

Fear of Failure

College students, living in a relatively free environment, enjoy a substantial degree of autonomy. Sometimes, problems of low morale can prevent a student from exercising the autonomy necessary to maximize his or her own learning and growth. In academic settings, acceptant interventions have long been relied upon to help such students "find" themselves after emotions have blocked learning.

> Paul, a college student, comes to the counselor without an appointment and says that he is feeling desperate. He feels he is under much tension, he cannot face social groups, his hands sweat, and so on. An appointment is given for the following day and the student comes in for his first interview. This initial interview commences as follows (phonographic recording):
>
> *Consultant:* Well, now, yesterday I sent you off before we really got started talking. This will be a good time when we can talk things over. Do you want to tell me what's on your mind?
>
> *Client:* Yes. I told you that I experienced—uh—excessive tension whenever —uh—my personality to any degree is concerned, that is, whenever I— uh—when any issue was at stake, even if small, it's—uh—exceedingly gotten worse, and as I told you it's become quite unbearable, and I really have to do something about it, because I'll make a perfect flop of my college career. I can't waste my father's money.
>
> *Consultant:* You really feel it's interfering a lot with your college career?
>
> *Client:* Tremendously, oh, tremendously. I'm—uh—in some subjects I'm failing which I wouldn't fail, I'm sure of, if I wasn't feeling this way, and I'm so despondent and I haven't got any morale at all. *(Pause.)* As examples, I can't get up, I told you I couldn't get up to a blackboard and illustrate problems which I knew very well, and when I was called I was so tense that I couldn't think straightly and—uh—it seems all out of proportion—this tension.
>
> *Consultant:* In what way?
>
> *Client:* I said I couldn't even go into a restaurant without feeling tense, which seems very queer, but I—uh—that's the problem I'm confronted with nevertheless. *(Pause.)*
>
> *Consultant:* You feel you've gotten to a point where you've just got to do something.
>
> *Client:* Yes, I have to, definitely. It's been going on, I should say—I can recall I was twelve years old, the first time, when I was asked to read a— a—composition that I did. I was rather proud of it, and when I got in front of the class, why—uh—my hands started shaking like anything, and I had to sit down. I was extremely humiliated, too.
>
> *Consultant:* You felt very much humiliated.
>
> *Client:* Very much so.
>
> *Consultant:* In what way?
>
> *Client:* In the fact that I felt abnormal, because everybody else could do it and I couldn't.[5]

Paul is sufficiently distressed about the situation as to be eager to talk about it. With the supportive listening of the consultant, Paul is able to move toward a more focused definition of his problem. He learns that the character of his tensions, related to feelings of low self-worth, is out of line with the actual demands of the situations he faces. Through this insight, Paul is able to trace his feelings to an earlier, unrelated experience. Having knowledge of the problem's source, he is able to work toward its resolution.

Lack of Confidence

Low morale and reduced self-worth can stem from relations with parents and friends if the client feels duty bound to fulfill their expectations, yet is unable to do so. Although power/authority dynamics may have caused the problem, the intervention that helps resolve it may focus on morale/cohesion aspects. Once self-confidence has been increased, the client may be able to grapple with the basic problem.

Ginger, a sixteen-year-old, above-average student, exemplifies this. In a group consultation session:

> . . . the leader mentioned she looked depressed, and while she denied it, she seemed willing to talk if the leader was interested.
> After a little coaxing Ginger described herself as feeling that "I don't really exist." Everything she did was for other people—although, she quickly added, what they wanted was the right thing, so she did not mind. She said, "I would probably do them anyway, but they won't let me decide." She described her parents as genuinely concerned but very covertly making demands on her, at the same time denying that they were making demands.
> She talked about her Sunday-school group, how kids in it were wasting time, not doing anything in particular, and how she felt that she could not make them change. Essentially, Ginger felt powerless with both her friends and her parents, fulfilling their demands, living a life over which she had no control, unable to be angry because she was only being asked to do things that were for her own good.
> Ginger's twisting a piece of paper, her expression of sadness which her face assumed when she did not know she was being watched, her helplessness, all disappeared when she began to express her anger, resentment, and frustration—feelings she had never felt comfortable in expressing because they seemed "wrong" and "I feel guilty because they only try to do what is right for me." As they talked about the ways her parents gain (in pride, satisfaction) from her successes, she began to see that their statements of selflessness were not entirely true, and she began to feel that she could now express more of her resentment at their pressures upon her.[6]

Two weeks later Ginger told the consultant she had talked with her Sunday school class about her criticism, and they had responded to her suggestions. She also had been able to talk with her parents about their expectations regarding her school and social life. The consultant concludes:

> The issue of resentment and demands continually occurs with young people, who often bury their anger because they feel guilty about it, as Ginger did. Demands are often covert, understood, or they are covered over with disclaimers of any gain for the person making the "legitimate expectation"

demands. However, with Ginger and many others, the inability to comment directly on demands made on them creates a general state of confusion and helplessness, and often a vague feeling of emptiness, of being a form existing for, and conforming to, outside pressures, with no existence within itself.[7]

Shyness

Shyness is a problem that is receiving an increased amount of attention, and a number of approaches for relieving it are under experimentation. One approach, which is applicable to any focal issue, can be illustrated by demonstrating its use with shyness.

Psychotheatrics is an acceptant intervention that breaks new ground. By comparison with psychodrama, in which a professional director supervises the client's reenactment of his or her focal issue and uses auxiliary egos to support the client in playing out his or her problem, there are three quite different kinds of psychotheatrics, all of which are distinguished from psychodrama.

In *playwright psychotheatrics,* the client is the author of his or her own drama. He or she directs the cast in how to understand the drama and provides the supervision for its enactment. By doing so, the client lives out his or her own problem but in such a way as to gain deeper understanding of what is going on among the principal characters in order to resolve the focal issue.

Spectator psychotheatrics is a variation of the same basic theme, but, except for the role of client, is more like psychodrama. A group of alcoholics, for example, may enact the focal issue of one member whose real-life drama is being portrayed by the person authoring and directing the entire activity. The others take parts in the drama. In the end critique, which is called *coalescence,* they can connect the experience to situations arising within their own lives. By comparison with psychodrama, the others are similar to auxiliary egos, but with the twist that all of them share in common the same basic problem and therefore all of them stand to gain benefits from their participation. The client acquires the same benefits as in playwright psychotheatrics.

The third form is called *environmental psychotheatrics.* Now the client authors and directs a dramatic enactment in which he or she is depicting how and what would result from implementation of the ideal solution to his or her own problem.

There are three phases in the total sequence that make up any one of the three versions of psychotheatrics. The first is preparing the drama. The second is the client-directed enactment. The third is the discussion of the play as a coalescence, meaning critique and generalization by each participant of what has been learned.

The professional in charge supports the preparation, enactment, and coalescence, but the initiative throughout remains wholly in the hands of the client.

Psychotheatrics can be applied in dealing with any focal issue. The following illustrates its use in a morale/cohesion setting where the client wants to develop better relationships with those around him.

Jeffrey, a client in a day treatment center, was engaged in counseling about his main fear—that of "getting along with people." In formulating a problem to work on in a psychotherapeutic situation, he described his inability to go to a neighborhood teen dance and ask a girl to dance.

Jeffrey said, "They might laugh at me; the girl might say 'no.' Then what do I do?" I decided this was the situation to confront if Jeffrey was ever to realize his goals. If he could get through that door at the dance, then many other doors might open up for him.

. . . By putting this situation into action, I felt we might be able to break through the impasse. Stress about the situation should be reduced if Jeffrey could experience both negative and positive outcomes. Demystifying the unknown could render it powerless.[8]

Two colleagues of the counselor in the treatment center acted as Jeffrey-player and Denise-player, a girl with whom Jeffrey wanted to dance. After sketching out the situation, the counselor helped Jeffrey direct the action.

I first told Jeffrey to direct the situation in which he would go up and ask Denise to dance, and to have it be the worst possible situation he could imagine. Jeffrey, sitting on the edge of his chair, subjectively directed the action, and objectively watched it take place. The worst possible situation to Jeffrey was having himself stutter when he asked the woman to dance, then having her make fun of him by saying, "No, I don't want to dance be-cause I don't like people who stutter and who have 'zits.' "

Next I had Jeffrey direct the best possible situation, and he readily did. This time he did not stutter and the woman happily accepted. Everything was very smooth. Next I had Jeffrey direct a scene midway between the worst possible and the best possible situations.[9]

The same scene was repeated a number of times with many variations in the possible sequence of events and outcomes with positive consequences for reducing Jeffrey's fears.

After talking for a while, it became clear that this situation that had been vital just a few minutes before was now a "joke" and no longer fearful. Jeffrey had been desensitized.[10]

This is a new and innovative approach for dealing with focal issues. It holds much promise for aiding clients to address and resolve problems through better understanding of self and others.

Loneliness

When the client is facing an immediate crisis, telephone counseling permits the person to contact quickly a professional for help.

Whenever a caller presents a specific difficulty, the staff member's interest increases. Results are tangible, some sort of resolution is possible within the period of one call. Common experiences leading to the typical crisis call

are loneliness, confusion, anxiety, and depression, while the typical problems fall under four categories: self, others (sexuality), parents, school. The
following example comes from Number Nine's phone log.

10:00 p.m. Girl, Jane called. 16 years old. She was very lonely and afraid
to talk, but wanted to. She says she can't relate to people, and feels withdrawn. She said she feels like she's falling off a cliff backwards and can't
feel anything. She talks about animals and really digs them, but all of a
sudden, after talking for 45 minutes she just withdrew, and wouldn't talk
anymore.[11]

In time, the crisis counseling led to the consultant's assisting through extensive acceptant interventions. Telephone counseling continues to provide quick
access to persons in crisis and it is often enough to swing the balance away from
impulsiveness and emotion toward logical analysis and rationality, at least
until further help can be provided.

Despair

Numerous people have resorted to drugs as an avenue of escape from life.
However, handled in an accepting way, the drug experience may provide insights that restore a sense of self-worth. An example is fifteen-year-old Sara,
who tried LSD out of a sense of despair and began what evidently was a "bad
trip." Her friends took her to a crisis center, where several consultants assisted
by encouraging her to express the thoughts and feelings she was experiencing.
Many of these thoughts and feelings had been "buried." They concerned matters
of sex, both in aspects of her childhood upbringing and most recently with a
boyfriend who had rejected her, wishes for greater intimacy with her parents,
guilt about physical exposure, and so on.

Sara's account of what she felt during her trip (taped when she returned
two weeks later) shows the importance of setting in transforming an initial
negative set.

"I was feeling very depressed, and I had tried to kill myself, so I thought
I'd just become an acid head or speed freak or something. I expected it to
be like going crazy and I was surprised it turned out so different, because
of the state of mind I was in. Maybe it was the surroundings. I'll never forget
what happened in that room, because it's been so important to me . . ."

At first Sara huddled in the corner and cried out in Spanish, her negative
language which she had not used regularly for years.

"Mike Samuels I love you. I need you. I want to die." Yvonne was called
in because she is Spanish also, and Jerry and Billy, two other staff helpers,
also came. Sara repeated those phrases in a common trip sign of a wish
(in this case for love, closeness, and sexual pleasure) and fears and guilt
associated with satisfying it (punishment by dying), which indicates that the
conflict is not being resolved. Yvonne encouraged Sara to express the feelings she blocked and work through a fantasy solution, which will then be
vividly remembered as the experience which resolved the conflict.

Sara was afraid and in need of support and security. She was on such a regressed level that the most meaningful support would be physical contact with a surrogate mother (of either sex). Yvonne took this role, telling her not to be afraid and bathing her hands and feet with a wet handkerchief. Yvonne saw her withdraw slightly, and took this as a sign that she was working on negative feelings about touching her body. It is easy to build rapport with someone who is tripping, even when the guide and tripper have never met before, because the tripper relates to people mainly as fantasy versions of parents and other important figures in his life.

Mothering is best when it is physical and direct. Words are confusing and often not understood, because the tripper may regress to a period before language. The integrity and self-awareness of the guide in this role is critical. He or she must move with the tripper, not seeking power or advantage over him because people on psychedelics are usually sensitive to such maneuvers . . . A mother surrogate, whose love is more unconditional than the original, can undo some of the damage in people who are much more fearful than Sara. The trip out of psychosis, while much longer, can be similar and demands the same kind of patience from the guide-mother.

Once contact is made, the guide can tune into the conflict the tripper is experiencing. There are only a small number of themes which make up the human condition, though they exhibit infinite variations. Since they involve sexuality, guilt, union with parents, or desire for closeness and intimacy, the guide can test for the relevant theme by suggesting phrases which relate the tripper's words or actions to possible sources of the conflict; he can then judge from the reaction whether the supposition is correct. If the theme suggested by the guide is not relevant the tripper will simply ignore it, since LSD frees one almost totally from social games and polite conversations. Under acid all relationships relate directly to central needs.[12]

Sara's report of her experience in retrospect includes the following.

When she came back two weeks later, she was beaming and smiling, wearing colorful clothes and a bright rainbow shawl. As she thanked us for the experience, her face was as radiant as it had been during the trip, in sharp contrast to the subdued demeanor before and immediately after it. Her account validated our impression of the significance of the trip, and of the amount she had uncovered and learned to accept about herself.

She ends her narrative with these conclusions:

"Right after the trip I didn't really know what I had done, but felt guilty anyway. When I woke up it was so different. Then I started reconstructing things, and I realized it was true, that's your subconscious and that's how you feel. I started feeling that we really have to live to satisfy ourselves. Not be selfish you know, but you can't satisfy anyone if you're not satisfied yourself. That's my main goal now. Before, I was so afraid of being hurt that I built this wall and made myself a prisoner in it. I've changed now. Like before I'd just nod. My feelings have been blocked and sterile. I couldn't communicate with people. Like I wanted to shout 'I love you' or 'I just want to hold your hand' or something like that, but I couldn't because I was so restrained. We have only one of those things we call lives, and we breathe and walk around and things like that, and poof, it's gone. As far as I'm concerned there's nothing else, as far as positive proof is concerned, so I'd better make sure I make something of it, enjoy myself."

The trip intervention turned what was intended as an act of self-destruction into an opening-up peak experience. Because of her tremendous insight and capacity to integrate learning, Sara has since been freed to trust people more and to express herself without drugs, and she has no desire to trip again. Through counseling and group experience at Number Nine, she continues to relate her insights to her everyday life. She contacted her parents and told them about what she is doing and about some of the feelings she was holding back. She visited home, and her family agreed that she could continue to live in New Haven in a residential job-corps program.[13]

This process of nonjudgmental, understanding-based acceptance permitted Sara to rediscover buried thoughts and feelings. By talking and acting them out, she was able to assess and to replace them with functional ways of thinking and feelings that are basic to sound adult adjustment.

Gordon offers an acceptant-consultation strategy useful to teachers dealing with classroom relationship problems. First the teacher decides "whose problem it is." The problem belongs to the child if it impedes learning but has no deleterious impact on other students or the teacher. It is the teacher's problem if the student's behavior impedes either the teacher's effectiveness or the classroom learning opportunities of others. In the first case the child-as-client is dealt with through acceptant interventions. Confrontation is the intervention approach in the latter case.

An example of acceptant intervention concerns a student having difficulty finishing a school project. The consultant, a classroom teacher, is talking with a girl about producing the school paper.

Client: I'll never get the paper out. I think I'll quit.

Consultant: (Silence, nods)

Client: I've been here since three this afternoon. Everybody else split. They seem to think because I'm the editor that I have to do all the work. That's a bummer.

Consultant: Uh-huh.

Client: Ellen didn't get the typing done and Maryanne still has to do those layouts—and look at that mess over there that Steve calls the sports page.

Consultant: (Nods)

Client: (Pause) The problem is that everybody is waiting for somebody else to do something. We need a list of things that have to be done and the order they must be done in. That way everybody will be able to see what the next job is and who has to do it.

Consultant: I see.

Client: I can make the list at home tonight. See you tomorrow.

Consultant: Right.[14]

Encouraged by this nonjudgmental attitude of acceptance, the client discovers a personal solution and is freed from the tensions that were negatively impacting morale a moment before.

Walling Off Emotions

For years, an author had been unable to establish a realistic basis of adjustment even though her psychiatric treatment had been extensive. Depression led to drinking, drinking led to further withdrawal in a series of ever-deepening cycles. While past treatment had involved conversational efforts, the new format, predicated on a nonverbal acceptant approach, was calculated to assist the client in experiencing her emotions more directly, with acceptant interventions provided on a nonverbal basis.

In expressive therapy interventions, the client expresses himself or herself by using media with which he or she has little or no prior experience—clay modeling, water colors for painting, or dancing either by oneself or with others. Whatever the medium, the client must deal with it in an expressive way, and as a "primitive" artist because it is an unfamiliar form. He or she does not have a programmed way of response, stereotyped or stylized over the years. Such neutral media for artistic expression can be used in conjunction with a consultant who aids the expression of buried emotions by helping the client feel it is "safe" to reveal his or her feelings. In the following example, the author/client learned to get in touch with her emotions through a variety of methods.

Her first experience was with dance therapy. She went through a practice session believing that she was doing well. However, the instructor's evaluation was "Professorial, knows it all." Apparently, expressiveness was lacking. The following passage is the client's description of the consultant's facilitative efforts.

> The next hour J. had me lie down on the floor and close my eyes. I was to feel my body touching the floor, the back of my head, my shoulders, my arms, my back, my buttocks, my thighs, my legs, my heels. Then I was to open my body to the air, to let it touch me all over, let it caress me. As I was lying spread-eagle fashion, J. said all the parts of my body where the air was touching my skin. She then put on a record, and asked me to imagine that the music was flowing over me. Music soon turned into waves; I saw myself at the edge of the ocean; waves were lapping over me, washing me back and forth. I felt like crying.
>
> It seems to me now that it took me a long time to cry, to be angry, to be sad, to be sensuous. I had always *felt like* crying, being angry, or being joyful. I had screened myself from perceiving motion and emotion and regarded the former as merely useful or necessary, the latter as an uncomfortable hindrance at best, a weakness at worst. At first, after an hour of beating in anger on a beat-up bed, of shouting, of moving sensuously, of dancing with exhilaration, I felt rather guilty, even though I thought I had repudiated prudishness.[15]

Later, the consultant provided acceptant support while the client enacted her recollections of anger and rage.

Anger caused us more trouble in acting out than anything else; perhaps, I should rather say rage. What is so frightening is not only the realization of one's destructiveness and one's fear of retaliation, but also the terror of losing control and of never regaining it. Let me illustrate. I dislike myself worse when I felt in myself reactions, belief patterns, which consciously, I rejected years ago. They are residues of my mother's influence upon me that I experience as alien. I should add that some of my mother's *traits* in me do not provoke such self-dislike. I demonstrated to J. a childhood day when I was ill and my mother's reaction to my illness. I was the child in pain; I was the mother calming down the child. I stopped the acting-out, too petrified to go on. I felt I was entering a terrible darkness that I could not tolerate. J. told me that she would go into the darkness with me. Her words felt like the hand of my brother to whom I had clung when small and frightened.

I reenacted the scene and this time *played* it through. When the mother admonished the child to be quiet and not to make a fuss, the child stopped crying and went rigid. The mother continued saying: "See, there is not much the matter with you, you are quiet now." I felt the child get up and hit out at the mother, hitting to kill. Beating and trampling about, I saw a bloody body; as this image came, I felt sick with fear and collapsed sobbing. J. held me in a manner that conveyed to me that she believed the reality of my feelings, the pain, the rage, the fear and the grief. She was not afraid of these feelings in me, hence not afraid of losing control. Since this was so, I could let her take care of me.

It does not really matter whether or not this incident constitutes a memory of an event that happened—namely the child pleads for help, the adult denies the plea and hence the child's feelings, the child believes that in her rage over the denial she has killed her mother. What does matter is that this scene showed the essence of the child's relationship to her mother; a denial of emotion and its reality on the part of the mother; a cutting off of emotions and an underlying rage that is perceived as omnipotent by the child. It does matter that J. believed the emotions, accepted them as real and was not afraid of losing control. She provided me with the consolation and courage that my brother had given me, a help I could accept in the initial stages of the scene.[16]

The focal morale/cohesion issue has now become a power/authority issue, showing the close linkages between these two focal concerns.

Both clay and wood carvings were subsequently used to express in art form what the client had been unable to put into words.

Let me summarize: In the last few years I have learned to express my emotions in a way that is meaningful to me and to my friends. As the art work gave clearer expression to my emotions, I became more comfortable with myself. My life is taking on a new shape, I am beginning to know what I need and I feel surer of the ways to satisfy my needs. The need to dull emotions by alcohol disappeared. Expression of emotions is not restricted to working through a medium: clay, wood, or words; it is not a substitute for relationships to others. I can equally well express emotions through touch or words, for I have gained the assurance that whatever expresses me honestly is acceptable. Sculpture or a piece of writing are merely more durable and they may reach more people.[17]

Finally, the significance of the consultant's or the paraprofessional consultant's acceptant mode of relating, and of group support as well, is pointed out.

The art therapist need not be a person trained in artistic skills. It is best if she is a patient with artistic inclinations who is a little further along in her therapy—she has been there, she knows what mental illness feels like, she can encourage expression, she is not afraid of emotion. It is wise not to ask the patient to pursue a skill he had before therapy. If I had tried writing as a medium of expression, I could not have done anything with it, it had ceased to help me express myself; know-how and long habit had removed feeling expression from it.

Finally, it is important that several patients share an art activity, explore the possibility of new media, and share the enjoyment of their new discovery. An analogy with a supportive family describes the situation best; the therapists as parents encourage emotional expression and provide means for such expression; fellow patients like siblings participate in and enjoy together a common task. All members of the family support the achievements of each individual.[18]

Various nonverbal expressive modes for intervention seem to be quite useful in working through emotional difficulties when the client is blocked in some way from discussing his of her feelings directly with the consultant. In one respect, it is similar to play therapy as described earlier (Chapter 27) by Axline and Moustakas in connection with focal issues in the power/authority area. The consultant's role of nonjudgmental support makes it possible for clients to "be themselves" and thereby gain release from tensions. A significant difference lies in the client's attempt, as expressiveness increases, to translate this experience into some unique creative "product" of feelings that represents integrated-whole *outcomes* of therapy rather than fragmentary episodes within it.

GROUP (E-2-2)

Inappropriate use of power/authority, whether it be between persons of equal rank or between a boss and a subordinate, can result in problems involving issues of morale/cohesion. In the first example given, involving a team-building session, the consultant sought to ease antagonisms that group members were developing toward one another. In the second case, an organizational situation was so fraught with negative aspects of morale—i.e., frustration, antagonisms, internal conflict, suspiciousness, and hostility among work team members—that work was disrupted.

Interpersonal Tensions

As illustrated below, team building is one approach for investigating how feelings among team members influence their effectiveness. Interpersonal skills for dealing in a more constructive way with interpersonal tensions can also be developed.

> B is a drawling Texan who had the habit of accentuating points in the group by telling rather long and very funny stories ranging in dialect from Texan to Irish to Cajun to Jewish. Each story was followed by widely shared group laughter, although some group members, A in particular, appeared to be getting annoyed at the amount of group time being taken up by B. The group had discussed some of their reactions to B's storytelling behavior for about twenty minutes when the following interchange took place. [C denotes comments made by the consultant.]
>
> A (to B): It just seems to me that you might be more effective if sometimes you came right to the point. Some people might not enjoy your stories and might not understand what you were getting at.
>
> B: Didn't you enjoy them?
>
> A: Oh yes! I think they're great, I wasn't talking about me; I was thinking of other people who might not appreciate . . .
>
> C: Well how did you feel when B was telling his story?
>
> A: I felt he might be more effective if he came to the point more directly.
>
> C: That's what you thought, but how did you feel? Were you angry?
>
> A: Oh no!
>
> C: That's funny, you looked angry. Maybe irritated then?
>
> A: No.
>
> C: Even a little irritated?
>
> A: No.
>
> D: (In exasperation) For crying out loud! Then if it didn't bother you, why have you been kicking it to death for the last hour?
>
> A: I just felt that B would be more effective if . . .
>
> Postscript: Two sessions later, A admitted how much B's behavior had bothered him, and then added, "But now that I've come to know you, it doesn't bother me any more."[19]

Although the consultant tried to intervene early and allow the feelings to emerge, his initial attempts were unsuccessful. Oshry has summarized how feelings can influence problem solving in a team situation such as that exemplified above.

EFFECTS OF FEELINGS ON IDEAS

Feeling	Effects on Openness, Expression, and Experimentation with Ideas
A feels *competitive* toward B. In any group interaction, he is motivated to increase his own status and decrease B's.	1. A takes premature potshots at B's ideas, thus decreasing the opportunity for others to evaluate or build on B's ideas.

A is *irritated* by a persistent pattern of B's behavior. (For example, he is annoyed by B's domination of group discussion.)

2. *A* saves his best ideas for those times when *B* is not present.

3. *A* tends not to express incompletely conceived ideas, which in open discussion might have been productively developed, for fear that critical judgment might lower his status relative to *B.*

4. *A* tends to tune out *B* or to distort what *B* says.

A feels *unsure* of his own ability, which may in fact be equal to or greater than the ability of others in the group.

5. *A* prefers not to build on others' ideas for fear that his contributions will not be significant.

A feels *dependent* on his superiors' good will.

See 3 and 5 above.

6. *A* tends not to critically evaluate or alter in any way his superiors' ideas for fear this will threaten the relationship between them.

A likes *B* personally and wants him as friend.[20]

See above.

Frustrations, Antagonisms, and Suspicions

People tend to shy away from hostile and antagonistic emotions. The natural inclination is to leave a "hot" situation alone in the hope that it will cool off. When conflict is thus avoided or delayed, tensions escalate. Recall of problematic events becomes less factual and more emotional. In the next example it is likely the situation would have deteriorated further had not management provided an avenue for working through the destructive emotions.

At the Weldon Manufacturing Company, prescriptive interventions concerned with work study, incentive rates, and so on were having negative rather than their intended constructive effects on production. Suspicions, hostilities, and future-oriented fears were rampant among managers and supervisors. Morale was at low ebb. In an effort to address these problems, an acceptant kind of consultant intervention was "superimposed" on the first, or prescriptive, step.

This second intervention focused on "family groups." It started with the top team of the Weldon organization, but the consultants interviewed members individually in advance, partly to provide themselves with background but more significantly to explore and moderate or allay apprehensions—an acceptant intervention in itself—as well as to encourage hope for the future among prospective participants.

Here is how the situation appeared:

> It was believed at that time that progress potentially available through the various technical improvements was being blocked by the hostilities, suspicions, and fears of the Weldon managers and supervisors in their work relations with one another. Not that these had become worse, but just that they had not become better. It was felt, further, that these conditions among the higher-level people had their effects among the lower-level supervisors and operators as well. Coordination between the merchandising and manufacturing divisions remained poor and a constant source of difficulty. The plant managers and supervisors clearly were performing at a level well below their capacities.

Then group sessions of two to four days were scheduled. Each session commenced with a *problem census,* which is usually a catalytic intervention technique. Soon, strongly felt emotions both in regard to operations and toward one another were expressed.

> The training period ran from the evening of the first day through noon of the fourth day, and the work was continuous and intensive, with breaks only for meals, brief recreation, and sleep.
> The "program" was unstructured at the beginning, as is conventional in this type of training. The first evening discussion began with a problem census, often a rather neutral opening process but in this case one that very soon led to strongly emotional expression of concern.[21]

Acceptant interventions permitted long-suppressed hostilities and anxieties to be shared, and slowly it became possible to deal with human and mechanical barriers to organization effectiveness.

> By the following day the participants had begun to express their feelings toward each other quite directly and frankly, something they had rarely done in their daily work. As the discussion progressed it became easier for them to accept criticism without becoming angry or wanting to strike back. As they began to express long-suppressed hostilities and anxieties the "unfreezing" of old attitudes, old values, and old approaches began. From the second day onward the discussion was spontaneous and uninhibited. From early morning to long past midnight the process of self-examination and confrontation continued. They raised questions they had never felt free to ask before. Politeness and superficiality yielded to openness and emotional expression and then to more objective analysis of themselves and their relationships at work. They faced up to many conflicts and spoke of their differences. There were tense moments, as suspicion, distrust, and personal antagonisms were aired, but more issues were worked out without acrimony.[22]

Thereafter, more constructive interaction became possible, replacing the resistance that had been shown to the prescriptions of the first interventions.

INTERGROUP (E-2-3)

By their nature, the conditions under which low morale/cohesion is the focal issue between two groups make it highly unlikely that intervention will be sought. When two groups despair of coordinating effort, they tend to become more separately encapsulated and withdraw from one another. Each group may develop its own resources rather than rely on the other. When this occurs, a condition of autonomy becomes "natural," and thus neither group is likely to seek consultant assistance to deal with the morale/cohesion issues, even if an effective intervention could restore a circumstance of interdependence.

ORGANIZATION (E-2-4)

Lowered morale/cohesion can become a problem for the membership of an entire organization. At least two factors are involved in creating such conditions. One is organization trauma in which some critical event occurs. Members who previously had a strong group commitment feel a sense of loss and subsequently withdraw their identification from the organization. Consequences of this include apathy, indifference, or feelings of rejection.

Another cause of reduced morale/cohesion is more difficult to observe but no less important. It occurs when organization members experience a succession of small disappointments over a more extended period of time, with each disappointment causing participants to withdraw emotional commitments to some small degree. The cumulative effect over time of a succession of disappointments can have the same consequences for organization morale/cohesion as a single traumatic event.

Few documented examples of successive disappointments leading to morale/cohesion problems are available, but an acceptant approach for bringing about organization-wide relief from tensions associated with change is described by Levinson. One year previously, a consulting firm had prescribed a reorganization that resulted in the stripping of authority from many who had previously held significant positions. As a consequence, widespread depression and anger were generated.

Following the devastating effect of the reorganization of a company . . . and a subsequent year of turmoil, a consultant was asked to undo the situation. Initial interviews with the executives indicated the severity of the depression each was experiencing and provided information on the turmoil in the rest of the organization. Building upon a clinical understanding of depression following the experience of loss, an appreciation of the sense of responsibility the managers in the organization felt, the sensitivity of the new leadership, and important changes in external forces which the organization now confronted, the consultant recommended that the 100 top management people be brought together for a meeting to last several days. During this meeting, on the consultant's recommendation, the chief executive officer presented the history of the organization, its achievements, its present state, and its future potential, and indicated clearly what was happening in the outside environment and what drastic changes had to be made. This was followed by an opportunity for the 100 men, in small groups, to discuss and analyze what they had heard and to mourn the loss as well as to confront reality. While regretting the past, they could begin to see clearly what the future held and what kinds of adaptive efforts might have to be made.

The consultant's acceptant intervention permitted these managers to mourn—that is, to discharge the feelings associated with their giving up an attachment to extinct realities. The president's presentation in historical perspective of their situation provided organization members an opportunity to identify the emotion-provoking problem and thereafter to express their feelings of frustration, anger, and loss. The consultant's second-step recommendation (a catalytic phase) permitted study and shared perception of their new reality. Later still, freed from their counterproductive emotions, managers began to deal with the current organization situation in problem-solving terms.

They were then reconvened to hear presentations about future trends in their field, as well as in society at large, and to set in context what they were up against. They then had the opportunity to discuss and digest their impressions and to see how such forces related to them. On the basis of those small group discussions, they established priorities for action, coalesced them in large plenary sessions, and evolved a charter for their functional operations. Thus, they began to turn their aggressions outward on real problems, which they faced together, while working through their sense of loss and depression.[23]

Without the prior cathartic release from tensions, this new attitude of constructive desire to meet and master organizational realities would probably not have been possible. Furthermore, had this catharsis been experienced on a one-by-one basis or by only a few individuals, the absence of sharing would probably have minimized the change brought about.

Congruent with Levinson, Davis emphasizes that organization development efforts that focus on but limit themselves to promoting cathartic release among organization members are counterproductive.

There is no real growth—there is no real development—in the organization or in the individuals within it if they do not confront and deal directly with their problems. They can get together and share feelings, but if that is all they do, it is merely a catharsis. While this is useful, it has relatively minimal usefulness compared with what can happen if they start to relate differently within the organizational setting around task issues.[24]

His solution is to provide work teams with on-the-job support for problem-solving efforts *after* they have attended emotionally freeing sensitivity training sessions. In a certain sense, the sequences described by Davis and Levinson illustrate constructive follow-up intervention possibilities.

LARGER SOCIAL SYSTEM (E-2-5)

Acceptant interventions can contribute to the restoration or maintenance of mental health for larger social system members.

Trauma

Sometimes survivors or relatives of victims of a catastrophe, such as a mine cave-in, an airplane crash, or a natural disaster, experience great difficulty in regaining balance. Aroused emotions can be so intense that participants are unable to cope with them, so unbearable that they can "disappear" from consciousness. Calm returns. But the traumatic experience has not gone away: it has been buried. While the individual feels no immediate pain, the buried emotions may impact later behavior. Acceptant interventions in such traumatic situations can be used to reduce the likelihood of future adverse mental health consequences by enabling participants to talk about their feelings as soon as possible after the episode. If those who suffered the disaster can share their emotions with one another, then the distortions that might otherwise result may be reduced or entirely avoided.

The following incident exemplifies the beneficial results that can flow from emotion-releasing interventions. Tuckman was involved with a situation where forty-three school children had been in a bus accident. Five had been killed; only one person escaped hospitalization.[25] Tuckman's crisis team quickly intervened, but even then found that some children had blocked the accident from conscious thought, denying everything that had happened. Others had reactions involving guilt and uncontrolled anxiety. The Tuckman team provided the children an opportunity to face their losses and injuries by sharing with one another their feelings about what had happened. The consultants also worked with the victims' parents, teachers, and classmates in a similar manner. Cohesion returned and personal morale was restored with a minimum of emotional damage.

Other examples of emotional release in larger social systems involve customary, long-established acceptant intervention mechanisms. Examples include traditional mourning procedures where close friends comfort the person who has lost a loved one. A minister may also contribute, or friends of the deceased may come together and hold a wake where they have the opportunity to mourn together. In larger social systems as wholes, cathartic experiences of this kind occur at the time of the death or funeral of a respected and beloved leader.

Creating a Support Group

The majority of adults have not been hospitalized for mental health difficulties; yet for many, their ways of adjusting to the larger social system or the constraints of their present situations are characterized by various symptoms of mental illness. Such aspects include loneliness, isolation, and withdrawal. These isolated individuals may go unnoticed, even when suffering many of the same or similar problems that characterize those who are hospitalized.

Within a larger social system, families may be living in relative isolation from one another even though situated side by side. Moreover, where one or more of a family's members are away at work or school for a significant part of the day, a parent may be tending young children or spending all day in total solitude. Parents who find coping difficult and who do not maintain social contact with others may need to vent dissatisfactions in order to reestablish perspective. Depressed parents, who may benefit from active and acceptant support with accompanying opportunities for cartharsis, often remain unidentified unless a community consultant takes active steps to locate them.

> The choice of ten mothers for membership of the new group was made partly on their own relationships with one another and partly on the caseworker's assessment of their emotional needs and the stresses which seemed to be troubling them.
>
> Through her diagnosis of the mothers' needs she quickly recognized that what was necessary above all else was a group from which they could gain "support" for the strains and stresses of family life. These stresses were particularly heavy, and they were unable to derive from the neighbourhood the support which most mothers get from friends and relatives. "We are all in the same boat together and got to cope," as one member said.
>
> Her (i.e. the worker's) method was not to make plans for talks from visitors, nor arrange outings, nor, during the last nine months of the group when the members met in each other's homes, to fix up accommodation in the Meeting Rooms. The planning and organization she left to the members themselves. But it was certainly to encourage and facilitate activity and to make it easier for them to do the kinds of things which secretly they hoped for, but had not the energy or initiative to do without encouragement, such as the planning of a party or an outing with their families. Above all, it was to help them to make relationships which would be a source of support. When invited—and this happened on several occasions—the group worker joined the mothers and their families on special occasions such as a visit to the approved school to see one of the children, or a grammar school commemoration service in the Cathedral.[26]

Wilson summarizes the acceptant basis of intervention for these most impoverished mothers.

> The worker's method was not dependent on the programme. She welcomed and accepted the mothers as they were, encouraging them to feel comfortable and to feel free to talk about some of the things that they felt troubled about in themselves and their families. In the early days she dropped in for a chat in their own homes as well as meeting them in the group. Within the group, the worker regarded it as her job to ease the relations between the members themselves, so that they came more and more to a sense of mutual support. For the first six months the group met in the Meeting Rooms, but for the rest of the two years over which the work lasted it met in one or another of the members' homes. There was never a programme. The aim

was that they should enjoy one another's company enough to be able to give each other a sense of support and so to establish confidence in human relationships.[27]

The general outcome of the community worker's numerous interventions with individuals was the creation of an informal therapeutic community.

Building Self-Confidence

When mental health problems concerned with self-rejecting behavior become unmanageable, hospitalization is one recourse. Psychiatric hospitalization has been described as producing an unusual degree of dependency in that the patient is called upon to exercise minimal responsibility for himself or herself. When or if a patient eventually is released from hospital confinement, whatever degree of morale/cohesion he or she possesses may easily be shattered in an unprotected environment. A number of acceptant interventions are available within a halfway house, where the discharged patient is encouraged to build up realistic self-esteem as he or she seeks to cope with the everyday external world.

Clark and Jaffe describe conditions under which a therapeutic living community may be organized around strengthening the dynamics of morale/cohesion. Members of this live-in community are former mental patients. During hospitalization they had accepted being dependent upon prescriptive consultation and had either lost or failed to gain such social skills as are essential for self-confident living in the wider society.

The essential supportive climate was available in New Haven in the form of a transitional community, referred to as the New Haven Halfway House. Participants could interrelate with one another in a trusting, accepting, loving, and helpful way in order to build the confidence and skill essential for coping in real-world terms. The atmosphere of the house is described as follows.

> The pressures and problems a resident faces at the House are not so much authority problems, problems of dealing with a structure of rules and demands, than they are those of getting close to people, living together, and making personal decisions about the future and about methods. The burden of handling himself and getting along with others is placed on the resident, and he can neither blame his past, his illness, restrictive rules or external circumstances for his own failings in the House.[28]

Interviews with residents demonstrate how they reacted to the environment and its benefits.

> —People are supposed to unravel some of their problems. This is supposed to be a community, so you're not supposed to be evasive. Maybe people can help you if you come out of your shell. Most people try to work on their problems alone, but they find they need an understanding person to listen. The House gives people a responsive attitude to themselves, to know there's another life when they leave here. They're learning to accept other people,

so they can go out and accept others. The House is a lantern to show the way out.

—You go to the hospital because you feel nobody needs you and say to hell with life. I couldn't develop a relationship and didn't feel wanted. Here I find I can contribute, so relating is a two-way street. People listen to me and sometimes they accept it. It makes me somebody because they need me.

—You act like yourself here. You don't have to be phoney. I don't feel I have to put on shows or acts. Like if I get mad, I won't be threatened with being put back into the hospital. I feel no pressure, strain, or anything.[29]

The residents-as-clients recognize from their own direct experience the morale/cohesion-building aspects of learning to accept and support one another and the importance of this for coping with outside life.

The backup consultation mode provided by the house director was primarily catalytic. Her routine administrative responsibilities included such things as the assignment of chores, collecting rent, and so on. When conflict arose she frequently mediated the differences as well as reinforced the rules or norms of the House. University students who also lived in the House as part of their learning of clinical dynamics provided the former hospital patients a basis of comparison and reality-checking data. This also is in the catalytic mode.

The Santa Barbara Psychiatric Foundation is a similar community created to provide its members, themselves also recently released from a mental health institution and still "patients," with cohesion-building opportunities necessary for the growth and development of self-confidence.[30] The New Haven House and Santa Barbara Foundation together verify the importance of acceptant interventions for reestablishing self-esteem.

"Deep Dive" Therapeutic Environments for Disturbed Persons

Communities have been created to help more severely disturbed persons by providing a milieu within which these clients can "work themselves through" their subjective experiences. The character of this "milieu as an acceptant intervention" can be contrasted with the help-giving values characteristic of the New Haven Halfway House, which mostly accepts residents after their release from mental hospitals.

In London's East End, the Philadelphia Association (P.A.) leases Kingsley Hall, an old settlement house.

Madness, especially the form known as schizophrenia, is seen by members of the P.A. as a response to a family or other interpersonal situation where contradictory demands make the person feel that no response he makes is right. The schizophrenic child has lived in fear of irrational, punitive behavior by his parents and feels prohibited from pointing it out. Such a person never is able to feel at home in a world which is perpetually fearsome and inconsistent. At best the child learns to face the world with a false self of either rigid conformity or bizarre eccentricity which shields him from destruction by the hostile world. But when life gets too stressful, the fears and desires that he has been holding back burst out; he breaks down and goes mad. Support for this theory has come from several quarters of the United States.

Laing and his group see madness as a natural coping mechanism in an intolerable living situation, much as a fever is a sign that the body is combatting disease. The mental hospital, by simultaneously treating the patient as if he is sick, by not allowing him to experience the integrative possibilities of his madness, and by trying to stop the process with drugs and social reinforcement techniques to reduce the "symptoms," further cuts off the patient from experiencing things which are his own, not the expectations and demands of those around him. The patient thus is once again in a situation like that of his family. His madness is usually an attempt to assert his autonomy by fleeing a family which has never allowed him any experience that is his own, by always telling him what to do.

At Kingsley Hall the individual's rebellion is supported, and he is allowed to experience his autonomy. There are no rules, and nothing is prescribed as conventional. There are people available to help one go through the experience, but only if asked. The hope is that undergoing a period of madness, in a place where one is helped not to fear oneself and where others understand and sanction the process, can often lead to a natural resolution.[31]

While both the halfway house and Kingsley Hall milieux constitute acceptant interventions through community organizations, Kingsley Hall is intended for people with more severely impaired functioning. While a halfway house can offer positive and active support, the Kingsley Hall situation can respond best to an individual's unique needs once help has been sought.

Summary

Acceptant interventions appear to be particularly applicable to problems on the low-morale/cohesion end of the scale. This suggests that the acceptant mode of intervention helps a person unload burdensome thoughts and reactions and enables the client to reorient his or her thinking toward a more objective appraisal of the surrounding situation. The common-sense aspects of this dynamic are suggested by such phrases as "getting it off your chest," "getting it out of your system," or "having a good cry."

Miniature social systems that provide a supportive environment and nurture the self-esteem of members can sometimes deter certain of the more severe mental health problems and strengthen the individual as he or she seeks to cope with the realities of the larger social system. Other-than-residential acceptant interventions can be made available to individuals immediately after they suffer traumatic experiences. Such timely interventions help to reduce the likelihood that more serious emotional problems, such as loss of self-esteem, will occur.

Notes

1. M. S. Schwartz and G. T. Will, "Intervention and Change in a Mental Hospital Ward," in W. G. Bennis, K. D. Benne, and R. Chin, eds., *The Planning of Change* (New York: Holt, Rinehart and Winston, 1961), p. 568. Reprinted by permission.

2. Ibid., p. 573.

3. C. R. Rogers, *Counseling and Psychotherapy* (Boston: Houghton Mifflin, 1942), pp. 56–57. Reprinted by permission.

4. R. T. Golembiewski, S. B. Carrigan, W. R. Mead, R. Munzenrider, and A. Blumberg, "Toward Building New Work Relationships: An Action Design for a Critical Intervention," *The Journal of Applied Behavioral Science* 6, no. 2 (1972): 135–48. Reprinted by permission.

5. Rogers, *Counseling and Psychotherapy*, pp. 66–67.

6. T. Clark and D. T. Jaffe, *Toward a Radical Therapy: Alternative Services for Personal and Social Change* (New York: Gordon and Breach, Science Publishers, 1973), p. 190. Reprinted by permission.

7. Ibid., p. 191.

8. R. D. Allen and N. Krebs, *Psychotheatrics* (Sacramento, CA: Garland STPM Press, 1979), p. 47.

9. Ibid., pp. 48–49.

10. Ibid., p. 49.

11. Clark and Jaffe, *Toward a Radical Therapy*, p. 156.

12. Ibid., pp. 92–93.

13. Ibid., pp. 96–97.

14. T. Gordon, *T.E.T. Teacher Effectiveness Training* (New York: Peter H. Wyden, 1974), pp. 62–63.

15. U. Mahlendorf, "Experiential Therapy," in J. L. Carleton and U. Mahlendorf, eds., *Man for Man: A Multidisciplinary Workshop on Affecting Man's Social and Psychological Nature through Community Action* (Springfield, Ill.: Charles C Thomas, 1973), pp. 318–19. Reprinted with permission.

16. Ibid., pp. 320–21.

17. Ibid., p. 326.

18. Ibid., p. 327.

19. B. I. Oshry, "Clearing the Air in Human Relations," *Business Horizons* 9, no. 1 (1966): 40.

20. Ibid., p. 41.

21. G. David, "Building Cooperation and Trust," in A. J. Marrow, D. G. Bowers, and S. E. Seashore, *Management by Participation* (New York: Harper & Row, 1967), pp. 95–96.

22. Ibid., pp. 99–100.

23. H. Levinson, *The Great Jackass Fallacy* (Cambridge, MA: Division of Research, Harvard University Press, Graduate School of Business Administration, 1973), pp. 166–67. Reprinted with permission.

24. S. A. Davis, "An Organic Problem-Solving Method of Organizational Change," reproduced by special permission from *Journal of Applied Behavioral Science* 3, no. 1 (1967): 4.

25. C. Safran, "How Mental First Aid Can Pull You through a Crisis," *Today's Health* 51, no. 9 (1973): 67–68.

26. R. Wilson, "Difficult Housing Estates," *Human Relations* 16, no. 1 (1963): 36–37. Reprinted by permission.

27. Ibid., p. 38.
28. Clark and Jaffe, *Toward a Radical Therapy,* p. 231.
29. Ibid., p. 231.
30. L. Carlton, "The Therapeutic Community and the Workshop," in J. L. Carleton and U. Mahlendorf, eds., *Man for Man: A Multidisciplinary Workshop on Affecting Man's Social Nature through Community Action* (Springfield, Ill.: Charles C Thomas, 1973), pp. 329–33.
31. Ibid., p. 241. M. Barnes and J. Berke, *Mary Barnes: Two Accounts of a Journey into Madness* (New York: Ballantine Books, 1971).

29

**ACCEPTANT
INTERVENTIONS**

Norms/
Standards

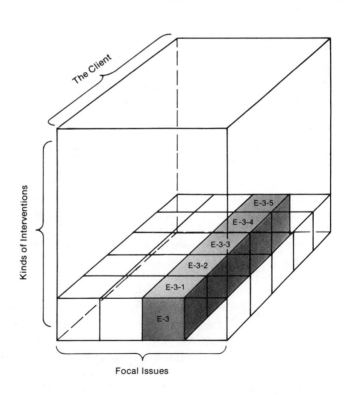

Focal Issues

Norms and standards sometimes resist change because they are reinforced by feelings and emotions rather than by logical justification. Any effort to change norms/standards that disregards these emotional underpinnings is likely to prove unsuccessful. Therefore, such an intervention should identify and focus on the critical issue that is provoking the emotions aroused in relation to a particular norm or standard.

The two examples below demonstrate the acceptant intervention strategy as used to aid people to work through their emotions and feelings prior to the change of norms/standards at the organization-wide level.

ORGANIZATION (E-3-4)

Norm-based emotions may be corporate-wide. For example, even though management may claim, on a public-relations level, that it desires to deal with its plant's union representatives in a solution-seeking way, more deeply rooted and widely diffused antiunion attitudes may repeatedly surface to stifle the effort. Under these circumstances the problem cannot be solved simply by working with the management bargaining committee (the organization's representative in negotiations with the union), for committee members can move in a problem-solving direction *only* when they are confident of management's support at all levels.

Norm Formation

An example of an organization-wide acceptant intervention for setting new norms and standards of conduct is reported by Blake and Mouton.[1] The entire management team engaged in a cathartic experience prior to union-management bargaining. A series of one-day conferences was held with approximately 100 members of management. The purpose of these meetings was to identify feelings about the union through answering a key question, *Can* better relations between union and management be achieved?

Participants discussed this question in three *diagonal slice* groups. The plant manager, operations superintendent and the personnel chief "led" the discussions. Their goal was promoting a true exploration of feelings rather than guiding the discussion toward predetermined conclusions. Consultant interventions focused discussions in each group on a basic question: What are your attitudes toward the union? These interventions occurred repeatedly as the discussions unfolded, particularly at points where participants were voicing fears and anxieties and needed reassurance that these feelings were acceptable. To promote either clarification of thinking or differentiation of ideas, other interventions restated, rephrased, or reflected comments made. When the consultant, who had no vested interests in management attitudes toward the union, reflected the attitudes aired, the echo effect permitted management to hear themselves talk.

Group after group came to recognize the one-sidedness of their viewpoints as well as the dead-end quality of hopelessness they connoted. How did this come about? Time and time again some member would eventually become impatient with the bitter feelings the others expressed and would ask other members to examine *why* they felt as they did. This phase of cathartic release seemed an essential prelude to the next step.

As deep-lying attitudes and feelings were identified, expressed, shared, and explored, constructive concepts began to surface. The groups realized that improvement in union-management relations can only occur when subjective attitudes that block problem solving are eradicated or at least given an experimental adjournment in the minds of management.

Though no single generalization was reached at all conferences, the following newsprint summary of the consensus reached at one conference gives the gist of what transpired. It was concluded that:

> Regardless of what the union officers are, personality-wise, and what their history has been, the only way for bringing about a resolution of conflict is through treating them as *officers,* according them the dignity and respect that people who have been duly elected should receive. Our role is to meet these people and to search for whatever conditions of cooperation and collaboration are possible.[2]

Cathartic release had permitted an organization-wide norm regarding warfare relations with a union to be replaced by a new norm that guided management in building a more problem-solving relationship. Thereafter it was possible for the management's bargaining committee to take a more collaborative stance toward the union. This eventually led to the solution of many problems that had become chronic stand-offs.

Shifting a Norm

Another approach to organization norm setting starts from the premise that organization life in modern times is fear provoking, characterized by high levels of member distrust. If change is to occur, it is necessary to help organization members shift their trust levels upward so they may interact not according to implicit role requirements and norms of defensiveness, but rather out of spontaneous feelings or problem-solving requirements. The intervention may rely heavily on emotional release—i.e., helping participants "let down their guard." Described by Gibb[3] under the acronym of the TORI (Trust, Openness, Realization, Interdependence) Community, one such approach aids participants to experience all the others simultaneously.

Nonverbal activities are organized or undertaken spontaneously in order to engage participants in uncustomary modes of relating. The approach is designed to create a clearer communication than words often convey. As old norms begin to break down, a contagion effect is produced. Aroused feelings can be expressed, talked about, and worked through. Acceptant interventions stimulate activities that range from several people collaborating in lifting and rocking another person, to touching and feeling one another while blindfolded, to Indian wrestling, and so on. One person might lead another who is blindfolded on a walk, helping the other experience his or her surroundings by smell and feel rather than through words or sight. Engaging in such activities automatically violates old norms of "keeping your distance," being formal, and staying in role. A new sense of closeness and mutual dependence, which is not necessarily experienced in conversational interaction between people, is communicated.

Gibb describes the new norms and standards of conduct he believes this emotion-freeing intervention produces. One response is deep interpersonal acceptance, as indicated in such terms as being personal, people-oriented, intimate, and close. Individuals become more authentic, transparent, honest, available, assertive, and direct. Rather than controlling others, individuals become more accepting, less intrusive, less manipulative, more collaborative, and more sharing. He points out that following these organization-building experiences makes it possible to use the climate of high trust and acceptance for initiating problem-solving activities that continue to be carried out in the "each to all" community setting.

Different interpretations regarding the impact of TORI nonverbal activities are possible. One is that physical contact serves to reduce participants' inhibitions. Another is that under a no-words convention, and within the overall TORI environment, it becomes easier for a participant to communicate acceptance of others. In any case, there are risks that can hardly be anticipated and obviated unless the particular consultant has previously gained deep understandings of individual participants.

> As part of a development effort in a company, thought to be a wise course to "open people up," a trainer undertook encounter experiences that involved having the executives touch each other and engage in activities that brought them physically closer to each other. Two executives, whose latent homosexual impulses (unconscious and well controlled) could not tolerate such closeness, had psychotic breaks, and had to be hospitalized.[4]

LARGER SOCIAL SYSTEM (E-3-5)

Trade associations and other professional meetings have certain characteristics that make them temporary as contrasted with permanent or enduring communities. Even so, they exemplify models of a larger social system (actual or potential), because people are associated in an exchange of information as well as in resolving matters regarding food, clothing, and shelter.

Such a temporary social system has characteristic properties, often involving sociometric networks of friends who cohere versus strangers who are isolates with either no real membership status or only a minimal one. As a result, those who have already established friendships maintain their interaction but do not expand it; and those who are strangers have little or no contact and, therefore, can only profit from the meeting's formal presentations, exhibits, and so on.

Acceptant interventions are useful in preparing people to be more emotionally expressive and responsive to one another when attending such meetings, for individuals characteristically interact according to norms of formality and distance rather than informally and with intimacy. Part of the warm-up for breaking away from conventional norms and embracing new ones engages people in positive emotional experiences with one another. Similar procedures are used in organization growth situations. Gibb[5] describes typical procedures used in large space, often without furniture to impede the interaction. An acceptant consultant may start things off by engaging participants in a mingling experience. People move along in two circles, traveling in opposite directions. As one person passes the next, introductions are exchanged, with each person telling something about himself or herself that ordinarily would not be discussed with a stranger. This kind of sharing creates "instant" warmth and mutual friendliness. A second activity might involve participants sitting on the floor in pairs, or in small five- or six-person clusters, with participants looking intently at one another in silence. After a few minutes, participants talk about what each "saw" in looking at the other, and how each felt being able to look but not talk. Participants usually make remarks that are pleasant and intimacy producing. A basis for liking the other person is established, and new functional norms replace conventional norm-based formality to permit free and easy exchange in the temporary community.

Summary

Generalizations about changing norms and standards through organization-wide catharsis include the following. First, an organization is a reference group for its individual members—no one member really can change his or her attitudes until other members are ready to change theirs. The impracticality, for example, of using acceptant interventions to solve *organizational* problems on a *one-to-one* basis is apparent. In the management-ideology case discussed earlier, for example, each individual, in working through his own feelings with a consultant, might have come to the same end point in terms of altered feelings toward the union. But without a basis for *sharing* these feelings with others in order to reach a new consensus, each person would probably have felt compelled to get his emotions and feelings back into line with the perceived norms of his reference group rather than shifting to a new and more constructive basis.

A second generalization concerns the source of the intervention when norm changing is involved. Usually, it is more feasible for the intervention to be introduced by an outsider-insider consultant combination. An outsider can be emotionally neutral, whereas an insider is expected to share a common membership norm. The insider is more likely to be treated as "one of us" and may be putting his or her career on the line by getting *out* of line. Organization members—initially at least—usually presume that the outsider consultant has no personal axe to grind. Accordingly, the insider can be a consultant to the outsider, who in turn is in a better-informed position to be a consultant to the organization.

A third generalization relates to norms that traditionally have been regarded as representing the "rational man" concept of management. Behavioral science has shown us that feelings and emotions can sometimes overwhelm logical analysis of facts and data and cause people to hold irrational positions. When feelings and emotions can be identified and worked through *prior* to attempting to deal logically with a problem, it becomes possible to bring about the kind of development needed for more effective functioning of the organization.

This review of acceptant interventions in the context of norms/standards suggests several significant conclusions. First, because norms and standards are aspects of behavior difficult to define in operational terms, they are rarely regarded in consultant activity as being maintained and perpetuated by existing emotions and feelings. Therefore, modes of intervention other than the acceptant approach are generally relied upon to bring about changes in norms/standards. Prescription, for example, rather than being an effective intervention, may unwittingly block norm changing although the norms/standards focal issue has been accurately identified.

Second, when an individual deviates from group norms, he or she is likely to experience feelings of rejection. When the problem is experienced in this way, it becomes a morale/cohesion issue for the person involved rather than being experienced as a consequence of norm deviation.

Notes

1. R. R. Blake and J. S. Mouton, "The D/D Matrix," in J. D. Adams, ed., *Theory and Method in Organization Development: An Evolutionary Process* (Washington, D.C.: NTL Institute for Applied Behavioral Science, 1974), pp. 9–10. (Originally published Austin, Texas: Scientific Methods, Inc., 1972.)
2. Ibid.
3. J. R. Gibb, "The TORI Experience as an Organizational Change Intervention," in W. W. Burke, ed., *Contemporary Organization Development: Conceptual Orientations and Interventions* (Washington, D.C.: NTL Institute for Applied Behavioral Science, 1972), pp. 109–26. J. R. Gibb, *Trust: A New View of Personal and Organizational Development* (Los Angeles: The Guild of Tutors Press, 1978).
4. H. Levinson, *The Great Jackass Fallacy* (Cambridge, Mass.: Harvard University Press, 1973), p. 164.
5. Gibb, "The TORI Experience."

ACCEPTANT INTERVENTIONS

Goals/
Objectives

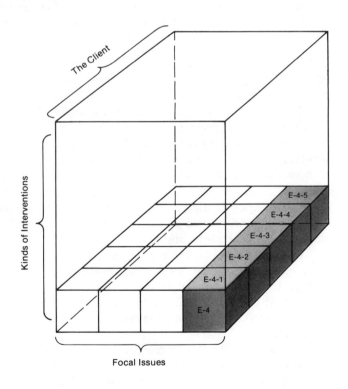

Acceptant interventions are rarely relied upon when the focal issue involves establishing or changing goals/objectives. Acceptant interventions might be applicable, however, to goal clarification or to reality testing in terms of already established goals. An example of supportive counseling for low-ability students regarding their high goal aspirations in colleges was reported by Burck and Cottingham. This is an instance where aspirations and ability were contradictory to one another. While desire is an important component of success, it is not sufficient to produce a positive outcome when the aspirant lacks the abilities to support his or her expectations.

This intervention in academic counseling took place at Florida State University. It involved thirty-five of forty students who had been classified as having this basic contradiction of ability and expectations. The thirty-five who volunteered for the counseling experiment were divided into a control group, which did not receive counseling, and an experimental group.

The experimental group received counseling, which extended over an average of 4.52 sessions per student. The acceptant character of the counseling is shown in the following.

> Care was taken not to covertly or overtly persuade any client that he should change his [or her] educational aspiration. The only information about the study which the [student counselors] had was that certain characteristics of students interested in medicine, dentistry, law, and engineering were being investigated. [Counselors] were not aware of [students] being chosen because of their relatively low ability.[1]

This kind of passive, but supportive, counseling apparently had the effect of aiding the students in the experimental group to come to grips with the contradiction between their ability levels and their aspirations. No change was apparent in the control group, which was matched with the experimental group in every important respect, except for the intervention.

A follow-up study three years later led to the interpretation of the findings, however, that the counseling had no long-term effects. The school performance of both the experimental and control groups, in terms of grade-point average, remained about the same. Even without intervention, appropriateness of aspirations of the control group had also shifted so that at the end of three years the experimental and control groups were indistinguishable in terms of the relationship between aspirations and ability.

Viewed in a short-term perspective, this intervention appeared to have been successful in the sense that aspirations became more appropriate to ability. Even without intervention, however, congruence came about as a function of college experience in the control group, suggesting again that the impact of interventions should be evaluated on a longer time line than that usually employed.

The same kind of incongruence between goals and abilities (or resources) may occur at the group level. In many work groups, goals and objectives are established by the boss. Therefore, when failure to realize the objective occurs, or when frustrations in attempting to achieve the goal are experienced, the resultant focal issue is more likely to be the power/authority rather than the goals/objectives (E-4-2) aspect of the situation.

In the intergroup context, it is rare to find any kind of intervention, whether acceptant (E-4-3) or otherwise. The concept of *superordinate* goals/objectives—that is, goals that could be pursued with high commitment by otherwise separate groups—is not a concept sufficiently developed to enter into the thinking of participants. Even though two or more groups may in fact share a formal goal that could be best achieved through intergroup collaboration, the focus is likely to be on the distinctive properties or goals of the two groups. When these become incompatible, power/authority rather than goals/objectives is the focal issue.

Focal issues that invite acceptant intervention at the organization level (E-4-4) do not involve goals and objectives either—if this can be inferred from the absence of acceptant interventions. The setting of objectives for organizations is likely to be seen "naturally" as a top-down activity. Therefore, the line membership of an organization is unlikely to feel a sense of loss or depression associated with the failure to realize organizational goals. Accordingly, consultant interventions to deal with feelings of loss or failure are improbable.

Acceptant interventions with a goals/objectives focal issue are also absent at the larger social system level. Rarely does the membership of a larger social system participate in the setting of system-wide goals, and no sense of emotional loss can be experienced for failing to meet goals that do not exist. Although in some larger social systems there is a concept of national planning, this planning is normally of a strategic economic character. Thus, achievement is dependent on technology rather than on behavior of people as a whole, precluding the need for acceptant interventions in the event of failure.

Again, in larger social systems that within living memory have been created on ideological as well as socioeconomic grounds, the "crisis"[2] may come many years later as the group's pioneers, themselves the creators of the ideology-referenced goals/objectives, recognize that the newer generations are drifting away from commitment to such goals. Problems such as these tend not to be approached in the goals/objectives focal issue area of acceptant intervention. Rather, if addressed at all by that mode, they are viewed as individual or senior citizen group problems linked with tendencies to idealize the past and mourn its, and their, passing from relevance.

Notes

1. H. D. Burck and H. F. Cottingham, "The Effective Counseling Low-Ability High-Aspiring College Freshmen," *Journal of College Student Personnel* (September 1965): 280.
2. M. E. Spiro, *Kibbutz: Venture in Utopia* (Cambridge, Mass.: Harvard University Press, 1956).

31

ACCEPTANT INTERVENTIONS

Summary and Implications

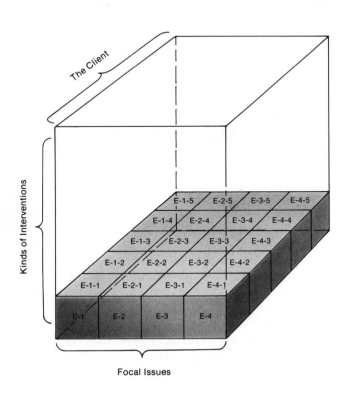

Focal Issues

The ability to express feelings and emotions freely and appropriately is basic to psychological health and behavioral effectiveness. Blocked emotions can cause many difficulties in thinking, decision making, and problem solving; resulting tensions and anxieties may lead to physical illnesses.

An important aspect of consultation involves interventions in which the client is assisted in clearing up emotional blockages in order to engage in more objective problem solving. Acceptant interventions bring about the unblocking step through a process of catharsis, intended to trigger a free flow of emotions.

The use of acceptant interventions to activate a cathartic process is most valuable when the client feels weak in the sense of being unable to deal in a constructive manner with whatever obstacles are preventing him or her from taking appropriate actions. This does not necessarily mean that the client is *weak* on some absolute scale of strength, but only relative to the obstacles impeding progress in focusing on and dealing with problem issues.

WHAT AN ACCEPTANT CONSULTANT DOES

An acceptant consultant helps the client think through his or her situation in a manner that relieves the blocking aspects and ensures that the client retains a sense of personal "ownership" in resolving problems. This is accomplished in two ways. (1) The consultant gives passive support by attentive listening and nonevaluative responses. He or she avoids a partisan stance and suspends all judgments regarding what the client is saying or doing. (2) The consultant may intervene more actively by creating conditions under which the client experiences emotional release, but he or she does so in a nonprescriptive way. Again, this kind of intervention avoids a partisan orientation and provides the client a sense of support by implying that any action is acceptable regardless of its contents.

LIMITATIONS

Two possible limitations are of sufficient importance to be emphasized. One is that the client, after working through and relieving his or her emotions via a cathartic process, may come to *accept* the circumstances that caused the problem rather than take the initiative to correct them.

A second pitfall is possible when disturbed emotions extend beyond one's personal and subjective experience to interpersonal or intergroup relationships. The person who goes into catharsis "in public" after having become accustomed to doing so within private acceptant intervention situations may arouse hostile reactions. In a hostile social climate, cathartic release may be so contrary to a tradition of resolution via aggression as to be impractical.

WHY IS THE CATHARTIC PROCESS HELPFUL?

The answer to this question has many facets:

1. By seeking to define his or her problem to an acceptant listener, the client is able to gain a fuller perspective on the problem, which lessens the earlier sense of uneasiness.

2. By exploring the content of subjective experiences, emotional tensions associated with insufficiently examined situations may be reduced.

3. An acceptant intervention permits the client to explore concepts in his or her own experience and to learn a language and set of concepts to which words may previously never have been attached. By finding words and concepts to characterize these dimensions of experience, the client may be assisted to see in more precise terms the extent to which his or her emotions are appropriate to the situation and the extent to which these responses are untenable in the light of operating circumstances.

4. By working backwards to identify presumed causes for present problems, the client is able to pinpoint what is really causing what and therefore is in a better problem-solving position.

5. When a client is able to connect things that previously had seemed separate or disparate, the insights gained can reduce tensions associated with earlier apparent contradictions.

6. By sorting out his or her various feelings, the client may be assisted to see in more specific and concrete terms exactly what aspects of his or her circumstances are producing anxiety.

7. By testing in words the consequences of an anticipated action, tensions and fears associated with the real-life action may be reduced.

POSSIBLE CLIENT BENEFITS FROM ACCEPTANT INTERVENTIONS

Successful acceptant interventions may result in the client:

1. Experiencing improved self-acceptance.

2. Enjoying greater spontaneity.

3. Developing the capacity, through learning how to talk with himself or herself, to deal in more objective terms with emotional problems that may arise in the future.

4. Reactivating and experiencing in a more healthy way emotions that may previously have been repressed or denied.

5. Developing an increased ability to experience reality-based emotions appropriate to the given circumstances.

6. Formulating more objective definitions of the problem or situation faced, thereby increasing his or her problem-solving capacity.

Theory and Technique of Consultation

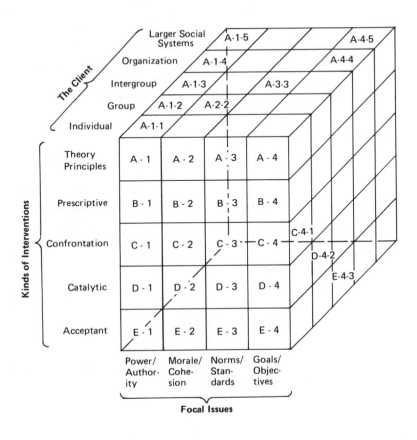

A systematic and comprehensive study of the interventions described in previous chapters provides a useful framework for determining what kind of approach will work best with which type of client in any particular situation. Conclusions drawn throughout this book as to the appropriateness of each intervention mode to specific client problems are summarized in Table 32.1.

Table 32.1 When different kinds of interventions are appropriate

Intervention	Key Words	When Indicated
Theory/principles	Insight	Client(s) is ready to shift to a science-oriented basis of problem solving.
Prescription	Giving answers	Client(s) has thrown up his or her hands or is on the ropes, unable to exercise sufficient initiative to move.
Confrontation	Value clarification	Values, often hidden, are having negative effects.
Catalytic	Information exchange	Poor communication has resulted in ignorance that blocks effectiveness.
Acceptant	Emotional release	Pent-up feelings are blocking thought and action so that needed initiatives cannot be taken.

Other theoretical and technical issues dealt with in this final chapter comprise a day-to-day guide for the practicing consultant. Integration, application, and implementation of the information available here may lead to greater consultant success and enhanced client performance and satisfaction.

PHASES IN CONSULTING

Since consultation takes place over time, it is both helpful and convenient to speak of phases of consultation from entry to exit.

The use of such a longitudinal model is limited, however, by two important considerations: (1) the focal issue addressed by the intervention, and (2) the consultation mode required by the situation or preferred by the consultant. Nonetheless, certain generalizations are possible, and exceptions to them can be introduced to clarify individual differences in the phases of consultation as a function of these two considerations.

After the definition of "who is the client?" has been reached, major phases of consultation may be identified. We know, however, that these phases are not always executed as a linear progression. Sometimes one step is completed but another not taken, or one step happens with such lightning speed that its occurrence is not easily detected. Given these limitations in any logical breakdown of the consulting process, there are certain benefits in evaluating the broad phases of consultation. There are four major phases.

Entry

A consultant may contact a potential client or be contacted, and few generalizations can be made as to how this comes about. The contact may arise from a chance acquaintance, as when a student in a class or seminar comes to see him- or herself as a potential client for a consultant's services. Such a contact may be generated from the yellow pages. In some instances, contact is made based on word-of-mouth between persons in different firms who speak with one another and share information as to help received or not received from specific consultants. An overture may follow a journal article written by the consultant, or reference to his or her work in one of the magazines or journals read more or less routinely by many executives and managers.

In any event, once contact has been made, the next steps involve the consultant in making a preliminary inquiry as to the nature of the interest, the character of the problem, or the reasons for the inquiry. If these turn out to be within the consultant's competence, then one of two things may happen.

The first is that the consultant is invited to visit the site in order to make the acquaintance of one or more persons in the client system, or the client may visit the consultant in his or her office. Then further discussions take place as to the business, professional, or personal character of the problem. Alternatively, these considerations may come up as a part of the first conversation, particularly those salient aspects of the relationship, including consulting fees, time frames, schedules, etc.

Contracting

In recent years, it has become common to speak of contracting between the consultant and the client system. The use of this term is not as formal as in other areas such as when contracts are signed for the delivery of goods or services. More often than not, a discussion takes place in which mutual expectations are set for what is to occur, particularly in the short term. This development of mutual expectations is referred to as the *contract,* although it is uncommon for such a contract to be written. A feature of most shared expectations between consultant and client is the understanding that the terms of the contract may shift radically as the consulting process unfolds.

Diagnosis

Beyond entry and contracting, it is difficult to be specific as to what the next activity entails, except that a common next step involves diagnosis of the problem the client is concerned about, either as an individual, as a team, or as an intact organization. Even here, however, the possibility of generalizing is restricted.

The consultant may reject the client's definition of the problem as "given," and consultation may proceed or end at this point. Alternatively, the client's definition of the problem may be taken as a starting point, with the consultant telling him- or herself that as experience with the client develops, the definition of the problem will inevitably take several turns before the real problem comes under scrutiny.

There are at least two radically different approaches to the methodology of diagnosis. One involves the consultant in interviewing or administering measuring instruments and then reaching conclusions as to the felt problems or real problems confronting the client. This is followed by suggestions and recommendations as to approaches that might be useful in dealing with these problems.

Quite the opposite, however, is the notion that the consultant's job is best carried out when he or she teaches the client to carry out the diagnosis after acquiring skills in utilizing primarily behavioral science knowledge for investigatory purposes. One of the more common approaches in which the consultant engages the client in learning the skills of diagnosis involves the Grid.

The Grid is a set of theories of leadership that center upon the exercise of power and authority. The strategies of power and authority can be examined from the standpoint of a given individual, or from the standpoint of a team, or in its exercise between groups that need to collaborate. How it is exercised throughout the hierarchical system of the organization also can be analyzed and evaluated.

Various ways of exercising power and authority can be described and have been used to design instruments that, once learned and understood by managers, can be employed for diagnostic purposes. Thus, how a boss operates a team is subject to assessment by the team itself through the use of instruments. Customarily each member completes each instrument alone. Then team members together compare how each has answered the instrument. Generalizations as to how leadership currently is being exercised and what its positive and adverse consequences are from the standpoint of promoting or inhibiting effective teamwork can then be dealt with. As the next step, team members agree on what would be the sound basis for exercising leadership. This ideal formulation is then compared with the actual situation. Planning is the next step in eliminating the gap between demonstrated and desired performance.

An examination of the exercise of leadership and membership can be further refined with instruments based on an evaluation of the degree of participation, involvement and commitment, conflict resolution, trust and respect, utilization of objectives for organizing effort, and so on.

Thus, the situation is significantly different when the consultant accepts responsibility for diagnosis or serves the client system as the facilitator through interviews and questionnaires and then reports the conclusions about the diagnosis back to the client system. In one case, the client has learned the skills of diagnosis and analysis; in the other, the consultant retains this responsibility.

Planning

Once a problem(s) has been identified, the next step is "what to do about it?" Planning courses of action may be done by the consultant alone, by a consulting team, by the consultant with the client, or by the consultant with the client plus others. In other words, it cannot be projected in advance as to how the planning will be done or who will be involved. This is partly determined by the consultant's style, partly by the client's concept of how consultation can best be applied to his or her situation, and even possibly partly by organization politics, such as, "We had better get Mr. Smith in on this, or he will not support the conclusion."

Implementation

Implementation follows once a plan is in place. Plans are more or less worthless unless they provide the basis for concrete actions intended to solve identified problems. However, the linear sequence frequently breaks down at this point. An established plan of action may not be tenable in the light of application efforts. It is then necessary to either revise the plan or discard it. Indeed, the effort to apply an unworkable plan often tells the consultant that the diagnostic phase has been inadequate. The return step may be back to the diagnostic phase. No matter how often this cycle occurs, plans are the basis for actions, and taking action is the next phase in this formal approach to the process of consultation. The action research model presented in Chapter 20 is a more accurate way of depicting this multistep process than is a straight linear progression model.

If participants have themselves used instruments to evaluate their problems and formulate strategies for solving them, it follows that the need for further consultation in implementation may be unnecessary. However, if the consultant has carried the responsibility for diagnosis, it is likely that he or she will be looked to for leadership during this phase.

Critique and Evaluation

A final step of critique and evaluation is carried out to determine the extent to which the original diagnosis was correct. If the diagnosis is correct, then the evaluation is in terms of the extent to which the planning for change has resulted in successful implementation. If further steps are needed, then redesigning ways to strengthen implementation (to meet the problem-solving objectives established in an earlier phase) may take place. The effort may start again if the diagnosis was wrong.

This outline of steps from entry to exit would be incomplete were the reader left with a notion that all that is involved is one diagnosis of one problem, with one effort to plan changes necessary for solving it, and with one implementation, followed by one critique. Rather, consultation in any complex system is multi-faceted, involving not just one sequence but possibly hundreds and thousands of sequences, sometimes over many years. Indeed, on occasion a change strategy that is implemented by the line management itself can become a way of life, with only occasional periods of review and testing by the consultant with the client of new possibilities for increasing effectiveness.

WHEN CONSULTANTS CONTRACT WITH THEIR CLIENTS

Any relationship is based on expectations. Sometimes these are made explicit through formal contracts, comprising either written or verbal agreements. Often, expectations are difficult to express and are left undefined, or at least unstated and informal. In consultation, the preparation of contracts usually represents an effort at mutual understanding of what is to be achieved, at what expense, and under what terms. Most importantly, contracting can help both the consultant and client crystallize expectations for what the relationship is to be. In this way, unwitting violation of unstated expectations can be reduced, and the consultant is freed from untenable demands.

A major limitation in contracting is that the client may never have experienced many of the kinds of consultation approaches possible; in other words, at the beginning of the consultation, the client does not understand what will occur in the relationship. Under these circumstances, words, whether spoken or written, mean little. By the time a contract is possible, it is unnecessary, for client expectations as to what the consultant can do and consultant understanding of client needs have been clarified and crystallized into an acceptable basis of intervention.

One effective approach to contracting involves stating in contractual terms what the relationship *will be at the beginning* and leaving it open for repeated negotiation as to what it will be as the relationship advances. As experience builds, such expectations are continuously clarified as part and parcel of the consultant's work by process of renegotiation. Some consultants maintain that this process of clarification is inherent in effective consultation and therefore is not some additional aspect brought about by contracting. Others see the importance of renegotiation as an additional component that can keep both parties conscious of what is taking place and ready to identify and explore previously unexamined alternatives.

The character of a contract varies with the strategy of consultation, whether cathartic, confrontational, etc. What follows is a description of contract preparation from each of these major orientations.

Contracting under a Theory/Principles Approach

At the outset, a theory/principles consultant finds it difficult to be specific with the client as to what "contributions" can be expected from the intervention. The difficulty arises from the unique characteristics of this mode of intervention. It is the only approach calculated to be educational in character—i.e., the consultant aids the client to gain theory-based understanding of his or her situation through insights that enable the client to take systematic problem-solving steps. The particular theories and principles the client may need to learn make contract writing difficult. While there is widespread understanding of how education can benefit understanding, many adults have been "turned off" by school-based learning and have yet to participate in experiential or other relatively new modes of education.

Yet the outlines of contract writing are fairly clear. Points that the theory-and-principles consultant makes in approaching contract preparation are summarized as follows.

1. Agreement is reached on the major problem(s) to be approached via the client's learning pertinent theories.

2. The method of teaching (whether teacher-tell, case, programmed instruction, instrumented learning) is specific, and one or more modes of intervention for assisting the client to apply these theories and principles in solving designated problems are also discussed. Assistance in evaluating or assessing the extent to which theory-based learning and implementation will have contributed to his or her situation may also be offered.

3. Additional areas that might benefit from a similar approach may be anticipated and noted for study at some future time as the basis for further work.

The theory/principles consultant has a basis for anticipating the work hours to be involved in theory and principles learning, expenses for learning materials, and the on-site support necessary in assisting the initial educational or implementation phase of the consultation. Support during more extended implementation activities is more difficult to specify in precise terms.

Contracts, whether in words or in writing, can strengthen the process of theory/principles intervention in useful ways. The activity involved in negotiating a contract helps the client reach realistic expectations as to what the consultant will or will not do. The likelihood of future misunderstandings and disappointment can be reduced this way, and the consultant gains additional insight into the client's present worries, doubts and reservations, unwarranted enthusiasm, excessive dependency, and so on. These observations can be useful in diagnosing how best to proceed in dealing with the client.

A second value of the contract is that the client can place limits on the consultant's activities or sphere of influence. By the same token, if what the client is prepared to agree to is viewed by the consultant as inherently unproductive, the consultant need not accept. By pretesting the viability of the situation, a sound footing is assured at the outset.

A third advantage of theory/principles contracting is its flexible character. The renegotiation possibilities are completely open; terms can be renegotiated whenever either party wishes to do so. For example, a client who might initially have wanted to go slow may, upon experiencing the benefits, see merit in speeding up. Correspondingly, one who starts by dealing with surface problems may gain the security and convictions essential for grappling with deeper issues.

A major limitation of unprogrammed renegotiation, though, is that it predisposes the consultant toward interacting with the client in terms of felt needs. Since the client does not recognize his or her own *latent* needs, they may never be considered. Also, initiatives by client or consultant to renegotiate might be viewed by the other party as attempts to violate the contract, and so provoke resistance. Even so, without necessarily agreeing to a felt-needs basis for contracting, the theory/principles consultant can define with the client certain areas of freedom to exercise professional judgment and to help the client become effective by discovering and solving real—though previously unrecognized—problems.

The Prescriptive Contract

The prescriptive approach is the easiest of the interventions to characterize in contract terms. This is because prescription is closely aligned with the everyday experiences people have had as they interact with experts and authorities on various topics. The prescriptive consultant might say to the client, "I would like to start with your definition of the problem and then study the situation from my point of view. In due course I will provide you a review of my findings and recommendations for action. I will expect to provide you with solutions for the situation that you now face."

By this approach the consultant is in a somewhat better position to indicate the amount of time (and therefore expense) required to study the situation, to prepare a report, to provide advice, and possibly to supervise implementation of the plan.

The key to crystallization of client expectations is in the consultant's readiness to take initiative, to exercise judgment, and to give answers. Since initiative taking, the exercise of judgment, and giving answers are characteristic of relationships in modern society, the client has little difficulty in understanding this contract. What he or she may not understand when agreeing to a contract is the future reluctance he or she is likely to feel toward acting on the recommendations offered.

The Confrontation Contract

The confrontational consultant faces problems in contract writing that are similar to those in acceptant consultation. Since the client usually is inexperienced with this kind of an approach, he or she is not really in a position to exercise judgment as to exactly what the consultant should contribute. After the client has had sufficient experience, it is less necessary to prepare a contract: either the relationship is terminated or continued.

Nonetheless, at the beginning of their relationship the consultant can do something to specify what he or she expects to contribute. For example, the consultant might say, "I see it as my job to aid you to examine and, to whatever degree you find it appropriate, to change the basic assumptions and values that underlie your behavior. I do not see it as my job to judge the soundness or rightness of the values and assumptions you hold. Once I have assisted you in recognizing them, my task is to offer whatever additional help can be provided through aiding you to explore the consequences of that conduct on your situation.

"You should not necessarily expect me to accept your definition of problems you face or your interpretation of their causes. At times you may find my interventions personally threatening—not that this would be my intention—and you may experience resentment when I challenge you on what I observe your values and assumptions to be.

"I intend to be as open and responsive to your reactions as I am capable of being. You can expect that I will do my best to provide you with concrete and specific evidence as to rationales of the interventions I make, or interpretations of consequences that I report to you from them.

"I do not see it as my job to tell you what to do or to offer advice as to alternative or possibly better courses of action."

The confrontational consultant often explains in advance that until the client reveals the values and assumptions implicit in his or her everyday activities, the consultant cannot point out what kinds of values and assumptions will be challenged. Thus an experiential basis for interpreting this contract is lacking. Once values have been revealed and challenged, though, the client is in a position to appreciate the character of the consultation and to enter into contract writing dependent on his or her readiness to engage further in this approach.

The Catalytic Contract

Preparation of a contract is somewhat easier for the catalytic consultant than for the consultant who works along acceptant lines, for clients more readily understand the catalytic mode—it is more within the purview of what goes on in their everyday relationships. For example, a person who has a problem expects in everyday contacts with others to be asked what the problem is and perhaps to receive help in clarifying it. The principal effect of a consultant's catalytic intervention impinges on the client's perception of the problem, not through "telling" him or her what it is, but through aiding the client to test his or her view of the problem.

A major difference between everyday boss-to-subordinate interactions and the catalytic approach is that the consultant's help often comes through introducing techniques and procedures of data gathering for perception building *that are not in everyday use by the client.* The consultant's expertise, in other words, enables the client to check his or her perception of the situation in ways he or she might eventually have been able to grasp, at a slower pace, even without catalytic perception-building interventions. With new information the client may be prompted to act differently and often more effectively.

The catalytic consultant might suggest contract expectations in the following way. He or she might say, "The way I see my possible contribution is this: First I want to understand your problem as you define it. Once I am aware of this, I will either gather additional data that will help you to check out your definition of the problem, or I will assist you in designing measuring procedures through which you can test your definition of the problem. I will offer whatever procedural help—such as helping a meeting run smoothly—that may be asked of me in terms of your interpreting the data or your figuring out its implications for your dealing with the situation.

"If the data that are gathered lead to verified or altered perceptions, you may want me to work with others in helping them see the situation differently. I am prepared to do this under the circumstances that you authorize."

A case study of contracting within catalytic assumptions is provided by Weisbord. He goes into some detail about strategies for designing a "fluid" consultant "job description," in this case called a *contract*. This job description covers expectations about consultant-client relations where the consultant operates according to the view that ". . . he hires me to consult to him while he is working on his problem, helping *him* to achieve a better diagnosis of what has happened and what steps he must take to improve things."[1]

According to Weisbord, the client already is grappling with a situation that makes life difficult and which has three main components:

1. Organization crises due to people leaving, excessive absenteeism, cost control problems, budget difficulties, "boss" pressures, interpersonal and intergroup conflict.
2. "Significant others" to the client, who number among his or her sore spots.
3. Personal matters, such as uncertainty that "what I have is what I want."

Bypassing categories (1) and (3) above, the client initially nearly always seeks guidance on how to deal with the "significant others" category. Helping a client cope in a better way with more pertinent organization-related problems— for example, those listed under (1)—is the consultant's "bread and butter" business. How does he or she go about it? By ". . . gathering information, becoming aware of the deeper meanings, making choices . . ." that in the process help the client to:

1. Solve the immediate problem.
2. Gain insight into his or her own coping style.
3. Acquire greater coping skills.

What kind of contract do you build with a client in pursuit of these kinds of outcomes? First of all, the client has a right to know what the consultant expects to do in terms of time invested in:

1. Interviewing or survey sampling (done anonymously).
2. Organizing data.
3. Meetings with the client.

The purpose of the job description is to clarify new expectations whenever the situation shifts in any significant way. Thus the contract may be for two hours, a day, or a year, always subject to renegotiation on a moment-by-moment basis and subject to cancellation on twenty-four-hours' notice, the proviso being a face-to-face meeting first.

Most significant in understanding the catalytic aspects of consultant-client relationship as described by Weisbord are the following features.

1. Reacting to his perceived problem, the client sees the intervention as helping him to gain understanding and control over it.
2. Designation of who, when, where, and "why," with the "why" being the client's rather than a "joint" definition or the consultant's task to answer.
3. Diagnosis, based on some kind of collected information; the test of "good" data being that those who contribute it "will recognize it as critical to their lives together when I collate it and hand it back."[2]

Most of what has been described in this consultant-client relationship is based on catalytic assumptions, although not completely so for Weisbord recognizes that under some eventualities either the client or the consultant may compel a "test" of the relationship. These tests, which lead either to deepening the relationship or terminating it, seem more confrontational in character since they promote an "emotion-provoking" exchange. Presumably more basic values and assumptions are being challenged; and when these challenges are successful, the client may come to a new definition of his or her situation, as uncovered values and assumptions put the problem in a radically altered perspective.

A broader example of a catalytic approach is provided by the Tavistock Institute of Human Relations in one of its first projects at the Glacier Metal Company. Solutions to a number of consultant-client relationship issues were incorporated into the contract in terms of which consultant interventions could be made.

To whom should the consultant team be responsible? This issue was resolved by having the consultant report to the Works Council, a permanent union-management body that for some years had been providing a basis for resolving grievances. The Council was an elected representative body that was neither management controlled nor worker dominated. The Works Council delegated a project subcommittee as its source of contact with the Tavistock consultants. It was agreed that only public information would be gathered.

Consultants can and do gather information at one level and feed it to another higher level, where it is acted upon. This strategy weakens rather than strengthens management. It reduces boss-subordinate communication and often creates defensiveness, withholding of data, and so on.

The Research Team avoided creating any suspicion of gathering secret information on the premise that the only real value is in information that can be freely discussed. In terms of projects, only those projects were undertaken that had the general approval of the people likely to be affected by the results.

Catalytic aspects of the interventions to preserve the nonsecrecy pledge with individuals or groups were based on the Research Team acting only in an advisory or interpretive role. As they said, "Nothing will be done behind anyone's back. No matter will be discussed unless representatives of the group are present or have agreed to the topic being raised."[3]

The Tavistock consultants, in other words, were governed by ground rules that put them in a catalytic role relative to helping with the operational problems of the company.

The key strategy in writing a contract is to convey to the client that the consultant's contribution is in assisting in problem definition through approaches to data gathering and data interpretation. This is in contrast with exercising initiative to impose a problem definition on the client or give the client "answers" as to what should be done to rectify the situation.

Contracting under an Acceptant Orientation

The character of the consultant-client relationship involved in the acceptant mode of intervention is nowhere better described than by Rogers:

> The counseling relationship is one in which warmth of acceptance and absence of any coercion or personal pressure on the part of the counselor permits the maximum expression of feelings, attitudes, and problems by the counselee. The relationship is a well-structured one, with limits of time, of dependence, and of aggressive action which apply particularly to the client, and limits of responsibility and of affection which the counselor imposes on himself. In this unique experience of complete emotional freedom within a well-defined framework, the client is free to recognize and understand his impulses and patterns, positive and negative, as in no other relationship.[4]

Because each such relationship is a unique one, acceptant consultation makes contract preparation difficult. Few clients have had prior experience with it or have experienced it in everyday life. They do not know what to expect, and words from the consultant do little to clarify the situation. Only after they have had experience with this approach does it become possible to talk meaningfully about it. Nonetheless some value may come from trying to be explicit. The consultant might say, "In many relationships the 'expert' takes the initiative to assist the one seeking help to resolve the problems for which help is being sought. Other consultants share the initiative with the client in a give-and-take way. It would be my desire that the initiative in our relationship always remain in *your* hands. I will offer whatever help and assistance I can contribute through aiding you to exercise initiative in dealing with your situation. I will do my best to understand what you are experiencing. For me to understand in a manner that will be helpful to you, it is important that I absorb what you are seeking to communicate, and that I do so in a nonevaluative, nonpartisan manner. In this way, it may be that our relationship will offer you the kind of safety that makes it possible for you to explore your own experience so as to gain deeper insight into why you feel as you do; and, further, to see opportunities of change that may not have been as apparent in the past. I may suggest experiments useful to you in entering into an experience, but the initiative for taking part, and for interpreting that experience is yours.

"As we go along you may come to experience your situation in a new light, and in turn this may have a significant bearing on how you relate to others. It might be that by speaking to them I could help them to see your altered situation.

But then the initiative would be shifting from you to me. The alternative is that you retain initiative by communicating to them your altered situation as you now or later conceive it. If you wish, I can offer help in providing a safe place to engage in these kinds of interactions with people who are significant to you."

This kind of statement is only the beginning of a contract. Much more is understood than is spoken, in the sense that the client appreciates not being told in a directive, advice-giving way what he or she should start or stop doing in order to deal with the problem.

Summary

The contract is one way in which the consultant and client can mutually develop a basis of interaction: the client thus has prestart expectations as to what he or she will gain from the process of consultation, and the consultant has a foundation for a period of work with the client.

At the outset of a consultative relationship, acceptant, confrontational, and theory/principles consultants encounter difficulty in "explaining" the character of their intervention, for their modes of intervening usually are not within the client's realm of experience. In the initial contact it is desirable, if at all possible, to demonstrate the character of intervention rather than to rely on explanations of what can be expected. Of these three, the theory/principles consultant has the easiest time in presenting a demonstration. For purposes of internalization he or she can administer instruments on the spot, present theory for using data, and feed back the data, thus giving the client some idea of what to expect and an indication of understandings necessary and progress possible in resolving larger problems. The acceptant consultant faces the difficulty of encouraging the client to express feelings freely. If a client is ready to talk, this is no problem; but if he or she resists doing so, the consultant faces the more difficult task of illustrating to the client how they might relate with one another. The confrontational consultant's difficulty is that usually he or she needs to spend some time pinpointing the client's values and assumptions *before* demonstrating to the client how consultant challenges might help him or her become more objective about the situation at hand.

The prescriptive consultant can explain quite easily, on the basis of an expert approach to the problem, what he or she intends to do and how he or she intends to go about doing it. If the consultant's credentials make sense and his or her presentation demonstrates understanding of the client's problems, then a contract between them is not difficult to prepare.

The consultant who uses a catalytic approach gains acceptance by discussing some aspect of data gathering and then demonstrating its use. In this way, the client can check out whether or not the data make sense in the light of his or her own situation, and on this basis decide readiness to take additional steps.

The idea of working out a psychological contract to guide intervention is often advanced as an important aspect of the catalytic approach to consultation. As described by Kolb and Frohman, its characteristics are as follows.

Once the entry point has been selected, the consultant and the client system, through the entry representative, begin to negotiate a contract. In its use here, the word "contract" implies more than a legal document agreed upon at the outset of the project. The contract will define if and how the succeeding stages of the planned change process will be carried out. The emphasis is on a continuing process of sharing the expectations of the consultant and the client system and agreeing on the contributions to be made by both parties. Mark Frohman has listed 10 areas in which agreement over expectations is important in order to develop an effective working relationship: (1) the consultant's and the client's goals for the project, (2) broad definition of the problem (to be redefined as the relationship progresses), (3) relationship of the problem to the overall system, (4) client resources and abilities applicable to the problem, (5) consultant resources and abilities applicable to the problem, (6) broad mode of approach to the problem, (7) nature of the consultant/client relationship, (8) expected benefits for the client, (9) expected benefits for the consultant, and (10) ability of one party to influence the other.[5]

TEAM CONSULTATION

Team consultation assumes a number of forms and variations in reported case studies appearing throughout the intervention literature. Two fundamental considerations seem to be important in consultant team formation and in the comparison of team intervention approaches to individual interventions.

Interdisciplinary Team Formation

One consideration in team formation is organizational complexity. Organizations are such complex wholes that a full and complete diagnosis of an organizational situation is possible only when multiple skills of diagnosis are employed. Thus, one consultant might be disciplined in the financial area, the second in technological considerations, and the third in the behavioral science area. Using their various skills simultaneously, the interdisciplinary team works toward diagnosing the conditions prevailing with an organization, then collaborates in developing a joint assessment. Many more significant variables of organization can be brought under scrutiny and examination through the combined expertise of team members.

Team Consultation for Cross Checking

An alternative to interdisciplinary team composition is found in teams where two or more consultants work together for the primary purpose of providing a system of checks and balances. The attempt is to increase the validity of the diagnosis by having at least two observers. Each consultant can evaluate what is learned from his or her own point of view and in comparison with what the other person is learning. Perceptions, observations, and conclusions are shared and discussed in order to maximize both accuracy and objectivity.

Sometimes data for the organizational diagnosis is collected in two-on-one interviews, where consultants interview key executives simultaneously. The benefit of this is that one consultant can follow up leads generated by the other consultant's inquiry. Alternatively, the second consultant can fill in blind spots that the first consultant may not recognize. Based on his or her information, each is able to check with the other to test the implications of what was discussed after the interview is completed.

Thereafter it is much more common for two or more consultants to separate, each conducting interviews on a one-to-one or one-to-group basis. The team then confers with one another to test what has been learned, to give one another leads as to what is being heard, and to discuss areas of investigation that might merit increased emphasis. Where this approach is used, it is desirable that team members interview in the same organization subsystem. Direct comparisons of reports by groups and individuals operating in the same culture can then be made. Discrepancies can be identified and resolved.

Sometimes interviewing is done sequentially, with one consultant following the other. Usually the interviews are staggered in some way, i.e., Person A being interviewed by Consultant 1 on Day 1 and by Consultant 2 on Day 3. The advantage of this is that the second consultant can focus inquiry in a much more critical way by virtue of what has been learned from Person A on Day 1 and from many other contacts by both consultants on Days 1 and 2. These second sequence consultations many times have the purpose of validating conclusions being developed but not yet finalized. In some instances only one or a very few persons are in a position to give ultimate information that would validate or invalidate the consultant's analyses.

An apparent limitation in the second approach is more hypothetical than real. With consultants serving as listening posts for one another and with the possibilities for double checking, it is important that they be oriented toward diagnosing in the same subject area. The concern is that if members of the consulting team are oriented toward the same discipline, they may be limited in what they can see, hear, or learn; therefore their diagnosis is likely to be similarly limited. Further analysis shows that this concern is not necessarily a legitimate one.

An example of an evident computer problem demonstrates the utility of the cross-checking team. A problem in utilizing the computer within the financial operation is generally not related to the computer per se, but is rather a problem of poor planning, inadequate involvement of the user, conflicts within the computer group, etc. All of these create the "computer problem," which is merely symptomatic of the real human effectiveness issues residing beneath the surface. To diagnose the problem as one of inadequate computer knowledge or skills is to disregard or misdiagnose the deeper issues involved. Defining the problem in terms of the presented problem is far less likely to be valid than seeing the problem as a symptom of difficulties resulting from the ineffective mobilization of human resources.

Viewed from this perspective, diagnostic work in consulting is related to cutting through the problem as presented by the felt needs of the client and identifying causative factors for the deeper-lying problems beneath the surface.

If the barriers to organizational effectiveness are truly represented by obvious surface issues, the solution is one of mobilizing available resources within the firm or beyond it in order to make up for knowledge deficiencies. In doing so the organization is depending on technically knowledgeable people to provide answers or to teach capable persons to absorb technical information as a basis for more effective problem solving. In either case, this use of outsiders does not involve consultation. Rather a specific skill is being brought into the organization on either a temporary or permanent basis just as happens when an organization decides to enter a new area and employs persons who are competent to exercise leadership within that area.

TEAM CONSULTATION DYNAMICS

Consultant teams themselves are subject to certain potential barriers to their effectiveness, which need to be understood and dealt with in order to avoid the inherent constraints that otherwise are created by their presence.

Internal Dynamics

When two or more individuals join together in a collaborative effort, the very act of doing so creates potential tensions between them that can reduce their effectiveness. These are so well known as to be self-evident, and what follows is simply a review of basics.

Hierarchy. A consulting team can be organized in a boss-subordinate manner, that is, with a Number 1 and a Number 2, or it can operate in a collegial manner within an atmosphere of equality based on interdependence. All of this is dependent not only on the skills of the participants, but also on their personal needs for dominance or operating in the follower or supportive role. Generally speaking, it can be said that a consulting team should have the expertise to be able to carry out the assignment in an effective manner. Therefore it is to be expected that equality, based on interdependence and reinforced by sound qualification, creates a better consulting basis than one premised on a hierarchy of 1 and 2.

The exception to the above is when a member of the consulting team is new to consultative work and is not fully qualified. Under these conditions, he or she needs the support and help that could come from something approaching a boss-subordinate relationship, particularly so if the relationship is open, candid, and based on trust and respect, rather than on being given directions and expected to exercise responsibilities for implementation only.

Personal needs for dominance, priority, or "looking good" in the eyes of the client are likely to have negative effects on prospective outcomes. Such needs are likely to reduce the effectiveness of the consulting team unless they can be openly discussed by the consultants themselves in a manner that will eliminate any adverse impact they may create.

External Influences. Influences from persons within the client system can also create problems for a consultation team if the client shows a preference for one or another person in the team. If the preferred consultant accepts this influence, he or she is likely to have a disrupting effect on the rest of the team. On the other hand, if the presumed preference is not based on ability or experience, but is limited to personal preference and the consultant confronts this issue directly, he or she can many times eliminate this source of tension and prevent it from having a disrupting effect on the consulting team.

The many factors involved in the effectiveness of a consulting team go beyond what has been said here, but these points offer major considerations in determining when a consulting team may be more effective than an individual consultant. Other studies are available, including an important one by Fritz Steele.[6]

INTERNAL AND EXTERNAL CONSULTANTS

The history of external consultants is very long, but in recent times can be traced to the turn of the century when the management consulting firms emerged on the scene. The external consultant served a genuine need: to bring information that was outside of the organization into the organization by prescribing new solutions for long-standing problems. Up until World War II, this consultation tended to be on the technological, financial, structural, and/or manufacturing side of the organization. After the war, the subject matter of consultation was vastly expanded. It came to include individual behavior, group dynamics, organization culture, and so on.

Then a new trend developed in the 1960s. It involved designating certain organization members as internal consultants. The internal consultant was a line or staff person who was relieved of other duties and assigned responsibility for bringing more effective ways of managing through better decision making and problem solving into organizational use.

Strengths and Limitations of External and Internal Consultants

There are advantages and limitations in both the internal consultant role and the external consultant when intervening on organization life.

External Consultation. One of the main strengths of the external consultant is that he or she has the opportunity of dealing with many organizations. What is learned by intervening in one organization can be brought to bear on comparable problems existing in other organizations.

Another benefit that external consultants enjoy is that they can be in contact with managers at all levels of an organization. In other words, an external consultant can work with the chief executive officer or the president, as well as with department heads or supervisors. He or she can do so because, not being a member of the organization, he or she does not hold a position in the hierarchy and therefore is free from hierarchical constraints. To confront a person of rank with an aspect of his or her own behavior that may have consequences for the organization may be threatening, but it cannot be rejected out of hand on the premise of insubordination.

A third advantage is that he or she is in a better position to make high-risk interventions. A high-risk intervention is one in which a significant member of the firm is confronted in a straightforward way with negative implications of decision making. The advantage to the organization is that if the diagnosis is valid and the intervention is done in an effective manner, potentially great benefits are derived by the organization. Should the intervention be wrong or, even if valid, rejected, the consultant can be terminated. The advantage to the firm is that it does not have to maintain continuity with the consultant. The advantage to the consultant is that, having other clients, he or she is not thrown into the ranks of the unemployed by having one client relationship terminated.

One of the limitations, at least in the case of many external consultants, is that they do not have the continuity with the firm that otherwise might be of benefit from the standpoint of increasingly deeper consultant insights into real needs. The lack of continuity is one of the main limitations, but it has its balancing benefits from the consultant having many clients and therefore being able to bring learnings from one setting into another.

The Internal Consultant. By virtue of having organization membership and sometimes over many years, internal consultants may have a deep and detailed knowledge of what actually goes on in a firm, including the hidden politics and the subtle but unstated agreements, collusions, and so on. As such, the internal consultant is in a more fully informed position regarding organization barriers to effectiveness than is likely to be possible for an external consultant. The insider can make interventions based on his or her knowledge that might not be credible if made by someone without such knowledge. Furthermore, the internal consultant has the likelihood of greater continuity of working with members of the same organization over an extended period. Under these conditions, interventions are possible on a continuing rather than on an interrupted basis.

Of the several disadvantages that are encountered by internal consultants, the most important is related to holding membership in the hierarchy. Since many, if not most, internal consultants are staff and assigned to the personnel function, it is difficult for the consultant to work effectively at ranks higher than his or her own reporting relationship. The reason is that if an internal consultant, whose membership is in the personnel function, were to challenge persons of higher rank, he or she would run the risk of arousing negative feelings and appearing insubordinate.

Linkages between Internal and External Consultants. One of the arrangements that permits organizations to benefit from both internal and external consulting is through external-internal consultant cooperation. This solution is close to an optimal basis for bringing consultation help to bear on solving real needs. Some of the advantages to be derived by organizations arranging the collaboration between external and internal consultants include the following.

The internal consultant, knowing the situation more intimately than the external consultant, can aid the external consultant to gain insight as to what goes on in the organization. Thus, the external consultant's knowledge of the organization is deepened through insight that can be made available to him or her by the internal consultant.

By virtue of his or her continuity, the internal consultant can aid the organization through implementation of agreed-upon next steps. A third basis of collaboration is that the internal consultant may see important confrontations that need to take place, but by virtue of his or her position in the hierarchy, it is unsound to attempt such prescriptions or confrontations. Nonetheless, the internal consultant can create the conditions under which the external consultant can implement these interventions. In other words, the external consultant can often do work in levels of the hierarchy that are off limits to the internal consultant.

An illustrative example of this approach involved internal and external change agents joining forces to propel a traditional county jail toward institutionalization of major reforms at the Berkshire County (Massachusetts) House of Correction.

At the request of the County Sheriff, the University of Massachusetts School of Education at Amherst agreed to explore new systems for delivering educational and other services. A project director from the university worked closely with a correctional officer assigned by the jail during a three-year project designed to create new programs and new processes for developing and carrying out these programs. The product of their intervention was the "Model Education Program," designed to provide inmates a viable alternative to spending their days "watching television and assisting in menial institutional work."

Gluckstern and Packard define their roles and activities throughout the three years of the project.

> In the first year of the project, the external change agent's job involved diagnosing the system, establishing . . . credibility within the jail, establishing communication with the different groups and constituencies there, and educating them about the nature of the change process. . . . [Work of the internal change agent] involved helping and monitoring the outside change agent as she tried to gain access to information, subgroups, and individuals within the jail.
>
> During the first year these two change agents, along with the staff that was gathered to assist them, began the work of creating *vehicles for institutional change.* They worked with inmates and officers to articulate specific needs and develop programs to meet them.

To do this, they formed committees, discussion groups, and task-oriented work groups. . . . The participatory aspect of the process defined a democratic collaborative approach to change, which set an example to the jail to revise its traditional autocratic structures.

In the second year of the Model Education Program, the two change agents functioned as co-workers busy with the administrative operations of these many new programs. . . .

During this period, a Governance Board was established composed of inmates, correctional officers, jail administrators, and Model Education Program staff. The Governance Board was charged with considering grievances and approving new programs. Though at the beginning it had little real power, it did not take long for it to become a focal point in the jail and establish an expectation for more democratic administrative procedures.

The third year was a time of transfer of roles and the stabilization of the organizational changes that had been accomplished. . . . The external change agent prepared to leave and took on an increasingly marginal role functioning more as a consultant and advisor. Meanwhile the internal change agent began to function as a new kind of administrator. . . . By January 1976 . . . the jail had secured its own sources of funding to maintain the programs that were underway.[7]

This intervention demonstrates how internal and external change agents can work together to bring about lasting institutional change. At the onset of this intervention, "The jail was authoritarian and repressive, and inmates were treated like children without even the smallest responsibility in the running of their own daily lives. It was an environment that fostered passivity, resentment, alienation, and paves the way for the continuation of a lifestyle of crime." Through the combined and concerted efforts of these change agents, coupled with the sheriff's commitment and client's participation, positive organizational change is reported to have occurred.

BURNOUT

An adverse reaction experienced by some in the helping profession is burnout. The word itself explains the phenomenon: a feeling of energy having been consumed and with little or no additional energy available for further effort. Burnout is also known in other than helping professions, but it is most conspicuous among those who directly involve themselves in aiding others.

If burnout occurs, it does so to a significantly lesser degree when an individual is in a line assignment, where power and authority are available to exercise control over the situation.

What Causes Burnout?

Different explanations have been offered for the appearance of burnout, including the following.[8] First there is a sense of idealism and commitment. The consultant exercises his or her efforts with clients to truly rectify difficulties, and a desire to be helpful is genuine and deep-seated.

A second condition is the experience of failure or disappointment in the degree of success realized. A considerable gap is felt to exist between aspiration and actuality. The consultant's perception of results achieved is beneath his or her expectations.

A third condition is a sense of frustration, but the specific cause of the frustration cannot be targeted. The "cause" is not definable or identifiable in the manner that the consultant might, if he or she were able to pinpoint it, be able to do something to remove it.

The consultant may experience a sense of entrapment as a fourth condition. Aspirations to contribute are present, but results are less than had been desired. Frustration deepens, and the consultant comes to feel a sense of disappointment. The disappointment does not induce a "why try more" reaction, but rather a sense that no amount of effort is likely to fundamentally alter the situation. Burnout is well underway.

It is probably true that persons consulting under certain Grid styles are more likely to become burnout victims than others. Three burnout prone styles can be specified.

Certain Grid Styles Predisposed to Burnout

The 9,9-oriented consultant prefers a consultative mode based on openness and give-and-take collaboration. He or she may fail to aid the client to make the hoped-for progress. The same is true of a 9,1-oriented consultant who, however, is more likely to "lash out" and to discharge frustration, though even this is of little help to the client. Consultants whose fundamental orientation with clients is paternalistic are possibly the most susceptible. Some reasons for this follow. One is that if the consultant has a clear sense of what he or she would like to see the client accomplish, but the client does not respond in an obedient manner and the desired results are not achieved. Furthermore, the paternalistic consultant cannot apply pressure of the sort commonly associated with the line exercise of power and authority. The result is that feelings of frustration become apparent, but they cannot be expressed in the same manner as when the person who feels responsible can "chew out" those who are resisting his or her influence. The frustration has to be lived with without being made explicit. Disappointment creeps in, but idealism as to the desirability of being helpful is not diminished. The paternalistic consultant experiences burnout.

Many of the "true" causes of frustrations in the kinds of situations being described are embedded within the culture surrounding the client. The constraints within such cultures make it impossible for movement to occur in spite of the fact that direction of movement is well recognized and both logical and valid. Because the culture does not support this movement, the frustration and lack of progress seem to mount.

What Can Be Done About Burnout?

Any number of suggestions have been offered on how to avoid burnout, or when it has occurred how to restore a sense of involvement and commitment.

Many of these recommendations deal with symptoms, however, and there is no clear evidence that any of them contain the solution to the problem. Recommendations include reducing client load, taking more frequent vacations, reducing the work day through the consultant taking responsibility for line activities and in this way engaging in activities that are distinctly different from those experienced in the consultant role.

One antidote to burnout is through deeper understanding of the conditions responsible for it. When a consultant understands these dynamics, he or she is less likely to be vulnerable to its insidious influences. But even here logical insight into the problem is sometimes of little consequence. Other recommendations are even quite gratuitous—more sleep, more exercise, etc. None of these recommendations is of demonstrated utility in checking or reducing burnout.

CONSULTANT PREFERENCES AND "NATURAL BENT"

Many consultants have personal preferences and predispositions that influence their choices or govern their tendencies to intervene in a certain way. Often these influences are unrelated to a client's real needs. Interventions based on consultant preferences and predilections such as these, rather than on a valid diagnosis of the requirements for addressing the client's situation, are of less value than when they are targeted to the client's unique needs. The Grid framework, introduced in the discussion of theory/principles interventions and referenced earlier in this chapter, can be used to illustrate.

Many considerations determine an intervention's effectiveness. Nevertheless, a single Grid-style orientation, given that it is sufficiently constructive so as not to rule out consideration of other intervention modes that at some time may become pertinent, can serve to structure the use of an entire range of consultation skills, as illustrated below.

Table 32.2 Intervention preference by grid style of consultant

Consultant's Intervention Preference	Consultant's Probable Grid Style(s)
Theory/principle	9,9 (and 9,1)
Prescriptive	9,1 (and paternalism)
Confrontation	9,9 (and 9,1)
Catalytic	5,5 (and "statistical" 5,5)
Acceptant	1,9

Intervention Mode	Grid Style	When
Theory/principle	9,9	The client can approach and probably solve his or her problems based on systematic insight and be in a better position for contending with similar future problems.
Prescriptive	9,9	The client has reached the point of impasse, hopelessness, or despair, and yet action is imperative to avoid further negative consequences.
Confrontation	9,9	The client's problem can only be brought into focus and resolved through the client's coming to recognize in his or her behavior the cause of his or her problems.
Catalytic	9,9	By enriching the client's perceptions of the situation, the consultant assists him or her in taking fundamental rather than superficial action.
Acceptant	9,9	The consultant helps the client to relieve immobilizing tensions and thereby to unblock barriers that have prevented constructive action.

Sometimes the intervention mode is more related to 9,1 assumptions on the part of the consultant than to the problem-solving needs of the client.

Intervention Mode	Grid Style	When
Theory	9,1	The consultant is certain that theory represents the one and only way for the client to solve his or her problem.
Prescriptive	9,1	The consultant is determined that an action he or she sees as valid be taken and is ready to use whatever pressures are necessary and available to get the client to take the action.
Confrontation	9,1	The consultant derives gratification from creating conflict (or hostility).

A special case of relying on prescriptive intervention can arise out of a consultant's paternalistic orientation.

Intervention Mode	Grid Style	When
Prescriptive	Paternalistic	He or she insists, and often correctly, that the client take the recommended action "for his own good," even though the client may not see it that way.

In contrast, the 5,5 consultant assumptions lead to the following:

Intervention Mode	Grid Style	When
Theory	5,5	The consultant presents theory not for its usefulness but because he or she thinks the client wants it.
Catalytic	5,5	The consultant responds to the client's felt needs, even when it is clear to him or her, privately, that the realistic solution would entail an alternative definition of the problem.
Acceptant	5,5	The consultant reacts in terms of the client's felt needs without being convinced in his or her own thinking that this is the best thing to do.

When the consultant is oriented in the 1,9 direction:

Intervention Mode	Grid Style	When
Catalytic	1,9	He or she intervenes in an effort to please the client.
Acceptant	1,9	He or she approaches a client in this manner because high concern on the personal dimension is his or her sole way of feeling helpful.

The 1,1 consultant:

Intervention Mode	Grid Style	When
Acceptant	1,1	The consultant takes a passive, listening posture not out of supportive orientation toward the client but from lack of interest.

These various intervention modes as evaluated according to Grid-style orientations specify a particular consultant's "legitimate" interventions. When examined as a broad array of alternatives, however, the approaches also make it possible to distinguish between sound interventions and interventions that have inherent weaknesses.

Any consultant whose predilections are other than 9,9 is faced with a dilemma. For example, if his or her orientation is 1,9, would it be better to stay in that mode and concentrate on situations where an acceptant mode would be appropriate, disregarding other modes? Or would it be better for the consultant to try to acquire 9,9 flexibility so as to be able to intervene in an effective way regarding whatever specific issue the client has to resolve? A decision to remain within the 1,9 mode leads toward specialization, whereas resolution in terms of the 9,9 alternative promotes a generalist orientation.

Another way of looking at consultant effectiveness is provided in Table 32.3. Warrick and Donovan[9] surveyed twenty well-known OD experts as well as fifty industry and government internal OD practitioners and compiled a composite picture of the requirements for effective organization consultation as shown below.

Four critical skill areas, including knowledge, consulting, conceptual, and human, are identified in this schema. Specific requirements are listed in each of the four major categories. The original text provides further information which may facilitate the scoring and evaluation process.

While a perfect score is 200, norms suggested by Warrick and Donovan indicate that a consultant's readiness is excellent if his or her score is 90 or above. (See Table 32.3 for specific criteria and scoring instructions.)

This approach has some value as a survey instrument, yet we know that many of the listed skills are of critical importance and some of lesser importance. For example, poor knowledge of organization behavior, behavioral sciences, management, and training technology lowers a respondent's score by only 16 points, yet these deficiencies are critical relative to some of the others, i.e., a good sense of humor, or report writing. The other limitation in the use of this instrument is for self-assessment, which is known to be distorted by self-deception. Such an instrument used as a framework for analysis, or as the basis for feedback by experienced colleagues, may prove quite valuable.

OVERRELIANCE ON VARIOUS INTERVENTIONS

Any intervention mode, if relied upon exclusively, can sooner or later prove ineffective. A "permanent" acceptant mode, for example, can result in the client's becoming so comfortable and accepting of his or her situation, after having been assisted in working through disturbed emotions toward it, that in effect the client becomes satisfied with existing circumstances and loses desire to deal with the source(s) of the problem.

The weakness of a perennial catalytic mode is its shallowness. A catalytic consultant can aid the client to recognize problems, ones that he or she would be likely to overlook without such an intervention, and can then help the client place them in priority order for action. Such listing may promote the confidence necessary for solution seeking on a step-by-step basis. Yet it is a common observation that this kind of "bridging," even though it aids a client to see aspects of the situation that previously were less visible, rarely helps the client learn to independently diagnose "novel" problems. The consultant becomes a crutch; and as the client gets more help, he or she becomes "weaker."

A risk in a too-long-continued confrontational mode is that of "uncovering" client weaknesses without offering him or her ways to overcome these failings. The dramatic character of even one such exposure—not to mention a series— can be traumatic to the client. He or she can no longer repeat the past and yet

Table 32.3 Survey of organization development skills

Knowledge Skills	Consulting Skills	Conceptual Skills	Human Skills
☐ Organization development	☐ Proposal writing	☐ A sound philosophical base concerning human behavior, management, organization behavior, learning behavior, and organization development	☐ A genuine caring for people
☐ Organization behavior (individual, group, intergroup, and whole organization behavior)	☐ Marketing programs and ideas		☐ A positive attitude
	☐ Diagnosing organizations		☐ Self-awareness
	☐ Synthesizing data		☐ Self-discipline
	☐ Report writing		☐ Good rational/emotional balance
☐ Behavioral sciences, management	☐ Problem solving	☐ A systems view of organization and the environments in which they operate	☐ Integrity
☐ General business (accounting, finance, marketing, management information system, budgeting, etc.)	☐ Team building		☐ Helping skills (understanding, empathetic, good listener and coach, good at checking out perceptions, assertive. Good at giving and receiving feedback)
	☐ Conflict resolution		
	☐ Process consultation	☐ An ability to visualize, design, and manage long-range programs, training interventions, and follow-up programs	
	☐ Training and development skills		
☐ Training technology	☐ An ability to identify and respond to an organization's real needs		☐ Sensitivity to organizational needs
☐ An awareness of current developments in OD	☐ An ability to quickly adapt to changing situations	☐ An ability to understand and communicate theories, principles, models, and ideas	☐ Leveling and confronting skills
	☐ An ability to quickly establish client trust and rapport		☐ Persuasiveness and persistence
	☐ An ability to obtain lasting results	☐ An ability to innovate	☐ A willingness to take risks
			☐ An ability to successfully handle stress and frustration
			☐ A good sense of humor
			☐ An ability to model and practice healthy behavior

OD Skills Evaluation

Evaluate yourself on each of the OD skills by placing the appropriate answer in each box. Total your scores, divide by two, and compare the result below.

1 = Poor   2 = Below Average   3 = Average   4 = Good   5 = Excellent

is unable to see what alternative actions may be possible. This can be an ultimate kind of defeat.

A weakness of never-ending prescription is that the client is given answers without having learned to think through and to define the problem. Thus, as with catalytic interventions, the client may become ever more dependent on continual instruction "from the outside." He or she may completely surrender personal will on a more or less permanent basis, letting the consultant dictate the strategy and actions of daily life.

An unvarying theory-based approach may encourage the client to become too absorbed in intellectual activity, not as a tool for solving problems, but rather as an end in itself. As Kingsbury[10] has mentioned, to the extent that the client can "talk" theory and keep it at a high level of abstraction, it is unnecessary for him or her to take needed actions. Intellectualizing is, in a certain sense, a means of problem avoidance rather than problem solving.

WHEN TO USE DIFFERENT INTERVENTION MODES

Each intervention mode used in consultation has been pictured as a dominant strategy for given kinds of situations. For a contemporary consultant who is not at the leading edge of his or her field, one approach or another *is* the customary and dominant approach. Yet what was appropriate in an earlier phase of a consultation may be superfluous at a later stage—something else is required if the client is to take another forward step. And, indeed, there is no basic reason why combinations of approaches may not be employed sequentially as the client's situation evolves.

Not all modes are equally compatible with one another, even when used on a "well-intended judgment" basis by the same consultant with the same client. Some of the more compatible combinations of approaches are discussed below.

Following Theory/Principle

Although the need for any other kind of intervention may be stimulated by a theory-based approach, prescription is the least probable. Since sound theory provides the client a basis for predicting the source of his or her own actions and for anticipating their consequences, he or she should not need to be "told" by another how to solve problems.

The most probable intervention following theory-based interventions is confrontational in character. Now that the client has an intellectual and emotional basis for insight into the situation, he or she is motivated to take those actions necessary to focus and resolve personal problems. But older values continue to exert a constraining influence. Confrontation can assist the client in rejecting what he or she "knows" to be outmoded values.

Theory-based interventions also may lead to catalytic interventions in the sense that assistance in perception building may be needed to see a complex problem more clearly. Alternatively, an acceptant intervention may aid the client to relieve, focus, express, and work through tensions that were triggered by the theory but were not known about prior to the theory-oriented discovery of them. The resulting catharsis is then of a bridging character, enabling the client to reestablish his or her emotional equilibrium before attempting to move forward.

Following Prescription

Regardless of how "right," prescription can and often does increase the client's tensions and block effective problem solving. This is particularly so whenever the prescription goes against the grain of the client's history or dramatically shifts interpersonal social or working relationships. After such a prescription, a shift of intervention mode may be necessary so that the client can explore, express, and work through the emotions and tensions it aroused. If this shift in intervention mode does not happen at an appropriate time—i.e., when the emotional tensions in the client are at their peak—it is likely to prove ineffective. Once emotions become crystallized or submerged, the client is likely to be more resistant to expressing emotions and therefore would avoid responding to the kind of intervention that would promote this approach. In this case, the only real possibility of further progress is confrontation, sometimes at a deep level.

Sometimes the consultant is no longer acceptable to the client after his or her prescriptive interventions have had such disturbing effects. Then catharsis, if introduced at all, comes about through the intervention of a second consultant, most often not connected in any way with the first.

Following Confrontation

Because a confrontational intervention can have a jolting effect and because it may bring a client face-to-face with problems in ways that prevent him or her from indulging in defensive rationalization, it can cause the client to see disabling personal weaknesses, sometimes for the first time. Once a client is disturbed by self-admission that personally held values and beliefs are unjustified, he or she may "spill" emotions. This overflow of emotions is one way of relieving the discrepancy between the need to maintain a false front and the relief possible through self-confession. The consultant then may shift from a confrontational to a cathartic basis in order to help the client reestablish emotional equilibrium.

There is the possibility of catalytic intervention when a confrontational mode has not provoked emotional expression but has brought about a major cognitive shift in the definition of the problem. Thereafter the consultant may deal with the client in a catalytic way, aiding him or her in perception building in order to explore action alternatives unavailable under the old definition of the problem.

Prescription also may follow confrontation. Once confrontation has produced a values reassessment, the client may wish to alter conduct yet may have little or no understanding of what new action might constitute a sounder alternative. The consultant may provide direction by telling the client what to do to solve his or her problem and keep the client at it until the new solution becomes sufficiently well established to be maintained without assistance.

Following Catalytic

This combination is the same as acceptant, but the sequence is in reverse. Should a catalytic intervention stir feelings of anxiety, fear, anger, or even uncertainty, it is natural for the consultant to back off from perception-building activities and provide the sympathetic support necessary for a client to work through his or her tensions. The interaction is likely thereafter to return to a catalytic basis. In this sense an acceptant intervention within a catalytic sequence is likely to be an interruption of data flow rather than a shift away from the perception-building process.

Following Acceptant

Under circumstances where emotional tensions are blocking problem-solving initiative, *only* the acceptant approach stands any likelihood of being able to reduce those tensions sufficiently to permit the problem itself to be examined. The most likely mode to follow, once catharsis has relieved the tensions within the system, is a catalytic approach. The catalytic orientation, which itself is in the nonevaluative and nonjudgmental direction, responds to the felt needs of clients. It is therefore emotionally more neutral but consonant with the sympathetic, supportive, warm relationship engendered earlier by acceptant interventions. Furthermore, a catalytic intervention following an acceptant one moves the client forward at the client's own tempo, permitting him or her to control the terms, means, and pace of the intervention. It is less likely to stir up new anxieties that would make it difficult for the client to build on progress already made.

By comparison, the confrontational approach is likely to jolt the client and to stir resistance by violating his or her expectations of sympathetic support founded upon experience of the consultant's attitudes in earlier interventions.

The prescriptive solution also is at odds with the support and encouragement characteristic of the acceptant mode, particularly when the prescribed action places the client in a new internal conflict or "forces" him or her to take an action adverse to colleagues or subordinates. A theory-based approach is possible, but less likely, for after tensions have been relieved there often is a need for immediate action and insufficient additional time to shift to a systematic problem-solving approach.

THE FUTURE OF CONSULTATION

Because of the importance of dealing more effectively with the numerous serious problems that confront modern society, it is probable that consultation is still in its infancy. As greater skill is acquired in helping clients solve their problems, consultation will become a more and more relied-upon means of assistance.

Prescriptive consultation, except in dealing with highly technical problems having little or no human content, is the least likely to expand. The weaknesses inherent in it are obvious. The catalytic approach is growing at a faster rate than it has in the past, even though its contribution is generally only of temporary value.

In order, the two fastest growing approaches are likely to be confrontational and theory-based consulting. Acceptant consultation is of importance in any situation where the client is unable to deal with personal problems because of a debilitating emotional overload. Only by the emotional release that catharsis can provide does the client stand any real prospect of coping in a problem-solving way with the difficulties being encountered. However, the attention given feelings in the late 1960s seems to have produced a boomerang effect in the recent past, with this approach now being seen as soft. The confrontational mode is of potentially high significance because the client can thus be assisted to face realities that he or she otherwise might never come to recognize.

Theory-based consultation holds the greatest promise for problem solving in the future. Once the client has learned theory and internalized it, he or she is released from dependence on others for assistance in solving problems and, thereafter, further consultation is unnecessary, at least in the domain of activity defined by the theory. Two current weaknesses of theory-based intervention should be pointed out. First, a client must devote substantial time to the learning of theory in order to permit its internalization. This relatively slow process can turn clients away from the theory-based approach in a world where time is at a premium. The other limitation is that very little work has yet been done in terms of converting the rich store of academic theories for functional use. Years of effort will be required to bring this conversion about, even though the strategies for such conversion and for internalization have been well established.

Once this happens, however, theory-based interventions can be replaced by theory-based teaching in the home, in the classroom, and on the job, such that consultation's instructional role can eventually be taken over by broader strategies of education.

Notes

1. M. Weisbord, "The Organization Development Contract," *OD Practitioner* 5 (1973) : 2. Reprinted by permission.
2. Ibid., pp. 1–4.
3. E. Jaques, *The Changing Culture of a Factory* (London: Tavistock, 1951), pp. 13, 14.
4. C. R. Rogers, *Counseling and Psychotherapy* (Boston: Houghton Mifflin, 1942), pp. 113–14. Reprinted by permission of the author and publisher.
5. D. A. Kolb and A. L. Frohman, "An Organization Development Approach to Consulting," *Sloan Management Review* 12, no. 1 (1970): 55. © 1970 by the Industrial Management Review Association. All rights reserved.
6. F. Steele, *Consulting for Organizational Change* (Amherst: University of Massachusetts Press, 1975), pp. 1–202. See particularly chapter 7, "Teamwork in Consultation," pp. 109–38.
7. N. B. Gluckstern and R. W. Packard, "The Internal-External Change-Agent Team: Bringing Change to a 'Closed Institution,'" *The Journal of Applied Behavioral Science* 13, no. 1 (1977): 45, 46, 47.

8. M. Lauderdale, *Burnout.* Austin, Texas: Learning Concepts, 1982. See also J. Edelwich, and R. Brodsky, *Burn-out, Stages of Dissolutionment in the Helping Professions.* New York: Human Sciences Press, 1981, and C. Maslach, and A. Pines, "The Burn-out Syndrome in the Day Care Setting." *Child Care Quarterly* 6, no. 2 (1977): 100–13.

9. O. Warrick and T. Donovan, "Surveying Organization Development Skills," *Training and Development Journal* 33, no. 9 (1979): 22–25. Copyright 1979, Training and Development Journal, American Society for Training and Development. Reprinted with permission. All rights reserved.

10. S. Kingsbury, "Dilemmas for the Trainer," in W. G. Dyer, ed., *Modern Theory and Method in Group Training* (New York: Van Nostrand Reinhold Co., 1972), pp. 107–15.

33

Consultant as Entrepreneur

Up to this point, the study of consultation, for the most part, has focused on its professional aspects with much attention placed on accurately diagnosing the focal issue, ensuring that the intervention is with the correctly identified client, and that the intervention itself is congruent with the focal issue and with the client's perceptions and understandings as well. Because of the intricacies and subtleties involved, the professional side is a source of unending fascination, but there is a business side as well. The result is that a consultant only can be successful when the professional side is supported by the business arrangements through which consultation takes place.

The solo consultant, or consultants in a small firm, is in fact an entrepreneurial businessperson, just as is the medical doctor who sets up his or her own practice, or the dentist who joins with others to establish a dental clinic. This means a host of decisions must be made that are not directly concerned with consultation itself but have a significant impact on its success.

A consideration here is what model the consultant has in his or her mind when thinking about what he or she is to be engaged in providing. Two models are identified below.

VENDOR MODEL

A consultant may see himself or herself as selling services in a way that is comparable with any other service available in the market place. Then, he or she sees the situation as involving selling, advertising, and various forms of promotions, cold calls, free demonstrations, and so on. If the consultant sees services in this way, he or she is more likely to provide a range of services to meet whatever felt needs are expressed when a client requests services.

PROFESSIONAL MODEL

A professional model is a consultant with expert competence. He or she sees providing services according to professional standards. Under these conditions different guidelines prevail with regard to marketing, advertising, and promotions. The consultant is more likely to restrict him- or herself to making the services available known. Under these conditions, the consultant's fee structure is presumed to be fixed, and negotiation is usually considered inappropriate except under the conditions where a very large service is to be provided over a very long, extended period of time.

Under the professional model, consultants expect to be paid for services provided, without regard for demonstrations or other promotional services.

These two models are quite different ways of conducting a consultation business. They result in different amounts of expense, different fee structures, and so on.

The consultant entrepreneur needs to be clear as to which model is to constitute his or her basic approach. Then it becomes possible to plan the operations side of the business.

OFFICE

One decision is related to the location from which the consultation service will be undertaken. This can be a home office or an office in a building, etc. Part of this decision relates to the extent the consultant intends to offer services by clients coming to his or her location in comparison to his or her going to the location where the consultation is to be conducted. The obvious point is that office space is expensive, and unless the new consultant is able to anticipate earnings to cover this expense, he or she may be exposed to unrealistic and unbearable financial obligations.

TELEPHONE

The consultant usually needs to be in touch with clients and vice versa by telephone. This is not as simple as it seems. If the consultant is a one-person operation, he or she is absent during periods of outside consultation or unavailable during inside consultation and therefore unable to answer.

An answering service can be retained, but there are also limitations in this. An answering machine may be purchased, but this also puts a period of silence between the caller and the person to whom the call was placed. Such silent periods can have adverse implications for effective consultation.

SECRETARY

A secretary can contribute to effective consultation in many ways beyond writing letters and proposals, answering mail and the telephone, etc. He or she can be called on to transfer calls based on judgment as to whether the consultant's activities will be adversely affected or not, or can promise an answer as to when the consultant will be able to respond. As with an office, a secretary is potentially an expensive support system, and the entrepreneur's earnings may not justify the overhead.

FEE STRUCTURE

The consultant charges for service rendered. The fee structure reflects this. But, how does one establish a fee structure?

One common way of doing so is to take the following steps.

1. Prepare some statement of annual earnings anticipated from consultation, projected on a net basis, usually related to what the person might be expected to earn from full and continuing employment.
2. Anticipate the amount of billings called for to provide this income after meeting expenses by estimating overhead to be borne before salaries of personal earnings can be realized.
3. Calculate the number of anticipated consultation days.
4. Once expenses are identified and number of paid consulting days specified, it

becomes possible to subtract them from what would have to be earned in order to arrive at net earnings.

5. It is then possible to compute what fee structure would be necessary to satisfy overhead, and thereafter to earn the net anticipated based on the forecasted number of paid consulting days.

These are simple and yet basic steps that consultants often postpone, sometimes to their misfortune. The postponement is due to the feeling or hope that to earn something is better than to earn nothing, and to set fees low is better than to price one's services out of the market. Nonetheless when intuitive feelings like these are relied on, the consultant may come to the end of a period discovering that his or her business is significantly less profitable than necessary for staying afloat. By going through these steps, sometimes repeatedly, it becomes possible to avoid at least some of these pitfalls.

A supplemental way of setting fees is to learn from practicing consultants how they go about setting fees. This is a question other consultants are sometimes reluctant to answer. They may answer with hesitation but when the reason for the question is posed, they are more likely to be helpful. Once this information is known, it then becomes possible to test what one would necessarily develop as his or her fee structure in terms of what is likely to be in line with competition.

Still a different way of setting fee structures is to discuss this question with companies who employ consultants. These may be persons to whom one does not intend to offer consultant services, or they may be persons whom one is hoping to be able to serve. Many clients and organizations are prepared to provide this information in order to establish a basis of equity and help a consultant get underway.

The important point is for the consultant to see him- or herself from the standpoint of being in business and, therefore, having the requirement of operating an effective consultancy from a business point of view.

CONSULTANTS ENTER THE FIELD IN MANY DIFFERENT WAYS

There are many different ways of getting into a career of consulting. No one method is better than any other, and all need to be given consideration by those who seek to launch their consulting careers. The prerequisite, of course, is technical competence in the subject matter for which the consultation is offered. Nothing can substitute for that. A computer consultant, for example, needs to be on top of computer technology just as much as a behavioral consultant needs to be on top of behavioral science theories and techniques for giving help.

Beyond competence there are few other prerequisites. The real problem is, "How do I get started?" There are several ways enumerated briefly below.

1. Train with an established consultant as an apprentice, offering assistance to the client under his or her guidance. As experience is built, then one can launch out on his or her own.

2. Join a consultant firm as a junior. Here the same principle applies. The consulting firm needs persons who can do specific aspects of consulting, but who are not as yet capable of assisting clients as generalists. Consulting firms are aware of the need of juniors for experience. They are equally aware that many persons join consultant firms for the purpose of gaining experience before launching on their own, not for lifelong employment.

3. Offer your services based on your awareness of some human problem the potential client is facing. Here one may have a competence that matches a need he or she know a client is facing. This knowledge can be gleaned from newspapers, casual conversations, and even through interviews. A positive or direct approach in which help-giving services are offered is often the key to consulting assignments.

4. Author articles giving clinical case studies of your experiences as an internal consultant. Many persons have given internal consultative help either as a formal assignment or in an informal way. Whichever is the case, one is building the skills essential for helping others, and in doing so is preparing him- or herself to start an independent career. Articles that demonstrate competence in consultation are similar to formal announcements of one's availability.

5. Ask a consultant friend to refer a prospect to you. Many consultants are more than fully engaged and unable to meet all of their client requests. An established consultant who is aware of your own credentials is often willing to make contact with a client in your behalf.

6. Join one of the consulting networks. There are associations of consultants that take different forms. Some are "professional" in character and seek to enroll as members those who meet minimum competence criteria. Others are associations of interested people, and no particular prerequisites of competence and experience are involved in membership. By joining associations or networks of consultants, one gains access to the experience of others in the consulting area and finds out how they go about working with clients. Additionally, one may make acquaintances who are prepared to give assistance by way of introductions. Thirdly, one learns of organizations and of the kinds of consulting services they are seeking. All of these can be helpful in getting started.

7. Cold calls can sometimes result in gaining an assignment. A cold call is one in which the would-be consultant simply makes an appointment or arrives unannounced at a location requesting an interview. Then he or she can tell persons within the organization of his or her interest in being retained as a consultant. Cold calls are not easy for many, but when a person is capable of making contact in this way he or she gains direct access to potential users of his or her services.

8. Advertising is a way that a person can make his or her services known within the community of users. Advertisements make one's availability known and specify one's primary area of competence.

9. Start a firm by employing established consultants. Many times association with others is a useful way of getting started in the consulting field. The reason is that several people who join together are able to provide a wider range of help-giving services than any one member may be capable of offering. A person may not have had experience as a consultant and yet may have the kind of managerial experience that makes it natural for him or her to start such an organization. As experience with established consultants develops, such a person may begin taking direct assignments.

10. Attend trade associations and societies that are attended by firms and organizations that employ consultants. Many such trade associations, functional interest groups, and so on conduct annual meetings. Most of them enroll any person who wishes to attend on the basis of paying tuition or a fee. The consultant attendee can make acquaintances with persons representing a large number of organizations, firms, or establishments. By joining in discussions, one may come to learn of difficulties to which his or her consultative skills may be applied.

Two additional considerations should be mentioned. One is the graduate student who is about to enter employment. The other is the mature manager or executive who is interested in shifting his or her career.

Many of the suggestions already offered are possible entry paths. In addition, one further possibility is involved through the graduate student consultation practicum. What happens is that graduate students enroll in a practicum, giving consultative services as a practice activity in his or her graduate program. This kind of practice activity has led to a number of graduate students being retained by the firm or organization in which they originally completed their practicum. In other words, a practicum is a potential launching pad for paid consultation services.

The mature manager or executive wishing to shift careers and to move into consulting is likely to encounter very few difficulties. This is partly because his or her experience is valuable and partly because he or she has, through the years, come to know consulting firms that are on the lookout for competent persons who can add strength to the services they provide. Beyond that, there are associations of retired persons who wish to remain active and who find consultation an excellent way of doing so.

Given such a wide range of problems for which help is sought and so many different ways for people to enter the consulting field, it might be thought that practices of consultation are so diverse and unique that consultation is a performing art rather than an applied discipline. By seeing the entire field in a coherent way, however, it is evident that an underlying order provides the formulations for an applied science of consultation.

Author Index

Subject Index